G000075725

ANGLO-SAXON TOWNS
IN SOUTHERN ENGLAND

ANGLO ~ SAXON TOWNS
In Southern England

Edited by
Jeremy Haslam

Phillimore

1984

Published by
PHILLIMORE & CO. LTD.
Shopwyke Hall, Chichester, Sussex

© Jeremy Haslam, 1984

ISBN 0 85033 438 1

Printed and bound in Great Britain by
THE CAMELOT PRESS LTD
Southampton, England

CONTENTS

LIST OF FIGURES

LIST OF PLATES

1. Wiltshire. Vertical aerial photograph of Cricklade
2. Wiltshire. Vertical aerial photograph of Malmesbury
3. Langport, Somerset
4. Saxon London. Milk Street excavations, 1977
5. Saxon London. Arch of re-used Roman tiles
6. Saxon London. New Fresh Wharf, 1975
7. Seal of Bath Abbey
8. Two-light window, possibly late Saxon, now in the Bath Abbey collection

FOREWORD

Most of the chapters in this volume were written in late 1980 or early 1981, and represent the thinking of the various authors at that time. The inevitable difficulties in the assembly and production of a multi-author volume of this nature have to a certain extent penalised those contributors whose views may have been modified in the intervening period. Nevertheless, the value of these chapters as a whole lies in the fact that they have for the first time brought together disparate strands of evidence relating to a wide area, and have set out models or hypotheses which should for some time to come provide a stimulus for the acquisition and synthesis of new evidence. It is perhaps therefore appropriate that the publication of this book marks the 50th anniversary of the publication of Carl Stephenson's *Borough and Town* in 1933, whose arguments against the existence of towns in the Anglo-Saxon period have since exercised the minds of generations of urban historians.

It is a pleasure here to recall the co-operation I have had with the contributors, as well as their patience while the volume was in the press. I must also thank my wife Claudia for preparing the index (amongst other traditionally wifely tasks), and Noel Osborne, Editorial Director of Phillimore and Co., Ltd., for his encouragement from the beginning.

Bradford-on-Avon
February 1984

JEREMY HASLAM

INTRODUCTION

*The thorough analysis of a small area must always possess a greater value
than the partial examination of a large one.*

J. H. Round (1882, 245)

The object of this book is to gather together between two covers the results of some
of the most recent work on the development of early medieval towns in southern
England. The emphasis is on the post-Roman and pre-Norman periods, though in the
nature of things evidence from the Roman period on the one hand, and from post-
Conquest sources (such as Domesday Book) on the other hand, must also be utilised.
Most of the towns which are now recognised as having developed so successfully in
the Anglo-Saxon period grew up either in virtually abandoned (and certainly
non-urban) Roman places or on altogether new sites, in response to forces which arose
from the existence of a new social order. Quite apart from the question of 'continuity'
from Roman (or, indeed, pre-Roman) to Saxon, the interest of these places lies in the
fact that at an early stage this new social order moulded the landscape—and the towns
within this landscape—in ways which to a large extent are still visible on the ground
today, and whose processes and stages can be begun to be reconstructed from later
documentary, cartographic and excavated evidence. The rapid expansion of knowledge
produced by much recent work on the archaeology, topography and history of early
medieval towns, which has been engendered to a considerable degree by recent
large-scale state sponsorship of the excavation of threatened urban sites and associated
research, has provided both the necessity and opportunity for a general synthesis,
which it is hoped this book will provide.

A combination of these various classes of the physical and historical evidence is,
as Martin Biddle has remarked (1976, 101–3), already producing its own distinctive
contribution to early urban studies, the most notable of which is perhaps *Winchester
in the Early Middle Ages* (M. Biddle [ed.]1976). It is intended here to bring together
some of the less widely available results of this recent research, and to provide as
balanced an account as the evidence permits of both the physical and documentary
sources available to reconstruct this development. It is hoped that from this will
emerge some patterns of general significance which will themselves lead to the
formation of useful models, or conceptual formulations, against which new evidence
can be tested.

Recent work on either groups of towns or individual towns has not been duplicated
in this volume. The towns of Sussex have been discussed recently by David Hill (1978),
and those of Cornwall by M. Witherick (1967) in a paper which anticipates some of
the methods and conclusions of several of the authors in the present volume. Of
individual towns, Winchester (not considered in detail here) has provided a model
in many senses: in the wealth of evidence relating to its early development, and in the

comprehensiveness with which much of this evidence has been discussed and published (Biddle [ed.] 1976; Biddle 1964–75; 1973; 1976). Southampton, both its earlier phases at *Hamwic* (Addyman and Hill 1968, 1969; Holdsworth 1980; Keen 1975; and Hodges 1981), and its later phases on its present site (Platt and Coleman-Smith 1975), has also had a considerable amount of attention. The origins of the latter settlement are, however, cast in a new light in Philip Holdsworth's chapter in this volume. Bristol, a town of late Saxon origin, not discussed in this book, has also had its recent account (Lobel and Carus-Wilson 1975). This gap is to some extent filled by the account of recent work at Gloucester, although its connections were perhaps more with Mercia than southern England. London, similarly north of the Thames, is a further case where recent historical and archaeological work, mainly undertaken since the publication of the short yet important survey by Biddle and Hudson (1973), was seen to require an extended account.

The emphasis of the present volume is therefore to expound what may be described as an 'archaeological' approach, in which the physical evidence (whether archaeological or topographical) is combined with relevant historical (including numismatic) and geographical data to reconstruct the processes which determined the early development of towns. This approach has affinities with those methods used by historical geographers, though in several important respects shows fundamental differences from them. For instance, for R. E. Dickinson, it is the present pattern of the townscape which is the central object of study. While the urban geographer recognises both stages and formative processes in the historical development of a town, nevertheless the 'final object of study, and that to which all else is subordinated, is the depiction and inter-pretation of the settlement of today' (1961, 2). Similarly for H. Carter the study of historical geography provides 'essential depth to the unravelling of the complex contemporary situations' (1976, 222). In short, the geographical approach only values the past insofar as it elucidates the present. On the other hand, it could be said that the archaeological approach values the present primarily insofar as it provides evidence about structures, situations or processes in the past.

The work of the geographers, however, contains certain ideas which could with profit be used in the archaeological approach to the history of towns. One of Carter's criticisms of Conzen's work on the topography of towns is that his approach to town plan analysis is merely descriptive: it is 'not theoretical-deductive but essentially empirical-inductive' (1976, 150)—a criticism which could be levelled at much archaeo-logical work, in towns as elsewhere, in the medieval period. The emphasis on model-building by geographers as well as prehistorians, not to mention scientists in general, is now a matter of common procedure. That it does not seem to have been applied to processes which have a traditionally 'historical' dimension is perhaps more the result of a lack of an agreed methodology rather than to a basic inappropriateness. If a model is to be of use as a tool, it must purport to describe and explain a wide range of phenomena: in other words, models derived from archaeological or topo-graphical data must, in common with others, consider patterns which can be shown to be repeated (or not repeated) within a group. This need to 'substitute generality for the scholarly study of the unique' (Carter 1976, 148), notwithstanding J. H. Round's dictum quoted at the beginning, is all the more pressing in view both of the increas-ing amount of archaeological data being produced, and of the almost unlimited amount of topographical data still available in present townscapes, recent town plans or earlier documents. The student of the development of historic towns has indeed much to learn about the value of model-building and the classification and grouping of observed phenomena, while at the same time preserving, where appropriate, the sense of the unique situation and the unrepeatable process or series of events in the past which have always been the preserve of the strictly historical approach.

This introduction is not the place to set out an exhaustive agenda for future work on early towns, though it is hoped that this will to a large extent emerge from both the evidence and conclusions set out in the various chapters in this book. The historical context of urban development, using a number of different kinds of evidence, has been explored elsewhere; for instance in three papers by Henry Loyn (1961a, 1961b, 1971), and in papers by Mary Lobel (1976), Martin Biddle (1976), James Campbell (1979), and Nicholas Brooks (1979). It might not be inappropriate, however, to discuss further three possible avenues for further research involving closely interrelated themes, which are all followed to some extent by the various authors in this volume, but which have not until recently had the attention they deserve.

Firstly, it is necessary to see urban settlements, in both their spatial and functional aspects, as part of wider patterns of settlement development and landscape utilisation. This involves seeing them, amongst other ways, as points within a hierarchy of settlement types. For later periods this is, of course, the well-digested subject matter of the geographer, its bibliography growing as rapidly as the diversity of approach and methodology. However, geographers do not as a rule appear to venture into fields such as the subject of pre-Conquest towns where there are few if any quantifiable or measurable constants, and where relationships and even general processes are hard to demonstrate. Students of early towns must, however, retain the geographer's perception of towns as places which are constructed as they are, or which played their particular roles—whether unique or otherwise—through being enmeshed in wider political and/or economic systems. The phenomenon of settlement shift, applicable to towns as well as to villages, is one where this perception is all-important.

A further aspect of the wider relationship of towns to the landscape is their position as settlements within a system of tenurial or territorial units such as manors, parishes and hundreds, as well as groups of hundreds, shires, tribal territories and kingdoms. The relationship for instance between early towns and their parishes, whether intra-mural or extra-mural, is one which has received some attention in individual cases, but little systematic analysis. The generalisations (not all of them in the writer's view entirely convincing) derived from Alan Rogers' detailed study (1972) of the parishes of two Midland towns (Nottingham and Stamford) demonstrate both the complexity and the importance of the subject. Several studies in the present volume have, however, attempted to describe and draw some conclusions from these patterns. The systematic analysis of the relationships of early urban places to these administrative units, as well as to larger ones such as hundreds or shires, or within earlier land units such as Roman villa estates or town territories, would also provide much evidence for the continuity, or its absence, between the Roman and Saxon periods of either settlement or land use. Such evidence is of particular importance in ascertaining the role which certain settlements may have performed within structures of authority. As with every other aspect of the study of early towns, an analysis of the individual instance or of merely localised phenomena is only the first step, however essential, in the appreciation of the wider pattern, from which alone can be derived meaningful historical generalisations.

A second important aspect of early urban studies is that of the reality, status and function of places which may loosely be described as 'proto-urban'. One currently persuasive model of early urban development in England is of the growth in the middle Saxon period of relatively large centres on coastal sites ('ports-of-trade') performing specialised economic functions under the direct control of the king, which can be contrasted with essentially non-urban inland sites which, where they were not purely agricultural, were characterised by a 're-distributive' economy. This has recently been forcefully stated by Richard Hodges (1982), but also forms a general paradigm operating on implicit and explicit levels in much recent discussion by historians and archaeologists alike. The growth of 'market towns' is thus seen as the result of general processes, as well as particular forces such as the royal foundation of burhs, operating only from the late 9th century onwards. (This theme is enlarged upon by Grenville Astill in Chapter 3.) A sharply defined contrast such as this has two main effects. While it tends to illuminate a particular class of evidence it also tends to obscure, like a torch-beam on a dark night, other phenomena for which the evidence is not so clear. Secondly, by its very nature it is exclusive, having the often consciously accepted implication that places which do not show clear evidence of having a 'market' economy were never truly urban.

As will be clear from various chapters in this book, however, a common feature of the landscape of much if not most of southern England (as indeed of Midland England as well) was a series of small multi-functional settlements which developed around royal (and occasionally monastic) central places as a direct result of their essentially non-agricultural roles. These places must have developed such characteristics at a period well before c. 800 A.D., and there is good reason for supposing that they would have acted as true market centres, albeit under royal control and possibly jurisdiction. It also seems clear that the 'planted' towns, almost invariably defended burhs, of the late 9th and early 10th centuries were not only the exception numerically, but were also fitted into, and to a greater or lesser extent came to modify, an existing and securely established system of such 'proto-urban' central places within large estates.

These settlements may be described as 'proto-urban' not only because they can often be shown to have developed characteristics which by the 10th or 11th centuries may be recognised as being truly urban, but also because before this they were central places with administrative, 'redistributive'/market and ecclesiastical functions which set them apart from neighbouring purely agricultural settlements. A recent study of such phenomena in Ireland (so tantalising in that such useful discussion is based on so little systematically analysed evidence) has led R. A. Butlin (1977) to the identification of several such proto-urban settlements at royal or monastic centres. Similarly J. Campbell has pointed out (1979, 120–1) the relationship between these significant places and early royal and ecclesiastical as well as monastic centres, though again adducing all too few examples to uphold this thesis.

This dichotomy between proto-urban and urban centres may even reflect more a conceptual and semantic division rather than a model purporting to describe real situations. The danger of definition is that it sets apart phenomena which in reality may be closely connected. The artificiality of this semantic trend is perhaps indicated by the inadequacy of the conceptual definitions of a town which have been advanced by various writers. Thus M. W. Beresford (1967, 273) has advanced lawyers' tests for 'borough' status, which as Biddle has remarked (1967, 99–100) are not anyway applicable to pre-Conquest towns. Biddle himself (*ibid.*), following C. Heighway (1972) and Continental practice has suggested that urban status can be defined through the possession of several objective characteristics which can be listed. F. M. Stenton has asserted that an Anglo-Saxon town should have possessed a market, a mint, fortifications, tenements and open fields (1971, 527-8). Similarly H. R. Loyn has asserted that it should have possessed 'a market, a mint, special tenure and special jurisdiction' (1961, 9).

While all these characteristics are discussed more fully by their respective authors, and although Biddle, for instance, has urged a flexibility of approach, the fact remains that these are all exclusive definitions. The very existence of such 'bundles of criteria', as with the concept of the basic dichotomy between a redistributive and market economy, often presupposes the premise—which is always implicit if not actually explicit—that the absence of a key defining characteristic relating to a particular place implies that that place was not truly urban. In short, such characteristics may well describe early towns in their maturity, but in a period when the survival of evidence is anyway haphazard their absence cannot be used to demonstrate that a place was not urban.

Similar reservations should indeed be made with regard both to documentary sources, such as Domesday Book or the Burghal Hidage, as well as numismatic evidence, which are often taken as systematic or exclusive lists. They may well supply valuable positive evidence concerning early towns, but the fact that certain places are either not mentioned in these documents or do not show evidence of having had, for instance, a mint or a market, cannot legitimately be taken as demonstrating that they were not boroughs or fortified burhs, or did not mint coins. The absence of evidence has all too often been regarded as positive evidence for the absence of a phenomenon or course of events. In reality, however, the absence of evidence is only evidence for the absence of evidence. The central contention of my own chapters in this volume (Devon and Wiltshire) is that many places had been undergoing a long process of proto-urban and indeed urban development, of rise and of shifting fortunes, which had passed virtually unrecorded in objective or measurable terms before the Domesday survey, for instance, was ever written.

Perhaps a more realistic approach towards a true characterisation of urban places is firstly that of Susan Reynolds, who has suggested (1977, ix-x) that any town should show two main characteristics: that its population should have been engaged in non-agricultural pursuits; and that it should be a distinct social entity. The first of these is somewhat unsatisfactory: since some, possibly most, of the inhabitants of the majority of towns in the Saxon and medieval periods did engage in work on the land, this definition becomes difficult to apply. The second is perhaps more helpful, and foreshadows the approach of R. A. Butlin (1977, 12-13) who has characterised a town as a settlement 'whose function and inhabitants exhibit traits, be they cultural, religious, administrative or ceremonial, sufficiently distinctive to distinguish them from predominantly rural forms of settlement and occupation'.

The conclusion that any sharply defined distinctions between urban and non-urban places are likely to be more illusory than real, or to obscure rather than illuminate, povides some support for suggesting that the development or urban places in the Saxon period is in general a process of continuous development than of abrupt change. In other words, the development into urban places of many of the settlements which can be recognised as towns by the later Saxon or early Norman periods was not only the end result of forces which had been in operation since at least as early as the 7th century, but had also begun long before the plantation on new sites of the urban burhs of King Alfred and Edward the Elder in the decades around 900 A.D. These burhs, though they are numerous, form a distinct class of settlement which in terms of numbers is probably the exception rather than the rule.

The earlier examples of these places, at least in southern England, which may be referred to as proto-urban settlements appear from the 7th century onwards, and can be recognised by their possession of some or most of the following distinctive characteristics:

1. they are located on distinctive topographical sites
2. they may have been fitted into an already existing agricultural system
3. they are usually central settlements of large royal estates, the sites of *villae regales*
4. they were the centres of routeway networks
5. they usually formed the administrative heads of hundreds, groups of hundreds, or other large land units
6. they usually possessed a minster church
7. they often show a clear topographical relationship to earlier settlement foci (Roman villas or larger settlements, or to Iron Age or early Saxon hill-forts)
8. they are sometimes the sites of early battles, or were recorded as places raided by Viking armies.

These characteristics are not descriptive of the places themselves, but are rather the signs by which such places can be recognised. This list is merely at this stage an attempt to highlight a phenomenon which requires further study. But the fact that settlements showing many of these characteristics consistently form the nuclei of places which in the later Saxon or medieval periods become true urban settlements suggests that, as both elements in the developing landscape and as social phenomena, they are of more importance than is suggested by merely calling them 'pre-urban nuclei' or by attempts to devalue their economic functions by describing them as 'redistributive'.

The third aspect of research on early urban development which has not been as systematically employed as it could is what might broadly be described as 'topographical evidence'. As with 'town histories' there have been many 'town topographies', though only a few can claim any lasting significance. Varieties of approach have been advocated and tried. As with much urban history and archaeology in general, however, real insights have seldom been pursued to the point of becoming general historical statements, primarily through a failure to place these developments in contexts of more widespread patterns and processes. Only by a comparison of topographical observations from different places can repeated patterns be established and the subject placed on a proper scientific footing.

But perhaps the basic assumptions—or rather belief—of those who have utilised topographical evidence, is that the systematic analysis of physical evidence represented by topographical material can, independently of other disciplines, by itself provide valid evidence from which historical processes can be inferred. Since indeed topographical material comprises the surviving evidence of spatial patterns which have resulted from past processes, it must be a valid assumption that such processes can be deduced from this evidence when it is analysed properly. As with the evidence from numismatics or place-names, or from archaeology itself, it can (and must) free itself from history and become a discipline from which historical syntheses can themselves be created. It is not without interest that a similar assertion, though with a slightly different subject matter in mind, has recently been made by Peter Fowler (1977, 59–60); and this assumption has perhaps been born out by the results of the paper by Martin Biddle and David Hill on the development of Alfredian burhs (1971).

These ideals can, however, only be achieved by the systematic application of agreed methods and stated objectives, not merely to one town but to a series of, and eventually to all early towns. It is only when repeated and contrasting patterns have been recognised over wide areas that this data can stand alongside and be combined with that from other disciplines—whether derived from the study of coins, place-names, documents or archaeological excavations—to produce larger syntheses.

This time has not yet arrived. But if one result of this book has been to show that it is indeed the time at least to take a determined step along the path to a synthesis of all available evidence from groups of as well as individual towns, then the work of its various authors will not have been in vain.

BIBLIOGRAPHY

Addyman, P. V. and Hill, D. H. (1968 and 1969), 'Saxon Southampton: a review of the evidence', pts. 1 and 2, *Proceedings of the Hampshire Field Club* 25, 61–93; 26, 61–96.

Beresford, M. W. (1967), *New Towns of the Middle Ages*.

Biddle, M. (1964–75), 'Excavations at Winchester', interim reports 1–10, *Antiquaries Journal* 43–55.

Biddle, M. (1973), 'Winchester, the development of an early capital', in H. Jankuhn, W. Schlesinger and H. Steuer (eds.), *Vor-und Früh-formen der Europäischen Stadt im Mittelalter*, Vol. I, 229-261.

Biddle, M. (1976), 'Towns', in Wilson, D. M. (ed.), *The Archaeology of Anglo-Saxon England*, 99-150.

Biddle, M. (ed.) (1976), *Winchester in the Early Middle Ages*, (Winchester Studies 1).

Biddle, M. and Hill, D. H. (1971), 'Late Saxon planned towns', *Antiquaries Journal* 51, 70-85.

Biddle, M. and Hudson, D. (1973), *The future of London's past*, Rescue publication 4.

Brooks, N. P. (1979), 'England in the ninth century: the crucible of defeat', *Transactions of the Royal Historical Society* 5th series, 29, 1–20.

Butlin, R. A. (1977), 'Urban and proto-urban settlements in pre-Norman Ireland', in R. A. Butlin (ed.), *The development of the Irish town*.

Campbell, J. (1979), 'The church in Anglo-Saxon towns', in D. Baker (ed.), *The church in town and countryside* (Studies in Church History, 16), 119-35.

Carter, H. (1976), *The study of urban geography*, 2nd edition.

Dickinson, R. E. (1961), *The West European city*, 2nd edition.

Fowler, P. (1961), *Approaches to archaeology*.

Heighway, C. M. (1972), *The erosion of history: Archaeology and Planning in Towns* (C.B.A.).

Hill, D. (1978), 'The origins of the Saxon towns', in P. Brandon (ed.), *The South Saxons*, 174-89.

Hodges, R. (1981), *The Hamwih Pottery*, C.B.A. Research Report 37.

Hodges, R. (1982), *Dark Age Economics: the origins of towns and trade A.D. 600–1000.*

Holdsworth, P. (1980), *Excavations at Melbourne Street, Southampton, 1971-6*, C.B.A. Research Report 33.

Keen, L. (1975), ' *"Illa mercimonia que dicitur Hamwih"*: a study in early medieval urban development', *Archaeologia Atlantica* 1, 2, 165-190.

Lobel, M. D. (1976), 'Some reflections on the topographical development of the pre-industrial town in England', in F. Emmison and R. Stephens (eds.), *Tribute to an antiquary*, 141–64.

Lobel, M. D. and Carus-Wilson, E. M. (1975), 'Bristol', in M. D. Lobel (ed.), *Historic Towns Atlas*, i.

Loyn, H. R. (1961a), 'Boroughs and Mints, A.D. 900-1066', in R. H. M. Dolley (ed.), *Anglo-Saxon Coins*, 122-135.

Loyn, H. R. (1961b), 'The origin and early development of the Saxon borough with special reference to Cricklade', *Wiltshire Archaeological Magazine* 58, 7-15.

Loyn, H. R. (1971), 'Towns in late Anglo-Saxon England: the evidence and some possible lines of enquiry', in P. Clemoes and K. Hughes (eds.), *England before the Conquest*, 115–28.

Platt, C. and Coleman-Smith, R. (1975), *Excavations in medieval Southampton 1953-69*, Vol. I.

Reynolds, S. (1977), *An Introduction to the History of English Medieval Towns.*

Rogers, A. (1972), 'Parish boundaries and urban history: two case studies', *Journal of the British Archaeological Association* 3rd series 34, 46–64.

Round, J. H. (1882), 'The Domesday of Colchester', pts. 1-4, *The Antiquary* 5, 244–50; 6, 5–9, 95–100, 251–6.

Stenton, F. M. (1971), *Anglo-Saxon England*, 3rd edition.

Witherick, M. E. (1967), 'The medieval boroughs of Cornwall—an alternative view of the origins', *Southampton Research Series in Geography*, No. 4, (University of Southampton) 41-60.

Chapter One

THE TOWNS OF KENT

By Tim Tatton-Brown

Introduction

WITH THE EXCEPTION OF CANTERBURY, very little has been written about the Anglo-Saxon towns of Kent. Even in recent years when many of the Anglo-Saxon boroughs in England have been re-examined, the early towns of Kent have for some reason been left to one side. This may partly be because Kent was not included in the Burghal Hidage document, or because Kent was not within the Danelaw and so had no Viking boroughs. However, there is other evidence for the late Saxon towns, particularly in early charters and in Domesday Book, and it is time that the eight to 10 pre-Norman towns of Kent were examined as a group. This chapter will look at the 10 towns in Kent that are most likely to have been boroughs before 1066. They are: Canterbury; Rochester; Sandwich; Fordwich; Dover; Romney; Hythe; Milton; Faversham; and Seasalter. Domesday Book lists seven of these boroughs, of which two are called *parvus burgus* (Fordwich and Seasalter); an eighth borough at Dover (only called a *villa*) is also implied. Domesday Book also lists Faversham and Milton Regis (two already very ancient royal demesnes) as having markets, and, as will be shown below, both places were incipient boroughs by 1066 at the very latest. Wye and Sarre (Hawkes 1970, 191) which may also have qualified as Saxon boroughs are not included, however.

Much discussion has taken place concerning the criteria for urban status in the Anglo-Saxon period, and it is not proposed to go into all the details here. However, Biddle (1976, 100) has defined 12 criteria. These are set out in tabular form on the next page in relation to the 10 Kent towns mentioned above.

It will be seen, therefore, that except for Faversham, Milton and Seasalter, many of these criteria apply, though the evidence comes almost entirely from documentary sources such as Domesday Book. One day, when a great deal more area-excavation has been carried out in these towns (Canterbury and Dover are, of course, exceptions), it may be possible to fill in more details on the Table. Thanks to the recent work of Stuart Rigold (in Parkin 1973, 118, n. 7) and others, a great deal more is now known about the Kentish mints, and it is now possible to state that minting probably started in Dover under Athelstan (924–39), in Limen under Eadgar (959–75), in Romney under Ethelred (the 'Unready') (997–1003), and in Sandwich, under Edward the Confessor (1042–66). Mints had, of course, existed in Canterbury from the 7th century (perhaps the first post-Roman mint in England starting here as early as 630), and in Rochester from at least the 9th century, and Athelstan's decree records seven moneyers in Canterbury and three in Rochester (Whitelock 1979, 420). It is also just possible that there was a late Saxon mint at Fordwich, since a moneyer is mentioned in a

TABLE I

	Canterbury	Rochester	Sandwich	Fordwich	Hythe	Romney	Dover	Faversham	Milton	Seasalter
1. Defences	X Roman	X Roman					X Roman			
2. Planned streets	X	?	X		X	X	?			
3. Market(s)	X	X	X		?	?	X	X	X	
4. Mint(s)	X (7)	X (3)	X	?	X	X	X	—	—	—
5. Legal autonomy	X	X	X	X	X	X	X	?	?	X
6. 'Central place'	X	X								
7. Dense population	X	X	X	X	X	X	X			
8. Diversified economic base	X		?	?						
9. 'Urban' house-plots	X	X	X	?	?	?	?			
10. Social differentiation	X	X								
11. Complex religious organisation	X	X	X		?	?	X			
12. Judicial centre	X	X	?		?	?	X			

charter of 1111 (Urry 1975, 137). On the question of the legal status of the towns, Kent has the unique group of towns called the Cinque Ports (only Hastings is outside the county) and it is quite clear from Domesday Book and the *Anglo-Saxon Chronicle* that the origin of the special status of these ports is pre-Norman. Dover, the head port, and Hythe, Romney and Sandwich were all doing 'ship-service' for the last Saxon kings. It is also of interest to note that Sandwich and Fordwich were both liberties in their own hundreds (clearly a special status) and that Seasalter was a liberty in no hundred.

Domesday Book, though disappointing in what it does report for Kent, indicates a fairly dense population in seven of the boroughs. Ballard (1904, 4) divided them into three main categories: the county boroughs (Dover, Canterbury and Rochester) and the quasi-county boroughs (Sandwich, Romney, Hythe and Fordwich); Seasalter with no burgesses he calls a 'simple borough'. However, the Domesday information is so incomplete that one can only really summarise it with little comment as did Darby and Campbell (1971, 545-54). The main numerical facts are as follows:

Canterbury: 438 burgesses, 142 *mansurae*, 15 *hagae*, 4 *domus*.
Sandwich: 383 *mansurae hospitatae*, 32 *mansurae*.
Hythe: 231 burgesses.

Romsey: 156 burgesses
Rochester: 80 *mansurae,* 10 *hagae,* 17 *domus,* 3 *mansiones,* 5 burgesses.
Fordwich: 96 *mansurae terrae* (1066) and 73 *mansurae terrae,* 6 burgesses, 7
            mansurae (1086).
Dover: 29 *mansurae* (very incomplete).

Despite the incompleteness of this information, the surviving town plans
(and topography) of these towns also suggest that the above order (except for
perhaps Dover) is probably correct, that in 1066 Canterbury and Sandwich were by
far the most populous towns in Kent, and that Rochester, the 'second' town of Kent,
was only the fifth or sixth largest in population.

Chronologically, and in part geographically, the towns fall into six groups. It is
proposed in this study to deal with them in the order given below as this is probably
the order in which they originated.

(a) Canterbury and Rochester—Roman walled towns, seats of the earliest
      7th-century bishops in England; centres of Roman road patterns.
(b) Sandwich and Fordwich—Middle Saxon trading settlements with *-wic*-
      place-names.
(c) Dover—fortified minster site with a natural harbour, later an important late
      Saxon seaport with a mint.
(d) Romney and Hythe—late Saxon trading seaports with mints, rebuilt on new
      sites as planned towns as a result of natural coastal change.
(e) Faversham and Milton Regis—*c.* 6th-century *villae regales* on north coast
      tidal inlets; later seaports with markets.
(f) Seasalter—unique archiepiscopal borough with no burgesses, probably the
      centre of a salt and fish industry.

It is very striking that every one of these places, except Canterbury, was directly
related to the sea, though today many of them are not. This is because all the Kent
coastline has been, and still is being, greatly altered by erosion, longshore-drift and
silting. Until comparatively recently little attempt had been made to try to understand
the physical geography of the Kent coast in past times, but recent work by the Soil
Survey of Great Britain near Sandwich (Fordham and Green 1973) and particularly
in Romney Marsh (Green 1968) has allowed for the first time a much more complete
understanding of ancient coastlines in the marshland areas (e.g., Cunliffe 1980).
Figure 1 attempts to show the marshland coastlines of Kent as they were developing
between the 8th and early 11th centuries. During this period the Romney Marsh
area, the Wantsum area and the Medway–Swale area were large areas of mainly
unreclaimed marshland dissected by numerous small creeks and channels, and it is
against this background that the origins of the Anglo-Saxon towns of Kent must
be studied. Because the coast was always changing, the positions of the natural
harbours changed and so one often sees a movement of the town itself, for example,
Old Romney to New Romney or West Hythe to Hythe. This is, of course, not unique
to Kent, and exactly the same thing can be seen at Southampton with the movement
from the *Hamwic* site (Biddle 1976, 112).

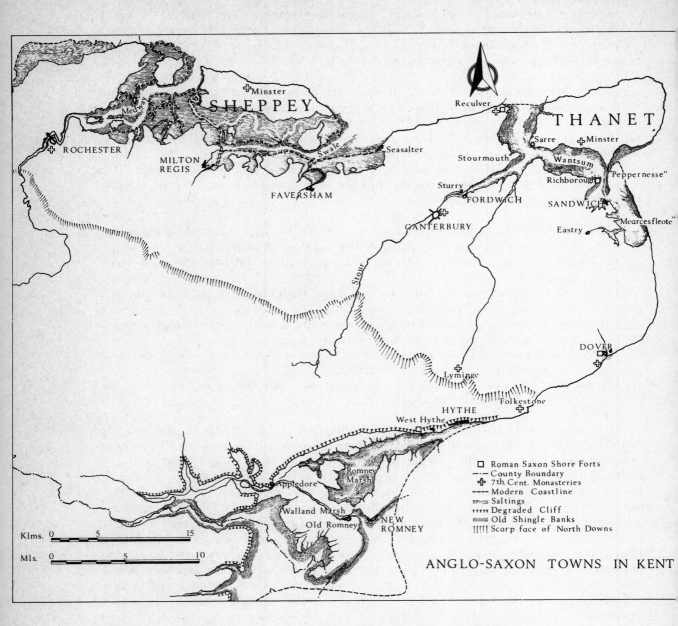

1. Map of Anglo-Saxon towns in Kent with ancient coastlines

Canterbury

Canterbury has many claims to being one of the earliest and best documented of the Anglo-Saxon towns in England, and historians such as Stenton (1971) and Loyn (1962) have often quoted the evidence from Bede and early charters to show that it must have been a densely packed urban centre by the early 9th century. In the very early Saxon period Canterbury has had claims advanced for it of continuity of occupation from the 5th to the 7th centuries, largely because of the discovery by Frere (1966) in small excavations of some 5th- and possibly 6th-century occupation. More recently, larger area-excavations in Canterbury have thrown doubt on the idea of continuity (Tatton-Brown 1980) and it has been shown that there was almost certainly a clear break in occupation in Canterbury between the middle of the 5th and the middle of the 6th centuries. The break is represented by the complete decay of all Roman streets and buildings and the covering of the ruins by layers of black soil (humus). Even outside the city walls the Roman roads were abandoned and right to this day it has been difficult to trace the Roman roads in the first mile or so around Canterbury. It seems very likely therefore that Canterbury was largely avoided by the earliest Anglo-Saxon (or Jutish) invaders, and that re-occupation of the walled area only started again a century or so later (i.e., in the later 6th century) when Aethelberht was not only king of Kent, but also 'Bretwalda'. In fact, the most likely reasons for this re-occupation was the arrival in 597 of St Augustine and his followers. Before that Aethelberht must have spent most of his time travelling between his various *villae regales*—places like Milton, Faversham, Sturry, and Eastry. With the revival of Roman Christianity, an old Roman town filled with ruined flint and brick buildings (as opposed to the timber buildings of the early Saxons) was an ideal place to re-occupy, and as Bede tells us this is just what St Augustine did, though Pope Gregory in Rome may have planned for him to use London rather than Canterbury.

Recent large-scale excavations have shown that the south-eastern area of Canterbury (Fig. 2) was quite densely occupied in the 7th century by *grubenhauser*; of which more than 30 have so far been found. Some of these huts may date from the late 6th century, but almost certainly no earlier. It seems very likely, therefore, that while St Augustine and his followers were rebuilding churches and converting the people, many of them were also moving into the walled area of the city and building huts among the ruins. This then is the most likely time for the re-occupation of Canterbury on a large scale, but despite this Canterbury in the 7th century can hardly have been called urban in any strict sense. It was certainly an important ecclesiastical centre (particularly after the arrival of Archbishop Theodore of Tarsus and Abbot Hadrian in 669), but only in the early 8th century (in Bede's time, when he calls it a *metropolis*) is it likely to have become a town with markets and a fairly dense 'urban' population. There was certainly a very early mint here, but only after the new series of silver pennies, which we (mistakenly) call *sceattas* started to be minted (many almost certainly in Canterbury) from the late 7th century would an international trade have really got going. It is at this period that completely new trading centres like Sandwich and Fordwich (see below) would have come into existence.

Throughout the 8th century Canterbury must have been expanding, and though little archaeological evidence for buildings of this period has yet emerged, quite a

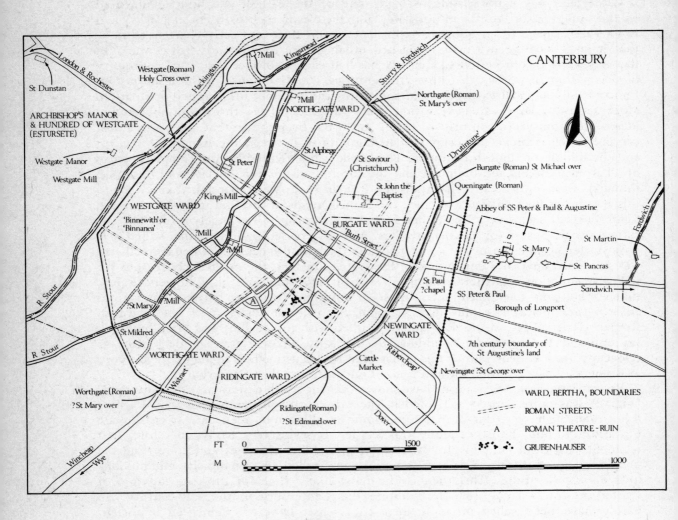

2. Anglo-Saxon Canterbury

large number of *sceattas* and several very finely-worked objects have been found. It appears that by this date *grubenhauser* were giving way to buildings still constructed of wood, but leaving fewer traces behind in the ground. The post-holes are smaller, and some buildings may well have been constructed on ground-beams. A charter of 762 (Sawyer, No. 1182) which is a grant of land near the Quentingate to St Augustine's Abbey, also mentions a 'forum' near the Queningate which is perhaps the area now known as Lady Wooton's Green. In 754 the *Anglo-Saxon Chronicle* says that Canterbury was burnt down, but this must have been only a temporary setback as the later 8th century sees Canterbury as the most important mint in England for Offa's new silver pennies. These new coins, which remained virtually unchanged for the next 500 years, were struck by all the archbishops of Canterbury from 766–923, as well as by the king, and only after 824 did the main Mercian mint move from Canterbury to London. With the rise of Wessex as the major power in England, however, Canterbury was once again an important mint, and the city was ruled by under-kings of the Wessex royal house who had a major mint here. As Professor Dolley (1964, 17) puts it: 'By the end of the third decade of the ninth century silver pennies were being issued in England on a quite considerable scale. The bulk were struck at Canterbury, but the mint at Rochester was already a respectable affair'.

Archaeologically, the 9th century in Canterbury is a very shadowy time, as virtually no material remains of this century are known from the city. This is, of course, the time when Viking raiders, and later large armies, were disrupting the county and clearly Canterbury suffered considerably. The *Anglo-Saxon Chronicle* records 'great slaughter' in 842 at 'Cantwic'; though this may refer to Quentovic, the context makes Canterbury a far more likely candidate. If so, this is the only time Canterbury is called a 'wic' (see below). The *Chronicle* also records 350 ships in 851 coming to the mouth of the Thames and storming Canterbury and London. Several 9th-century charters also survive which give us a few fascinating clues about the city at this time. The charters imply that parts of the city were fairly densely occupied as there was a need for a two-foot 'eaves-drip' between houses (Sawyer, No. 1204, and Stenton 1971, 527), while other areas of land inside the city walls must have been used for pasture or arable. Areas of 6, 10, 14 or 30 acres are mentioned, the latter being a grant of Cenwulf of Mercia to Archbishop Wulfred in 814 (Sawyer, No. 176) of 30 *jugera* at 'Binnan Ea'. This must be nearly the whole of the area south-west of the High Street between the eastern branch of the Stour and the city walls (Fig. 2). A *port* (i.e., market) is also mentioned at this time at Canterbury as well as a burh, and hence the people are called variously *portware* or *burhware*. There is also a unique reference to the *cnihtengild* (Sawyer, No. 1199), which is the earliest recorded guild in England (Stenton 1971, 527). Another charter (Sawyer, No. 287) of 839 probably refers to land just to the north-west of the later church of St Alphege (Fig. 2). In this charter 14 acres within the walls of Canterbury 'with a meadow of the Abbot of St. Augustine's on the west and the River Stour flowing between' is mentioned, and Ward (1951, 16) equates this land with another charter of 832 (Sawyer, No. 1268) which mentions two weirs on the River Stour, presumably fish weirs. Finally, a charter of 804 (Sawyer, No. 160) gives six acres pertaining to the church of St. Mary in the west part of the city to the abbess and nuns of Lyminge as a refuge. This church is described as being on the west side of the Stour (Fig. 2), but this may be a mistake and the church referred to could be the large church of St Mildred's which still stands and is certainly Anglo-Saxon in origin, though as Dr. Brooks points out (pers. comm.) there were almost certainly two different churches (Potts 1943, 19–22). In the 11th century the church belonged to St Augustine's abbey and the monks may well have re-dedicated it to St Mildred after they had brought the saint's body to Canterbury in 1030 (Ward 1941, 67; Radford 1970, 237).

Throughout the 7th, 8th and 9th centuries Canterbury was, of course, a very important ecclesiastical centre (Brooks 1977), with two foci, firstly at the cathedral in the north-eastern part of the city, and secondly at St Augustine's abbey, with its line of churches (similar to the lines of churches in the city of London, Winchester and elsewhere) just outside the city walls on the east, and close to the main road leading into the Burgate. The abbey (originally called the monastery of St Peter and St Paul) was initially a royal and ecclesiasical mausoleum, but burial at the cathedral started in the middle of the 8th century, by which time the abbey had perhaps become more famous as the most important centre of learning in the country. The arrival of Abbot Adrian from Italy in 669 had set this side of the monastery in train, and for nearly 200 years it must have been one of the greatest centres of scholarship in northern Europe. The Viking incursions of the middle of the 9th century would have put an end to this golden age, but a century later the abbey was again prosperous, and Archbishop Dunstan re-dedicated a rebuilt and enlarged abbey in 978 (Davis 1934, 38).

The 10th and early 11th centuries saw the flowering of many burhs in southern and eastern England, so that Canterbury was only one among many towns in England, albeit still the most important one in Kent. However, its mints, which were once the most important in England, now ranked a long way behind those of London, York, Winchester, Lincoln, Chester, Thetford, and Exeter, though Canterbury with its seven moneyers in Aethelstan's decree of the early 10th century is second to London with eight, followed by Winchester with six, and Rochester with three. This decree (Whitelock 1979, 420) also says that of the seven moneyers here, four were of the king, two of the (arch)bishop, and one of the abbot (of St Augustine's).

Excavations have also shown that in the 10th century Canterbury was a large and important trading centre (as well as a religious one), and though few complete structures have yet been found, pottery and some fine objects, including a very fine recently-found Anglo-Scandinavian knife (Graham-Campbell 1978, 130–3), indicate a prosperous population with wide trading contacts. More important information comes from the charters; of particular interest are charters of 923 (Sawyer, No. 1629) and 1002 (Sawyer, No. 905) which mentions a house plot between *Burh Straet* (now Burgate Street) and *Se Lictun* (the cemetery of Christ Church which must have been on the south side of the chapel of St John the Baptist, east of the cathedral, Fig. 2). These charters also mention various plots of land just outside the eastern walls of the city and in particular the *Hrythera Ceap* or *Rytherceap* (the cattle market) and *Portmanna* land. It is quite clear that this area just outside the eastern city walls was already used for a series of markets. Later medieval documents (Urry 1967, 108) indicate that *Ryther Ceap* was a name that survived to the 15th century and was used in particular for the street now known as Dover Street. A cattle market in this area was still operating until 1955, over 1,000 years after it is first mentioned (Fig. 2). The cattle market was, however, not the only market, and it is very likely that the whole area outside the eastern walls between the Worth Gate and the Northgate was a large open area used for a variety of markets. There were also oat and salt markets in this area in the 12th century (Urry 1967, 108–9). The two extra-mural suburbs of Wincheap (probably Wain-market) and Longport are also two street markets which must be late Saxon in origin. Wincheap is still to this day very wide in its central section, while St Augustine's abbey was granted the right to hold a market in 1103 (Davis 1934, 64) in Longport. Longport, however, was mentioned in Domesday Book, so this was probably a confirmation of earlier rights.

The medieval street plan of Canterbury must also go back well before the Norman Conquest. Some streets like *Burh Straet, Wistraet* (probably Castle Street now), and *Drutintune* (Old Ruttington Lane now) are mentioned in pre-Conquest charters and it seems fairly certain that the medieval street plan was substantially complete by the later 10th century. This street plan, which bears no resemblance to the Roman one, appears to have the cathedral as a primary focus, and the roads from Burgate, Northgate and Worthgate all meet in an open area just outside the cathedral precincts (called a 'forum' in the 12th century and the Buttermarket after 1700— Urry 1967, 108). Dr. Nicholas Brooks (1977, 495) has suggested that the north-eastern corner of the Roman walled area may have been an inner burh and that it may even have been fortified with an earthwork and timber defences on the south and west. This is an attractive idea which could be reflected in the street pattern around the cathedral, but as yet there is no archaeological evidence to either confirm or disprove the theory. Dr. Brooks also points to the 9th-century references to the *innan burhwara* and the *utan burhwara* which may refer to the communities inside and outside this smaller burh rather than the Roman city walls. The second major element of the street plan is the High Street which leads from the West Gate (almost certain a Roman gate) to St George's or the Newingate, a 'new gate' in the eastern city walls. Historical and documentary evidence (Brooks 1977, 495) perhaps suggest an early 10th-century date for this element and the 'planned' lanes leading off this main street and off *Wistraet* (Fig. 2). This has yet to be confirmed by archaeological evidence.

Finally, something should be said of the churches of late Saxon Canterbury, although again, more archaeological work is still very necessary. In the 12th century there were 22 parishes and parish churches in the city, and though many were definitely post-Conquest foundations, perhaps as many as half of them, particularly those associated with the city gates, were probably pre-Conquest in origin and associated with a pre-Conquest ward system, though the parochial system is almost certainly post-Conquest. There is a strong evidence to show that the original churches of the Holy Cross, St Mary Northgate and St Michael's were built on top of the Roman Westgate, Northgate and Burgates respectively. Less certain is the evidence for the churches of St George's, St Edmund's and St Mary (later St Mary de Castro) being originally above the Newingate, Ridingate and Worthgates. It is also known that a group of six wards (uniquely called *bertha* at Canterbury) were in being by the mid-12th century at the latest (Urry 1967, 92–6) and that they were based on the six gates and had areas of land inside and outside the city walls. Only in the Westgate area is it complicated by the proximity of the archbishop's great manor and hundred of *Estursete*. It is possible, that, as in London, these wards were late Saxon in origin and represent the way in which the city's walls were manned in time of danger (Brooke 1975, 168). This may be the way the city held out against the Danes for three weeks in 1011 before treachery by one of the inhabitants let them in.

Apart from the churches above the gates and the churches at St Augustine's and the cathedral, at least five other churches in Canterbury may have been in existence before the Conquest. St Martin's and St Mildred's are certain (see above), while St Peter's, St Alphege's and St Dunstan's may be foundations of the early 11th century by the archbishop, perhaps Aethelnoth (1020–38) who brought St Alphege's body back to Canterbury and set up new shrines in the cathedral to the two newly-canonised late Saxon archbishops, Dunstan and Alphege. St Dunstan's church, the centre of another extra-mural suburb, was certainly in existence by 1085 when Lanfranc, the first Norman archbishop, gave it to his new foundation of St Gregory's (Woodcock, 1956). The main street between this church and the Westgate, which was also the road to London, may also have been used for a market which would have been under the archbishop's control.

There is evidence from several charters of the presence of the king's reeve in Canterbury before the Norman Conquest. It is clear that the city was an important town when William the Conqueror arrived here soon after the battle of Hastings in 1066 and received his submission. By this time many of the plots (*hagae*) along the main streets had tightly-packed houses on their frontages and open areas of ground behind. The boundaries of these plots, which are first known about in detail in the 12th century (Urry, 1967) must have continued with little change until the present century. The major re-developments of these areas which are now taking place, are also enabling a few of these plots to be examined in detail by area-excavation.

In the later medieval period, Canterbury had large tracts of rural land outside the walls on the south and east (Fig. 3). On the west and south-west the archbishop's great rural manor and hundred of *Estursete* (later called Westgate) came right up to the city wall and River Stour. It is highly likely that the rural area on the south and east already belonged to the city before the Norman Conquest, and though the parochial system was not at this time yet in existence, the manorial system certainly was. In this rural area were the later medieval manors of Northgate, Caldecote and Wyke (part of Westgate manor), Longport, and to the south the small group of Dungeon, Staplegate, Stuppington and Dodingdale (Fig. 3). These manors may be divided into three main groups: to the north the area between the river and the Roman road to Sandwich belonged to the archbishop and Christ Church. The eastern boundaries with Fordwich and Odo of Bayeaux's park of Wickham may well have been altered soon after the Norman Conquest. Then to the south of the Sandwich road and continuing originally as far as the Roman road to Dover was St Augustine's great manor of Longport. The area of this manor, which lies south-west of the road to Dover probably only became part of it in the early 12th century after the hospital of St Lawrence had been built here. Finally there are the small group of non-ecclesiastically owned manors between the road to Dover and the road from Wincheap to Hythe. These manors were almost certainly given soon after the Norman Conquest to Norman knights, and for a time were connected with the royal castle, hence the name 'Dungeon' (Dane John) for one of them. In the period before the Conquest it must have been one royal manor. In the late 11th and 12th centuries the parochial

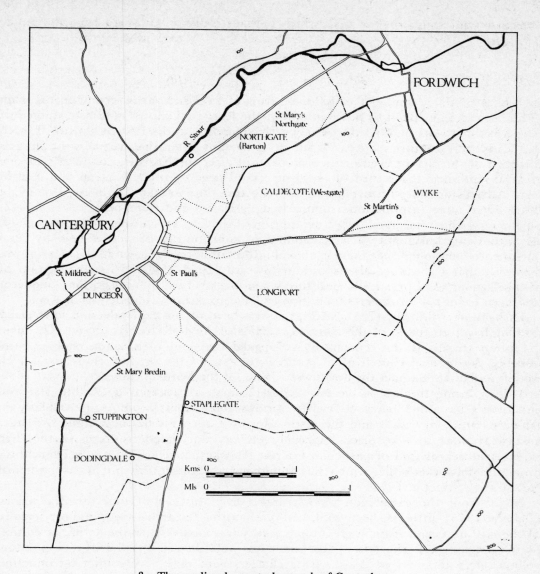

3. The medieval county borough of Canterbury

system would have been imposed on the area and St Mary Northgate and St Martin's parishes covered the northern extra-mural areas, St Paul's covered the Longport area and St Edmund's Ridingate (and after its demise St Mary Bredin) and St Mildred's covered the southern area (Fig. 3).

The pattern of roads in this area, showing the main routes radiating out from Canterbury, is also of interest. The earliest medieval roads, however, are those in north-east Kent which run north-east to south-west. Initially some of these roads bypassed Canterbury on the east, which perhaps indicates they are pre-7th century in origin.

Rochester

Rochester, the second city of Kent and from 604 the site of the second post-Roman bishop's seat in England, is possibly one of the least well-known and least studied of Anglo-Saxon towns in England. A few early references to its first bishops in the 7th and early 8th centuries are recorded in Bede, but after that virtually nothing is recorded of the city or even of its bishops until after the Norman Conquest. The one great exception is the record of its unsuccessful siege by the Vikings in 885, and of King Alfred's arrival with a relieving army. After the Norman Conquest, Domesday Book gives some information (summarised in Darby and Campbell 1971, 550–2) on the city which hardly allows a description of the late Saxon town to be attempted. As with Canterbury quite a large number of contributory properties held by rural manors are mentioned, but there is no real information on the town itself. It is known, however, that the cathedral, its bishop Siweard (1058–75), and its small group of secular canons were practically destitute when it was siezed by William the Conqueror and given to his half-brother, Odo, bishop of Bayeaux, who was made earl of Kent.

Excavation within the city has so far always been on a small scale, and so virtually nothing has been found of the material remains of Anglo-Saxon Rochester. The main exception to this is the remains of an apsidal east end of a Saxon church, quite possibly the original church of St Andrew (or one of the original churches), which were found in 1888 under the north-west corner of the Norman cathedral (Livett 1889, 261–78). During the last 20 years a series of small excavations by Arthur Harrison and others has done much to clarify various topographical points, particularly in relation to the city walls and the castle. However, the time has now come for larger area-excavations to take place, especially on any uncellared frontages to the High Street. One recent find of particular interest (Hawkes, *et al.,* 1979) is of a 7th-century bronze metalworker's die, which was found in a 12th-century pit in the garden of No. 30 High Street in 1976.

Apart from the excavation reports and a brief history of the cathedral priory (Oakley 1975), little has been published summarising the archaeology and topography of the city in recent years. A great opportunity was missed when the definitive edition of the Anglo-Saxon charters of Rochester was published in 1973. This disappointing volume gives the text of 33 surviving charters with only a very brief introduction (Campbell 1973). The best topographical and archaeological accounts of the city were all published over 80 years ago. These were the work of Hasted (1798, IV, 45–191), Payne (1895), Livett (1895), and St John Hope (1898 and 1900), and are still of much value today. This present account will try to summarise what can be inferred about the Anglo-Saxon town.

The original walled circuit of Rochester (Fig. 4) encloses the relatively small area of 23½ acres (*cf.* Canterbury with 130 acres) and recent excavations (Harrison and Flight, 1968) suggest this circuit dates from the early 3rd century. This small Roman town, called *Durobrivae* and situated just to the east of a Roman bridge on Watling Street over the River Medway, was probably, like Canterbury, abandoned by

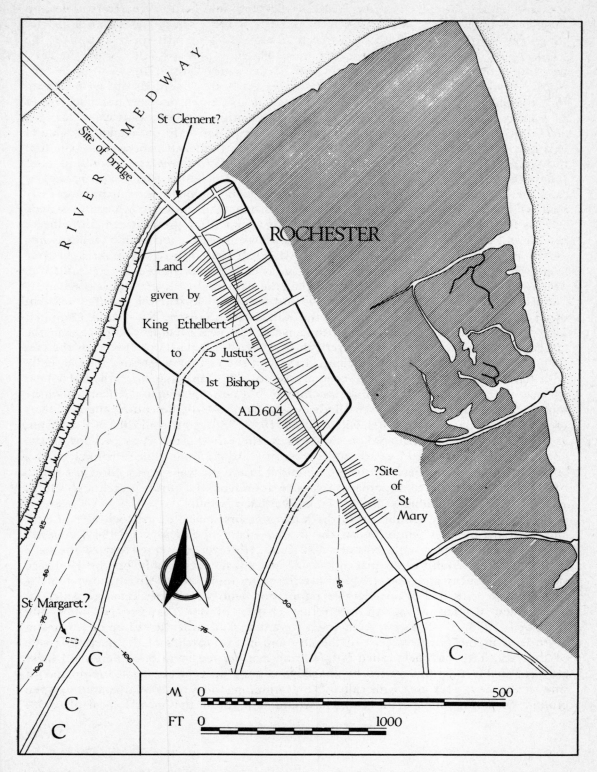

St Clement?

RIVER MEDWAY

Site of bridge

ROCHESTER

Land

given by

King Ethelbert

to   Justus

1st Bishop

A.D. 604

?Site
of
St
Mary

St Margaret?

C

C

C

C

M   0   500

FT 0   1000

4. Anglo-Saxon Rochester with marshland as it was in the mid-19th century. (N.B. In figures 1 to 13 contours are in feet, c=early Saxon cemetery)

the middle of the 5th century. An early Saxon inhumation cemetery (Meaney 1964, 134–5), which perhaps dates from the 5th or 6th century was found a quarter of a mile south-east of the city suggesting some sort of settlement nearby in the 'Dark Ages'. Another inhumation cemetery which is perhaps 7th century in date, was found over a quarter of a mile south of the south gate of the city in the area nearly opposite the later church of St Margaret. Both cemeteries are well beyond the city walls, but close to the later roads leading to Canterbury and Borstal. Neither of them was necessarily related to a settlement within the city walls (*pace* Hawkes *et al.* 1979, 384, who has not located the cemeteries correctly on her Fig. 2). In 604 it is known from Bede (III, 3) that King Aethelberht built and endowed, for the first bishop Justus, a new cathedral inside the walls of *Hrofescaestir*. This and later references in Bede, which call it the *castellum* of Rochester (Bede, IV, 5) suggest that the city may have been a virtually empty shell at the time, and that the early bishops' hold on the *castellum* was a precarious one until the early 8th century. Bede tells us how Justus had to abandon the see for a time after the death of Aethelberht in 616 and that there was a gap in the succession after the second bishop was drowned at sea in 627. In 633, Bishop Paulinus, who had fled from Northumbria, became bishop here and both he and his successor, Ithamar, were buried in the cathedral. This is of particular interest as it shows that the cathedral at Rochester was receiving burials long before Canterbury. Both this and the original grant by King Aethelberht of all the land in the southern part of the walled area (Sawyer, No .1 and Campbell 1973, No. 1) may suggest that the Roman city was nearly empty. More gaps in the episcopal succession occur in the later 7th century, and Bede (IV, 12) records the fact that Aethelraed, king of the Mercians, destroyed the city of Rochester in 676. Only with the arrival of Tobias on the scene as bishop (692–726) does the cathedral appear to have entered a new era. Tobias was buried in a new *porticus* of St Paul which he himself had added to the church (Bede, V, 23) and east of the church there appears to have been a lay cemetery (Hawkes *et al.* 1979, 386), so the minster in Rochester, as with many other Anglo-Saxon minsters in the 8th century, was perhaps at last going through a period of peace and prosperity. At the same time it is likely that a large settlement would have grown up around it inside the walled area, though nothing of this settlement, except perhaps a *sceatta* found on the priors' gatehouse site in 1976 (Harrison and Williams 1979, 27), has yet been found.

In the 9th century trouble from the Vikings is first heard of at Rochester in 842, and with the Vikings wintering on the nearby island of Sheppey in 854 Rochester would once again have entered uncertain times. However, the epic story of the siege in 885 with a Viking camp placed outside the town (presumably on the landward side, to the south) and the arrival of a relief army under King Alfred shows that by this time the city had a considerable population who were determined to hold out inside their Roman walls. An interesting charter of 868 (Sawyer, No. 339, and Campbell 1973, 30–2) shows Aethelraed I granting Cuthwulf the bishop of Rochester more land in the northern part of the city and in the marshes of the north-east side of the city. Two channels called *Pirigfiat* and *Scipfiat* are mentioned here, and these are presumably tidal inlets used by the ships coming up to a beach on the north-east side of the city. This area, still called 'The Common' today, was a large area of open ground bordering the marshes, which would have been the most logical place for large markets to have been held (Fig. 4). The charter also mentions *Liabingescot* (presumably a house) and *Doddinghyrnan,* which is mentioned in several other earlier charters as well as later documents, and is perhaps the lane leading from the crossroads in the centre of the town to the cathedral (Ward 1949, 41). Another charter of 850 (Sawyer, No. 299, and Campbell 1973, 25) mentions a half-acre plot outside the eastern walls of the city of Rochester, and a nearby church dedicated to St Mary the Virgin. This church, which is not heard of again, was perhaps destroyed by the Vikings. Its exact site has yet to be located, but it is just possible that it may have been near the early cemetery and related to it (Fig. 4). The church of St Margaret, which dates from at least the 11th century, may be related in a similar way to the early cemeteries outside the south side of the city. Hasted (IV, 174) even mentions a 'Saxon coronet' found in St Margaret's churchyard in the late 17th century. One other church which may also be late Saxon in origin is that of St Clement which was situated just inside the West Gate on the north side of the High Street. This church was already in ruins in Hasted's time (IV, 154) and its site is now covered by the modern dual carriageway. Its situation close to the end of the bridge is probably not fortuitous.

From the early 9th century Rochester had a mint, and it is clear that despite the Vikings the city was an important *port* (market) as well as a burh throughout the century; so much so that Aethelstan's law code in the early 10th century records three moneyers in the city. Rochester was obviously helped during this period by having its strong Roman walls which must have been in fairly good condition at the time. The account of the siege in 885 gives some information about the city and the camp built by the Vikings outside, but makes no mention of the bridge. It seems very likely, however, that this famous bridge, which must have had stone piers built by the Romans, was in use at the time. Dr. Nicholas Brooks (1971, 69-84) has suggested that 'bridgework' in Kent was perhaps first introduced by Offa in 792. If this is so, Rochester bridge, the most important in Kent, would certainly have been rebuilt, not only for crossing the river, but also for stopping Viking ships from getting into the upper Medway. An early 12th-century account of bridgework at Rochester in the *Textus Roffensis* (Lambarde 1570, 344) does, however, give the impression that the bridge was in use in the latest Saxon period, suggesting that it must have been restored by the early 11th century at the latest. The *Textus Roffensis* account says that the bridge was 431 feet long with nine piers (presumably the Roman ones restored) and with wooden planking in between. The upkeep of each section was the responsibility of different manors of the king, the archbishop of Canterbury, and the bishop of Rochester (these manors are specified in detail in the *Textus Roffensis*), and it is probable that these were the people who restored the bridge during the 9th or 10th centuries. A new study of the early documentary evidence relating to the bridge is, however, long overdue.

By the 10th century Rochester must have acquired the street plan it still has today (Fig. 4). This consists of a main street leading from the bridge into the town through the West Gate, and following the long axis of the Roman-walled area to leave by the East Gate. The only other major streets within the walled area are the street leading from the South Gate (later King's Head Lane and College Yard) to the place that is perhaps to be identified with the *Doddinghyrnan* of the charters (see above), and the street leading from the North Gate to *Doddinghyrnan* (later Cheldergate or Pump

Lane). This rough crossroads in the middle of the city was clearly a central point and some of the charters suggest that the street (called Broad Gate) between here and the North Gate was extra wide and may also have been used for a *port* (market). The names Broad Gate and Cheldergate are rare occurrences in Kent of the use of the Scandinavian word *gaet* for a street. Broad Gate was also the street connecting the city with the marshes and sea creeks and hence with the main harbour area. There were also a few side lanes leading off the main street though only in the northern part of the city did they survive into the later medieval period. One feature which might have been expected, but of which there is no sign in the later street pattern, is an intra-mural street to allow easy access to the walls. Of particular interest, however, are the series of long narrow plots of land (late Saxon *hagae* perhaps) which front on to the High Street (Fig. 4). Some of these plots were later shortened on the south by the Norman castle ditch and the cathedral priory, while others may have existed before 1066 outside the city walls beyond the East Gate where their late medieval descendants are shown on Speed's map of 1610. It is significant that both of the main roads from the south join Watling Street before it reaches the East Gate in this eastern suburb. The road to the south gate, passing St Margaret's church is only of minor importance.

The later medieval borough of Rochester took in a considerable rural area around the walled city, the southern boundary being two miles south of the East Gate well up the dip slope of the Downs. The city also had jurisdiction over the whole of the course of the River Medway below the high water mark as far as its mouth at Sheerness. These boundaries as well as this very ancient right may go well back before the Norman Conquest, and are similar to those at Sandwich, Fordwich and New Romney (see below).

The period at the end of the 10th century and the early 11th century of the weak rule of Aethelraed ('the Unready') again saw the disruption of trade by the Danes. The *Anglo-Saxon Chronicle* tells how King Aethelraed laid waste the diocese of Rochester in 986 and how the Danes sailed up the Medway to Rochester in 999 and won a battle there against Kentish levies. More disruption is likely to have occurred in the years 1009–12 when a Danish army was moving up and down the Thames, but Rochester itself does not this time seem to have been laid waste or burned. However, the cathedral was clearly at a very low ebb at the Norman Conquest and only with the appointments of Lanfranc as archbishop and Gundulf as bishop of Rochester and the founding of a new Benedict priory did the cathedral, and the city with it, once again see prosperity.

Sandwich and Fordwich

Neither Sandwich nor Fordwich were Roman towns, and both places were almost certainly founded on virgin sites near good natural harbours as new trading settlements in the middle of the 7th century. They were perhaps typical of a new type of settlement (many of them having place-names ending in *-wic*) that were appearing on both sides of the North Sea and English Channel littorals at this time (Reynolds 1977, 24–7). All these sites were situated on navigable rivers or beside natural harbours, and the most important examples in England are London (*Lundenwic* in an 8th-century reference) and York (*Eoforwic*). Other well-known English examples are Swanage (*Swanawic*), Norwich, Ipswich (*Gipeswic*), Dunwich, Harwich, perhaps Greenwich, and best known of all from excavation, *Hamwic* (Southampton) (Biddle 1976, 114-7). On the Continental side, there were sites at *Sliaswich* (Schleswig), Brunswick, and Bardowick, but the two most famous sites were Quentovic (near Boulogne) and Wijk-bij Duurstede (at the mouth of the Rhine), and it is of interest that some of the earliest references to these places are in the early *Lives of Saints*. For example, it is recorded that St Boniface crossed the Channel from London to Duurstede in 716 and from London to Quentovic in 718, while Willibalde crossed from *Hamwic* to Rouen in 720 (quoted in Loyn 1962, 80). Earlier than this, in 679-80, St Wilfred's *Life* mentions both Duurstede and Quentovic, and in 664-5 St Wilfred arrived at Sandwich on his return from the Continent after being consecrated bishop of Northumbria (Colgrave 1927, 25 and 28). This is the earliest reference to Sandwich and only a few years later a charter of King Hlothhere in 675 mentions Fordwich (Sawyer, No.7). It is also in the time of Hlothhere that a law code first mentions in Kent a *wīc-gerēfa*, i.e., the reeve of the trading settlement, and it seems likely that the Frisians and the Men of Kent were at this time first setting up new inter-national trading centres which would become the first true Anglo-Saxon towns. Excavation of the earliest levels at Sandwich (and Fordwich) is now needed to confirm this and to see whether a similar wealth of imports as those found at *Hamwic* were also brought here.

Sandwich is not heard of again until the advent of the Vikings, and, as with Rochester, it appears by the middle of the 9th century to have become an important trading centre. In 851, the *Anglo-Saxon Chronicle* says that King Athelstan and his ealdorman, Ealhhere, fought the Vikings in ships, and destroyed a great host at Sandwich, captured nine ships and drove off the rest. This Viking army had just, for the first time ever, spent the winter on the Isle of Thanet and both this island and Sheppey off the north Kent coast (Fig. 1) made ideal secure winter bases for early Viking armies.

The site of Sandwich was very similar to that of *Hamwic* (Southampton). It was situated beside a large open seaway, the Wantsum, that once surrounded the Isle of Thanet (Fig. 1). This seaway also joined the estuary of the River Stour, at the head of which was Fordwich, and like the Solent this had a double tide. The Wantsum had been important since Roman times at least, the Saxon Shore forts of Reculver and Richborough were built at either end of it in the later Roman period. During the 5th and 6th centuries the Wantsum was the most important haven on the east coast of England. The *Anglo-Saxon Chronicle* records the arrival in 449 of the semi-legendary Hengest and Horsa at Ebbsfleet (*Heopwinesfleot* or *Ypwinesfleot*). This was part of the Wantsum between Richborough and Minster (Fig. 1) and was an ideal haven well protected from the English Channel by shingle banks (Hawkes in Cunliffe 1968, 224-31). It is described in Bede (I, 25) when St Augustine and his monks arrived here in 597. A rising sea-level, erosion and changing conditions of silting had meant that by the 7th century Richborough was probably an unsuitable place for beaching ships and so a new site at Sandwich would have come into being (Fig. 5). This was directly paralleled in the Solent by the sites of *Clausentum* and *Hamwic* (Biddle 1976). Richborough, however, with its strong walls was probably still used as a burh in time of

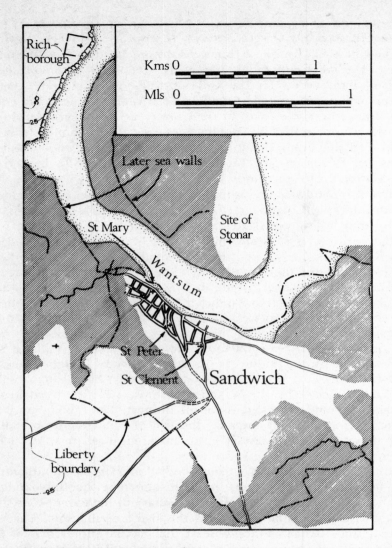

5. Anglo-Saxon Sandwich. (N.B. In this and all subsequent figures in this chapter, north is at the top, and dark lines beside streets represent early post-medieval built-up areas. Shaded areas are marshland reclaimed at a later date)

trouble and some evidence of middle Saxon occupation has been found there (Cunliffe 1968, 251). The new site clearly takes its name from the sand bank at the south end of the Wantsum on which the new *vicus* was situated (geologically this is Thanet Sands and brickearth/loess). To the east was the large area of open water (now the Lydden Valley) that was protected from the open sea by an offshire shingle bank. In the later medieval period this bank was engulfed by another shingle bank which had moved northwards and westwards towards the earlier Stonar bank, virtually blocking the eastern entrance to the Wantsum (Robinson and Cloet 1953).

The famous charter of Cnut (Sawyer, No. 959), in which the port of Sandwich is confirmed in 1023 as belonging to Christ Church, Canterbury, mentions that Sandwich had all the revenues of the haven on both sides 'from Pepernesse [the northern tip of the shingle bank] to *Meacesfloete*, so far as a taper axe can be thrown from a vessel afloat at high water'. *Meacesfloete* must have been the name for the area of open water south-east of Sandwich in what is now the Lydden Valley. The boundary implied in the place-name is presumably the boundary between the Eastry and Cornilo hundreds, which was an early boundary between the lands of Christ Church (on the north) and St Augustine's abbey (Fig. 1). This area was progressively reclaimed from the sea from the 12th century onwards, but in the 7th to 11th centuries was presumably the main haven for Sandwich in which many of the Viking leaders and later Saxon kings assembled their large fleets of ships, for example Anlaf's 93 Viking ships in 994, Aethelraed's vast fleet to oppose Swein in 1009, or Edward's fleet in 1046.

Sandwich's connection with Christ Church, Canterbury, probably goes back to the late 10th century, although the charter of King Eadgar (Sawyer, No. 808) 'on the prayer of Archbishop Dunstan' is almost certainly a forgery. The charter of Aethelraed, however, of 979 (Sawyer, No. 1636) may well be genuine. This was confirmed in 1023 by Cnut (see above) and at the same time Minster (to the north) with Stonar (on the shingle bank opposite Sandwich [Fig. 5]) was given to St Augustine's, sowing the seeds for intense rivalry between the two great Benedictine houses over toll rights in the Wantsum channel. In fact only a few years later, in 1038, Christ Church temporarily lost Sandwich to St Augustine's (Sawyer, No. 1467), but by 1040 they had got it back again, and St Augustine's were being advised to make their own harbour at Minster ('in front of Mildred's acre').

The liberty of Sandwich was a hundred in its own right (Fig. 5), and the early town was situated on the sand bank at the north-western end of this area. To the east and south was an area of higher ground within the liberty used early for arable farming (it was later part of the manor of Sandown). All the earliest streets in Sandwich (Fig. 5) run north-west to south-east, and the only way to reach Sandwich by land in the Saxon period was from the south (Fig. 5). Once the marshland area to the west had been drained in the 12th and 13th centuries, new causeways brought the roads from Canterbury and Woodnesborough into the town on the west, and a New Street with a man-made canal alongside it (The Delf) was constructed on the south (Fig. 6). Later still, in the 14th to 15th centuries, a new defensive rampart and ditch with masonry gates was built around the city. This finally cut off the two original routes into Sandwich from the south. Without excavation, it is impossible to date closely the more regular pattern of streets on the north-west (around St Mary's church). It is clearly earlier than the 12th century, and E. W. Parkin (1970, 220–1) has suggested that both St Mary's parish and St Clement's are Norman suburbs. However, Domesday Book gives 383 houses in the town implying that these 'suburbs' were already in existence. Parkin (*op. cit.* above) has also shown how the water front (Strand Street) has been moved forward in the 14th century, and 13th-century stone houses can still be seen today on the old line. Excavations have never taken place here, but if carried out the known waterlogging of the area would make them as important as any of the recent waterfront excavations in, for instance, London, Dublin, or King's Lynn— particularly as the medieval documentary evidence, some of which is published

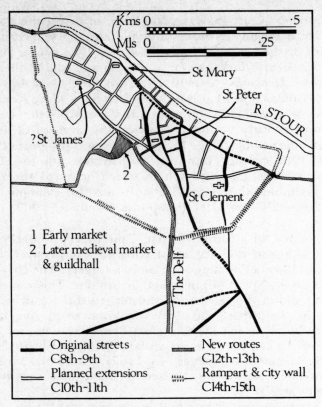

6. Topographical development of Sandwich

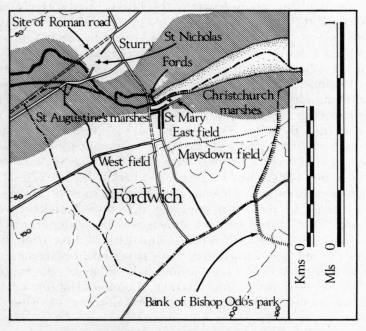

7. Anglo-Saxon Fordwich. (N.B. Marshland area shaded)

(Boys 1792), is also very rich. The period at which Sandwich was at its greatest was between the 11th and 13th centuries, and this is the period which now needs to be enlightened by archaeology.

Fordwich, which in its earlier history had many aspects in common with Sandwich, was always small in size because of its proximity to Canterbury. For much of its life it was indeed the seaport for Canterbury, and many medieval documents show stone and other materials for building the cathedral being shipped in through Fordwich until the end of the 15th century. However, in the middle and later Saxon periods it must have been a place of considerable importance, and toll-charters of 747 and 761 (Sawyer, Nos. 1612 and 29) imply that Fordwich was already receiving many ships in the mid-8th century. By the 9th and 10th centuries other charters (e.g., Sawyer, No. 1654) speak of *hagas* and meadows near the town, and just before the Conquest Domesday Book says there were 96 *mansurae terrae* in the town. In 1055 Edward the Confessor granted all his lands in Fordwich to St Augustine's (Sawyer, No. 1092), which Domesday Book records as comprising two-thirds of the borough. The other third, which was once Earl Godwin's, passed to Odo, bishop of Bayeux, who also granted it to St Augustine's (in about 1075) with King William's consent. Odo also carved out for himself a park (a detached portion of Wickham manor, and also mentioned in Domesday Book) on the east side of the liberty of Fordwich (Fig. 7), which almost certainly took in some land originally belonging to Fordwich. This park, Trenley Park, was still a detached portion of Wickham (breaux) parish in the 19th century. Domesday Book also says the archbishop had seven *masuras terrae* in the borough which did service to St Augustine's in the time of King Edward. Lanfranc had by 1086 taken this service away and a later document (Woodruff 1895) says this was ship-service (*servicum ad mare*), a reminder that Fordwich was also a Cinque Port which was later attached to Sandwich.

The importance of the whole of the Wantsum channel and the Stour estuary in the Anglo-Saxon period cannot be overstressed, and apart from the rights of Sandwich over the channel at the eastern end (see above), Fordwich had very similar rights over the whole of the Stour estuary. In fact, an inquest of *c.* 1272 in the Fordwich Custumal (printed at the end of Chapter IX, Woodruff 1895) says, 'the franchise (includes) water which ebbs and flows as far as Stormouthe, and by land on both sides of the water as far as a man standing in a boat at high tide can throw an axe of vii lb. called a Taperaxe upon the land'. This is very similar language to the Edward the Confessor charter at Sandwich and it is thus very likely that the original franchise at Fordwich also goes back to the Confessor's time. The other important early and middle Saxon port on the Wantsum was at Sarre, opposite the mouth of the Stour and at the point where the two tides met. Very little is known of this site, and it may also be a middle Saxon trading port like Fordwich and Sandwich.

The later medieval landward boundary of the liberty of Fordwich (Fig. 7) is perhaps different from the Anglo-Saxon boundary because apart from Odo's park which impinges on the east, the 13th-century Custumal (Woodruff 1895) says that the liberty of Fordwich extended over parts of the surrounding 10 parishes. Within the liberty, later medieval documents suggest a large three-field system around the town (presumably open fields), with drained marshland area on the east and west belonging to Christ Church and St Augustine's respectively. The built-up area of the later

medieval town was small, though a few medieval houses and a court hall, rebuilt in
c. 1544, still survive. The church (which perhaps contains a little late 11th-century
work) is surprisingly close to the waterfront, suggesting that it is built on reclaimed
land, but excavation work alone will now add further information to the early history
of the site. As in the case of Sandwich, this has yet to be carried out.

Dover

Dover is one of the most perplexing of all the late Saxon towns in Kent. At the
time of the Norman Conquest it was clearly the most strategically important seaport
in south-east England, and the very first page of Domesday Book starts with a long,
but very unsatisfactory, account of the place. Although only 29 *mansurae* are
mentioned, and the place is only called a *villa*. It does, however, list a guildhall and
four churches, and it is quite clear that Dover was already a borough and the head-port
of a group of south-east coastal towns doing ship-service for all the late Saxon kings.
As with Sandwich, there are various pre-Conquest accounts (in 1036, 1051 and 1066)
of the harbour being used as a royal base, and Domesday Book specifies that in
exchange for exemption from 'sac and soc' the burgesses had provided Edward the
Confessor with 20 ships for 15 days each year, each ship containing 21 men. It also
states that the town was burnt in 1066, but that by 1086 it had clearly recovered
completely and was flourishing. The rebuilding of the huge early Norman church of
St Martin-le-Grand was certainly underway before 1086. Among other strange little
details, a mill at the entrance
to the harbour (presumably a
tidal mill) is mentioned which
had been built after 1066 and
which damaged nearly all the
shipping that entered the port
(Fig. 8).

It is certain, therefore, that
Dover was an important town
in the early 11th century, but
when it became a town is
uncertain. Perhaps the best
evidence available at the
moment is the mint starting
at Dover before the middle
of the 10th century (perhaps
under Athelstan). This is the
earliest of the mints in the
Cinque Port towns and suggests that from the middle of
the 10th century at least,
there was a sizeable trading
community here. Where this
community lived is by no

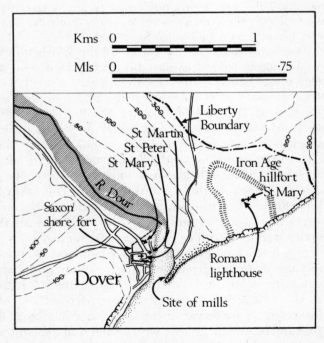

8. **Anglo-Saxon Dover**

means certain, but it is more than likely that in the first instance they were in the shell of the old Roman-Saxon shore fort which Brian Philp's recent excavation has now so convincingly uncovered. On the east side of the area enclosed by the walls and towers of the Saxon shore fort is the open square of the medieval market-place and this is by far the most likely site for the 10th-century houses and market, particularly as the area was flanked on the west by the very ancient minster church (founded by King Wihtred in the 690s) of St Martin (Rigold 1968 and 1977b, 73). Two of the other churches mentioned in Domesday Book were perhaps St Peters (later a parish church) on the north side of the market square, and St Mary's church (another later parish church) which was perhaps just inside the as yet unlocated northern walls of the Saxon shore fort.

The fourth church mentioned in Domesday Book must have been the great church of St Mary (de-Castro) situated on top of the hill just east of the Roman lighthouse (and inside the later castle). This exceptional building is now generally agreed, on architectural grounds (Taylor 1965, 241–7), to have been built in the late 10th or early 11th centuries. Excavations beside it (in 1961–3) found part of an early inhumation cemetery (Biddle 1970, 264–5), but no real evidence of a Saxon settlement (let alone a burh) in the area. Nevertheless, the building of this great church on the hilltop site does suggest that this area (inside a probable Iron Age hill-fort) may have been a late Saxon burh. It may also have been Harold Godwinson's 'castle' of c. 1064. Perhaps by this time the walls of the Saxon short fort were so decayed that a more defensible site in the very troubled years of the early 11th century was needed, and the Iron Age hill-fort (as at Old Sarum in Wiltshire) would have been an ideal site. More excavation in this area is, however, needed to demonstrate this.

The very complicated topography of the inner estuary of the River Dour on the east side of the Saxon shore fort was partly unravelled by Stuart Rigold a decade or so ago (Rigold 1970b), and it is possible to estimate the approximate position of the late Saxon harbour (Fig. 8). Longshore drift was clearly already forming an outer shingle spit on the south-east, and the east wall of the Saxon shore fort (if it ever existed) must have disappeared early in the Saxon period, leaving an inlet here which later developed into the market-place. The suburb of Dover below the castle on the east side of the estuary (later the parish of St James) was probably already in being before the Conquest, and it is possible that St James Street with some of its side and back lanes is pre-Conquest in origin. Excavation at the waterlogged western end of this street may well produce some very interesting early buildings at a future date, and perhaps indicate the exact size of the late Saxon inner harbour (the extent of the harbour shown in Fig. 8 is largely hypothetical). Later in the medieval period, the whole of this area silted up, and the harbour moved progressively south-westwards down the coast.

Romney and Hythe

Only in the last decade or so, since the publication of the Soil Survey Bulletin (Green 1968), has the evolution of Romney Marsh been properly understood, and even now only a 'preliminary statement' has been published giving the main outlines of that evolution (Cunliffe 1980a). Much detailed work has yet to be done, not least in relation to the topography of the two late Saxon boroughs in the area, Romney and Hythe.

In the late Roman period a large river with several tributaries, the Limen, appears to have flowed from the Weald (with its many iron-working sites) due east to an estuary in Romney Marsh proper (Fig. 1). Above the mouth of this estuary on the northern side, was situated the Saxon shore fort now called Stutfall Castle; its original name which is given in the 3rd-century *Antonine Itinerary,* was *Portus Lemanis.* From the 4th century onwards, this estuary appears to have progressively silted up, and by the later Saxon period a new estuary had apparently been formed at Romney which was probably by then the mouth of the Limen. This new estuary appears to have cut off the head waters of the Limen near Appledore, and once this had been achieved the estuary was clearly large enough to allow the Viking fleet of 892 to sail up it at least as far as Appledore. The other estuary near Hythe, though much reduced by the end of the Saxon period, was clearly an important natural harbour throughout the Saxon period. Various charters dating from the 8th to the 10th centuries relating to the reclamation of the area have been partly elucidated by Ward (1931, 1933a and b), and it seems likely that the earliest major Saxon settlement was situated inside the Roman-Saxon shore fort. With progressive silting up, the settlement seems to have moved to 'Sandtun', a site on an old shingle bank mentioned in charters of A.D. 732 and 833 (Sawyer, Nos. 23 and 270). The last vestiges of this site, a few cottages at a place called Sampton, near Botolphs Bridge (perhaps also a significant place-name), are just on the edge of the sand and shingle bank (Ward 1931), and quite a large amount of 10th- and 11th-century pottery has been found in a sand pit nearby. Later still the site may have moved to West Hythe before its final eastward move to Hythe. The name of the Anglo-Saxon port here was also probably 'Limen' as coins of Eadgar (959–75) give this name as the name of the mint. However, which of the many sites was actually 'Limen' at this time is uncertain. It could have been either Stutfall Castle, 'Sandtun', West Hythe, Hythe, or even Lympne, though this latter site was probably only a new Norman castle site built on the cliff top after 1066, and taking its name in turn from the earlier Saxon site below. Both Lympne and Saltwood Castles (above Hythe, Fig. 9) were early Norman castles belonging to Christ Church, Canterbury, and with Lanfranc's reorganisation of the temporalities, Lympne went to the archdeacon of Canterbury and Saltwood to the archbishop himself. It is interesting that all four parish churches in Hythe (St Michael Ashe, St Nicholas, St Leonard and St Mary) were always only chapels-of-east to Saltwood. Of these only St Leonard's survived after the massive depopulation of the later 14th century, but even this did not become a separate parish from Saltwood until 1844 (Dale 1931, 63). Similarly the town did not break free from the archbishop until 1575 when it received a new charter and the archbishop's bailiff became the first mayor.

The late Saxon town of Hythe was perhaps at its present site by Cnut's reign (*c.* 1036—see Sawyer, No. 1221—Dr. Brooks, however, says this is a 12th-century forgery) as Halfden at this time is recorded as giving Hythe and Saltwood to Christ Church, Canterbury. At about the same time Hythe, like Dover and Sandwich, was doing ship-service and enjoying special royal privileges. In Domesday Book 231 burgesses are recorded, and it, of course, became one of the original Norman Cinque Ports. Later, Hythe, like the other early towns, was a liberty in its own hundred.

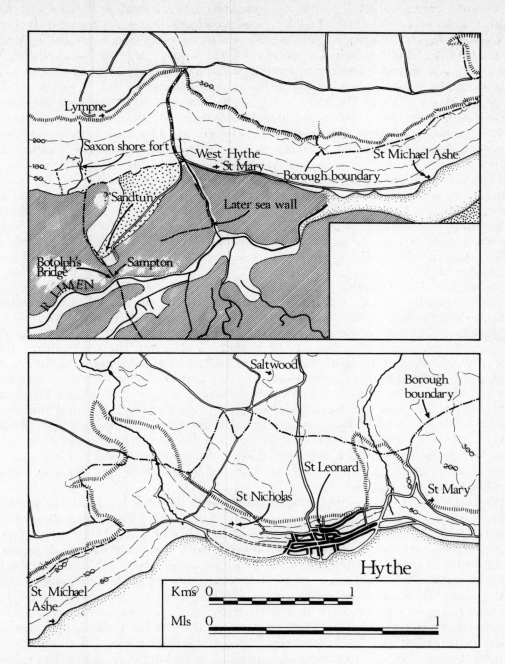

9.   Anglo-Saxon Hythe. (N.B. The left-hand side of the lower figure overlaps the right-hand side of the upper figure. Marshland area shaded)

The topography of Hythe with the long thin area of its liberty stretching from Sandtun nearly to Folkestone (Fig. 9), is of particular interest. It contains the parish of West Hythe, but Lympne (and the Saxon shore fort) had been cut out of it (probably after the Norman Conquest). By the end of the medieval period, the urban area had shrunk to the area around St Leonard's (Fig. 9), but this shrinkage is known to have taken place mainly in the later 14th century due to plague and the silting up of the harbour. In 1400, after a great fire had destroyed over 200 houses in the town, there was even talk of abandoning the town altogether, and Hythe had clearly reached its lowest ebb. However, between the 11th and 13th centuries the town was flourishing, and it is likely that a fairly densely populated 'urban' area extended in a narrow strip along the steep hillside above the shoreline between the churches of St Michael Ashe and St Mary. Fieldwork and excavation in this area is, however, necessary to prove this, and one of the problems of working in the area is the amount of landslipping that has taken place since the Roman period. Recent excavations at Stutfall Castle (Cunliffe 1980b) have highlighted this. It is also important now that the largely unpublished material from 'Sandtun' (mostly in the British Museum) is examined again before a much-needed excavation is carried out on the site.

The elucidation of the past topography of the town and port of New Romney relies even more heavily on the work of the Soil Survey (Green 1968). Unfortunately, both of the relatively recent accounts of the early history of Romney (Ward 1952, and Parkin 1973) have made major errors in the interpretation of the topography of this part of the marsh. Neither of the authors understood the true nature of the Rhee wall (a 13th-century artificially cut channel), and hence a non-existent channel through the Walland Marsh is postulated. The original mid- to late-Saxon estuary does, however, show up very clearly on the Soil Survey map as 'Calcareous Marshland' (Green 1968, 40, Fig. 20; Cunliffe 1980a, 48, Fig. 21) (Fig. 10), and this shows that the settlement of Old Romney was on the south side of this estuary. The planned town of New Romney of c. A.D. 1000 (see below) was, however, situated on a shingle bank that projected into the northern side of this estuary, and it is clear that the estuary had already silted up around Old Romney by this date (Fig. 10), necessitating the move to the new site.

It is possible that Old Romney in the middle Saxon period was already an important trading settlement, but it is more probable that Lydd with its Saxon basilical church (Livett 1930, 72) and associated manor and hundred of Langport (a long market, presumably on the shore protected by shingle bank that later became Dungeness) was the original trading settlement in the area. It may have been a *wic*, but excavation only can resolve this. The origin of New Romney, on the other hand, is now much more certain. It is clear that it was a newly-planned town (Beresford 1967, 459) and Stuart Rigold has shown convincingly from the evidence of the mint at New Romney that the town was probably planted on the site in Aethelraed's reign (the earliest coins are of the 'long-cross' type, 997–1003) with a mint, market-place and probably the regular grid of streets (Rigold, n. 7 in Parkin 1973, 118). The market, a wider street, was probably at the east end of the present main street (just east of St Martin's church in Fig. 10), and the mint, which lasted at least until Henry I's time, must have been close by. Again, excavation is needed to find out more details; in this

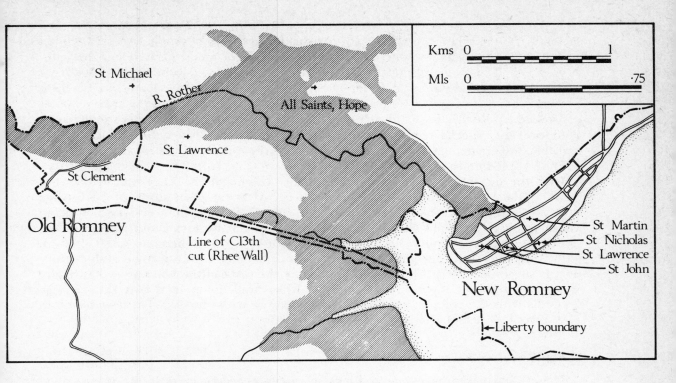

10. Anglo-Saxon Romney, with 'Calcareous Marshland' (the original Saxon estuary of
the River Rother) shaded

connection it should be borne in mind that all pre-1287 levels lie under a 2-3ft. layer of shingle and silt that covered the town as a result of the great storm at this date.

The land around New Romney had belonged originally to the nunnery at Lyminge (Sawyer, No. 21), but by the 10th century the nunnery had gone (presumably destroyed by Vikings) and all its property had passed to the archbishop. It is he who would have planned the new port and borough here in c. A.D. 1000, with the king's permission. In 1052 it was already recorded in the *Anglo-Saxon Chronicle* as having an important port for ships. By the time of the Norman Conquest it was clearly flourishing, and was the first place to be 'disciplined' by William after the battle of Hastings. Domesday Book also shows a relatively large borough here, though the details are uncertain. Eighty-five burgesses are recorded from the archbishop's manor at Aldington, 21 burgesses from the archbishop's knight's fee manor of Langport, and 50 burgesses from what had been the bishop of Bayeux's manor of Langport. The knight in question was Robert of Romney, the first of the Norman rulers of the town. Domesday Book also incidentally mentions ship-service to the king, and as with Dover, Sandwich and Hythe it became one of the original Cinque Ports. By about 1300, the town was at its height with 12 wards, five parish churches, a hospital, and a cell (the priory) of Pontigny abbey being recorded. At the same time the liberty boundaries of New Romney in the form in which they survived until the 19th century (Fig. 10) had clearly been established. This remarkable area (Scott Robertson 1880), which had extended as a thin strip from the open sea with the town and haven of New Romney at one end, to a large open marshland area west of Appledore at the other end, included the whole of the line of the Rhee Wall (or the 'lande betwene the walls' as it is called in a description of the liberty in 1565—Scott Robertson 1880, 269), and a larger area around Old Romney (Fig. 10). This area was clearly, in the 13th century, the area of water controlled by the town, and is similar to the areas of water controlled by Rochester, Sandwich, and Fordwich (see above). It is more than likely, therefore, that special rights over this area also go back to just before the Conquest, and that the original liberty covered the whole of the estuary of the River Rother from west of Appledore to the mouth near the new town (Fig. 10).

With the digging of the new channel along the line of the Rhee wall in the 13th century, the boundary would have been moved. After the great storm of 1287 when the course of the Rother was changed to its present line (along the west side of Walland Marsh passing Rye), the channel quickly silted up till disputes about whose responsibility it was led to an official enquiry in 1565 (Scott Robertson 1880, 270-1). After this, the significance of the Rhee wall was gradually lost until some 19th-century writers suggested it was a Roman sea wall. Only the work of the Soil Survey has finally once again resolved this, showing that the Rhee 'wall' is, in fact, two 13th-century sea walls with the compacted silts of the channel in between, and that it was built in two stages before and after 1257 (Green 1968, 40).

Milton Regis and Faversham

These two places have many things in common. They were both ancient royal demesnes situated just off Watling Street beside north coast tidal inlets (see Figs. 11 and 12). Both were almost certainly *villae regales* whose origins can be taken back to the 6th century. At Faversham, in a field significantly known as the King's Field, was one of the richest Anglo-Saxon pagan cemeteries in the whole of Kent (Meaney 1964, 118). Unfortunately, the cemetery was cut through by the railway from 1855 onwards and virtually no proper records of its contents survive. There is, however, a remarkable collection (mostly in the British Museum) of gold and garnet jewellery as well as of many other items which almost certainly came from this area (Jessup 1974, 12), and this clearly shows what a rich settlement Faversham was and how much vital information has been lost. If any site in Kent could be compared to Sutton Hoo, it is surely Faversham.

An important group of pagan Anglo-Saxon material has also come from Milton (or Middleton). Unlike Faversham with its one large cemetery, however, Milton had five or more distinct cemeteries (Rigold 1970, 3), at least one of which has produced some fine jewellery. Both Faversham and Milton have also produced many scattered Roman occupation and cemetery sites. Some of these sites are beside Watling Street, while others are beside the tidal inlet near the later Anglo-Saxon settlement (Philp 1965). If there is to be any continuity proved between the latest 5th-century Roman and the earliest 'Jutish' sites in Kent, it is most likely to be at sites like these, and not at Roman towns like Canterbury.

The place-name Faversham is said to be derived from *faefersham* 'the village of the smith', the word coming from the Latin, *faber* (Gelling 1978, 80). Does this imply

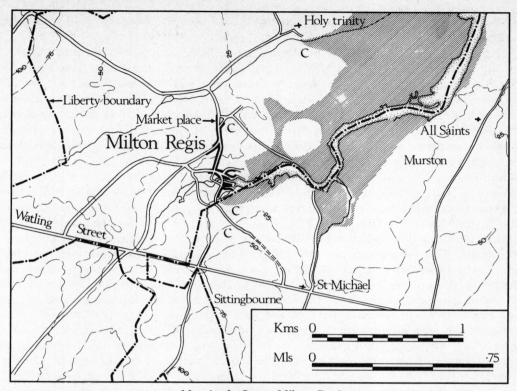

11. Anglo-Saxon Milton Regis

12. Anglo-Saxon Faversham. (N.B. Marshland areas shaded)

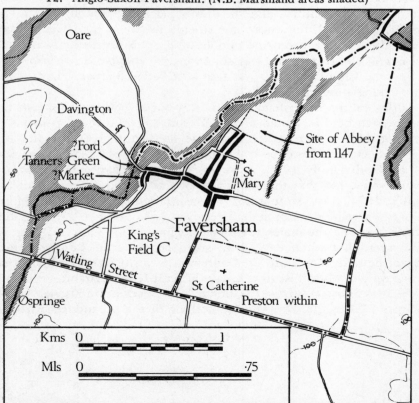

late Roman smiths who have a connection with the 6th-century gold and garnet jewellery?

On the eve of the arrival of St Augustine in 597, Aethelberht is most likely to have used *villae regales* such as Milton, Faversham, Sturry, and Eastry (Hawkes 1970) as his main centres (Fig. 1), not least because they were natural havens for the ships (like the Sutton Hoo vessel) that were his most important means of communication. Of these *villae regales* only Milton and Faversham appear to have become proto-towns.

During the 7th and 8th centuries, the importance of these sites must have continued, though excavations to find the middle Saxon settlements have yet to be carried out. The hoard of 20 early 8th-century *sceattas* from Milton (Hawkes and Grove 1963, 23; Rigold 1977a, 43), and a middle Saxon loom weight from Faversham (Grove 1955, 208) are as yet tantalisingly the only evidence for these. By the early 9th century the great royal demesne at Faversham was clearly being divided up, and charters of 811–15 (Sawyer, Nos. 168, 169, 170, 177, 178 and 1617) show Cenwulf of Mercia granting land 'in the region suburban to the King's *ton*' to Wulfred, archbishop of Canterbury. This is presumably why there was later a very complicated system of parish boundaries with many detached portions 'within' and 'without' Faversham right up to the present century (Ward 1934). The rectangular area of Preston Within, with its own separate church, in the south-eastern part of the later municipal borough (Fig. 12) is in all probability part of the estate given in 811 to Wulfred. The name Preston is just 'the priests' *ton*'. Are these priests perhaps the monks of Christ Church, Canterbury? Ospringe, Luddenham and Davington as well as Preston were also probably parts of the royal estate that had been parcelled out before the Norman Conquest.

At Milton the pattern is not similar, but the attack by the Danes in 893 (as recorded in the *Anglo-Saxon Chronicle*) shows that Milton, too, was an important royal settlement in the 9th century, and that both places were well on the way to being urban centres, if, indeed, they were not already so, when their trading patterns were disrupted by the Vikings. From the middle of the 9th century onward Viking attack along this part of the Kent coast was common; the *Anglo-Saxon Chronicle* states, for example, that the Isle of Sheppey was first attacked in 835, and that it was the winter base for the Viking army in 855 (Fig. 1).

In the 10th century Faversham at least was once again an important royal centre, at which Athelstan held a council in 930. Despite this, however, it seems that neither Faversham nor Milton were quite towns at the Norman Conquest. Milton would certainly have been in disarray as it had last been attacked and burned as recently as 1052 by Earl Godwin. By 1086, however, Faversham had a market worth £4, and Domesday Book implies that there was also one at Milton as well as at Hythe (Darby and Campbell 1971, 554), so that both towns again were on the verge of urban status, though it was Faversham, once it had received King Stephen's royal abbey in 1147, which actually became the major town and a Cinque Port limb of Dover. It should be noticed, however, that when Faversham got a charter from Edward I, he ratified its customs from the time of Edward the Confessor (Beresford and Finberg 1973, 128).

The topography of Milton Regis is today difficult to understand, because the ancient town has been swallowed up by the much later roadside industrial town of Sitting-bourne (Rigold 1968, 11). However, something of the pre-industrial topography can be gained by studying the 18th-century maps (Rigold 1970, 3 and Fig. 1). These show (Fig. 11) that Milton had three separate parts: the isolated church on the north-east; the triangular market-place (with its surviving late-medieval timber-framed court hall in the middle), roughly at the centre of the town; and running south from this the street to the port area at the end of the tidal inlet off the Swale, the channel dividing the Isle of Sheppey from the mainland (Fig. 11). All this suggests a once much larger town and that the site of the earliest settlement, the *villa regis*, was perhaps near the the church. Just to the south of the church was a 6th-century pagan cemetery (No. 2 in Rigold 1970, 18), and another early cemetery underlies the later market-place (Rigold 1968, 12; No. 1 in Rigold 1970, 18). The best recorded of the Anglo-Saxon cemeteries (No. 3 in Rigold 1970, 18), which lies to the south of the port on both sides of the track, and which contained the very fine 'Vallance' disc-brooch (stolen from the Dover Museum in 1967) is certainly 7th century in date. It seems probable that this cemetery related to the expanding trading settlement. The triangular market-place to the north is presumably the one implied in Domesday Book, and late Saxon in origin. Again, it is important that excavation should be carried out in the town, particularly in the area between the church and the market-place, largely built on in recent years, so that the growth of the Anglo-Saxon settlement may be understood.

In turning to the topography of Faversham, it is also imporant to look at pre-industrial maps, and here Jacob's fine map of the borough in his *History of Faversham* (Jacob 1774) is very useful indeed (Fig. 12). Is is clear that the original axis of the town is the street running roughly parallel to Watling Street (today called West and East Streets) which presumably crossed the head of the Faversham tidal inlet at a ford, today the site of Stone Bridge. To the west of this, two tracks lead off up Davington Hill, one running north-west to Oare (on another tidal inlet), and the other to Luddenham and Teynham. To the east, the track continues to Graveney and Seasalter. Connecting this track with Watling Street are three other tracks. One heads diagonally from Ospringe (now Ospringe Road and South Road) with another track (now St Ann's Road) joining it. A second track, Preston Street, runs more directly between the two main east-west streets, while a third (Love Lane) which runs along a ridge forms the eastern boundary of the later borough. Between St Ann's Street and Preston Street, and not far south of West Street, is the King's Field, the site of the great Anglo-Saxon cemetery. It seems likely therefore that the earliest part of the town was in the area between the King's Field and the head of the tidal inlet centring on West Street and its back lane, Tanner Street.

The very wide Court Street and its continuation, Abbey Street, which connected the site of the great royal abbey (founded by King Stephen in 1147) with East and West Streets, may only date from the 12th century. It was certainly the site of the large later medieval and post-medieval street market, hence the greater width of the street. The Domesday market was perhaps at Tanner's Green, where the old Guildhall stood until 1571 (Jacob 1774, 61). East of Court Street is the parish church, which also perhaps only dates from the 12th century, and on the west back lanes connect Court Street with the later medieval quays on the tidal inlet. It is interesting that documents dating from Edward III's time still speak of the 'Old' and 'New' town (Jacob 1774, 15).

The area of the later municipal borough, which in origin is presumably pre-Norman, is triangular in shape and is bounded by a stream and the tidal inlet on the north-west, Watling Street on the south, and an almost straight line on the east. This area, which was largely good arable land until the 19th century contains the parishes of Faversham Within and Preston Within. As has already been shown, Preston was probably cut out of this area in the early 9th century. The surrounding hundred of Faversham, which was later divided into 18 parishes perhaps represents the full extend of the original royal estate (Hasted 1798, VI, 317), just as the great hundred of Milton perhaps also represents the original royal estate there.

Seasalter

This is perhaps the most puzzling of all the towns in Kent. In Domesday Book it is called a *parvus burgus* belonging to the archbishop's kitchen and held from the monks (of Christ Church) by Blize. A church and eight fisheries were also recorded (Darby and Campbell 1971, 554). Domesday Monachorum (Douglas 1944, 90) does not mention the archbishop, but tells us that 'Saesealtre est burgus monachorum et de cibo et proprie de coquina eorum'. At this time a certain Blittaere held it from the monks, and it is also recorded that the manor is in no hundred. It was still a liberty not in any hundred until the 19th century (Hasted 1798, VIII, 499). No burgesses, however, are mentioned, so what sort of borough does it represent? The most important clues are first its name, Seasalter, which suggests that it was closely connected with the marketing of salt, and that it supplied the archbishop and the monks with food, presumably seafood—hence the eight fisheries mentioned in Domesday Book. The fact that, like Fordwich and Sandwich, it was a liberty on its own also suggests that it had a special status.

Topographically, Seasalter is a small parish a few miles north-east of Faversham (Fig. 13) which must, at some time in the middle Saxon period, have been cut out of the north-west corner of the Blean, a royal forest. On the east it is bounded by Whitstable Street (the main street of the post-medieval town of Whitstable), while on the south-west there was a large marshland area (drained and protected by a sea wall in the 14th century—Thompson 1956, 47). In this area (Fig. 13) were presumably situated the *salinae* (salt works) which gave the borough its name, though strangely enough no salt works are mentioned at Seasalter in Domesday Book, while seven are recorded for Whitstable and four for Graveney. Salt working is, however, mentioned at Seasalter in two 8th-century charters (Sawyer Nos. 123 and 125). Fieldwork and excavations in 1955–6 (Thompson 1956) were able to show that 13th-century salt works existed in Graveney marshes, Hernhill marshes, and in the Seasalter level (Fig. 13). Graveney marshes, which are close to Seasalter, have also produced the famous 10th-century boat (Fenwick 1978) which was deeply buried in marsh clay on the edge of an old tidal creek. On the north Seasalter has been considerably eroded away, and it is quite likely that the Saxo-Norman borough and the church recorded in Domesday Book may have been destroyed by the sea. Hasted (1798, VIII, 503) records that a great storm in 1779 uncovered the foundations and surrounding graveyard of a church on the beach to the north of Seasalter, which may have been the centre of the borough. However, the 13th-century chancel of an

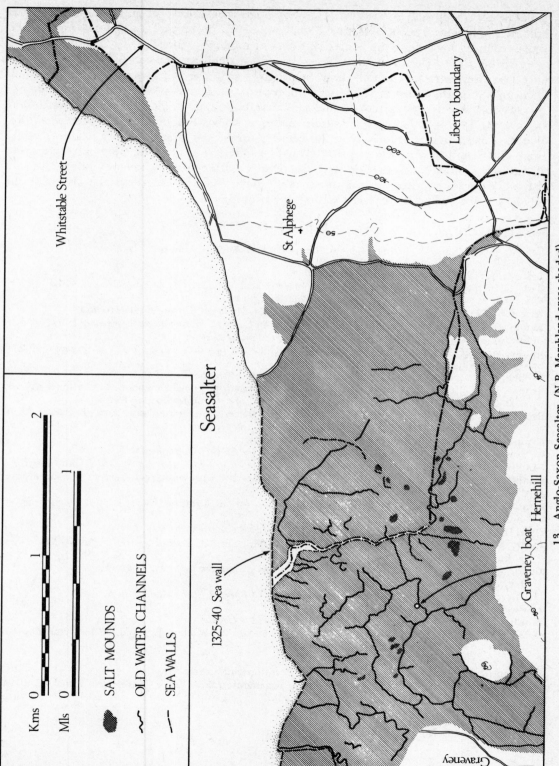

Whitstable Street

St Alphege †

Seasalter

Liberty boundary

1325–40 Sea wall

Graveney boat

Hernehill

Graveney

Kms 0   1   2

Mls 0   1

▮ SALT MOUNDS

∿ OLD WATER CHANNELS

– – SEA WALLS

13. Anglo-Saxon Seasalter. (N.B. Marshland areas shaded)

isolated parish church dedicated to St Alphege (the nave was pulled down in 1845) still exists further south, and this equally may be the centre of the old borough; it must certainly have been the centre of the later medieval village.

It seems likely therefore that Seasalter was a small late Saxon borough where salt and fish were traded, which had been given by the king to the archbishop of Canterbury, perhaps in the 9th or 10th century. It is just possible that the dredging of oysters, which was later to make Whitstable famous, had already started here before the Norman Conquest, which makes a suggestion of R. H. Goodsall (1938) that the name Whitstable is Norman-French for *huitre staple* (oyster market) rather than Old English for 'white post' (Ward 1944, 53) quite plausible. Oysters were apparently found in association with the nearby 10th-century Graveney boat. The salt, fish and oyster market would presumably have been situated on the shore at the north-western end of the present Whitstable High Street.

BIBLIOGRAPHY

Abbreviations: *Arch. Cant. = Archaeologia Cantiana*

Ballard, A. (1904), *The Domesday Boroughs.*
Bede, *A History of the English Church and People* (trans. and ed. by L. Sherley-Price, 1955).
Beresford, M. W. (1967), *New Towns of the Middle Ages.*
Beresford, M. W., and Finberg, H. P. R. (1973), *English Medieval Boroughs—A Handlist.*
Biddle, M. (1970), 'The earthworks around St Mary-in-Castro', *Archaeological Journal*, 126, 264–5.
Biddle, M. (1972), in Heighway, C. M. (ed.), *The Erosion of History.*
Biddle, M. (1976), 'Towns', in Wilson, D. M. (ed.), *The Archaeology of Anglo-Saxon England*, 99–150.
Boys, W. (1792), *Collections for a History of Sandwich in Kent, etc.*
Brooke, C. N. L. and Keir, G. (1975), *London 800-1216, The Shaping of a City.*
Brooks, N. P. (1971), 'The development of military obligations in eighth- and ninth-century England', in Clemoes, P., and Hughes, K. (eds.), *England before the Conquest*, 69–84.
Brooks, N. P. (1977), 'The ecclesiastical topography of early medieval Canterbury', in Barley, M. W. (ed.), *European Towns, their Archaeology and Early History.*
Campbell, A. (1973), *Anglo-Saxon Charters I, Rochester.*
Colgrave, B. (1927), (ed.), *The Life of Bishop Wilfred by Eddius Stephanus.*
Cunliffe, B. W. (1968), (ed.), *Fifth Report of the Excavations of the Roman Fort at Richborough.*
Cunliffe, B. W. (1980a), 'The evolution of Romney Marsh: a preliminary statement', in Thompson, F. H. (ed.), *Archaeology and Coastal Change*, 37–55.
Cunliffe, B. W. (1980b), 'Excavations at the Roman fort at Lympne, Kent, 1976–8', *Britannia* XI, 227–88.
Dale, H. D. (1931), *The Ancient Town of Hythe and St Leonard's Church.*
Darby, H. C. and Campbell, E. M. J. (eds.) (1971), 'Kent', in *The Domesday Geography of South-East England*, 483–562.
Davis, W. H. (1934), *William Thorne's Chronicle of St Augustine's Abbey, Canterbury.*
Dolley, R. H. M. (1964), *Anglo-Saxon Pennies.*
Douglas, D. C. (1944), *The Domesday Monachorum of Christ Church, Canterbury.*
Fenwick, V. (1978), *The Graveney Boat.*
Fordham, S. J., and Green, R. D. (1973), *Soils in Kent II (Deal).*
Frere, S. S. (1966), 'The end of towns in Roman Britain', in Wacher, J. S. (ed.), *The Civitas Capitals of Roman Britain*, 87–100.
Gelling, M. (1978), *Signposts to the Past.*
Goodsall, R. H. (1938), *History of Whitstable, Seasalter and Swalecliffe.*
Graham-Campbell, J. (1978), 'An Anglo-Saxon ornamented knife from Canterbury, Kent', *Medieval Archaeology* 22, 130–3.
Green, R. D. (1968), *Soils of Romney Marsh.*

Grove, L. D. A. (1955), 'Archaeological notes from Maidstone Museum', *Arch. Cant.* 69, 208–10.

Harrison, A. C., and Flight, C. (1968), 'The Roman and medieval defences of Rochester in the light of recent excavations', *Arch. Cant.* 83, 55–104.

Harrison, A. C., and Williams, D. (1979), 'Excavations at Prior's Gate House, Rochester, 1976–7', *Arch. Cant.* 95, 19–36.

Hasted, E. (1797–1801), *The History and Topographical Survey of the County of Kent* (2nd edn.).

Hawkes, S. C. (1970), 'Early Anglo-Saxon Kent', *Archaeological Journal* 126, 186–192.

Hawkes, S. C., and Grove, L. D. A. (1963), 'Finds from a seventh-century Anglo-Saxon cemetery at Milton Regis', *Arch. Cant.* 78, 22–78.

Hawkes, S. C., *et al.* (1979), 'A seventh-century bronze metalworker's die from Rochester, Kent', *Frumittelalterliche Studien* 13, 382-92.

Jacob, E. (1774), *The History of Faversham.*

Jessup, R. F. (1974), *Anglo-Saxon Jewellery.*

Lambarde, W. (1570), *A Perambulation of Kent.*

Livett, G. M. (1889), 'Foundations of the Saxon cathedral church at Rochester', *Arch. Cant.* 18, 261–78.

Livett, G. M. (1895), 'Medieval Rochester', *Arch. Cant.* 21, 17–72.

Loyn, H. R. (1962), *Anglo-Saxon England and the Norman Conquest.*

Meaney, A. (1964), *A Gazetteer of early Anglo-Saxon Burial Sites.*

Oakley, A. (1975), 'The cathedral priory of St Andrew, Rochester', *Arch. Cant.* 91, 47–60.

Parkin, E. W. (1970), 'Perambulation of Sandwich', *Archaeological Journal* 126, 220–1.

Parkin, E. W. (1973), 'The ancient buildings of New Romney', *Arch. Cant.* 88, 117–28.

Payne, G. (1895), 'Roman Rochester', *Arch. Cant.* 21, 1–16.

Philp, B. (1965), *Excavations at Faversham, 1965.*

Potts, R. V. (1943), 'St Mildred's church, Canterbury: further notes on the site', *Arch. Cant.* 56, 19–22.

Radford, C. A. R. (1970), 'St Mildred's church', *Archaeological Journal* 126, 237.

Reynolds, S. (1977), *An Introduction to the History of English Medieval Towns.*

Rigold, S. E. (1968), 'Two types of court hall', *Arch. Cant.* 83, 1–122.

Rigold, S. E. (1970a), 'Three Anglo-Saxon disc-brooches', *Arch. Cant.* 85, 1–18.

Rigold, S. E. (1970b), 'The Roman haven at Dover', *Archaeological Journal* 126, 78–100.

Rigold, S. E. (1977a), 'The principal series of English *sceattas* and a check list of English finds of *sceattas*', *British Numismatic Chronicle* 47, 21–52.

Rigold, S. E. (1977b), 'Litus Romanum—The shore forts as mission stations', in Johnston, D. E. (ed), *The Saxon Shore.*

Robinson, A. H. W., and Cloet, R. L., 'Coastal evolution in Sandwich Bay', *Proceedings of the Geologists Association* 64, 69–80.

St John Hope, W. H. (1898), 'The architectural history of the cathedral church and monastery at Rochester', *Arch. Cant.* 23, 194–238.

St John Hope, W. H. (1900), 'The architectural history of the cathedral church and monastery at Rochester', *Arch. Cant.* 24, 1–85.

Sawyer, P. H. (1968) (ed.), *Anglo-Saxon Charters, an Annotated List and Bibliography.*

Scott Robertson, W. A. (1880), 'The Cinque Port liberty of Romney', *Arch. Cant.* 13, 261-80.

Stenton, F. M. (1971), *Anglo-Saxon England* (3rd edn.).

Tatton-Brown, T. W. T. (1980), 'Canterbury's urban topography; some recent work', in P. Riden (ed.), *The Medieval Town in Britain* (Gregynog seminars in local history, I, Cardiff), 85–98.

Taylor, H. M. and J. (1965), *Anglo-Saxon Architecture*, 214-7.

Thompson, M. W. (1956), 'A group of mounds on Seasalter level, near Whitstable', *Arch. Cant.* 70, 44–67.

Urry, W. (1967), *Canterbury under the Angevin Kings.*

Urry, W. (1975), 'A list of Fordwich burgesses in A.D. 1111', in McIntosh, K. (ed.), *Fordwich, the lost port*, 136–8.

Ward, G. (1931), 'Sand Tunes Boc', *Arch. Cant.* 43, 39–48.

Ward, G. (1933a), 'The river Limen at Ruckinge', *Arch. Cant.* 45, 129–32.

Ward, G. (1933b), 'The Saxon charters of Burmarsh', *Arch. Cant.* 45, 133–141.

Ward, G. (1934), 'The topography of some Saxon charters relating to the Faversham district', *Arch. Cant.* 46, 123–36.

Ward, G. (1941), 'The age of St Mildred's church, Canterbury', *Arch. Cant.* 54, 62–8.

Ward, G. (1944), 'The origins of Whitstable', *Arch. Cant.* 57, 51–5.

Ward, G. (1949), 'A note on the Mead Way. The Street and Doddinghyrman in Rochester', *Arch. Cant.* 62, 37–44.

Ward, G. (1951), 'Dudda's land in Canterbury', *Arch. Cant.* 64, 13–19.

Ward, G. (1952), 'The Saxon history of the town and port of Romney', *Arch. Cant.* 65, 12–25.

Whitelock, D. (ed.) (1979), *English Historical Documents* I (2nd edn.).

Woodcock, A. M. (1956), (ed.), 'Cartulary of the priory of St Gregory, Canterbury', *Camden Third Series*, 88.

Woodruff, C. E. (1895), *History of the Town and Port of Fordwich*.

Chapter Two

THE TOWNS OF SURREY

By Martin O'Connell and Rob Poulton

THE BOUNDARIES of the modern administrative county of Surrey differ in a number of respects from those of the historic county (Fig. 15) which were almost identical with those suggested by Domesday Book. The most significant changes are those in the north, where, firstly a large area of the old county now forms part of Greater London, and, secondly, the district of Spelthorne (formerly part of Middlesex) is now included in Surrey. The following review of the evidence from Saxon towns covers the whole of the area within both the historic and administrative counties. An exception is, however, made in the case of Southwark which is more logically considered with London (Chapter 9).

Some general points with regard to the topography and geology of this area must be made (Fig. 14 gives the geology, while the main hills and rivers form the background to the other county maps). Four major natural areas may be defined (*cf.* Atkins and Salnow 1975, 1–17; Lloyd 1962, 401–5). In the north the London basin includes a relatively fertile area of London Clay interspersed with river gravels, and the infertile region occupied by Bagshot sands. The southern boundary of these lands is clearly defined by the North Downs, which are quite wide in the east, but narrow considerably to the west. This chalk outcrop forms a barrier to easy north-south communications, with a corresponding emphasis on its river and dry gaps.[1] Between the Downs and the Weald is an area dominated by Lower Greensand deposits, but with considerable variation both in relief and fertility. Finally, the Wealden Clay occupies much of the south of the county and must have been comparatively thinly populated in the Saxon period. The almost empty wilderness suggested by Domesday Book (only two places are named within the Weald) is, however, undoubtedly misleading (Sawyer 1976), as Brandon's essay (1978) on the South Saxon *Andredesweald* indicates.

The transition from Roman to Saxon Surrey is as yet imperfectly understood, but before considering this difficult phase some of the major elements of the Roman period of occupation should first be briefly summarised (Fig. 15). Two principal highways crossed the county and belonged to the important road network that was probably developed soon after A.D. 43, radiating from London. The roads linked London with Silchester and Chichester (Stane Street). Other roads that passed through Surrey were probably a later development and included the London to Brighton and London to Lewes roads. These two routes connected the capital of the province with the south coast and the rich corn-growing region of the South Downs as well as forming a link with the iron-working communities of the Weald (Margary 1967). Two posting stations have been found on the line of Stane Street in Sussex at Hardham and Alfoldean, and two more are thought to have existed on

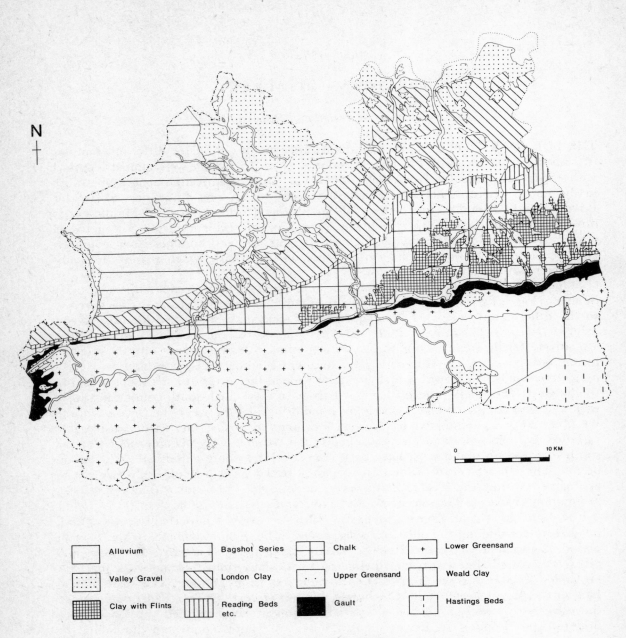

14. Surrey: major geological divisions

Legend:
- Alluvium
- Valley Gravel
- Clay with Flints
- Bagshot Series
- London Clay
- Reading Beds etc.
- Chalk
- Upper Greensand
- Gault
- Lower Greensand
- Weald Clay
- Hastings Beds

N

0   10 KM

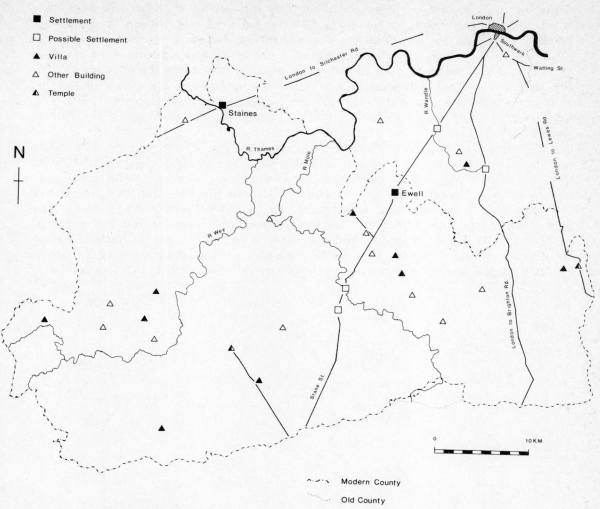

- ■ Settlement
- □ Possible Settlement
- ▲ Villa
- △ Other Building
- ◮ Temple

15. Surrey: principal Roman remains

the section of Stane Street in Surrey. Various sites have been suggested, but probably the two likeliest put forward are Burford Bridge and Merton (Neale 1973). Roadside settlements are thought possible at Croydon and Dorking where Roman material has been found. More recently excavations at Dorking have produced evidence of Romano-British occupation close to the line of Stane Street proposed by Margary (V. Ettlinger, pers. comm.).

No cantonal capital is known in the area considered, and the only settlements that show signs of urbanism are Ewell and Staines. At Ewell the site straddled Stane Street, covering an area estimated at 6 hectares (15 acres) (Sheldon and Schaaf 1978, 68). Frere (1975, 4–7) classifies Ewell as a small town, but Sheldon and Schaaf's description of a 'roadside village' seems more appropriate on available evidence. There is no indication of deliberate planning or an organised street pattern, and although Pemberton (1973, 86) has suggested that the settlement was enclosed his evidence is by no means conclusive. A Romano-British community appears to have been still in existence at the end of the 4th century, and possibly lasted into the 5th century. The first indication of a Saxon presence consists of a large 6th-century mixed inhumation and cremation cemetery within the area of Roman settlement (Morris, 1959). This suggests that there was no continuity of organised settlement between the Roman and Saxon periods.

At Staines (Fig. 16) the evidence is both more substantial and complex. The place is referred to as *Pontes* in the *Antonine Itinerary,* suggesting the existence of more than one bridge—presumably one across the Thames and the second across the Colne—and from its inclusion in the same document it seems probable that the site enjoyed the status of a posting station (Crouch 1976, 72-3). Recent excavations have demonstrated that the settlement developed during the later 1st and 2nd centuries on a small raised area of gravel, and was centred on the London to Silchester road, close to the bridge across the Thames. No evidence of formal planning has been found, but at least one internal street has been postulated (Crouch 1976, 74). It seems likely

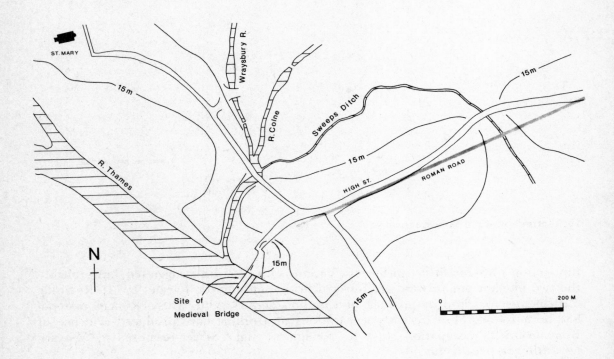

16. Staines: town plan, based on the O.S. first edition. The medieval bridge rather than its early 19th-century replacement is shown

that Staines was a centre for the production of lead-glazed pottery in the 1st and 2nd centuries, utilising the Thames for the distribution of the ware eastwards (Arthur 1978, 298–301). A period of contraction and decline followed in the 3rd century when flooding affected the occupied area to the south of the main street; soon afterwards much of this land was used for agricultural purposes. Although the character of the settlement had probably changed in the late Roman period there is still evidence of occupation and rebuilding in the 4th century (Crouch 1978).

It is now certain that a Saxon community was present at Staines in the 5th century, but not clear how it related to the late Roman settlement. Finds include two early 5th-century Saxon spearheads, at least three possible *grubenhäuser* together with early Saxon pottery and a 5th- or 6th-century iron-working area (Crouch 1978, 186). It is not possible to be certain whether this settlement began before or after the formal separation of Britain from Rome. Morris (1973, 109) has suggested that the early Saxon cemeteries at Croydon and Mitcham indicate the presence of communities deliberately settled to safeguard the approaches to London. The same explanation may well apply to the early Saxons in Staines, as also, perhaps, at nearby Shepperton, where an early 5th-century cemetery has been discovered at Upper West Field (Longley and Poulton, forthcoming).

Staines can be considered to have enjoyed urban status at least by the beginning of the 13th century and had elements of urbanism before that date. Although the area to the south of the main road was again subject to flooding in the early Saxon period, and, indeed, reverted to agricultural land between the 9th and 12th centuries, recent work indicates that the High Street remained the centre of occupation throughout the Saxon period. The parish church of St Mary is situated some distance to the north-west of the town and occupies a small area of high ground which was known as Binbury in the 14th century. This place-name (*cf.* Smith 1956,59–60) may well refer to the manor house believed to have stood in the vicinity, the presence of which could explain the siting of the church. It is not known when this area was first occupied, but some degree of settlement is attested in the 14th century (Reynolds, 1962, 16).

The discovery of imported red-painted pottery from the Continent (Pingsdorf Ware) and an 11th- to 13th-century wharf (Crouch 1976, 114 and pers. comm.) point to the early commercial development of Staines with its dependency on through traffic along the major route ways of the Thames and the London road. The settlement had a market before 1218, and the market area occupied a site close to the bridge across the Thames. Staines did not enjoy borough status in the Middle Ages, and the 46 burgesses mentioned in the Domesday account of the manor were probably based at London (Campbell 1962, 131). Nevertheless, the number of burgesses provided by Staines must reflect the relative importance of the community and also demonstrates a significant link between it and the capital (Jones, forthcoming).

The above discussion of Staines has in the interests of clarity anticipated the argument, and it is now necessary to return to the early Saxon period (Fig. 17). The archaeological discoveries are almost entirely funerary. They indicate that the earliest settlements lie in an arc drawn around London, and that settlements in the centre and south of the county only developed from the 6th century onwards. For the period after the coming of Christianity archaeological evidence is extremely sparse,

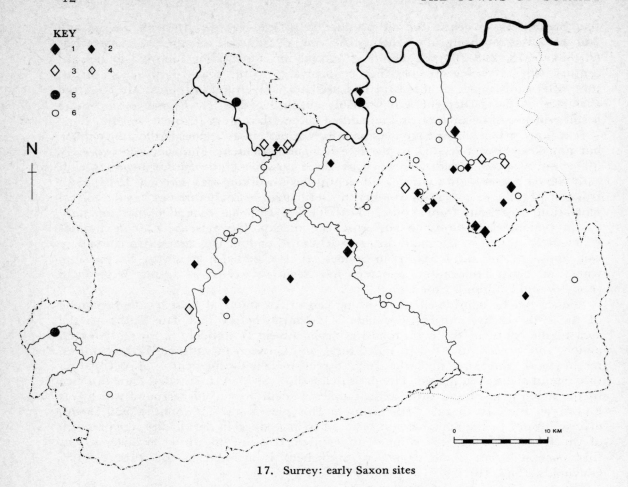

KEY

17. Surrey: early Saxon sites

	No. of Burials	
Inhumation	More than 10	Less than 10
Inhumation Cemetery	1	2
Inhumation + Cremation Cemetery	3	4
Settlement Site 5		Unassociated Find 6

as is the documentary evidence. In these circumstances it is not surprising that in the early and middle Saxon period no site shows any convincing evidence for urban status. In the later period the evidence improves, though remaining fragmentary, and a number of places may be identified as possible sites of Saxon towns, using a variety of approaches to the problem.

Contemporary written evidence for Saxon towns in Surrey is extremely slender. The Burghal Hidage (Hill 1969; Biddle and Hill 1971) lists only *Escingum* in Surrey. The name has long been accepted as referring to Eashing (Fig. 20) and the exact site of the burh has now been identified there (Aldsworth and Hill 1971). It effectively occupies a defensively strong promontory site, ill-suited for commercial purposes, and in view of its short existence (see below) is therefore probably a fort, rather than a town. The site is now open land.

Domesday Book suggests that two places were towns—Southwark (considered in Chapter 9) and Guildford (*see also* Staines, above). Guildford is not described in any detail in Domesday Book. For our purposes the important information is that 'King William has 75 sites, whereon dwell 175 men. Before 1066 they paid £18 0s. 3d.; now they are assessed at £30; however, they pay £32' (translation from Morris [ed.], 1975, 1). Domesday Book makes no mention, however, of the mint known to have existed from the silver pennies of kings from Ethelred (or possibly Edward the Martyr) to William Rufus (Guildford Corporation 1957, 5 and 32-3). This evidence clearly suggests that in the 10th and 11th centuries Guildford was a commercial centre. The problem now is to relate this documentary and numismatic evidence to the topography of the town.

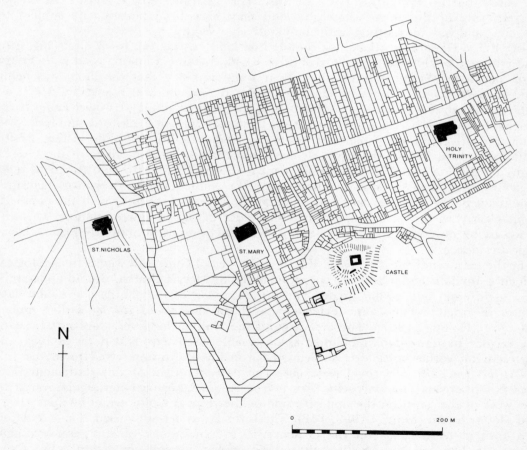

18. Guildford: town plan, based on the O.S. first edition

Figs. 18 and 19 illustrate and interpret the plan of Guildford as it appeared in the mid-19th century. In essentials this plan is unchanged from that shown in 1748 on Richardson's 'Ichthnography of the town of Guildford' (figured in Sprules *et al.* 1911, opposite 548). The main elements of that plan are a main thoroughfare (High Street), which leads to a bridge crossing the Wey, with long narrow plots fronting on to it on both sides. These plots are limited on either side by North Street and by Sydenham Road with its continuation, Castle Street. This last seems to form an intrusive element in an otherwise coherent plan. Since the castle is almost certainly late 11th century in origin (Renn 1968) this means that the plan is that of the late Saxon town.

In 1606 a reference to the 'highway called the North Town Ditch'[2] indicates the process of transmutation to North Street, while the South Town Ditch preceded Sydenham Road. The major missing part of this enclosing ditch is probably indicated on Richardson's map as a path through Holy Trinity churchyard, which is also the only place where the ditch has been observed, during building work (Sprules, *et al.* 1911, 5, 47). Clearly Guildford must formerly have had an earthen bank on the inside of the ditch, but no evidence survives of this.[3] The ditch probably did not exist on the western side of the town where the land may have been marshy and subject to flooding, and was not built on until comparatively recently.

In 1275 a Dominican friary was founded on land outside the town ditch (Fig. 19). The entrance to this was from Woodbridge Road,[4] making a linking road with Friary Lane necessary. Since at this early date it seems unlikely that the ditch was being used as a road, this suggests that a road already existed which was, in effect, an 'intra-mural' street, which was probably also the original status of Friary Lane. If so, it is likely to have been an integral part of the Saxon plan of Guildford, and it may be compared to those at Winchester or, more aptly, Lydford (Biddle 1976, 27–9). Guildford, then, has all the main elements discerned as characteristic of the Wessex burhs of the 9th and 10th centuries: a main thoroughfare with side streets at right angles to it, leading to an intra-mural street, the whole within a defensive enclosure. Cumulatively the documentary and topographic evidence, together with the parallels, point clearly to the town's origin as a single act of Saxon town planning. It must, however, be observed that at no point can this hypothesis be supported by archaeological evidence.

In the circumstances it is ironic that the one area of Guildford where archaeological evidence for late-Saxon activity is forthcoming, St Mary's church, should apparently have a different and earlier origin. The present tower of the church is probably late Saxon in origin, while some evidence has been discovered for an earlier timber structure (Holling 1967). The area around the church, however, does not fit with the regular pattern of plot boundaries observable elsewhere, and it seems likely to represent an earlier nucleated settlement, probably the one referred to in the will of Alfred (*c.* 880) as a royal residence. The date of origin of this settlement is at present unknown. The only clue lies in the Anglo-Saxon cemeteries discovered to the west of the town on the opposite side of the river at Guildown (Lowther 1931) and Mount Street (Morris 1959, 142). The former was certainly used as an execution site until at least 1043 (on the evidence of a coin in one of the graves) though continuity between the two uses is not necessarily implied since the focus of the execution site was almost certainly a barrow.[5]

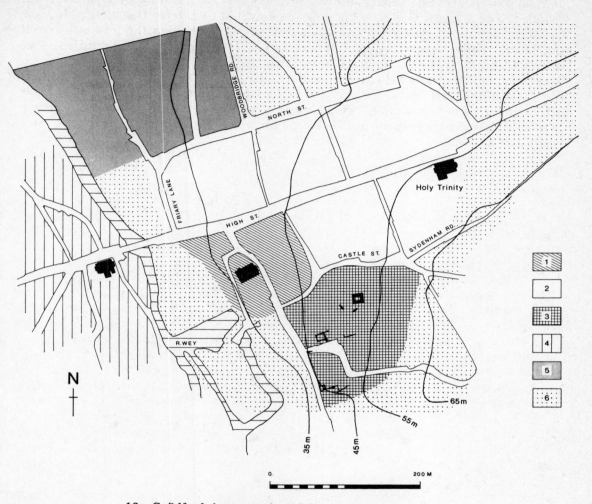

19. Guildford: interpretation of the development sequence

KEY

1. = Primary settlement around St Mary's church
2. = Area of late Saxon planned town
3. = Area of Norman castle
4. = Suburb of St Nicholas (13th century and later)
5. = Precinct of Dominican friary (founded *c.* 1275)
6. = Area of principally post-medieval development

It should be emphasised that the above interpretation is in many respects a tentative one

Finally we must ask when, and therefore by whom, the burh of Guildford was founded. The Burghal Hidage is probably to be dated to *c.* 919 (Hill 1969). In view of the proximity of Guildford and Eashing it seems likely that the former replaced the latter, which means, unless the list was anachronistic when published, that Guildford must have been founded some time after that date. Equally it cannot be later than the first coins minted at Guildford, that is 991 (or possibly 975–9). Edward the Elder (899–924) and Athelstan (924–39) have both been associated with burh development. The connections are, however, tentative and hypothetical, and we cannot in this instance distinguish between them, nor, indeed be certain that a later king is not involved.

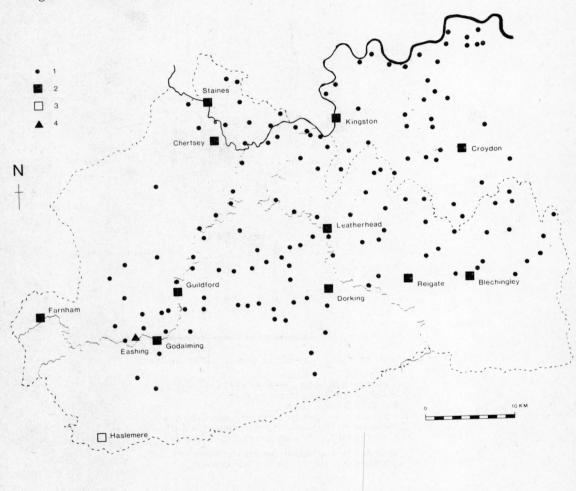

20. Surrey: Domesday Book Settlements

KEY

1. = Settlements named in Domesday Book
2. = Domesday settlements which were towns in the medieval period
3. = Haslemere, a medieval borough, not named in Domesday Book
4. = The burh of Eashing

No other place in Surrey has contemporary evidence for urban status. However, it seems advisable, when so few sources survive, to examine carefully any possible approach. In the medieval period at least 12 towns (excepting Southwark) are known in this area (Fig. 20). Is there topographical or archaeological evidence for an earlier development for any of these? For the 10 towns which lie in the modern adminstrative area of Surrey there is no need to discuss the question in detail. Staines and Guildford have already been examined, and for the others O'Connell (1977) has recently reviewed the evidence and, in brief, found it lacking. While most of these towns were found to have some evidence for pre-Conquest origins, in no case did this amount to an indication of urban or proto-urban status. At Reigate (or more accurately, Cherchefelle) recent excavations (Poulton 1980 and forthcoming) have, perhaps, modified that impression.

The modern and medieval town of Reigate (Fig. 21) is clearly planned around the castle, built in the late 11th century, and excavations in the town have revealed no material earlier than the 13th century (Woods 1974). In Domesday Book, however, the manor in this area is rubricated under Cherchefelle, and that settlement has been thought to be located near the parish church, some 0.5km. distant from Reigate town centre. This has now been confirmed by recent excavations at the Old Vicarage site (Fig. 22), which have uncovered features dated by the pottery and an archaeomagnetic date of 950 to 1150 (at single standard error) to the Saxo-Norman period. The pattern revealed is one of a complex of rubbish pits, post-holes and indications of minor industrial working. This is clearly de-limited by plot boundaries marked on the east by a ditch, on the north by shallow gullies, and on the west by five pits in a line, which obviously respect a boundary not traceable by excavation. The plot must surely have fronted on to Church Street. Long narrow plots with intensive utilisation of the

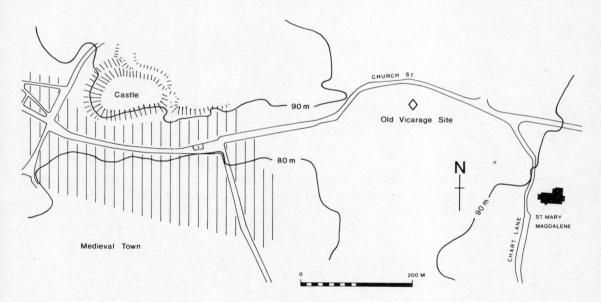

21.   Reigate: town plan, based on the O.S. first edition.

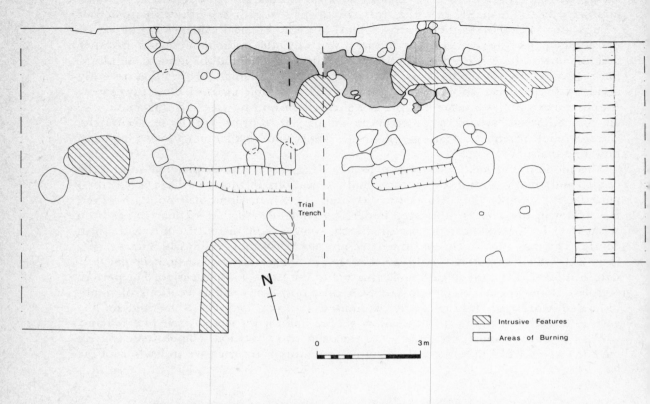

22. Old Vicarage site, Reigate: plan of the features of Saxo-Norman date

backlands are normally characteristic of urban settlement. The settlement could, of course, belong to the immediate post-Conquest period, but there is here at least a suggestion that Cherchefelle was an urban or proto-urban site in the late Saxon period. The manor was one of the wealthiest in Surrey according to Domesday Book, and it would have been well placed, with good north-south and east-west lines of communication, to act as a market with the Weald as its hinterland.[6]

Turning now to the areas of the historic county now in Greater London, two places have a claim on our attention. Croydon is the site of an archiepiscopal palace from at least 1273, but though it has an early-Saxon cemetery (Morris 1959, 137–9) and some mid- and late-Saxon occupation material (Drewett 1974), there is nothing indicative of major settlement in this period. Kingston is notable as a royal site where six kings were crowned in the period 902 to 958. It is first mentioned in 836 or 838 when it was the scene of an important meeting between King Egbert and Archbishop Ceolnoth (Garbett 1911, 487). At the time of Domesday Book the manor was clearly an important one with a population of perhaps 400 (calculated as in Lloyd 1962), and therefore was probably a main settlement of some size. It must be emphasised, however, that none of the documents refers to Kingston as a burh and it is possible that this was simply an estate on which there was an important royal residence.

Against such a view one can point to the certainly Saxon origins of the church (Finny 1929), the discovery of a plot boundary of late Saxon origin off Thames Street (Hinton 1977), and the possible signs of rectangular planning in the area east of the medieval bridge. There is, however, no evidence that this last is of late Saxon date, and though Kingston would fit nicely into the known pattern of late Saxon towns (Hill 1981, 136-7), the question must remain open, particularly in view of the absence of a mint and the lack of evidence for defences.

The above discussion, then, shows that one town, Staines, has indications of continuity from the Roman period; that the same town together with Kingston and Cherchefelle are possible urban places in the late Saxon period; and that Guildford is our only certain example of a late Saxon town. The siting of all these places is similar, with a bridge or ford across a major river at a point where important routes meet. Cherchefelle is apparently an exception, but it, in fact, occupies a dry, rather than a river, gap.

This extremely sparse distribution of sites can be compared to that of the known medieval towns (Fig. 20), when the large gaps have apparently become filled in, with the exception of the thinly-settled areas of the Bagshot Beds and the Weald. It may be suspected that many of these sites were settlement foci and market centres at a rather earlier date. Any such assumption is, however, at present unverifiable, and its likelihood depends on our views of the extent of late Saxon settlement. In this context Sawyer's (1976) arguments for the intensity and completeness of rural settlement must be noted.

Clearly the central problem here is to define the characteristics by which we recognise a town. As Hill (1978) has justly remarked, if Stenton's criteria of defences, a mint and a market are all necessary then discussion of the subject can hardly begin. But however loose the definition, the fundamental problem remains on the one hand that there is a paucity of documentary evidence, and, on the other, that the archaeological evidence has frequently been destroyed by later development or, if not, has not received the large-scale excavation needed to elucidate its importance. This means in turn that a heavy (possibly excessive) reliance on topography is necessary not only to identify the details of the plan, but also for overall classification. While critical appraisal of the written sources may yet reveal new information, the primary hope for improved knowledge of the Saxon origins of Surrey's towns must be excavation, of which there has so far been little.[7]

Whatever new knowledge is gained it is doubtful if it will alter the general conclusion that in this period in Surrey town life is of minor importance. This point is emphasised by a comparison with Sussex which has at least six late Saxon boroughs (Hill 1978), of which two, Chichester and Lewes, are two to three times as big as Guildford, which is presumably Surrey's largest town with a population of perhaps 750 (Lloyd 1962).

This circumstance cannot be understood without reference to the importance of London (Chapter 9). The proximity of that town must have tended to stifle the development of towns in this area,[8] especially as Surrey is an entirely inland county, separated from the ports of the south-east coast by the Weald. The point is emphasised by the fact that all the Saxon towns of Sussex are on coastal sites. This is surely reflected by the figures in Domesday Book which suggest that, excluding Southwark, the urban element in the population is only 5 per cent. of the whole.

ACKNOWLEDGEMENTS

We should like to thank the following for help and advice: Kevin Crouch and Phil. Jones (both Staines); Shirley Corke (Guildford); Marion Hinton (Kingston); David Williams (Old Vicarage Excavations, Reigate); and David Bird (general discussion and advice).

NOTES

1. It is normally assumed that the North Downs have a long history of use as a ridgeway. Turner (1980) has now demonstrated that positive evidence for this function does not exist at any period.

2. Guildford Muniment Room, L.M. 349/21. Many other documents of the 17th century use similar phraseology. The documentary evidence and its relevance to the topography of this area will be more fully considered in Poulton and Woods, forthcoming.

3. Manning and Bray's (1804, *1*, 12–13) remarks on the existence of a stone wall, parts of which were visible, surrounding the town, which they regard as the castle wall, may indicate that the bank was surmounted by a wall.

4. Norden's Map of Windsor Park (Poulton and Alexander 1979, 6), dated 1607, clearly shows the position of the entrance.

5. We owe this interpretation of the Guildown cemetery to D. Bird and D. Hill.

6. It may be instanced that Worth, deep in the Sussex Weald, with its superb pre-Conquest church (Taylor and Taylor 1965, *2*, 691–2), is assigned to Cherchefelle in Domesday Book.

7. There has, however, been little opportunity in recent years, partly because so much destruction of the early levels had already taken place.

8. Bird, *et al.*, 1975, conveniently indicates the truth of this dictum over a longer period of history. Chapter 5 advances similar arguments for the effect of Winchester on urban development in Hampshire.

BIBLIOGRAPHY

Aldsworth, F. G. and Hill, D. (1971), 'The Burghal Hidage—Eashing', *Surrey Archaeological Collections* 68, 198-201.

Arthur, P. (1978), 'The lead glazed wares of Roman Britain', in Arthur, P. and Marsh, G. (eds.), *Early Fine Wares in Roman Britain*, British Archaeological Reports 57.

Atkins, J. E. and Sallnow, J. (1975), 'Geology, geomorphology and climate of Surrey', in Salmon, J. E. (ed.), *The Surrey Countryside*, 1975.

Barley, M. W. (ed.) (1976), *The Plans and Topography of Medieval Towns in England and Wales*, C.B.A. Research Report 14.

Biddle, M. (1976), 'The evolution of towns: planned towns before 1066', in Barley (ed.), 1976.

Biddle, M. and Hill, D. H. (1971), 'Late Saxon planned towns', *Antiquaries Journal* 51, 70-85.

Bird, E., *et al.* (1975), 'The Archaeology and History of Surrey', in Salmon, J. E. (ed.), 1975.

Brandon, P. (1978), 'The South Saxon *Andredesweald*', in Brandon, P. (ed.), *The South Saxons*.

Campbell, E. M. J. (1962), 'Middlesex', in Darby, H. C. and Campbell, E. M. J. (eds.).

Canham, R. (1979), 'Excavations at Shepperton Green, 1967 and 1973', *Trans. London and Middlesex Archaeological Society* 30, 97–124.

Crouch, K. (1976), 'The archaeology of Staines and the Excavation at Elmsleigh House', *Trans. London and Middlesex Archaeological Society* 27, 71-134.

Crouch, K. (1978), 'New thoughts on Roman Staines', *London Archaeologist* 3, No. 7, 180–86.

Darby, H. C. and Campbell, E. M. J. (eds.) (1962), *The Domesday Geography of South East England.*

Drewett, P. L. (1974), 'Excavations in old town Croydon, 1968-70: a middle Saxon to post-medieval occupation sequence', *Surrey Archaeological Society Research Vol. 1*, 1-46.

Finny, W. E. St L. (1929), 'The Saxon church at Kingston', *Surrey Archaeological Collections* 37, 211–19.

Frere, S. S. (1975), 'The origins of "small towns"', in Rodwell, W. and Rowley, T. (eds.), *The Small Towns of Roman Britain*, British Archaeological Reprint 15.

Garbett, H. L. E. (1911), 'Kingston Upon Thames', in Victoria County History: *Surrey* 3, 487–516.

Guildford Corporation (1957), *The Borough of Guildford 1257-1957*: catalogue of an exhibition.

Hill, D. H. (1969), 'The Burghal Hidage: the establishment of a text', *Medieval Archaeology* 13, 84-92.

Hill, D. H. (1978), 'The origins of the Saxon towns', in Brandon, P. (ed.), 1978.

Hill, D. H. (1981), *An atlas of Anglo-Saxon England.*

Hinton, D. (1977), 'Kingston: excavations in 1976: 4 Thames Street', *Surrey Archaeological Society Bulletin* 134.

Holling, F. W. (1967), 'The early foundations of St Mary's church, Guildford', *Surrey Archaeological Collections* 64, 165–8.

Jones, P. (forthcoming), 'Saxon and Saxo-Norman Staines', *Surrey Archaeological Collections.*

Lloyd, C. W. (1962), 'Surrey', in Darby and Campbell (eds.), 1962.

Longley, D. and Poulton, R. (forthcoming), 'The Saxon cemetery at Upper West Field, Shepperton', *Transactions of the London and Middlesex Archaeological Society* 33.

Lowther, A. W. G. (1931), 'The Saxon cemetery at Guildown, Guildford, Surrey', *Surrey Archaeological Collections* 39, 1-50.

Manning, O. and Bray, W. (1804), *The History and Antiquities of the County of Surrey*, 3 vols.

Margary, I. D. (1967), *Roman Roads in Britain*, revised edition in one volume.

Morris, J. (1959), 'A Gazetteer of Anglo-Saxon Surrey', *Surrey Archaeological Collections* 56, 132–58.

Morris, J. (1973), *The Age of Arthur.*

Morris, J. (ed.) (1975), *Domesday Book: Surrey.*

Neale, K. (1973), 'Stane Street (Chichester–London) the third mansio', *Surrey Archaeological Collections* 69, 207–10.

O'Connell, M. (1977), 'Historic towns in Surrey', *Surrey Archaeological Society Research Volume* 5.

Pemberton, F. (1973), 'Prehistoric and Romano-British settlement in Ewell', *London Archaeologist* 2, No. 4, 84–6.

Poulton, R. (1980), 'Cherchefelle and the origins of Reigate', *London Archaeologist* 3, No. 16, 433-8.

Poulton, R. (forthcoming), 'Excavations at the Old Vicarage site, Reigate', to be published in *Surrey Archaeological Collections.*

Poulton, R. and Alexander, M. (1979), *Guildford's Dominican Friary: Recent Excavations*, Guildford Museum.

Poulton, R. and Woods, H. (forthcoming), 'Excavations on the site of the Dominican friary at Guildford in 1974 and 1978', *Surrey Archaeological Society Research Volume* 9.

Renn, D. F. (1968), *Norman Castles in Britain.*

Reynolds, S. (1962), 'Staines', *Victoria County History (Middlesex)* 3, 13-32.

Salmon, J. E. (ed.) (1975), *The Surrey Countryside.*

Sawyer, P. H. (1976), 'Early medieval English settlement', in Sawyer, P. H. (ed.), *Medieval Settlement.*

Sheldon, H. and Shaaf, I. (1978), 'A survey of Roman sites in Greater London', *London and Middlesex Archaeological Society Special Paper* 2.

Smith, A. H. (1956), *English Place-Name Elements—* (English Place-Name Society 25 and 26).

Sprules, D. W. *et al.* (1911), 'Guildford borough', *Victoria County History (Surrey)* 3, 547-70.

Taylor, H. M. and J. (1965), *Anglo-Saxon Architecture.*

Turner, D. J. (1980), 'The North Downs trackway', *Surrey Archaeological Collections* 72, 1–13.

Woods, H. (1974), 'Excavations in Reigate, 1974', *Surrey Archaeological Collections* 70, 79–95.

Chapter Three

THE TOWNS OF BERKSHIRE

By Grenville Astill

THE ARCHAEOLOGICAL CONTRIBUTION to the discussion about urban revival in southern England between the 8th and 10th centuries has consisted almost exclusively of the identification and characterisation of two types of site, the coastal trading site and the burh (e.g. Biddle 1974, 1976). While this approach has made, and no doubt will continue to make, fundamental revisions in our ideas of urban development, it is only recently that a broader view has been taken in an attempt to set this essentially archaeological material into a framework of contemporary economic and political developments (Hodges 1977, for what follows). However, this has been done in such a way that the two site-types become the physical manifestations of two different economic systems. To put it crudely, the port of trade existed within one system which gradually changed into another, this represented by the burh.

Thus it is argued that in the 8th century the personal nature of kingship was an important determinant of the economic system. The king was at the centre of a redistributive network which he controlled. It was from such control that he derived his pre-eminent position as a dispenser of largesse (*cf.* Duby 1974, 48–72; Grierson 1959). Periodic access to the products of long-distance trade was essential for the maintenance of kingly prestige, and these items were gained through the coastal trading sites such as *Hamwih*. In this scheme the fortunes of the ports of trade were tied to the personal needs of the king, who supervised the exchanges and maintained this privilege by restricting the activities of alien traders within his kingdom.

This redistributive system changed with the change in the king's position. From the 830s the king assumed a more distant yet more powerful role, which was associated with the expansion of the Wessex kingdom and the consequent need for a larger administration. This administration allowed a greater control over the country, enabling Alfred and his successors to build and man a 'planned scheme of national defence' in response to the Danish incursions (e.g. Brooks 1971). This scheme, however, was also designed to exploit the resources of the kingdom. The burhs were intended as market centres as well, and attempts were made to control trade and to channel it into these foundations, facilitated by the proliferation of a stable, royally-controlled coinage. Thus the change in the king's authority destroyed the purpose of the port of trade and its system, and heralded the development of the English state and a market economy.

The mechanisms which brought about these changes cannot be explained more precisely: it is only possible to characterise the situation in the 8th century and compare it with that of the 10th century. There is, however, a distinct disadvantage in concentrating first on the coastal trading sites and then on the burhs. Although this approach has the virtue of emphasising the difference between a redistributive and a market economy, it nevertheless makes the change appear extremely harsh and unconvincing. There is the basic problem of what happened to the economy (and how it was organised) between the decline of *Hamwih,* perhaps by the early 9th century, and the inauguration of the burhs in the 880s (Cherry and Hodges 1978). We therefore lurch from one type of economy and settlement form to another without explanation.

Much of the trouble still lies in our definition of urbanism. Continued use is made of criteria which can only depict a town in its maturity (e.g., Biddle 1976, 99-100; Phythian-Adams 1977, 33-36; Schledermann 1970; Wheatley 1972). Thus classes of site at the top of the settlement hierarchy such as the burhs are readily identifiable, but it is more difficult to recognise the equally important subsidiary settlements.

A possible starting point might be to establish the relationship of the port of trade with the interior. That a connection did exist can be seen from the occurrence of middle Saxon imports on settlement sites in southern England, and from the wide distribution of Ipswich ware (Hodges 1977, 201; Dunmore *et al.* 1975, 59-60). A comparison between the faunal assemblages from rural and urban settlement sites in Denmark demonstrates the dependence of long-distance trading ports on the interior, and this is also probably the case with *Hamwih* (Randsborg 1980, 54-59; Bourdillon 1979; Coy 1980). Yet it is not known whether this dependence on surplus coming from the interior was cause or result of long-distance trade. Nor is it known how the internal redistributive exchanges were organised.

The importance of central places for such exchange has received a certain amount of attention, and may be relevant for this period. Such places may only assume the status of exchange centres at particular times, for instance when the king was present.

It would be wrong, however, to place too much stress on the necessity of a royal presence in order for surplus to be exchanged. By the ninth century the royal right to *feorm* had been granted to lay as well as ecclesiastical lords; the maintenace of law and order was delegated in a similar way, and this, too, must have occasioned the transference of surplus on a more regular basis than was the case it if were solely dependent on the presence of a peripatetic king (Sawyer 1978, 175, Duby 1974, 45). The Church in its own right was also heavily involved in long-distance trade, and periodic 'markets' at monastic institutions, for example at major festivals, may well have provided alternative loci for such redistribution, as indeed has been suggested in France (Lombard-Jourdan 1970). Some minsters, as repositories for the relics of venerated saints, were important centres for the religious life of the country and as such were clearly capable of providing the occasions for exchange to take place (Rollason 1978; Sawyer 1978, 238-40).

The fact that such exchange centres could exist within a redistributive as well as a market economy might provide a link between the two very different economic systems which are currently being proposed for the Saxon period. Such centres would have existed lower down the settlement hierarchy, at the places where surplus would need to have been gathered under both systems.

Although these places did not perform the 'mature' urban functions of the burhs, nevertheless they shared certain identifiable attributes which set them apart from wholly agricultural settlements and gave them a certain status as 'central places' of local political and juridical units, as royal residences and as ecclesiastical centres. In other words the importance of these places would be recognisable in the 8th as well as the 10th century.[1] It is interesting to note that Tait appreciated that urban and royal settlements often shared the same functions (1936, 14). Having postulated the existence of these centres and suggested their potential importance in the transition from a redistributive to a market economy, it is quite a different matter adequately to characterise them (*cf.* Everitt 1974).

However, it is possible to gain some insights from looking at a section of the Wessex interior, Berkshire, with these problems in mind. The historic county has seen very little extensive excavation in its urban centres. Most work has been done in Abingdon, Newbury and Wallingford, but little has changed since the last general surveys in 1975 and 1978 (Rodwell 1975; Astill 1978). Insufficient material has been recovered from redevelopment to gain an impression of the extent of the towns during the whole medieval period. The archaeological data is greatly augmented by surveys of the early history of the county, based on documents and place-names, against which we can set the evidence for urban growth (e.g., Stenton 1913; Gelling 1973-76). The following therefore can out of necessity only be a review of existing information to provide an agenda for future work.

Compared with other counties of Wessex, historic Berkshire was formed comparatively late: the first mention of the shire is in 860. The fact that it took its name neither from a royal estate, like other Wessex counties, nor from a burh, like the Mercian shires, but from a wood (Berroc) indicates the unstable history of this area between the late 7th and 9th centuries (Gelling 1973-76, 838-47). The area to become Berkshire was disputed territory between Mercia and Wessex for most of this time, and was clearly peripheral to both kingdoms (Stenton 1913, 19-29). Indeed it has been suggested recently that the area comprised two distinct regions which were only united in the reign of Offa. Between 672 and 675 there is mention not only of an under-king of Wessex called Cissa who, to judge from his endowment of a monastery at Abingdon, controlled west Berkshire, but also of a province called Sonning, which stretched over what is now east Berkshire, and was therefore probably part of the middle Saxon Kingdom (Gelling 1973-76, 839-44). Gelling suggests that the boundary of the two areas lay south-west of Reading, within the belt of parish names ending in *-feld* (1973-76, 835-36, 841).

This certainly implies that, even if one accepts that the areas south of the Thames maintained a political unity focussed on Silchester in the 5th and 6th centuries, this arrangement was ignored in the subsequent land divisions, for the old territory was split down the middle (Myres 1969, 89; Biddle 1975, 330, 334-35; but *see also* Dickinson 1977, 408; Fulford and Sellwood 1980; Astill forthcoming). The fact that the area comprised two provinces which continued after the rest of Wessex had been grouped into shires argues against the existence of a single central place for the whole area and for a more diffuse system (which lasted for a longer time than anywhere else in Wessex) where the central functions were performed periodically by royal or monastic settlements.

It would, however, be wrong to assume that friction over Berkshire implied that the area was devastated, or that being peripheral it was isolated. Metcalf's recent work on *sceatta* distributions (1972) suggests that some of these coins, particularly the 'bird and branch' variety, may have been minted in the Oxford region, perhaps at Dorchester, in the 720s and 730s. Metcalf (1977) sees this as a 'frontier' mint which may indicate the transacting of long-distance trade on the border of Aethelbald's Mercian kingdom.[2] Inter-kingdom exchange between Wessex and Mercia is also hinted at in the provenances of the 'Southampton' and 'Midlands' types of *sceatta*; and contacts with the south-east are shown by the occurrence of 'London connected' varieties in the southern Midlands (Metcalf 1974a, 1977).

This admittedly sparse evidence for the penetration of long-distance trade inland is nevertheless a useful corrective to the current view that it was mostly conducted at the coast. Certainly the *sceatta* finds from the Abingdon/Dorchester area imply an exchange centre in the vicinity and this is confirmed at a slightly earlier time by Arnold's recent work. His identification of high quality and prestige goods in burials in the upper Thames area and Kent show these areas to have been redistribution centres, which were centrally controlled in the late 6th and early 7th centuries, for both prestige goods and raw materials (Arnold 1980, 91, 96, 138-39).

Dorchester (Oxfordshire) has been suggested as one of these potential centres within the upper Thames region. The importance of the late Roman occupation and the possibility of the settlement continuing as a focal point for the surrounding area into the 6th and 7th centuries has recently been reconsidered, and there now appears to be the likelihood of a break between the sub-Roman occupation and the evidence for reorganisation in the 6th or 7th centuries (Bradley 1978; Rowley 1974). Nevertheless, the repeated importance of Dorchester as a centre in the 5th century and again in the 7th century is impressive, but may in each case be for totally different reasons. Arnold's arguments about the need to control resources at times of scarcity may partially explain the attraction of the decaying Roman town as a pool of raw materials rather than as a civic centre (1980, 101; and *cf.* Myres 1978).

Dickinson has published the archaeological evidence for Dorchester as a royal centre in the early 7th century, and she argues that this status was acknowledged in *c.* 635 when it was created the diocesan centre for Wessex (1974, 25-35). Despite the withdrawal of the episcopal centre of Wessex to Winchester by the 660s, Dorchester's sporadic importance as a bishop's seat was recognised in 675-85, and again in the late 9th century.

The combination of a royal and an ecclesiastical centre at Dorchester would seem to make it a clear candidate as a centre for redistribution. The evidence of its possible assessment at 100 hides and its association with Thame and Banbury in a triple hundred has been taken to indicate that Dorchester could draw upon a large estate and was an early centre of administration (Cam 1933, 13-25; Lobel 1962, 3).

Both Chadwick (1905, 233-37, 249-58) and Cam (1932) have argued that a manor which had the rights of a hundred attached to it (and often gave its name to the hundred) was once in royal hands, and that this arrangement commemorated 'an earlier form of organisation, namely a district dependent on the king's tun, which was administered by a king's reeve' (Cam 1932, 371). It is also significant that such an arrangement is sometimes recorded in Domesday; dues and services that had anciently been rendered at the king's tun were described as a 'night's farm', the amount needed originally to support the royal household for a day (Lennard 1959, 128-34 ; Darby 1977, 357-58). Clearly the king's tun would form an important locus for exchange, a role that would have been reinforced by the presence of an ecclesiastical foundation (*cf.* Rahtz 1979, 4–21).[3]

The case of Dorchester illustrates the kind of attributes which could be expected from a place which was performing 'higher order' functions and which placed it above the ruck of rural settlements. The royal presence is important in that it concentrates and redistributes the surplus from the district, and offers an opportunity for recourse to justice in the folkmoots (an important function of such a centre was the exchange of information). All this was carried out under the umbrella of royal protection, and that too, as Bede realised, was important for the spread of Christianity, and must have been an important influence in the location of early minsters (Campbell 1979, 120–22).

This combination of political, administrative and ecclesiastical functions may provide a useful tool with which to identify other potential centres. In terms of development Abingdon has similarities with Dorchester. There was an extensive settlement here during the Roman period, and Abingdon and its environs have produced material which appears to extend from the 4th to the 6th centuries and suggests it, like Dorchester, had become a focus for early Saxon settlement (Biddle *et al.* 1968; Miles 1974).

In *c.* 670 a west Saxon noble, Hean, founded a monastery at Abingdon, the predecessor of the great Benedictine house. The monastery was endowed by the sub-king Cissa and also by King Ine, and when the area passed into Mercian hands it received protection from Aethelbert (Stenton 1913). There is some debate about the authenticity of the tradition that this monastery was originally founded on Boar's Hill (where there is the place-name *abbendun*) and then moved to the present site by the river, which was previously known as *Seukesham* (Gelling 1957; Biddle *et al.* 1968, 32, 34, 41; Gelling 1973–76, 433–34).

On reconsidering the evidence, Mrs Lambrick concluded (Biddle *et al.* 1968, 26–28) that the tradition of Cilla, Hean's sister, founding a nunnery at Abingdon was authentic, and that it was located near the present parish church of St Helen. The first documentary references to the nunnery, as a *monasterium* in 995, imply it had become a minster and, moreover, that it was a royal foundation. Mrs Lambrick believed the *parochia* of this minister to be coterminous with the extent of the three royal hundreds of Hormer, Sutton, and Ock, and Stenton was prepared to see Abingdon as a centre for hundredal administration by the 9th century (Biddle *et al.* 1968, 26–34; Stenton 1913, 47). There is thus sufficient evidence to regard Abingdon as of some religious and political significance at this time, and indeed perhaps earlier. The importance of Abingdon as a centre on the southern border of Mercia in the early to mid-8th century is shown by local *sceatta* finds around the settlement suggesting that this frontier zone was involved in mobilising resources for long-distance trade (Metcalf 1972).

Within the county it is possible to identify further settlements with the same 'central place' attributes. Wantage appears to have been a centre of a royal estate where Alfred was born *c.* 849. The settlement gave its name to the hundred, emphasising its function as a collecting and administrative centre. It was also the site of a minster church (Page and Ditchfield 1924, 319; Ordnance Survey 1973, 57).

Another potential centre in the Vale of the White Horse was Shrivenham, a royal estate with a dependent hundred. The church, recorded at Domesday with the very large endowment of five hides, was probably a minster (Page and Ditchfield 1924, 542; Ordnance Survey 1973, 57). Five other settlements share these characteristics:

Cookham—minster in the mid-8th century, a royal estate with a dependent hundred (Astill 1978, 23);

Reading—a royal vill by 870, a dependent hundred and a minster by the 10th century (Astill 1978, 75);

Kintbury—a royal settlement with a dependent hundred and a minster documented in 931; 10th-century coins found in the churchyard (Page and Ditchfield 1924, 206);

Lambourn—a royal settlement c. 889, with a dependent hundred; mention of a minster in 1032 (Astill 1978, 37; Stenton 1936, 231–32);

Thatcham—a royal settlement with a dependent hundred, with a minster (Kemp 1967–68; Astill 1978, 87–88).

Consideration should also perhaps be given to those settlements which had some, but not all, of the attributes. If Cam's arguments about the early significance of the royal manor attached to a hundred can be accepted, then three further places ought to be candidates for 'centres'.

Blewbury—a 100-hide estate in 944, an hundredal centre until the 12th century (Gelling 1973–76, 810; Anderson 1939, 201, 216–17);

Bucklebury—a royal manor and centre of a Domesday hundred, a *villa regalis* (Anderson 1939, 206; Myers 1954, 98);

Compton—a royal manor and centre of a Domesday hundred (Anderson 1939, 215).

Similarly those royal estates with minsters, like White Waltham and Faringdon (no longer regarded as the place of Edward the Elder's death), should be included, as should Sonning, the site of a great minster at the heart of a massive estate of the bishops of Ramsbury (Page and Ditchfield 1923, 223, 176, 4, 489; Gelling 1973–76, 366; Huggins 1975).

The sheer number of these potential centres, most of which may have been in existence by the 9th century, indicates the degree to which the county was already being exploited. This is particularly evident from the surviving Saxon charters, especially those with boundary clauses; these show much of west Berkshire had been divided into estates, which were clearly being extensively worked by the 9th century. Arguing from the laws of Ine and some charter material, Sawyer sees large portions of the landscape as fully exploited a century earlier (1978, 144–45). While this cannot be documented specifically for Berkshire, it is perhaps significant that Gelling's study of place-names implies that some of the 9th-century estates have a much greater antiquity (Gelling 1973–76, 801–12).

The main point is that parts of the county were able to produce sufficient surplus to sustain periodic 'fairs' at these centres. Thus the trade in prestigious items would be underpinned by a trade in utilitarian goods, prompted by their scarcity in some areas.

In this respect it is interesting to note the distribution of the centres. Most were in the north-west, the area described in the surviving charters as one of large estates. Moreover, some, for example Wantage, Faringdon, Bucklebury, and Shrivenham, were located on the boundary between two differing ecological zones, the most obvious of which are the Vale of the White Horse and the chalk downland. If the evidence of Domesday can be seen as relevant for the 9th century, the Vale, judging from the

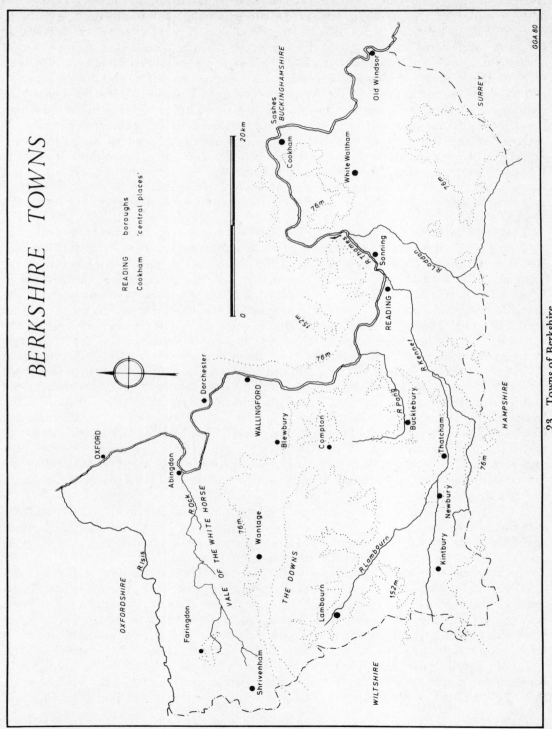

23. Towns of Berkshire

wic names and the high proportion of meadow, was an area of dairy farming and arable, while the Downs were devoted to sheep grazing (Ditchfield and Page 1906, 307–8; Gelling 1973–76, 915, 943; Sawyer 1965, 162). Settlements such as Wantage therefore were able to draw on the resources of two contrasting regions. Other settlements may have had access to similarly diverse areas via the rivers by which they were sited—Cookham, Abingdon, Kintbury, Lambourn, Thatcham, and Bucklebury.

The early charter bounds make frequent mention of trackways and Roman roads, implying that these remained in use during this time. Indeed this could be assumed from the fact that many of our sites are located near nodes in the communications system: at the crossings of navigable rivers (Cookham, Abingdon, and Kintbury), or where Roman roads intersected with routes across the Downs and Vale (e.g. Wantage, where the road is known as the Portway). The convergence of routes and the place-name, as well as the existence of a royal estate and the slim archaeological evidence, might suggest that a similar centre existed at Wallingford before it was created a burh.

Compared with the western half, east Berkshire was less intensively exploited at this time. The few Saxon charters suggest a settlement pattern of enclosures and clearings within a wooded area (Gelling 1973–76, 646–47). This impression of sparse settlement is to a certain extent confirmed by the information in Domesday. Population appears to have been low, particularly in the area of acidic soils of the Bagshot Beds, where there was a high proportion of woodland and forest (Campbell 1962, 243–65, 285). The small size of the population might also be reflected in the apparent absence of both minster churches and royal centres. The great contrast between the two parts of the county could be as much a result of their belonging to different political groupings until the 9th century, as of basic differences in geology and agricultural potential. It is significant that none of the centres in the east are situated in the wooded areas. Most, like Cookham and Sonning, are further north, on the banks of the Thames. Virtually the whole of the east of the county was administered from Cookham in the group known as the 'Seven Hundreds of Cookham and Bray', which Cam suggested was of pre-Conquest origin (1933). This arrangement may underline the undeveloped character of this area, as it was necessary to call upon the resources of virtually half the county in order to sustain the centres at Cookham and Sonning.

If the hypothesis that these centres played an important role in the transition from a redistributive to a market economy is correct, it must be shown that they either remained in existence throughout the Danish incursions or revived soon after so that they continued to exercise a local influence on the economy.

The activities of the Danish army which over wintered at Reading in 870–71 are only known in the barest outline, but it appears that most of the county suffered some disruption. There was certainly a break in the monastic routine at Abingdon between 871 and *c.* 928, and this dislocation was probably experienced at other minsters, particularly as Stenton is at pains to stress that Abingdon was similar to other foundations not yet having achieved the eminence it was to possess from the late 10th century (Stenton 1913, 30–38). However, it is difficult to be certain that some minsters recovered from these attacks; some are documented as minsters in the late 9th and 10th centuries which does suggest they continued to function

(Kintbury, Sonning, Thatcham, and ? Reading). It would however be mistaken to regard the fate of the exchange centre as being inextricably bound to that of the minster. Royal involvement in both the economic and judicial areas may have enabled the settlements to survive, or recover quickly to perform their trading functions. Indeed the combination of royal and ecclesiastical interests in these places ensured that they continued. They could operate without the royal presence because the minster's demands were virtually constant, as they could survive on the royal requirements should the monastery fail. During the 10th century meetings of the witan were held at Abingdon (926), Cookham (990s), and Wantage (997). The ability of these centres to continue to exist is to a certain extent confirmed by their Domesday entries which set them apart from other, rural, settlements; and from the medieval documentation which records them as either markets or boroughs [Abingdon, Wantage, Cookham, Reading, Lambourn, Thatcham, Faringdon (Rodwell 1975, 33–35, 117, 163; Astill 1978, 4, 8)].

It was into this framework of secondary trading centres that the burhs were set. The chief documentary source, the Burghal Hidage, mentions two sites in the county, Wallingford and Sashes, the former interpreted as a town, the latter as a fort (Hill 1969; Robertson 1939, 247, 496; Brooks 1964).

Wallingford is first mentioned in a charter of *c.* 895 (Gelling 1973–76, 535). The impressive remains of the rectangular rampart and the grid of streets, so similar to the arrangements of other Wessex burhs, have been taken as evidence that this site was a *de novo* creation of Alfred's (e.g. Biddle 1976, 124–34; Hinton 1977, 37). The Burghal Hidage reference and that in Domesday to 'the eight virgates of the king' have been used to support the view that the burh was a deliberate foundation (Stenton 1971, 529). However, as Lobel has observed such small estates were by no means unusual for the county, and that it 'need mean no more than the fortification of an existing settlement' (1976, 149). The pre-10th century material from the town certainly points to a pre-burh settlement here.[4] That Alfred chose a site what was well suited to both his military and economic purposes is without doubt (*cf.* Radford 1978, 148). Located on a gravel terrace in a strategic position north of the Goring gap, Wallingford was a focus of communications. The place-name emphasises the importance of the river crossing here, although Gelling notes the mention of a *Welingaford* in the charter bounds of Cholsey and Moulsford (*c.* 895), which she tentatively locates 800m. south of Wallingford bridge (1973–76, 535–36). In the 11th century, and probably earlier, the most important route for Wallingford was east-west, leading to Wantage and Abingdon, and giving access to the Vale and the Downs.

Wallingford, with its 41 defended hectares, was the second largest burh in Wessex; it needed the resources of 2,400 hides to defend it. It is important to consider whether the potential for defence outlined in the Burghal Hidage was achieved, and if so whether on a permanent or occasional basis, and what this implies in terms of economic development. The evidence for Wallingford has conflicting aspects. Sawyer, following Chadwick, noted the correlation between the Burghal Hidage figure for Wallingford and the size of the Domesday county (2,400, 2,473 hides) and suggested that the assessment of the shire was determined by the size of the burh (1978, 227). If this was the case, then the arrangement must relate to a time when Sashes, the other burh in the county and needing 1,000 men to defend it, had gone out of use.

Domesday also records a large number of rural manors with attached properties in Wallingford; many of these manors were in Oxfordshire (Campbell 1962, 275). This may commemorate the area from which men were recruited to defend the burh: in Wallingford's case this went beyond the borders of Berkshire, which suggests that at the time of Alfred (when the Wessex boundary had been pushed further east) the military catchment area was different, and perhaps larger, than the county.[5]

Work carried out in other Wessex burhs, particularly Winchester, suggests that the street system was integral with the defences, and that an important element in the plan was the 'wall street'. Biddle argues that this arrangement allowed quick movement for defensive purposes, and emphasises 'the initially military purpose of the Wessex burhs' (1976, 130). Certainly this explanation of the scale and type of planning of the burhs is more convincing than arguments about the rehousing of an existing population or the expectation of rapid growth; but it still leaves unanswered the question as to whether these arrangements were made for a permanent or seasonal occupation. In Winchester's case a military presence is assumed, and the growth of population and the development of craft specialisation was rapid and permanent; but as Biddle says 'that city was probably exceptional and may provide no sure guide to the situation elsewhere' (1976, 131).

Brooks (1979, 18) has emphasised that some kind of garrison must have existed in the burhs, to judge from the *Chronicle* references concerning men who held permanent residences in burhs. The contributory properties which were held by thegns in 1066 and the mention of 15 acres on which the *huscarles* were settled might reflect such a practice. Brooks has also stressed the scale of the military demands set out in the Burghal Hidage. His comparison between the total garrison for the Wessex burhs (27,071) and the estimated Domesday population (*c*. 560,000) shows that almost one in five adult males was required for military service (Brooks 1979, 18–19). Wallingford's need for 2,400 men may have taken a slightly higher proportion—some 8 per cent. of the county's population in 1086.

If these demands were fulfilled, the arrangement would indeed represent 'a major colonising enterprise, a significant redistribution of population from countryside to essentially new towns' (Brooks 1979, 20). Yet, even if we assume that all this number were permanent residents, it is doubtful whether the whole of the intra-mural area would have been occupied. The Domesday population of Wallingford is reckoned at 2–3,000, and it can be shown that the built-up area did not extend over the whole of the defended area in the late 11th century (Campbell 1962, 275). It should not be forgotten that the burhs, with their regular spacing over the kingdom of Wessex, were not only designed as garrisons, but also as refuges for the rural population.

It is nevertheless necessary to separate the military and economic functions of the burh. While burhs like Wallingford may have had street grids similar to Winchester's and therefore perhaps saw similar military arrangements, it does not follow that they experienced Winchester's rapid economic development. For example, the burh may only have been a bustling centre of population in the periods when the full garrison was present. This seasonal occupation would not, in the initial phases, affect the burh's economic development. The settlement could have continued to perform the quasi-urban functions of a central place without being recognised as a town. It is not therefore, perhaps, to be expected that the burhs were densely populated, at least in the initial stages of their development.

It is however important to recognise the efforts made by Alfred's successors to control and administer trade which encouraged a growth in the urban functions of the burhs. The laws of Edward the Elder, Athelstan and Cnut all give clear evidence of the importance they attached to transactions being peaceful and being witnessed, and the best location for such activity was within the burh—hence the insistence (later to be modified) on the need for all exchanges to take place within a borough under the supervision of a royal official (Loyn 1961, 130-3).

Allied to the attempt to channel trade into the boroughs was the creation of mints within them, and the reform of the coinage. Athelstan's Grately decrees authorised the setting up of mints in *ports* and burhs, and Wallingford may have received its first moneyer as a result of this law code (Loyn 1961, 124-28). However the first coin which can testify to a mint in Wallingford comes from the reign of Edgar prior to his coinage reforms of 973. It is clear that by this time Wallingford had become the county town of Berkshire, and indeed remained the only mint for the area until the Confessor's reign (Dolley and Metcalf 1961, 145, 150).

Domesday confirms Wallingford's importance for the area, and reiterates and amplifies the main features of the town which were noticeable a century before. Described separately and heading the entries for the county, Wallingford possessed a mint, and there is mention of a Saturday market, as well as 22 Frenchmen who no doubt illustrate the extensive trade that was carried on in the town. The existence of smiths gives some indication of the diverse economic base which a settlement of this size and nature must have had. The heterogeneous nature of the tenure also illustrates the vast number of interests present in the town. The area over which the town exercised economic influence extended either side of the Thames, judging from the distribution of contributory properties and the royal carrying services to and from Blewbury, Reading, Sutton Courtenay, and Benson recorded in Domesday (Ditchfield and Page 1906, 325).

During the 10th century, then, Wallingford can be regarded as a major town by virtue of its market, defences and mint, Stenton's urban criteria (1973, 528). The pre-eminence of the town must be seen entirely as a result of a royal initiative, at first conceived in military terms, but quickly expanded as a means of controlling the economy. The later history of the town points to the success of this venture, and even the Danish devastation in 1006 does not seem much to have checked its progress.

Royal initiative took more of a military character at Sashes, where a burghal fort was constructed on an island in the Thames. Its location, if Brooks's identification is accepted, is particularly interesting. It was of some strategic importance, being sited on the probable river crossing of the Silchester–St Albans road (Brooks 1964, 79-81). Sashes is classified as a burghal fort because there is no evidence that it was permanently occupied, and it failed to develop into an urban settlement. Cookham is 0.5km. west of Sashes, which forms a kind of bulwark between the settlement at Cookham and the river. It has been suggested that forts like Sashes would have 'withered after performing their defensive function to be replaced by adjoining or nearby marketing centres, themselves capable of fortification and further growth' (Loyn 1971, 126). Cookham is a candidate for such a marketing centre by virtue of being the possible site of a royal palace in the reign of Ethelred II and possessing a new market at Domesday.

But is the proposed sequence of a burghal fort with the subsequent growth of a market centre the right one? Market and fort may equally have existed simultaneously, and some of the urban functions that were combined in other burhs (e.g. defence and an exchange centre) were divided between Cookham and Sashes. The area around Cookham was one of early Saxon settlement; indeed, it has already been suggested that Cookham was in existence prior to the building of Sashes fort. The presence of an 8th-century minster at Cookham, which was also the centre of an extensive hundred, implies that it could have been a local exchange centre. The siting of the fort at Sashes could have been designed to protect an already existing settlement which continued to develop after Sashes had fulfilled its purpose. The survival of Cookham as a marketing centre is indicative of the economic expansion of the 10th and 11th centuries, and it is possible that the market continued into the high medieval period, for by 1225 Cookham had become a borough (Astill 1978, 323–24).

The quickening of the economy during the late Saxon period saw the continuation of the minor marketing centres despite the growth of the burhs. As is well known, the laws of Athelstan and Cnut recognised and legalised the existing practice of small-scale trading which took place elsewhere than in the royally-controlled boroughs. In Berkshire the role of these small centres was of particular importance as the county was only served by one large borough, Wallingford. Indeed some of the secondary centres which can be identified might be compared, in economic function at least, to the group of small boroughs in Somerset and Wiltshire during this period (Hill 1978, 217–22). The main difference is that none of the Berkshire examples had a mint. This need not be too disturbing; Metcalf has noted that in Ethelred II's reign the agriculturally rich region of the Thames valley was not serviced by any mint (apart from the small one at Reading) between Wallingford and London. Clearly the lack of mints does not indicate a low level of economic activity in this area (Metcalf 1978, 183–84).

The lack of specific evidence for the secondary centres means we can only surmise that most continued and moreover flourished in response to the acceleration of the economy. However this can be documented for Reading where, despite a Danish attack in 1006, the town continued to develop. Two coins, both found in Scandinavian collections, testify to the existence of a mint at Reading in 1044–46, and Domesday records it as having borough status (Dolley 1961; Van der Meer 1962; for a doubtful third coin, Thompson 1956, 121). This is certainly confirmed by the rest of the Domesday entry with the mention of 29 *hagae* and an equal number of *masurae* attached to a large estate. The output of the mint appears to have been small, and may mark an attempt by the Confessor to exploit more fully the resources of his large estate at Reading. If the distribution of contributory properties is an index to the economic influence of a borough, then Reading's was extremely limited.

Settlements similar to Reading, but without a mint, existed on other royal estates. By the time they are recorded in Domesday, these places have two common characteristics: a large rural estate, and a smaller arrangement of enclosures or *hagae* which to a certain extent are regarded as being indicative of urban status at this time. Round certainly realised this in his discussion of Domesday, and considered whether Faringdon, Thatcham, and Windsor should be regarded as towns (Ditchfield and Page 1906, 313). These places did not have a separate borough jurisdiction, but, as Stenton has pointed out, this aspect was not inherent in the Anglo-Saxon conception of the borough (1973, 534).

It has already been suggested that Thatcham and Faringdon were established as exchange centres before the foundation of the burhs, and the recognition that they differed from rural settlements in Domesday merely confirms that they continued to function as such in the 11th century and indeed beyond, for they became boroughs in the 14th and 12th century respectively (Rodwell 1975, 117; Astill 1978, 87–88).

The case of 'Windsor' is different. In the past it has been assumed that the Domesday reference relates to New Windsor, but until the later 12th century it is difficult to distinguish between New and Old Windsor in the documentation. It is perhaps more justifiable to regard all mentions before 1100 as relating to Old Windsor as there is no definite evidence that the settlement of New Windsor existed before that date (Astill 1978, 69). Old Windsor was a large royal estate of 20 hides, with 25 *hagae,* which suggests that it was a place which had pretensions to urban status. In 1065 Old Windsor is recorded as the site of a royal residence. The results of Dr Hope-Taylor's excavations between 1953 and 1958 are not known in detail, but interim accounts suggest that Old Windsor achieved this status in the 9th century. The site underwent a drastic change at this time which has been interpreted as signifying a systematic exploitation of the area, consonant with a reorganisation of the estate to cater for a large household (Wilson and Hurst 1958, 183–85). It is this type of increased exploitation of resources on royal sites which has been regarded as a preliminary to the establishment of a small market.

However it is clear that by the late 10th century the stimulus for the foundation of market centres could be provided by people other than the king. Whereas royal power was critical in providing the necessary prerequisites such as defences and a mint for the development of a town in the late 9th and early 10th centuries, the small 'boroughs' founded on royal estates a century later did not require such a sophisticated structure in order to function as secondary centres, and therefore did not need specifically royal support. This was probably the case in Ethelwold's refounding of Abingdon abbey in the 950s, which attracted numerous benefactions and juridical powers, particularly within Berkshire, ensuring that the institution not only had an important religious influence, but an economic one as well. The necessity of maximising their own resources and attracting and profiting from traders to the abbey is illustrated by the digging of a new channel for the Thames to allow traffic to continue up and down the river. In addition, the existence at Domesday of 'ten merchants dwelling in front of the door of the church' at Barton is interpreted as a small trading community which, living close to the abbey, provided the nucleus for the development of the medieval borough (Rodwell 1975, 33–35).

Whereas most of the marketing places mentioned appear to have evolved from pre-existing central places, this does not seem to have been the case with Newbury. Although it is sited where the Oxford–Southampton route crosses the Kennet (which may explain the 9th- and 10th-century coins there), there is no definite evidence of an important settlement here until Domesday (Peake 1931, 215). The manor of Ulvritone, now lost, had 51 *hagae* attached to it. The large increase in the assessment between 1066 (£9) and 1086 (£24) perhaps implies that the trading element attached to the manor was a deliberate creation in the years before the

Conquest (Astill 1978, 49–52). Round interpreted a charter, earlier than Domesday, which mentions tolls as indicating a market (Ditchfield and Page 1906, 314).

The mention of *hagae* has been regarded as important in signifying the urban status of these particular settlements. It should be said however that some doubt has been cast on this interpretation because, although it can be shown that legally the *hagae* were attached to the settlements mentioned, there is no proof that they were located there. It has been suggested, for instance, that the *hagae* were in fact located in the well established boroughs like Wallingford and Reading, and that the entry under settlements like Faringdon and Newbury implies that these places were really 'rural manors' (Campbell 1962, 273–74). In the absence of other evidence, it is impossible to say which interpretation is correct, but it should be noted that many of these places functioned as centres before Domesday and that they became medieval boroughs after, suggesting that they retained their importance during the whole period under consideration.

A similar argument could be used for those places which were unexceptional in Domesday and yet shared this history of a centre before and after, for example Wantage (a borough in the 12th century), Kintbury (a market in 1267), and Lambourn (a borough in the late 12th century) (Rodwell 1975, 163; Astill 1978, 4, 8).

The Archaeological and Topographic Evidence

In an attempt to chart the development within towns this section should consider such important themes as the existence of late Roman and early Saxon settlements as potential foci for the later towns, the internal arrangements within towns and their size, as well as discussing the evidence for buildings, both public and private. It is unfortunate that the lack of data prevents us from discussing adequately any of these topics for individual settlements, let alone on a comparative basis.

For example there is frequently no archaeological evidence to locate precisely many of the early monastic and royal centres which we have identified from documentary sources, and often few clues can be gained from place-names or cartographic material. Their identification stems from the assumption that the present churches stand on the same sites as their predecessors (e.g. White Waltham, Sonning, Kintbury), supported in some cases by another perhaps unwarranted assumption that the cruciform post-Conquest churches with crossing towers might contain material or commemorate the plan of an earlier structure (as at Lambourn, Faringdon, Shrivenham, Wantage, and Blewbury: Pevsner 1966, 139, 90, 163, 217, 252).

Where scatters of earlier material are recorded, it is impossible to assess their significance for later settlement. For example Roman pottery recovered from limited areas at Lambourn and Old Windsor gives no indication of the status or date of the settlement at these places. On the basis of the density of finds (including building materials and cemeteries) recovered from a wide area, and the proximity to routes, large settlements have been postulated in the late Roman period for Wantage, Wallingford, Reading and Abingdon (Rodwell 1975, 13, 33, 163, 155; Biddle *et al.* 1968; Simpson 1973; Astill 1978, 77). It has been suggested that these settlements remained as important nuclei for the continued settlement of the area in the 5th and 6th centuries. Although unconvincing for the most part, the clearest evidence for this comes from Abingdon where the earliest phases of the Anglo-Saxon cemeteries may be contemporary with the latest Roman occupation (Biddle *et al.* 1968, 27, 41; Avery and Brown 1972).

The data from Wallingford and Reading is less satisfactory; most finds neither occur in sufficient quantity nor can be dated precisely enough to suggest even that occupation there was continuous, let alone that the importance of the site remained undiminished in the early Saxon period. Similarly the partial evidence from Cookham and Sonning cannot be used to give a reliable indication of the time span for the associated settlements (Meaney 1964, 45, 52).

The non-cemetery evidence for the existence of these local centres is equally unsatisfactory. Most of it relates to the churches. At Wantage there were two churches standing side by side until the older, smaller church was demolished in 1850. Part of a 10th-century cross-shaft was recovered from the rubble, which might confirm the location of the minster (Piggott 1934). Although many sites have been suggested for the palace where Alfred was born, no archaeological evidence is available to locate it.

There is a tradition of a 9th- or 10th-century minster at Reading. This is assumed to have been on the site of St Mary's on the grounds that there is a Minster Street nearby, and that a hoard of 9th-century coins was found in St Mary's churchyard (Slade 1969, 3). Similarly the discovery near Helenstow in the 10th century of the Black Cross of Abingdon, illustrated in a 13th-century chronicle of the abbey, is now interpreted as an open work disc-headed pin, perhaps of the 8th century. Mrs Lambrick regarded this as indicating the existence of a monastery near St Helen's at this time (Biddle *et al.* 1968, 27–8). During the restorations of 1873 some earlier, but undated, foundations were uncovered in the south aisle (Rodwell 1975, 35). More recently sunken-featured buildings of early or middle Saxon date have been recorded in the area round St Helen's church (Rahtz 1976, 408).

A pre-burh settlement at Wallingford has been assumed from the cemetery material which dates from the 5th, 6th, and perhaps the 7th centuries, and from the unusual orientation of St Leonard's church in the south-east corner of the burh (Leeds 1938). Although first documented as late as 1122, the church is not orientated on the same alignment as the defences, even though it is less than 5m. from this dominant topographic feature. This may imply that the church was founded before the construction of the burghal defences (Rodwell 1975, 157). Beresford and St Joseph also noted that some parish bounds did not respect the town defences, but enclosed areas of the surrounding countryside, and interpreted this as possible evidence for an earlier settlement (1979, 196). The cutting across the western defences demonstrated that the bank sealed a plough soil (which of course may indicate Roman rather than Saxon activity) (Durham *et al.* 1972). The trench through the northern defences produced early and middle Saxon pottery from the body of the bank; this again supports the idea of a pre-burh settlement (Brooks 1965–66, 17).

Street Plans

The lack of archaeological work in these towns means that our interpretation of the topography can only be extremely tentative. This is particularly true of our

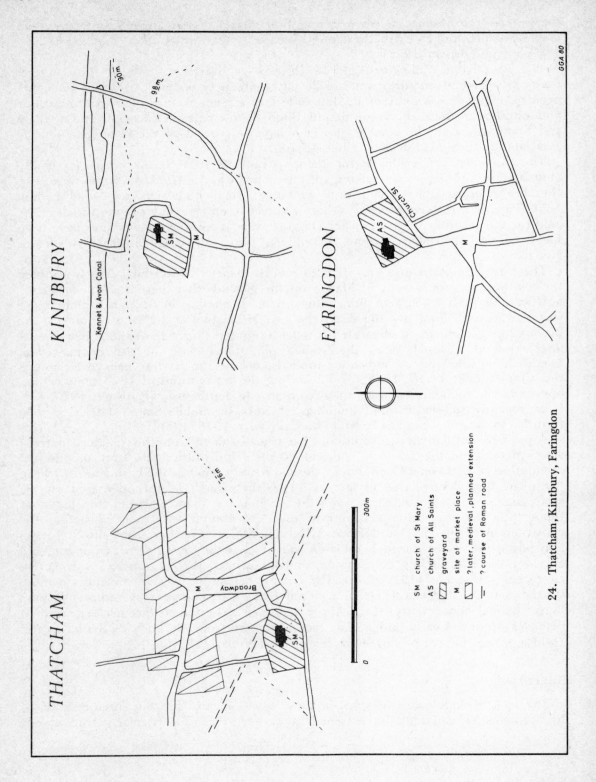

24. Thatcham, Kintbury, Faringdon

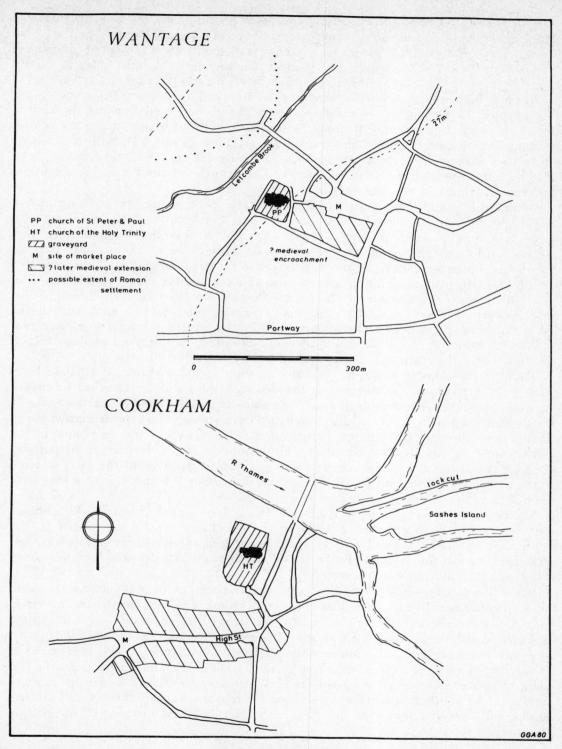

WANTAGE

PP   church of St Peter & Paul
HT   church of the Holy Trinity
    graveyard
M   site of market place
    ? later medieval extension
•••   possible extent of Roman
         settlement

Letcombe Brook

PP

M

? medieval
encroachment

Portway

0   300 m

COOKHAM

R Thames

lock cut

Sashes Island

HT

M   High St

GGA 80

25. Wantage, Cookham

knowledge of the Saxon topography, for many places maintained an urban status and underwent considerable rearrangement in the post-Conquest period. The evidence for the earlier disposition of these settlements then is limited, and in all probability distorted by these later changes. Consequently in most cases it is only possible to make the most basic statements about their early physical character.

In most instances the church, usually a minster, had a dominant influence on the topography. In Faringdon, Wantage, Kintbury, Lambourn, and Reading the church faced the market-place, and in doing so emphasised the church's important role in trading. In the case of Thatcham and Cookham (Figs. 24 and 25), both settlements close to a Roman road, there are no open spaces by the churches: the market-places may have been moved as part of the medieval replanning of the boroughs, and in the process the original open areas built over.

Within this group Lambourn and Reading have more distinctive and informative street patterns. It has already been stressed that Lambourn lay at the centre of a large economic and administrative area, and that it was the probable site of a Saxon palace, judging from the reference in Alfred's will. The earliest part of Lambourn's plan appears to be the oval bounded by streets (Fig. 26). Within this area stands the late medieval church and the site of a medieval manor house, replaced in the 19th century by Lambourn Place, now demolished (Page and Ditchfield 1924, 252). There is a tradition that the Saxon palace stood in this area. During the redevelopment of most of the ground within the oval some Saxon pottery was recovered, although no structural evidence was noted, but this is not surprising as the building of the Place and its gardens had greatly disturbed the area.

There is also some topographic evidence to support the tradition of a palace here. Firstly the market-place is adjacent to the oval area near the church and is reminiscent of other market-places outside the precinct gates of Saxon foundations. Secondly it seems that the southern part of the churchyard has encroached on to the market-place. If this were the case, the church stands on the line of where the south side of the circuit ought to run. It thus would have stood looking on to the market, perhaps by the gate into a 'royal complex', in a similar position to churches at the gates of some burhs such as Wareham and Oxford. It is indeed possible that the oval area may have been defined by a bank.

Saxon pottery has also been recovered from sites outside the oval. In addition earthworks to the north and north-east of the church might be related to the settlement. In 1934 a small trench was cut through the northern earthworks, but produced inconclusive results (Peake 1936). Both sets of earthworks have now been built over, but no finds were recovered.

While Lambourn, then, may illustrate one arrangement of a royal residence and marketing centre, Reading provides another. Reading was first mentioned by Asser in c. 870 when the Danes overwintered 'to the right of the royal vill' in a camp with a rampart which they built between the Thames and the Kennet (Slade 1969, 1–3). The Saxon borough and the 9th-century settlement, with one church mentioned at Domesday, is thought to be centred on St Mary's (Fig. 27). The church faced the Old Market, at the junction of the roads from Winchester to Oxford and from London to Bath. The southern encroachment of the churchyard, causing the bend in Minster Street, obscures the important position of St Mary's at the crossing of the routes,

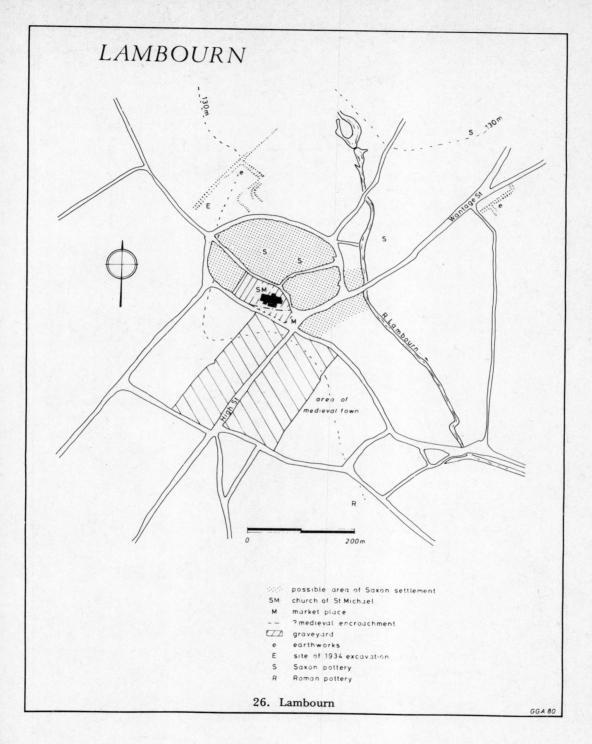

26. Lambourn

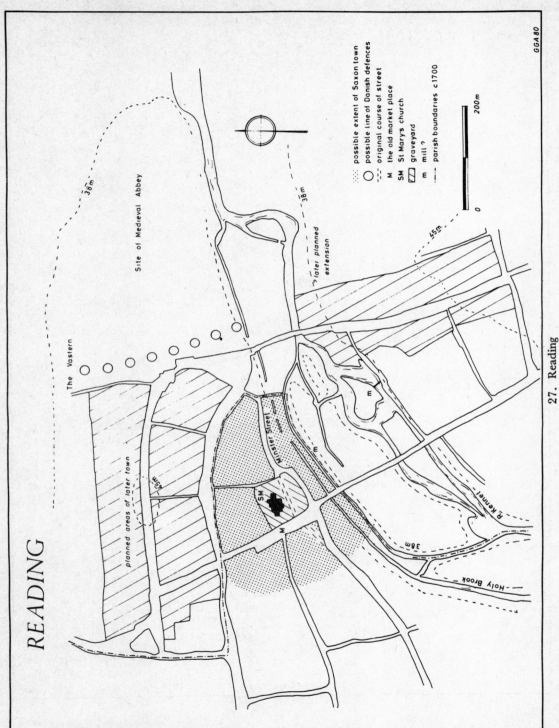

27. Reading

facing the original market-place. Despite the recent development of much of the area of the early town there is insufficient Saxon material to estimate the extent of the settlement. However, some indication of this might be afforded by the unusual eastern course taken by the parish boundary of St Mary's. This peculiar digression may reflect the eastern boundary of the Saxon borough, and could have determined the curving shape of the parallel streets which were laid out in the 12th or 13th centuries (Astill 1978, 77).[6]

The most likely site for the Danish wintering camp would be on the defensive gravel ridge slightly to the west of, and overlooking, the confluence of the Thames and the Kennet. This prominent position was chosen as the site of Henry I's abbey, and the west precinct wall may have followed the line of the camp's defences. The north end of the wall ended at water meadows by the Thames, known as the Vastern, an Old English word meaning stronghold. This could refer to a structure at the north end of the Danish rampart (Gelling 1973-76, 174). The skeletons of a man and a horse, and (? associated) 9th-century sword were found in the Vastern in 1831 (Wilson 1976, 402). Residual Saxon pottery has been recovered during excavations at Reading abbey, but this may relate to an earlier settlement (Slade 1975–76, 61). The occupation of this area to the east of the Saxon town might explain the origin of the double focus which characterised the medieval town.

The documentary evidence for Abingdon could imply that this settlement too had a double focus. If the tradition of a 7th-century nunnery at Helenstow is taken with the evidence of the Black Cross, then the settlement had two ecclesiastical centres 500m. apart, one at St Helen's, the other at Hean's abbey.

The topography of the town, however, points to an early centre round St Helen's, overlooking the confluence of the Thames and the Ock (Fig. 28). Two streets, West and East St Helen's Streets, radiate from the church, and Mrs Lambrick suggested that one or possibly two more streets followed the same pattern (Biddle et al. 1968, 28). Recent excavations near St Helen's have produced early or middle Saxon structures, and the possibility of West St Helen's Street following the line of an early Roman track has been raised (Rahtz 1976, 408; Parrington 1974, 38). Yet St Helen's does not face on to an open market area and neither is it near the ford across the Thames. The road from the ford leads into the other major topographic feature of the town, the sub-rectangular market-place. This lies immediately outside the gates of the abbey and must have been the focus of activity for the traders mentioned in Domesday. Indeed, with the increasing importance of the abbey from the 10th century this area must have become the economic centre of the town.

The most dominant feature of Wallingford's topography remains the sub-rectangular defences (Fig. 29). It is difficult to compare exactly the length of wall inferred from the Burghal Hidage and the actual perimeter. The earthworks of the castle have obscured the north-east course of the defences, and a recent cutting has shown that the crest of the surviving bank is a product of erosion of the outer face of the bank and deposition on its tail, so that the original crest would have been at least 1.5m. further out (Durham et al. 1972). The 3,016m. of the Burghal Hidage must have included the river frontage, and Hinton has recently suggested that the modern boundary of the borough, in describing an area of the east bank of the Thames, commemorates a Saxon bridgehead designed to control and block the river, reminiscent of Charles

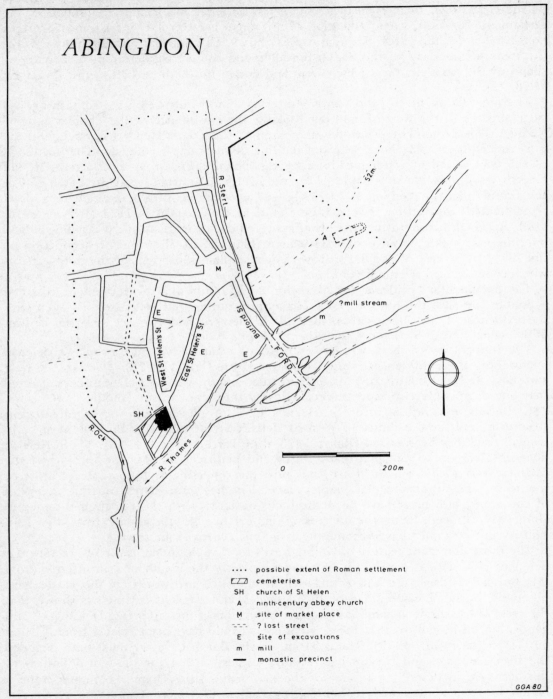

ABINGDON

possible extent of Roman settlement
cemeteries
SH   church of St Helen
A   ninth-century abbey church
M   site of market place
?   lost street
E   site of excavations
m   mill
      monastic precinct

GGA 80

28. Abingdon

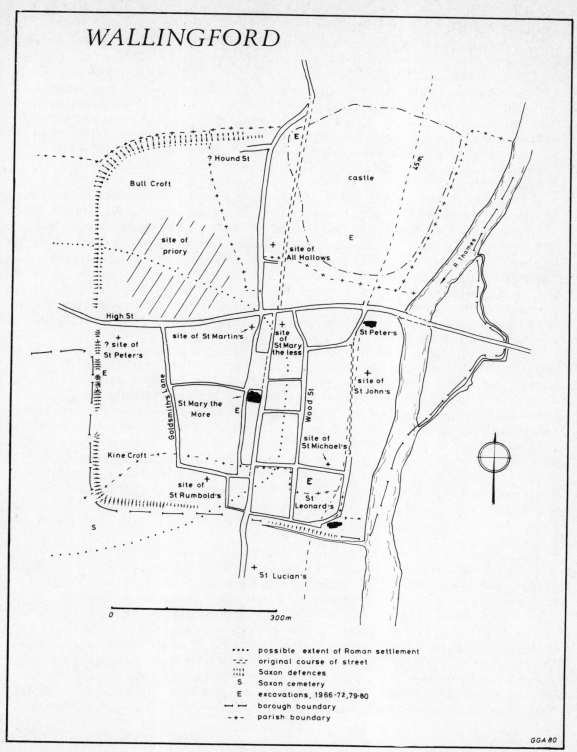

WALLINGFORD

29. Wallingford

the Bald's defensive measures in north Francia, and also the arrangement of London
and Southwark (Hinton 1977, 37).

Two cuttings have been made through the banks, one in the west section in Kine
Croft, the other in the north under the castle earthworks. Both showed a two-phase
pre-Conquest sequence. A primary bank, of gravel revetted with turves and stabilised
with vertical timbering at the castle, and of turf in Kine Croft, is presumed to
represent the Alfredian defences. Early and middle Saxon pottery was recovered
from the northern bank, along with two 9th-century sherds. The excavator however
has more recently written that the defences cannot be dated more accurately than to
the post-Roman period, and questions whether they could, in fact, have been
constructed earlier than Alfred's reign (Durham *et al.* 1972; Wilson and Hurst 1967;
Brooks 1979, 17).

In the late Saxon period the north bank was raised with material from the
enlargement of the ditch, and a stone wall built on the crest of the bank, similar
to the sequence at Wareham. This second bank was also noted at Kine Croft.
Subsequent excavation at the castle apparently confirmed the existence of an
original timber gate, but the results have not yet been published (Simpson 1973, 8).
The ditches associated with the banks have not been found: their continued use at
the castle prevented this, and only the lip of a ditch was observed at Kine Croft.
Modern suburban development and the road system around the defences prevent us
from discovering whether the burh had a multiple ditch system, as at Lydford,
Cricklade, and Wareham.

Although the town gives the impression of having a gridded street system, it is
difficult to know which elements are original. None of the streets can be dated (*cf.*
Hinton and Hodges 1977). It is usually assumed that the main axial streets have
remained in their original position. However the western extension of the castle
defences is normally regarded as causing a shift of the main north–south route to the
west. A recent excavation near St Mary the More has provided some evidence for the
existence of the west market street in the 11th century (B. Durham, pers. comm.).
This suggests there was, at that time at least, a back-street arrangement similar to
that at Winchester. If this is the case, there is a possibility that the back street
continued into the northern half of the burh, and indeed still exists as Castle Street.
Thus when the original north–south street was destroyed by the castle extension, a
new road was not created, but the original back street was brought into use as the
main thoroughfare.

Excavations at Oxford have shown that the alignment of some main streets
did not remain constant (Hassall 1971, 17). The slightly curving course of Wallingford's other main street, High Street, particularly in the east, might suggest that
it had moved to the north. The evidence is extremely tenuous; the well-preserved grid
to the east of the market goes badly out of alignment before it reaches High Street
(e.g. Wood Street). These lanes could have been laid out after the rest of the grid, and
perhaps after High Street had been moved. The other scrap of evidence concerns
the location of the three churches of St Martin's, St Mary the Less and St Peter's.
All three churches face on to a north–south street, but they are also set back a similar
distance from High Street, as though all three might have overlooked the original
High Street and thus stood at a crossroads.

The intra-mural, or wall, street, so important for the military function of the burhs, can only be traced in the south-east as St Leonard's Lane. Herbert however thinks Hound Street, a lane giving access to Bull Croft from Castle Street, followed the inner line of the northern defences (1971, map I).[7]

As regards the subsidiary street pattern, the grid of streets in the south-east quarter might be contemporary with the defences. Wood and Thames (before it was realigned in the 1760s) Streets are parallel with the market street and the east-west lanes divided the space into rectangles of approximately the same area. The 16-pole module which Crummy suggests was used in the planning of the Wessex burhs could apply to the east-west dimensions of this grid, but it appears inapplicable anywhere else in the town (1979, 153). To the west of the market the 'grid' is less complete and less regular. Goldsmith's Lane for example is not aligned with the other streets in the southern half of the burh, and could be later.

It is impossible to reconstruct the street patterns in the northern half of the burh: tracks are mentioned in the 1548 survey of the town, but these cannot with any certainty be located on the ground (Field 1915; 1916).

It is equally difficult to estimate the degree to which the area within the defences was occupied. At Domesday 491 plots were recorded, eight of which were destroyed to make way for the castle in the north-east. The 1966–68 excavations produced a sequence along the original north street of timber and stone buildings dated between the late 10th and 13th centuries, and some ovens interpreted as corn driers (Wilson and Hurst 1967, 284; 1969, 255). The 1972 excavations in the outer ward of the castle also found parts of timber structures belonging either to the Saxon burh or to the early castle (Simpson 1973, 14). In 1980 a three-phase sunken-featured building was excavated to the west of the market-place. Although a complete plan could not be recovered, the structure appeared to have plank walls supported on the inside by vertical posts with its gable-end parallel with the market-place (B. Durham, pers. comm.).

An index to the extent of the town would be the number and distribution of the churches. Only one church is mentioned in Domesday, although four priests are recorded. None of the surviving churches have pre-Conquest work (although there is herringbone work in the north wall of St Leonard's). There were however 10 churches in the town by the mid-12th century, and it is assumed that many of these were Saxon foundations. In many cases the precise location of these churches is unknown; the discovery of cemeteries is assumed to indicate the presence of a church. Most of the churches were in the south-east, and this must have been the most densely occupied part of the town. However, the earliest features found in a small excavation close to the site of St Michael's were two pits, dated to the 12th or 13th centuries (Weare 1977, 206).

It is doubtful whether the western half of the town was so intensively settled. The only church in Kine Croft was St Peter's which was probably a chapel by the west gate, and watching briefs in the area have produced no pottery earlier than the 12th century (Durham *et al.* 1972). It is also significant that there was sufficient space in the north-west quarter of the town for the establishment of a Benedictine priory there in the late 11th century (Ditchfield and Page 1907, 77–79).

Tenth-century Wallingford, then, like Cricklade may have had empty spaces within the area, spaces perhaps intended as camping areas for the temporary garrison.

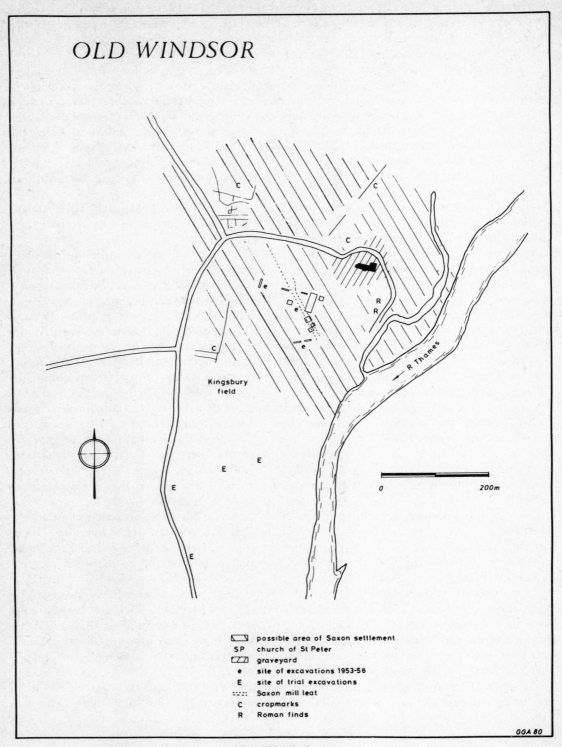

OLD WINDSOR

Kingsbury
field

R Thames

0   200m

possible area of Saxon settlement
SP   church of St Peter
graveyard
e   site of excavations 1953-58
E   site of trial excavations
Saxon mill leat
C   cropmarks
R   Roman finds

GGA 80

30. Old Windsor

1. Wiltshire. Vertical aerial photograph of Cricklade showing the shape of fields and the extent of ridge and furrow determined by the alignment of the Saxon and Norman defences.

2. Wiltshire. Vertical aerial photograph of Malmesbury.

3. Langport, Somerset. Vertical aerial photograph taken by the R.A.F. in 1947 showing the burh on the medieval town in the centre and flooding of the levels to north and south.

4. Saxon London. Milk Street excavations, 1977: typical stratigraphy of the Saxon period, showing: A, underlying 2nd-century mosaic; B, dark earth of the late Roman and Saxon periods; C, 10th-century buildings along Milk Street (off the top of the picture).

5. Saxon London. Arch of re-used Roman tiles uncovered after wartime bombing at All Hallows Barking church, Tower Street. The view, looking N, is from the ?*porticus* into the nave.

6. (*overleaf*) Saxon London. New Fresh Wharf, 1975: stakes of probably late 9th- or early 10th-century foreshore, covered by a raft of rough timbers as base for the late 10th-/early 11th-century embankment of the river (off the picture to the right).

7. Seal of Bath Abbey from a document of 1159-75 (Harl. ch. 75A. 30). The matrix is believed to be 10th century (Cat. of Seals in the M.S. Dept. of the B.M. no. 1437). (Actual size)

8. Two-light window, possibly late Saxon. Now preserved in the Bath Abbey Collection. (Scale one-eighth)

Nevertheless, the presence of St Lucian's church outside the south gate indicates the growth of a southern suburb by 1122.

The site of Old Windsor is mostly deserted and therefore the little that can be said about its topography is largely the result of excavation (Fig. 30). Documentary evidence confirms the existence there of a royal palace between 1061 and 1107, after which the royal household moved to New Windsor Castle. The interpretation of the archaeological material must be tentative because it is dependent on interim reports. It is however clear that a small, middle Saxon settlement around the church underwent a drastic change in the early 9th century, a process which may mark the creation of a royal palace. A large mill and a stone building were constructed, and pollen analysis suggests this period of occupation was associated with a greater exploitation of the surrounding area. Both buildings were destroyed in the early 10th century, but were replaced (Wilson and Hurst 1958, 183–85).

The extent of this royal complex is unknown: none of the larger buildings one would expect from a royal site such as halls were discovered; neither has the 'town' of 25 *hagae* been located. Trial excavations to the south of Kingsbury fields failed to produce occupation deposits. The mill leat may have acted as a boundary to the settlement, although geophysical survey has identified archaeological features beyond the leat, but as yet these are undated. To the north-west of the excavations crop marks have been seen which may indicate the position of the rest of the settlement (Astill 1978, 69–71).

It could be argued from the Domesday evidence that Newbury was an 11th-century foundation, and that the 'lost' manor of Ulvritone was its rural predecessor. The topography of the town gives the impression of a well-integrated settlement (Fig. 31). The two southern roads join before crossing the Kennet, and then continue as a single, wide road—Northbrook Street—giving the town a distinctive 'Y' plan. The core of the town is clearly around the river crossing. This is where the church, the market-place and the 12th-century castle were located, but it is difficult to tell whether this reflected the 11th-century arrangement. Excavations took place at Bartholomew Street in 1972–76 and 1979, and in Cheap Street in 1972–76. At 143–45 Bartholomew Street two phases of agricultural activity, perhaps dating from the 10th or early 11th century, were succeeded by the construction of timber buildings and property boundaries in the 11th century. The excavator, Alan Vince, interprets this as clear evidence for the laying out of the town along Bartholomew Street, and a similar sequence could be surmised from the other excavations (Vince 1980; Ford 1976; 1979).

It is, however, difficult to reconstruct the plan of the town centre in the 11th century prior to the building of the castle. The triangular market-place is sited at the gates of the castle. Vince has plausibly suggested that originally the market-place was rectangular and extended west to the church, and that part of it was later built over. Judging from its straightness and the evenness of the tenements (particularly on the east side), Northbrook Street could have been laid out at one time and it is possible that this was not part of the original street pattern. The 11th-century town may have just been focussed around the roads and church on the south bank of the Kennet.

As regards the kind of buildings that stood within the towns of Berkshire, very little can be said. Our knowledge of the religious complexes is limited to that at

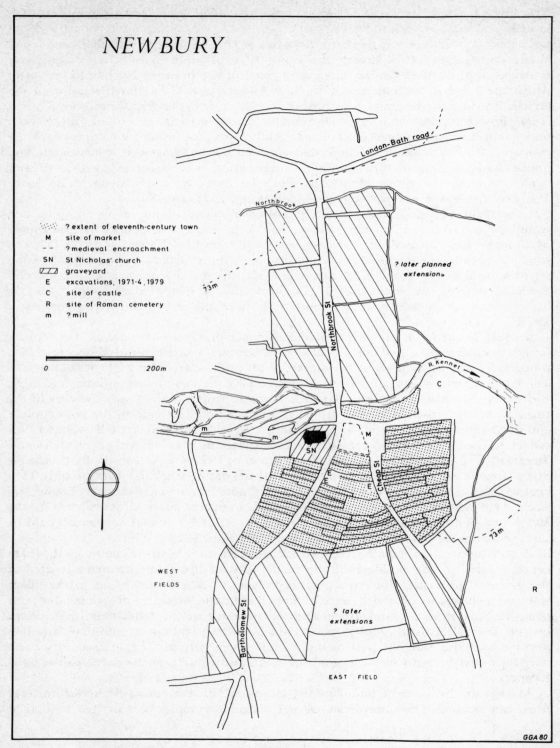

NEWBURY

? extent of eleventh-century town
M   site of market
--   ? medieval encroachment
SN   St Nicholas' church
     graveyard
E   excavations, 1971-4, 1979
C   site of castle
R   site of Roman cemetery
m   ? mill

0   200m

London-Bath road

Northbrook

? later planned extension

73m

Northbrook St

R. Kennet

C

m
m
SN
M

E
E   E

Cheap St

73m

WEST FIELDS

Bartholomew St

? later extensions

R

EAST FIELD

GGA 80

31. Newbury

Abingdon. There is a description of Hean's monastery in a corrupt chronicle of the mid-13th century, but, despite this, the account of the buildings is regarded as having some veracity. The church is described as 120 feet long, with an apse at both the west and east ends. The site was enclosed by a wall, which served as a cloister walk: it had gaps between it and the individual living quarters of the monks, where they ate, drank and slept. Each cell had a chapel attached to it; there is however no parallel for these separate buildings. The complex was described as being under the cellar range of the medieval abbey.

The same chronicle provides an account of Ethelwold's church which is suspiciously similar to that of Hean's, although the two buildings must have been different. Mrs Lambrick has also discovered that by 977 the church had a porticus on the north, and by the 11th century had another on the east. In 1091 part of the church collapsed, and the description implies that it had a central tower with a chapel forming the east end of the church and that the chapter house was immediately south of the tower. A refectory, cloister dormitory and perhaps a kitchen can also be inferred (Biddle *et al.* 1968, 42–47; Cramp 1976, 215–17).

In 1922 excavations took place under the guidance of C. R. Peers and A. Clapham with the intention of exposing the Norman, and perhaps the Saxon, abbey. The results were never published, but Biddle has compiled an account of the work from the fragmentary record. Under the Norman church fragments of walls were recovered which were assumed to belong to the same Saxon church. The building was about 60m. long and 15m. wide with a round apse at the east end which Clapham interpreted as the central chamber of a ring crypt; he dated this east end to *c.* 960. Biddle, however, notes the similarities of plan and proportions to the church at Cirencester, and suggests a 9th-century date: it therefore could not be Ethelwold's foundation. If Leland was correct in thinking Ethelwold's church to be further north, there is thus a possibility that there was more than one church within the 10th-century monastic enclosure.

The excavations showed that the cemetery to the south of the Norman church contained Saxon burials. Structures were not recovered in this area, nor to the north of the church. Biddle, on the analogies of Wearmouth and Jarrow, thus thought the 10th-century claustral complex was south of this cemetery (Biddle *et al.* 1968, 60–67).

The only other buildings for which information is available are the mills. The large mill at Old Windsor is the only one to be excavated in the county. It was driven by a leat over 6m. wide and 3–4m. deep. Judging from the names of fields within the Thames meander (the 'Great and Little Mill Ditch'), the channel was over 1,100m. long and was cut across the bend in the Thames. The mill itself had three vertical wheels, and nearby was a stone building with glazed windows and a tiled roof. This building and the mill were destroyed in the early 10th century when the leat was filled in. The leat, however, was re-cut to drive a horizontal-wheeled mill which continued in use until the early 11th century (Wilson and Hurst 1958; Astill 1978, 70–71).

Abingdon abbey also seems to have had a number of mills. In the time of Ethelwold there were two, and monks dug a new mill stream which must have extended as far as St Helen's church (Biddle *et al.* 1968, 47). The abbey was also involved in river management in the early 11th century in an attempt to preserve the volume of river traffic which passed by the town. A stretch of the Thames was silting up, making it increasingly difficult for merchants to get up to Oxford. The abbey considered the amount of traffic to be sufficiently large and remunerative to justify digging a new channel for the river (Davis 1973, 263).

Domesday provides the only record of mills in the other towns, but in some cases the numbers are an index to their economic importance. Reading for example had six mills which must have been situated on the Kennet (Campbell 1962, 269–71).

Our review of the urban potential within Saxon Berkshire has demonstrated the unusual development of the county compared with some counties in Wessex. The fact that it was on the periphery of both the Wessex and Mercian kingdoms in what was the formative period for the other shires of Wessex, and that it was a union of two contrasting areas, might in part explain this difference. From a superficial point of view urban development in Berkshire seems more akin to the later Mercian counties which were dominated by one large town. Yet this would be merely looking at the top of the settlement hierarchy, whereas the approach adopted here has sought to demonstrate that such an attitude may lead to a distorted view of town growth in some areas in the Saxon period and fails to set the development of later medieval urbanism in its proper context.

NOTES

1. There is an interesting discussion concerning the commercial potential of these places in Harmer (1950, 356 ff.). *Cf.* F. Neil's comments about the commercial origins of burhs in Rahtz (1979, 10–12).

2. A similar 'frontier' distribution might be seen on the present southern boundary of Berkshire between 735 and 740 when Aethelbald had annexed the county (Metcalf 1974b).

3. For the archaeological evidence of a possible middle Saxon royal collecting centre, *see* Wade, 1980.

4. It is interesting to note that recent evidence suggests that an earlier settlement could exist at the site of a 'new' town in that other period of plantation, the 12th century (Owen 1980).

5. I am grateful to Jeremy Haslam for pointing out that the military catchment areas shown by the contributory burgesses of Wallingford and Oxford might alternatively illustrate a pre-Alfredian, overlain by an Alfredian, arrangement.

6. Phythian-Adams has also offered a similar interpretation of Reading's topography (1977, 31, 38).

7. I am grateful to Dr. Herbert for allowing me to cite evidence from his unpublished thesis.

BIBLIOGRAPHY

Anderson, O. S. (1939), *The English Hundred-Names: The South-Western Counties*, Lund.

Arnold, C. (1980), 'Wealth and social structure: a matter of life and death', in Rahtz, P., Dickinson, T. and Watts, L. (eds.), *Anglo-Saxon Cemeteries, 1979*, B.A.R. 82, Oxford, 81–142.

Astill, G. (1978), *Historic Towns in Berkshire: an archaeological appraisal*, Reading.

Astill, G. (forthcoming), 'Excavation at Grim's Bank, Aldermaston, 1978', *Berkshire Archaeological Journal*.

Avery, M., and Brown, D. (1972), 'Saxon features at Abingdon', *Oxoniensia* XXXVII, 66–81.

Beresford, M. W. and St Joseph, J. L. (1979), *Medieval England: an aerial survey*, 2nd edn., Cambridge.

Biddle, M., Lambrick, Mrs, and Myres, J. N. L. (1968), 'The early history of Abingdon, Berkshire and its abbey', *Medieval Archaeology* XII, 26–69.

Biddle, M. (1974), 'The development of the Anglo-Saxon town', *Settimane di studio del centro italiano di studi sull'alto medioevo*, 21, 204–30.

Biddle, M. (1976), 'Towns', in Wilson, D. M. (ed.), *The Archaeology of Anglo-Saxon England*, London, 99–150.

Biddle, M. (1977), 'Hampshire and the origins of Wessex', in Sieveking, G., Longworth, I. H. and Wilson, K. E. (eds.), *Problems in Economic and Social Archaeology*, London, 323–41.

Bond, C. J. (1979), 'The reconstruction of the medieval landscape: the estates of Abingdon abbey', *Landscape History* I, 59–75.

Bourdillon, J. (1979), 'Town life and animal husbandry in the Southampton area, as suggested by the excavated bones', *Proceedings of the Hampshire Field Club and Archaeological Society* 36, 181–91.

Bradley, R. (1978), 'Rescue excavation in Dorchester-on-Thames 1972', *Oxoniensia* XLIII, 17–39.

Brooks, N. P. (1964), 'The unidentified forts of the Burghal Hidage', *Medieval Archaeology* VIII, 74–90.

Brooks, N. P. (1965–66), 'Excavations at Wallingford Castle, 1965: an interim report', *Berkshire Archaeological Journal* 62, 17–21.

Brooks, N. P. (1971), 'The development of military obligations in eighth- and ninth-century England', in Clemoes, P. and Hughes, K. (eds.), *England Before the Conquest*, 69-84.

Brooks, N. P. (1979), 'England in the ninth century: the crucible of defeat', *Transactions of the Royal Historical Society* 5th series 29, 1-20.

Buckley, D. G. (ed.) (1980), *'Archaeology in Essex to A.D. 1500'*, C.B.A. Research Report 34, London.

Cam, H. M. (1932), *'Manerium cum hundredo*: the hundred and the hundredal manor', *English Historical Review* 47, 353–71.

Cam, H. M. (1933), 'Early group of hundreds', in Edwards, J. G. (ed.), *Historical Essays in Honour of James Tait*, Manchester, 13–26.

Campbell, E. M. J. (1962), 'Berkshire', in Darby, H. C. and Campbell, E. M. J. (eds.), *The Domesday Geography of South-East England*, 239-86.

Campbell, J. (1979), 'The church in Anglo-Saxon towns', in Baker, D. (ed.), *The Church in town and countryside*, Studies in Church History 16, 119-35.

Chadwick, H. M. (1905), *Studies on Anglo-Saxon Institutions*.

Cherry, J. and Hodges, R. (1978), 'The chronology of Hamwih: Saxon Southampton reconsidered', *Antiquaries Journal* 58, 299–309.

Coy, J. (1980), 'The animal bones', in Haslam 1980, 41–51.

Cramp, R. (1976), 'Monastic sites', in Wilson, D. M. (ed.), *The Archaeology of Anglo-Saxon England*, London, 201-52.

Crummy, P. (1979), 'The system of measurement used in town planning from the ninth to the thirteenth centuries', in Hawkes, S. C., Brown, D. and Campbell, J. (eds.), *Anglo-Saxon Studies in Archaeology and History*, I, B.A.R. 72, Oxford, 149–64.

Darby, H. C. (1977), *Domesday England*, Cambridge.

Davis, R. H. C. (1973), 'The ford, the river and the city', *Oxoniensia* XXXVIII, 258–67.

Dickinson, T. M. (1974), *Cuddesdon and Dorchester-on-Thames*, B.A.R. 1, Oxford.

Dickinson, T. M. (1977), 'British antiquity', *Archaeological Journal*, 134, 404–18.

Ditchfield, P. and Page, W. (1906), *Victoria County History (Berkshire)* 1, London.

Ditchfield, P. and Page, W. (1907), *Victoria County History (Berkshire)* 2, London.

Dolley, R. H. M. (1961), 'A note on the Anglo-Saxon mint of Reading', *British Numismatic Journal* 30, 70–75.

Dolley, R. H. M. and Metcalf, D. M. (1961), 'The reform of the coinage under Eadger', in Dolley, R. H. M. (ed.), *Anglo-Saxon Coins*, London, 136–68.

Duby, G. (1974), *The Early Growth of the European Economy*, London.

Dunmore, S., Gray, V., Loader, T. and Wade, K. (1975), 'The origin and development of Ipswich: an interim report', *East Anglian Archaeology* 1, 57–67.

Durham, B., Hassall, T., Rowley, T. and Simpson, C. (1972), 'A cutting across the Saxon defences at Wallingford, Berkshire 1971', *Oxoniensia* XXXVII, 82–85.

Everitt, A. (1974), 'The Banburys of England', *Urban History Yearbook*, 28-38.

Field, J. E. (1915-1916), 'A survey of Wallingford in 1550', in *Berkshire, Buckinghamshire and Oxfordshire Archaeological Journal* 21, 82–85 and 22, 21–25, 46–49, 82–84.

Ford, S. D. (1976), 'Excavations in Newbury town centre, 1971–74, Part 1', *Transactions of the Newbury District Field Club* 12, No. 4, 21–41.

Ford, S. D. (1979), 'Excavations in Newbury town centre, 1971-74, Part II', *Transactions of the Newbury District Field Club* 12, No. 5, 19–40.

Fulford, M. G. and Sellwood, B. (1980), 'The Silchester ogham stone: a reconsideration', *Antiquity* 64, 95-99.

Gelling, M. (1957), 'The hill of Abingdon', *Oxoniensia* XXII, 54–62.

Gelling, M. (1973-76), *The Place-Names of Berkshire, Parts 1-3* (English Place-Name Society 49-51).

Grierson, P. (1959), 'Commerce in the Dark Ages: a critique of the evidence', *Transactions of the Royal Historical Society* 5th series, IX, 123–40.

Harmer, F. E. (1950), '*Chipping* and *Market*: a lexicographical investigation', in Fox, C. and Dickins, B. (eds.), *The Early Cultures of North-West Europe*, Cambridge, 335–60.

Haslam, J. (1980), 'A middle Saxon iron-smelting site at Ramsbury, Wiltshire', *Medieval Archaeology* 24, 1-68.

Hassall, T. G. (1971), 'Excavations at 44–6 Cornmarket Street, Oxford, 1970', *Oxoniensia* XXXVI, 15–33.

Herbert, N. M. (1971), 'The borough of Wallingford, 1155–1400', unpublished University of Reading Ph.D.

Hill, D. H. (1969), 'The Burghal Hidage: the establishment of a text', *Medieval Archaeology* 13, 84–92.

Hill, D. H. (1978), 'Trends in the development of towns during the reign of Aethelred II', in Hill, D. (ed.), *Ethelred the Unready*, B.A.R. 59, Oxford, 213–26.

Hinton, D. A. (1977), *Alfred's Kingdom. Wessex and the South 800–1500*, London.

Hinton, D. A. and Hodges, R. (1977), 'Excavations in Wareham, 1974–5', *Dorset Natural History and Archaeological Proceedings* 99, 42–83.

Hodges, R. (1977), 'Trade and urban origins in Dark Age England: an archaeological critique of the evidence', *Berichten van de Rijksdienst voor het Oudheidkundig Bodemonderzoek* 27, 191–215.

Huggins, R. M. (1975), 'The significance of the place-name *Wealdham*', *Medieval Archaeology* XIX, 198–210.

Kemp, B. (1967–68), 'The mother-church of Thatcham', *Berkshire Archaeological Journal*, 63, 15-22.

Leeds, E. T. (1938), 'An Anglo-Saxon cemetery at Wallingford, Berkshire', *Berkshire Archaeological Journal* 42, 93–101.

Lennard, R. (1959), *Rural England 1086-1135, A Study of Social and Agrarian Conditions*, Oxford.

Lobel, M. D. (1962), *Victoria County History (Oxfordshire) 7*, London.

Lobel, M. D. (1976), 'Some reflections on the topographical development of the pre-industrial town in England', in Emmison, F. and Stephens, R. (eds.), *Tribute to an antiquary*, London, 141–64.

Lombard-Jourdan, A. (1970), 'Y'a-t-il une protohistoire urbaine en France?' *Annales Economies Sociéties Civilisations* 25, 1121–42.

Loyn, H. R. (1961), 'Boroughs and Mints A.D. 900–1066', in Dolley, R. H. M. (ed.), *Anglo-Saxon Coins*, London, 122–35.

Loyn, H. R. (1971), 'Towns in late Anglo-Saxon England: the evidence and some possible lines of enquiry', in Clemoes, P. and Hughes, K. (eds.), *England before the Conquest*, Cambridge, 115–28.

Meaney, A. (1964), *A Gazetteer of Anglo-Saxon burial sites*, London.

Metcalf, D. M. (1972), 'The "Bird and Branch" *sceattas* in the light of a find from Abingdon', *Oxoniensia*, XXXVII, 51–65.

Metcalf, D. M. (1974a), 'Monetary expansion and recession: interpreting the distribution patterns of seventh and eighth century coins', in Casey, J. and Reece, R. (eds.), *Coins and the Archaeologist*, B.A.R. 4, Oxford, 206–23.

Metcalf, D. M. (1974b), '*Sceattas* found at the Iron Age hill fort of Walbury Camp, Berkshire', *British Numismatic Journal* XLIV, 1–12.

Metcalf, D. M. (1977), 'Monetary affairs in Mercia in the time of Aethelbald', in Dornier, A. (ed.), *Mercian Studies*, Leicester, 87-106.

Metcalf, D. M. (1978), 'The ranking of boroughs: numismatic evidence from the reign of Aethelred II', in Hill, D. (ed.), *Ethelred the Unready*, B.A.R. 59, Oxford, 159–212.

Miles, D. (1974), 'Abingdon and region: early Anglo-Saxon settlement evidence', in Rowley, T. (ed.), *Anglo-Saxon Settlement and Landscape*, B.A.R. 6, Oxford, 36–41.

Myres, J. N. L. (1954), 'The Anglo-Saxon period', in Martin, A. F. and Steel, R. W. (eds.), *The Oxford Region*, Oxford, 96–102.

Myres, J. N. L. (1969), *Anglo-Saxon Pottery and the Settlement of England*, Oxford.

Myres, J. N. L. (1978), 'Amulets or small change?', *Antiquaries Journal* 58, 352.

Ordnance Survey (1973), *Britain before the Norman Conquest*, Southampton.

Owen, D. M. (1980), 'Bishop's Lynn: the first century of a new town?', in Brown, R. A. (ed.), *Proceedings of the Battle Conference of Anglo-Norman Studies*, 2, 141–53.

Page, W. and Ditchfield, P. (1923), *Victoria County History (Berkshire)* 3, London.

Page, W. and Ditchfield, P. (1924), *Victoria County History (Berkshire)* 4, London.

Parrington, M. (1974), 'Small excavations in Abingdon, 1973', *Oxoniensia* XXXIX, 34–43.

Peake, H. (1931), *The Archaeology of Berkshire*, London.

Peake, H. (1936), 'Trial excavations at Lambourne Place', *Transactions of the Newbury and District Field Club* 7, No. 2, 109–12.

Pevsner, N. (1960), *The Buildings of England: Berkshire*, Harmondsworth.

Piggott, S. (1934), 'A Saxon cross shaft fragment from Wantage', *Transactions of the Newbury District Field Club* 7, No. 3, 149–50.

Phythian-Adams, C. (1977), 'Jolly cities: goodly towns', *Urban History Yearbook*, 30–39.

Radford, C. A. R. (1978), 'The pre-Conquest boroughs of England, 9th–11th centuries', *Proceedings of the British Academy* 64, 131–53.

Rahtz, P. A. (1976), 'Gazetteer of Anglo-Saxon domestic settlement sites', in Wilson, D. M. (ed.), *The Archaeology of Anglo-Saxon England*, London, 404–52.

Rahtz, P. A. (1979), *The Saxon and Medieval Palaces at Cheddar*, B.A.R. 65, Oxford.

Randsborg, C. (1980), *The Viking Age in Denmark*, London.

Rigold, S. E. and Metcalf, D. M. (1977), 'A check-list of English finds of *sceattas*', *British Numismatic Journal* XLVII, 31–52.

Robertson, A. J. (1956), *Anglo-Saxon Charters*, Cambridge.

Rodwell, K. (1975), (ed.), *Historic Towns in Oxfordshire: A Survey of the New County*, Oxford.

Rollason, D. (1978), 'List of saints' resting places in Anglo-Saxon England', *Anglo-Saxon England*, 7, 61–94.

Rowley, T. (1974), 'Early Saxon settlement in Dorchester', in Rowley, T. (ed.), *Anglo-Saxon Settlement and Landscape*, B.A.R. 6, Oxford, 42–56.

Sawyer, P. H. (1965), 'The wealth of England in the eleventh century', *Transactions of the Royal Historical Society* 5th series, 15, 145–64.

Sawyer, P. H. (1978), *From Roman Britain to Norman England*, London.

Schledermann, H. (1970), 'The idea of the town', *World Archaeology* 2, 115–27.

Simpson, C. (1973), *Wallingford: The Archaeological Implications of Development*, Oxford.

Slade, C. F. (1969), 'Reading', in Lobel, M. (ed.), *Historic Towns*, 1, London.

Slade, C. F. (1975–76), 'Excavation at Reading Abbey 1971–73', *Berkshire Archaeological Journal* 68, 29–70.

Stenton, F. M. (1913), *The Early History of the Abbey at Abingdon*, Oxford.

Stenton, F. M. (1936), 'St Frideswide and her times', *Oxoniensia* I, 103-12, reprinted in Stenton, D. M. (ed.), *Essays Preparatory to Anglo-Saxon England*, Oxford, 1970, 224-33.

Stenton, F. M. (1971), *Anglo-Saxon England*, 3rd edn., Oxford.

Tait, J. (1936), *The Medieval English Borough*, Manchester.

Thompson, J. D. A. (1956), *Inventory of British Coin Hoards*, Royal Numismatic Society Special Publications, No. 1.

Van der Meer, G. (1962), 'A second Anglo-Saxon coin of Reading', *British Numismatic Journal*, 31, 161-62.

Vince, A. G. (1980), *Bartholomew Street, Newbury. A Preliminary Report on the Archaeological Excavations of 1979*, Newbury.

Wade, K. (1980), 'A settlement site at Bonhunt Farm, Wicken Bonhunt, Essex', in Buckley, D. G. (ed.) (1980), 96-102.

Weare, T. J. (1977), 'Excavations at Wallingford, 1974', *Oxoniensia* XLII, 204-15.

Wheatley, P. (1972), 'The concept of urbanism', in Ucko, P. J., Tringham, R. and Dimbleby, G. W. (eds.), *Man, Settlement and Urbanism*, London, 601-37.

Wilson, D. M. (1976), 'The Scandinavians in England', in Wilson, D. M. (ed.), *The Archaeology of Anglo-Saxon England*, London, 393–403.

Wilson, D. M. and Hurst, J. G. (1958), 'Medieval Britain in 1957', *Medieval Archaeology* II, 183–85.

Wilson, D. M. and Hurst J. G. (1967), 'Medieval Britain in 1966', *Medieval Archaeology* XI, 262-3

Wilson, D. M. and Hurst, J. G. (1969), 'Medieval Britain in 1968', *Medieval Archaeology* XIII, 255.

Chapter Four

THE TOWNS OF WILTSHIRE[1]

By Jeremy Haslam

Introduction

WILTSHIRE HAS BEEN DESCRIBED by Maitland as 'the classical land of small boroughs'; it certainly had more of these boroughs than any other county by the time of Domesday (Darby 1977, 296–7, 368). These 'petty boroughs' may have been, in comparison with the huge towns of Midland and eastern England, relatively small, and as elements in the total settlement landscape of the south-west they may have been less distinct from the surrounding countryside. But already by the early 10th century (and as this chapter will suggest, rather earlier) they were important focal points of administrative and economic activity, and must have possessed physical as well as social characteristics no less 'urban' than those shown by many of the larger urban places of the period.

There are 10 places in the county which are variously described in Domesday Book either as boroughs, as having burgesses or a market, or as being liable to payment of the third penny, from which it can be inferred that these were urban places certainly in the early 11th century and very probably the 10th century. These places are: Bedwyn, Bradford-on-Avon, Calne, Cricklade, Malmesbury, Marlborough, Salisbury (Old Sarum), Tilshead, Warminster, and Wilton.[2]

There are two, possibly four, other places not so described, which share so many of the characteristics of these Domesday boroughs as to suggest that by the later Saxon period they, too, had developed into truly urban places. These are: Amesbury, Chippenham, and possibly Westbury and Downton.

It is proposed to discuss the topographical and historical characteristics of these places in such a way that common features—of their lay-out, their historical development, and their wider spatial and temporal relationships in the historical landscape—can be compared. From these comparisons it should be possible to make valid inferences about early urban development over an area which forms a significant portion of the area of Saxon Wessex.

There are perhaps four other important types of evidence around which more inferential arguments suggesting urban status and development can be woven. These are, firstly, the record of the Burghal Hidage document of the early 10th century, which mentions four places in the county: Chisbury, Cricklade, Malmesbury, and Wilton.

It is not in doubt that most of those places mentioned in the Burghal Hidage which were not merely re-fortified hill-forts were already—or at least were very soon to become—truly urban places in the early 10th century (Loyn, 1961; Biddle, 1976a). As will be discussed further below, Chisbury, the only re-fortified Iron Age hill-fort

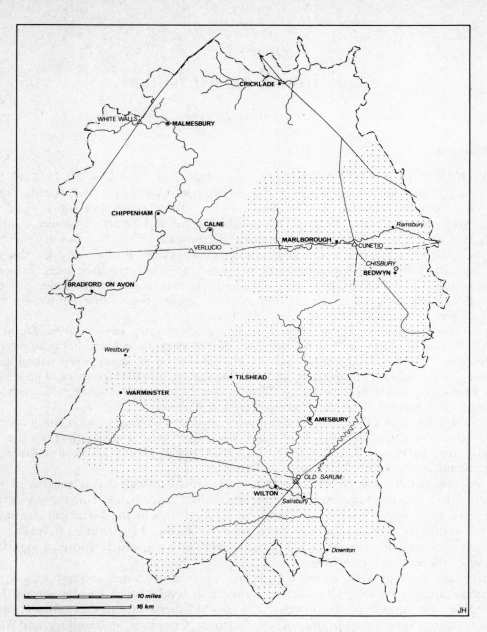

32. Wiltshire, showing Saxon towns (bold capitals) with other places mentioned in
the text

in this list, stands in close topographical and historical relationship to Bedwyn at its foot, and the two must be considered together.

The second line of positive evidence is the existence of pre-Conquest mints, which are known from the following places: Bedwyn, Cricklade, Malmesbury, Marlborough, Salisbury (Old Sarum), Warminster and Wilton.[3]

As Professor Loyn (1961) (amongst others) has pointed out, the evidence from mints is one of the most direct indications of royal control of the type of economic activity which is a necessary characteristic of urban life, whether found in defended or undefended settlements. In particular at Wilton and Old Sarum, the existence of closely dateable mint signatures and moneyers is important evidence for their development in the early 11th century.

A third type of evidence, the topographical features shown by a place or group of places, is seldom one which has been applied systematically to groups of the smaller towns. It will be shown below, however, that many of the places mentioned above have topographical characteristics which suggest that both in their siting and their layout they were regularly ordered (as distinct from planned) settlements, and, secondly, that many of these features are common to a group of places which share a common historical development. The topographical patterns shown particularly by Wilton, Chippenham and Calne suggest the association of a market-place, a minster church, an area set aside as an enclosed (possibly fortified) royal residence, and an area for other houses, which together form a complex of features which can possibly be taken back to the 8th century. As will be shown, these observations appear to reinforce conclusions about the development of these places that can be drawn from other kinds of evidence.

A fourth type of evidence, though it is one which is not directly indicative of urban status as such, is the part which a place has played in the historical landscape. The evidence is complex, involving both spatial and temporal connections. In this chapter, therefore, this evidence, insofar as it relates to all 15 of the places already mentioned above, can only be examined briefly. Nevertheless, the relationships described below show quite clearly, firstly, that without exception these urban places developed at or near the centres of royal estates, most of which are recorded as being 'ancient demesne' in Domesday Book and were therefore probably in royal hands in the early years of the formation of the West Saxon kingdom. It is suggested that these places developed their urban characteristics as a direct result of their role as central places on these royal estates at a period which was arguably somewhat earlier than the period (the 10th century) most commonly accepted for the beginning of the general growth and spread of urban institutions in England. And, secondly, these estate centres were generally directly related (albeit with links which become dimmer in the more distant past) to estates and/or central settlement locations which can be taken back through the early Saxon to the Roman period, and in some cases back to the pre-Roman Iron Age. Bradford-on-Avon, which is the site of an Iron Age hill-fort, a large Roman villa and cemetery, an early Saxon river crossing and battle site, an early 11th-century royal and subsequently monastic estate centre, and a Domesday borough, is perhaps the clearest example of a pattern of continuity from the Iron Age to the present, both in the central settlement and in its larger territory. It is argued below that this pattern is shown (with variations) by most of the other places mentioned in this chapter.

Bradford-on-Avon

Of all the places discussed in this chapter, Bradford-on-Avon is probably the one which shows the best archaeological and historical evidence for suggesting that the later-Saxon urban place has developed on or very near the site which was the focus of its immediate area from the Iron Age onwards. The physical focus of this site was the natural ford, described as 'braden forda be afne' in the *Anglo-Saxon Chronicle* in 652. On the edge of the steep hillside overlooking the ford was the Iron Age hill-fort of Budbury (Figs. 35 and 36), excavated in 1969 (Wainwright 1970). Immediately to the north of this was a substantial Roman villa, discovered and partly excavated in 1977. It must be from this villa, and from a probable settlement around it, that the many burials, pottery and coins found in the vicinity derived.[4] Though there were no obvious indications of continuity of occupation in the villa into the 5th century, it seems likely that the estate of which it was clearly the centre survived to become the Domesday hundred and parish with little change. The northern boundary of this land unit is still formed by the disused Roman road between Bath and *Verlucio* and, although further work is necessary to document it in detail, its western boundary (now the county boundary) is contiguous with the area formerly dependent upon Roman Bath. An element in the early post-Roman organisation of this estate is indicated by the village of Cumberwell to the north of Bradford, whose name suggests a settlement of Welsh or British origin (Smith 1956, i, 119).

The later history of Bradford also suggests that the settlement focus shifted from the villa on the hill to around the ford in the valley early in the Saxon period. Bradford was the site of a battle, presumably at the river crossing, in 652. Most commentators have regarded this as a battle between Britons and Saxons (e.g., Jones 1859, 9–10; Major 1913, 54; Oman 1938, 287; Hunter-Blair 1956, 36), but the description of this battle as a 'civil war' by Aethelweard (Whitelock 1979, 164, n. 5) suggests the possibility that it was fought between Saxon and Mercian forces. Since the latter had, as a result of the battle of Cirencester in 628, gained Bath and its territory (Stenton 1943, 44, 66), they might be expected to have wished to extend their control over a further stretch of the Avon and into the neighbouring estate.

Bradford was thus, in the mid-7th century, already probably a settlement, a focus of routeways over a comparatively large river, and the centre of an estate (presumably in royal hands) whose boundaries were in all probability the same as those of the later *parochia*. These conclusions are further strengthened by the foundation there of a minster church (*monasterium*) by Aldhelm before 705, which must have been established to serve, and possibly convert, an already existing population. There are indeed grounds for suggesting that the siting of this church was governed by the existence nearby of a pagan, and latterly, Christian, religious site at the holy well. At Wells (Somerset), a minster church of the same period was similarly sited near the holy wells, which has been described as one of the several places in the Celtic west of 'pagan veneration which were dedicated and perhaps adapted as baptismal foci during the Christian conversion' (Rodwell 1980, 39).

Bradford was certainly the centre of a royal estate by 1001, when it was given by Ethelred to the nuns of Shaftesbury as a refuge for both the nuns and the bones of Edward the Martyr from the Danes (Gem 1978, 109–10).[5] The writer does not now

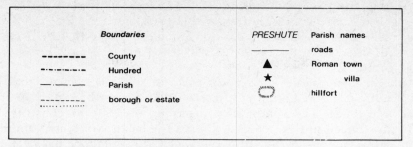

33. Symbols used in Figs. 34–56. Parish boundaries are based on the Tithe Award maps, *c.* 1840. Boundaries in towns are based on those shown in the first edition 1 : 2500 O.S. maps, augmented by earlier evidence where indicated in captions. Contour plans of towns at two or four metre intervals are from surveys by Wiltshire County Council

34. Bradford-on-Avon area showing bounds of charter of 1001

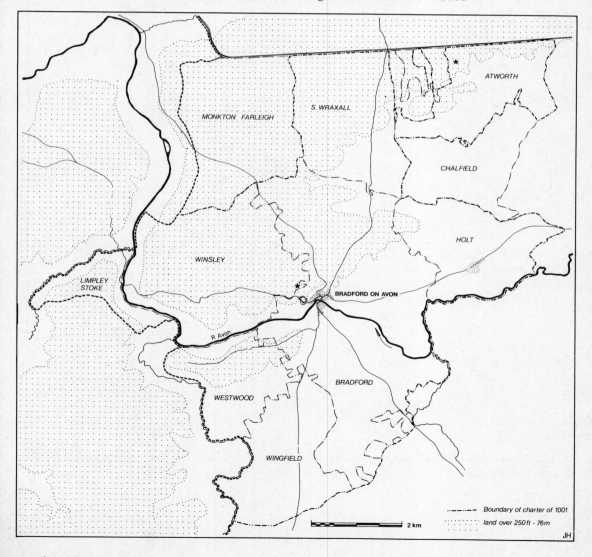

consider that this implies that Bradford was fortified (*cf.* Haslam 1976, 10). It is, however, in a less strategic position than Shaftesbury itself. The references in the charter must mean that it was deemed more suitable in being further from the coast, referring perhaps directly to the events of 998 when the whole of Dorset was overrun by the Danish army.

It seems likely, furthermore, that it was as a result of these events that the Saxon churches at Bradford and at Limpley Stoke (on the western boundary of the estate—*see* Fig. 34) were built. The controversy regarding the date of construction of the church at Bradford need not be rehearsed here. The balance of recent opinion favours a late Saxon date (Taylor 1973, 165), for which the inference has been made that

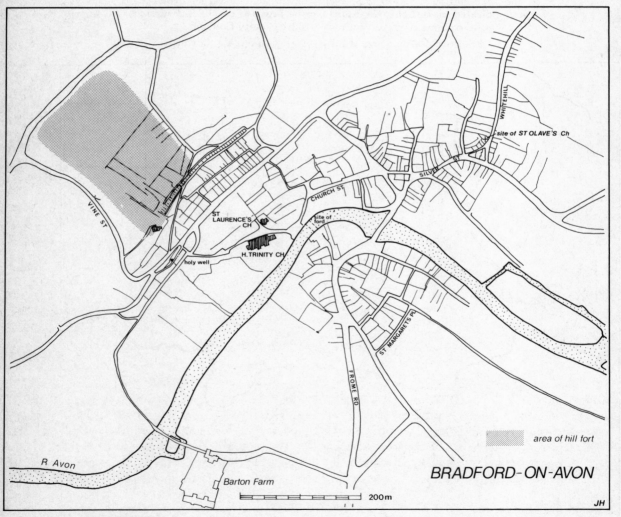

35. Bradford-on-Avon

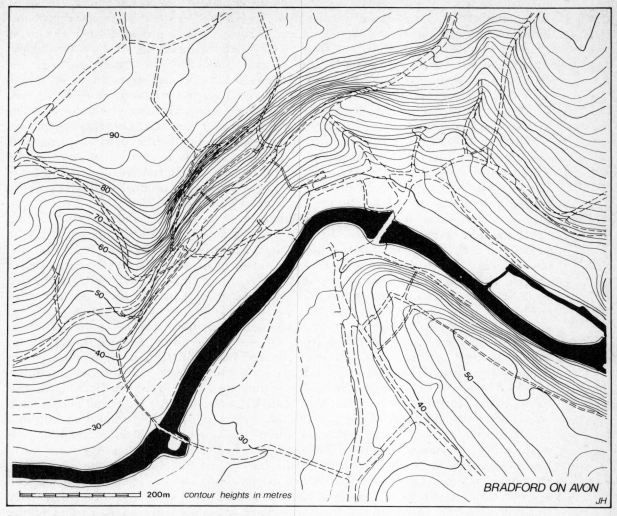

36. Bradford-on-Avon, contours at 2m. intervals

the context for its construction lies in the acquisition of Bradford by Shaftesbury abbey (Haslam 1976, 9; Hinton 1977, 24; Gem 1978, 110). Some strength is given to this by the consideration that the Saxon chapel is not on the site of the parish church. Since (as Gem [*ibid.*] has pointed out) the latter is most likely to mark the site of the minster church of St Aldhelm, the chapel must therefore have had some specialised function unconnected with a parochial role—a fact which also explains its temporary 'loss' among later buildings. This conclusion strengthens a suggestion made by H. M. Taylor (lecture at Bradford, 1975) that the chapel could have served as a reliquary chapel for the bones of Edward the Martyr, for whose safekeeping the Bradford estate had, according to the charter of 1001, been given to the nuns of Shaftesbury.

The physical development of Bradford is relatively easily discernable from its topography (Fig. 35). To the south of the ford a marked spur forms an arm of dry land, surrounded on three sides by river or marsh, which provides one of the few crossing places of a wide, often flooded and presumably originally marshy valley. The ford was in use until the early 19th century, though it was replaced by a bridge a little way upstream in the 14th century. It has already been suggested (Haslam 1976, 10), that the earliest settlement was concentrated on the northern end of this spur south of the ford, a suggestion strengthened by the concentration of early settlement at the heads of similar spurs at river crossings at, for instance, Calne, Chippenham, and Wilton (below). A comparison with the topography of these places also suggests the possibility that a discrete area of land on this spur, which survives in the 19th-century townscape (*see* Fig. 35), could have been an enclosure containing the Saxon royal *villa*. This would place it at the centre of an original settlement whose southerly limit may be marked by the presence of St Margaret's Place.

The ecclesiastical focus of the settlement was, however, clearly always on the northern side of the river, possibly reflecting, as suggested above, the existence of a pagan and early Christian religious site around the holy well. The 8th-century minster church was most likely on the site of the chancel of the present (Norman) parish church. It seems probable that the monastic precinct of Shaftesbury abbey, associated with St Lawrence's church, would have occupied at least part of the lower slopes of the hillside to the north of the church.

At a relatively early date, however, settlement must have spread—or shifted—along an early routeway to Chippenham from the northern end of the ford up the hill to the north-east. Its most likely course followed Church Street, the Shambles, Silver Street and White Hill. The site of St Olave's church, its dedication suggesting a mid-11th-century date, shows how far settlement must have reached along this route. It also, furthermore, suggests that some Viking settlement after, and perhaps as a consequence of, the raids of the late 10th and early 11th centuries was concentrated at Bradford (as well as probably at other similar early centres), possibly even augmenting its status and function as a developing urban place. A similar early routeway northwards from the ford can be traced past the church to the north-west. Its line is marked by footpaths, though partly obscured by 18th-century terraced housing, and continues up modern Wine Street to the top of the hill. Other early routeways to the south of the ford must have included the road to Frome to the south-west, and a pathway to the south along the crest of the spur which marks the site of the early settlement.

Bedwyn, Chisbury, Ramsbury, and Marlborough

These four places lie close together near the Kennet valley in eastern Wiltshire (Fig. 36a). It will be argued that in the late Saxon period their development can only be understood when their roles as high-order settlements are considered as being essentially complementary.[6]

Chisbury is a late Iron Age hill-fort (Cunliffe 1973, 431) whose inclusion (as *Cissanbyrig*) in the Burghal Hidage suggests that its defences were probably refurbished to form an element in King Alfred's systematic fortification of Wessex

36A. The area around the early estate centres of Bedwyn and Ramsbury. The Saxon royal multiple estate probably stretched approximately from the Ridgeway on the north and west to the county boundary on the east and south-east, and possibly comprised an area formerly dependent on the Roman town of Cunetio. The late Saxon centre of Marlborough subsequently developed on a new site within this early royal estate, probably as a burh in the early 10th century as a replacement for a hilltop burh at Chisbury.

(Brooks, 1964 75–9). This conclusion appears to be strengthened by the presence of a small medieval chapel dedicated to St Martin, at present quite isolated, at the eastern entrance of the defences. It is difficult to suggest a context for the construction of this, other than as the successor of a chapel placed by, or possibly over, the gateway of the Alfredian burh. The probable abandonment of the hill-fort in favour of settlement at Bedwyn at its foot in the early 10th century[7] suggests that the chapel is of late 9th-century origin.[8]

Immediately to the south of Chisbury lies Bedwyn. Detailed arguments have recently been set out by the writer (Haslam 1980, 58–64) suggesting that Bedwyn was the site of an early *villa regalis* at the head of a large estate which occupies roughly the catchment area of the Bedwyn stream. It is probable that it was in existence as such by the mid-7th century, and was early on provided with a minster church.

The writer has also argued (*ibid.*) that Ramsbury, which lies in the Kennet valley to the north of Bedwyn, was also an early *villa regalis,* with presumably a minster

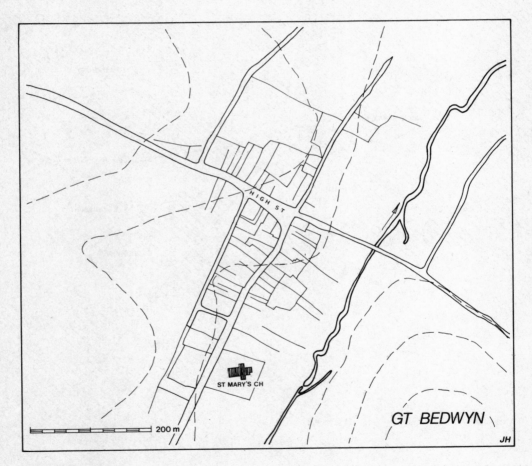

37. Great Bedwyn

church, which had developed at an early date by transference of royal power from the late Roman fortified town of *Cunetio*, only six kilometres to the west.[9] This development is suggested as providing the context both for the presence at Ramsbury in the early 9th century of a large-scale iron-smelting industry using innovative techniques, with which were associated exotic imports (lava querns), as well as for its later choice as the seat of a bishopric in A.D. 909.

Unlike Ramsbury, however, Bedwyn certainly became a small town by the 10th century, whose chief interest lies in the survival of guild statutes of the early to mid-10th century.[10] By the mid-11th century it possessed a mint, and had 25 burgesses at Domesday. It seems likely that the location of the royal burh at Chisbury was

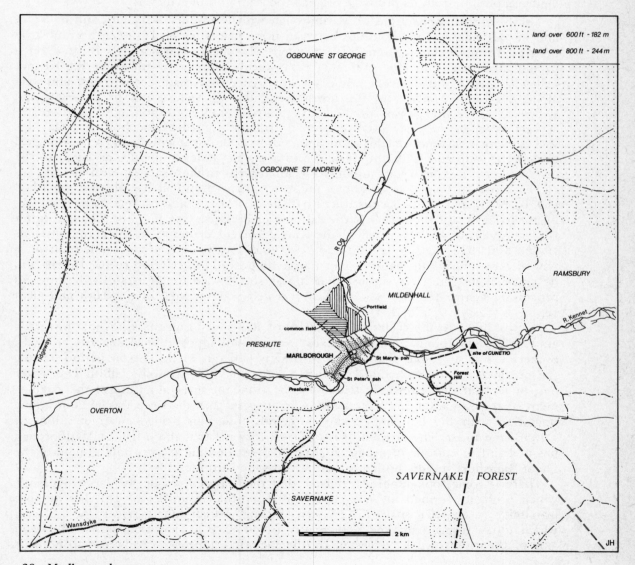

38. Marlborough area

governed as much by the fact that it lay on a royal estate as by its central position within the defensive system as a whole. Although Bedwyn's development as a town and the choice of Ramsbury as the bishop's seat in the 10th century must have reflected the importance of this burh, the writer has already argued (Haslam 1980, 63 and n. 144) that their respective roles should be considered more a consequence of their status as royal residences at the heads of large estates from a rather earlier period.

The topography of Bedwyn (Fig. 37) is uninformative. St Mary's church, which is presumed to be the site of the early minster, is some way removed from the focus of the present village. It is clear that the settlement has shifted, possibly in the early medieval period, from its probable original focus around the church.

The historical connections of Marlborough with Ramsbury, Chisbury and Bedwyn, and in particular the relationships between these places in the 10th century, must be inferred from similar patterns of settlement elsewhere. Marlborough is sited on a prominent broad spur, for the most part steeply sloping, overlooking the Kennet valley (Figs. 39 and 40). The advantage of its site, with easy access to east and west along the Kennet valley, to the north along the Og valley, and to Salisbury and Winchester over the Downs to the south, must in part be responsible for its greater success as an urban place over Bedwyn. It will be argued below, however, that this success, which becomes steadily more apparent in both documentary and archaeological evidence during and after the 11th century, is due at least initially as much to the historical circumstances surrounding its foundation as to these geographical factors.

The most striking feature about the town is, as Brentnall has already remarked (1950, 275), that its two constituent parishes, St Mary's and St Peter's, have clearly been carved out of the earlier parochial unit of Preshute (see Fig. 38). That the latter was in royal hands (it was called the King's 'ancient demesne' in the Hundred Rolls [*ibid.,* 300, 313]) suggests that the town was a deliberate urban foundation on a new site by one of the later Saxon kings. Its position in relation to the Downs and its situation by the river suggest that it was so founded to act as a distribution and processing centre for the wool industry which was growing in the 10th and 11th centuries (Sawyer 1978, 233).

Its proximity to the ecclesiastical centre of Ramsbury suggests a possible historical context for its foundation. Recent excavation and topographical analysis at Wells, Somerset, has suggested that a new town was laid out in the Saxon period outside the precincts of the cathedral established there in 909 (Rodwell 1980). The writer has, in fact, argued elsewhere (Haslam 1981) that the integral nature of the arrangement of town, market and Saxon cathedral suggests that the town was laid out in one operation with the building of the cathedral, both thus being new foundations of Edward the Elder. The possibility is thus put forward that the origin of Marlborough lies in a similar episode of urban creation at the same time as the establishment of the see of Ramsbury in 909, both again initiated by Edward the Elder.

There is some topographical evidence that this was centred on St Mary's church,[11] which probably formed the church of the new urban foundation. This lies in close proximity to an open space (The Green) through which runs a street (Herd Street) which today forms a marked hollow way (*see* Fig. 40). That this formed the main axis of the new town is suggested by the fact that approach roads lead to both its

CASTLE

COLDHARBOUR LA

BLOWHORN LA

KINGSBURY ST

THE GREEN

ST MARY'S CH

HIGH STREET

PORT MILL

ST PETER'S CH

R Kennet

200m

approx. area of
e. 10th cent. burh

MARLBOROUGH

JH

39. Marlborough

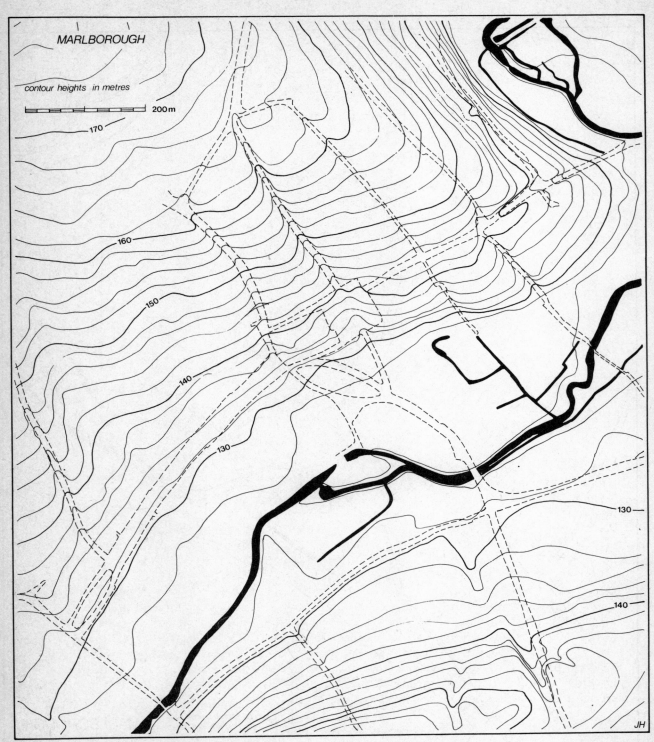

MARLBOROUGH

contour heights in metres

200 m

170

160

150

140

130

130

130

140

JH

40. Marlborough, contours at 2m. intervals

northern and southern ends, the latter across a bridge and probable causeway over a low-lying area of the river valley. There is some archaeological indication for the existence of defences to the west of the church, the presence of the defended burh appearing to be enshrined in the place-name 'Kingsbury'.

The area to the north-east shows several other streets lying parallel to Herd Street, connected by a central east/west street. Although these streets could constitute what remains of an original planned lay-out, it seems more likely that this pattern is the result of continued growth over a period of time. The name 'New land' was given to the eastern part of this area in the 12th century, with a new church and parish (St Martin's) created for it in 1254 (Brentnall 1950, 300–2).[12] Archaeological evidence of 11th- or early 12th-century occupation on the south-western side of the town (immediately north of St Peter's church) indicates that the town expanded considerably during the Norman period. It is to this period, therefore, that we should attribute both the creation of this new 'suburb' to the east of the original burh (though extra-mural expansion eastwards before the Conquest need not be ruled out), as well as the creation of a new wide market street to the west with its own church, the whole development forming a new parochial unit, probably as a consequence of the establishment of the Norman castle further to the west.

Marlborough thus provides a sharp contrast with the small town of Bedwyn: the former was a new foundation on a geographically advantageous site, while the latter was the result of an 'organic' development of proto-urban and urban functions at an ancient royal estate centre, perhaps encouraged by the proximity of the royal burh at Chisbury. Possibly the clearest demonstration of the suitability of Marlborough's site, and therefore of the reality of the economic factors which governed its choice, lies in its subsequent success both as a market town and as an industrial centre in the medieval period.[13] This contrast is further demonstrated by the fact that while Bedwyn has no clear cut area of arable and common town fields, those of Marlborough form a distinct entity to the north of, and topographically closely related to, the early nucleus of the town, the arable portion being called Portfield (see Fig. 38). Though this area is (perhaps rather surprisingly) not included within its original parish (St Mary's), it is clear that, like the town itself, it has been carved out of the king's 'ancient demesne' of Preshute. From this it can be inferred that this area formed an 'endowment' made by the king for the support of his newly created borough in the early 10th century.[14]

The developing relationship of these four settlements throughout the Saxon period is thus of great interest, showing a process of settlement development throughout the Roman and Saxon periods which involved several major shifts of both administration and population foci. The evidence suggests the formation of two royal estate centres at Ramsbury and Bedwyn at some time after the end of the Roman period in succession to *Cunetio,* both of them developing as proto-urban ceremonial, administrative and redistributive centres. In the late 9th century this pattern was augmented by the re-use of Chisbury hill-fort as a royal 'public burh'. In the early 10th century, however, the pattern was broken by the splitting of urban and ecclesiastical functions between the new town of Marlborough and the bishopric at Ramsbury by Edward the Elder in 909, with the (presumed) abandonment of the royal burh at Chisbury, but with the continuing focus of proto-urban if not by now truly urban functions at

Bedwyn. Soon after the Norman Conquest Marlborough became, as a result both of the construction of the royal castle there and of its more suitable geographical position, the dominant economic focus, inhibiting any nascent tendencies for urban growth at either Ramsbury or Bedwyn.

Calne

Calne is first recorded in the will of King Eadred (d. 955), when it was given to Winchester (Whitelock 1979, 555). However, a life of St Swithun (d. 862) written by

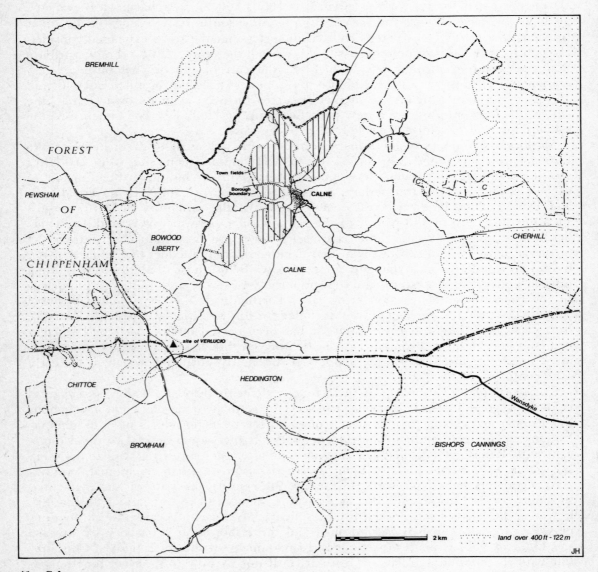

41. Calne area

Wulfstan in c. 1000 speaks of a prisoner being in the care of the chief magistrate of the district or hundred who lived in the king's villa ('regia . . . villula') at Calne (Marsh 1904, 14). It was clearly in this *villa regia* that the witan of 978 was held in which Bishop Dunstan miraculously escaped the collapse of the floor of a two-storeyed building—presumably the hall of the king's residence. A second witan is also recorded as being held at Calne in 998 (*ibid.*, 16). The existence of an early minster church at Calne, while not specifically mentioned in early documents, can be inferred from the exceptionally large holdings of the church in 1086, which amounted to 11 hides in all (Darlington 1955, 32).[15]

By the middle of the 9th century, therefore, Calne was already the site of a *villa regalis,* the centre of a large royal estate and hundred which was administered by, and under the jurisdiction of, a royal reeve. It was furthermore in all probability the site of a minster church which may well have been a late 7th- or (as at Bradford and several other royal centres) an early 8th-century foundation. Its urban character, certainly evidence by the time of Domesday, must have developed at an early date as a direct result of the concentration of these functions at one place (a process discussed further below).

The position of Calne in relation to the parish and hundred boundaries (Fig. 41), as well as to the earlier settlement pattern, is also of some interest. The Domesday hundred of Calne, on whose northern side the town lay, comprised several units, which include the Roman town of *Verlucio* in its south-western corner. The latter lies near the meeting points of three other ancient royal estates besides Calne: Chippenham to the north-west; Melksham to the south-west; and Bishops Cannings to the south-east. There is no evidence for any continuity of occupation at *Verlucio* into the 5th or later centuries, and it seems likely that the immediate area around the former Roman settlement and its attendant villas, occupying a watershed area of poor soils, must have reverted to the waste and forest out of which, as Bonney has recently suggested (1972, 178), they were probably carved. The present pattern of the distribution of royal estate centres around *Verlucio,* of which Calne is the nearest, is perhaps best explained by the fragmentation into smaller units of the presumably large territory dependent both administratively and economically upon *Verculio* soon after the formation of the West Saxon kingdom, each with a *villa regalis* at its centre. The writer has already argued (Haslam 1980, 60–61) for the operation of similar processes in the estates around the Roman town of *Cunetio.* That Bishops Cannings formed part of this larger area is suggested by the fact that the manor held one house in Calne at the time of Domesday, and by the fact that Chittoe is a chapelry of Bishops Cannings rather than Calne.

Calne provides one of the clearest instances among all the Wiltshire towns of the preservation of early features within the present townscape. The nucleus of settlement must have been round St Mary's church, which presumably occupies the site of the early minster. The church is centrally placed at the end of a low spur of land surrounded by streams on three sides. To the south, an open space (The Green) is separated from the church by a roughly equilateral area, occupied now (and clearly defined in the 19th century) by houses. This area is itself bounded to the north by Kingsbury Street. The association of these distinctive topographical features with the place-name 'Kingsbury', which means 'the king's burh or fortified house' (P-N

Wilts, 256) suggests the possibility that this discrete block of land represents the area occupied by the former royal *villa*—a conclusion considerably strengthened by the same associations of similar topographical features and the Kingsbury place-name in, for instance, Wilton.[16]

The early lay-out of the settlement might therefore have comprised the church, the royal residence, and an open space, all surrounded by land on the sides and

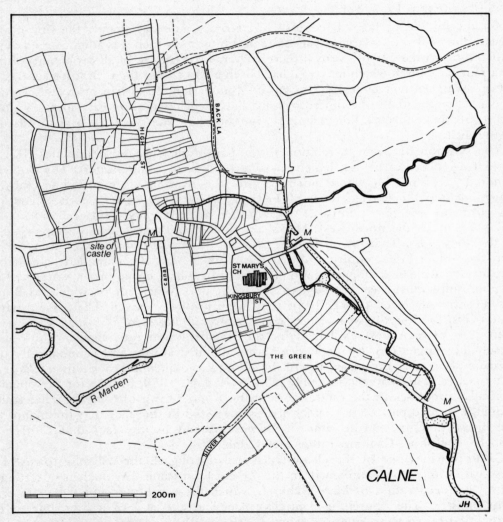

42.   Calne, with boundaries and other details from map of Calne by T. Cruse, 1828

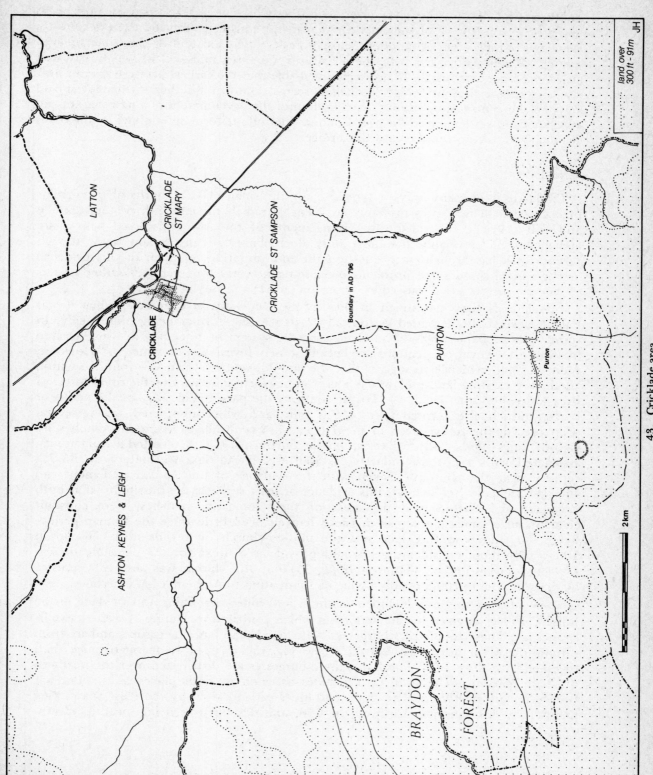

LATTON

CRICKLADE ST MARY

CRICKLADE

CRICKLADE ST SAMPSON

Boundary in AD 796

PURTON

Purton

ASHTON . KEYNES & LEIGH

BRAYDON

FOREST

land over
300 ft - 91m

JH

2km

43. Cricklade area

southern end of the spur given over to houses (Fig. 57).[17] There is no reason, given the probable existence of the royal residence and minster church by the 8th century, why this arrangement should not closely reflect that existing at this time or even earlier. Closely associated with these features are three mills, all of which may well be of pre-Conquest origin. It also seems probable that the earliest bridge was at or near the site of the present bridge, though it seems doubtful whether settlement spread beyond the central spur around the church until the development of a new market and its associated settlement in the post-Conquest period, its form determined by the roads leading from the northern end of this bridge.

Cricklade

Cricklade is in many ways a type site for the small class of burhs of rectangular plan created on new sites probably by King Alfred in the later 9th century (Biddle and Hill 1971).[18] The defensive arrangements of the town, discussed below, are archaeologically probably the most fully documented of any Saxon burh, though recent work has brought into question the interpretation of much of this evidence and has highlighted some problems concerning its early topography.[19] Other aspects of its early history are discussed by Thomson (1961) and Loyn (1963).

Cricklade is first mentioned in 903 in the *Anglo-Saxon Chronicle*, when it was either successfully defended or not in existence—the former being more likely. In spite of its probable origin as an element in the system of defence of Wessex initiated by Alfred, its royal connections are only obscurely revealed in documents.[20] However, there is some evidence to suggest that the late 9th-century town was founded within an already existing land unit which was from an early date part of the royal forest of Braydon (Thomson 1953, 6). To the south of the parish (Fig. 43) lies the parish of Purton, which also formed part of this unit, and which numbered among several properties in the forest given in the 7th and 8th centuries to Malmesbury abbey by various kings (*ibid.*, 5-6).[21] Excavations at Purton itself have revealed a Roman villa associated with a pottery industry, as well as a pagan Saxon cemetery of the 7th century near the church.[22] Taken with the evidence of the Roman settlement and villa at Cricklade (see below), this evidence at least suggests the possibility that both Cricklade and Purton, and the areas of their respective parishes, were constant elements in a landscape whose divisions had changed little since the Roman period. Since the church at Cricklade was the mother-church of a wide area (Thompson 1961, 1-2) these considerations would provide a context for the plausible though neglected suggestion of Thomson (*ibid.*, 65) that the church was already a minster by or soon after *c.* 700, possibly owing its foundation to Aldhelm of Malmesbury.

Some idea of the area included in the 1,500 hides pertaining to Cricklade in the Burghal Hidage is given by the area from which contributory burgesses were drawn in Domesday. These totalled 33 burgesses, with one house and one garden, and are from various places in north-east Wiltshire (*see* Fig. 45). It is of some significance that, together with those of Malmesbury, these burgesses are distributed over the northern third of Wiltshire. The total of the hides assigned to both places in the Burghal Hidage is very nearly equal to the 3,000 hides of land given by the West Saxon king Cenwalh to his kinsman, Cuthred, in 648, and described as being 'near Ashdown'

(Whitelock 1979, 164). Since Ashdown was the area of the Berkshire Downs to the north of the River Kennet (O.S., 1966), this suggests that the burghal areas of these two places, presumably apportioned in the late 9th century, preserved and were merely a division of a very much more ancient land unit which must have comprised the whole of the northern part of Wiltshire north of the River Kennet and the Roman road betweeen Bath and *Verlucio*.

The topography of Saxon Cricklade has been greatly elucidated not only by a series of excavations on various parts of its defences (described below), but also by a growing appreciation of the scale of Roman activities in the area. Excavations by the writer in 1975 within the north-west corner of the defences demonstrated the existence of an extensive and long-lived (1st to 4th centuries A.D.) village settlement previously hinted at from finds of Roman pottery in the area (Radford 1972, 94–5). This settlement was apparently associated with a large villa situated near the High Street,[23]

It is probable that this villa settlement was itself associated with a river crossing and causeway forming the foundation of the present road running northwards from the town, giving access to Ermine Street. The demonstration by F. T. Wainwright (1960) that the line of Ermine Street over the river had become lost immediately after the end of the Roman period suggests that an easy alternative route and crossing point of the Thames and its valley, represented by this causeway, was then available. Continuity of the settlement site at Cricklade after the 5th century can be neither demonstrated nor reasonably postulated. However the connections of this routeway both to the north and the east, with Ermine Street (whose preservation implies continued use throughout the Saxon period) suggest its continued local importance as a crossing point of the river and its valley, and provide the context for the siting there of the Alfredian burh in the late 9th century.

Both the position and the lay-out of the burh were thus determined to a large degree by already existing topographical features, which included the north gate and possibly the church, an earlier routeway approaching the river crossing from the south-west (the present Bath Street), and another routeway possibly approaching from Purton to the south. The lay-out of the defences, however, represents the closest approach of any new Alfredian burh to a perfect rectangle, in spite of the fact that its precise disposition was apparently further determined on the north and east sides by the edge of firm ground represented by the 80m. contour (*see* Fig. 44), and on the south side by a steep-sided though shallow valley.

The results of the excavations by the writer on the south-west corner of the defences in 1975,[24] when analysed with the results of previous work on the defences (Radford 1972), have shed some new light on both the topography of Cricklade and the lay-out of Saxon burhs in general. It is clear from the evidence of all the excavations to date that the construction of the defences in the pre-Conquest period falls into three main periods.

Firstly, an earth and clay bank some 6m. in width, which was probably supported and strengthened in front by a timber palisade, was further strengthened by the construction outside the bank of a triple-ditch system comprising two smaller ditches and a wide outer ditch, separated from the bank and from each other by wide berms. A double-ditch system has been put forward as the norm of Saxon

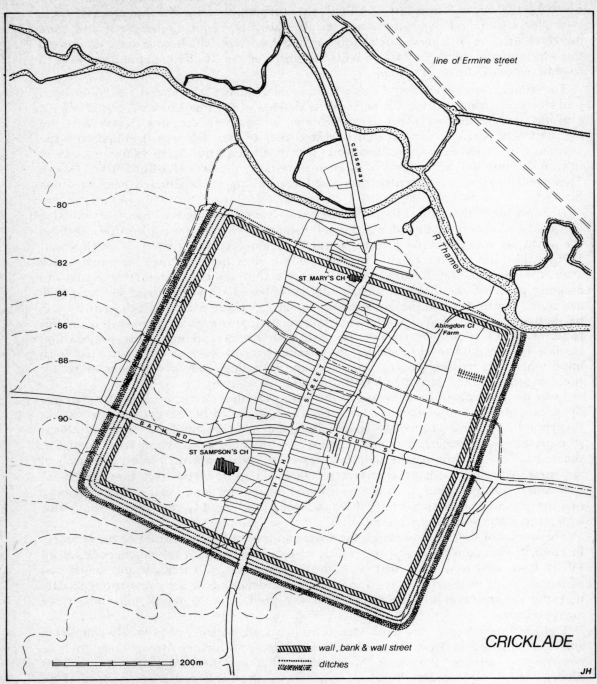

line of Ermine street

Causeway

R Thames

ST MARY'S CH

Abingdon Ct Farm

BATH RD

HIGH STREET

CALCUTT ST

ST SAMPSON'S CH

//////// wall , bank & wall street

··········· ditches

200m

CRICKLADE

JH

44. Cricklade, with boundaries from Tithe Award map, 1841

burhs, including Cricklade, by Biddle (1976a, 129); however, the feature described by Biddle as the outer Saxon ditch at Cricklade was demonstrated in 1975 to be a later ditch dug around the earlier burh in probably 1144. These results suggest the possibility that other burhs might well have been provided with a triple- rather than a double-ditch system, increasing the resemblance of their fortifications to those of Roman military camps.

Inside the bank was a narrow walkway of laid stones worn smooth over what must have been an appreciable period, the whole about 1.5m. in width, which must have acted as an intra-mural or 'wall' street—a feature well documented archaeologically as being characteristic of the layout of Saxon burhs in general (Biddle and Hill 1971, 73, 76; Biddle 1976a, 130). It was clear that this walkway was no later than the construction of the bank. The fact that turf used in the construction of the bank had been removed from the area of the bank and ditches, but still remained under the stones of the walkway, even suggests the possibility that the walkway had been laid out *before* the bank and ditches were constructed. This feature has been found in nearly every section cut across the bank, and on all four sides of the defences,[25] confirming its importance as an integral part of the lay-out of the whole defensive system of the burh.

A possible additional element in the initial lay-out of the burh was a feature found in two places on the inside of the eastern and western sides of the defences. This consisted of a 1m. wide line of stones running parallel to the bank and walkway about 5m. inside the latter. What this feature represented—whether the base of a wall or another flat stone walkway—is problematical; however, one likely interpretation is that it defined the inner edge of a zone around the inside of the defences which remained in royal hands to enable the proper military function of the defences to be maintained.

The second period is marked by the insertion of a new stone wall, of about 1.2m. thickness at the base, into the front of the bank, replacing the original (probably decayed) timber palisade. Though there is no positive dating evidence for this feature, its construction should most probably be viewed in the context of a general strengthening of existing defences by King Ethelred in the late 10th or early 11th century, in response to renewed Viking attacks, a programme which involved both the refurbishment with stone walls of other urban burhs such as Wareham and Christchurch, and the construction of 'emergency burhs' on hilltops, such as South Cadbury and Old Sarum (see below) (Radford 1972, 106; Hill 1978, 223-5).[26] At the same time as the construction of the front wall another was probably added to the upper part of the back of the bank to act as a rear revetment to a walkway along its top.

The third period in the defensive sequence is marked by the complete and deliberate destruction of the front and rear walls—an episode which has not hitherto been recognised at Cricklade. The two inner ditches were either partially or completely filled with stones, and the destruction deposits from the wall piled on the inner berm. The rear wall was similarly pushed down the back of the bank. Similar deposits have been observed in all earlier trenches across the defences, but incorrectly interpreted.[27] The archaeological evidence of the systematic destruction of the wall, the deliberate infilling of the ditches, and the fact that these processes can be shown to have taken place on all four sides of the defences, demonstrates that this was the result of a deliberate act designed to destroy the defences as a functioning system. Similar phenomena have been observed at South Cadbury (Alcock 1972, 201), as well as the defences of other burhs such as Wareham, Christchurch, Lydford, and probably Cissbury and Old Sarum (Haslam, forthcoming). This widespread, and therefore arguably systematic, episode of destruction can in the writer's view be best interpreted as a deliberate policy on the part of the Danish Cnut, after he became king in 1016, of the razing of existing defences to consolidate his position in the area in which he himself had fought. Significantly, however, the mint at Cricklade still produced coins throughout his reign. It was therefore not town life, or the towns themselves, which were destroyed, but only their defences.[28]

Several conclusions can be drawn from these excavations and other evidence about the original lay-out of the town. The existence of the intra-mural walkway or wall street demonstrates that the existing streets must have formed part of a system of internal streets which, like those at Winchester, were arguably laid out in a single operation designed to sub-divide the land inside the defences 'for the apportionment of land and for ease of movement on interior lines' (Biddle 1976b, 27), and that both this process and the lay-out of the defences must be considered as comprising one operation. It is indeed possible that the lay-out of the intra-mural walkway on open ground provided the initial grid around which the bank and ditches were subsequently constructed. The poor performance of Cricklade as an urban place in medieval and later times has meant that many of the internal streets have since become lost. The 1975 excavations showed furthermore that much of the land inside the defences on the western side of the town, and probably therefore on its eastern side as well, was open ground throughout the life of the burh.

A further problem on which some light has been thrown by excavation is the position of the west gate. Attempts have been made to show that it was situated in the centre of the western defences, in an equivalent position to the east Gate (Thompson 1961, 68; Radford 1972, 88-9). However, various lines of evidence suggest that the original gateway was probably under the present line of Bath Road.[29] The existence of a hypothetical extra-mural market outside the supposed centrally placed west gate (Radford 1972, 89, 99) must in consequence also be discounted. The so-called 'hollow way' leading to it from the river is, in fact, a mid-12th-century defensive ditch.

The present St Mary's church by the north gate is also very probably an element in the pre-Conquest topography of the burhs. Agruments have been given by Drs. Taylor and Thompson (1965 and 1966) for suggesting that the north chapel of the church was built on the site of the gatehouse of the burh, though doubt has been cast on this by Radford (1972, 106-7). The writer has argued elsewhere, however (Haslam 1981), that it is indeed of pre-Conquest origin, and represents a chapel either newly constructed or rebuilt (or re-dedicated) as a result of the acquisition in 1008 of the area of its later parish by Abingdon abbey (which is also dedicated to St Mary). There is, furthermore, some evidence for supposing (*ibid*) that the land unit represented by this parish was of rather earlier origin, serving some sort of defensive function for the north walls and gate, rather in the manner of the wards of London and Canterbury, possibly from the initial stages of the formation of the burh.

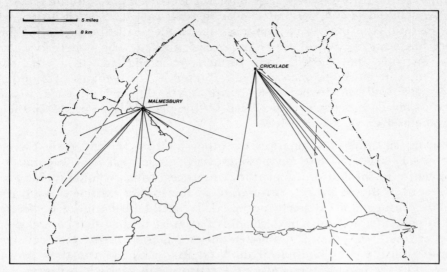

45. Domesday manors with property in Cricklade and Malmesbury

Malmesbury

As with most other places discussed in this chapter, the existence of an urban place at Malmesbury by the 10th century is the end result of its development as a settlement focus from well before the Saxon period. Little excavation has taken place in the town, but the early records of the abbey, together with the relationship of Malmesbury to the surrounding parishes, can begin to establish these settlement patterns.

One important element in this pattern is the early relationship of Malmesbury to Brokenborough. There is some evidence to suggest both the existence at Broken-borough of an early *villa regalis* and, furthermore, of the existence of an Iron Age hill-fort at Malmesbury itself, the two bearing a similar relationship to the hill-forts and *villae regales* at, for instance, Amesbury, Bedwyn, Bradford, Warminster, and Wilton. This relationship is suggested firstly by the account of the abbey's origins in the *Eulogium Historiarum* which represents stories current in the abbey in the 14th century (Watkin 1956, 210, n. 21).[30] This exhibits several features which, bearing as they do a close resemblance to more recent ideas concerning post-Roman settlement history, merit rather more serious attention than has been given to them in the past. The salient features of this account are, firstly, that the Irish monk, Maeldulph, came (in the early or mid-7th century) to a fortified *castellum* called Caer Bladon, the later Malmesbury; secondly, that this fortified place was only sparsely inhabited at that time, and was the site of a former British 'city'; and, thirdly, that this place stood in some relationship to another, probably fortified, centre named Caer Dur, the king's residence, now Brokenborough.

As for the first of these observations, there is some evidence that Malmesbury was indeed an Iron Age hill-fort. Its site, surrounded by steep slopes on all sides except a narrow ridge of land to the north-west, is nature's gift to defence-conscious man. A more concrete indication of Iron Age defences is provided by an observation of J. M. Moffat, who noted (1805, 101) that near the east gate 'at a small distance from the base of this wall (the town wall) about six feet underneath the surface of the earth, a substance has been discovered, which has been supposed to be a vitrified matter, and it has been imagined that the place was formerly encompassed with a vitrified bank or vallum'. This can most reasonably be interpreted as the remains of a timber-framed limestone slab wall which had been burnt *in situ*. Further evidence of the former existence of bivallate defences is provided by the peculiar topography of the medieval defences themselves, discussed below.

This being so, the re-occupation of other hill-forts in the early Saxon period (Fowler 1971) suggests that Malmesbury itself could well have become a military or tribal centre in the 5th or 6th centuries, a process which would provide the context for the record in the *Eulogium Historiarum* of the former existence of a British 'city', in the 7th century only sparsely occupied. It would furthermore be reasonable to suggest, in view of the similar pattern shown at most of the other centres discussed in this chapter, that a *villa regalis* developed out of this tribal centre on a new but nearby site, possibly on the consolidation of the West Saxon kingdom in the 7th century. As such it would have formed the centre of a territory either closely reflecting or directly continuing the early Saxon, or even the Iron Age, tribal territory. This would place in context the reference to Brokenborough as this royal centre, its name Caer Dur not so much showing the existence of another hill-fort (as Gomme thought, 1887, 422), but rather the presence of a fortified royal residence or burh.[31]

Some support is given to this model of early settlement development around Malmesbury by later evidence. In 956 Brokenborough was the centre of a large royal estate of 100 hides which was given to Malmesbury abbey by King Eadwy (Sawyer 1968, No. 629; Finberg 1964, No. 275), of which part had probably already been given by King Ine to Aldhelm (Darlington 1955, 88–9). The precise area comprised in this grant of land is uncertain, but must have included the modern parishes of Brokenborough and much, if not all of Crudwell, Charlton, Garsden, and Lea (*ibid.*; Grundy 1920, 42–53), as well as the area of the two Malmesbury parishes (Fig. 46). The parishes of Great and Little Somerford may well also have comprised part of this large royal estate.[32]

The probable early development of the royal centre at Brokenborough allows the foundation of the monastic establishment by the Irish monk, Maeldulph, in the mid-7th century to be placed in its proper context. William of Malmesbury suggested that Maeldulph 'was attracted by the solitude of woodland which surrounds the place',[33] but the foregoing considerations suggest that his choice of site and his reasons for coming were governed, firstly, by its proximity to the royal centre and by its defensive potential, and, secondly, by the consideration that, occupying as it must have done a central position in a relatively populous place, it would have been an ideal place for a Celtic missionary enterprise.[34] Furthermore, the relationship already suggested between the royal centre at Brokenborough with the hill-fort at Malmesbury provides one more instance of a pattern already noted by Alcock (1971, 326) of the association of early monastic establishments with pre-existing fortresses,[35] and of the possession of such places by the monastic founder by direct royal gift.

These royal connections have a further implication. Malmesbury provides an interesting parallel for the phenomenon noted in Irish examples of the siting of monastic establishments on the borders of kingdoms (Riain 1972). The Wiltshire-Gloucestershire border must in the 7th century have formed the boundary between the West Saxon and Mercian territories (the Hwicce from the early 7th century)—its disputed status at that time shown by the grants of land to Malmesbury in the later 7th century by both Mercian and West Saxon kings. It is not impossible that both

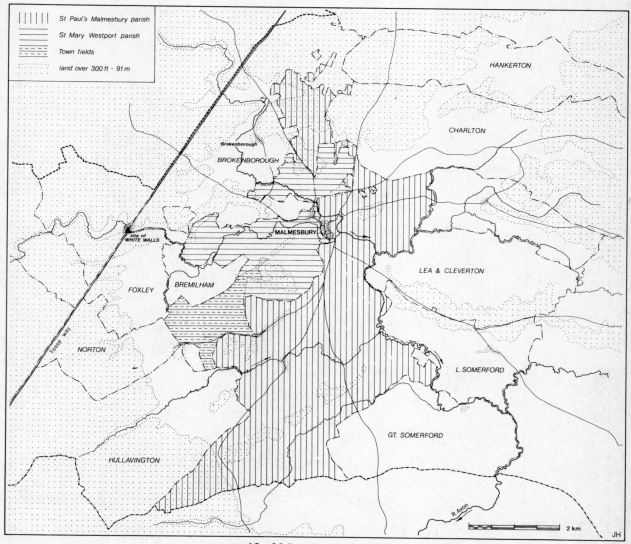

46. Malmesbury area

Maeldulph's initial choice of site, and in particular the growth of Aldhelm's expanded monastic establishment, were directly encouraged by the West Saxon kings to stabilise this outlying area of their kingdom. Indeed, William of Malmesbury himself noted that Aldhelm obtained special privileges for Malmesbury, Bradford and Frome lest conflicts between the kings of Mercia and Wessex should jeopardise the future of the monastery (Watkin 1956, 211).

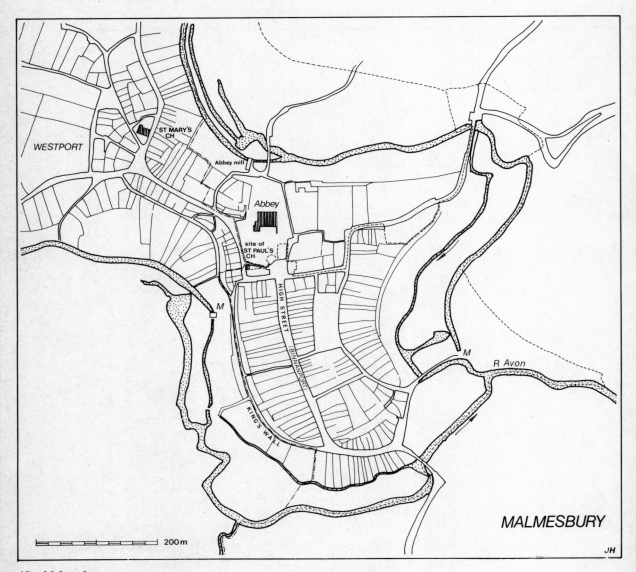

47. Malmesbury

The subsequent history of the monastery has been told already (*ibid.*). It is reasonable to suppose, however, that quite early in its life the monastic establishment must have attracted around it a considerable service population of miscellaneous students, craftsmen, traders, and other providers who constituted what may be described as a proto-urban settlement, becoming a focus of local if not regional trading activity and of small-scale industrial production.[36]

By the later 9th century, however, the Danish threats to Wessex led (as is suggested by the inclusion of Malmesbury in the Burghal Hidage) to the choice of Malmesbury, very probably by King Alfred, as a fortress to form an element in his systematic defence of Wessex. Its site, one of the factors which determined the presence of the monastery more than two centuries earlier, marked it out as being of great defensive potential. It must be inferred that the earlier Iron Age defences around the edge of the hilltop were refurbished, a process in all likelihood accompanied by the laying-out of at least some of the streets and the division of the interior space into *hagae,* whose boundaries must be reflected in the rectangular property divisions within the town observable to this day (Fig. 47). Malmesbury must have been both a fortress and a new urban creation, and is similar in plan to those other promontory fortress sites at Shaftesbury, Lydford, and Lewes.

It is not impossible, however, that some of these features—in particular the line of the central spinal street, the position of the three main gates, and the monastic precinct boundary—already formed elements in the topography of the earlier settlements. The roads entering the town through presumably long-established entrances to the north-west and north-east both turn southwards before meeting at the northern end of High Street, at which point is a market cross. It seems likely that this pattern developed well before the period of Alfredian urban restoration, and reflects the passage of well-used routeways around the outside of an already established monastic precinct, as well as the possible presence of an early market-place outside the monastery gate.

It is also possible that the former existence of bivallate defences of the Iron Age hill-fort is reflected in the present topography. The outer ends of properties within the town and the crest of the slope around all the sides of the town are marked by a common line, which is presumed to mark the crest of the inner bank re-utilised in the late 9th century. Outside this line, however, and lower down the slope, is a second line which marks another break in slope. On the south side this line is marked by a wall forming the boundary of extra-mural properties fronting on to the lower High Street, on the west side by the outer edge of the small street now called King's Wall, and on the east side by the edge of a similar, though unnamed, pathway running southwards from the east gate. Although these apparently double topographical features could be a fortuitous result of the relatively precipitous slopes, they could on the other hand reflect the adaption in the late Saxon period of an earlier bivallate defensive system. The paths or streets on both the east and west sides of the defences could on this interpretation be seen as the intra-mural streets running inside an outer bank.

The history of the various churches in Malmesbury is bound up with the early development of the monastery, and is not easy to discern. The available evidence has been discussed by Watkin (1956, 227–8), and suggests the presence of several subsidiary churches or chapels within the precinct, numbering at least four before the Norman Conquest. There was a further chapel dedicated to Our Lady which was referred to by Leland as being built in the town ditch to the west of St Paul's church. The church of St Paul was the parish church in the medieval period (to be succeeded after the Dissolution by the remains of the abbey church), and there is no reason to doubt that this was the principal church of the original Alfredian burh. In view of its site within the probable original monastic precinct, however, it seems possible that its origin could be even earlier. Its parish, occupying a large area of land around the town

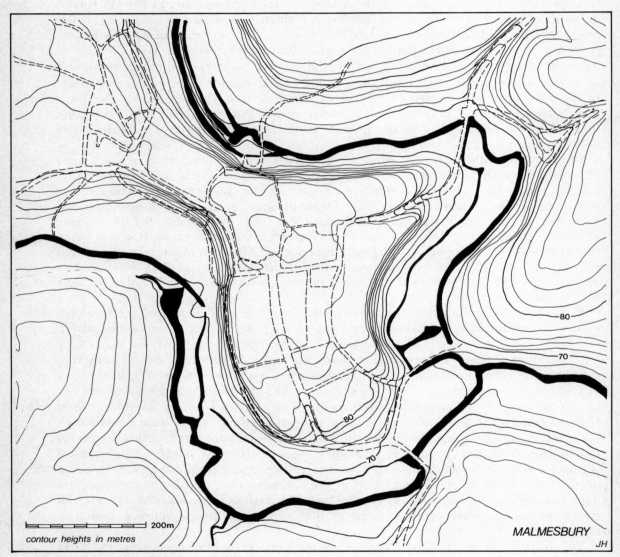

contour heights in metres   200m

MALMESBURY

JH

48. Malmesbury, contours at 2m. intervals

(Fig. 46) is closely associated topographically with that of St Mary Westport, suggesting that the two originally formed one unit, with the latter divided from the former at some later date.[37] This unit shows every sign of having been divided off from a larger territory, in this case very probably the royal estate which was still, in the late 9th century, centred on the *villa regia* at Brokenborough. This, in turn, suggests the possibility that the original parish unit of the town (comprising the present St Paul's and St Mary Westport parishes) was created by royal endowment on the establishment of the burh by King Alfred in the late 9th century.[38]

These suggestions seem to be strengthened by the disposition of the town fields, most of which lie at present within St Mary Westport parish. In the medieval period the area cultivated exclusively by the burgess community comprised various large fields ('magnae bruerae') among which was one called *Portmannesheath*.[39] This 'port' element in this name suggests a Saxon origin for the use of the land by the property-holders of the Saxon burh.[40] The charter of Athelstan granting these lands to the townspeople for services rendered may be spurious, but all the foregoing arguments suggest at least the strong possibility that some if not all of these lands were, in fact, set aside for the exclusive use of the original *burhwara* at the same time as the formation of the parish of the burh church on the creation of the burh by King Alfred.[41] It thus seems intrinsically likely that the tradition in this charter of the gift of lands to the town may indeed have had some basis in fact, and that it recorded the gift of part of the royal estate to the town (though possibly even earlier than the 'Athelstan tradition' would assert), the whole estate later given *in toto* to the monastery by Eadwy.

In spite of its hilltop location therefore, Malmesbury appears to have become a successful urban centre in the 10th and 11th centuries. It was an important minting centre from the reign of Edgar, and is the only mint recorded in the Wiltshire Domesday. Its success must have been due as much to the already long-established role of the monastery as both consumer and provider of food and commodities as to the continuing interest of Alfred and his successors in its fortunes.

Tilshead

The only definite indication of the existence of urban functions at Tilshead is the mention of 66 burgesses attached to it in Domesday Book. It was, however, part of the ancient demesne of the king, liable, like others, for the *firma unius noctis*. Its estates, assessed at 40 ploughs, was the same size as Warminster and Amesbury, and rather larger than Calne. It is difficult to reconstruct the extent of this estate, although it must have occupied most of the central area of the upland chalk downs, probably bounded on its edges by those parishes extending into the downland from centres in surrounding valleys—the Wylye to the south, the Avon to the east and north, and the Pewsey Vale to the north-east. The greater part of this central area is co-extensive with the Domesday hundred of Dole, which spans the lower reaches of the (later named) River Till. It is possible that other neighbouring upland parishes to the west (Chitterne and Imber) also formed part of this original royal estate.

It can be inferred, therefore, that as the site presumably of a *villa regalis* Tilshead was the place of central importance within this area of the chalk uplands, and as such would have shown many of those administrative functions—economic, legal and

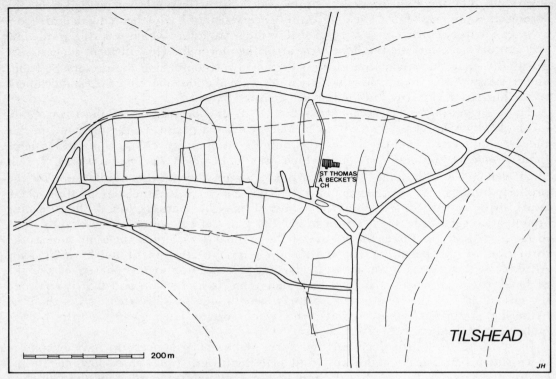

49. Tilshead, with boundaries from Inclosure Award map

ecclesiastical—shown by other better-documented centres. The evidence pointing to the importance of the woollen industry in Saxon England (discussed below) suggests that the specifically urban functions of Tilshead—whether the burgesses recorded in Domesday book lived there or elsewhere—must therefore have arisen out of its role as both a collection and distribution centre for both the wool and the sheep produced on the surrounding open downland.

There is little indication in the present topography of Tilshead of either the density of occupation at this period or of the lay-out of individual properties. The later Saxon period must have represented the peak of its fortunes, from which it seems to have declined steadily. It seems probable, however, that some of the present long boundaries between the main street and two back lanes (*see* Fig. 49) must mark some of the initial land divisions within the early town.

Warminster

The town of Warminster is a further instance of the early concentration of urban development at a Saxon royal estate centre of some antiquity. In Domesday it was an ancient demesne of the king, and supported 30 burgesses. There is some evidence

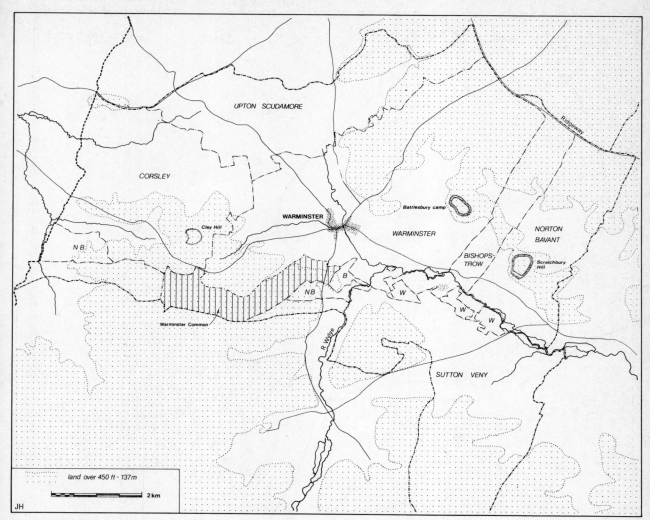

50. Warminster area

that the Domesday hundred (which was the same as the modern hundred [Rogers 1965, 1]) preserves the extent of the original royal estate centred on Warminster (Fig. 50). Most of its constituent parish churches were daughter churches of that at Warminster and the pattern of parish boundaries shown in Tithe Award maps shows close connections between them.[42]

This estate contains three Iron Age hill-forts: Cley Hill, Battlesbury, and Scratchbury camps. Finds of Roman coins, and of possibly pagan Saxon weapons, together with

51. Warminster, with boundaries and other details from Inclosure Award map, 1783

horse and human skeletons from Battlesbury in particular,[43] suggest its continuing (though doubtless intermittent) role throughout the Roman and early Saxon period as a military focus. Though the relationship of the later royal estate and its *villa regalis* to these earlier features are not so clear cut as, for instance, at Bradford, Amesbury, and Wilton, it could nevertheless be concluded that this *villa regalis* developed on the present site of Warminster early in the period of the formation of the West Saxon kingdom. The antiquity of this estate is suggested by the further possibility that the minster church at Warminster owes its origin to St Aldhem. He was certainly responsible for the foundation of the minster churches at the adjoining royal estate centres of Frome and Bruton, to the west and south-west. Furthermore, William of Malmesbury records the tradition that, as bishop of Sherborne, Aldhelm preached at Bishopstrow,[44] one of the constituent villages of Warminster hundred, whose church is dedicated to him. The intrinsic likelihood that the origin of both the village name and church dedication lies in a historical event suggests that by this time St Aldhelm had already founded a minster church at the centre of the estate of which Bishopstrow was one component, either (as at Bradford and Frome) before the beginning of his episcopate in 705, or else immediately afterwards.

As in the case of Calne and Wilton, the topography of the town suggests both the site of the royal residence and the lay-out of settlement immediately around it. The church of St Denys lies at the highest point of a raised area of land between two small streams which surround it on almost every side (Fig. 51).[45] A portion of this area (defined by the 375ft. [115m.] contour) is also occupied by the present Manor Farm, immediately to the south-east of St Denys's church. This was formerly called Warminster Court, and was in the hands of the Maudit family, the lords of Warminster, soon after the Norman Conquest (Daniel 1879, 115), and is thus likely to mark the site of the earlier Saxon royal residence.[46] This suggestion is further strengthened by its position so near to the site of the early minster church. Around this area, which takes up much of the available space on the higher ground between the streams, the single surviving street formed by Church Street and Silver Street must have formed the axis of the early settlement. Properties along this street must have backed on to the royal residence to the north and east, on to the small stream to the south, and on to low-lying land to the west.

A recent excavation to the north of Emwell Street[47] has shown that this street (whose properties backed on to the same stream as those along the south side of Silver Street) was being developed from the late 10th century onwards for small-scale industrial use.[48] Assuming that occupation along Emwell Street is secondary to that along Silver Street, it seems likely that the latter was developed during the 10th century if not somewhat earlier.[49] The identification of this Saxon nucleus thus provides a pattern of the close topographical association of the royal residence, the borough and minster church, and Saxon occupation—a pattern which can also be inferred from the topography of Calne, Chippenham, and Wilton, discussed elsewhere in this chapter. Later Saxon and early medieval development must have been concentrated round the bridge over the River Were to the east, with a further new urban development to the east of this, probably as a result of the grant of a market to the town in 1204 (Haslam 1976, 63).

Wilton and Old Sarum

For reasons which will become apparent, Wilton and Old Sarum must be considered together as being the two main focal points in an area which has been one of the most significant foci of settlement in Wessex throughout the Saxon period. The development of urbanism in these two places can only be understood by examining their changing roles in the settlement pattern during this period, a process which with the growth of New Salisbury in the 13th century and the subsequent eclipse of urban functions at both Old Sarum and Wilton is one which is among the most complex and interesting in the south of England.

In the Iron Age the hill-fort of Old Sarum, lying in a commanding position between the rivers Bourne and Avon, must have been in many senses the focus of a wide area. On it later converged several Roman roads, a large Roman settlement probably developing on a site in its shadow closer to the river (R.C.H.M. 1980, xxviii). The hill-fort, nevertheless, gave the settlement its name (*Sorviodunum*), which has been perpetuated throughout the Saxon period.[50] The Anglo-Saxon penetration of this area is well documented both in the *Chronicle* and, more recently, in numerous archaeological finds (*ibid.*, xxviii-xxix). The battle recorded at *Searoburh* in 552 indicates the continuing importance of the hill-fort as a military if not also an administrative or tribal focus of its region. Indeed, it seems at least possible that the manifest attraction of this area for the Saxons lay in the existence of a working system of administration and land utilisation preserved from, and around, the Roman settlement at *Sorviodunum*.

It is in this context that the rise of royal Wilton, and its assumption as the capital place of the later shire, must be placed. Royal charters were signed at Wilton in 838 and 854 (James 1962, 7). It was certainly the chief place of the present county by the end of the 8th century, and of the Wilseatan (whatever area this covered) very probably by the end of the 7th century (Young 1942, 28-9; Darlington 1955; P-N Wilts, xvi-xvii). This evidence points to the conclusion that it became the local royal administrative centre on the consolidation of Saxon power in the area in direct succession to the tribal base at Old Sarum.[51] These necessarily brief arguments suggest that the royal palace complex at Wilton, described above as centring on Kingsbury Square, has an origin possibly as early as the early 7th century. These conclusions certainly fit in with the development of settlement patterns within and around the royal Forest of Grovely, which occupied the ridge immediately to its west, and whose eastern bounds were drawn along the western defences of the town (Grundy 1920, 571-3). Bonney has argued (1972, 180-1) that the woodland comprising the later forest was formed by regeneration of land abandoned by Iron Age and Roman settlements consequent upon their movement into the valleys. He has also suggested, however (lecture, 1980) that Wilton itself does not fit neatly into the pattern of surrounding settlements and parishes, and has observed that it is an intrusion into a landscape already settled and divided up by the earlier Saxon period.[52]

These observations suggest that the royal vill at Wilton was a 'planted' settlement, and that the existence or development of the forest on the Grovely ridge, and its suitability as a royal hunting ground, was either the immediate cause or the immediate consequence of this development. This conclusion is strengthened by the position of Wilton at the junction of two valleys, on a gravel ridge surrounded by marsh or rivers, suggesting a conscious choice, for specific reasons, of a site combining regional accessibility with local inaccessibility. A similar conclusion can be drawn from the relationship of Chippenham to surrounding settlements (see above), and from its position on a similarly distinctive site.

An ecclesiastical presence must also have developed at Wilton at an early date. There are various intermittent references to the formation of a monastic establishment of some kind at Wilton from the early 9th century onwards (Hoare 1825, 60–67, 78–80; Nightingale 1906, 2; Darlington 1955, 30). According to a 15th-century poem setting out the history of the nunnery, King Ecbert founded a nunnery for 13 sisters in 830, dedicated to St Mary. This was said to have been the successor of a chantry built in commemoration of Alemund by Weohstan, the first recorded Ealdorman of Wiltshire in c. 800 (Hoare 1825, 60–61). Alfred is said to have refounded the monastery dedicated to St Mary, removing it 'from its former situation to the site of what had previously been the royal palace', and giving it the title of Abbey (ibid., 78).

Although the author of the V.C.H. has dismissed this account out of hand (Crittall 1956, 231), its underlying authenticity appears to be borne out by independent evidence shown by the topography of the centre of the town. It preserves, in particular, a record of the close relationship between the main monastic church, dedicated to St Mary, and the royal residence; it is precisely this same relationship which is demonstrated in the proximity of the present St Mary's church and the king's burh' or royal palace, shown by the place-name 'Kingsbury', discussed in more detail below.[53] If it is accepted that these accounts are genuine, St Mary's church would by the end of the 8th century have been a minster church of some importance— reflecting the regional importance of the villa regalis. In view of this late 7th-century origin of minsters at other places discussed in this chapter, its origin could well be taken back to the early days of the conversion of Wessex in the 7th century.

The close association of St Mary's church and royal palace is further indicated by the burial there of two, possibly three, of Edward the Elder's daughters, together with his second wife. Edgar's charter of 974 suggests that Edward refounded the monastery (Hoare 1825, 85), but since most of the 9th- and 10th-century kings seem to have had a finger in the monastic pie (ibid., 78) it is difficult to know precisely what this means. It is possible, however, that both this episode (and perhaps also Alfred's earlier 'refoundation') mark the provision of a new minster church separated from the earlier monastery (included in consequence within the precincts of the royal palace) to provide a parish or burh church for the developing urban community in precisely the same way, and for the same reasons, that the New Minster was provided at Winchester (Biddle [ed.] 1976, 314). The close interest of Edgar in the monastery at Wilton (his daughter, Edith, was associated with the monastery for most of her life), suggests furthermore that the move of the monastery from a position either within or attached to the royal palace to the site some 300m. to the east, where it remained until the 16th century, was the direct result of the reformation of the monastery by the king and Bishop Dunstan, probably before 974.

From the late 9th century to beyond the Norman Conquest both the functional and spatial relationships between Wilton and Old Sarum become close, and are highly illuminating for any study of urban origins and development. In 871, a month after his accession to the throne, Alfred fought and lost a battle against the Danes at Wilton. There is some evidence to suggest that it was at this time that the strategic importance of Old Sarum in relation to the old-established royal site at Wilton was appreciated anew, and its defensive potential once again utilised. Wilton formed one of the places mentioned in the Burghal Hidage, being assessed at 1,400 hides (Hill 1969, 90). However, of all the places mentioned in this document, Wilton has the least adequate defences, whether artificial or natural, a fact which has led the author of the *V.C.H.* to suggest some link between Wilton and Old Sarum (Hill 1962, 52–3). It is thus intrinsically possible that it was Old Sarum rather than Wilton which formed the original fortification in King Alfred's initial scheme for the defence of Wessex. This suggestion is strengthened by the evidence of a document noticed by Colt Hoare (1812, i, 224) which records the re-fortification of Old Sarum by King Alfred. It reads: 'I Alfred, king and monarch of the English, have ordered Leofric Earl of Wiltunshire not only to preserve the castle of Sarum (? *Searoburh*), but to make another ditch to be defended with palisades, and all who live about the said castle, as well as my other subjects, are immediately to apply to this work'.[54] Whatever might have been the provenance or the form of this document, its genuineness is suggested by the appearance in it of those elements which would be expected in such an undertaking: the use of ditch and palisade defences, the summons to the earl (shire reeve) of the county, and the nature of the re-fortification as a public enterprise.

There is nothing, however, to suggest that the provision of defences at Old Sarum implied the creation there of an urban place, although coins of Athelstan and Edgar have been found inside the defences (Shortt 1965, 9; R.C.H.M. 1980, xxix).[55] The topographical evidence described below suggests that urban development was concentrated at Wilton, then as later a far more accessible and well-watered site. The inclusion of Wilton in the Burghal Hidage document, furthermore, shows that this must have been a development no later than the reign of Edward the Elder. Whether this document relating to Old Sarum is genuine or not, it certainly describes a development—or at least part of a series of developments—which can be recognised as occurring in other places in southern England, in which an initial non-urban (presumably Alfredian) hilltop fortress was succeeded by a topographically distinct urban development, with or without defences, on a new and more accessible site.[56]

The Alfredian origin of the burh at Old Sarum provides a context for its use as an 'emergency burh' during the period of renewed Danish hostilities in the early 11th century. In 1003 Swein 'led his army into Wilton, and they ravaged and burnt the borough, and he betook him then to Salisbury'. It was either in anticipation, or as a direct result, of this event that the moneyers moved from Wilton to Old Sarum (Dolley 1954; Hill 1962, 53).[57] There is good evidence from other fortresses constructed at this time that the existing defences of the hill-fort must have been strengthened or reconstructed.[58] One, and possibly two phases of post-Roman defences have been identified archaeologically, but in view of the lack of dating evidence or other diagnostic archaeological features it would be a mistake to identify these firmly with this episode.[59]

It is possibly to this phase of burh construction (or equally possibly to the preceding Alfredian phase) that several features discernable in the Norman period can be ascribed. Firstly, the area of the hill-fort and burh was by the time of Domesday quite clearly a royal enclave surrounded by lands belonging to the first bishop (Benson and Hatcher 1843, 41; Hill 1962, 51–2; R.C.H.M. 1980, xxix-xxxi). In his gift of these lands to the bishop, probably before the Conquest (Hill 1962, 52), the king must have reserved for himself the old royal burh—a conclusion which provides the context for the unusual interest which William I took in Old Sarum both as the site of a castle and a cathedral.

Secondly, there are suggestions that there was already by the end of the Saxon period a church or chapel dedicated to St Mary inside the burh, within the precinct of the later castle (Benson and Hatcher 1943, 12). The evidence is somewhat confusing, as Musty and Rahtz have already pointed out (1964, 131–3), but the possibility should not be overlooked that this, or another of the several churches recorded as being in Old Sarum (*ibid.*), was the church of either (or both) the 9th- or the early 11th-century burh.[60]

Thirdly, it appears that there was a church placed over the east gate dedicated to the Holy Cross, which was observed by Leland in 1540 (Stone and Charlton 1935, 174). Though there are no references to it earlier than 1236 (Hill 1962, 60) it is highly probable that this is a further example of that group of churches which were placed over or by the sides of gates of Saxon burhs.[61] The late 9th- or early 10th-century origin of a similarly-placed chapel at Chisbury, argued above, at least suggests the possibility that the church at Old Sarum could have owed its origin to the period of fortress creation by King Alfred.

The historic core of Wilton is situated on a low spur of river gravels which is never more than 2–3m. above the rivers Wylye and Nadder which surround it on three sides.[62] It has been described as a 'promontory burh',[63] though its topography is by no means as marked as that of other promontory burhs such as Shaftesbury and Lydford. An earlier attempt by the writer to see parallels in its plan to those rectilinear burhs such as Cricklade (Haslam 1976, 67–9), must, in view of the discussion below, be considered inappropriate.[64]

For various reasons, it is likely that the historic core of the town lies around Kingsbury Square (Fig. 52), which contains an open 'market' area, space around this for houses, and St Mary's church. Evidence already set out suggests that this church is on the site of an early (presumably 7th-century) minster church, and a 9th- and early 10th-century nunnery. The present Kingsbury Square is, furthermore, adjacent to an area which is clearly shown on a plan of *c.*1568 (James 1962, 28) as being a discrete area of enclosed land set in the central part of the spur between the rivers to the north and south. The association of this area with the 'Kingsbury' place-name, and the parallel to this arrangement at, for instance, Calne (discussed above, and further below), suggest that this area was the site of the royal palace, the 'king's burh', which has been suggested above was certainly in existence by *c.* 800 and very probably considerably earlier.

Converging on to this central area are two roads leading from the north-east and south-west over a succession of bridges. There is no reason to believe that these are not the direct successors of roads, probably constructed over causeways with frequent small bridges over the various branches of the rivers, which formed the original entry and exit points to this royal palace complex (Fig. 52). It seems quite likely, though it has yet to be demonstrated, that the areas on either side of these roadways could have been the site of early 'suburban' development, the proximity to flowing water facilitating industrial activities such as flax retting, cloth fulling, or tanning.[65]

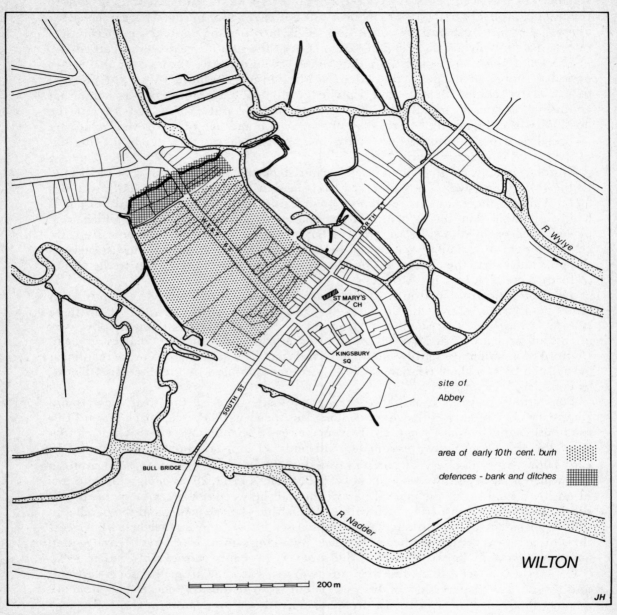

52. Wilton

To the north-west, along the low ridge of the spur, lies a wide street bounded to the north-west by bank and ditch defences,[66] which topographically forms an area separate from the royal palace complex described above. The courses of the roads approaching Wilton from the west and north-west (Fig. 52) are clearly determined by a gate at the centre of these defences. The boundaries of the properties still discernable along this street lie at right-angles to it, running back at least part way to the river channels on either side. It is uncertain whether any purpose-built defences were constructed at these sides (to the north-east and south-west of West Street); field-work suggests that a marked ditch to the south-west may have been a canalisation of the river for defensive purposes, but its date is uncertain.[67] The topographical evidence thus suggests that this area was a new urban development, laid out as a discrete unit next to the early palace complex and provided with new defences in a single operation.

No excavations have been undertaken in this area, and no dating evidence obtained in the two trenches cut across the defences. It is suggested, however, that in view of Wilton's inclusion as a fortress in the Burghal Hidage document, this defended area was added to the earlier undefended nucleus either in the period of Alfredian fortress and town building in the late 9th century, or else by Edward the Elder in the early years of the 10th century. Arguments already given suggesting that Old Sarum was used as the original Alfredian fortress implies that this defended area in Wilton was a new urban development of Edward the Elder, arguably before 911 when he began his Midland campaign. This conclusion also fits in with the pattern argued by the writer (in Chapter 8 below) for the development of Barnstaple, Totnes, Kingsbridge and Plympton (Devon) as fortified urban centres founded by Edward the Elder, to replace the Alfredian fortresses of Pilton and Halwell. Topographically, and also in the writer's view in the manner of its origin, this is a remarkable parallel for the town at Langport (Somerset), though the development along the long causeway there is secondary to an earlier hilltop fortress rather than to an undefended royal palace nucleus, as at Wilton.

It is clear that subsequent to the focus of Old Sarum as a tribal 'capital' in the 5th and/or 6th centuries, Wilton developed as the central settlement in both the area and the region, and as an important royal residence. Ideally sited for both regional and local trade, it cannot have failed to have become a relatively sizeable settlement which by the 9th century must have been at least proto-urban in character. It is thus unlikely that the creation of the Alfredian fortress at Old Sarum could have led to much if any urban development there—a conclusion borne out by the topographical evidence at Wilton of a phase of urban expansion in the early 10th century. Wilton must have developed rapidly as an urban centre throughout the 10th and 11th centuries, helped no doubt by the popularity of the nunnery in its midst. This seems to be confirmed by the mention in a charter of King Edmund in 940 of a *haga* in Wilton granted as an appurtenance of an estate at Wylye (Sawyer 1968, 469; Finberg 1954, No. 254)—the earliest mention of an urban *haga* in charters. A charter of Edgar, furthermore, grants to the monastery two hides of land 'juxta civitam sitas', which Regenweard the merchant formerly held, including also a mill, a church and 16 acres of pasture on the common meadow (Hoare 1825, 85). This again is one of the few direct pieces of evidence, firstly, for the existence in the 10th century of common fields attached to early urban communities, and, secondly, for the fact that these fields must have been, as they clearly were in the medieval period in many places, divided up in some way between the burgesses and/or the occupiers of *hagae*. It also emphasises that these 'town fields' were owned by, and in the gift of, the king rather than the burgesses as a group, which is a reminder of the origin of the town as a royal foundation attached to a royal vill.

In itself the creation of an 'emergency burh' at Old Sarum in 1003, and the move there of the Wilton moneyers, does not necessarily imply either that urban activities ceased at Wilton (in spite of its recorded destruction) or that Old Sarum necessarily became an urban place. The fact that the moneyers stayed at Old Sarum rather than moving back to Wilton after the end of Aethelred's reign does, however, suggest that probably from this time some of the functions of royal administration centred at Wilton—in effect the residence of the shire reeve—were transferred to Old Sarum on a permanent basis. The continuation of the mint there throughout the 11th century can be seen at least in this case as more of a convenient administrative arrangement than a demonstration of its urban status. Such settlement as there was in the period up to the Norman Conquest need have consisted of no more than a small service population gathered around the hall of the shire reeve, inside the defences. Since archaeological evidence for settlement outside the east gate is only of the Norman period and later (Stone and Charlton 1935; Musty and Rahtz 1964), it must be concluded that any truly urban development at Old Sarum ·began in the 'suburbs' (i.e., outside the earlier burh) only as a consequence of the construction of the castle and cathedral inside the former burh from the Norman period onwards.[68] In contrast, the urban functions of Wilton can have been only momentarily disrupted by the destruction of the town in 1003. That new moneyers began working there from the beginning of the reign of Cnut even suggests the possibility that the new king pursued a policy of urban restoration and renewal. Wilton subsequently developed through the early medieval period to become by any standards an important town, until its urban functions (together with those of Old Sarum) were gradually usurped by New Salisbury from the early 13th century onwards.

*   *   *   *   *

There are two, possibly four, other places in Wiltshire which are not described in Domesday Book as having burgesses, mints or markets, but which yet have some claim to be regarded as urban places by the later Saxon period. The two most certain ones are Amesbury and Chippenham, and the two less certain are Westbury and Downton. Amesbury and Chippenham were both part of the royal demesne in Domesday, both paying the *firma unius noctis,* and can be considered, therefore, as being the head places of royal estates which were ancient by the time of Domesday.

Westbury had none of these characteristics except in being the central place of a large parish which was also a Domesday hundred. A little to the east of Westbury, and at the centre of this land unit, lies the Iron Age hill-fort of Bratton, a relationship apparently enshrined in the name 'Westbury'.[69] As with Amesbury, Bedwyn, Bradford, Warminster, and Wilton, it is possible to see Westbury as an early Saxon, possibly royal, estate centre, continuing by more or less direct succession the role formerly played by the hill-fort.[70] Although early- to mid-Saxon pottery has been found at Westbury (Fowler 1966), any urban or indeed proto-urban characteristics are difficult to demonstrate before the 13th century—though probably more through the non-survival of relevant evidence than anything else.

Similarly, Downton was also the centre of a large royal estate which was probably given to the bishops of Winchester in the late 7th or early 8th centuries (Crowley 1980, 19–28). It has been suggested that Downton itself probably succeeded a large Roman villa as an estate settlement (*ibid.*, 23), a development which would certainly place in context the middle or late Saxon pottery found there (Rahtz 1964). However, without the stimulus of the royal presence after the 8th century, arguably of some importance in the special development of other settlements, it is uncertain whether this estate centre would have developed any recognisable proto-urban or urban characteristics.

Amesbury

Amesbury has been well served by several recent historical studies (Pugh 1947–8; Pugh 1956; Chandler 1978–9; Chandler and Goodhaugh 1979; Hinton 1979), which have dealt with most aspects of its development. Although Domesday Book gives no indication of any recognisable urban characteristics, there are some grounds for suggesting that it developed at an early date as an important proto-urban settlement, and that by the end of the Saxon period it would have been as 'urban' as any of the smaller places so far considered.

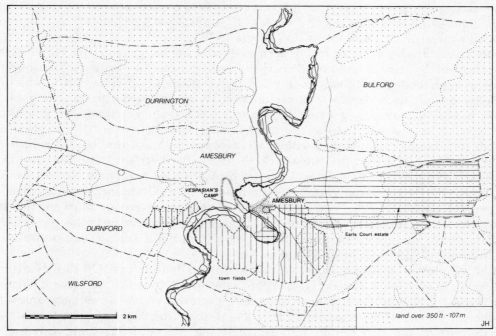

53. Amesbury area

It seems clear that Amesbury's early significance was due to its role as a central place from the Iron Age if not rather earlier. It is first mentioned as *Ambresbyrig* in King Alfred's will (P-N Wilts, 358-9), from which fact two important points emerge. Firstly, as the central settlement in a royal estate, Amesbury was an administrative, judicial and economic centre, the site of a *villa regalis* and very probably a minster church. The area administered by this estate centre, in both secular and ecclesiastical matters, was probably the whole of the Domesday hundred (Hinton 1979, 27), though the royal demesne by the time of Domesday probably covered only the area of the parish itself with that of Durrington to its north (Fig. 53). The royal estate also included a large area of woodland to the south and south-east (Pugh 1947-8, 101-2).[71] It has also been suggested (Hinton 1979, 27) that the existence of an early minster church was responsible for the stories recorded by Geoffrey of Monmouth of an early monastery at Amesbury (Chandler 1978-9, 6).

Secondly, the name *Ambresbyrig* shows with little doubt that the settlement at Amesbury was in some way connected with the hill-fort ('Vespasians camp') immediately to its west. The development of royal administrative centres in direct and arguably casual relationship to hill-forts shown at, for instance Wilton/Old Sarum, Warminster/Battlesbury, Bradford/Budbury, and Brokenborough/Malmesbury, suggests that a similar process could well have operated in the case of Amesbury and 'Vespasian's camp', and that the hill-fort itself would in the early Saxon period have been re-used as some sort of military and/or territorial tribal focus. The wider incidence of this pattern of development lends some support to suggestions (admittedly somewhat speculative) that the hill-fort was re-occupied as one of a number of permanent garrison points of the forces of Ambrosius Aurelianus, the commander of British forces in the 460s and 470s (Morris 1973, 100).[72]

The royal vill at Amesbury is thus seen as developing in probably the 7th or possibly even the 6th century at a convenient river crossing near the formerly garrisoned and possibly re-defended hill-fort, as the central settlement of a territory which was probably at that time already well established. Its gradual acquisition throughout the Saxon period of economic, administrative, ecclesiastical and ceremonial functions must have given rise eventually to a proto-urban and latterly a truly urban place, even though its administrative and to some extent economic roles would always have been overshadowed by Wilton to the south. It is likely therefore that (as Hinton has suggested, 1979, 28) both the royal palace, probably surrounded by its own ditch and bank, and the early minster church would have been sited around the bridgehead and the present parish church, with any associated settlement grouped around this focus along the road approaching from the east. There are, however, no clear topographical indications of the lay-out of this early settlement complex such as can be postulated for instance at Wilton, Calne and Chippenham.

It is in relation to this pattern from the abbey, founded in 979 shortly after the assassination of King Edward (Pugh 1956; Hinton 1979), must be placed. There has been considerable controversy over its precise location, which is even now unresolved. On the one hand, Hinton argues (1979, 24-5) that since the monastery was not an integral part of the community into which it was placed, it lay some distance from the present church on the later abbey site (to the north-east), and quotes as a parallel the separation of the monastery at Bradford from the parish church (see above). This

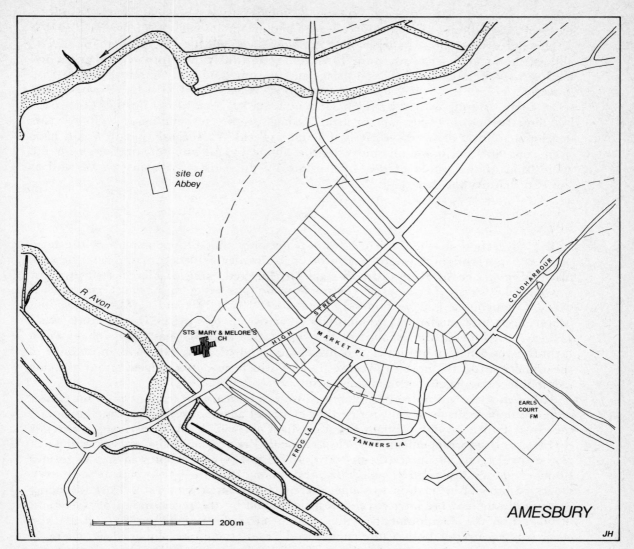

54. Amesbury, with boundaries and names from map by T. Flitcroft, 1726

view is perhaps given some support by the suggestion made above in the case of Wilton
for the move of the monastic house from its original position in close association with
the royal palace and earlier minster church to a new site, either in the early 10th
century or more probably during the reforms of Edgar and Dunstan in the 970s. However, Chandler has argued (1979, 14) that the original monastic church and conventual
buildings were grouped around the present parish church (near the presumed site of the
royal palace), and that on the re-foundation of the nunnery in 1177 new buildings

were constructed on another site, the old buildings on the original site being rebuilt to accommodate a house of male religious, who had moved in by 1189.

This latter suggestion fits with other topographical and historical observations. The abbey held no land of its own in the town, and seems likely therefore to have originated in close association with the royal palace and presumed minster church. The suggested move in 1177 to the new site can, furthermore, be associated with the growth of the town to the south, with the lay-out of a new market area whose northern approach lay directly opposite the gate or lane leading to the new nunnery.[73] Though this development cannot be dated, it is not unreasonable to suggest that it would have been consequential upon this move of the nunnery, and not unconnected with the acquisition of the whole of the royal estate by the earls of Salisbury by the end of the 12th century (Pugh 1947-8, 74-5).

Chippenham

The suggestion in the evidence from Domesday that Chippenham was the head place of an early royal estate is reinforced by earlier evidence. Asser describes the place of marriage of King Alfred's sister to Burgred, king of Mercia (which event was recorded in the *Anglo-Saxon Chronicle* in 853) as being 'in the *villa regia* which is called Chippenham (*Cippanhamme*)' (Whitelock 1979, 189 and n. 8). He describes Chippenham in a similar way when it was taken over in 878 by the Danish army (*ibid.,* 195, n. 10). Indeed, the account of this occupation suggests that Chippenham was a favourite residence of the king and his family, and of some strategic importance in the royal control of most of Wessex—factors which no doubt singled it out as being a desirable winter camp for the Danish army.

Although there are no earlier references to it, it is clear that from early in the Saxon period Chippenham must have formed the centre of a large royal estate which included the royal Forest of Chippenham and Melksham (Fig. 55). This forest, which extends southwards from Chippenham to include Roman *Verlucio* as well as the western parts of the royal estate of Calne (Grant 1959, 407-14, 446-7), occupies an area of former Roman villa estates centred on *Verlucio* (Bonney 1972, 178). As has already been suggested (above) in relation to Calne, there is thus some reason for at least advancing the hypothesis that the later royal forest developed by the regeneration of waste and woodland on the abandonment of these estates after the Roman period, and that the royal estates around both Chippenham and Calne therefore remained as workable estates (with a shift of estate centre to new sites) in possibly direct continuity from a situation existing in the Roman period. These places would thus have taken over the role of *Verlucio* as regional administrative centres at an early date, in the same manner as has been suggested for Bedwyn and Ramsbury in relation to Roman *Cunetio* (Haslam 1980, 58-64) and as can also be suggested between Roman White Walls and Brokenborough.

This seems to be supported by the topography of the estate appurtenant to Chippenham. The Domesday manor occupied a tract of land mainly to the west of Chippenham (Ford 1976) (Fig. 55). To the north of this lie the manors of Kingston St Michael and Kingston Langley,[74] whose names suggest that they formed part of the ancient royal estate centred on Chippenham.[75] This whole area, together with the present parish of Langley Burrell, was known at the time of Domesday as *Lang-leah* (Ford 1976; Jackson 1858, 38), its extent coinciding with an area of lighter soils on the Kellaways sands and surrounded by Oxford clays (Ford 1976).

Chippenham itself must thus have acted as an early estate centre and, by inference from its later role as the centre of a hundred, the administrative centre of a large area. The details of its relationship with surrounding places has indeed suggested to Ford (*ibid.*, 15) that it 'was not sited on any known medieval agricultural settlement and had no appurtenant field systems of its own'. While there is no positive evidence of an early minster church (the royal marriage recorded in 853 could have been held in a separate palace chapel), its presence at Chippenham can be regarded as likely.

That Chippenham may have originated as an early 'planted' settlement is reinforced by its distinctive topography. Its site on a pronounced spur of land, surrounded by the River Avon on three sides (Fig. 56), is in many significant respects similar to the sites of other royal vills discussed in this chapter such as Bradford, Calne, and Wilton. As in the case of these other places it is approached by a route along the crest of the

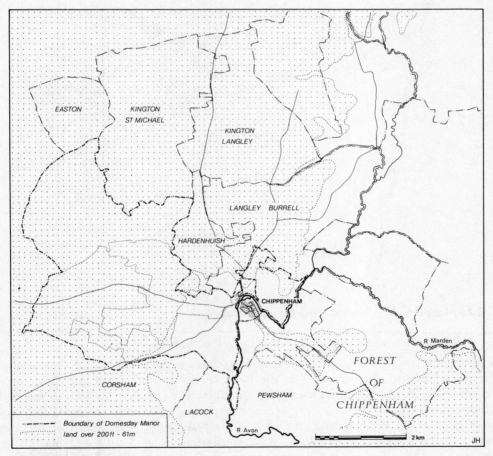

55. Chippenham area

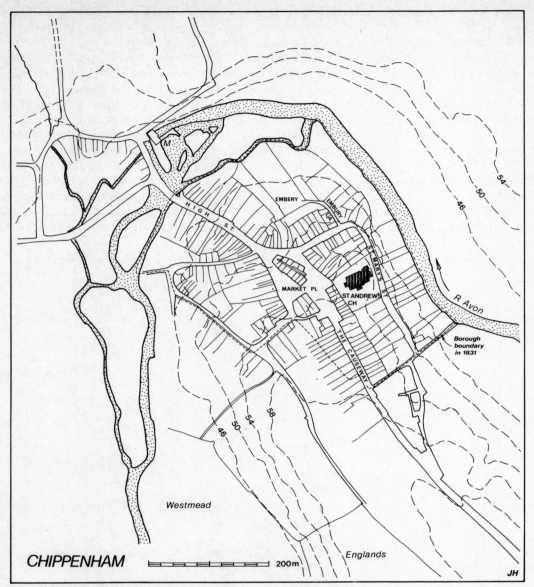

56. Chippenham, with boundaries from map by T. Powell, 1784

spur (from the south-east), and by several routes from the north which converge at the
northern end of the river crossing at the head of the spur.[76] The built topography of
the centre of Chippenham is closely comparable in particular to Calne and Wilton.
In Chippenham, as at these other places, the principal church is associated with an
open area or market-place, together with a discrete area to the north of the church,
surrounded by streets. By analogy with similar areas at Calne and Wilton which
are probably the sites of royal palaces (both being associated with a Kingsbury

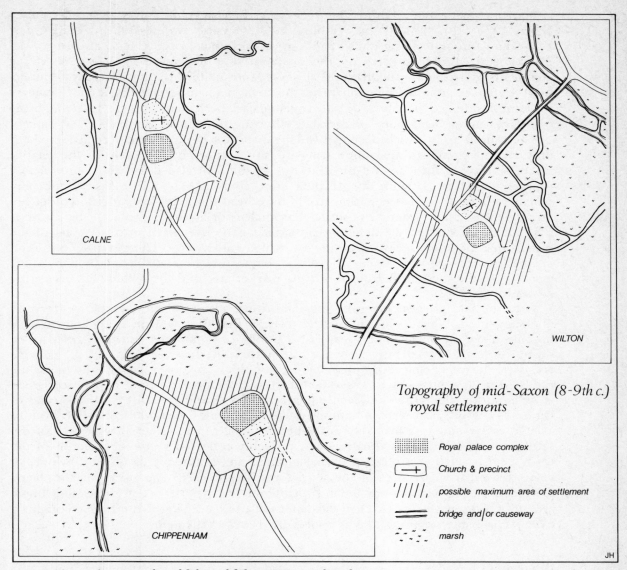

CALNE

WILTON

CHIPPENHAM

Topography of mid-Saxon (8-9th c.) royal settlements

Royal palace complex

Church & precinct

possible maximum area of settlement

bridge and/or causeway

marsh

JH

57. Conjectural topography of 8th- and 9th-century royal settlements.

place-name), this area in Chippenham was possibly also occupied by the royal palace. This was certainly in existence by the mid 9th century, which suggests (again by analogy especially with Wilton) that all these features were, together with areas of occupation surrounding them on the north and west sides (Fig. 57), probably established by this time if not rather earlier. The existence of this royal 'burh'—consisting as at Cheddar probably of a hall and ancillary buildings surrounded by a bank and ditch defence—is supported by the description of an area east of St Mary's Street as abutting on to 'the ditch of *Imburi*' in an early-13th-century deed of Stanley abbey (Ford 1976, 16). 'Imburi' or 'Ymburi' in Old English is suggested by Ford (*ibid.*) as meaning 'around the burh'. A field also called Imburi, later Emery, also lay to the rear (north) of the burgages on the northern side of Cook Street. In view of the arguments given below suggesting that there were neither Danish nor Saxon 'public-burh' defences around Chippenham in this area, it seems likely that these references to Imburi refer to defences of the royal 'palace-burh', and can be taken as being equivalent to the 'Kingsbury' place-names surviving at, for instance, Wilton and Calne.

The Danish army which occupied Chippenham in 878 must have been attracted not only by the administrative importance of this settlement, but also by the relative inaccessibility of the site and by its status as the central place within a presumably prosperous estate. The brevity of their stay, from 878 to 879, suggests that any tangible effect of their occupation would have been limited to the addition of hastily dug defences either around the settlement nucleus or across the spur to the south of the church. In view of the defensive potential of the river itself on three sides of the settlement, the latter seems to be the most likely alternative. There is little indication in the present topography to suggest a course for these defences, though a line marked by the southern edge of both the market area and the churchyard seems the most probable.[77]

Both the fate of these defences and the history of the town in the 10th century are ill-documented. What seems certain, however, is that Chippenham is unlikely to have become a Saxon burh, in the sense of a public or communal urban fortified place set up by the king. Attempts to see a 'grid pattern' in the street plan (Ford 1976, 16) are quite unconvincing. Any observable regularities are suggested here as being the result of a 'lay-out' which was established well before the time of Alfred. Urban growth during the 10th and succeeding centuries would (in spite of the silence of Domesday Book) have been a natural result of its central position in relation·both to a large estate and to a probably developed regional route system. The growth of the settlement at this time is, furthermore, probably reflected in the acquisition of the town fields, called Westmead and Englands, on the southern side of the town. They were assarted from the area of the royal forest (Ford 1976), the name Englands being derived from the Saxon word 'Inland' ('Hinlond' in the 13th century) meaning 'home ground' (Jackson 1857, 34). Their existence must reflect the growth of the community from its probably original status as a specialised royal settlement.

*   *   *   *   *

Discussion

The 11 places discussed in this chapter which show some evidence for the development of urban functions before the end of the 11th century form a sufficiently large sample to enable some preliminary conclusions to be drawn about the development of urbanism in the Saxon period. It has been the intention to show that it is only through the detection of patterns that it is possible to construct developmental models to explain all the observed phenomena.

The development of urbanism in this period can best be categorised by suggesting five different stages. Whether they represent real stages in the organisation of society as a whole or of urban places in general, or whether the changes between the stages merely reflect convenient breaks in the surviving evidence, is a matter for continuing discussion.[78]

1. Primary phase: 7th–later 9th century.
  (a) Proto-urban development around royal *villae,* which acted as re-distributive and administrative centres; as loci for industrial activity (e.g., Ramsbury); as ceremonial ecclesiastical centres (with early minster churches and/or monastic establishments).

        Amesbury, Bedwyn, Bradford, Calne, Chippenham, ? Downton, Ramsbury, Tilshead, Warminster, ? Westbury, Wilton.

  (b) Proto-urban development around monastic centre of Malmesbury, though this itself developed in close relationship to *villa regales* at Brokenborough).

  Wilton possibly combines both (a) and (b).

2. Late 9th century.
  (a) Phase of Alfredian fortification and urban creation:

    Cricklade: functioned as a defended frontier town; on a royal estate but probably not at estate centre. The only Alfredian 'new town' in Wiltshire.

    Malmesbury: re-fortification of old defences, and formal structure given to earlier proto-urban settlement.

    Old Sarum; Chisbury: non-urban hill-forts near *villae regalis* (Wilton and Bedwyn).

  (b) Possible temporary Danish fortification at Chippenham.

3. Early 10th century (Edward the Elder, between 899–910).
  (a) Foundation of possible fortified new urban centre at Marlborough, concurrent with ecclesiastical development at Ramsbury (*c.* 909). Disuse of Chisbury as fortress.
  (b) Planned and fortified urban development at Wilton, or extension of earlier nucleus.

4. 10th century.
  (a) Growth and consolidation of all the above urban centres. Formation of mints at many places.

    Probable reformation of monasteries at Wilton and Malmesbury (*temp.* King Edgar), encouraging growth as pilgrimage centres; creation of of Amesbury monastery, having similar effect.

  (b) Possible special status of Old Sarum as non-urban administrative centre.

5. Early 11th century.

    Programme of re-fortification by Æthelred, affecting Cricklade and Old Sarum (possibly also other places such as Chisbury, Caesar's Camp (Amesbury), Malmesbury. Destruction of defences, certainly at Cricklade, by Cnut. General effects of these events on urban development uncertain, but possible phase of urban renewal by Cnut (e.g., Wilton).

The places of group 1, suggested as having proto-urban characteristics at an early date, must be considered further. The evidence already summarised for each of these settlements makes possible the construction of a model describing the general development of proto-urban and urban places which appears to embrace all the observations and relationships already made. In the early post-Roman period it can be suggested that in the break-up of the Roman administrative system in the 4th and/or 5th centuries, and with the emergence of the Saxons as the dominant force, the Roman administrative centres were replaced by large self-sufficient agricultural estates ('multiple estates'), with administrative centres on new sites which took over the local and regional administrative roles of the former Roman settlements. For instance, it has already been suggested that *Sorviodunum* gave place to Wilton, *Cunetio* to Ramsbury and/or Bedwyn, *Verlucio* to Calne and Chippenham, White Walls to Brokenborough, and Bradford villa to Bradford itself. Most, if not all, of these Saxon settlements were on new sites, some closer to their 'parents' than others. The precise period when they originated after the 5th century is unclear, but they had probably formed as *villae regales,* or royal administrative centres, by the consolidation of the West Saxon kingdom in the 7th century.

The role of the church must have been of some importance in the later stages of this process. The fact that all known early minster churches in the county were sited at these royal centres suggests a deliberate policy of moulding the ecclesiastical administration around a framework of royal administration which was already securely established by *c.* 700. As has been pointed out by D. Hinton (1979, 27), the fact that King Ine's late-7th-century laws made provision for the payment of an annual tax to the church suggests that 'the church at which this payment was made was likely to be attached to the royal residence where the secular taxes were paid'.

It can also be suggested that these places were from the beginning specialised non-agricultural centres, which in some cases (such as at Wilton and Chippenham) were fitted into an already existing, and probably ancient, agricultural system consisting of villages surrounded by their appurtenant fields. This conclusion appears to be strengthened by the fact that many of these places were sited in distinctive topographical positions on relatively inaccessible spur sites, themselves surrounded by rivers and originally marshy valleys (in particular, Bradford, Calne, Chippenham, Warminster, and Wilton), and commanding crossing places of these rivers.

These settlements may be described as 'proto-urban' not only because they developed (at least in Wiltshire) into truly urban places in the later Saxon period, but also because even at an early date (before the 9th century) it can be suggested that they had—or their inhabitants performed—distinctive functions which were essentially non-agricultural. As sites of royal palaces and minster churches they must have been centres of high levels of both consumption and production, both, for instance, documented archaeologically in the large iron-smelting site of the early 9th century at Ramsbury (Haslam 1980), which was associated with imported lava querns.[79] Given the high level of agricultural production on royal estates from an early date (argued by Sawyer 1978, 144–49), they must have been centres through which the proper utilisation of the resources of the estates were organised. They were the focal points for the creation and collection of the real wealth of the ruling power: agricultural production. They were the places from which surpluses were distributed and to which dues and food rents were paid, thus naturally becoming the centres of lines of communication—a situation which their often close relationship with Iron Age or Roman centres suggests was no new development in the early Saxon period. The development of centralised administrative and economic functions at these places would certainly have been enhanced by the siting of minster churches at them from *c.* 700 onwards.

The evidence thus suggests that these *villae regales* were, from early in the Saxon period, the foci for non-agricultural population concentrations: they were administrative, fiscal, and religious and ceremonial centres. It also seems likely that they would have been the centres at which the increasing royal control of trading transactions, involving as it did the provision of witnesses, was to be concentrated. These places thus fall into that class of proto-urban settlements 'whose function and inhabitants exhibit traits, be they cultural, religious, administrative or ceremonial, sufficiently distinctive to distinguish them from predominantly "rural" forms of settlement and occupation' (Butlin 1977, 13). A similar development of proto-urban settlements, some of them around royal sites, has been recognised in Ireland (*ibid.*).

A parallel course of development in the period up to the end of the 9th century can be seen at Malmesbury. It has been suggested above that the rapid rise in importance of the monastery from the mid-7th century was due in large measure to its origins as a royal foundation, placed on the borders of the West Saxon and Mercian kingdoms in close relation to a *villa regalis* (Brokenborough), and fostered during the later 7th and succeeding centuries by royal gifts of land. Though there is little concrete evidence, either of the economy of the monastic establishment or its size at any period, it must be considered as the point around which a sizeable settlement must have been attracted, and which must have functioned not only as a religious, but also as a nascent urban community, having economic links with a wide area of northern Wiltshire and southern Gloucestershire. There is every reason for believing that Malmesbury would have developed in similar ways to contemporary Irish monasteries, whose rapid growth in the 7th and 8th centuries produced some sites which became proto-urban settlements, if not actual urban communities, situated at regionally accessible places (Butlin 1977, 20–25; Norman and St Joseph 1969, 97–8; Hughes and Hamlin 1977, 19–36). Some of these developed, furthermore, out of royal sites (Butlin 1977, 20–21).

As has been described above, a significant feature of some of these places (most clearly shown at Wilton, Calne and Chippenham) is the preservation in the present topography of a lay-out which is arguably as early as the beginning of the development of these settlements. This consists of the close association of a church, an open 'market' area, and a discrete area whose proximity in Wilton and Calne with the place-name Kingsbury suggests was an area occupied by the royal palace, around which is space for further settlement—the whole complex centrally placed on a raised spur of land bounded by a river or rivers (*see* Fig. 57). There is no evidence that these places were defended with the kind of public work so characteristic of later Saxon burhs,[80] although it is very likely that the palace complexes would have been provided with their own defences. The early association, for instance, of the palace and minster church at Wilton, both in existence by *c.* 800, suggests that these topographical survivals could preserve the form of these settlements from the 8th, if not even from the later 7th century.

From the late 9th century onwards, this pattern of the comparatively straightforward development of proto-urban settlements around royal and ecclesiastical centres is disrupted by the imposition of new patterns which involved the creation of new towns on new sites. These are represented in Wiltshire by the large burh at Cricklade, with Malmesbury refounded on an earlier proto-urban site, both in the late 9th century. New towns were founded at Marlborough and Wilton in the early 10th century, both probably provided with defences, the latter as an extension to an earlier royal centre. It has been suggested above that Marlborough developed in parallel with the henceforward non-urban high-order ecclesiastical site at Ramsbury, the combined functions of both these places—of defence and economic and religious activity—overshadowing similar functions formerly shown at Bedwyn and Chisbury. It is of some significance that the high-order religious and economic functions were probably combined in one place at Wells, Somerset (Haslam 1981). The growth of the earlier proto-urban centres which were not directly affected by these developments was encouraged not only by the increase in the size and complexity of later Anglo-Saxon society in general, but also by such purely historical forces as the attempts by the 10th-century kings in particular to control and augment their revenue, and to enforce the 'king's peace' by the suppression of fraud through the limitation of trading transactions to boroughs, by the production of coinage and the control of mints, and by the promotion of legislation requiring trading transactions to be vouched by witnesses (Loyn 1961, 128–9).

It has, however, recently been suggested by D. Hill that the development of these small towns in Somerset and Wiltshire, all of them on royal estates, is the result of the deliberate setting-up of a market and/or mint on the royal estates by the king 'as a form of improvement to increase his limited revenues' (Hill 1978, 217-22). While this may be true for those new urban foundations at Cricklade, Wilton, or Marlborough, the evidence already adduced suggests that with these exceptions the towns at least in Wiltshire were not new 'foundations', but rather places whose development was characterised by an organic, though not necessarily even, growth from proto-urban into urban status over a considerable period. The difficulties in attempting to point to particular 'urban' attributes in such places as Amesbury, Bedwyn, Bradford, Calne, Chippenham, Tilshead, or Warminster at any particular period before the time of Domesday must militate against the idea that, with those few clear exceptions apart, the origin of any of the Wiltshire towns lies in an episode of deliberate 'urban' formation.

NOTES

1. I am grateful to a number of people for help of various kinds in the writing of this chapter. Bob Smith and John Chandler have provided information on Warminster and Amesbury respectively, and the latter has given other assistance with references. Desmond Bonney has provided information concerning *Sorviodunum*. My wife has also spent long hours typing a much-corrected manuscript.

2. This evidence is described and tabulated by Darby (1977) and further discussed by Darlington (1955).

3. A complete list of mints and moneyers is given in Shortt 1947 and 1948. Further reference to mints in this chapter are to these papers, unless otherwise stated.

4. The villa was excavated by Wiltshire County Council (monograph forthcoming), and earlier finds reported in *V.C.H.* (Wilts.) ii (1957), 45, and *W.A.M.* 53 (1950), 137–8; 56 (1956), 390–1; 61 (1966), 95–6. The nearest villa is at Atworth.

5. The charter is printed and translated by Paffard (1952).

6. The association of these places has been commented on as a phenomenon by Aston and Bond (1976, 60), but not explored in any detail.

7. Arguments showing that the Alfredian system of fortresses was superseded by a new system created in the early 10th century by Edward the Elder are given in Chapter 8.

8. Examples of other churches near or over gates or burhs—St Mary's church, Cricklade, and the church of the Holy Cross, Old Sarum—are discussed below.

9. This process is in many ways similar to the shift from *Sorviodunum* to Wilton, and from White Walls to Brokenborough, discussed below.

10. Translated in Whitelock 1979, 605–6.

11. It is intended to discuss the evidence for the development of the town in some detail at a later date.

12. This new parish, itself carved out of Preshute, was amalgamated with the older St Mary's parish in 1565 (Brentnall 1950, 302). It is not clear, therefore, where the eastern boundary of the latter would originally have been drawn.

13. The moneyer working at Bedwyn in the 1060s was transferred to Marlborough after the Norman Conquest.

14. *Cf.* n. 41 below on the origin of the town fields of Malmesbury.

15. Susan Pearce has shown how those churches with large land holdings in Domesday Book are likely to represent early minster churches (1978, 93–121).

16. Both Canon Jackson (1853, 172) and Marsh (1903, 11) (following Jackson) have suggested that the site of the royal residence is to be identified with that of the castle on the western side of the town. The arguments against this are precisely those supporting the arguments suggested here.

17. It is perhaps of some significance that the limits of the latter are marked by the borough boundary.

18. The others, Wareham and Wallingford, are considered elsewhere in this volume.

19. The historical aspects of the town, in both their local and national setting, have been well served in recent studies (Thomson 1961; Loyn 1963). Earlier excavations are described by Radford (1972). An interim report of the 1975 excavations is published in Schofield and Palliser (eds.) 1981, 28–30.

20. In his discussion of the royal connections of late Saxon towns in Wiltshire and Somerset, Hill suggests (1978, 217–22) it is one of the few burhs not founded on ancient royal demesne.

21. Thirty manentes in Purton were given by Cadwalla of Wessex to Malmesbury in 688 (Finberg 1964, 69, No. 185). This was taken away by Offa in the late 8th century, but sold back to Malmesbury by his son, Ecgfrith (*ibid.*, 72, No. 196), and confirmed by later kings (*ibid.*, 74, No. 204).

22. Wiltshire County Council Libraries and Museums Service, *Cricklade and Purton District Plan, a report on Archaeology*, November 1979, p. 10.

23. I am grateful to M. Stone for this information. The existence of a cemetery just outside the western defences suggested by Radford and hailed as the 'most important contribution made by the present series of excavations' (1972, 95) must be discounted. The burials are, in fact, cut into the upper filling of a Saxon ditch and through layers containing 12th-century pottery (*ibid.*, 87–8 and 86, Fig. 10).

24. Publication forthcoming in *W.A.M.*

25. It has, however, been consistently misinterpreted in Radford's report as a 'wall' or 'revetment' to the rear of the bank. His further regards the intra-mural street as being a scatter of stones at the rear of the the bank, a feature which can, however, be more satisfactorily regarded as the tumbled remains of a rear wall destroyed in period 3 (see below).

26. The necessity for this programme is suggested for instance by the inadequacy of the defences of Shaftesbury in the late 10th to early 11th centuries, which can be inferred from the grant of Bradford to the nuns in 1001 as a refuge from the Danes, and by the ease with which Wilton was sacked in 1003.

27. The destruction deposits of the rear wall have been interpreted (Radford, 1972) as the metalling of the intra-mural street; those of the front wall have also been represented as 'deliberate settings of stones' on the berm.

28. See the suggestion made in relation to Wilton, below, that Cnut was indeed responsible for a phase of urban restoration after 1016 (*see* p. 128).

29. This evidence will be discussed in the forthcoming excavation report.

30. This is published in the Rolls Series 1857, i, 225, and quoted and discussed by Gomme (1887, 423), though more to prove his theory of the Celtic origin of Malmesbury corporation than to establish the facts of settlement history.

31. The shift of centres of authority suggested here is completed by including White Walls, a Roman small town situated some 4km. west of Malmesbury in a position on the Fosse Way midway between Bath and Cirencester, a position similar to *Verlucio* which is midway between Bath and *Cunetio*. Archaeological evidence from White Walls is lacking, but field evidence indicates a sizeable settlement. The local shifts of foci of authority from Malmesbury (Iron Age) to White Walls (Roman) to Brokenborough (early Saxon) to Malmesbury (late Saxon) is remarkably similar to the shifts shown around *Cunetio, Sorviodunum* or (for the Roman and Saxon periods) *Verlucio*.

32. There is a need for more work on the bounds and early relationships of the constituent parts of this estate.

33. *de Gestis Pontificum Anglorum* (Rolls Ser.), 334, quoted in Watkin 1956, 210.

34. A conclusion also suggested by Darlington (1955, 25).

35. Among other examples Alcock has suggested (1971, 219) that the Iron Age and early post-Roman hill-fort at Cadbury-Congresbury was also the site of a monastery founded by Congar in the 6th century.

36. Some of these themes have been discussed by Rahtz (1973) and by Campbell (1979, 121). The absence of any archaeological excavation at Malmesbury makes these possibilities somewhat hypothetical, though they are suggested by the more concrete evidence from other monastic settlements of the period.

37. St Mary Westport was certainly in existence by 1177 (Watkin 1956, 218), and there is a possibility that the suburb of which it is the parish church began to develop in the pre-Conquest period around an extra-mural market area, perhaps significantly now called Horsefair.

38. The Tithe Award states, though, that Brokenborough, Charlton and St Mary Westport parishes formed one entire parish before the statute of 13 and 14 Charles II, forming a single district for the paying of tithes. However, St Mary Westport must have had a parish of its own before the 17th century, and there is no reason to reject the conclusion that it is early.

39. *Registrum Malmesburiense* (ed. J. S. Brewer and C. T. Martin 1880). The topography of these fields requires further elucidation. The area of the town fields in existence in the 19th century (*see* Fig. 46) is probably only a fraction of their original extent.

40. This conclusion is supported by the occurrence of the Portfield at Marlborough, suggested below as being the fields originally made over for the use of the inhabitants of the early 10th-century town. Similar names occur as Portmanneit (later Portmeadow), Oxford (Salter 1936, 26, 35–6), and Portfield, Stamford, comprising the major part of the parish of the main town church (Pythian-Adams 1977, 70–71). Charter evidence from Wilton (below) shows that the 'town fields' there were in existence in the 10th century.

41. The coincidence of the area of the town fields—i.e., that area used exclusively by the burgesses—with the parish of the main church has been seen hitherto as typically a Midlands phenomenon (Rogers 1972), though is shown for instance by both Southampton and Exeter. The writer has suggested (Haslam, forthcoming, a) that the creation of the double field system at Cambridge is the result of the reservation of parts of a larger royal estate by the king as the 'town fields' on the formation of burhs on the north and south banks of the river, the first by Offa in the late 8th century, the second by Edward the Elder in the early 10th century, by processes analogous if not entirely similar to those shown at Malmesbury.

42. These aspects are discussed more fully in Rogers (1965, 13, 47, 55, 78–9).

43. Described in *V.C.H. (Wilts.)* 1, i (1957), 118 and 270, and *W.A.M.* 42 (1923), 368–73; 43 (1926), 400; 47 (1935), 285; 52 (1948), 218.

44. *Gesta Pontificum Anglorum*, Rolls Series (1870), 304–5. Its name is said to derive from the miraculous growth of ash trees from his pastoral staff (*P-N Wilts.*, 151).

45. Finds of foundations and burials in a field about 100m. west of this church have led to undemonstrable speculations that this is the site of an 'earlier church built by the Saxon kings' (Daniel 1879, 152).

46. The royal residence was certainly in existence in the early 10th century, and as argued above, probably on this site from the early Saxon period (Rogers 1965).

47. Called Back Lane in a map of the town of 1783.

48. Information kindly made available by the excavator, Bob Smith.

49. This evidence modifies considerably the hypothesis of a 12th-century origin for this area put forward earlier by the writer (1976, 63).

50. Dūnon=fort; the Anglo-Saxon for Old Sarum was *Searoburh*: *Searo* being a descendant of British *Sorvio*, and *burh* a descendant of *dūnon* (Rivet 1970, 79). 'Salisbury' is a modification of the Saxon word, and 'Sarum' its medieval contracted form. The Roman town was probably sited at the river crossing to the south-west of the hill-fort. I am grateful to Desmond Bonney for this information.

51. See further examples discussed below.

52. The early boundaries of neighbouring villages, of the territory of the early town, and of the later monastic possessions, are somewhat obscure and require further elucidation. They are not, therefore, discussed in detail here.

53. That the present St Mary's church is the site of the earlier monastery is, however, largely inferred from its topographical proximity to the 'kings burh'. It only became the parish church in the 16th century, through amalgamation of several smaller urban parishes, though this in itself suggests its earlier importance.

54. Colt Hoare describes this as being taken from 'some ancient manuscripts in the Bodleian and Cotton Libraries', but gives no further reference. Later searches have failed to find a source for this document (Irving 1859, 296). It seems highly unlikely, however, that Hoare would have deliberately manufactured this evidence.

55. The assertion by the R.C.H.M. (1980, xxix) that Old Sarum was not settled before *c.* 972 at the earliest, on the basis of its non-mention in a charter referring to a road running past it, cannot in the writer's opinion be maintained, even though it may support the present arguments.

56. In Wiltshire this can be recognised at Chisbury, Bedwyn and Marlborough, and is discussed more fully by the writer with reference to Barnstaple, Totnes, Plympton, and Kingsbridge (Devon), in Chapter 8.

57. D. Hill has pointed out (1978, 223) that Old Sarum was thus a true 'fluchtburg', though, as will be argued below, his assumption that the burh church and 'town' were outside the walls at this time cannot be sustained.

58. See n. 26 above relating to Cricklade.

59. Montgomerie has suggested (1947, 134-5) that evidence recovered in 1914 demonstrated two periods of heightening of the original Iron Age fortifications before the Norman period. The detail of recording, however, does not allow an independent assessment of these conclusions. Rahtz and Musty have demonstrated a phase of pre-Norman and post-Roman strengthening of the defences, though here again there is no dating evidence (1960, 366, Fig. 9, layers 10 and 15-18 in trench B). This refurbishing could belong equally to the 5th to 6th centuries, the late 9th century, or the early 11th century.

60. This possibility (which requires closer examination) is increased by the more concrete example of the church provided for the Aethelredian burh at South Cadbury (Alcock 1972, 200).

61. The medieval references state that it is either over, beyond (*ultra*), or outside (*extra*) the east gate (R.C.H.M. 1980, 12), so the evidence is somewhat equivocal.

62. Observed by the writer in construction work near Kingsbury Square in 1976.

63. *W.A.M.* 67 (1972), 176.

64. Wilton is also described as a 'large *de novo* burh' by Hassall and Hill (1969, 189, Fig. 1), and the supposed rectilinear elements in its plan remarked on by Biddle and Hill (1965, 81). All of these descriptions give a misleading impression of both its site and its topographical and historical development.

65. See, for instance, the existence of flax retting near the late 8th-century causeway to the south of Oxford, described by Durham (1977, 200-1).

66. For short interim notes on excavations across these defences see *W.A.M.* 66 (1971), 191; 67 (1972), 175–6.

67. It is probable that it was constructed during the civil wars of the 12th century, during which Stephan built a 'castle' at Wilton in 1143. A similar episode of 'castle'-building at Cricklade in 1144 consisted of the construction of new defences around the whole of the earlier Saxon burh (Haslam 1976, 18).

68. This view is, however, contrary to that of the R.C.H.M., who have concluded (1980, xxix), in the face of a massive lack of evidence, that by the Norman Conquest Old Sarum was one of the 'most advanced trading centres' in the shire. The topography and course of development of this new royal borough is outside the scope of this chapter, but has been briefly discussed by Hill (1962, 63–5), and the R.C.H.M. (1980, 12–13).

69. 'West of the burh'. *P-N Wilts.* (149) derives its name from its proximity to the western border of the county. However, since Westbury is not a burh, it is difficult to accept this derivation.

70. This role may, however, have been performed by Edington, which lies almost directly underneath the hill-fort. This estate was mentioned in King Alfred's will (Whitelock 1979, 536), and was, as *Ethandum,* the scene of Alfred's victory over Guthrum.

71. At least one of the major components of the Domesday manor can be recognised in the later topography. The sheriff of Wiltshire (Edward of Salisbury, the progenitor of the earls of Salisbury) at that time held a small estate which was 'recently accumulated and probably compact' (Pugh 1947–8, 71–2). It can be suggested that this estate was that shown in the Tithe Award map as surrounding the suggestively-named Earl's Court Farm, shown on Figs. 53 and 54.

72. This question has recently been discussed by J. Chandler (1978–9) who has suggested that 'the appearance of Ambrosius (in Geoffrey of Monmouth's history) is doubtless an echo of an Amesbury legend based on the etymology of Ambresbury' (1979, 69). This, however, still begs the question of the origin of the name 'Ambre' or 'Ambri'.

73. I owe this suggestion to John Chandler.

74. By the 19th century these formed the single parish of Kingston St Michael.

75. Both of these were the subject of grants by the king in 934 and 940 (Sawyer 1968, No. 426; Finberg 1964, 86), the latter signed at Chippenham. Various other estates in the north-west and north-east were also the subject of royal grants: Grittleton in 940 (Finberg 1964, 85; Sawyer 1968, No. 472), and Christian Malford, also in 940 (Finberg 1964, 86; Sawyer 1968, No. 466). It is not certain whether these formed part of the earlier royal estate centred on Chippenham.

76. This area is now dominated by the railway, to whose construction may be attributed the creation of New Street. This latter street has clearly replaced the routeway to the north along Old Street. The suggestion that this New Street is the successor of 'le Newestrete' mentioned in 1406 (*P-N Wilts.*, 89; Haslam 1976,15) can therefore be discounted. This route, and the one to the west (Bath Road), both start on the 46m. contour, which also marks the outside limit of occupation on the southern side of the river.

77. Ford (1976, 16) has suggested that the Danish fortifications completely enclosed the central area on the top of the spur. However, his proposed course fits rather awkwardly with the present topography, and assumes furthermore that the Imburi place-names refer to these works.

78. An attempt was made by the writer (1976, 97–101) at a similar classification, but this must be considered inadequate. Its deficiences were due to the lack of appreciation, firstly, of the role that royal estate centres must have played in early proto-urban or urban development, and, secondly, of the importance of the distinction between the roles of King Alfred and his successor, Edward the Elder, a subject enlarged upon in Chapter 8.

79. The former is also well documented archaeologically at Wells, Somerset, in the finds of exotic imports of the 8th century and a Frisian coin (Rodwell 1980; Haslam 1981).

80. The postulation of the existence of defences at Bradford and Calne by the writer (Haslam 1976, 10 and 13) now seems unlikely.

BIBLIOGRAPHY

Abbreviations

P-N Wilts: The Place-Names of Wiltshire, by Gover, J. E. B., Mawer, A., and Stenton, F. M.,
English Place-Name Society, Vol. XVI, 1970.
V.C.H.: Victoria County History.
W.A.M.: Wiltshire Archaeological and Natural History Magazine.

Alcock, L. (1971), *Arthur's Britain*.
Alcock, L. (1972), *By South Cadbury, is that Camelot . . .*
Alcock, L. (1977), 'Aspects of the warfare of Saxons and Britons', *Bulletin of Board of Celtic Studies* 27, 413–24.
Aston, M. and Bond, J. (1976), *The Landscape of Towns*.
Benson, R. and Hatcher, H. (1843), *Old and New Sarum or Salisbury*.
Biddle, M. (1976a), 'Towns', in Wilson, D. M. (ed.), *The Archaeology of Anglo-Saxon England*, 99-150.
Biddle, M. (1976b), 'The evolution of towns: planned towns before 1066', in Barley, M. W. (ed.), *The Plans and Topography of Medieval Towns in England and Wales*, C.B.A. Research Report 14, 19-32.
Biddle, M. (ed.) (1976), *Winchester in the Early Middle Ages* (Winchester Studies, 1).
Biddle, M. and Hill, D. H. (1971), 'Late Saxon planned towns', *Antiquaries Journal* 51, 70-85.
Bonney, D. J. (1972), 'Early boundaries in Wessex', in Fowler, P. J. (ed.), *Archaeology and the Landscape*, 168-186.
Brenthall, H. C. (1950), 'The origins of the parish of Preshute', *W.A.M.* 53, 294–310.
Brooks, N. P. (1964), 'The unidentified forts of the Burghal Hidage', *Medieval Archaeology* 8, 74–90.
Butlin, R. A. (1977), 'Urban and proto-urban settlements in pre-Norman Ireland', in Butlin, R. A. (ed.), *The Development of the Irish Town*.
Campbell, J. (1979), 'The church in Anglo-Saxon towns', in Baker, D. (ed.), *The church in town and countryside*, (Studies in Church History 16), 119-35.
Chandler, J. (1978–9), 'Three Amesbury legends', *The Hatcher Review*, No. 6, 12–23.
Chandler, J. (ed.) (1979), *The Amesbury Millenium Lectures*.
Chandler, J. and Goodhaugh, P. (1979), *Amesbury: History and Description of a South Wiltshire Town*.
Crittal, E. (1956), 'Abbey of Wilton', *V.C.H. (Wilts.)* 6, 231-41.
Crowley, D. A. (1980), 'Downton hundred', *V.C.H. (Wilts.)* 11, 1-104.
Cunliffe, B. W. (1973), 'Iron Age and Roman periods', *V.C.H. (Wilts.)* 1, ii, 408-67.
Daniel, J. J. (1879), *The history of Warminster*.
Darby, H. C. (1977), *Domesday England*.
Darlington, R. R. (1955), 'Anglo-Saxon Wiltshire', in *V.C.H. (Wilts.)* 2, 1-34.
Dolley, R. H. M. (1954), 'The sack of Wilton in 1003 and the chronology of the "Long Cross" and "Helmut" types of Ethelred II', *Nordish Numismatisk Unions Medlensbled*, 152-6.
Durham, B. (1977), 'Archaeological investigations in St Aldate's Oxford', *Oxoniensia* 42, 84-203.
Finberg, H. P. R. (1964), *The early charters of Wessex*.
Ford, W. J. (1967), 'A survey of the archaeology of the Chippenham area', Wiltshire County Council Library and Museum Service (limited circulation).
Fowler, P. J. (1966), 'Two finds of domestic Saxon pottery in Wiltshire', *W.A.M.* 61, 31–7.
Fowler, P. J. (1971), 'Hillforts, A.D. 400–700', in Hill, D. and Jesson, M. (eds.), *The Iron Age and its Hillforts*, 203-213.
Gem, R. (1978), 'Church architecture in the reign of King Ethelred', in Hill, D. (ed.), *Ethelred the Unready*, B.A.R. 59.
Gomme, G. L. (1887), 'The history of Malmesbury as a village community', *Archaeologia* 50, 421–38.
Grant, R. (1959), 'Royal forests', *V.C.H. (Wilts.)* 4, 391-457.
Grundy, G. B. (1920), 'Saxon land charters of Wiltshire, 2nd series', *Archaeological Journal* 27, 137-47.
Haslam, J. (1976), *Wiltshire Towns, the Archaeological Potential* (Devizes Museum).

Haslam, J. (1980), 'A middle Saxon iron-smelting site at Ramsbury, Wilts', *Medieval Archaeology* 24, 1–68.

Haslam, J. (1981a), 'Wells and Ramsbury: a further look at urban origins', *Current Archaeology* VII, 188.

Haslam, J. (1981b), 'A "ward" of the burh of Cricklade', *W.A.M.* 76, 77-81.

Haslam, J., forthcoming (a), 'The origins and topography of Cambridge', *Proc. Cambs. Antiquarian Society*.

Haslam, J., forthcoming (b), 'Cnut and the defences of Wessex burhs'.

Hassall, J. M. and Hill, D. H. (1970), 'Pont de l'Arche: Frankish influence on the West Saxon burh?' *Archaeological Journal* 127, 188–95.

Hill, D. H. (1978), 'Trends in the development of towns during the reign of Ethelred II', in Hill, D. H. (ed.), *Ethelred the Unready*, B.A.R. 59, 213-26.

Hinton, D. (1977), *Alfred's Kingdom*.

Hinton, D. (1979), 'Amesbury and the early history of its abbey', in Chandler, J. H. (ed.), *The Amesbury Millenium Lectures* (Amesbury), 1979.

Hoare, R. C. (1812), *Ancient Wiltshire*.

Hoare, R. C. (1825), *History of modern Wiltshire*, 2, pt. 1.

Hughes, K. and Hamlin, A. (1977), *The modern traveller to the early Irish church*.

Hunter-Blair, P. (1956), *An introduction to Anglo-Saxon England*.

Irving, G. V. (1859), 'On the earthworks at Old Sarum', *Journal of the British Archaeological Association* 15, 291–302.

Jackson, J. E. (1853), 'Calne', *W.A.M.* 24, 166–219.

Jackson, J. E. (1857), 'On the history of Chippenham', *W.A.M.* 3, 19–46.

James, M. K. (1962), 'The borough of Wilton', *V.C.H. (Wilts.)* 6, 1-36.

Jones, W. H. (1859), 'Bradford-on-Avon: general history of the parish', *W.A.M.* 5, 1-88.

Loyn, H. R. (1961), 'Boroughs and Mints, A.D. 900-1066', in Dolley, R. H. M. (ed.), *Anglo-Saxon Coins*.

Loyn, H. R. (1963), 'The origin and early development of the Saxon borough with special reference to Cricklade', *W.A.M.* 58, 7–15.

Major, A. (1913), *Early wars of Wessex* (reprinted as 2nd edn., 1978).

Marsh, A. E. W. (1903), *A history of the borough and town of Calne . . .*

Moffat, J. M. (1805), *History of the town of Malmesbury . . .*

Montgomerie, D. H. (1947), 'Old Sarum', *Archaeological Journal* 104, 129–43.

Morris, J. (1973), *The Age of Arthur*.

Musty, J. and Rahtz, P. A. (1964), 'The suburbs of Old Sarum', *W.A.M.* 59, 130–54.

Nightingale, J. E. (1906), *Memorials of Wilton*.

Oman, C. (1938), *England before the Norman Conquest* (8th edn.).

Ordnance Survey (1966), *Map of Britain in the Dark Ages*, 2nd edn.

Paffard, J. H. P. (1952), 'Bradford-on-Avon: The Saxon boundaries in Ethelred's charter of A.D. 1001', *W.A.M.* 54, 210–18, 372.

Pearce, S. M. (1978), *The kingdom of Dumnonia*.

Pugh, R. B. (1947–8), 'The early history of the manors of Amesbury', *W.A.M.* 52, 70–110.

Pugh, R. B. (1956), 'The Abbey, later Priory, of Amesbury', V.C.H. *(Wilts.)*, III, 242–59.

Phythian-Adams, C. (1977), 'Rutland reconsidered', in Dornier, A. (ed.), *Mercian Studies*, 63–86.

Radford, C. A. R. (1972), 'Excavations at Cricklade, 1948-63', *W.A.M.* 67, 61-111.

Rahtz, P. A. (1964), 'Saxon and medieval features at Downton, Salisbury', *W.A.M.* 59, 124–29.

Rahtz, P. A. (1974), 'Monasteries as settlements', *Scottish Archaeological Forum* 5, 125–35.

Riain, P.O. (1972), 'Boundary association in early Irish society', *Studia Celtica* 8, 12–29.

Rivet, A. L. F. (1970), 'The British section of the Antonine Itinerary', *Britannia* 1, 34–82.

Rodwell, W. J. (1980), 'Wells, the cathedral and city', *Current Archaeology* VII, No. 2.

Rogers, A. (1972), 'Parish boundaries and urban history: two case studies', *Journal of the British Archaeological Association*, 3rd series 35, 46–64.

Rogers, K. H. (1965), 'Warminster hundred and Warminster', *V.C.H. (Wilts.)* 8, 1-5, 91-135.

Royal Commission on Historical Monuments (and trs. after Rogers) (1980), *Ancient and historical monuments in the city of Salisbury* 1.

Salter, H. E. (1936), *Medieval Oxford* (Oxford Hist. Soc. Vol. 100).

Sawyer, P. H. (1968), *Anglo-Saxon Charters, an Annotated List and Bibliography.*

Sawyer, P. H. (1978), *From Roman Britain to Norman England.*

Schofield, J. and Palliser, D. (eds.) (1981), *Recent archaeological research in English towns* (C.B.A.).

Shortt, H. de S. (1947), 'The mints of Wiltshire, from Eadgar to Henry III', *Archaeological Journal* 104, 112–28.

Shortt, H. de S. (1948), 'The mints of Wiltshire', *Numismatic Chronicle* 6th ser. 8, 169–87.

Shortt, H. de S. (1965), *Old Sarum* (D. of E. guide)

Smith, A. H. (1956), *English Place-Name elements* (English Place-Name Society, 25 and 26).

Stone, J. F. S. and Charlton, J. (1935), 'Trial excavations in the east suburb of Old Sarum', *Antiquaries Journal* 15, 174–92.

Taylor, H. M. (1973), 'The Anglo-Saxon church at Bradford-on-Avon', *Archaeological Journal* 130, 141–71.

Thomson, T. R. (1953), *Bradon Forest* (Cricklade Historical Society).

Thomson, T. R. (ed.) (1961), *Materials for the History of Cricklade.*

Thomson, T. R. and Taylor, H. M. (1965) and (1966), 'St Mary's church, Cricklade', *W.A.M.* 60, 75–84; 61, 38–42.

Wainwright, F. T. (1960), 'Ermine Street at Cricklade', *W.A.M.* 57, 192–200.

Wainwright, G. J. (1970), 'An Iron Age promontory fort at Budbury, Bradford-on-Avon, Wiltshire', *W.A.M.* 65, 108–166.

Watkin, A. (1956), 'Abbey of Malmesbury', *V.C.H. (Wilts.)* 3, 210-30.

Whitelock, D. (ed.) (1979), *English Historical Documents* I (2nd edn.).

Young, G. M. (1942), 'Saxon Wiltshire', *W.A.M.* 59, 28–38.

Chapter Five

THE TOWNS OF HAMPSHIRE[1]

By David A. Hinton

SINCE IT WILL SOON BE 900 YEARS since William the Conqueror ordered that information about his kingdom should be gathered together at Winchester, it is appropriate to begin a survey of Hampshire towns with the Hampshire section of Domesday Book. The shire's three boroughs do not appear as a separate entry at the beginning or elsewhere. They are variously described: Twynham (Christchurch), with the entries of the other manors held by the king in *Egheite* hundred; *Hantone* (Southampton) on a separate folio at the end of the Hampshire section, preceding the Isle of Wight entries; and Winchester not at all. Information on Winchester was available, however, and presumably it was intended to include it on the blank folio at the beginning of the Hampshire section. The collation was never made, but much of the information that it would have contained survives nevertheless within the Winton Survey, the subject of a major recent publication (Biddle [ed.] 1976).

There were other Hampshire places which Domesday acknowledged to be more than just ordinary rural settlements, although not boroughs in their own right. Basingstoke had a market worth 30s., Titchfield had one worth 40s., with toll. Both these were owned by the king. So, too, was a market worth £8 at *Neteham,* a manor in the hundred of the same name. The modern Neatham is on the outskirts of Alton, another manor within the *Neteham* hundred; it was held in 1066 by Queen Edith, and by the abbot of the New Minster in 1086, but 'he had received it unjustly, in exchange for the King's house, because the house was the King's [own]. Of this same manor, the King holds 5 hides, as part of his farm . . .' (*V.C.H.* I, 470). The skulduggery which this entry disguises was the seizure by the king in 1069–70 of land in Winchester owned by the New Minster, which he needed for his palace, and for which the community received Alton and *Clere* in exchange (Biddle [ed.] 1976, 292). Alton had been a royal demesne, like *Neteham* manor, until 1069–70, so the market of *Neteham* may have been physically within the Alton manor, but remained financially attached to *Neteham* because this was the hundredal manor, and the market a hundredal right (Britnell 1978). The alternative is to assume that the obviously well-established market was moved from a site in Neatham to one at Alton at some time after 1086. Transfers of this sort did occasionally occur; moreover the large Roman site now known to underlie Neatham may have been the reason why market rights existed in the area. Another such hint of continuity arises at Andover, near which is a Roman crossroads settlement at East Anton, and another at Havant, also a Roman crossroads site (Hughes 1976, 8–9). Neither of these places has a market attributed to it in Domesday Book, although by 1205 Andover had acquired borough status, and Havant a market.

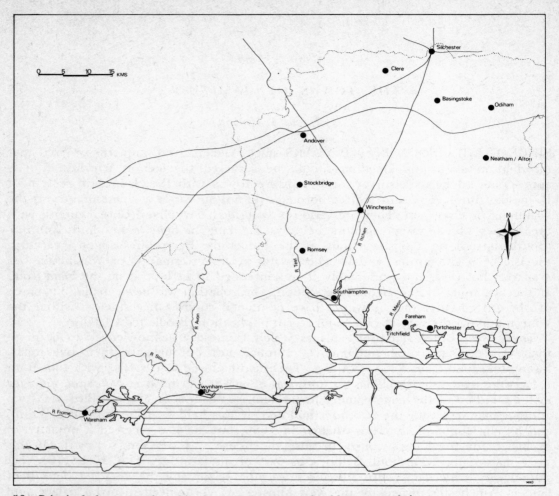

58. Principal places mentioned in the text, Roman roads, ridgeways and rivers

Another place which was later to have a market was Kingsclere, which is in Domesday Book as *Clere*, a royal estate and hundredal centre with rights of toll in 1066. Right of toll does not necessarily imply a market (Britnell 1978, 190), but seems likely in this case. It is, of course, a well-known failing of Domesday Book for historians that it does not record all the markets that existed. There was no need to mention them specifically if the dues from them were incorporated as part of an estate's overall assessment total. So there may well have been markets at other centres, particularly at head manors of hundreds, and these may not appear in historical records for some centuries; since they were ancient rights, no charter needed to be granted to them. A good example is Andover, which had a charter for its guild in 1175, and subsequent municipal privileges. But there is no market grant, presumably because the market already existed. It may well have been there in the 11th century (Spaul 1977, 9, 48).

Although Winchester does not have its own entry in Domesday Book, it is not unmentioned. Many rural manors had properties in Winchester attributed to them, such as the two *hagae* worth 65d. which *Wallope* had, or the seven *hagae* of *Cladford* worth 10s. These were Winchester properties which for historic reasons paid their rent into the rural manor's assessment: they serve to show how town and country were still inter-related. Later in the Middle Ages, no townsman would have acknowledged such rural ties. There are similar entries for Southampton, and even the very small Twynham (Christchurch) had two messuages which were attributed to the (presumably neighbouring) manor of *Bortel* in the same hundred. Such entries can cause problems, for their locations are not always made clear. Thus at Somborne on the east side of the Test Valley, William de Ow's manor, previously owned by Tol the Dane, had nine *mansiones* of burgesses which paid 12s. 2d. (*V.C.H., I,* 491), and on the west side at Houghton the bishop had three burgesses worth 30d. (*ibid.,* 462). These 12 burgesses are causing controversy, for whereas it is usually assumed that they lived in Winchester (e.g., Biddle [ed.] 1976, 384), Professor Rosalind Hill has recently claimed that they actually lived on the Test at Stockbridge (1975, 94; 1976, 79), which was therefore already a small borough by 1086, within William de Ow's Somborne manor. Stockbridge was not directly mentioned in Domesday Book, unless it is the one-hide manor of *Stoche,* which is not otherwise located (Hughes 1976, 130), but it was certainly part of Somborne in the late 12th century when a weekly market in 'Lestrait' was granted with Somborne lands to William de Briwere (Hill 1975, 94), the first indisputable reference to urban characteristics at Stockbridge. But if Stockbridge was already a borough, would a specific market grant have been necessary? As has been suggested above, it was not needed for Andover. Perhaps it can be said that Stockbridge was, like Kingsclere, given a market grant in the 12th century to safeguard a non-royal owner's right.

One further reason for assigning an early borough to Stockbridge is a handful of coins of Ethelred II's reign struck with the mint name *Brygin*: these are *first hand* types, i.e. attributed to A.D. 979–85. It used to be thought that *Brygin* might mean Bridgnorth, but a die-link with Shaftesbury firmly places *Brygin* in the south of England: Bristol and Stockbridge are both possibilities.[2] Also unlocated is *Bric* which occurs on *last small cross* types, probably of 1009–10. Coins of Cnut with *Bri, Bric,* etc., are more firmly attributed to Bristol (Grinsell, *et al.* 1973, 13). Professor Hill was readier than numismatists (e.g., Metcalf 1978, 160) to reject a mint at Stockbridge, but it is perhaps more likely that Bristol is designated: the *Brygin* coins are too early in the reign to be attributed to an 'emergency' mint, so somewhere developing as a trading settlement is preferable to a place originating as a defensive burh, which is how Professor Hill would see the origin of Stockbridge (1976, 79). Furthermore, a mint there might have taken its name from its manor, Somborne, rather than from the subsidiary settlement at the bridge. One must further assume that William de Ow's 14-hide Somborne estate was separated from the king's between the 980s and 1066, for the king would certainly not have permitted a private mint, even if he could tolerate a private borough. Such a division is perfectly possible, although there is no other evidence for it, and the larger Hampshire estates have a high survival rate of Anglo-Saxon charters (some 80 per cent. of those rated at 12 hides or over: Aldsworth 1973/4, 56).

The possibility of a small, privately-held borough at Stockbridge therefore remains unproven: only archaeological evidence can establish whether the causeway on which 'the Street' is built belongs to the Roman period and was re-used by the Anglo-Saxons, or was constructed in the 12th century. It would, however, have been the only privately-owned borough in 11th-century Hampshire—even the bishop of Winchester apparently did not have a borough on such valuable manors as Fareham on the south coast. Recent excavations there have produced evidence of late Saxon occupation around the church (Holmes 1978), but it is impossible to characterise the pits and gullies found as being specifically 'urban'. The place was ideally located for a market centre, because of its position for road and navigable river communications. Indeed, the failure of the burh at nearby Portchester to develop as a town should have provided an excellent opportunity for an alternative place to develop in its stead, as Barnstaple did from Pilton, or Totnes from Halwell. If Fareham was not a borough, why should Stockbridge have been?

Despite the lack of an entry in Domesday Book, there may have been markets in the 11th century in such later towns as Andover, Odiham, Fareham, and Romsey; but it is doubtful if archaeology could ever prove the case, for the Saxon evidence is usually too vestigial, as at Fareham. Nor could a 'market' be proved merely on the evidence of neatly laid out streets and tenement boundaries. The 7th-century site at Chalton (Champion 1977) is a corrective to any assumption that a rural settlement is disorganised, an urban one alone orderly. Assemblages of material are not characteristic of one or the other: there is no clear-cut qualitative difference between the late Saxon pottery and other finds from Southampton (Platt and Coleman-Smith 1975, II) and those from Portchester (Cunliffe 1976). The former can boast a pre-Conquest coin hoard, but there is more pottery, of better quality and imported from as many different places, at the latter. One should regard as cautionary also the material from Mr. J. Fairbrother's site at Netherton in north Hampshire (Fairbrother 1976, 3–11). Here the crucibles and other debris are exactly what would be expected from a community of small craftsmen establishing themselves in a 'proto-urban' environment: the number of coins found could easily be taken as evidence of transactions at a market-place. But Netherton was a manorial site, and remained so throughout the ensuing centuries.

The Netherton assemblage is certainly likely to prove richer, in quantity and in quality, than any from Twynham (Christchurch), even though the latter was both a 10th-century burh and an 11th-century Domesday borough. The many excavations that have been carried out there in recent years are being collated by Mr. K. Jarvis, and his forthcoming monograph will reveal how scanty is the 10th- and 11th-century evidence other than that of the defences. This is not really surprising, since it can never have been a place of much significance. Domesday mentions a mere 39 houses, and Twynham is one of the few boroughs in England which is not known to have had a mint, at least for a brief period, for no coins can be attributed to it. So insignificant does it appear to have been that it may have been reckoned as a rural vill rather than as a borough in the Hampshire assessment. Professor P. H. Sawyer has noted that the total Hampshire assessment for Domesday was 2,588 hides, and that this figure is significantly close to the 2,550 hides which the early 10th-century Burghal Hidage ascribes to Winchester and Southampton, if added together. Other counties show that this correlation was not mere chance (Sawyer 1978, 227). So neither Portchester, which had no burgesses, although it had been a burh, nor Twynham, which did have burgesses, seems to have counted towards Hampshire's 1086 assessment. In part, Twynham's insignificance must be because of its location. Its catchment area inland was a poor one, much of it comprised of heathland. But the Avon and Stour valleys provide stretches of better land, and some prosperity might have been expected on their account. There is a remarkable contrast in scale of economic activity between Twynham and Wareham, the next burh along the coast. Wareham had the same disadvantage of heathland to its north and south, yet was important enough to have had two moneyers in the early 10th century, and 285 houses in 1066.

The defensive systems at Twynham and Wareham must have been very similar. The discovery that the latter's extant banks had had a stone wall added to the crest at some date before the 12th century (R.C.H.M. 1959, 126–8), and quantities of stone found in the ditch fills at Christchurch, indicate that Twynham had had a similar wall (Jarvis, forthcoming). The north bank at Christchurch defended by a double outer ditch may have been matched by a double ditch on the west and east sides of Wareham, but this has not been proved by excavation (R.C.H.M. 1970, 324). At Portchester, it appears that the Roman ditches were left in their silted-up condition until the early medieval period, when only the inner ditch was recut: 'a few sherds of gritty medieval cooking pots' in the primary silt are the evidence for the date (Cunliffe 1977, 9–10). It is perhaps surprising that there is nothing

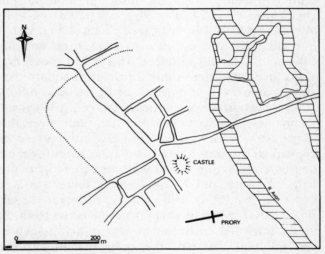

59. Twynham (Christchurch). Principal streets; the dotted line shows the probable course of the defensive bank (after Penn 1980)

to suggest late Saxon ditches at this burh, especially since Winchester, another re-used Roman site, probably had a double ditch around at least a part of its circuit in the late Saxon period (Biddle [ed.] 1976, 274–5).

Portchester of course developed differently from the other burhs in Hampshire, never apparently becoming a borough despite its transfer from episcopal to royal ownership in 904 (Cunliffe 1976, 2). By 1066, the estate named after Portchester was divided into four holdings, the small part retained by the king being part of his Wymering manor, and presumably therefore on the wooded fringes of the territory. The rest was in three separate manors, one of which included the fort (Hughes 1976, 116–7). The excavations have suggested that the *caput* of that manor was within the Roman walls: the evidence is the foundation of substantial timber buildings, and of a square stone structure that may have been a bell-tower-cum-chapel, since it had burials round it (Cunliffe 1976, Fig. 29); an impressive establishment for someone who, at any rate by Domesday, was a freeman of no great standing in the kingdom. As has already been noted, there seems no obvious geographical reason why a borough should not have flourished at Portchester, perhaps adjacent to the defensive area, as at Shaftesbury (*see* Chapter 7), but instead its activity was limited to that of a manorial centre. Nevertheless, it is worth remarking that the finds from the excavations reveal the fort area to have been a centre of wealth, creating opportunities from which an urban centre might be expected to have developed.

Even Southampton does not show as much evidence of urban activity as might be expected. The material record, discussed above, is unimpressive, and Domesday records only 76 (or 79) houses in 1066. But Domesday also records that the number of inhabitants rapidly increased after the Conquest, with an influx of both French and English settlers, presumably taking advantage of the port's position for communication with Normandy. As for a mint, there are no coins identified as having been struck there after *c.* 1025. The physical extent of the town is dealt with elsewhere in this volume by P. Holdsworth (*see* Chapter 11), but it should be noticed that it was quite a small area that appears to have been enclosed by the early ditch system—some 300 metres by 200 metres. This is not much bigger than the area within the Roman walls at Portchester—some 200 metres square. Its size would certainly help to explain the apparent lack of importance of late Saxon Southampton.

The overall picture which 11th-century towns in Hampshire therefore provides is surprisingly unbalanced. In size and everything else, the dominant place was Winchester, which seems to have suppressed the growth of potential rivals. This appears at any rate to be the explanation for the difference between the urban picture in this county and effectively all others in the south. Particularly there is a contrast with Wiltshire and Dorset, where there was a relative multiplicity of urban places, explained by Dr. D. Hill as being deliberate royal plantations intended to compensate financially for loss of royal demesne land (1978, 222). In Hampshire, this policy would surely have led to boroughs and mints at such royal demesne centres as Basingstoke and Odiham. Instead, the only certainly-known Hampshire mint was Winchester, except for the one at Southampton, which was actually closed down in the 11th century. This is another reason why it seems unlikely that there was ever a mint at Stockbridge, so close to Winchester.

It is easy enough to accept that to further the royal policy of fostering Winchester, rivals in the sphere of minting were prevented from being in close proximity. Southampton perhaps kept its mint during the 10th century for historical reasons, since it was probably there that coins had first been struck in Wessex. Twynham and Portchester, the other Hampshire burhs in the early 10th century, were never allowed to have moneyers, nor was a potential substitute for Portchester, such as Fareham or Titchfield. This cannot have been simply lack of demand, which as has been suggested could account for Twynham if the Wareham evidence is disregarded, for the south coast fringe was one of the wealthiest zones in England (Darby 1977,

Fig. 72), and supported a string of boroughs and mints in Sussex, from Chichester to Hastings.

If royal protection of Winchester prevented alternative mints being established in Hampshire, it is not unreasonable to suppose that the same policy restricted the number of places that were boroughs with legal status, to ensure that most large-scale transactions in the shire had to be accounted for in front of the king's reeve at Winchester. This would probably have been a more significant check on the growth of the Farehams, the Basingstokes and the Andovers than the lack of minting facilities. Deliberate late Saxon concentration on Winchester would explain the different urban pattern of the later Middle Ages in Hampshire. After *c.* 1140, the English kings had no particular regard for Winchester. Before the end of the 13th century, a network of small boroughs had been established in Hampshire which was certainly no less dense than that in the neighbouring counties. There was no major change in the economic base which promoted this: instead Hampshire, like other counties, was allowed to develop in the 12th and 13th centuries an urban pattern according to the demands of the market; it seems that under the Anglo-Saxon kings this was not the case, for Winchester benefited from their special protection.

If Winchester dominated Hampshire in the 10th and 11th centuries, it is appropriate enough that it should have dominated recent archaeological thinking about English towns and their origins. A seminal article on town planning stemmed from long consideration of Winchester's evidence (Biddle and Hill 1971), and has culminated in the first volume of *Winchester Studies* (Biddle [ed.] 1976). Even in Winchester, however, all the details of the town's plan are not certain. It is assumed, for instance, that the High Street was laid out on the lines which it still largely retains, and was about 40ft. (8m.) wide. It is narrower at 'The Pentice' in the middle of the town, because a short strip on the south side of the street was encroached upon by the royal palace in *c.* 1070 (*ibid.*, 282).[3] It is as possible, however, that the street was widened on its south side, and that only the palace's and the Nunnaminster's frontages remained unaltered. A frontage change in the principal street at Oxford is known to have occurred (Hassall 1971, 17, 33), and Wareham's main street frontage on the east side was certainly well forward of its present line in the 11th century (Hinton and Hodges 1977, 82). So it could be that Winchester's was widened, to provide more space for the market, the king and the Nunnaminster both refusing to co-operate. This could only be tested archaeologically; but it is worth noting that such uncertainties can exist even in a town so thoroughly investigated as Winchester. No opportunity to look at a High Street frontage site has presented itself since the St George's Street excavation of 1955–62, when only a few medieval rubbish pits were located (Cunliffe 1964, Fig. 9).

It is not only in the sphere of town planning that the Winchester excavations have been important. The opportunity to investigate a whole range of sites has been taken, so that the results will eventually produce a range of evidence from cathedral, bishop's palace and Norman castle down to parish churches and artisan housing (Biddle 1973). There is also information on the suburbs, with occupation datable from as early as the 9th century found at the West Gate (Collis 1978, 162). Otherwise, the data from the suburbs are 10th and 11th century, and later, with 'dirty' trades such as butchery and leather-working taking place. As inside the town, parish churches were established, St Paul's being built over an area previously occupied (*ibid.*, 265). Such earlier occupation may be evidence of settlements distinct from the city, later incorporated into it administratively (Biddle [ed.] 1976, 264–5). Until some pre-9th-century evidence from these sites is found, however, there seems no reason to think that they functioned other than as normal suburbs, for instance as farmsteads.

The splendidly detailed evidence that Winchester's documents and archaeology provide has thrown up many lessons, questions and problems applicable to other towns. It is, for instance, worth noting how little weight is placed in the reconstruction of Winchester upon parish boundaries. Changes in these were so frequent that extreme caution is rightly used in any argument that depends upon them for establishing early features (e.g. Biddle [ed.] 1976, 300). In 1143, for instance, some large-scale alterations may have been made (*ibid.*, 332). For this reason, it would perhaps not be wise to make too much of the problem of the parishes in Southampton which the new theory of the burh boundaries presents (*see* Chapter 11). Dr. C. P. S. Platt assumed that the churches of St Michael and St John were both post-Norman foundations, because they are French dedications, St Michael being the patron saint of Normandy (Platt and Coleman-Smith 1975, 20). But St Michael is a very common Anglo-Saxon dedication, too; an excellent example is the surviving church tower at Oxford's north gate—and it is close to the postulated north entrance to Southampton that St Michael's there would have stood. At Winchester, the east gate was dedicated to St Michael *c.* 994 (Biddle [ed.] 1976, 330). Southampton's St John was perhaps not a gate church at the south end of the burh. St John is not a frequently found Anglo-Saxon dedication, and its parish does not neatly bisect the burh, but has Bugle Street as its western boundary. This suggests that it may be a later sub-division of St Michael's. Both have eastern boundaries between French and English Streets. Perhaps St Michael's lost some territory here to Holy Rood, when that church was established in the newly-important English Street, with All Saints and St Lawrence. There is no documentary or archaeological evidence for the foundation of any of these; entries in Domesday Book referring to ownership of churches in *Hantone* are not explicit about their location (*see* Fig. 60).

No very large church should be expected in pre-Conquest Southampton, since the old minster at the mid-Saxon site, St Mary's, remained the 'mother-church' for the whole area (Crawford 1944–47, 149). This impeded church development in the new burh, although many such new burhs were provided with minsters: the New Minster at Winchester may have been built with the needs of the burh's inhabitants in mind (Biddle [ed.] 1976, 314). Elsewhere, existing minsters retained their rights. There is reason to think that there was a minster at Twynham before the site became a burh (Hase 1975); but no separate parish churches ever augmented the ecclesiastical provisions for the townsfolk. At Wareham, by contrast, several such establishments developed, despite the presence of St Mary's minster. Two at least were pre-Conquest foundations: St Martin at the north gate, which has an Anglo-Saxon nave and chancel; and St Andrew (Holy Trinity) at the south end of the burh, indirectly referred to in Domesday Book (Penn 1980, 110–11). There is also a St Michael, inconspicuously located in a lane behind West Street. It is possible that St Michael originally stood beside the west gate, and was forced to take up less desirable premises when the castle was inserted into the south-west corner of Wareham (Hinton and Hodges, 1977 82). (*See* Fig. 61).

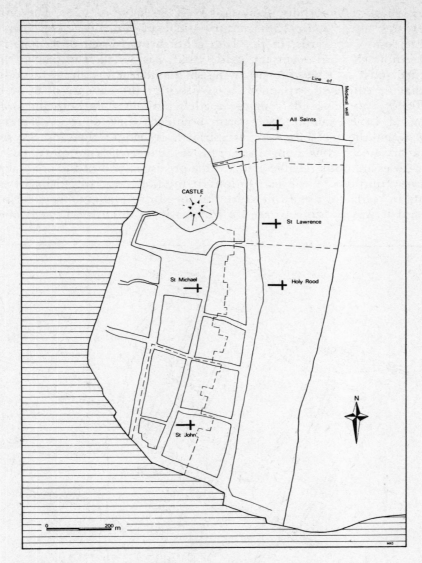

60. Southampton. Principal streets, medieval parish churches and
parish boundaries (after Platt and Coleman-Smith 1975)

The 18th-century Wareham parish boundaries reveal a complicated pattern, of
which two aspects are worth noting. Firstly, the boundary of St Martin's for a short
length runs along Dollins Lane—which excavations have demonstrated to be a fairly
late arrival within the street plan (Hinton and Hodges 1977, 82).[4] Secondly, the
St Andrew's boundary partly follows Pound Lane, which marks the line of the
castle's inner bailey. It is now known from the excavations that the castle had an

outer bailey, marked by Trinity Lane and West Street (*ibid.*, 78). The ditch of this outer bailey was filled in the 13th century and it presumably passed from castle to domestic use soon afterwards. In the 18th century the former outer bailey area was part of St Andrew's parish—yet the castle itself was a detached part of St Mary's. The inference must be that the earlier parish boundary was along the outer bailey line, and that St Andrew's expanded its territory at the expense of St Mary's when the outer bailey was removed from the castle's perimeter. In both the Dollins Lane and the Pound Lane examples, the parish boundary runs along a street which was not extant when the parishes were established. It cannot therefore be said that a parish boundary which runs along a street proves that street's antiquity. Post-medieval parish boundaries are not a reliable guide to the precise extent of the original parish.

The primary purpose of the excavations at the north end of North Street next to Dollins Lane in Wareham was to measure the speed of development of an area within the burh, and it was possible to see how increasingly intensive use was made of the

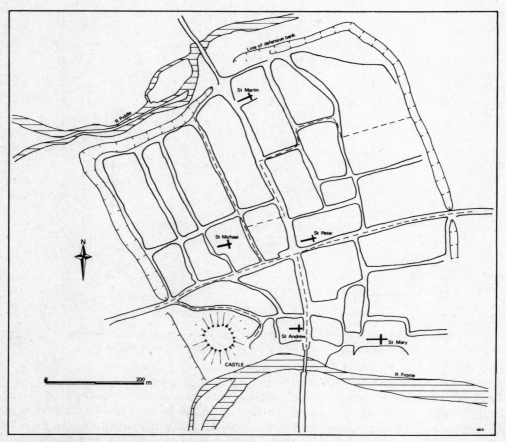

61. Wareham. Principal streets, parish churches, and parish boundaries as in the 18th century

site during the course of the 10th and 11th centuries. This process presumably reflects the growth of commercial activity in the town—just as the Brooks Street sites in Winchester demonstrate the growth of *Tannerestret*, which was fully built up by the middle of the 11th century (Biddle [ed.] 1976, 276), although there were still open plots in it until well into the 10th century. That Tanner Street, a side road set well back from the best commercial area, both grew more rapidly and was more intensively used than the Wareham site is another measure of Winchester's exceptional development. North Street was one of the major axial roads in Wareham, although the site excavated was not close to the crossroads at the centre of the town, where presumably the most sought-after premises would have been located. Winchester had a great advantage in the form of running streams, carefully channelled through the lower part of the town to supply the cloth-workers, dyers, tanners, etc. (*ibid.*, 282–5). Wareham has no springs or water-courses, sited as it is on a peninsula. The apparently wooden-lined gullies and the clay-lined cistern found in North Street clearly show the importance of making use of rain-water (Hinton and Hodges 1977, 58–9), but Wareham could not hope to match Winchester's industrial potential. Nor could Southampton. There also were no flowing streams, and throughout its history, therefore, the town did not develop its own industries. Here then is a further clue to Southampton's small size in the pre-Conquest period.

Southampton was, of course, to flourish—and wane—in the later Middle Ages on the strength of its trade with France, Spain, and the Mediterranean. As we have seen, it began to grow immediately after the Conquest, as new settlers took advantage of the new links with Normandy. It would be wrong to exaggerate these new opportunities, for there would always have been local coastal trade, and trade with France; but it has long been accepted that the greater volume of English trade in the 10th and 11th centuries was with Flanders, the Rhineland and the north of Europe, for which London and east coast ports were better placed (Sawyer 1979, 233). Winchester perhaps flourished not just because it was creaming off trade profits which should have been Southampton's, but because it was able, helped by its royal and ecclesiastical connections, to draw in silver for its mints and other products by the overland routes from London and areas to its north and east, its *chenictes* (Biddle [ed.] 1976, 335) trading in return wool and textiles gathered from the sheep of Wessex, which were presumably the chief source of the wealth of the chalk downlands which Domesday Book can be made graphically to reveal (Darby 1977, 167, 224–5). It is difficult to make this more than speculative, although Winchester's links with Flanders can be demonstrated (Biddle [ed.] 1976, 462). There were people in Winchester with Continental Germanic names (8 per cent. of the total) before 1066: some of these were French names, but many were Flemish (*ibid.,* Table 7 and p. 464). Trade may not have been the reason for their presence, however. Nor should the Southampton link be ignored altogether: the southern suburb at Winchester is taken to reflect the importance of the route to the port (*ibid.*).

That fluctuations in trading patterns may have had a major effect on Southampton becomes more apparent when the mid-Saxon port is considered. In particular, one of the most valuable pieces of recent work has been the analysis of the imported pottery, revealing that little of it originated in the Rhineland, as used to be thought. The great majority came from northern France, although the Low Countries perhaps provided a significant component (Hodges 1980, 55-6; 1981). The pottery demonstrates that the mid-Saxon port, like its medieval successor, depended primarily on its French trade. Detailed study of the *Hamwic* glass finds is showing that there are many unusual features in the assemblages, suggesting that it was at the very least in a 'different area of distribution from Scandinavia, and even Kent' (Hunter 1980, 71). This is research of very great importance, and one of its contributions will be to compare the sources of the glass with those of the pottery. At present, it is enough to say that they are not incompatible.

The possibility that trading fluctuations can not only be recognised as long-term factors, but may be identified within the short-term, is one which has been taken up in a recent article on *Hamwic* which breaks new ground in its analysis of the data assemblages (Cherry and Hodges 1978). This paper is important to medieval archaeology as much for its application of computer and seriation techniques as for its results, which suggest three fairly distinct phases of activity on the site, instead of a steady process of development, prosperity and decay. That the port's effective abandonment took place in the 9th century, not the 10th, is a convincing argument based both on the coin data and on the pottery.[5] It would argue that there was a considerable lapse of time before the new Test-side *port* was established, which is seen as serving a different, 'market', economy (*ibid.*, 307). This would help to explain the new *port's* smaller size. Abandonment of the peninsula can never have been absolute, of course—the survival of St Mary's 'old minster' is proof of that, and Southampton had two moneyers attributed to it in King Athelstan's laws. It is not, however, known where they operated: it could have been within the old Roman fort at Bitterne, which is for many the preferred location of the king's vill (e.g. Hase 1975), since it was later the centre of the bishop's manor, a royal gift. It was from the stone remains at the fort that the estate known as *Stanham* on which *Hamwic* stood was probably named (Crawford 1944-47, 150).

It is some years since Dr. Hill proposed that the early 10th-century burh of *Hamtune* was sited on the River Itchen at Bitterne (1967), because the length of the Roman wall defence corresponds with the length that 150 hides were needed to maintain. That only a small burh was needed at Southampton is presumably indicative of the port's decline. The new discoveries about the defended circuit on the Test-side site do not, of course, preclude that the early 10th-century burh was on the Itchen, where it would be better placed to prevent passage up-river to Winchester: the Test-side site could, as Hill originally postulated, be a slightly later development. Roman walls were, of course, also used at the Portchester and Winchester burhs.

So far as we know mid-Saxon Southampton was not fortified. (A ditch on the west side was found in 1982 by Southampton City Museums Services, however.) Some provision for protection may have been provided by the king's vill, if it was a physically separate entity. Dr. A. R. Rumble has warned against making that assumption too readily (1980, 12), for mentions of it in charters may refer to the whole estate, not to a small enclosed area like the Roman fort. Even if Bitterne was the burh site in the early 10th century, it cannot be assumed that it played a similar role in the 8th century. On the other hand, a *sceatta* coin and graves (Hodges 1977, 192) suggest some activity within its walls.

It would be valuable to have more information about post-Roman—and, indeed, about Roman—use of the Bitterne area. The discovery of a disc-brooch dated to the late 5th century by Dr. M. Welch (in Cunliffe 1976, 205) and of undated graves (Cotton and Gathercole 1958, 30) opens possibilities of some function for the site which may have helped to influence the location of the port on the opposite side of the Test. Similarly, the recent discovery and excavation of a late 6th- and 7th-century cemetery immediately adjacent to the Twynham burh at Christchurch (Jarvis 1979) may help to explain both the location of the burh and the reasons for the importance of its minster (Hase 1975). At Wareham, an early minster is known both from archaeological and historical information (Hinton and Hodges 1977, 81–2), and may well have influenced the choice of the place as a burh. The Portchester excavations have produced a record of great activity within the fort before it became a burh (Cunliffe 1976, 121–3), and Winchester's mid-Saxon use may be related to the large number of cemeteries, and presumably therefore of settlement, nearby (Biddle 1973, 237). Nor is it only the recorded burhs which have such antecedents. Basingstoke, already discussed as a place with a Domesday market, had an important early Anglo-Saxon site in the immediate vicinity, currently (1980) being excavated at Cowdery's Down, which has many substantial rectangular buildings (Millet 1980). There is a concentration of Anglo-Saxon settlements and cemeteries around Andover, another later Hampshire borough (Davies 1979, 178). There was a 6th- and 7th-century cemetery at Alton (Hughes 1976, 24). Titchfield, another market, has a church which may well be a 7th-century minster (Hare 1975). Of course there are other major Anglo-Saxon sites which did not have important successors above or adjacent to them—Chalton (Champion 1977) and Droxford (Aldsworth 1978) are the most obvious—so that the Stockbridge Down cemetery does not make an early borough of Stockbridge (Hill 1937). Nevertheless, there is a corpus of information here which has grown strikingly in the last two decades, and which may help us to understand why certain places were to emerge as significant in their area in the Middle Ages.

Some of these places had been important in the Roman period, and of them it is more appropriate to speak of a re-emergence. Roman markets at Havant, Andover and Neatham/Alton have already been mentioned. Certain of the Roman walled sites could have remained in some form of continuous use: the Portchester sequence is equivocal, the excavator seeing it as unbroken (Cunliffe 1976, 122), others as interrupted in the 5th century (*see* Hinton 1980). The Bitterne evidence is inadequate, but there is no reason to suppose that occupation was maintained through the 5th century. At Silchester, doubt has recently been cast upon one of the few objects dated to the post-Roman era, a stone with ogham cut on it (Fulford and Selwood 1980). Abandonment by at least the middle of the 5th century is probable on the present evidence. That the administrative boundaries of the Roman site had any bearing on later organisation in the area is unlikely (Hinton 1980).

Of Winchester, it must still be said that the evidence of continuity is ambivalent. Even though some of the pottery excavated may be 6th century in date, there is too little of it to deny the possibility of an occupation interval of as much as a century (Biddle 1975, 303). It is splendid that the full report on the Lankhills cemetery has now been published (Clarke 1979), with a wealth of information opening, for instance, discussion about the decline in Romanised life that may have been taking place from as early as the middle of the 4th century (*ibid.*, 346). There are two groups of graves which seem to stand apart from the others: the first makes its appearance *c.* 350, and gradually thereafter loses its separate identity; the other contains six graves attributable to the late 4th or early 5th century. A strong case is made that the former were administrators, aliens from the Danube (*ibid.*, 383–9), and the latter Anglo-Saxons, with particular affinities with people around the Upper Thames Valley (*ibid.*, 396–8). Whether the second group would have been numerically strong enough to make any real impact upon the natives must be a moot point: did they affect the composition of later Wessex, or did they integrate as rapidly as their Danubian predecessors, so that there would have been no element still recognisable as Germanic in the neighbourhood of Winchester by the time that the next Anglo-Saxon migrants arrived—whenever that may have been? There is a long gap between the early 5th-century dates at Lankhills and inside Winchester, and the late 5th-century dates at the Kings Worthy cemetery (Biddle 1973, 237), always providing that these dates are reliable, and do not result from too much compression of the late Roman chronology.

Even if there were some activity within such sites as Winchester in the 5th and 6th centuries, no-one would claim that urban life was maintained. The volume of overseas trade that took place despite the lack of towns in the early Anglo-Saxon period should not be underestimated, however. Studies such as that by Dr. C. J. Arnold (1979) emphasise the number of imported objects that the south coast was able to attract to itself in the 6th and 7th centuries, especially Kent, Sussex, and the Isle of Wight. In particular, Arnold would see the islanders acting as middlemen, before their conquest by Caedwalla of Wessex: thereafter, Southampton replaced the Island as the place where rich goods were landed (1979, 286, 343). No single large centre emerged on the south coast before Southampton at the end of the 7th century, nor did it have imitators. Kent, for instance, seems to have utilised a number of small harbours—Sarre, Dover, Fordwich, Richborough, Reculver, Sandwich, and Canterbury, the last being accessible to small vessels (*see* Chapter 1). Why did Wessex concentrate on a single port to the extent that it appears to have done? Was it because of the royal centre at Winchester, just as Ipswich in East Anglia may have served Rendlesham (Biddle 1976, 114–7)? This places an emphasis on Winchester which can be overstated: there is not, for instance, an exclusive tradition of royal burial there (Hinton 1980), and the shire was dependent on Southampton, not Winchester. Furthermore, the shire was perhaps not always the most important element in the composition of Wessex, since Sigebeorht retained it when deprived of the rest of his kingdom (Rumble 1980, 12).

Is there then a clue to Southampton's mid-Saxon pre-eminence in Wessex in the particular nature of what was being handled there? Gold, glass and garnets do not require the same physical facilities, such as large storage sheds, that barrels of wine and bales of textiles, wool and hides require. The goods passing through *Hamwih* are largely 'invisible' to archaeologists, but the enormous quantities of bones suggest that animal products played a major part. Even slaves and hunting dogs involve specialist organisation: they have to be fed and watered while awaiting a boat. The conquests of Caedwalla and Ine enlarged the potential catchment area of Southampton, which would have increased substantially the volume of traded products available to it. This as much as direct royal stimulus and control would be the catalyst for a large, specialised port. For Kent, and to a lesser extent, Sussex, show that a re-distributive system under the king's control did not necessitate a single 'port-of-trade' (as Hodges 1977, Fig. 9, 1). He could operate as successfully through a network of smaller ports. It follows, therefore, that the size of Southampton needs some further explanation, which the sheer bulk of the trade may provide. The non-political motifs on the Southampton coinage (Metcalf 1977, 90) are a corrective to over-emphasising royal regulation of every aspect of the port's affairs. There is no doubt that the suggestion (Hodges 1977, 208–10) that *Hamwih* should be regarded as a 'port-of-trade', different in nature from later medieval ports which were dependent upon a regular network of internal markets, is stimulating, but the immediate dynamic for its establishment may have been the mundane requirement for large, permanent warehousing facilities.

We are left, therefore, with a sequence of urban developments in Anglo-Saxon Hampshire which cannot be matched in other counties. Of the two Roman sites, one, Silchester, was not to re-emerge as a town, its local role being taken over by Reading (Astill 1978, 75). There is the interesting possibility that markets at some smaller Roman sites led to continuity of preferred settlement location in their neighbourhood. Winchester reappears in the historical record in the middle of the 7th century, but was soon overshadowed as an urban place by Southampton, where there flourished in the mid-Saxon period an international *mercimonia*. This may not be unique in England, for it may have been matched in size by Ipswich, and perhaps London—but it is unique in archaeological terms, for the extent to which the data from it can be recovered. It is the site from which most can be learnt about the origins of urban development in a pre-market economy. Only in the 10th and later centuries in England is a market network, served by a series of small boroughs, seen to emerge. And here, too, Hampshire seems exceptional, since Winchester apparently retarded the development of lesser centres. It was only well after the Norman Conquest that Hampshire's urban history conformed to the general pattern of southern England.

NOTES

1. This chapter, at the Editor's suggestion, includes an excursus upon Wareham, Dorset, and omits detailed consideration of Winchester and Southampton, the county's two most important pre-Conquest settlements. Southampton is considered more fully by P. Holdsworth in Chapter 11.

2. But probably not Bridport, as Hill 1976, 79: *see* Dolley (1955–7), 93.

3. It is difficult to see why the destruction of the palace in 1141 should have caused a permanent encroachment, as Biddle (ed.) 1976, 282, f. n. 4.

4. Crummy (1979, 153) claims that a 16-pole unit of measurement can be seen in the Wareham 'grid' plan. Since there is no uniformity in the distances between the side streets, and since it is also assumed that the streets are contemporaneous, this contention seems invalid.

5. Here and elsewhere (1977, 194), Dr. Hodges has placed the decline of *Hamwic* as early as 'the first or at the most second decades of the ninth century'. His own computer analysis does not really support this. It has three groups (Cherry and Hodges 1978, 305). The absolute dating of the final group depends on Tating ware of *c.* 800, and on the only coin in the third group of pits, a penny of King Ceonwulf (796–821). But such a coin would remain in circulation long after it was minted: its terminal minting date is not the same as its terminal date of deposition. The same is, of course, true of the Tating ware sherds. It may indeed be that the seriation does not cover a long timespan (*ibid.*, 306), but the third group has no *starting* date. The *finishing* date can, therefore, lie decades later, and this is more in line with the *Hamwic* coin finds shown on Fig. 1, several of which date to the middle years of the 9th century. It still remains much more likely that *Hamwic's* trade was disrupted by the Vikings in the 830s–870s than by nebulous political and economic factors in the 800s–820s (as Cherry and Hodges 1979, 307).

BIBLIOGRAPHY

Aldsworth, F. G. (1973/4), 'Towards a pre-Domesday geography of Hampshire—a review of the evidence'. Unpublished B.A. dissertation, University of Southampton.

Aldsworth, F. G. (1978) 'The Droxford Anglo-Saxon cemetery, Soberton, Hampshire', *Proc. Hampshire Field Club and Archaeological Society* 35, 93–182.

Arnold, C. J. (1979), 'Anglo-Saxon social structure: the cemeteries of the Isle of Wight.' Unpublished Ph.D. thesis, University of Southampton.

Astill, G. C. (1978), *Historic towns in Berkshire: an archaeological appraisal*, Reading.

Biddle, M. (1973), 'Winchester: the development of an early capital', in Jankuhn, H., Schlesinger, W., and Steuer, H. (eds.), *Vor-und Früh-formen der europäischen Stadt in Mittelalter*, Vol. I, Göttingen, 229-61.

Biddle, M. (1976), 'Towns', in Wilson, D. M. (ed.), *The Archaeology of Anglo-Saxon England*, London, 99–150.

Biddle, M. (ed.) (1976), *Winchester in the Early Middle Ages*, Oxford.

Biddle, M. and Hill, D. (1971), 'Late Saxon planned towns', *Antiquaries Journal* 51, 70-85.

Bourdillon, J. and Coy, J. (1980), 'The animal bones', in Holdsworth, P., *Excavations at Melbourne Street, Southampton, 1971-76*, C.B.A. Research Report, 33, 79–120.

Britnell, R. H. (1978), 'English markets and royal administration before 1200', *Economic History Review* XXXI (2), 183-96.

Champion, T. C. (1977), 'Chalton', *Current Archaeology* 59, 364–71.

Cherry, J. F. and Hodges, R. (1978), 'The dating of Hamwih: Saxon Southampton reconsidered', *Antiquaries Journal* LVIII, 299-309.

Clarke, G. (1979), *The Roman cemetery at Larkhills*, Oxford.

Collis, J. (1978), *Winchester Excavations 1949-1960. Volume II*, Winchester.

Cotton, M. A. and Gathercole, P. W. (1958), *Excavations at Clausentum, Southampton, 1951–1954*, London.

Crawford, O. G. S. (1944–47), 'Bitterne after the Romans', *Proc. Hampshire Field Club and Archaeological Society* XVI, 148–55.

Crummy, P. (1979), 'The system of measurement used in town planning from the ninth to the thirteenth centuries', Hawkes, S. C., Brown, D. and Campbell, J. (eds.), *Anglo-Saxon Studies in Archaeology and History* I, B.A.R. 72, 149-64.

Cunliffe, B. W. (1964), *Winchester Excavations 1949-1960. Volume I*, Winchester.

Cunliffe, B. W. (1976), *Excavations at Portchester Castle. Volume II: Saxon*, London.

Cunliffe, B. W. (1977), *Excavations at Portchester Castle. Volume III: Medieval*, London.

Darby, H. C. (1977), *Domesday England*, Cambridge.

Dolley, R. H. M. (1955–57), 'A probable new mint in Shropshire', *British Numismatic Journal* 28, 92–9.

Fairbrother, J. (1976), *Netherton, Hampshire: Interim Report*, City of London Archaeological Society.

Fulford, M. and Selwood, B. (1980), 'The Silchester ogham stone: a reconsideration', *Antiquity* LIV, No. 211, 95–99.

Hare, M. J. (1975), 'The Anglo-Saxon church of St Peter, Titchfield', *Proc. Hampshire Field Club and Archaeological Society* 32, 5–48.

Hase, P. (1975), 'The development of the parish in Hampshire'. Unpublished Ph.D. thesis, University of Cambridge.

Hassall, T. G. (1971), 'Excavations at 44–46 Cornmarket Street, Oxford', *Oxoniensia* XXXVI, 15–33.

Hill, D. H. (1967), 'The Burghal Hidage—Southampton', *Proc. Hampshire Field Club and Archaeological Society* XXIV, 59-61.

Hill, D. H. (1978), 'Trends in the development of towns in the reign of Ethelred II', 213-27, in Hill, D. H. (ed.), *Ethelred the Unready*, B.A.R., 59, 213-26.

Hill, N. G. (1937), 'Excavations on Stockbridge Down 1935-36', *Proc. Hampshire Field Club and Archaeological Society* 13, 246–59.

Hill, R. (1975), 'The Manor of Stockbridge', *Proc. Hampshire Field Club and Archaeological Society* 32, 93–101.

Hill, R. (1976), 'The Borough of Stockbridge', *Proc. Hampshire Field Club and Archaeological Society* 33, 79–88.

Hinton, D. A. (1980), 'Hampshire's Anglo-Saxon origins', in Schadla-Hall, R. T., and Shennan, S. J. (eds.), *The Archaeology of Hampshire: from the Palaeolithic to the Industrial Revolution*, Winchester.

Hinton, D. A. and Hodges, R. (1977), 'Excavations in Wareham, 1974–5', *Proc. Dorset Natural History and Archaeological Society* 99, 42-83.

Hodges, R. (1980), 'The pottery', in Holdsworth, P. (ed.), *Excavations at Melbourne Street, Southampton, 1971-76*, C.B.A. Research Report 33, 40-58.

Hodges, R. (1981), *The Hamwih Pottery*, C.B.A. Research Report 37.
     1971-76, C.B.A. Research Report 33, 40–58.

Hodges, R. (1981), *The Hamwih pottery*, C.B.A. Research Report 37.

Holmes, A. G. (1978), 'Excavations at 33 High Street, Fareham, Hants', *Rescue Archaeology in Hampshire* 4, 44–59.

Hunter, R. (1980), 'The glass', in Holdsworth, P. (ed.), *Excavations at Melbourne Street, Southampton, 1971-76*, C.B.A. Research Report 33, 59–71.

Jarvis, K. (1979), 'Christchurch, 235–36 in Medieval Britain in 1978', eds. Webster, L. E. and Cherry, J., *Medieval Archaeology* XXIII, 234–78.

Jarvis, K. (1983), *Excavations in Christchurch 1969–1980*, Monograph 5 of the Dorset Natural History and Archaeological Society.

Metcalf, D. M. (1977), 'Monetary affairs in Mercia in the time of Aethelbald', in *Mercian Studies*, Dornier, A. (ed.), Leicester, 87-106.

Metcalf, D. M. (1978), 'The ranking of the boroughs: numismatic evidence from the reign of Aethelraed II', in Hill, D. (ed.), *Ethelred the Unready*, B.A.R., 59, 159-212.

Millett, M. (1980), *Excavations at Cowdery's Down, Basingstoke*, Basingstoke.

Penn, K. J. (1980), *Historic towns in Dorset*, Dorset Natural History and Archaeological Society, Monograph Series 1, Dorchester.

Platt, C. and Coleman-Smith, R. (1975), *Excavations in medieval Southampton 1953–1969*, 2 vols., Leicester.

Royal Commission on Historical Monuments (1959), 'Wareham west walls', *Medieval Archaeology* 3, 120-38.

Royal Commission on Historical Monuments (1970), *Dorset II South-East, Part 2*, London.

Rumble, A. R. (1980), 'HAMTUN *alias* HAMWIC (Saxon Southampton): the place-name traditions and their significance', in Holdsworth, P. (ed.), *Excavations at Melbourne Street, Southampton, 1971-76*, C.B.A. Research Report 33, 7-19.

Sawyer, P. H. (1978), *From Roman Britain to Norman England*, London.

Spaul, J. (1977), *Andover: an historical portrait*, Andover Local Archives Committee.

Victoria County History (Hampshire and the Isle of Wight) vols 1-5, 1905-12.

Chapter Six

THE TOWNS OF SOMERSET

By Michael Aston

Introduction

IN ANY SURVEY OF PLACES recorded in the Anglo-Saxon period Somerset is bound to appear of great importance. It has the third highest number of place-names recorded in Anglo-Saxon charters (after Kent and Worcestershire) (Hill 1974, 71, Fig. 17), and formed a significant part of the important Saxon Kingdom of Wessex. It has an impressive group of late-Saxon monasteries on the edge of the floodlands at Glastonbury, Muchelney and Athelney, the Saxon see of Wells, and the royal interests in Athelney and Cheddar, as well as its share of burhs recorded in the Burghal Hidage. In distribution maps of Anglo-Saxon mints, 'ports' or burhs it appears as dense as any other county in England (Hill 1974, 5).

It is perhaps surprising, therefore, that Saxon sites have been so little studied in the county. Of course Glastonbury has been dug over a number of years (Aston and Leech 1977), and more recently there have been the excellent excavations of the Saxon royal palaces at Cheddar (Rahtz 1979). But as yet there has not been any systematic attempt to view the Saxon period as a whole, with the result that the Saxon towns in the county have suffered from this general lack of study, with the laudable exception of the work of David Hill.

This chapter, therefore, cannot be any more than a general statement of what is known so far, with, as the reader will soon note, a monotonously regular plea that 'little is known' and 'more work needs to be done'. For Somerset towns the statement which Martin Biddle made generally in 1976 still applies: 'There could scarcely be a more difficult moment at which to attempt a survey . . ' and 'No account can in these circumstances be more than an interim statement, marked by hypotheses and suggestions rather than by deduction from a solid and extensive basis of observed fact' (Biddle 1976).

Any work on historic towns of any period in Somerset was rare until recently. Despite the pioneer work of Savage in 1954 little attempt was made to survey generally the development of urban centres in the county until the mid 1970s. Outside Ilchester (and Bath) no archaeological excavation (beyond attention to major medieval features such as abbeys and castles) was undertaken until the late 1960s. In common with other areas of the country, concern was then expressed for the destruction of evidence being caused by re-development projects in historic town centres (Heighway 1972), but only one 'implication report' was produced (for Taunton, *see* T.R.E.C. 1975) before the general survey carried out by Aston and Leech in 1977. This was the first attempt to gather documentary, topographical and archaeological evidence together for the towns in the county. However, the nature of its genesis, as a tool for planning, and as an outline policy for a rescue archaeology unit, curtailed the amount of discussion which was needed if it was to form the introduction to historic urban studies in Somerset.

Most towns in the county have some sort of historical account and the more recent ones take some cognisance of archaeological data (Bush 1977, Wedlake 1973). The *Victoria County History* of the county was only restarted in 1967 under the able direction of Dr. Robert Dunning, but the slow pace of its compilation and the rigid framework within which the research is carried out has meant that few towns of Saxon origin have so far been covered (Vol. III 1974, Ilchester, Somerton, Langport; Vol. IV 1978, South Petherton and Crewkerne); it will be some years before others are dealt with. There is nevertheless in Somerset, as in other counties, a wealth of early topographical writing and sources of documentation which can be sifted for information about particular places. While the Somerset Record Society has not published documentary material relating to pre-Conquest towns, the general articles on such sources as the Burghal Hidage (Hill 1969) (Table II), and Domesday Book (Darby and Finn 1967) (Table III) deal adequately with Somerset material. For the former source there are specific articles on Axbridge (Batt 1975) and Lyng (Hill 1967).

TABLE II

The Burghal Hidage—Somerset (after Hill 1969)

Every pole of wall = 4 men   1 pole = 5½ yards

	hides	∴ men	poles	suggested length of defences (yds.)
Axbridge	400	400	100	550
Langport	600	600	150	825
Lyng	100	100	25	137½
Watchet	513	513	128	704

TABLE III

Domesday Book 1086—Somerset (after Darby and Finn 1967)

	Recorded burgesses, *domus* or *masurae*	Third Penny	Market	Domesday Mint	No recorded rural population
Axbridge	/	/	—	—	/
Bath	/	/	—	/	/
Bruton	/	/	—	—	—
Frome	—	/	/	—	—
Ilchester	/	/	/	—	/
Ilminster	—	—	/	—	—
Langport	/	/	—	—	/
Milborne Port	/	/	/	—	—
Milverton	/	/	/	—	—
Taunton	/	—	/	/	—
Watchet	—	?	—	—	—
Yeovil	?	—	—	—	—

Recent archaeological work on the Saxon towns in the county must include the important excavations by Leslie Alcock at South Cadbury where evidence of re-fortification of the hill-fort with a stone wall and gateway in the late Saxon period was shown. Other excavations have been less conclusive. No evidence for Saxon occupation has yet been found in excavations at Axbridge or within the Burghal Hidage defences at Lyng (Leach 1976) or Langport. At Taunton (Leach forthcoming, a) the evidence is enigmatic; despite a series of small but widespread excavations little is known of the form or even the precise whereabouts of the Saxon town. At Ilchester (Leach 1982) the evidence is not much better. As a result of excavations in 1974, 1975 and 1980 much new information has been gathered for the Roman period, but little has been discovered of the Saxon town.

Excavations elsewhere have only indirectly influenced our ideas on the early towns. Work at Glastonbury, on the edge of the abbey precinct, has shown some sort of defensive activity in the mid-Saxon period; while at Wells, Warwick Rodwell has postulated an embryonic Saxon street and property pattern based on the alignment of the earlier cathedral building (Rodwell 1980). The catalogue of our lack of knowledge is disheartening. So far, except at South Cadbury, no clear evidence of Saxon defences has been found in any Saxon town in Somerset. No plans of complete Saxon buildings or properties have been recovered and no definitely datable streets have been excavated, although on the Westgate site at Taunton a paved road pre-dating the Norman castle was probably in use in the 11th century. No plans of pre-Conquest religious buildings in towns are known, neither is anything known of the fortifications and buildings which may exist at such sites as Athelney. The splendid royal palaces at Cheddar, however, show the potential of some of these sites in this period (Rahtz 1979). To this enormous lack of knowledge of archaeologically recorded structures must be added the lack of previous topographical work. Axbridge and Lyng have already been mentioned, and some consideration was given to the matter by Aston and Leech (1977). However, it is a sad reflection on the study of Anglo-Saxon archaeology in Somerset that any consideration of the exceptionally well-documented and historically very important site at Athelney had to wait until this latter publication.

The selection of places in this survey of Saxon towns in Somerset has been made on the basis of well-recognised criteria. In 1976 Biddle listed these under 12 headings: (1) defences; (2) a planned street system; (3) market(s); (4) mint; (5) legal autonomy; (6) role as a central place; (7) relatively large and dense population; (8) diversified economic base; (9) plots and houses of urban type; (10) social differentiation; (11) complex religious organisation; (12) judicial centre. For Somerset, however, little can be said for most of these categories. Headings 5/7/8/10/11/12 rely on archaeological and documentary evidence which does not exist for Somerset towns; as yet (2) and (9) can be guessed at from topographical rather than more reliable archaeological evidence, and even the existence or otherwise of defences (1) is often largely conjectural. This leaves markets (3) and mints (4) and the town's role as a central place (6). The importance of the latter will be discussed below, but Domesday Book, and a few earlier accounts, record markets and the existence or former existence of mints. Possession of a mint has been rated by a number of authors as an indication of town status—'Of all the possible tests of borough status the possession of a mint is in many ways the most satisfactory and complete' (Loyn 1961, quoted in Biddle 1976).

TABLE IV
Pre-Conquest Mints

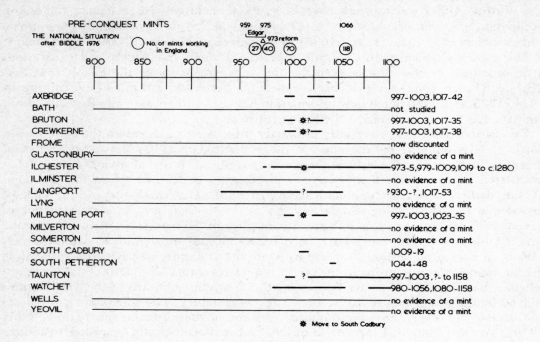

* Move to South Cadbury

By the time Domesday Book was compiled certain criteria were used which in some cases must reflect pre-Conquest circumstances. The author has followed Stenton, and Darby and Finn in recognising the payment of the third penny to the king as an indication of borough status, although this leads to the inclusion of minor places such as Milverton which may be of limited significance. Places in Somerset with mints, markets or burgesses were, however, clearly urban in 1086, although they may not have been so 50 years earlier. Inevitably a number of places have been excluded on the basis of the above definitions, while others have been included which are doubtful in character. As will be seen in the following account, Wells, Glastonbury, Somerton, Ilminster, Frome, Milverton, and Yeovil cannot be considered seriously as Anglo-Saxon towns, but each developed into a locally significant market town in the Middle Ages. The evidence is better, but still marginal, for Bruton, Crewkerne, and South Petherton, but Lyng may never have been more than a fort. On the basis of such criteria a number of other places in the county perhaps should have been considered. It is likely that further documentary work or archaeological excavations at such places as Shepton Mallet, North Petherton, or even Bridgwater, may prove them to be of a greater significance in the Saxon period than is thought at the moment.

This survey, therefore, deals with 18 places in Somerset (not including Bath, which is discussed in Chapter 12) which have some claim to be considered as towns in the

TABLE V

Urban Attributes of places in Saxon Somerset

	(1)* Defences — Burghal Hidage	(2) Planned Street System	(3) Market — Domesday 1086	(4) Mint — Pre- and Domesday 1086	(5) Legal autonomy — Burgesses 1086	(6) Role as a Central Place	(7) Large and dense population	(8) Diverse Economic Base — King's 3rd Penny 1086	(9) Plots and houses of urban type	(10) Social differentiation	(11) Complex Religious org. — Minster	(12) Judicial centre
Axbridge	√ √			√	√32			√				
Bath	√ √	√		√100s / √	√178-192			√			√	
Bruton				√	√5-17			√			√	
Crewkerne		? grid	√48s 8d	√							√	
Frome								√			√	
Glastonbury	√	?	√£11								√	
Ilchester	√ √	? grid	√20s	√	√108			√			√	
Ilminster	√ √	?									√	
Langport		? grid		√	√39			√				
Lyng	√										?	
Milborne Port		? grid	√60s		√56-67			√				
Milverton			√10s	√				√				
Somerton												
South Cadbury	√			√							√	
South Petherton			√50s	√	√64							
Taunton	? √			√				?√			√	
Watchet	√ √			√							√	
Wells		√									√	
Yeovil												

*Criteria after Biddle 1976

Saxon period. Of these, four (+ Bath) are recorded in the Burghal Hidage, and 10 (+ Bath) have recorded pre-Conquest mints. Three further places are included on the basis of Domesday Book, the assumption being that they may have been 'urban' in the pre-Conquest period. As well as the 14 places covered by these criteria, four other places are discussed which have some claim to be late Saxon urban places (Table II). Table V summarises Biddle's criteria and the factors discussed above.

GAZETTEER

Axbridge (Fig. 62)

Axbridge is situated on the shallow south-facing slope of the Mendips between the hills and the flat floodable land of the Somerset Levels. The present small town and the suggested site of the earlier burh are situated on *head* deposits between carboniferous limestone and extensive deposits of estuarine alluvium. It is not on the present course of the River Axe which flows westwards to the Bristol Channel a mile or so to the south. Topographical analysis suggests that the original settlement could have been situated on a tongue of land projecting into the marshland to the south along which Moorland Street now runs.

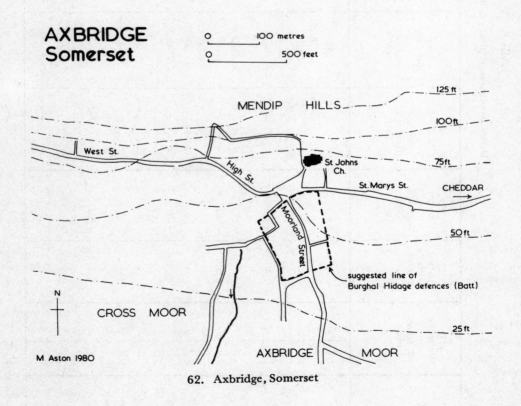

62. Axbridge, Somerset

The Levels are at 18–19ft. above Ordnance Datum, but the hills behind rise to over 800ft. Acess to the south is now by raised causeways but must have been by boat in earlier times. East-west movement was easy along the flatter lower slopes, but the only access northwards was through the hills, a half-mile to the west of the town. Two miles eastwards Cheddar Gorge provides easy access to the top of the Mendip plateau.

Considerable quantities of Romano-British pottery have been found in and around the present town. On the levels to the south a number of Romano-British farmsteads remaining as earthworks have recently been identified together with complexes of ditches and embankments (McDonnell 1979). The whole pattern is reminiscent of the Fenland and it seems likely that this part of the Levels was intensively exploited in the Roman period.

Axbridge is listed in the Burghal Hidage where 400 hides are attached to it (Hill 1969, 90). This would give a length of defences of 550 yards (500m.) (Batt 1975). It is described as a borough under the royal manor of Cheddar in Domesday (Round and Bates 1906) and receipts of the 'third penny' at that time suggest that there was probably an urban element of around 160 people (Darby and Finn 1967, 202). There had been a pre-Conquest mint briefly under Aethelred II (997–1003) and Cnut (1017–1040–2), but only 19 coins are known (Jones 1960–61). There has been much archaeological work in and around Axbridge, principally by the Axbridge Caving Group and Archaeological Society, whose members have carried out several small excavations and conducted watching briefs on a number of re-development sites in the town. This work has revealed Romano-British evidence and extensive finds from the important medieval town—but little of significance for the late Saxon town or the defences of the pre-Conquest fort.

Identification of the site and extent of the Burghal Hidage fort at Axbridge has formed the basis of considerable speculation. Attempts to fit 500 metres of defences around the town plan have been made by several people, but the most convincing is that suggested by Michael Batt (1975). Based on minor changes in level and property alignments, an area 100m. by 150m. is suggested, to the south of the market-place, centred on Moorland Street. Such an area would be aligned north-south between lower land to the west and east and marshland to the south. It would have been overlooked by the hills to the north and would have had easy access via the River Axe to the coast some seven or eight miles away. More importantly, perhaps, it would have controlled the road on the south side of the Mendips leading inland to the important Saxon royal centre at Cheddar (in the analagous position of Langport to Somerton—see below). The medieval centre of the town, with its church, developed outside the northern defences of the burh. The opportunity to test Batt's hypothesis has not yet been taken, although there are empty plots within the area of the suggested fort which could be excavated. Significantly no trace of Saxon occupation has been found within the present town.

Clearly the development of Axbridge must be seen in relation to the important royal palace complex at Cheddar. This was excavated by Philip Rahtz and shown to be occupied from the 9th to the 14th centuries with nearby important indications of a major Romano-British settlement (Rahtz 1979). Cheddar did not develop into a medieval town whereas Axbridge did; it is thus a possibility that Axbridge originated as the commercial and trading centre for Cheddar. This role could have been combined with military activities with the town providing outer defences for Cheddar and blocking access from the coast by both land and water. This separation of functions at different centres has been observed elsewhere in the late Saxon period and will be discussed below. The opportunity to test these hypotheses is available both in the open unexcavated areas within Axbridge and in the wealth of excavated material from Cheddar.

Bruton (Fig. 63)

Bruton lies in eastern Somerset on the southern edge of the former forest of Selwood (McGarvie 1978). At the time of Domesday it was in royal hands and had probably been the centre of a large royal estate. It lies on limestone and sand, on a south-facing gentle slope between the River Brue and low hills to the north. The Saxon town, however, may have been sited on the low oolitic limestone hill south of the river.

The Brue runs south-west at Bruton and the town is sited only a mile east of where the river breaks out into the flatter lower Lias clay lands in front of the Jurassic escarpment. The town is thus well hidden, but it has easy access routes up side valleys to north and south of the main Brue valley.

No finds of prehistoric, Roman or Saxon date have been made in the town, but one to two miles to the north is the important complex of sites on Creech Hill. Here there is a hill-fort on the edge of the escarpment overlooking the vale and the important Romano-Celtic temple on Lamyatt Beacon.

Bruton is not mentioned in the Burghal Hidage, but it had a mint and produced coins briefly in the reigns of Aethelred II (997–1003) and Cnut (1017–35). There were two Saxon churches, St Peter's, founded by Aldhelm in the 7th century, and St Mary's. In the 12th century an Augustinian abbey was founded near or on the site of St Mary's (Aston and Leech 1977).

By the time of Domesday, Bruton was a royal manor with five burgesses, but a further 11 burgesses rendering 23s., recorded at the adjacent manor of Pitcombe, were probably situated in Bruton. A further two burgesses were attached to Ilchester and Castle Cary manors. These 17 burgesses must have represented a small urban centre of around 85 people. There is no mention of a market or the mint which had existed, but 'the evidence suggests a small urban development in a rural setting' (Darby and Finn 1967, 201).

The present town consists of one long street lined with late medieval and post-medieval buildings on former medieval burgage plots. This plan is very regular with a back lane and the stream running parallel to the main street. Such a plan is more suggestive of an early medieval town plantation than a Saxon one and the probability exists that the earlier town was elsewhere (Aston and Leech 1977). The church of St Mary's lies on the other side of the stream on the edge of the former monastic precinct. If this church was in the Saxon town then it must have lain mostly on the south side of the stream. Later developments of the abbey precinct would have obscured any traces and necessitated the development of a medieval town to the north. The burgesses in Pitcombe in 1086 lend support to this suggestion since Pitcombe parish is over the Brue to the south-west of Bruton. Knowledge of late Saxon

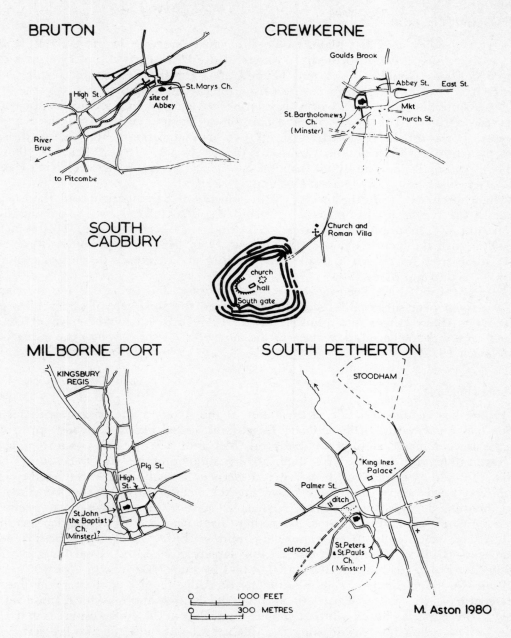

63. Saxon towns—Bruton, Crewkerne, Milborne Port, South Petherton

Bruton will only be increased when these hypotheses are tested by a planned series of excavations. Less seems to be known about Bruton than almost any other of the Saxon towns in Somerset.

Crewkerne (Fig. 63)

Crewkerne lies on a flat plateau of oolitic limestone with gently-shelving land to the east running down into the head-waters of the River Parrett. To the west a deep valley contains Gould's Brook and beyond are extensive deposits of fertile Yeovil sands. Access on to the plateau was easy from the east and south.

Crewkerne lies at the centre of a large former royal estate in existence by the end of the 9th century. 'The manor formed part of the ancient demesne of the Kings of Wessex. It was left by King Alfred (d. 899) to his younger son, Ethelweard (d. 922), but evidently reverted to the Crown of Wessex in 937. It was held in 1066 by Eddera, whom Round identified with Edith "Swan's neck", mistress of King Harold, and after the Conquest by William I' (Dunning 1978, a).

The church of St Bartholomew was a minster of Saxon origin and there was a mint at Crewkerne in the reign of Aethelred II (997–1003). It was re-opened under Cnut and was in use until the time of Harold I, i.e., c. 1017–38. This evidence, together with the mention of a market paying £4 in 1086 (Domesday Book) suggests that there may have been a small urban centre at Crewkerne in the pre-Conquest period (Round and Bates 1906).

No excavations have been carried out in the town, but fieldwork and an analysis of the town plan suggest that the church formed the west side of a rectilinear plan based on Abbey Street and Church Street. There are other parallel streets to the south, and a triangular market-place forms the centre of the town to the east (Aston and Leech 1977).

Frome (Fig. 64)

Frome lies on the west side of the valley of the River Frome on a steep limestone slope facing eastwards. It lies within a large parish called Frome Selwood on the edge of the former medieval forest of Selwood (McGarvie 1978). This was a royal estate in Saxon times with a monastery established by Aldhelm in the late 7th century.

By the date of Domesday, Frome may have been a small town. It rendered receipts from its 'third penny' and there was a market yielding 46s. 8d., but no burgesses are mentioned. This small urban nucleus existed within a large royal manor of predominantly agricultural status. There may have been a mint here in earlier times. 'There are other coins from a puzzling mint at FRO which could be Frome in Somerset' (Dolley 1960), but this is now largely discounted. By Domesday it is likely that Frome 'had practically ceased to be a borough' (Darby and Finn 1967, 204).

Frome's origins lie in the foundation by St Aldhelm of a monastery in the late 7th century. This was dedicated to St John the Baptist and may have stood on the site of the present church which contains fragments of Anglo-Saxon cross-shafts. Its siting on a spring line overlooking the valley probably initiated the lay settlement nearby. As yet there is no evidence of pre-Roman or Romano-British settlement in

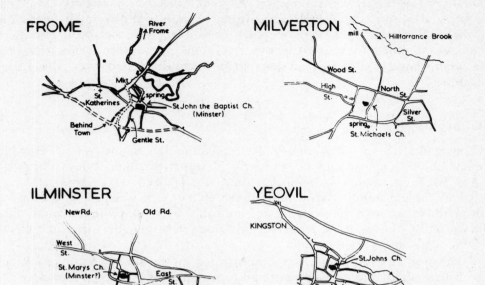

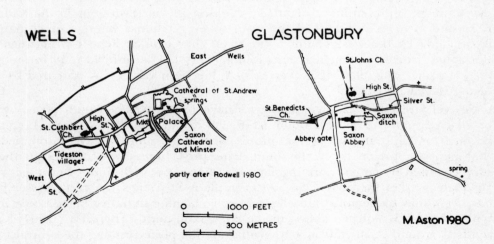

64. Saxon towns—Frome, Milverton, Ilminster, Yeovil, Wells, Glastonbury

the immediate vicinity but virtually no archaeological work has been carried out in the town.

Frome may, therefore, owe its origins as a late Saxon town to the existence of a monastery on a large royal estate. A small nucleus of traders could have been encouraged within the overall agricultural economy and a small centre developed at the abbey gate. Such a development seems to have occurred elsewhere in the country and will be discussed below. At Frome the venture seems to have failed by the 11th century, although an important town developed from the 13th century onwards.

Glastonbury (Fig. 64)

The inclusion of Glastonbury as a possible late Saxon town rests largely on topographical evidence and its similarity in status to other abbeys where late Saxon towns were founded. Glastonbury abbey was centred on a large estate already in existence in the middle Saxon period; the abbey itself was probably founded by the 7th century. A town, however, is not indicated by a pre-Conquest mint, the Burghal Hidage or by reference to burgesses or a market, although at the time of Domesday (1086) eight smiths are recorded.

Excavation at Glastonbury has concentrated on the abbey (Aston and Leech 1977). The debate about the development and topography of the Saxon monastery is beyond the scope of this chapter, but recent work has suggested a mid-Saxon origin (at least) for an enclosure within the extended medieval abbey precinct. The topography of the town outside the abbey's precinct consists of two main elements. The most regular part is the High Street with its lines of former burgages butting against the less regular precinct boundary in Silver Street. It is possible that this is a secondary development representing a planned extension as the town grew in the Middle Ages. A second element lies west of the main abbey gatehouse where a small market-place is situated. To the west of this is the small church of St Benedict. Between this and the abbey gate is a triangular area looking very like an infilled (and formerly larger) market-place. This plan, if it ever existed, has been very much obscured by burgages facing Magdalene Street.

Several larger late Saxon monasteries have towns attached with plans very similar to Glastonbury (Aston and Bond 1976, 74-7, and Fig. 14). At both Ely and Peterborough small triangular market-places with small churches were founded outside the monastic precincts in the immediate pre-Conquest period. Later these were supplemented by larger more regular town plan units with lines of burgages and more adequate market facilities. The best example is St Albans, where Professor Beresford has been able to demonstrate clearly town planning initiative being taken by Abbot Wulsin VI of St Alban's abbey in the late Saxon period (Beresford 1967, 326). This resulted around A.D. 950 in a triangular market-place forming the central feature of a small town with several roads being diverted into it. It is probable that the same thing happened at Glastonbury. Analysis of the largely unstudied mass of documentation relating to the abbey together with more extensive excavation may provide answers to such problems.

Ilchester (Fig. 65)

Ilchester is situated on the River Ivel where it is crossed by the Fosse Way. Its Roman name was probably *Lindinis* which may be translated as 'little Marsh', a description which fits the topographical situation well. The town lies on a very low mound running south from higher land to the north-west. This mound itself may be partly man-made; up to three metres of accumulated occupation debris has been recorded in the town. On all other sides the land is low-lying and still subject to periodic flooding. However, higher flood-free land lies not far away to the north and east; Roman roads ran in these directions as well as south to Dorchester in Dorset.

Some evidence of pre-Roman occupation has been found at Ilchester, but its main development occurred during the Roman period (Aston and Leech 1977). A Roman fort of about 12 hectares was established before the town was developed. Little is known of the street plan or buildings within the town, but it was later defended by a stone wall; it had extensive suburbs, and in the late Roman period it became the northern capital of the *Durotriges Civitas*.

In the Saxon period the town probably formed part of the large royal estate of Somerton (Dunning 1975, Fig. 7). It is probable that the Roman walls, suitably

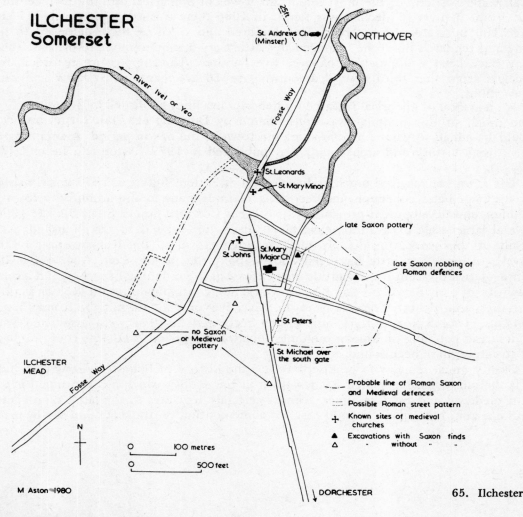

ILCHESTER
Somerset

St. Andrews Ch. (Minster)   NORTHOVER

River Ivel or Yeo

Fosse Way

St. Leonards
St Mary Minor

late Saxon pottery

St Johns
St Mary Major Ch

late Saxon robbing of Roman defences

St Peters

no Saxon or Medieval pottery

St Michael over the south gate

ILCHESTER MEAD

Fosse Way

- - - - Probable line of Roman Saxon and Medieval defences
.... Possible Roman street pattern
+ Known sites of medieval churches
▲ Excavations with Saxon finds
△ "   "   without   "   "

N

0 — 100 metres
0 — 500 feet

M Aston 1980

DORCHESTER   **65. Ilchester**

repaired, would have remained in use, but Ilchester is not mentioned in the Burghal Hidage. Nothing is known of the pattern of streets or the areas occupied in the late Saxon period, but a mint operating from the reign of Edgar (973) to 1280 gives some indication of its commercial importance. There are gaps in its operation, in the reigns of Edward the Martyr (975–79) and, after the Conquest, in those of Richard I and John, but from 1017 to 1023 there were seven or eight moneyers operating (Stevens Cox 1948). For a brief period it seems that the moneyers retreated to South Cadbury castle (Fig. 63) and minted coins there (1009–19) (Alcock 1972, 196: q.v., South Cadbury). A large number of churches are recorded in the Middle Ages, as at other important late-Saxon centres (e.g., Winchester, Exeter, Chichester), and some are likely to have been in existence before the Norman Conquest. Leland, in the 16th century, said that there had been four parish churches of which one remained, two were in ruins, and one had disappeared. Gerard in 1633 said there had been at least 10, while Stukely (1724) claimed that there had been sixteen. Clear references exist for six (Aston and Leech 1977). St Mary Major remains, as does St Andrews in Northover, a church with pre-Conquest origins, which is claimed to have been a minster (Dunning 1975). St Olaves, whose position is unknown, suggests a pre-Conquest dedication and possible Scandinavian connections.

Ilchester was one of the most important towns in Somerset until the 13th century, but from then on its decline was rapid. In 1086 there was a market worth £11 and over 100 burgesses are recorded. One hundred and seven of these belonged to the king and rendered 20s., one belonged to Castle Cary manor, and one to Bruton. There may have been a population of over five hundred. The mint is not recorded, but receipts from the 'third penny' amounting to £6 are mentioned (Darby and Finn 1967, 200).

A great deal of historical research on Ilchester has been published by J. Stevens Cox, and much of this material was consolidated by Dunning (1974a). Little, however, could be added to what was known of the town in the Saxon period. A summary of the town's history and archaeology was published in 1977 (Aston and Leech 1977, 67–75).

The town has received much archaeological attention. Before c. 1970 this consisted of the systematic collection and recording of finds made in and around the town in building and development projects by J. Stevens Cox and others. Since the late 1960s several larger-scale excavations have taken place, but little is so far published. As a result of this work considerably more is now known of the Roman phase of the town's history, but little has been added about the period from A.D. 400–1100. Finds of two 6th-century Byzantine coins, two Anglo-Saxon disc-brooches, and a small quantity of early Saxon pottery hint at occupation continuing after the Roman period, but the name Ilchester derives from the River Ivel or Yeo and not the Roman name *Lindinis*. Late Saxon pottery and a coin recovered in 1974 were associated with widespread cobbling of Roman buildings, but for the period A.D. 450–1066 no plans of structures have been found.

Clearly much remains to be discovered of the history of Ilchester. Along with Bath it is the only sizeable walled Roman town in the county which has continued in use into medieval and modern times. Almost certainly it relates to the late Saxon centre at Somerton, but equally a good case for some continuity of occupation can be made out for Ilchester from late Roman times onwards. Its importance at Domesday, together with the number of recorded churches, suggests that it was a prominent late Saxon town comparable to such places as Bath, Exeter, and Dorchester. Unlike these towns it subsequently declined so that now it is little more than a village.

Nevertheless, this decay represents an opportunity for archaeologists to examine a town's development in greater detail than may be possible elsewhere. Stray finds and the excavations conducted so far merely serve to emphasise the potential importance of Ilchester both as a multi-period settlement and as a long-lasting urban centre.

Ilminster (Fig. 64)

Ilminster has little or no claim to be a pre-Conquest town, but a market yielding 20s. belonging to Muchelney abbey is recorded in 1086 (Darby and Finn 1967, 209). It is also probable that Ilminster church may have been a minster before the Conquest (Dunning 1976).

The present small town is situated at the south-west corner of a large estate which was owned by Muchelney abbey by the late 10th century. The present impressive church has a cruciform plan and stands within a rough grid of streets and lanes. Adjacent, on the east and north-west sides are triangular market-places.

Ilminster probably developed as a small market centre adjacent to a minster and an agricultural settlement in the 11th century. It has no other obvious urban attributes at that time.

Langport (Fig. 66) (Plate 3)

Langport is situated on a prominent clay and limestone knoll in the middle part of the Parrett valley where it narrows to only 600 to 700 yards across. Both upstream

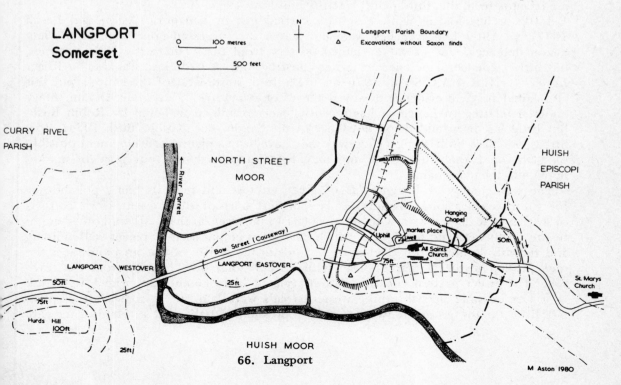

66. Langport

and downstream of the town there are extensive areas of the Somerset Levels which are still in part poorly drained. At Langport steep bluffs overlook the river and make an ideal crossing point, linking dry overland routes to east and west. It is likely that the town was founded to control this crossing and take advantage of tranship-ment facilities for land and water transport. To the west Hurd's hill, another clay knoll, rises to over 100ft.

Although no pre-Roman or Romano-British settlement has been found in Langport itself, there are extensive traces of Romano-British settlement in the immediate vicinity, especially to the east in the direction of Somerton (Leech 1976 and 1977).

Langport is first recorded as a burh in the Burghal Hidage with 600 hides assigned to it, giving a likely circuit of defences of about 825 yards. It was situated on the edge of the large royal estate at Somerton (Fig. 68) in the analogous position of Axbridge to Cheddar (q.v.). These defences could have run either around the steep hilltop, where excavations have been carried out (see below), or across the peninsular to the north-east. There is a massive bank here which runs from marsh to river and is c. 800+ yards long. This would seem to be the most likely candidate for the late-Saxon defences, although it has been interpreted as Civil War works.

By 930, under Athelstan, there was a mint at Langport. This was one of the earliest recorded in Somerset and it was still in production in the 11th century. It was producing coins under Cnut and Halfcnut (1017–42), but ceased operating under Edward the Confessor some time after 1050–53. At the time of Domesday (1086) Langport is briefly mentioned under the entry for the royal manor of Somerton (Round and Bates 1906). Thirty-four burgesses are recorded together with five rendering 38d. attached to North Curry manor nearby. This implies a population of perhaps 200 people, and while there is no mention of a market or a mint there are receipts from the 'third penny' (Darby and Finn 1967, 202).

Little archaeological work has been carried out in Langport (Aston and Leech 1977). In 1969 two trenches were cut across the suggested upper line of the late Saxon defences. One of these yielded pottery from the 11th to the 18th centuries, but little evidence of defences or other constructions. A large area was dug by Roger Leech (for C.R.A.A.G.S.) in 1976 on the hilltop, south-west of the church, but this also failed to yield evidence of any defences or structures of any date. Documentary material relating to Langport has recently been examined in detail by Robin Bush, but little has been added to knowledge of the Saxon occupation (Bush 1974). Bow Street, which is built along a causeway may have been a planned development possibly of 11th- or 12th-century date and may have supported the 'long port' or market implied in the place-name.

The topography of Langport is of great interest and suggests many possibilities for future excavation programmes. The highest part of the present town consists of a triangular-shaped area with steep slopes to the river on the south and other slopes to the north-west and north-east, which have been emphasised by recent wall-building and rubbish accumulation. The church stands in the centre of this area and faces the now infilled medieval market-place with its perennial water supply from the town well. The street pattern consists of a straggle of lanes coming up from lower land. It is just possible that the three western roads were laid out as some sort of plan, but little on the ground now gives this impression. To the east a rebuilt later gate surmounted by a chapel, Hanging Chapel, may stand near the line of Saxon defences, while to the west a gate is thought to have stood down the slope of Uphill. West of this hilltop the plan of the town is very different and today the change of level and functions within the town give each area a distinctive character.

Bow Street forms a direct east-west link across the valley and may be based on a causeway of uncertain date (but *cf.* Oxford where the causeway in St Aldates was of late 8th-century date). Burgage plots were laid out along this route with the river and water channels in place of back lanes, at the rear of the plots. While topographically the plan of this part of the town accords best with examples of medieval new towns the original function of the causeway in this pattern is of some interest. As has been mentioned already, Langport lies at the narrowest part of the River Parrett valley and it is tempting to see the construction of the fort as an attempt to control the river and the long distance routes running east-west which converge here. Was the causeway built in the Saxon period, or was it already in existence? Did the construction of the fort merely serve to emphasise the strategic importance of Langport? The excavations at the hilltop suggest that the fort was not built up in that area. It may be that the main settlement has always been at the bottom of the hill to the west or north-east. As in towns elsewhere only excavation in future is likely to give a clearer picture.

Lyng (Fig. 67)

Lyng lies on the east end of a marl promontory over two miles long and half-a-mile wide. This joins the 'mainland' at Buckland in Durston and is paralleled by a similar ridge to the south running through North Curry. There has been much alteration to

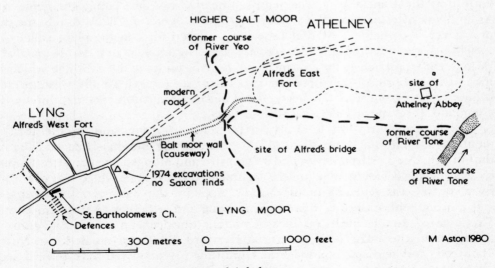

67. Lyng and Athelney

the landscape of the Somerset Levels hereabouts (Williams 1970), which has resulted in the shift of the confluence of the Rivers Tone and Parrett to the east, from the north of Athelney. The 25ft. contour indicates the extent of the flood-free land at both Lyng and Athelney.

Lyng is mentioned in the Burghal Hidage where 100 hides are assigned to it. This figure, which indicates defences of around 140 yards, only makes sense if much of the defensive circuit was provided by marshy floodable land around the end of the promontory. This has indeed been argued by Hill, who has also suggested the line of defences running across the neck of the promontory near St Bartholomew's church, where earthworks and breaks of slope can be seen (Hill 1967).

Lyng did not develop into a town. No mint, market nor burgesses are recorded, and the defensive circuit did not include a royal residence or early monastic or minster site. Recent excavations by Peter Leach (1976) failed to locate any late Saxon occupation. At the time of Domesday (1086) Lyng belonged to Athelney abbey (see below), but its situation between the large royal manors of North Petherton and North Curry suggests that originally this area belonged to one or other of these royal estates (Round and Bates 1906) and that the fort served a similar outlying defence function as Axbridge did for Cheddar. For the real significance of Lyng in the Saxon period, however, it is necessary to look at the nearby site of Athelney and the events associated with it.

In the spring of A.D. 878, Alfred, king of Wessex, withdrew to the Isle of Athelney and from there constantly engaged Danish raiding parties operating in his kingdom. The *Anglo-Saxon Chronicle* records that he built a stronghold (*geweorc*) there, and Asser states that it was surrounded by marsh. Today the Isle of Athelney is a low, long, natural marl mound with the Somerset Levels bounding it on all sides. Until alterations to the river courses nearby in the medieval period it was cut off from the 'mainland' to the west by the River Yeo.

From this base Alfred was able to defeat the Danes, and as part of the peace treaty Guthrum, the Danish king, was baptised nearby at Aller, taking the name Athelstan. As a thank-offering for this victory Alfred ordered, in 893, the foundation of a monastery at Athelney. At that time it was stated that 'in the place called Athelney, which is surrounded on all sides by very great swampy or impassable marshes, so that no one can approach it by any means except in punts or by a bridge which has been made with laborious skill between two fortresses (*arces*). At the western end of this bridge a very strong fort has been placed of most beautiful workmanship by the king's command' (Stevenson 1959, 79–80).

This latter description is clearly a reference to Lyng and to the fort which is mentioned somewhat later than Alfred's time in the Burghal Hidage. Thus it is clear that at Athelney, Alfred developed a defensive and monastic centre later supplemented by a bridgehead fort at Lyng on the 'mainland'. The bridge, which was over the former river course, was replaced in the Middle Ages by the Balt Moor earthwork which is still a prominent structure today linking Lyng and Athelney (Aston and Leech 1977). This idea of double burhs or forts defending a bridgehead was employed by Edward the Elder in the early 10th century at Hertford, Buckingham, Bedford, Nottingham, Stamford, and perhaps London and Cambridge; it may well have been based on the experience of defending Lyng and Athelney.

Lyng is thus of considerable importance in the Saxon period, not so much as an example of a Saxon town, since it never seems to have been urbanised to any degree, but rather as a demonstrable example of how a royal centre could be defended by outlying forts. Such an arrangement has already been suggested for Somerton at Langport (and perhaps Ilchester) and at Cheddar and Axbridge; others are clearly indicated elsewhere in southern England.

Milborne Port (Fig. 63)

Milborne Port is situated in the south-east of Somerset on a flat limestone peninsular projecting southwards with shallow steep-sided stream valleys to south and west.

Milborne Port was sited on the edge of a royal estate mentioned in Domesday Book. By that date 56 burgesses and a market paying 60s. are indicated on the royal manor, with five burgesses paying 3s. on the count of Mortain's manor. Other entries relate to appurtenant holdings—six burgesses attached to Abbas Combe rendering 50d. and two masurae attached to Goathill. These entries imply an urban centre of perhaps 350 people. Receipts from the king's 'third penny' are mentioned and so is the church of St John. This nucleus formed the centre of a large agricultural estate with numerous settlements in royal hands (Darby and Finn 1967). In pre-Conquest times there was a mint from 997 to 1003, which was re-opened under Cnut (1023–35). It had, like that at Ilchester, been moved to South Cadbury for some time as an emergency mint.

Little more is known of the town historically in Saxon times, but it is likely that the church was a minster. The architecture of the church of St John has been studied by Taylor and Taylor (1965, 424–28); it contains work of the 11th century.

There has been no systematic archaeological work in the town, and it is therefore not known how built-up it was in the Saxon period, how much of the street plan was developed, or if the site was defended at any stage.

Topographically the town poses interesting problems. The general arrangement of streets and properties is very regular (as are the surrounding fields) with orientations east-west and north-south. Pig Street and roads to the west form the main north-south axis, with the High Street and the lane to the church the east-west one. It is tempting to see this pattern and some of the property boundaries as a planned unit within which the church sits on the same alignment. However, only excavation can confirm whether any such planning took place in the Saxon period.

Milverton (Fig. 64)

Milverton lies in west Somerset on the margin between the fertile plain of Taunton Deane and the hilly country of Exmoor and the Brendon Hills to the west. It is situated on an easterly projecting spur with the wide valley of Hillfarrance Brook to the north, and streams to the east and south. The only level approach is from the west where there are extensive areas of meadow.

Milverton is not mentioned in the Burghal Hidage and it did not have a Saxon mint. By Domesday Book in 1086 no burgesses are listed, but there are indications that the place had burghal status. Oake is said to have had a house in Milverton in the same context as is seen at other towns (e.g. Bath) and there is reference to the 'third penny' for Milverton under the nearby royal manor of Brompton Regis. There was also a market rendering 10s. (Darby and Finn 1967). If this was a borough or the remains of a borough, it was surrounded by a large agricultural manor, clearly indicated in Domesday Book.

There have been no excavations in Milverton, but systematic collecting of surface scatters of pottery has been undertaken recently by Howard Davies in the town (pers. comm.) and this suggests that the earliest occupied area lies on the eastward projecting spur.

The present plan of the town consists of several streets aligned east-west crossed by two north-south roads across the spur. The High Street is now a relative backwater, just off the ridge top, but it is in line with the church on the highest point and has been diverted in recent times, around the garden of a large house. It is likely that this was the original street with perhaps side lanes to north and south. The other streets could have been developed and built up in the medieval period and later as the town grew. However, as elsewhere, only excavation can answer such questions. In this respect the large area to the east of the church represents potentially a great source of information about early Milverton (Aston and Leech 1977).

Somerton (Fig. 68)

Somerton is often claimed to have been a Saxon town, the shire town for Saxon Somerset and the 'ancient capital of Wessex'. The present town lies on a wide clay and limestone plateau and can be shown to have been founded in the 13th century (Dunning 1974b). Despite recent discussion as to a likely 'short-lived burh' site or the 'site for a fortified town' (Aston and Leech 1977) it seems unlikely that there was any urban nucleus at Saxon Somerton, although Dunning has argued that there might have been a pre-medieval centre north-west of the church—

> The town itself seems to have originated as a short-lived Saxon burh in the area north-west of the church, known as Bury in 1349. The abandonment of the original settlement centre probably dates from the creation of the new market and surrounding burgage properties south of the church before 1290. A new alignment of streets involving the creation of West Street and Broad Street gradually obliterated the original network, which comprised a direct east-west route north of the Vicarage and Church, with a junction or crossroads later providing access to the new market-place. There were 'ancient burgages' north of the churchyard in the 17th century in a street then referred to as East Street . . . (Dunning 1974b, 130).

This medieval town was situated on a wide eastward projecting spur with the steep-sided valley of the River Cary to the north and east and a deeply-cut stream to the south. The situation is similar to a number of Saxon town sites.

Somerton was an important royal estate in the Saxon period and at Domesday, and there was probably a royal house on the estate, perhaps at St Cleers farm (Dunning 1974b). The witan or Saxon royal council met here at least once, in 949. But Somerton is not mentioned in the Burghal Hidage and neither a mint, market nor burgages are recorded in the Saxon period. It is thus unlikely to have been more than a large royal agricultural holding; the real urban centre for Somerton was at Langport as is shown in the Domesday survey, although Ilchester may also be relevant to the estate (*see* Fig. 68).

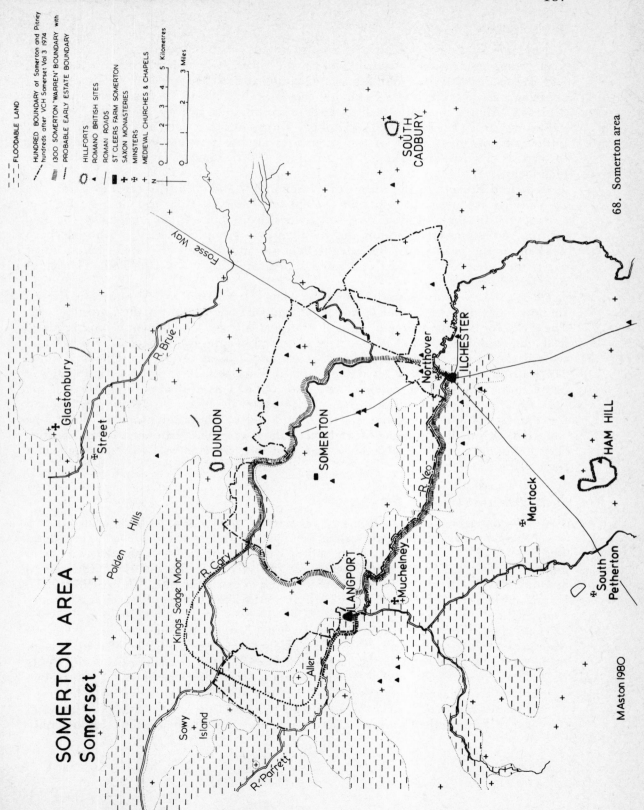

SOMERTON AREA
Somerset

FLOODABLE LAND

HUNDRED BOUNDARY of Somerton and Pitney hundreds after VCH Somerset Vol 3 1974

1300 SOMERTON 'WARREN' BOUNDARY with

PROBABLE EARLY ESTATE BOUNDARY

HILLFORTS

ROMANO BRITISH SITES

ROMAN ROADS

St CLEERS FARM SOMERTON

SAXON MONASTERIES

MINSTERS

MEDIEVAL CHURCHES & CHAPELS

Kilometres

Miles

Fosse Way

Glastonbury

Street

R. Brue

Polden Hills

DUNDON

SOMERTON

Northover

ILCHESTER

SOUTH CADBURY

HAM HILL

Martock

R. Yeo

Kings Sedge Moor

R. Cary

LANGPORT

Muchelney

South Petherton

Aller

Sowy Island

R. Parrett

68. Somerton area

M. Aston 1980

South Cadbury (Figs. 63 and 68)

The large hill-fort of Cadbury at South Cadbury in south Somerset has some claim to be considered in any discussion of Saxon towns. It was clearly never a successful late Saxon urban centre, but for a brief period it did have some of the functions of contemporary Saxon towns. The hill-fort at South Cadbury has been shown by Professor Alcock's excavations to have a continuous history from the Neolithic period onwards (1972, 194–201). Cadbury Hill stands as a detached oolitic limestone outlier off the west front of the Jurassic escarpment; to the west is the extensive lower Lias clay lowland. The hill rises to over 400ft., some 250ft. to 300ft. above the plain below.

Aethelred II came to the throne of Wessex in 978 and during his reign troubles with the Vikings restarted. In September 1009 or March 1010 he founded the burh of *Cadanbyrig* in the old Iron Age fort at South Cadbury as an emergency fortified centre. At the same time a mint was founded by a group of moneyers who had been working at the nearby lowland site of Ilchester and perhaps elsewhere. Later, under Cnut, the moneyers returned and some appear at Bruton and Crewkerne. The mint only lasted for a decade.

During the excavations under Professor Alcock from 1966 to 1970 no evidence was found of the mint at Cadbury, but good evidence was found for the burh defences. These ran for 1,200 yards and, using the Burghal Hidage formula, would have required 870 men to defend them. The defences consisted of a mortared wall of well-laid Lias slabs backed by a rubble core of local rock and a bank of earth, rubble and stone. The wall was four feet thick, but the whole defence was 20ft. deep. A south gateway contemporary with these defences was also found. This evidence is important as the only excavated example in Somerset of late Saxon defences. No evidence was found for domestic buildings within the fort, and indeed they are probably not to be expected. A cruciform-shaped trench may, however, have belonged to an abortive church building. By 1020 Cadbury had probably reverted to its present-day quiet rural character.

South Petherton (Figs. 63 and 68)

South Petherton, in south Somerset, has some small claim to be considered as a possible Saxon town. The early estate belonged to the crown in pre-Conquest times and in 1086. The church of St Peter and St Paul very probably originated as a Saxon minster serving the surrounding estates. It is likely that the thaneland referred to in Domesday Book may have related to a church in existence then (Thorn 1980, 294). However, there is no mention of a burh at South Petherton, and at Domesday only a large agricultural estate is indicated.

The village forms the centre of an extensive estate. Within this area there are widespread traces of Romano-British settlement, including probable villas at Bulsom Bridge and Mid-Lambrook and collections of Roman coins from Ben Cross and Fouts Lane. There was a large Iron Age and Romano-British settlement site at Stoodham overlooking the village and a reputed Saxon manor of King Ine in the valley below.

The tenuous evidence for a town rests on two small pieces of evidence. Firstly, in the reign of Edward the Confessor, there was a mint at South Petherton, although only two coins are known, dating from 1044 to 1048. Secondly, the topography of the present small town may indicate a small defended nucleus in the pre-Conquest period. South Petherton lies in a hollow, but locally the church and the centre of the village sit on a small but prominent spur facing eastwards with a stream below and appreciable slopes to east and south. There are traces of a hollow which could be a defensive ditch, west of George Lane. If this is so the rest of the defences would have run along Palmer Street.

There have been no excavations in the town, although a thorough history was recently completed (Dunning 1978b). Its status as an urban place in the Saxon period must for the time being be regarded as speculative.

Taunton (Fig. 69)

Taunton lies in the centre of the large fertile plain of Taunton Deane through which runs the River Tone. To the north lie the Quantocks and to the south the Blackdown Hills. The Saxon and medieval royal and ecclesiastical estate ran between the two, across the valley on a north-south axis (Darby and Finn 1967, 203).

The centre of the modern town stands on a low knoll of marl sloping gently northwards from The Mount, with extensive areas of alluvium along the valley of the Tone. North of the town the land rises gently towards Kingston St Mary, while locally the highest land is Haines Hill, south-west of the town centre.

Considerable evidence of early settlement has been found in this area with the important late Bronze Age enclosure and Iron Age hill-fort at Norton Camp (Norton Fitzwarren) indicating a pre-Roman 'central place' in the region. Some Romano-British settlements are known on the Tone valley and recently large numbers of cropmark sites have been identified around the town (Aston [ed.] 1977). There is no obvious predecessor in the Roman period unless the numerous finds at Holway, south-east of Taunton, indicate more than a 'large agricultural settlement'.

Taunton was a royal estate in the Saxon period, but in 904 it was purchased by Denewulf, bishop of Winchester (Bush 1977). It had been mentioned as early as 722 when the *Anglo-Saxon Chronicle* records that the place which Ine (king of Wessex 688–726) had built was destroyed by Queen Athelburga. It is, however, not clear whether this refers to a town, fort, palace or some other structure; it certainly cannot be taken as necessarily indicating a town at that date. The church of St Mary was traditionally founded by Frithogyth, wife of Ethelheard, as a minster in the 8th century. Taunton is not listed in the 10th-century Burghal Hidage, but there was a mint operating under Aethelred II from 997–1003; it continued until it was closed in 1158 in the reign of King Stephen (Bush 1977).

At the time of Domesday Book in 1086 a very large rural estate centred on a thriving town is indicated at Taunton, which Maitland has called 'the classical example of colossal manors' (Maitland 1897, 326). The town was the most important in the county after Bath and Ilchester. It had a market and a mint, each rendering 50s., and 64 burgesses paying 32s.; and it may well have had defences maintained by the manor (Thorn 1980, 297). Nineteen surrounding places paid dues to Taunton. It is likely that there were at least 300 or so people in the town at the time as well as large numbers in the settlements around (Darby and Finn 1967, 202). Taunton has had

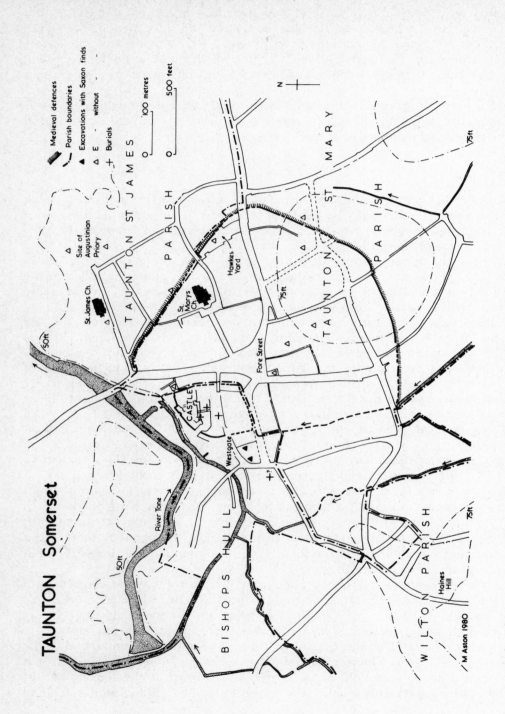

69. Taunton

a number of histories written about it. John Hunt examined much of the documentary material of the bishops of Winchester for the town in the Middle Ages, and recently a new history has appeared (Bush 1977), but little new material has been added for the Saxon period.

The same is not true for its archaeology (Aston and Leech 1977). Over the last 10 years a number of excavations have been carried out, under the auspices of the Taunton Research and Excavation Committee, which have greatly helped our understanding of the early history of the town. The results of these excavations are to some extent surprising, and in many ways pose more questions than they answer. Several sites have been excavated near to the site of the medieval Augustinian priory. Not surprisingly these did not reveal evidence of pre-Conquest occupation since they were beyond the medieval defences. However, two sites within the medieval town and another on the line of the eastern defences (Hawkes Yard) have also failed to reveal any occupation earlier than the early Middle Ages. Indeed, two of these sites (off Fore Street) show that the central area of the medieval town seems to have been fields and open country from the Roman period to the 12th century. On the corner of Fore Street and the High Street evidence of probable prehistoric occupation was found but no settlement of the Saxon period (Leach forthcoming, a).

Is there then any evidence for Saxon Taunton which is so clearly indicated in the documents? Many years ago when work was being carried out at the castle, a pre-Conquest rampart was found beneath the Great Hall (T.R.E.C. 1975). Alterations to the castle during the construction of the Local History Library revealed several skeletons, one of which was clearly beneath and therefore earlier than the castle wall. Other skeletons have been found in what was the castle outer bailey, although none was in a datable context. The skeleton under the castle wall has now been dated by C14 assay at A.D. 860 ± 70 (H.A.R. 2674). It has been suggested that these burials belong to the original site of a Saxon minster at Taunton (Minnitt and Murless 1979, 90). The only other evidence for Saxon occupation has come from areas to the west of, and underneath, the western defences of the later medieval town. Excavations in both 1973–4 and 1978 near the west gate of the castle, on the site of Benham's garage, have revealed some evidence of domestic occupation, albeit rather fragmentary. On this site a shallow natural valley showed evidence of Roman (?) field boundaries before progressive late Saxon and medieval flooding infilled it with deposits of waterlogged silts and organic material. A broad cobbled road of probable late-12th-century date led westwards over these deposits. Postholes of 11th- or 12th-century buildings were also found (Minnitt and Murless 1979, 93).

As yet it is difficult to interpret these finds, but they suggest that the area now occupied by Taunton town centre was fields in the Roman and post-Roman periods, although there must be prehistoric and Romano-British settlement not too far away. The large minster church founded by the 10th century, but possibly in existence by the 8th century, may well have stood somewhere in the area of the later castle outer bailey where so many burials have been found. The seat of the bishop's jurisdiction from the 10th century (and the royal centre before that) could have been sited nearby where, somewhat later, the keep and inner castle bailey were developed. So far the evidence, such as it is, indicates occupation to the west of the town centre. This area is well drained and above any flooding with good communications by land and water.

However, even with all the work that has been done, as at other towns, only much more archaeological research will provide clearer answers. In Somerset only at Taunton, and perhaps at Ilchester, are there any positive indications of what we might expect to find in a late Saxon town.

Watchet (Fig. 70)

Watchet lies on the north coast of Somerset near the north end of the Quantock Hills. To the west of the town the coast is much eroded, with cliffs 200ft. high at Daws Castle. The town itself is situated at the north end of a low northward projecting spur about fifty feet high. This has been considerably eroded by the sea at the north end, whereas the land rises steeply to the south to St Decuman's church. The River Washford runs across the north-west side of the town in a narrow alluvial valley, while on the east is a low-lying area, which may have been marshy in earlier times, but which is now infilled; the only easy access is from the south.

The small town of Watchet has been well studied over a long period and its local history is reasonably well known (Wedlake 1973). It is likely that Watchet has always been a port providing safe anchorage in the Bristol Channel. It is listed in the Burghal Hidage with 513 hides assigned to it in the early 10th century. This would give a line of defences of seven hundred or so yards. It was raided by Scandinavians in 918, 977, 988 and 997. There was a mint which is very well documented as a result of recent research. It was operating from the time of Aethelred II (980) until 1158, but

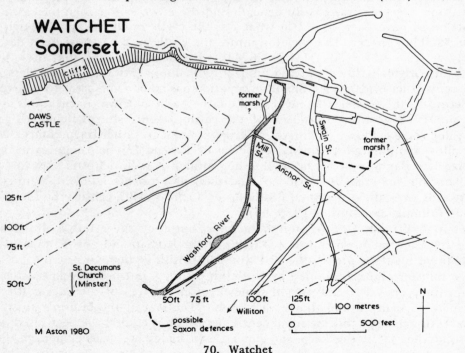

70. Watchet

there are gaps such as between 1056 and 1080. A single moneyer is recorded (1020–23) but there were two under Cnut (Blackburn 1974, 13–38). By the time of Domesday 1086, Watchet is recorded only as a small lay estate of agricultural character, but under the adjacent royal manor of Old Cleeve payment of the 'third penny' is recorded from four hundreds for which no borough is listed. Watchet lay within the area of these hundreds and it is possible that it was still 'a kind of borough in 1086' (Darby and Finn 1967, 199).

In the Saxon period Watchet was situated on the edge of the large royal estate of Williton with adjacent estates at Carhampton and Cleeve, also in royal hands, and possibly considered all as one unit; it is not clear if there was a royal house in this area. From earliest Christian times there have been churches on this coast, and St Decuman's, reputedly founded by the Celtic St Decumanus, may have been a minster church.

There has been no archaeological excavation in the town and there are considerable problems in understanding the topography of the Saxon burh. It is at least possible that the Iron Age site at Daws Castle represents the burh site, but in general the town seems a more likely candidate. The 700 yards of Burghal Hidage defences could enclose an area on the end of the promontory, which is possibly marked by a line of property boundaries, although the length might indicate a complete circuit rather than a promontory with natural defences. Only excavation can decide the matter conclusively. The interestingly named Swain Street runs along the low ridge of the promontory on which the town stands and, assuming that there were no defences on the cliff side to the north, the 700 yards of defences implied in the Burghal Hidage could easily be accommodated parallel to the river on the west, the marsh on the east, and in the vicinity of Anchor Street and Mill Street on the south.

It is likely that, like Axbridge and Langport, Watchet provided a defended market centre for an adjacent royal estate, but more historical and archaeological work needs to be carried out.

Daws Castle, Watchet

Excavations were carried out at Daws Castle by the Central Excavation Committee of the Department of Environment in early 1982. Remains of a stone wall and bank were found which have been dated by pottery to the late Saxon period.

It thus seems likely that the burh was at Daws Castle, although a lot of its perimeter has been eroded over the cliff in the last millenium. This does not preclude the possibility, however, that there was a late Saxon town under present Watchet, on the analogy of Pilton to Barnstaple and Halwell to Totnes.

Wells (Fig. 64)

Wells is not recorded as a borough in 1086 and it has none of the usual attributes recorded for urban centres in the Saxon period. Recent archaeological work, however, has suggested that a proto-urban centre may have been developing at Wells in the late Saxon period in a similar way to that at Glastonbury and elsewhere.

Wells lies in a large estate which had belonged to the church of St Andrew since the 8th century. Little evidence for Roman activity has been found in the area, but recent excavations (Rodwell 1980) have distinguished prehistoric and Romano-British settlement near to the springs which gave Wells its name. Somewhere in the vicinity of the east end of the cathedral there must be a substantial complex of Roman buildings. It is probable that the first church, a minster, was built by Aldhelm around A.D. 700. This became a cathedral in 909 when Edward the Elder made Athelm first bishop of Wells. Bishop Giso (1061–88) rebuilt many of the cathedral buildings, but the see was moved to Bath in 1088 by Bishop John de Villula, and the buildings demolished. This move to Bath may have been occasioned by the ordinance of 1075 under Archbishop Lanfranc whereby certain rural sees were to be transferred to towns. This process had begun in 1050 with the move from Crediton to Exeter, but was going on apace particularly in the 1070s and 1080s (Stenton 1947, 658–59). It perhaps demonstrates that in the late 11th century Wells was not considered a town—a situation indicated in Domesday Book where no market, burgesses nor mint are mentioned.

The new excavations to the south of the cathedral have shown that a building called 'The Lady Chapel by the Cloister' is certainly on the alignment of the Saxon cathedral, and may incorporate part of it. This alignment is different to the present cathedral and its surrounding buildings, but it is the same as that of the market-place to the west and some of the streets of the town.

The building of the present cathedral on its different alignment dates from about 1180; the basic outlines of the town plan are probably therefore earlier than the 12th century. It is on this basis that Warwick Rodwell has suggested that there may be elements of a late Saxon town plan at Wells based on the alignment of the earlier, Saxon, cathedral. It is thus possible that Wells developed, like Glastonbury and monastic towns elsewhere, as a market area outside the west side of a precinct. Further excavation, particularly within the town and around the market-place will help to clarify this suggestion.

Yeovil (Fig. 64)

Yeovil is now a large town on the south-east border of Somerset. The original nucleus is on an eastward-facing spur with stream and river valleys to north, east and south. There is abundant Romano-British settlement in the area, although none is known from under the town itself.

Yeovil has none of the attributes associated with Saxon towns elsewhere, and its inclusion in this discussion is based entirely on the evidence in Domesday Book. At that date no burgesses are mentioned, and it did not pay the 'third penny', but Round thought he could distinguish the beginning of a small town 'based on the recording of 22 masurae or households on the manor' (Round and Bates 1906). The manor was only held by a sub-tenant and had not been in royal hands before the Conquest. Nevertheless, it may possibly have been developing into a quasi-borough and should at least be noted (Darby and Finn 1967, 196–197).

No archaeological excavations have taken place in the town, but watching briefs on development sites have been carried out by the Yeovil Archaeological Society;

no pre-Conquest material has been recorded. The original town plan centres on the large church of St John's and the original urban nucleus could well have been to the south along the present High Street (formerly the Borough).

Discussion

Having thus surveyed the evidence for Anglo-Saxon towns in Somerset it remains to be shown how such places fitted into the general archaeological and topographical patterns of settlement in the county. In the only published general survey of Saxon towns, Martin Biddle has outlined a number of general themes which need to be discussed (Biddle 1976). Attention has been drawn to the legacy of Roman towns forming the basis for later urban centres in southern England. In Somerset (apart from Bath), Ilchester is the only obvious important late Saxon town with a clear Roman ancestry *on the same site*. In fact, this criterion of the 'same site' may not be strictly applicable, for two main reasons. Firstly, the attention of Roman scholars in the past has concentrated on walled Roman towns to the detriment of the large unwalled rural settlements which may have had some urban functions, and, secondly, such earlier centres need not be on the same site as the later towns if their *functions* are carried on elsewhere in the vicinity. As Biddle remarks, 'there are cases of settlement shift, a phenomenon of exceptional and to date little regarded importance in the evolution of English towns' (Biddle 1976, 110). An examination of non-walled Romano-British settlements in Somerset near to later centres suggests that several towns could have developed from pre-Saxon nuclei. Thus, there is a large open Romano-British settlement outside Taunton at Holway and there are villas and farmsteads (if nothing larger) under Axbridge, Glastonbury, and Wells, and Romano-British settlements near to Bruton, Crewkerne, Langport, Milborne Port, Somerton, South Cadbury, South Petherton, Watchet, and Yeovil. Indeed, a very high percentage of rural settlements in Somerset are near or on Romano-British sites, a situation which has led Roger Leech to suggest continuity of use of site and estate over wide areas of the county in the post-Roman period (Leech 1977).

Hill-forts are characteristically associated with settlement in the pre-Roman period, but in Somerset there is considerable evidence for post-Roman re-occupation of such sites (Fowler 1971; Burrow 1979). They must therefore be considered, along with the Roman sites, as precursors of the Saxon towns. As such, there is little obvious direct correlation and it depends on how near or far apart such sites must be before any significance can be postulated. As will be argued below this may not be the most useful way to look at such relationships.

By the late Saxon period, and particularly in Norman times (as indicated in Domesday Book), it is clear that towns have been founded principally on royal estates. This is the case with all of the towns cited above except the doubtful example of Yeovil, the probable ecclesiastical foundations at Wells and Glastonbury, and Taunton. The latter, which was owned by the bishop of Winchester, had, however, been a royal estate before it was sold in 909. Elsewhere the royal connection is perhaps an argument for accepting the otherwise doubtful cases of Bruton, Frome, Milverton, and Crewkerne.

For some places the royal connection is intimate, with Axbridge, Cheddar, Langport, Somerton, and probably Ilchester all on great royal estates, and places like Milborne Port, Lyng and Watchet all on the edge of extensive royal manors. It is perhaps odd, since these towns were so closely connected with royal estates, that when the Burghal Hidage was compiled some places were not included. A case in point is Ilchester, which was presumably still defensible at that date, since it clearly was in the early Middle Ages. Taunton would presumably also have been included had it not been granted away—it is very likely that it was defensible by this time.

So far this discussion has centred on the physical relationships between sites of different periods. Increasingly in archaeology, as in related disciplines, the examination of dynamic or functional relationships is seen to be much more significant in answering problems. It is now necessary to see Anglo-Saxon towns as functioning units and thence to examine their relationships to earlier, later and contemporary settlements if we are to see how they actually worked. In the economics of subsistence much of the basis of life for men and animals is produced by settlements in the countryside and few commodities need to be imported. Such items as salt and iron need to be brought in, and other luxury items have to be sought from time to time. These materials can be bought or bartered for at recognised centres at certain times of the week or year. Inevitably such sites form 'central places' for the settlements using them, although it is not necessary for the centres to be marked physically in the landscape. These places may not indeed have been of a permanent nature, or may have changed over time. Apart from marketing and trade, other functions—administration, judicial duties, religious provision, and perhaps defence of an area—are best carried out from 'central places'. Again some of these functions may be temporary, some may not be marked by physical and archaeologically recoverable features, and indeed they all need not be based in the same place.

It is now clear that after the collapse of the highly organised, market-orientated, money-using economy of late Roman Britain, much of the country must have reverted to a largely subsistence economy. Many Roman towns became probably no more than farms or villages working the land around—perhaps with continuity of settlement site, but not necessarily of function. Biddle has remarked that 'the growing realisation that towns could revert to non-urban settlements before re-emerging as urban places in later centuries has opened the way for an entirely fresh approach to problems of urban continuity' (Biddle 1976, 103). Only when trade and marketing again become necessary are markets re-established, and other services begin to be provided, even then the various 'services' do not seem to have always been in the same centre. Biddle remarks that Winchester and Southampton, in the 7th and 8th centuries, are 'two complementary settlements, the one royal, ecclesiastical, ceremonial, heir of an ancient and still lively dignity; the other bustling, crowded, commercial, outward looking . . .' (Biddle 1976, 114). At this time Southampton was a town, but Winchester clearly was little more than a royal palace and ecclesiastical centre within the Roman enclosure. Such divergence of function has been noted elsewhere in England in the Saxon period (Aston and Bond 1976).

In Somerset, Ilchester and Bath are the only Roman towns which can be shown to have been continuously occupied on the same site since the Roman period, and at Ilchester it is not clear whether its 'urban functions' lasted much beyond the 5th century. At a later date than has been indicated for Winchester, separate functions can be distinguished for some Saxon settlements in the county. Thus on the large royal estate at Somerton (Fig. 68) (a place which did not become a town until the 13th century) there is evidence of a royal residence, and a 'port' or market and transhipment point at Langport, itself a small urban unit carved out from the large surrounding agricultural estate, together with a fort for the defence of the surrounding countryside. Ilchester probably provided similar functions on the eastern edge of the Somerton royal estate. Somerton was also the hundredal meeting place in later times and may also have had a judicial function at this time. Northover, adjacent to Ilchester, probably had a pre-Conquest minster church and may therefore have been the religious focus (Dunning 1975). In earlier times, there are perhaps two or three sites which served as the 'central places' for this region. Excavation at South Cadbury has shown dense occupation of that hill-fort in the pre-Roman period, and at Ham Hill casual finds and previous small-scale excavations have indicated the importance of this very large hill-fort in prehistoric and Roman times. There is also a hill-fort on Dundon Hill, north of Somerton. Since this is in the centre of the Somerton region, this rather damaged site may be of potentially much greater significance than has been thought hitherto. Later, in the more developed economic systems of the medieval period, markets existed at Langport, Ilchester and Somerton, while there were others nearby at Glastonbury and elsewhere.

This example is mirrored less clearly at other places in the county. Axbridge can be seen as the commercial port, market and defended enclosure for the Cheddar royal estate with Cheddar housing the royal residence and minster church. At the west end of the county, Watchet may have provided similar functions for another royal estate at Williton and, although the evidence is not so obvious for Milborne Port, Bruton, and Crewkerne, each has elements of the same multi-function, multi-site arrangement. Finally at Lyng there may be another example. As has been shown the development of this site in association with Athelney is clearly shown in the document-ary evidence. In the late 9th century the nearby Taunton estate was still in royal hands and not far away were the royal estates of North Petherton and North Curry. Perhaps the Athelney complex could be viewed as a fortified base on the edge of one or two large royal estates with the other functions maintained at Taunton or North Petherton.

In pursuing this theme it is interesting to note the development and disposition around the county of the numerous 'minting' places. As Biddle has remarked 'the towns which came into being during the last century of the Anglo-Saxon state seem on the whole to have been the result of the general expansion of economic life and to have emerged more gradually. They were usually undefended and seem rarely to exhibit any degree of deliberate planning, as might be expected given their essentially uncontrolled genesis' (Biddle 1976, 137). In Somerset this suggestion best fits the evidence for the smaller places which have few or no other urban attributes in the Saxon period other than the possession of a mint. The best example is South Petherton, which has only a mint and a minster to recommend it, although Crewkerne, Bruton and Milborne Port also seem to be cases in point.

It can be suggested that in relation to the numbers developed in the Middle Ages there were only a few towns in Somerset before the end of the Anglo-Saxon period. By the time of Domesday Book a few places are either just beginning as urban centres (e.g., Yeovil) or are in decline from modest beginnings (e.g., Milverton) (Darby and Finn 1967). Somerset clearly shared in the general build-up of economic activity in Wessex in the 10th century and at least four places fall into Biddle's model of undefended markets with associated mints (Bruton, Milborne Port, Crewkerne, and South Petherton). South Cadbury clearly belongs to a class of redefended hill-forts, occupied, perhaps temporarily in the 11th century, because of fears of Danish invasion. It can be understood best as a well-defended substitute for Ilchester, but it is debatable whether 'temporary occupation' is indicated by the elaborate defences and building operations which seem to have been started (Biddle 1976, 140-1). The four forts (not counting Bath) listed in the Burghal Hidage are clearly in existence by the early 10th century. As we have seen, Lyng may have been a special case and this is reflected in the good information about its early development. The others (Axbridge, Langport, and Watchet) are best interpreted as outlying defences to some royal centre, controlling land route-ways or navigable rivers. Later, other commercial functions were added to them. We should perhaps see their origins in the troubled times of the late 9th century, but their main development during the 10th century. Excavations at Lyng and Langport suggest that their fort status did not necessarily mean a dense built-up appearance.

On the eve of the Norman Conquest a few centres may have been developing entirely in the form of permanently occupied markets. Aspects of such development can be seen at Glastonbury and Wells under the auspices of the abbey and the cathedral, but they may also have been going on at Frome, itself part of a royal estate. If so the degree of growth at these places must have been small to have remained undetected by the Domesday surveyors.

Since Somerton itself was clearly never an urban centre in the Saxon period this leaves Ilchester and Taunton as perhaps the most complex of the Saxon towns in the county. The development of Taunton is still largely unknown. It may have been an early town based on a large royal estate, with direct links to the sea, and supported by a rich agricultural region, or it could have been a minor development outside a royal palace site. Only future work, particularly archaeological excavation, is likely to clarify this problem. Ilchester on the other hand, though small in extent, clearly falls into the same class as the large towns of Roman origin across Wessex which became important late Saxon towns. It was probably connected to the Somerton estate, but its function must have gone well beyond acting as a mere subsidiary marketing and defensible centre. In common with Dorchester, Exeter and Winchester it had a mint, market and defences and a number of late Saxon churches, including at least one over a gate. We are reminded here that 'there can be little doubt that the urban parish church is one of the most important indicators of the growing importance of towns in late Anglo-Saxon England' (Biddle 1976, 133). Perhaps the dedication to St John of so many of the other churches in these towns also may be of significance.

With the exception of Ilchester and perhaps Taunton, the Saxon towns in the county can be depicted in two models of functional settlements (Fig. 71). Firstly, there is the large, usually royal, estate based on agricultural activities. Within this, there are numerous functions which can be carried on in the same or, more usually

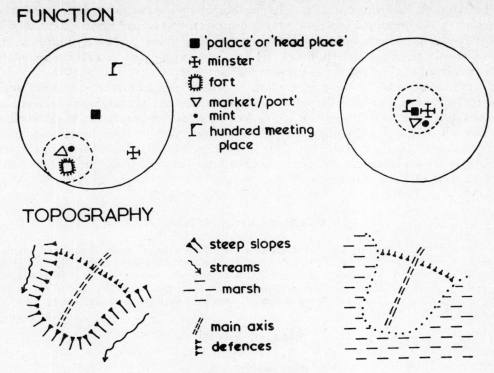

71. Function Topography

in *different* centres. These will include religious activities, judicial functions, defensive considerations, marketing operations and perhaps a 'port' for outside trading. Where any of these are combined a small town may exist; frequently this is on or near the edge of the estate. The addition of defences seems in some instances designed to block easy access from outside to some royal centre. Axbridge, Langport, Watchet, Ilchester and Lyng all fit into this model and should be seen as part of a wider pattern with other 'central place' activities going on elsewhere. The second model has, within the estate, a royal or ecclesiastical centre which has appended to it a market for trading goods. Other functions may also exist, but generally these will be in the *same* place. Crewkerne, Bruton, Milborne Port, South Petherton, Wells, Glastonbury, and perhaps Taunton fit into this model. To some extent this model is less complex and perhaps chronologically later than the first and over much of the country provides the settlement type for the 'new town' developments of the Middle Ages.

The commonest topographical situation of a Saxon town in Somerset, as elsewhere, is that of a promontory site. Many are small in extent or low in relief, but the use of poorly-drained land, streams or steep slopes was clearly an important consideration to the people selecting sites. The main 'land' access was usually from one direction only, and, where such places were defended, this is the side on which defences were constructed. Axbridge, Ilchester, Langport and Lyng have marshes on three sides, while streams and steep slopes define the extent of two or more sides of Milborne

Port, Milverton, Crewkerne, South Petherton, Watchet (with the sea), and Yeovil. The sites of occupation at Bruton and Taunton are too little known, although they are likely to have been defined by streams and/or rivers. South Cadbury is totally defensible within the earlier hill-fort. While little can be said of defence details even less is known of street patterns or property alignments.

It is perhaps unwise in the present state of knowledge of Saxon towns in Somerset to divide these basic models further, since as this account has no doubt demonstrated, and as Biddle wrote so tellingly in 1976, 'very few of the places are at all adequately documented in the pre-Conquest period and knowledge of their layout and growth can only come from excavation' (137). In Somerset we have gone little further than to identify the places, and these now need to be vigorously investigated if any understanding of them is to emerge.

ACKNOWLEDGEMENTS

I would like to thank Roger Leech for allowing me the free use of material gathered by him for our joint volume on the *Historic Towns of Somerset*. Steve Minnitt gave much help on the Saxon mints in Somerset, and Peter Leach of C.R.A.A.G.S. gave much advice and useful discussion on his work at Taunton and Ilchester in advance of publication. I am grateful to Barbara Brown for typing an obscure manuscript, Carinne Allinson for much help in checking references, and to Alan Wilson for work on the plate and plans.

BIBLIOGRAPHY

Alcock, L. (1972), *By South Cadbury is that Camelot . . .*
Aston, M. (ed.) (1977), 'Somerset Archaeology 1976', *Somerset Archaeology and Natural History* 121, 107–128.
Aston, M. and Bond, J. (1976), *The Landscape of Towns*, London.
Aston, M. and Leech, R. (1977), *Historic Towns in Somerset*, Bristol.
Batt, M. R. (1975), 'The Burghal Hidage—Axbridge', *Somerset Archaeology and Natural History* 119, 22–25.
Beresford, M. W. (1967), *New Towns of the Middle Ages*.
Biddle, M. (1976), 'Towns', in Wilson, D. M. (ed.), *The Archaeology of Anglo-Saxon England*, London, 99-150.
Blackburn, M. A. S. (1974), 'The mint of Watchet', *British Numismatic Journal* 44, 13–38.
Burrow, I. C. G. (1979), 'Aspects of hill-fort and hill-top settlement in Somerset in the 1st–8th centuries A.D.', unpublished Ph.D. Thesis, University of Birmingham.
Bush, R. J. E. (1974), 'Langport', in *V.C.H. (Somerset)* 3, 16-38.
Bush, R. J. E. (1977), *The Book of Taunton*, Chesham.
Darby, H. C. and Finn, R. W. (eds.) (1967), *The Domesday Geography of South-West England*, Cambridge, 196-205.
Dolley, R. H. M. (1960), *Anglo-Saxon Coins*, London.
Dunning, R. W. (1974a), 'Ilchester', in *V.C.H. (Somerset)* 3, 179-203.
Dunning, R. W. (1974b), 'Somerton', in *V.C.H. (Somerset)* 3, 129-53.
Dunning, R. W. (1975), 'Ilchester: a study in continuity', *Somerset Archaeology and Natural History* 119, 44–50.
Dunning, R. W. (ed.) (1976), *Christianity in Somerset*, Taunton.
Dunning, R. W. (1978a), 'Crewkerne', in *V.C.H. (Somerset)* 4, 4-38.
Dunning, R. W. (1978b), 'South Petherton', in *V.C.H. (Somerset)* 4, 170-98.
Fowler, P. J. (1971), 'Hillforts A.D. 400–700', in Hill, D. and Jesson, M. (eds.), *The Iron Age and its Hillforts*, 203-13.

Heighway, C. M. (ed.) (1972), *The Erosion of History—Archaeology and Planning in Towns*, C.B.A., London.

Hill, D. H. (1967), 'The Burghal Hidage—Lyng', *Proceedings of the Somerset Archaeological and Natural History Society* 111, 64-66.

Hill, D. H. (1969), 'The Burghal Hidage: the establishment of a text', *Medieval Archaeology* 13, 84-92.

Hill, D. H. (1974), 'The Anglo-Saxon town', unpublished Ph.D. Thesis, University of Southampton.

Jones, F. E. (1960-61), 'The mint of Axbridge', *British Numismatic Journal* 30, 61-9.

Leach, P. J. (1976), 'Excavations at East Lyng 1975', *Somerset Archaeology and Natural History* 120, 29-38.

Leach, P. J. (ed.) (1982) *Ilchester Vol. I: Excavations 1974-5*, Western Archaeological Trust Excavation, Monograph No. 3.

Leach, P. J. (ed.) (forthcoming), *Excavations in Taunton*, C.R.A.A.G.S., Bristol.

Leech, R. H. (1976), 'Romano-British and medieval settlement at Wearne, Huish Episcopi', *Somerset Archaeology and Natural History* 120, 45-50.

Leech, R. H. (1977), 'Romano-British settlement in south Somerset and north Dorset', unpublished Ph.D. Thesis, University of Bristol.

Loyn, H. R. (1961), 'Boroughs and Mints A.D. 900-1066', in Dolley, R. H. M. (ed.), *Anglo-Saxon Coins*, London, 122-35.

McDonnell, R. (1979), 'The Upper Axe Valley, an interim statement', *Somerset Archaeology and Natural History* 123, 75-82.

McGarvie, M. (1978), *The Bounds of Selwood Forest*, Frome Historical Research Group Occasional Papers No. 1.

Maitland, F. W. (1897), *Domesday Book and Beyond* (reprinted 1960).

Minnitt, S. and Murless, B. J. (eds.) (1979), 'Somerset Archaeology 1978', *Somerset Archaeology and Natural History* 123, 83-104.

Rahtz, P. and Fowler, P. (1972), 'Somerset A.D. 400-700', in Fowler, P. J. (ed.), *Archaeology and the Landscape*, London.

Rahtz, P. (1979), *The Saxon and Medieval Palaces at Cheddar*, B.A.R., 65.

Rodwell, W. J. (1980), 'Wells: the cathedral and city', *Current Archaeology* VII, 38-44.

Round, J. H. and Bates, E. M. (1906), 'Introduction and text of the Somerset Domesday', in *V.C.H.* (*Somerset*) I, 383-562.

Savage, W. (1954), 'Somerset Towns', *Proceedings of the Somerset Archaeological and Natural History Society* 94, 49-74.

Stenton, F. M. (1947), *Anglo-Saxon England*, Oxford.

Stevens Cox, J. (1948), *The Ilchester Mint* (privately printed).

Stevenson, W. H. (1959), *Asser's Life of King Alfred*.

Taunton Rescue Excavation Committee (1975), 'Taunton: History, Archaeology and Development'.

Taylor, H. M. and Taylor, J. (1965), *Anglo-Saxon Architecture*.

Thorn, C. and Thorn, F. (eds.) (forthcoming), *Domesday Book: Somerset*, Chichester.

Wedlake, A. L. (1973), *A History of Watchet*, Dulverton.

Williams, M. (1970), *The Draining of the Somerset Levels*, Cambridge.

Chapter Seven

THE TOWNS OF DORSET

By Laurence Keen

Introduction

RECENT WORKS on the Anglo-Saxon and medieval town (Biddle 1976; Reynolds 1977), while both accepting the difficulties faced in defining medieval urban places, offer conceptual or working definitions. Reynolds suggests that a town is a 'permanent human settlement with two chief and essential attributes': firstly, that a significant proportion of its population is involved in 'trade, industry, administration and other non-agricultural occupations'; secondly, that it forms a social unit more or less distinct from the surrounding countryside (Reynolds 1977, ix). Biddle, in offering 12 criteria based on Haase's compound concept of a town (1965), rightly proposes that the possession of one or more of them provides merely an indication which has to be considered more closely and suggests that 'a place needs to fulfil not less than three or four of these criteria to merit serious consideration as a town' (Biddle 1976, 100). The criteria offered are considered to be of differing importance. One, the role as a central place, has been selected by Ennen as the most consistent essential ingredient of the town, influenced by its cultural as well as political and economic standing in the region (Ennen 1979, 2). Nelson, however, has emphasised the fundamental importance of churches in the development of settlements since they provided a major focus for town life (1979, 103-4). Ennen has emphasised that the function and structure of a town, while always existing side by side 'never recurred twice in the same combination. In the particular variant of one time and place, they created the marked individuality which every town possessed' (Ennen 1979, 2).

Contemporary awareness and understanding of a town's particular role are difficult to establish, and one would expect that the more visible features of town life would mask less obvious economic, political and administrative roles. Such seems to have been the case in the early 12th century when William of Malmesbury's terminology stands in contrast to the administrative and fiscal parameters of the Domesday Book. Shaftesbury, which is listed along with Dorchester, Wareham and Bridport at the head of the Dorset entry, for William of Malmesbury *est vicus modo, quondam urbs* (*Gesta Pont.*, Bk. II, Ch. 86, p. 186). Sherborne, not singled out for special treatment in the Domesday Book *est viculus, nec habitantium frequentia nec positionis gratia suavis, in quo mirandum et pene pudendum sedem episcopalem per tot durasse saecula* (*ibid.*, Bk. II, Ch. 79, p. 75).

The essential rural character of these two settlements, both of which are of importance in the Anglo-Saxon period, is evident in almost every town in Dorset today. It must be of no surprise that William of Malmesbury observed what must have been a similar picture and so used the terms *vicus* and *viculus*. However many criteria may be found for the urban character of the settlements of the county, it is their ecclesiastical and royal connections, together with their rural character and role as market centres for agricultural regions, that emerge as being of major importance in the Saxon period. It is of interest to note that for fictional Casterbridge administrative functions appear less important than the relationship between the town and its region, which is expressed in terms as applicable to earlier periods as they were for late 19th-century Dorchester which was Hardy's model:

> Casterbridge was the complement of the rural life around not its urban opposite (Hardy 1929, 65).

> Thus Casterbridge was in most respects but the pole, focus or nerve-knot of the surrounding country life; differing from the many manufacturing towns which are as foreign bodies set down, like boulders on a plain, in a green world with which they have nothing in common. Casterbridge lived by agriculture at one remove further from the fountain-head than the adjoining villages—no more (*ibid.*, 70).

This essential relationship between towns and the areas they served is an aspect of urban history which is frequently neglected in individual town histories and regional studies. The potential of 'an intensive study of the ecclesiastical relations between the boroughs and their vicinities' was considered by Tait as necessary for the understanding of hundred courts. He referred especially to Dorchester and Wareham, where the relationship of parishes to the boroughs was of particular interest. Wareham, he observed, had several parishes which stretched beyond the ramparts, and thought it possible 'that the in- and out-parishes, as they were called, represented the single parish of one original church of Wareham, a parish which was too extensive to be included as a whole within the fortifications or even within the "liberties" of the borough' (Tait 1936, 55–6).

The study which Tait proposed has been started by the writer and some of the preliminary results are included here. This essay will first endeavour to consider the major settlements of Dorset within their 'vicinities', particularly within their ecclesiastical and royal framework. The major historical developments will be reviewed against this background and the internal organisation and structure of the towns will be considered. It is not the purpose here to consider every place in Dorset which might be described as a town during the Anglo-Saxon period, since, first, the documentary material available for such an approach has changed little since the meticulous research and extraordinary achievement of Hutchins and his editors Shipp and Hodson (Hutchins 1861–70); and, second, despite consistent and extensive support for archaeological investigation in Dorchester and Wareham, the understanding of the Anglo-Saxon town in Dorset (*pace* Biddle 1974, 203) has changed little 'under the accumulation of new facts'. Furthermore the thorough survey of published material is available (Penn 1980).

The towns selected for study are Sherborne, Shaftesbury, Wareham, Wimborne, Christchurch, Lyme, Beaminster, Dorchester, Gillingham, and Bridport. Where evidence is available the Roman background will be reviewed. The royal and ecclesiastical settlements will be considered in turn and then will be examined against the evidence for estates and *parochiae*. This examination will be followed by a review of 9th- and 10th-century settlement, the burhs and general topography, defences and street plans, and field systems. Churches will be considered briefly, and the evidence for mints and moneyers reviewed.

SETTLEMENTS AND ESTATES

The Roman Background

Of all Dorset towns Dorchester is the most likely candidate for a settlement which might provide evidence for continuous occupation from the late Roman through to the Anglo-Saxon period. As a major town the archaeological evidence for Roman occupation is extensive (R.C.H.M. 1970, 531–92). However, late Roman material is minimal within the town itself. It is from outside the town, at Poundbury to the west (Fig. 72), that Christopher Green's extensive excavations have revealed a 4th-century Christian cemetery containing small mausolea, two with painted plaster portraying men with staves. The cemetery was overlain by an agricultural settlement with corn-drying ovens, pits and timber buildings of post-Roman date. Two of the mausolea, which can perhaps be considered as *memoriae* (Thomas 1981, 238), were provided with paved thresholds and acted as the focus of this new settlement, while the other mausolea remained standing (Green 1977; 1979). Carbonised grain in two corn-dryers provide C14 dates of $360^{\pm} 80$ and $500^{\pm} 100$ (Keen 1979, 135), and both the absence of Roman pottery and the relationship with the underlying 4th-century cemetery suggest that the settlement belongs to the post-Roman period (Green 1979). While this evidence suggests a thread of continuity, occupation inside the town during the immediate post-Roman period has yet to be established. However, it is clear that the stone defences around the town survived in part and this fact no doubt would have helped any population to survive. The course of the defences is well established, except for part of the northern circuit. Later boundaries respected the line of the walls, and at least one small section survives (R.C.H.M. 1970, 542–3). More of its length once existed along the western side until it was demolished in the 17th century (Mayo 1980, xxxi).

Although the archaeological evidence for Dorchester in the post-Roman period may be a little tenuous, the place-name evidence provides more conclusive proof that occupation of some sort must have continued to allow elements of the Roman name *Durnovaria* to survive: the settlement was called *Dornwerecestre* in 833 (Mills 1977, 347–8; Thomas 1981, 253–62).

Evidence for Roman occupation at Sherborne is slight. A pavement discovered under the abbey church in the 19th century was thought to be Roman in date (Carpenter 1876–77, 137; R.C.H.M. 1952, 199), but no other Roman material has been found during recent excavations carried out to the north and west of the church. A few coins and occasional pieces of pottery have been found (Fig. 73), the main concentration being near Culverhays car park (Fig. 73, No. 2) (Bean 1951, 111; Farrar 1952, 108). The area around Sherborne (Fig. 74) has many Roman sites strung out along the valley of the River Yeo and on higher ground to the north (Leech 1977; Taylor 1970, Fig. 2), but the most important site for any attempt to unravel the history of settlement in the area is the large settlement at Pinford Lane (Fig. 73, No. 3). It has been suggested that a grid-pattern of Romano-British fields survives

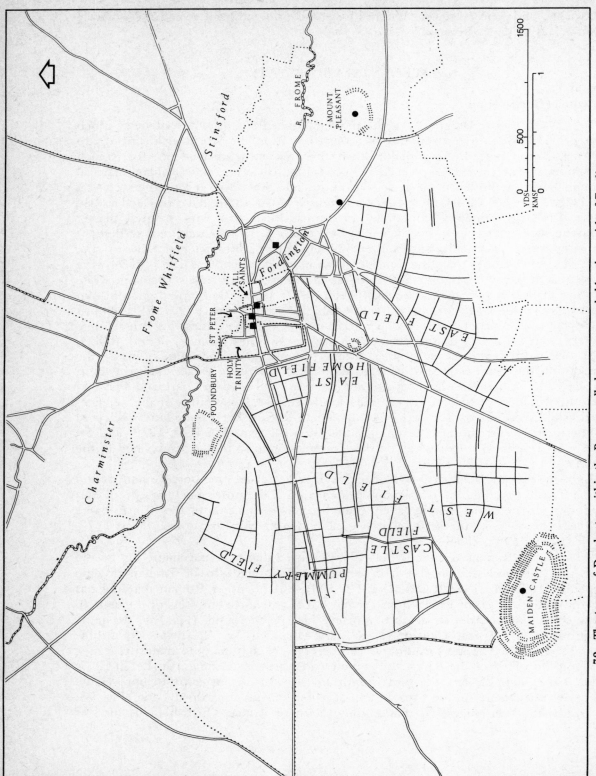

72. The town of Dorchester within the Roman walled area, surrounded by the parish of Fordington. The main divisions of the Fordington field system are taken from the Tithe map. For symbol key *see* Fig. 73

beneath the town and that the base measurement of the fields may be defined by the Trendle (Fig. 73, No. 16) where 'the missing Romano-British farmstead' in the line of settlement along the River Yeo valley might be found (Barker 1977, 127). There is no reason why Romano-British occupation should not be found at the Trendle, but there is no positive evidence to suggest that the grid-pattern is Romano-British in date. Indeed, it will be shown below that a much later date may be proposed.

Romano-British occupation has been located in the vicinity of the settlements at Beaminster (Fig. 75) (*PDNHAS*, 84 [1962], 112; *SDNQ*, 28 [1968], 320), Bridport (Fig. 75), Gillingham (Fig. 74) (*PDNHAS*, 73 [1951], 112; R.C.H.M. 1972, 35–6; Keen 1976, 56), but the limited evidence available suggests that Romano-British settlement is unlikely to have had any major influence on the later choice of site. At Wareham (Fig. 75), however, a significant quantity of Romano-British material has been found. There is a large body of evidence to suggest extensive occupation within the area of the later town and at a number of places in the vicinity during the Iron Age and Roman periods (R.C.H.M. 1970, 614; Radford 1978, 140), although a recent assessment of the evidence suggests that Roman Wareham might be two distinct sites, one in the north-west corner, the other around the church of Lady St Mary (Hinton and Hodges 1977, 81). From Wimborne Romano-British material is less plentiful (Farrar 1962, 109). Beneath the minster church a small fragment of tessellated pavement was discovered in 1961 (Farrar 1962, 106–9; R.C.H.M. 1975, 80, 85), but other evidence for a Roman building under or near the church is lacking. It is highly possible that this pavement, like that at Sherborne, is Saxon in date.

Royal Settlements

Of all Dorset settlements Dorchester, which gave its name to the shire, is of major importance. Settlement in the 8th century is attested by six or more *sceattas* presumed to have been found in the town (Rigold and Metcalf 1977, 39), five of which are in the County Museum (Gunstone 1977, Nos. 238, 239, 241, 244, 247). Two are of B.M.C. type 49 (Grierson 1958, No. 258; Gunstone 1977, No. 247), which Jesson has suggested were minted in Southampton (Jesson 1971; Keen 1975, 180). A gold finger-ring* found in 1877, decorated with free-standing filigree and biting animal heads, is probably late 8th or early 9th century in date (Hinton 1974, 16–17; 1975, 175). The existence of a settlement is further demonstrated by the account of the first arrival of the Danes in England (A.S.C., *sub anno* 789)—

> there came for the first time three ships of Northmen and then the reeve rode to them and wished to force them to the king's residence, for he did not know what they were: and they slew him.

Aethelweard's account adds the name of the reeve, Beaduheard, and the name of the *regia villa—in oppido quod Dorceastre nuncupatur* (Petrie 1848, i, 509). The port referred to is perhaps Weymouth: it is not necessarily Portland. Aethelweard's account is thought to have been based on a south-western version of the *Chronicle* (Stenton 1970, 110–13) and there is thus no reason to doubt Aethelweard's description of Dorchester as *regia villa*. That the settlement contained a royal residence, though a *villa regalis* need not necessarily do so (Rumble 1977, 188), is demonstrated by a long series of charters drawn up in the *villa regali* at Dorchester. Furthermore, it appears

---

*In a recent exhibition the provenance was given incorrectly as Dorchester, Oxon. (*The Vikings in England and in their Danish Homeland* (1981), C14, 50).

that the West Saxon kings were in the habit of spending Christmas in it, and perhaps Easter as well: B.C.S. 410 is dated 26 December 833; B.C.S. 451, 26 December 847. B.C.S. 508 was drawn up in 863; B.C.S. 510 was written on 26 December 864; and on 20 April, two days before the following Easter, King Aethelbert—

> with joyful heart laid this charter of freedom with his own hand upon the high altar at the monastery in Sherborne, in the presence of all the assembled brethren, both old and young, and also of his kinsmen, Aethelred and Alfred, and of his other councillors who were there with him, on behalf of himself during his lifetime, and for his two brothers, who were standing there present, and for the souls of King Aethelwulf, the father of all of them, and of King Aethelbald, their brother, whose body rests in the foundation (Robertson 1959, 21).

B.C.S. 520 is dated 868 *in loco qui appellatur aet Dornwaraceastre.* In 934 King Aethel-stan spent Easter in Dorchester and signed B.C.S. 738/9. In 937 he spent Christmas there with the witan: B.C.S. 716, 718, 719 are all dated 21 December. The location of the royal palace is unknown. It is perhaps to be found within the area of the Roman walled town and a likely site is under the medieval castle. However, it may have been at Fordington, as implied by the *-tun* suffix (Campbell 1979, 121).

Burials at three different sites in the vicinity of the town cannot be attributed with any certainty to the settlement (Fig. 72). A single 7th-century burial has been excavated at Maiden Castle (Wheeler 1943, 78-9), and two at Mount Pleasant (Wainwright 1979, 181-3). Nine or more graves, cut into chalk and found at Wareham House, about 850 yards to the west, may be similar in date. The cemetery seems to have been laid out regularly. The grave-goods—two iron knives, a double-sided comb, two ear-rings of silver wire, and coloured beads—are currently being examined by Christopher Green who has kindly provided the author with details (*cf.* R.C.H.M. 1970, 575, where the burials are considered to be Roman). The cemetery may probably relate to the early settlement at Fordington (see below).

Gillingham is mentioned in 1016, when King Edmund fought against the Danish army at Penselwood, near Gillingham (A.S.C. *sub anno*). It is possible that there was a royal residence since Archbishop Anselm met King William ('Rufus') there on 3 February 1094 (Douglas and Greenaway 1953, 659). The church at Gillingham had been given by the Conqueror to Shaftesbury abbey in exchange for one hide on which he built Corfe Castle (Darby and Finn 1967, 117), but it is highly probable that the church dated back several hundred years. Fragments of 9th-century decorated sculpture (R.C.H.M. 1972, 30) perhaps came from this church or the churchyard.

Ecclesiastical Settlements

Of the handful of settlements with major ecclesiastical establishments Sherborne is the most important. Indeed, as the seat of the bishopric founded in 705 to administer the West Saxon territory west of Selwood (Haddan and Stubbs 1871, 275-6) it was one of the most important ecclesiastical settlements in Wessex. Aldhelm was appointed the first bishop and there *ecclesiam . . . mirifice construxit* (*Gesta Pont.*, 375-6, 378); a building which William of Malmesbury claimed to have seen in the early 12th century: *ecclesiam quam ego quoque vidi* (*ibid.*, 378). It has been suggested that the *sedes episcopales* of the 8th and 9th centuries were centres of authority for wide areas, but were not necessarily at centres with a Roman past, and that the suitability of a particular site for a *sedes* was influenced by the presence of an estate sufficient to support a bishop. It seems likely, therefore, that the *sedes* at Sherborne was probably the centre of a large multiple estate (Campbell 1979, 119–20). The origins of this estate and early settlement thus require further examination.

The early history of Sherborne was examined in detail and with his usual thoroughness and perspicacity by Joseph Fowler (1951, esp., 30–4), who was of the opinion 'that the history of Sherborne went back well into the seventh century, and that the Church, Catholic and Roman, was established here for a considerable time previous to the appointment of Aldhelm, as bishop, in A.D. 705' (*ibid.,* 30). It seemed probable to Fowler that in 705 Sherborne possessed ecclesiastical status and that this was one reason why King Ine and Aldhelm selected the place as the centre of the new diocese. Fowler's standpoint was influenced by the grant of privileges *sedi pontificali Scireburnensis æcclesiæ* by King Cenwalch in 671 (B.C.S. 26). Fowler was well aware that the reference to the bishopric was only one of several errors which showed the charter to be a forgery. Mary O'Donovan has considered this charter in her edition and analysis of the Sherborne Cartulary, where she concludes that the main text cannot be based on any original. The document, although a manifest forgery, seems to belong to the pre-Conquest period since it would have been of little use after 1086 when the see was moved to Salisbury, although O'Donovan suggests that 'it is conceivable that the monks looked to the past to bolster up their sagging image' after the see was moved (O'Donovan 1972, 67–78). The grant was nonetheless still remembered in the late 14th to the early 15th century when *Rex Kenewalchus primus ecclesiam de Schirborn̄ roboravit privilegio suo et libertate* was recorded in the list of benefactors in the Sherborne Missal (Herbert 1920). However, the relationship between these documents and the record of one hundred hides of *Lanprobi,* granted by Cenwalch (B.L., Cotton MS. Faustina A.II, f. 24) is unclear, unless that, too, is a forgery undertaken with a view to establishing prestige and antiquity. The same kind of desire lay behind the 12th-century chronicler of Ely's writings, who endeavoured to establish a 'venerable antiquity for the privileges enjoyed by his church in his own day' (Miller 1951, 9).

Any discussion of the validity of the tradition contained in the texts rather than of the authenticity of the documents must be seen against events at this time. In the middle of the 7th century Cenwalch was leading a West Saxon westward expansion. He fought probably against the Mercians at Bradford-on-Avon in 652 (A.S.C. *sub anno*), and in 658 he fought the British *aet Peonnum,* and put them to flight as far as the River Parret (A.S.C. *sub anno*): the battle site has usually been considered to be Penselwood in Somerset. These events may suggest that the West Saxon victories were more political conquests than a start for the replacement of the existing population. It is likely that the British church continued to function under Saxon government and that the church had influence on later Christianity in Wessex (O'Donovan 1972, 29–30). That links with the British kingdom were not entirely severed is suggested by the grant (*c.* 710) by King Geraint of Dumnonia to Sherborne of five hides at Maker (Cornwall) (Gem 1976).

The identifications of *Lanprobus* of Cenwalch's grant, therefore, is of considerable importance for any discussion of the origins and early settlement of Sherborne. Finberg suggested that *Lanprobus* 'is the older British name of the monastic property

on which the town (of Sherborne) was afterwards built' (Finberg 1964, 98), but *pace*
O'Donovan (1972, 37) and Barker (1977, 127), the credit for this suggestion must go
to Baring-Gould and Fisher who, while linking Sherborne with *Lanprobi,* show that
place-name is the second only to record Probus (1913, 107); St Probus, in Cornwall
is the other (Padel 1976–77, No. 17 on Fig. 3). The prefix *Lan-* is of particular interest
since it relates to the elements *llan* and *lann,* which are found in a large number of
place-names in Wales and Cornwall (Thomas 1967, 47–8; Bowen 1954). These elements
are thought to derive from **lano-*, meaning 'flat space, cleared space' (Thomas 1971,
85, 87). Frequently, the element is found referring to a church standing in an enclosed
cemetery, combined with a personal name, most often that of the patron (Padel
1976–77, 15). It is perhaps significant that with only three exceptions all the monastic
communities in Cornwall mentioned in the Domesday Book, or in the Geld Inquest,
have names starting with *Lan-* (*ibid.,* 26).

The form of these settlements usually consists of earthen banks and ditches laid out
to form a circular or oval enclosure. However, the use of the Cornish *lan* is perhaps
more complex than the Welsh *llan*. In Cornwall particularly the element is found in
compounds which do not necessarily have any ecclesiastical significance (Thomas
1967, 48–9; 1971, 224). For Sherborne, therefore, if its early history is to be
elucidated and the possibilities of monastic forgeries discounted, even if the *lan* can be
identified, its ecclesiastical connections must be demonstrated independently.

Finberg's suggestion that *Lanprobus* lies beneath the town of Sherborne (see above)
has led Katherine Barker, in her enquiries into the origins of Sherborne, to look for
it there. She has identified the south-west to north-east arc of Hound Street (Fig. 73,
No. 4), together with the curving line of property boundaries today continuing north
of Newland and shown on a 1733 estate map as a narrow strip between the same
curving boundary and another a little way to the west, as a large enclosure which 'it
would seem highly likely . . . is to be identified with this *Lanprobi*' (Barker 1980.
230). Notwithstanding the fact that this strange curving element in Sherborne's plan
crosses linear east to west boundaries, which, it will be suggested below, possibly
belong to a post-Roman, probably early medieval field system, rather than being
consistent with a pre-Roman date proposed (Barker 1977, 127), Barker's interpretation
of this obvious topographical feature would carry more weight if conclusive evidence
for the curving boundary having continued to the west could be found. The 'shallow
gulley' located in excavations behind 60 Cheap Street is most unlikely to be part of
this boundary, indeed only the northern edge of the feature was found (*ibid.,* 127
and Fig. 33). A boundary, if it ever existed to the west of Cheap Street, might
reasonably be expected to survive in later boundaries, or more particularly, to have
its line fossilised in a road as proposed by Barker in the case of Hound Street. It is
possible, however, that such a boundary was obliterated by the monastic precinct.

A significant feature of an ecclesiastical *lan* is a chapel or church within an enclosure.
Barker has suggested that the Sherborne enclosure she identifies is subtended from The
Green, known to have been the site of a chapel dedicated to St Thomas the Martyr
(Fig. 73, No. 5). She proposes that the dedication perhaps replaces an earlier one
(Barker 1980, 230). Re-dedications in other urban contexts are well known, an
example occurring, for instance, at Winchester where the church dedicated to St Petroc
was re-dedicated to St Thomas the Martyr in the 15th century (Biddle [ed.] 1976,

330 and n. 10). However, the history of the Sherborne chapel dedicated to St Thomas the Martyr is recorded and suggests that it may have been newly built in the 12th century. A memorandum contained in the Sherborne Cartulary records the circumstances of the building of the church from its foundations, its endowment and consecration in 1177. It states that William Spyneuaus *ad commodum parochinorum suorum capellam sancti Thome martiris in loco qui dicitur Grene in honore eiusdem a fundamento construxit* (Fowler 1951, 131-2). Furthermore, in the list of William's works listed in the same Cartulary (ff. 67-8, quoted *ibid.*, 136-7) it is recorded, *quod preciosissimum est auriculare Sancti Thome martiris capellam etiam in honore Thome martiris construxit in loco qui dicitur Grene*.

If conclusive evidence for the enclosure identified by Barker is lacking, and if St Thomas the Martyr's chapel were an entirely new foundation of the 12th century, the argument that *Lanprobus* lies beneath the town of Sherborne loses much of its force. However, there is evidence, both documentary and archaeological, to suggest that there is another site which has more to commend it as the possible site of *Lanprobus*.

There are two papal confirmations of Sherborne abbey's property which provide a starting point for consideration of an alternative site. The bull of Pope Eugenius III, dated 1145, confirms among other properties *ecclesiam sanctæ Mariæ Magdalenæ iuxta castellum cum duabus capellis . . . Propeschirche et Stocland cum silvis et pratis et cum duobus molendinis* (Dugdale, i, 338-9). That of Alexander III, dated 1163, confirms *ecclesiam sanctæ Mariæ Magdalenæ sitam iuxta castrum Sherborne cum capellis sancti Michaelis et sancti Probi et omnibus pertinentiis suis* (*ibid.*, 339). The church of St Mary Magdalene, with its two (internal) chapels, near the castle, was no doubt the 'chapelle in a little close without the castelle by este' seen by Leland (*Itinerary*, i, 154). The position (Fig. 73, No. 7) is confirmed by a map of manors of north Dorset, made between 1569-70 and 1574 which shows 'St Magalenes' as a church on the south-east side of the castle (B.L. Add. MS. 52522; Tyacke and Huddy 1980, Pl. facing p. 32). The chapel of St Michael referred to in the 1163 bull was within the castle (Fowler 1951, 107). It would seem reasonable to propose that *Propeschirche* and the chapel *sancti Probi* are references to the same chapel and that both are probably connected with *Lanprobus*.

The order in which these buildings are listed gives an indication of the location for *Propeschirche* and St Probus's chapel (Fig. 73, No. 8). In the 1163 bull it follows that St Probus's chapel is near the castle. In the 1145 bull *Propeschirche* is referred to independently of St Magdalene's church, after the list of churches and vills. It is linked, however, with *Stocland*. *Stocland* is mentioned in the foundation charter of the reformed monastery, 998 (K 701): *Hoc est in ipsa Scirburna centum agelli in loco qui dicitur stocland et predium monasterii sicut Wlsinus episcopus fossis sepibusque girare curauit* (O'Donovan 1972, 218).

Stocland or *Stokland* is found in the Liber Niger of Salisbury cathedral which lists the tenants of Sherborne in 1377. The references are to *pratum de Stocland* (Nevill 1911-12, 341), *quatuor acras prati in Stokland,* and *iij acras terre in Stokland* (Nevill 1913-14, 172). Six acres in *Stocklande* appear in a 1614 survey of the manor of Sherborne (D.C.R.O. K.G. 1456, f. 49). The location of this land (Fig. 73), which appears to be meadow, is indicated on John Ladd's 1733 map of Lord Digby's manor of Sherborne (Fowler 1951, Pl. facing p. 73). *Stocklands* is the name of a group of fields north of Pinford Lane, immediately to the east of the castle. The acreage of the 10 fields to which the name refers amounts to some 48 acres. Since the 14th-century references are to meadow, it seems likely that, either the *Stocland* of 998 refers to a group of 100 fields of between three and six acres, the majority of which was given other names so that by 1733 only a minimum of 10 fields were so called, or that *agelli* were strips which were later enclosed.*

From the evidence outlined above it seems certain that *Propeschirche* is in the vicinity of the castle (Fig. 73, No. 6). If *Propeschirche* and St Probus's chapel are the same and may be identified correctly with *Lanprobus* it follows that the site of *Lanprobus* is to be found near the castle.

The archaeological evidence from the castle obtained by Mr. C. E. Bean's excavations during the 1950s and more recently by Mr. P. R. White show that important material lies beneath Bishop Roger's castle of the early 12th century. Both Bean (1955, 141) and White (*pers. comm.*) have found burials in levels earlier than the castle. They lie mainly to the west of the keep, alongside what is considered to be the main road into Sherborne before the castle was built. All the burials are cut into rock, although the tops of the graves were shaved off in Bishop Roger's levelling operations. Also earlier than the castle, but later than the burials through which it cuts, is a ditch with a maximum depth of three metres, which is found on the north side of the castle, along the west side, and turns by an obtuse angle under the south-west block to run underneath the hall (White, *pers. comm.*). This ditch may well belong to *Lanprobus*. No occupation debris has been found which can be assigned with certainty to the early settlement, except five grass-tempered sherds (Harrison and Williams 1979, 91, 98), which do not belong to the 12th-century groups and may be considered as residual material from earlier occupation of the castle site.

If this evidence points to the conclusion that the castle site is *Lanprobus,* three other factors might reinforce it: first, the fact that the old highway approaching Sherborne from the east ran through the site later occupied by the castle (Fig. 73), so avoiding the marshy ground which the modern A.30 crosses (J. H. P. Gibb, *pers. comm.*); second, the possibility that St Mary Magdalene's church belongs to an earlier settlement —by the time the castle was constructed it lay isolated outside, to the east of the castle, no longer serving the community which by then had moved away; and, third, the settlement would be advantageously situated on a natural spur (Fig. 74).

Aldhelm's cathedral, almost certainly beneath the present abbey, appears, therefore, to have been built on a new site. The inevitable conclusion is that by 705 the site of the earlier settlement *Lanprobus* was either deserted or was considered less suitable, but nevertheless its estate of 100 hides granted by Cenwalch was taken over by the new foundation.

For topographical reasons examined below it is likely that Shaftesbury was already a well-established settlement before King Alfred found and built an abbey *iuxta orientalem portem,* in which he placed his daughter Aethelgeofu as abbess (Asser, cap. 98). The abbey was well endowed with estates from 871 x 877 onwards (B.C.S. 531). However, the character of the settlement depends to a great extent on whether the site was in royal hands from an early date before Alfred in 878–9 founded the town, an event recorded by an inscription seen by William of Malmesbury (*Gesta Pont.,*

*For a further discussion on Stockland *see* Keen, 'The topography of Sherborne, Dorset—*Lanprobus*', *P.D.N.H.A.S.,* 103 (1981), 132–4: this writer cannot agree with the interpretation of Stockland as put forward by Barker in 'The Early History of Sherborne', *The Early Church in Western Britain and Ireland,* B.A.R. British Series 102 (1982), 77–116.

186; R.C.H.M. 1972, 57). The claim for a monastery earlier than Alfred's foundation rests on the interpretation of two charters (B.C.S. 107, 186) in the Shaftesbury Cartulary (Finberg 1964, 6, 85). B.C.S. 107 is a grant of *c.* 670/676 by Coinred to Abbot Bectune of *xxx manentes de aquilone rivus nomine Funtamel* [Fontmell], *ex meredie habet terram beatæ memoriæ Leotheri episcopi*. B.C.S. 186, *c.* 759, is a confirmation by Bishop Cyniheard of Winchester of the same estate which Bectune's successor, Abbot Catwali, a British name, had sold to Abbot Wintran of Tisbury (*E.H.D.*, 441–3; Wintran of Tisbury is mentioned in Willibald's *Life of St Boniface, ibid.*, 716). The fact that these charters were preserved at Shaftesbury make it likely that Shaftesbury was the original recipient and Bectune and Catwali were its abbots. If this is so Alfred's work was a refoundation (Gem 1976). It has been suggested, however, that since the estate in question presumably passed from Tisbury to Shaftesbury, which so came to possess the charters, the house ruled by Bectune and Catwali 'is left as mysteriously situated as ever' (O'Donovan 1972, 36).

The early history of Wareham is a little clearer and there is less disputable evidence for a Celtic element in the population. Five memorial stones of the 7th to 9th centuries are related to stones from Wales and the south-west of England (R.C.H.M. 1970, 310–12). The memorials, in the church of Lady St Mary, indicate a cemetery established in the 7th century and continuing into the 8th and 9th centuries to receive people with Celtic names. Radford has compared this arrangement with a Welsh *clas* (Radford 1970, 85).

Wareham has been considered to be a cross-Channel port in the early 8th century (R.C.H.M. 1970, 304). This reputation, which Hinton has recently questioned on the basis of the results of his excavations (Hinton and Hodges 1977, 81), rests on William of Malmesbury's accounts of Aldhelm waiting for favourable weather, and building a church in *Dorsatensi pagi ii milibus a mari disparatus, iuxta Werham, ubi et Corf castellum pelago prominet* (*Gesta Pont.*, Bk. V, Ch. 217, 363). Despite the description *iuxta Werham* Aldhelm's church has been taken to be Lady St Mary's in Wareham itself (R.C.H.M. 1970, 310). However, William of Malmesbury's long description of the church, which was in ruins when he wrote, suggests that the church was in the country, since shepherds frequently sheltered in it, and that no church in Wareham can be a candidate. Kingston, to the south of Corfe Castle, is perhaps a more appropriate site.

The burial in 802 of King Brihtric at Wareham (A.S.C. *sub anno* 786) suggests that a minster church probably existed there; it was no doubt this church that was part of the monastery which Asser records under the year 876 as being by the River Frome (Asser, Ch. 49). However, the history of this monastery, and consequently of any associated settlement, has been made difficult by those who consider that Aldhelm's monastery *iuxta fluvium qui vocatur From* dedicated to St John the Baptist (*Gesta Pont.*, Ch. 198, 346; B.C.S. 105) is not in Frome, Somerset, but Wareham (Lapidge and Herren 1979, 183, n. 26). The dedication to St John the Baptist makes this suggestion highly unlikely.

It seems probable, therefore, that a church existed at Wareham from the 7th century. No doubt the church would have provided a focus for settlement, but archaeological evidence is slight (Hinton and Hodges 1977, 81–2). No more than a few early sherds have been found, one probably of the 8th century (*ibid.*, 79).

An examination of the topography, unfortunately, yields no sign of the earlier settlement.

However negative the evidence, it is likely that what is now known as Poole Harbour, especially the Wareham Channel, might have been an important anchorage. In 998 and 1015 the mouth of the Frome is recorded (A.S.C. *sub annis*). Such anchorage would have necessitated services and hence settlement, surely placed strategically: the settlement cannot have been very far from Wareham.

The foundation at Wimborne of a double community, a phenomenon of the 7th to 9th centuries (Bateson 1899, 180; Cramp 1976, 206; Godfrey 1976, 344), is attributed to Cuthburh, King Ine's sister and wife of King Aldfrith of Northumbria (685–704) (A.S.C. *sub anno* 718). The monastery was founded before 705 when it is referred to *iuxta fluvium qui dicitur Winburna*, with Cuthburh as abbess (B.C.S. 114). Cuthburh had been abbess of Barking and is thought to have been the nun to whom Aldhelm dedicated *De Virginitate* (Lapridge and Herren 1979, 52). The community at Wimborne has a special place in the history of the West Saxon mission to the Continent since one of its nuns, his cousin Leoba, was persuaded by Boniface to become abbess of Bishcofsheim (Talbot 1954, 214; Gallyon 1980, 64–70); a letter from Leoba to Boniface written in or soon after 732 from Wimborne survives (Greenaway 1980, 44–5).

Of great interest is a description of Wimborne in Rudolf's *Life of St Leoba*—

> In olden times the kings of that [English] nation had built two monasteries in the place [Wimborne], one for men, the other for women, both surrounded by strong and lofty walls and provided with all the necessities that prudence could desire. From the beginning of the foundation the rule firmly laid down to both was that no entrance should be allowed to a person of the other sex. No woman was permitted to go into the men's community nor was any man allowed into the women's, except in the case of priests who had to celebrate Mass in their churches (Talbot 1954, 207).

There is no reason to suppose that Cuthburh's monastery was not on the site occupied by the present minster church. However, recent excavations by Peter Woodward in the vicinity of the church have not revealed any feature connected with the Saxon monastery, neither has his work elsewhere in the town revealed any pre-Conquest material (Keen 1979, 142–3).

The evidence for the early ecclesiastical settlement at Christchurch comes from documents of the later Augustinian community. There are three Anglo-Saxon charters, of 956, 985 and 1053 respectively, in the Christchurch Cartulary (B.L. Cotton Tiberius D.VI). Although they are issued to individuals rather than to the church at Christchurch, it is unlikely that there was a long period between the issuing of the charters and the granting of the estates to that church (Hase 1975, 184–5; K 458 [A.D. 956], K 647 [985], K 798 [1053]). In K 647 the beneficiary is described as *sacerdos,* and in K 798 *minister* raising the possibility that the individuals concerned may be connected with Christchurch.

However, of potentially far greater importance for providing details of the early church at Christchurch is the reference in the Cartulary to the churches which Ranulph Flambard pulled down to make way for his new church in the late 11th century: *Fregit vero episcopus illius loci primitivam ecclesiam novemque alias que infra cimiterium steterant cum quorumdam domibus canonicorum prope locum ecclesie cimiterii* (B.L. Cotton Tiberius D.VIa, f. 30v quoted in Hase 1975, 184). There were 24 canons at the time of Edward the Confessor (Dugdale, vi, 302) and they held large estates in Hampshire at the time of the Domesday Survey (V.C.H., *Hants.,* ii [1903], 152).

The references to the 'original' church and the nine other churches within the cemetery suggest that the complex was of considerable antiquity and perhaps British in origin. There is no documentary evidence to shed light on this possibility, nor is there any archaeological material to amplify the reference to the churches earlier than that built by Ranulph Flambard. However, the existence of a minster is demonstrated by the fact that it was taken over by Augustinian canons in *c.* 1150. While archaeological evidence for the early settlement around the ecclesiastical focus is lacking, it is important to refer to the pagan Saxon cemetery (Fig. 81) in the medieval suburb of Bargates to the north of the burh, excavated by Keith Jarvis. The cemetery consists of at least 30 inhumations and four cremations datable to the late 6th or 7th century (Jarvis 1980, 307-9). Without settlement evidence, however, it is impossible to suggest how this cemetery might relate to the presumed early ecclesiastical site.

There are two other settlements with ecclesiastical connections which need to be considered here: Lyme and Beaminster. The earliest reference to Lyme is in a charter, dated 774, whereby King Cynewulf grants to Æthelmod, bishop of Sherborne *unius mansionis terram . . . iuxta occidentalem ripam fluminis illius quod uulgo lim uocatum est. haut procul a loco ubi meatus sui cursum in mare mergit. quatinus illic prefatæ ecclesiæ sal conqueretur ad sustenationem multiformæ necessitatis. siue in condimentum ciborum. siue etiam ut in diuersis officiorum usıbus haberetur* (B.C.S. 224; the reading here is O'Donovan's 1972, 79). This grant was confirmed in Sherborne's refoundation charter of 998 (K 901), *et massam unam iuxta ripam maris quae dicitur æt Lim* (O'Donovan 1972, 218). O'Donovan's suggestion that the grant is of a small area of land suitable for a building (*ibid.,* 82) is possible although it seems much more likely that the area of land included a building (Niermeyer 1976, *mansus*). There is no archaeological evidence for the settlement.

Beaminster, with Portland, is included in a confirmation charter of Burgred, king of the Mercians. The charter is dated 872 and confirms a grant of 679 x 757 by Eafe, abbess of Gloucester to the church of Gloucester, *CXX cassatorum* (B.C.S. 535; Finberg 1964, No. 553). The estate later passed to Sherborne. Wulsige died here on 8 January 1001 or 1002 (O'Donovan 1972, 344-5; Gem 1975, 106), and it must be supposed that the bishops of Sherborne had a residence here.

It is uncertain when Beaminster came into the possession of Sherborne. A writ of the early 11th century addressed by Æthelric, bishop of Sherborne (1002-12) to a certain Æthelmaer is concerned with *scipscot* and refers to *prim hund hidun pe othre bisceopas ær hæfdon into hyra scyre* and mentions specifically the fact that his predecessors had 300 hides (Harmer 1952, 266-70; John 1964, 120-21). The 300 hides consisted of the hundred of Sherborne, Yetminster and Beaminster (Harmer 1952, 267) and John suggests that Sherborne's interest dates back to the reign of Edward the Martyr (975-8) (John 1964, 121). Unfortunately, there is no Anglo-Saxon material from Beaminster.

Ecclesiastical and Royal Estates and *Parochiae*

It is becoming increasingly apparent that if the early history of important settlements, or 'significant places' as Campbell prefers (Campbell 1979, 120), is to be understood, the settlements must be looked at against their relationship with the church and the Crown. This important relationship would appear to explain the 'remarkable foresight in choosing the sites of important future urban centres' in which the early English put their bishops (John 1970, 57). Campbell has investigated the connection of several *sedes episcopales* with estates (Campbell 1979, 119–20). Biddle's work at Winchester has shown that there the church dedicated to St Peter and St Paul was founded in the middle of the 7th century by Cenwalh of Wessex to serve an existing royal establishment, before Winchester became a bishop's see. This model applies also to Canterbury and Dorchester-on-Thames, and may also lie behind similar cases at Rochester, Felixstowe, Leicester, or Worcester. Biddle has argued that the availability of royal land is probably more important than the existence of royal centres (Biddle 1974, 210–12).

The connection between royal estates and the early monasteries needs to be considered, since if a model exists for those early monasteries for which documentary evidence survives it might reasonably be considered to apply to those early monastic communities for which little historical information is to be found.

Furthermore, the role of minsters (or because communal life is not necessarily implied [Hase 1975, 13; Lennard 1959, 402–3 for Dorset 'minster' place-names], more appropriately 'mother-churches') is especially important since it has been tentatively proposed that a mother-church was originally built in every *villa regalis* (Hase 1975, preface). The mother-church developed under royal control, and in the place where the royal *tun* also was 'often enough, in later centuries a real town grew up' (Campbell 1979, 121).

The lines of inquiry are inevitably complex, and there are pitfalls of interpretation at almost every step. However, the paths must be followed in the hope that the early history of the settlements examined here might be made clearer. A topographical study of ecclesiastical and royal estates is essential, therefore, if details of the associated settlements are to be elucidated.

The major difficulty facing any examination of estates is the identification of boundaries. A little confidence is provided by the fact that where boundaries are given in Anglo-Saxon charters and where they can be identified on the ground there is a very close, sometimes exact agreement with the manor boundaries marked on 16th- or 18th-century estate maps or described in documents, or with the earliest parish boundaries drawn on Tithe maps or Ordnance Survey maps. For all the estates examined below available documents or maps have been examined and the information obtained provides the basis for the boundaries drawn on the accompanying Figures, and also the evidence for the later discussion of the burhs.

Sherborne

The possible relationship between Cenwalch's 100 hides at *Lanprobus* and the hundred *agelli* mentioned in the foundation charter of 998, which has been examined above, must remain unresolved. It seems highly improbable, therefore, that the estate

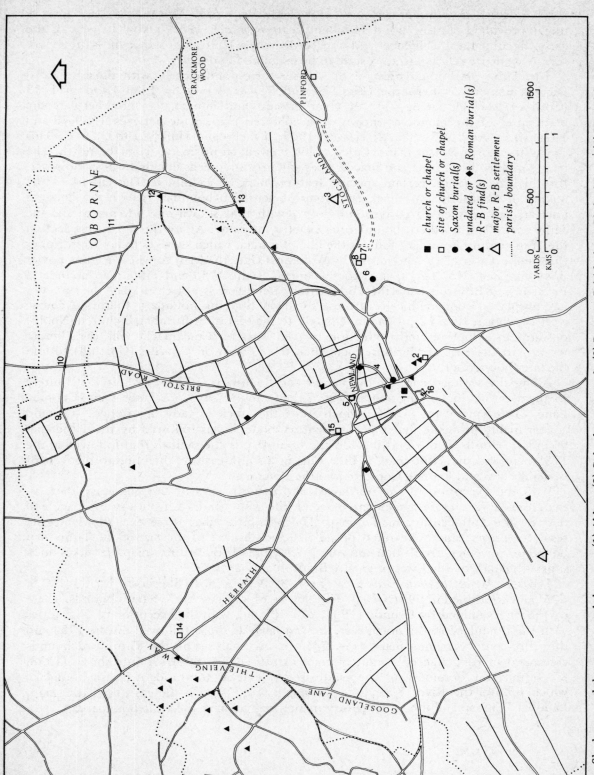

73. Sherborne and the area around the town. (1) Abbey; (2) Culverhays car park; (3) Romano-British site at Pinford Lane; (4) Hound Street; (5) chapel of St Thomas the Martyr; (6) the 12th-century castle; (7) St Mary Magdalen, site of; (8) possible site of the chapel of St Probus; (9) Upper Clatcombe Farm; (10) White Post Gate; (11) Lower Boyston Lane; (12) Oborne village; (13) St Cuthbert's church; (14) St Peter's chapel; (15) St Emerenciana's chapel; (16) Trendle. Main field divisions and town boundaries are taken from map of 1733 by John Ladd.

can be identified with any certainty. However, it is possible that retrogressive analysis might provide a starting point for identification (Bloch 1952, x-xiv). In view of the early documentary evidence and the settlement's later importance it is necessary for the evidence relating to the estate to be examined in detail.

The Tithe map boundaries for Sherborne correspond closely with those of Lord Digby's manor of Sherborne (Figs. 73 and 74) as drawn by John Ladd in 1733 (Fowler 1951, Pl. facing 73). Of great interest and importance, however, are the boundaries of the manor as shown on a coloured map, made between 1569-70 and 1574 (B.L. Add. MS. 52522; Harvey 1965; Tyacke and Huddy 1980, 56-7). This shows the north Dorset manors pictorially, viewed, surprisingly, from the north. The map contains distortions and inaccuracies and urgently needs detailed study. However, for this investigation certain specific features may be examined. The extent of the manor of Sherborne, in all except along its southern boundary where the detail is unclear, can be seen to correspond closely with that shown on Ladd's map and the Tithe map. The northern boundary is exactly the same. Along the north-east section the 16th-century boundary follows the line of a track which survives today from Upper Clatcombe Farm (Fig. 73, No. 9), by Whitepost Gate (No. 10) to where it joins Lower Boyston Lane (No. 11), that is to the north of the 1733 and Tithe map boundary. From Lower Boyston Lane the 16th-century boundary is not clear since the surveyor has misplaced topographical features. By deduction the boundary follows a course west of Oborne (No. 12), then immediately to the east of St Cuthbert's church (No. 13) onwards in a south-easterly direction to pass west of 'Crackmacke Hill' (Crackmore Wood), to the east of 'Pinforde', and then to the west of 'Gotylle' (Goathill) to join the later boundaries.

Along the western edge of the manor the boundary is ill-defined. It is definitely to the west of the curving course (Fig. 73) of the present Gooselands Lane, Coombe Lane, 'Thieveing Way' (1733), which joins the track already mentioned. It would appear highly probable that the 16th-century boundary is followed by the Tithe map boundary. South of the Yeovil Road the boundary is the same as that followed in the 1733 map and the Tithe map, it then runs in a south-easterly direction to the west of Bedmill Farm and Bedmill Copse to join the River Yeo.

With the exception of the north-east and eastern parts of the boundary there is, therefore, a very close agreement between the 19th- and 18th-century evidence and that of the 16th-century manor map. The possibility that these exceptions are the result of errors cannot be ruled out. To the south-west of the manor the Tithe map boundary diverges from that on the 1733 and 16th-century map. It takes in a substantial part of what was originally Bradford Abbas.

Ten *cassatae æt bradan forda* were given by Æthelstan to Sherborne in 933 (B.C.S. 695) and confirmed in 998 (K 701). The charter of 933 has Anglo-Saxon bounds. These have been examined by Grundy (1933, 250-53) and, with the exception of difficulties with the boundary in the north-east, are the same as those followed on the 1733 and the 16th-century manor maps (Fig. 74). In his analysis of the Thornford bounds contained in King Eadred's grant of eight *cassati* (B.C.S. 894), Grundy shows (1938, 87-9) that the boundary of the estate is the same as the modern parish boundary which follows the River Yeo along the north (Fig. 74). On the east, the Tithe map, Ladd's 1733 map and the 16th-century manor map all have the same boundary.

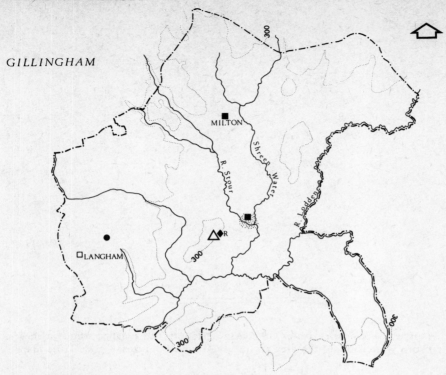

GILLINGHAM

74. Gillingham and its parish: boundaries from Tithe map. Sherborne and surrounding parishes: boundaries from Anglo-Saxon charters, 16th-century map of the manor of Sherborne and Tithe maps. Note, parish of Castleton omitted.

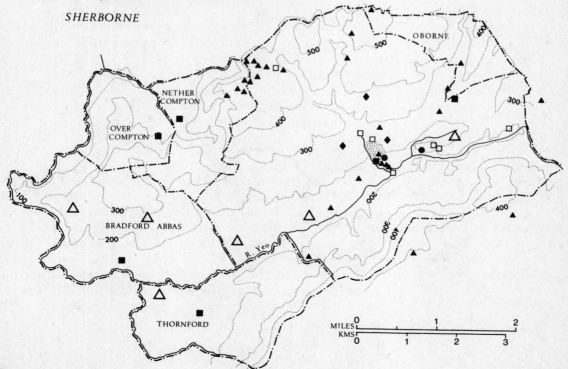

SHERBORNE

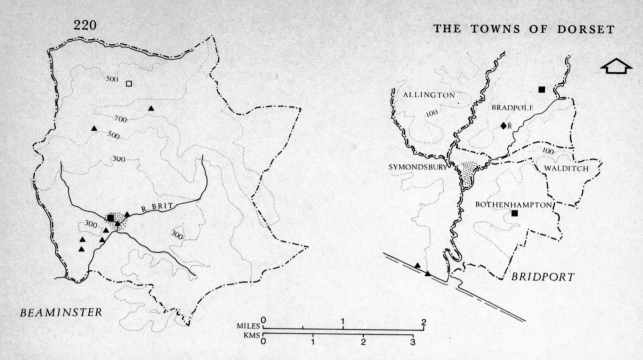

BEAMINSTER

BRIDPORT

ALLINGTON

BRADPOLE

SYMONDSBURY

WALDITCH

BOTHENHAMPTON

MILES
KMS

75. Beaminster and its parish: boundaries from Tithe map. Bridport and neighbouring parishes: boundaries from Tithe maps. Wareham and the area around the town: boundaries from Tithe maps

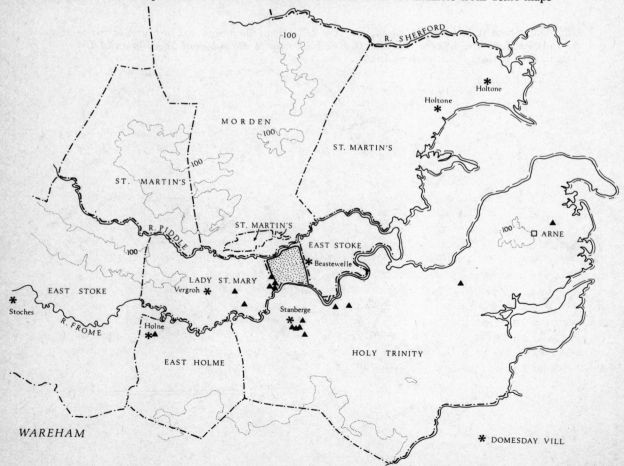

R. SHERFORD

MORDEN

ST. MARTIN'S

Holtone

Holtone

ST. MARTIN'S

ST. MARTIN'S

EAST STOKE

R. PIDDLE

ST. MARTIN'S

Beastewelle

LADY ST. MARY

Vergroh

ARNE

EAST STOKE

Stoches

R. FROME

Stanberge

Holne

HOLY TRINITY

EAST HOLME

WAREHAM

* DOMESDAY VILL

The difficulties with the Bradford Abbas bounds cannot be resolved easily by an examination of the bounds of Nether and Over Compton(Fig. 74), both of which formed part of Sherborne abbey's estate. Eight hides at Compton were given to the church of Aethelbert (860 x 866) (B.L. Cotton MS. Faustina A.II, f. 24) and eight *cassati* were confirmed in the 998 foundation charter. Nether Compton is not mentioned in the Domesday Survey and it seems likely therefore that it is included under Bradford Abbas: Over Compton is assessed at six hides. With no other evidence the Tithe map must be used, but for the eastern bounds of Nether Compton these follow the 1733 map boundary, and, as noted above, by deduction the 16th-century map also. In the north-east five hides at Oborne were given to Sherborne by Eadgar (970–5) (Robertson 1959, 104–7). Five *cassati* are confirmed in 998, and the Domesday Survey has five hides assessed: unfortunately, there are no bounds.

There are, therefore, significant details to show how the abbey's original *parochia* was extended by royal grant to include Thornford, Bradford Abbas, Compton, and Oborne (Fig. 74), all of which are out-hundred tithings of Sherborne hundred (Fowler 1951, 220). The inference to be drawn must surely be that the abbey's original endowment was a royal estate, remaining parts of which were later given to the abbey and added to the estate which they abutted. Indeed, the boundaries of Oborne suggest that its north-eastern extent was the limit of the original royal estate. It is interesting to note that in the Domesday Survey 27½ carucates did not pay geld (Darby and Finn 1967, 83): there is presumably a connection between these ungelded lands and the original royal estate.

The long curving line of track referred to above is of special interest and its relationship with the abbey estate appears to have particular significance. It is suggested that the track marks the boundary of the 100 hides which Cenwalch gave to *Lanprobus* (643 x 672) (Barker, *pers. comm.*). If this were the case it is difficult to explain the modest extension of the boundary on the north-west to include comparatively small blocks of land. The track forms the boundary with Oborne on the 16th-century map (see above and Fig. 73). If greater credibility could be given to the boundary as shown on the 1733 and Tithe map, the track would be unlikely to antedate the grant of 970–75, unless the track had its origins in the original royal estate before part of it was granted to *Lanprobus* or to the 8th-century monastery. However, if the track is a boundary line it may well have its origin in the 10th century. Abbot Wulfsige enclosed the monastic estate with hedges and ditches: *predium monasterii sicut Wlsinus episcopus fossis sepibusque girare curauit* (K 701). The question must remain open. Nevertheless, it is most likely that this track is part of the 'procession grownd' of about thirteen miles mentioned in the 16th century (*Itinerary*, i, 152n).

The settlement at Shaftesbury is difficult to place in the context of an estate. On the Tithe maps the settlement is surrounded by the parishes of St James and Cann, St Peter's parish jutting out into both (Fig. 76). One may reasonably suppose that if there were an old foundation, which seems highly probable, the later parishes reflect the extent of its *parochia*. A grant of 958 by King Eadwig to Wulfgar (K 470) of land *æt Sceaftesberi* contains Anglo-Saxon bounds, but the size of the grant, which Grundy placed within the town (Grundy 1938, 75), is not known because the manuscript has two blanks in front of *cassatos* (B.L. Harl. 61, f. 16v). However, *bytelesmor* in the bounds had been identified by Hutchins with 'Bytellesmore' (Fig. 77), near Holy Rood

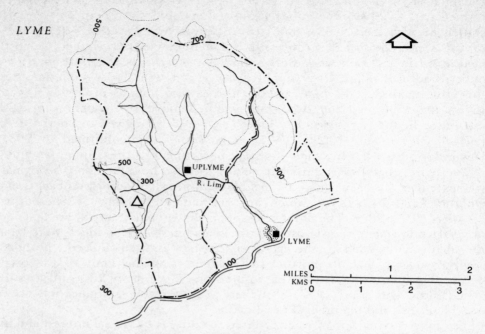

76. Lyme: boundary from Tithe map, and Uplyme, bounds of 938. Shaftesbury:
boundaries from Tithe maps

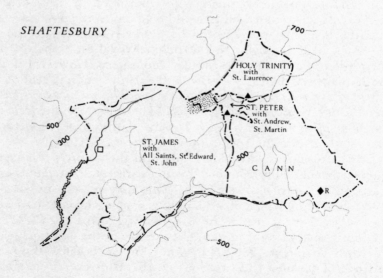

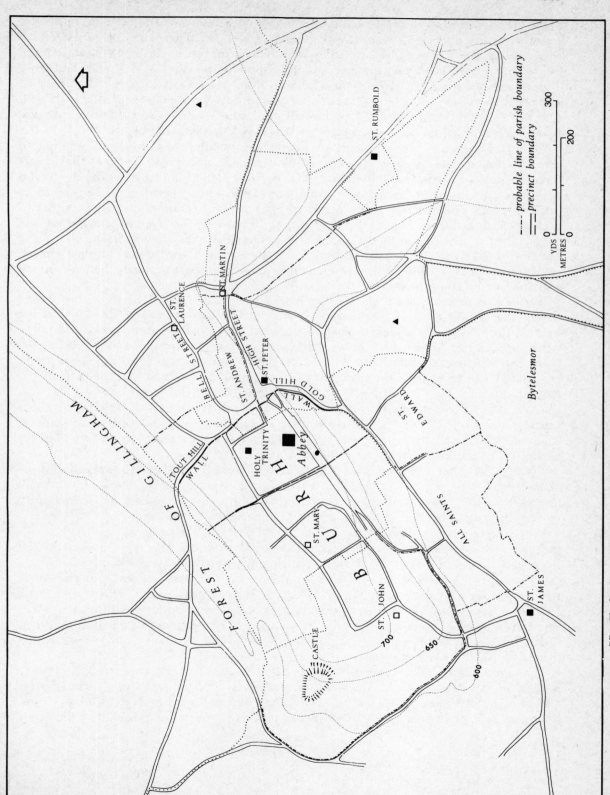

77. Shaftesbury. The burh on the top of the spur. Parish boundaries from Tithe maps

Mead in St James's parish (Hutchins 1868, 6): 'Buttlesmore' and 'Bytellesmore' are found in 1460 and 1476 respectively (*ibid.*, 89 and 91). The parcel of land came to Shaftesbury abbey at an unknown date and the charter was accordingly entered in the Shaftesbury Cartulary. The northern boundary of the parishes of St James and Holy Trinity as shown on the Tithe maps follows along its greater part the boundary of the royal forest of Gillingham (Fig. 76) as given in a perambulation of 1299 to 1300 (Drew 1952, 34–5). A coherent picture of the *parochia* is made difficult, however, by the presence of the later urban parishes which will be discussed below.

Wareham presents the problems of having no documentary evidence relating to the *parochia* of the original 7th-century church, combined with the fact that, apart from a length of Corfe Castle boundary (B.C.S. 868, 910, 10th century), the discussion of estate and *parochia* must rely solely on 19th-century evidence. Despite these difficulties an attempt has to be made to establish an idea of the original extent of ecclesiastical influence since this can supply evidence for a consideration of the 9th-century burh. It has been noted above that Tait has drawn attention to the possibility that the parish system represents 'the single parish of one original church of Wareham' (Tait 1936, 56): the challenge has remained for nearly half a century and must be taken up now.

The Tithe map evidence shows Wareham strategically placed between the Rivers Frome and Piddle (Fig. 75), a location perfectly described by Asser (Ch. 49). To the east of the town is a detached portion of East Stoke parish, and to the west is the parish of Lady St Mary which crosses the burh rampart in the south-west part of the town and which has a small area around the parish church (Fig. 78). East Stoke parish is situated to the west of the main part of the parish of Lady St Mary. North of the River Piddle is a large area of land with two large parts of St Martin's parish (Fig. 75), that on the east extending northwards as far as the River Sherford. Between the two separate parts of St Martin's a broad tongue of Morden parish extends southwards to surround two small detached parts of St Martin's parish: a small area of St Martin's surrounds the parish church within the town (Fig. 78).

South of the River Frome is a large area containing the vill of Stoborough and the chapelry of Arne, all of which is part of Holy Trinity parish, which also has a small area within the town around the church. The south-east boundary of Holy Trinity corresponds with the 10th-century charter boundaries of Corfe Castle.

What interpretation does this evidence offer? The two separate parts of St Martin's parish, with the small portions included in Morden parish, may reasonably be suggested to indicate that St Martin's parish once extended to cover the whole area as far as the River Sherford and to a boundary on the west beyond that shown on the Tithe map. To the south, the boundary of Holy Trinity parish with Corfe Castle follows a watercourse, and this is without doubt an early boundary feature. Westwards there are straight lengths of boundary which may be late features, and the parish of East Holme is probably a late development. Between the two rivers, the two separated parts of East Stoke parish offer no obvious interpretation.

It is immediately clear that the parish of St Martin's is the largest, Holy Trinity is next in size, and Lady St Mary is the smallest. Together these three parishes offer a shadow of the *parochia* of the early church, with the River Sherford as the northern boundary and perhaps part of the Purbeck ridge as its southern extent. The difficulty

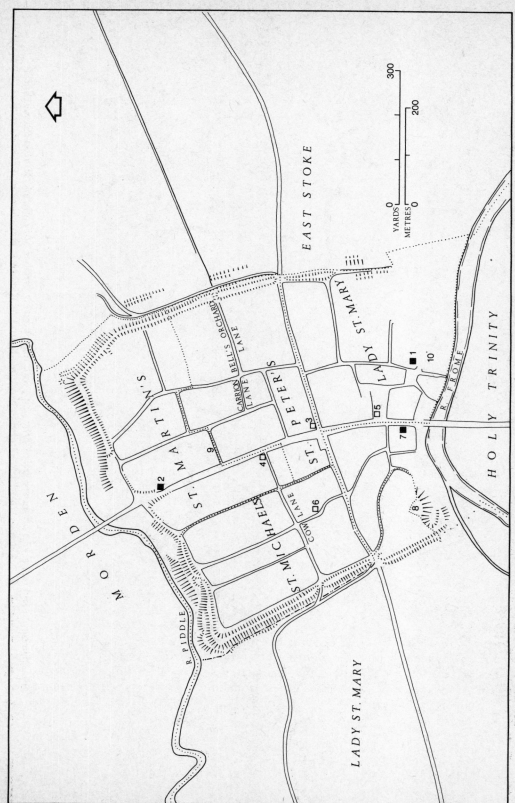

78. The burh of Wareham, with the boundaries of Lady St Mary and Holy Trinity extending across the defences and the urban parishes of St Michael's and St Peter's: St Martin's parish has larger areas outside. (1) church of Lady St Mary; (2) church of St Martin; (3) site of St Peter's; (4) site of All Hallows church; (5) site of St John's church; (6) site of St Michael's church; (7) Holy Trinity; (8) 12th-century castle; (9) Dollins Lane; (10) site of priory

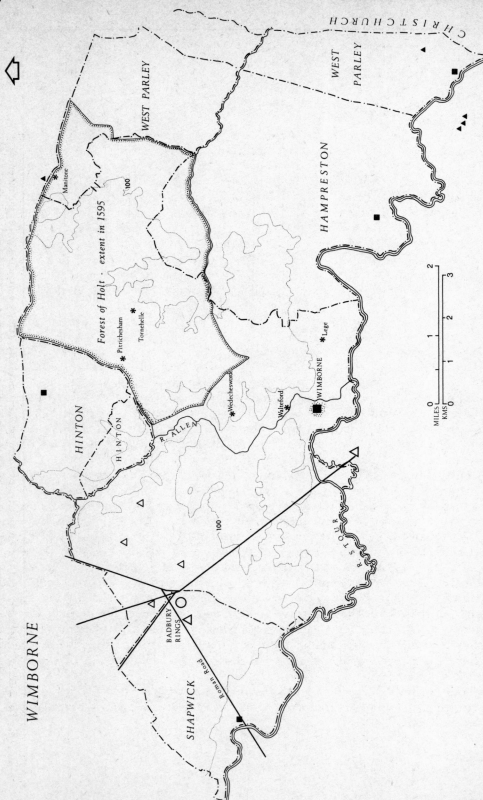

WIMBORNE

79. Wimborne and its parish: boundary from Tithe map, with neighbouring parishes of Shapwick, Hinton Parva, Hinton Martell, West Parley and Hampreston, all parts of Wimborne *parochia*.

is that one would perhaps expect the monastery of Wareham to have the largest parish. In its church (? of Lady St Mary) Brihtric was buried in 802; it was mentioned by Asser in 876; King Edward was buried there in 978; and its abbess, Wulfwyn, died in 982 (A.S.C. *sub annis*). In the absence of evidence to the contrary it may be deduced that the modest area attached to Lady St Mary was taken out of the much larger original *parochia,* the latest parts of which were taken over by the parishes of St Martin and Holy Trinity.

The monastery at Wimborne, founded in the late 7th or early 8th century has, unfortunately, left little information about its estate and *parochia.* Just as these details are obscure so, too, is its later history. King Ethelred was buried in the minster (A.S.C. *sub anno* 871), and King Sigeferth was buried there in 962 (A.S.C. *sub anno*). The account of the atheling Aethelwold's revolt in 900 records how he seized the residence at Wimborne and at Twinham, the king encamping at Badbury (Fig. 79), while Aethelwold stayed inside the residence at Wimborne with the gates barricaded. The atheling rode off to Northumbria, taking with him one of the nuns (A.S.C. *sub anno*). It may be presumed that the residence was a royal palace, and that Wimborne was part of a royal estate. Such a view is supported by the Domesday Survey which surveys Shapwick, Wimborne, Crichel, and Up Wimborne as a royal manor (Hutchins 1868, 159).

The boundary of Wimborne on the Tithe map surrounds a very large area (Fig. 79). However, this area is only part of the original *parochia* which included Shapwick, where the rectory belonged to the later College: Badbury Rings, where the king encamped in 900, is in the parish. Hinton, 'farm or estate belonging to the religious community' (Mills 1980, 146-7) may be included with confidence. In B.C.S. 818, a charter of 946 giving the bounds of Chalbury (Grundy 1934, 111-2), *to thare hina gemaere,* 'to the boundary of the community' (Mills 1980, 147) is mentioned. These bounds correspond with the northern boundary of Hinton, or with a small stretch of boundary in the north-west corner of the Wimborne bounds as shown on the Tithe map. The place-name, Hampreston, has the affix *preston,* 'priest farm' (Mills 1980, 225) which is probably a reference to lands originally belonging to the monastery. The western extent of the Christchurch *parochia* joins West Parley, and it seems reasonable to suppose that the two parts of West Parley were included in Wimborne's *parochia.*

The original *parochia* of Twinham (Christchurch) was considered briefly by Lennard (1959, 398-9) and has now been examined in depth by Hase (1975, 181-223). As for Wimborne the Tithe map boundaries of Christchurch parish (Fig. 80) include only part of the original *parochia,* which included the present parishes of Christchurch, Holdenhurst, Ringwood, Sopley, Milton, Hordle, Milford, Lymington, Boldre, Brockenhurst, the larger part of the parish of Beaulieu, and parts of Harbridge and Ellingham parishes. With the exception of Beaulieu, Harbridge, and perhaps Ringwood and Ellingham, the churches of all these parishes remained as dependent churches of Christchurch priory throughout the 12th century (Hase 1975, 189). The evidence for Christchurch is particularly important in showing the breaking up of the *parochia* into parishes before 1086.

Only the western part of the Christchurch *parochia* is shown on Fig. 80. It is significant that its western boundary joins the presumed eastern boundary of the Wimborne *parochia.*

If the reference to the atheling Æthelwold seizing the residence at Twinham in 900 implies a royal residence and, therefore, a royal estate, it is of some interest that as with the royal estate at Wimborne an enormous tract of country is involved. Furthermore, it seems reasonable to suggest that the royal estate was identical with the *parochia*.

In comparison the area of the parish of Lyme is miniscule (Fig. 76). It lies adjacent to an estate of six *mansae* given to one Æthelstan in 938 by King Æthelstan. The

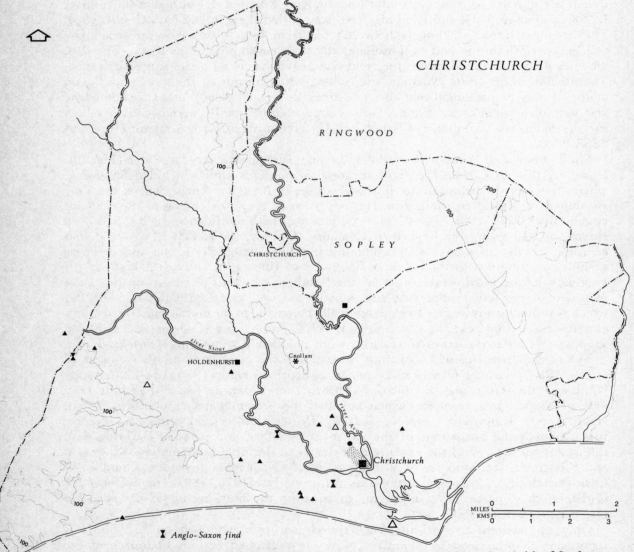

80. Christchurch and its parish: boundary from Tithe map. With the neighbouring parish of Sopley, this is only part of the original *parochia*.

estate was later transferred to Glastonbury abbey (B.C.S. 728; Watkin 1956, 577–8; Hart 1965, 160–61; for a discussion of the bounds, which are now shown to belong to Uplyme, Devon, rather than Lyme Regis, Dorset, *see* Fox 1970). The Tithe map parish of Lyme (Dorset) includes that area granted to Sherborne abbey in 774 (see above). Sherborne's more ancient rights led to the abbey founding a church there: it was mentioned in 1145 (Dugdale, i, 338). The importance of these coastal estates for both Glastonbury and Sherborne seems to have rested entirely on the salterns. A topographical examination of the Glastonbury estate and the parish of Lyme (Dorset) suggests that together they originally formed part of one, royal, estate.

Beaminster belonged to Sherborne abbey and the hundred is mentioned in the early 11th century. The early boundaries may well agree with those of the Tithe map (Fig. 75); certainly a substantial length of the boundary follows rivers, a fact which suggests an early boundary. The element *minster* in the place-name, perhaps as early as the first grant of 679 x 757, suggests that a church was established there at an early date. Whether it was founded by Gloucester abbey or later by Sherborne is a matter for speculation.

The importance of Dorchester as the centre of a royal estate is attested from the 8th century by the evidence reviewed above. The manor of Dorchester and Fordington was royal at the time of the Domesday Survey, and as part of the duchy of Cornwall it is still Crown land. The bounds of the manor as shown in the Tithe map (Fig. 72) correspond with those surveyed in 1607 (Bartelot 1915, 64–6): the length of these bounds common with those of Charminster are confirmed by the Charminster bounds of 1606 (D.C.R.O. *Lane* M5, p. 27 [1770]; Mills 1977, 339). The church of Fordington, which lies to the east of the town, is without doubt the earliest church. It has been suggested above that the royal residence was within the town or perhaps at Fordington itself. A royal residence at Fordington would demonstrate the close relationship between a *villa regalis* and a mother-church.

An examination of the plan of the streets and property boundaries between the centre of Dorchester and the western part of Fordington shows a series of curving property boundaries at the east end of High East Street, apparently continued along the line of modern Icen Way. The possibility that this curving line represents an earlier boundary related to the settlement at Fordington requires further investigation. If an earlier boundary may be established, the fact that it takes in part of the Roman walled town would serve to demonstrate an interesting relationship between Fordington and the walled town.

The royal manor of Gillingham, which takes in part of the royal forest, occupies a large area whose boundaries can be established only from the Tithe map (Fig. 74). The circumstances of the exchange with Shaftesbury abbey of the church for lands at Corfe have been considered above. The existence of a church earlier than the date of the exchange is confirmed by Anglo-Saxon sculpture and demonstrates the foundation of a church in a *villa regalis*. An important group of burials, numbering at least 100 and probably representing a sub-Roman Christian cemetery, which have been found near Langham (R.C.H.M. 1972, 35–6), would pay further investigation to establish the background to the foundation of the later church.

Ninth- and Tenth-century Settlement; the Burhs and General Topography

The examination of important settlements within their estate and *parochiae* has revealed very varying circumstances. However, it is possible to propose a tentative comparison on the basis of the size of estates and *parochiae* and the details of the settlements themselves.

It is apparent that the ecclesiastical influence is significant, and of interest that for Sherborne, Shaftesbury, Wareham, and possibly Christchurch, there is some evidence of British ecclesiastical settlement earlier than the Saxon monastery. Additionally, for Wimborne and Christchurch a royal residence is attested. The royal estates at Dorchester and Gillingham, both with royal residences, were evidently of importance, in particular, the former, which was the meeting place of the witan on several occasions.

TABLE VI

	British ecclesiastical settlement	Royal estate	Monastery	Monastic estate	Mother-church	Royal residence
Sherborne	X	X	X	X	X	
Shaftesbury	X		X	X	X	
Wareham	X		X	X	X	
Wimborne		X	X	X	X	X
Christchurch	?X	X	X	X	X	X
Lyme				X		
Beaminster				X	X	
Dorchester/Fordington ..		X			X	X
Gillingham		X			X	X

To what extent these places may be considered to be towns by the 9th century is extremely difficult to establish. It seems reasonable to suggest, however, that with the possible exception of Lyme and Beaminster, these settlements, with monastic houses and/or royal residences, possessed a focus which provided the basis for later settlement development and expansion. As central places within large estates, whether they were royal or monastic, these settlements had ingredients for the subsequent growth into a town. It would seem that the most influential characteristics for this growth were a royal or ecclesiastical interest because of the political, administrative, or economic roles that interest would initiate.

Between Dorchester and Sherborne, however, there is evidently a special and complementary relationship which may be taken back to King Ine (688–726), who founded a see at Sherborne in 705. The West Saxon kings are known to have stayed at their palace in Dorchester on many occasions during the 9th century. It is tempting to consider this as a direct result of the campaign against the Danes when the people of Dorset were directly involved under the leadership of Ealhstan, bishop of Sherborne (A.S.C., *sub annis* 840, 845). Dorchester, further away from central Wessex, may have been a little safer than Winchester, which was attacked in 860. In 864 King Aethelbert was in Dorchester with members of his family and his councillors and went to Sherborne to place his recent charter on the high altar. His father, Aethelwulf, had been buried in Winchester, but his brother, Aethelwald, was buried in Sherborne, where he, too, was to be interred. On the one hand, therefore, the estate of Dorchester had a royal palace and was the administrative centre, and on the other, Sherborne was the related episcopal centre where royal burials took place. As complementary settlements they have much in common with other settlements with the same relationships, examined by Biddle (1974, 214–6).

The establishment of fortified burhs provided a network with a minimum distance of 20 miles between sites and acted as an incentive for the growth of settlement within them. The burhs in modern Dorset, listed in the Burghal Hidage (c. 919) are. Wareham, Shaftesbury, Twinham, and Bredy (Hill 1969); Wareham being allocated 1,600 hides, Shaftesbury 700, Twinham 460/70, and 760 at Bredy. These figures give rampart lengths of 2,200 yards, 962½ yards, 206¼ yards, and 1,045 yards respectively.

Before considering the defences themselves in relation to settlement the dating of the system of burh defence and of the individual burhs needs to be examined. On the Continent some monasteries appear to have been fortified in the middle of the 9th century, for example, Angers in 851, St Omer in 846 (Hubert 1959, and Fig. 6.2, in Smith 1978). This is in contrast to the rebuilding of town walls and the construction of new fortifications which were not begun until the 860s by Charles the Bald (Brooks 1971, 81). This Continental development is paralleled by circumstances in Wessex where Brooks has noted 'fortress-work' reserved as one of the three burdens in West Saxon charters from the reign of Aethelbald (855–60). B.C.S. 451, signed in Dorchester in 847, grants land freed of all secular burdens *sine expeditione et pontis instructione,* lacking any reference to 'fortress-work'. B.C.S. 510 of 864, also given at Dorchester, similarly has no reference to 'fortress-work', but reserves *fyrde 7 brycge weorces.* In contrast B.C.S. 508, given in Dorchester in 863, grants land *libera ab omni regali servitio et omnium secularium servitate praeter expeditionem et pontis factionem et arcis munitionem.* All three burdens are reserved in B.C.S. 520 of 868 (Dorchester), B.C.S. 525 of 869 (Woodyates), and B.C.S. 564 of 891. The impression, therefore, is that the building of fortifications in Wessex may not have been exacted until the second half of the 9th century. Despite this late start the Viking invasions were successfully resisted. Brooks emphasises that 'the development of royal authority in England was directly connected with the successful enforcement of public works and general military obligations so that an adequate defence against the Vikings was provided' (1971, 84).

In his recent examination of England in the 9th century and particularly of the size of the Viking army, Brooks has shown that 'the army of 865 introduced a new tactic to Viking warfare' (1979, 9)—

> . . . the army of 865, like its successor on the continent from 879 to 892, moved each autumn to a fresh kingdom or district where it established a new camp for the following year. Moreover, the 'large army' of 865 did not as a rule construct new fortified camps. The sites chosen each autumn were not isolated island sites, but royal and administrative centres of the Anglo-Saxon kingdoms: York in 866–7, Nottingham in 867–8. York again in 868–9, Thetford in 869–70, Reading in 870–1, London in 871–2, Torksey in 872–3, Repton in 873–4, Cambridge in 874–5, Wareham in 875–6, Exeter in 876–7, Chippenham in 877–8 and Cirencester in 879–880. Most of these places were chosen by the army precisely because they already had defences (*ibid.*).

In the case of Wareham, Brooks's thesis confirms the inference contained in Asser's account of the Viking army leaving Cambridge and then *castellum, quod dicitur Werham, intravit* (Asser, Ch. 49). The description *castellum* would not have been used had Wareham been without fortifications. This view contrasts with Dr. Radford's recent examination of the evidence for Wareham, in which he concludes that by 876 no fortifications had been erected (Radford 1978, 140).

Brooks's review of the new tactics, coupled with the fact that estates had long since been bound to perform 'fortress-work', shows that considerable caution must be exercised in—

> . . . attributing to Alfred forts which happen to be first recorded in his reign or in that of his son. Archaeological dating of the West Saxon boroughs is seldom precise, and there is a dangerous tendency to label forts as 'Alfredian' where, as at Wareham, Wallingford and Lydford, the archaeological evidence only establishes defences as post-Roman. We should not rule out the possibility that some of the West Saxon boroughs that were in existence in the early tenth century were of Dark Age origin, and that others were the work of Alfred's immediate predecessors (Brooks 1979, 17).

It is also clear that the new tactics of the army of 865 demonstrate that the fortified centres had existing populations which, as Brooks has pointed out, were later to provide permanent garrisons.

The impressive defences at Wareham (Fig. 78), which enclose the town on its west, north and east sides, have been excavated (R.C.H.M. 1959). The excavations showed that the first phase of the defences consisted of a rampart with an outer face of timber and a ditch, dating 'from the end of the Roman period and possibly after *c.* 700' (*ibid.,* 137). In the second phase the bank was heightened with a stone wall set above the earlier rampart: this phase lies between the 8th and 11th centuries. The excavators concluded that the first phase represents the burgh which existed in the reign of Alfred, and that the second phase 'belongs to an unrecorded strengthening at some pre-Conquest date' (*ibid.*). However, they do not rule out the possibility that the Alfredian burh made use of pre-existing defences (*ibid.,* 123).

The relationship between the defences and the structure of existing settlement is of special interest. The relationship at Wareham between the burh and the parishes attracted Tait's attention in 1936. It has been shown above that the parishes of Lady St Mary, Holy Trinity and St Martin have their greater part outside the ramparts, with only a small area inside the defences (Fig. 75). This is in contrast to the later urban parishes of St Michael, All Hallows, and St Peter, which are confined within the burh (Fig. 78). This arrangement suggests that the parishes of Holy Trinity, St Martin and Lady St Mary had been established within the *parochia* of the mother-church and that the churches of all three parishes were already in existence before the construction of the defences. These circumstances may serve to suggest that a significant population existed in Wareham before the construction of the ramparts.

The extent of the burh at Shaftesbury, founded by Alfred in 880, according to an inscription seen by William of Malmesbury (R.C.H.M. 1972, 57; Radford 1978, 150), has always been a matter of speculation since no earthworks remain. It is clear, however, that the burh was sited on the spur with steep slopes on the north, west and south sides (Figs. 76 and 77). Taylor and Radford favoured a line to the west of the abbey for the burh defences (Taylor 1970, 188 and Fig. 19; Radford 1970, 87), a location adopted by the Royal Commission on Historical Monuments (R.C.H.M. 1972, 56), but Asser's description of the abbey being *iuxta orientalem portam* (Ch. 98) suggests that the burh defences could be to the east of the abbey. An examination of the street plan (Fig. 77) shows this to be a probability, since the main medieval streets, now the High Street, Bell Street, Gold Hill, and Tout Hill, indicate a plan distinctive to that of the street plan of the spur. Furthermore, the medieval walling along most of the length of the arc formed by Gold Hill and Tout Hill is the abbey precinct wall which was built no doubt after the abbess had received a licence to crenellate in 1368 (Parker 1859, 416). It is nonetheless strange that the wall, except for a very short length at the bottom of Gold Hill, does not agree with the western boundary of the parish of St Peter, which includes the ancient parish of St Andrew. This boundary lies many yards inside the precinct. The conclusion to be drawn from this fact must surely be that the boundary of the parish represents a boundary earlier than the abbey precinct wall and by deduction earlier also than the burh. Topographically this suggestion has much to recommend it since the main lines of communication, determined by natural factors, lie where the medieval town was and where the modern settlement is centred, in preference to the western spur which is but sparsely settled. Archaeological evidence for settlement is slight. Late Saxon pottery from beneath a late southern extension to St Peter's church at least demonstrates the use of part of the area to the east of the abbey from perhaps the 10th century (Keen 1976, 56–60; 1977).

Dorchester (Fig. 72) is not mentioned in the Burghal Hidage, but the surviving Roman defences and a mint which, according to the *Quadripartitus* text of the Grateley decrees (*E.H.D.*, 384), was established in the reign of Aethelstan (924–39), has always led it to be considered as a burh (Biddle and Hill 1971, 84): its location approximately halfway between the burhs of Bridport and Wareham lends considerable weight to this view. The earlier history of the settlement and its estate has been considered in detail above. It is suggested that the royal residence may have been within the Roman walled town or at Fordington itself, where the main settlement was around the church, which was the mother-church of the royal estate. The status of the church at Fordington is borne out by the fact that the later parish of Fordington has no authority within the walled town, as, for instance, do the earliest parishes at Wareham. If an early church of the royal estate was within the walled town one would expect the later parish to cross the line of the walls. The three parishes of Dorchester are confined within the walls. Tait's statement that the parish of Frome Whitfield extended into the walls (1936, 56) maintains a confusion about the extent of the borough initiated by Hutchins (1863, 415) and continued by Mayo (1908, 470). The three parishes of Holy Trinity, St Peter, and All Saints take up approximately equal third shares of the walled town. Such an arrangement suggests that the ecclesiastical division was made on one occasion. Together the evidence of the urban parishes and the earlier settlement history demonstrates that the burh, which was to succeed Fordington in importance as a settlement, was set up within the area of the Roman walled town which had remained apart from the settlement around Fordington.

Excavations by Hill have established the line of the burh defences at Twinham (Christchurch). The burh (Fig. 81) is situated on a gravel spur between the Rivers Avon and Stour; its defence, which lay across the north and along the west sides, consisted of a turf bank with multiple ditches. A later stone revetment located in several excavations is not precisely dated. Unfortunately, dating evidence for the earliest phases of the earthen bank is lacking. Late Saxon material has been found on many sites within the burh, but settlement evidence is limited to one six-post structure (Jarvis 1983, 38). A length of ditch, apparently earlier than the defences referred to above has been found by excavation and by augering parallel and to the east of the western line of defences (Aitken, *pers. comm.*). The date and purpose of this new discovery has yet to be determined.

81. The burh of Christchurch

The burh at Bredy (Fig. 82) is the most elusive and problematic of the Dorset burhs. Maitland's identification of Bredy as Little Bredy (1960, 578) was questioned by Symonds, who proposed, on numismatic grounds, that Bridport was a more likely candidate (Symonds 1922, 38–9). There is no good reason why Symonds's proposal should be questioned, even though, unlike the other major centres, Bridport has no known early settlement or estate history. It would appear from the parish boundary of the Tithe plan (Fig. 75) that the area of the burh was allocated from the royal manor of Bradpole (Tait 1936, 71). The burh, in a position similar to Twinham, occupies land between the Rivers Brit and Asker. No defences remain, but the line of a ditch cutting off the promontory has been established from documentary evidence (Short 1976). There have been attempts to investigate the interior of the burh, but so far no Saxon material has been uncovered (Bailey 1976).

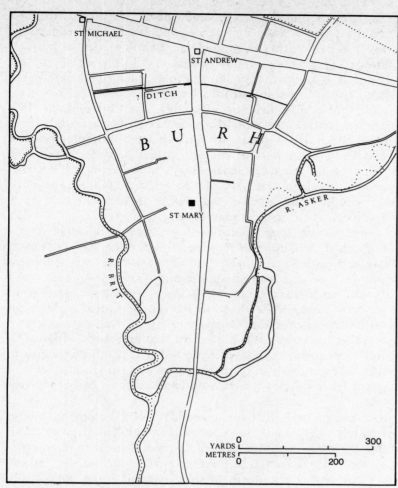

82. The burh of Bredy (Bridport)

The street plans of the burhs are seen as part of a deliberate royal policy of founding urban centres, and the rectilinear plan found in many burhs is considered 'to be a deliberate expression of the organisation and apportionment of the land for permanent settlement' (Biddle [ed.] 1976, 277). Wareham has such a rectilinear plan (Fig. 78) and has been used as a close parallel to Winchester (Biddle and Hill 1971, 70, 81 and Fig. 4). However, while a topographical analysis at Winchester has in part a firm basis as a result of much archaeological work, an analysis of Wareham's plan from topographical evidence alone is a somewhat dangerous exercise now that Hinton's excavations have shown that one element in the rectilinear street plan, Dollins Lane (Fig. 78, No. 9), is a development of the 13th century or later (Hinton and Hodges 1977, 82). Furthermore, where it can be demonstrated that settlements earlier than the setting-up of the burhs are likely to have existed, caution should be exercised lest elements of the lay-out of the earlier settlement were included within the burh. At Wareham there is sufficient evidence to show that the construction of the burh involved the replanning of an existing settlement. While the topographical elements associated with the castle (Fig. 78, No. 8) can be removed from the plan with reasonable confidence it is difficult to establish which elements might belong to the earlier settlement and which belong to the burh. The inherent dangers of analysis from topographical evidence has been shown by Hinton's excavations. However, it is of

interest that a major element in the rectilinear street plan, the west to east line of
Cow Lane, Carrion Lane, and Bell's Orchard Lane is continued to the east, through
a narrow gap in the east rampart, by a track and substantial bank and hedge. It is
difficult to consider this feature as being other than an element earlier than the burh.

The street plan of Dorchester (Fig. 72) contains certain rectilinear elements, but
the date of these is uncertain: it is noteworthy that the plan of the Roman streets
is different and that there is no known superimposition.

The three burhs, Shaftesbury (Fig. 77), Bridport (Fig. 82), and Christchurch (Fig.
81), have very similar plans: a central street on the main axis of the burh with a
number of small side lanes. Bridport appears to have been a completely new
10th-century foundation and the greater part of its plan probably reflects the new
street plan. Similarly, the plan of the burh at Shaftesbury, founded in the late 9th
century, no doubt demonstrates a substantial part of the original lay-out. The burh
at Christchurch, however, occupies the site of an earlier settlement and it is
consequently uncertain which elements in its plan may be original.

An examination of the burhs within their vicinities shows that Bridport (Fig. 75)
had little or no arable land attached to it and that Dorchester had none. No conclusion
may be arrived at for Wareham and Shaftesbury, but Christchurch had extensive
fields. Although Tait has pointed out that 'too much stress must not be laid . . . upon
the agricultural aspect of the Anglo-Saxon borough', since some boroughs 'were
practically as urban as a modern town, while those which retained most arable land
were often much less agricultural than they may seem since its cultivation was left to
a small number of burgesses' (Tait 1936, 73), it is important that any study of Dorset's
major settlements and burhs should attempt to investigate the evidence for agriculture.
If the available map evidence is examined, only in the areas around Dorchester and
Sherborne do details emerge of field systems which would appear to be early medieval
in date.

The very large open field system around Dorchester (Fig. 72), belonging to the
parish of Fordington, fortunately survived to be surveyed for the Tithe Award. The
map shows the East and West Fields on either side of the old Roman road towards
Weymouth. To the west of the town is East Home Field. Further to the west, north
of Maiden Castle is Castle Field, and to the north of that, straddling the old Roman
road towards Bridport, is Pummery Field. The remarkable feature of the groups of
strips making up all these fields is that an extensive system of long, slightly curving
parallel lines made up by the headlands and furlong divisions cross the field systems
from west to east. Equally remarkable is that a series of north-to-south headland and
furlong parallel divisions crossing the west-to-east boundaries is also apparent. In
several places to the south of the town tracks cross these boundaries without respect
to them or to the strips in the furlongs. The system is so extensive and regular that
it is clear that its results from a deliberate act of planning. Were no evidence of the
Iron Age/Roman field systems between Maiden Castle and Dorchester available it
would be reasonable to suggest that this system belongs to that period. However, a
recent analysis (Fig. 83) of all available aerial photographs by Caroline Wells shows
that the Iron Age/Roman field systems are very different (Wells 1981, Plan 4).
Since the medieval open field system, as shown surviving on the Tithe map, respects
the long, slightly curving boundaries it is evident that the system must be post-Roman

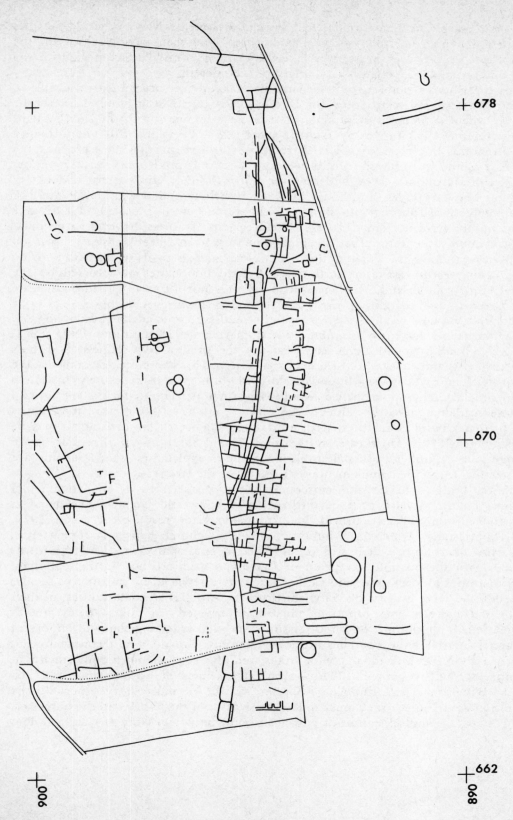

83. Aerial photographic evidence of Iron Age/Roman fields and settlement to the north of Maiden Castle

Reproduced by permission of the Dorset Archaeological Committee

and earlier than the medieval open field system. It is tentatively suggested that the system belongs most probably to the Saxon period and that, having regard for the historical evidence for Dorchester from the 8th century, a middle Saxon date for the system, laid out under royal authority, might be considered.

If this thesis is acceptable a quite remarkable example of survival is demonstrated. However, the analysis as proposed for Dorchester is tested again around Sherborne (Fig. 73), where a similar system emerges from an examimation of the field systems as shown on the 1733 survey by Ladd (Fowler 1951, Pl. facing 73). The difficulty arising from this Sherborne detail is that the west-to-east parallel lines crossing the higher part of the town have recently been interpreted as pre-Roman features similar to the south Dartmoor reaves, and that the north-to-south grid pattern laid out at an angle of between 63deg. and 65deg. is Romano-British in date (Barker 1977, 127). Unfortunately, aerial photographs showing field systems are not available for the area and excavations have not aided dating. Certain specific features, however, are similar to those around Dorchester: first, a number of west-to-east headlands are shown on the 1733 map to have tracks along them, some surviving as roads or footpaths today; second, both west-to-east and north-to-south field boundaries are crossed by the medieval road from Bristol. Neither west-to-east nor north-to-south field boundaries appear to cross any section of the estate boundary as discussed above, unless the boundary is a track or road. It is clear that the road system is ancient: the road from Marston Magna is referred to as a *herpath* in a charter of 938 (Grundy 1930, 103–4; 1939, 257, Road 59), and along its course are the sites of two chapels, St Peter's (Fig. 73, No. 14) and a chapel to St Emerenciana (No. 15). There is no reason why the north-to-south and west-to-east boundaries should not be part of the same field system —indeed, the Dorchester evidence would suggest this. The field system around Sherborne, which apparently respects the estate boundary, is therefore remarkably similar to that around Dorchester. With no dating evidence to the contrary it may be proposed that with the Dorchester system that around Sherborne is of middle Saxon date, here laid out under episcopal authority. Such an explanation would add another interesting feature to the complementary character of the two settlements.

Churches, both monastic and episcopal, have been seen to be of fundamental importance in the development of settlements which could later be considered as towns. Indeed, they clearly provided a major focus for town life (Nelson 1979, 103–4). Shaftesbury, Wareham, Wimborne, and Christchurch had early monasteries, so, too, did Sherborne, which was to become an episcopal centre. All the towns examined, with the possible exception of Lyme and Bridport, had mother-churches. The communities at Wimborne and Christchurch were replaced by minsters of secular priests, but the later history of Wareham is not known. These communities, in their governmental and economic functions, must have provided a stimulus for the growth of population. It should not be forgotten, however, that as resting places of important saints and their relics the churches attracted pilgrims who no doubt contributed to the fortunes of the individual communities and the settlements around them: at Sherborne, St Wulfsige and St Iuderware; at Shaftesbury, St Edward and St Æthel-geofu; at Wimborne, St Cuthbugh (Rollason 1978). At Shaftesbury especially the proliferation of urban parishes must reflect the wealth of the abbey and the burgesses. Unfortunately, the multiplication of parishes cannot be dated. Only at Wareham does evidence exist to suggest that at least two parishes, St Martin's and Holy Trinity, had been established before the setting-up of the burh. A detailed study of parishes in Dorset towns is outside the scope of this essay, but it is evident that, as elsewhere, such a study would help the understanding of urban development.

Architectural remains of Anglo-Saxon date are, unfortunately, not numerous. At Sherborne important Saxon work has recently been revealed and published in detail (Gibb 1975; Gem 1975). Nothing survives of the earliest buildings at Shaftesbury, Christchurch, and Wimborne. At Wareham, the church of Lady St Mary (Fig. 78, No. 1), destroyed in 1841-2, but fortunately recorded by plans and drawings, was one of the most important Anglo-Saxon churches surviving in England (Taylor and Taylor 1965, 634-7; R.C.H.M. 1970, 304-12). It is highly unlikely that the church dates to the time of St Aldhelm (*ibid.*, xliii-xliv, 310; Radford 1970, 85). As at Winchester, where the New Minster was dedicated in 903, the large and impressive church of Lady St Mary at Wareham may have been built especially 'to provide for the needs of the new burh and its rapidly growing population' (Biddle [ed.], 1976, 313-4).

The only urban parish church which may be dated structurally to the Anglo-Saxon period is St Martin's at Wareham (Fig. 78, No. 2), which is usually considered to be pre-Conquest in date (R.C.H.M. 1970, 312, Taylor and Taylor 1965, 637-9), but it could even be post-Conquest (Gem 1976). The church was probably longer originally (Keen 1979, 141), but its relationship to the ramparts of the town, particularly to the north gate, has been overstated (Taylor and Taylor 1965, 637; Hinton 1977, 77). The church is some way from the north rampart and gate, but of far greater significance is the fact that the analysis of St Martin's parish suggests that the church was in existence before the burh was constructed. If this is so, the surviving fabric may be considered as a rebuilding of an earlier church.

Moneyers and Mints

No review of the Dorset mints has been undertaken since the comprehensive survey published in 1872 (Warne 1872, 275-331). Recent work by numismatists, mainly on the coins in Scandinavian cabinets, has added significantly to the evidence available and altered points of detail about moneyers and attributions. While several important articles have been published (Blunt 1974; Dolley 1954, 1955, 1955-7, 1956, 1964) and much information is available in the volumes of the Sylloge of Coins in the British Isles, the results of Mr. W. Lean's recent research are not yet in print (Lean forthcoming). The following summary, which has benefited from Lean's unpublished data, is an interim statement to be superseded by Lean's work.

It is considered possible that some of the earlier kings of Wessex minted coins in Dorset (Symonds 1907, 160), but no mints are named until the reign of Æthelstan (924-39). In Æthelstan's Grately decrees (*E.H.D.*, 384), which Blunt suggests may have originated from an earlier set of laws now lost (Blunt 1974, 41), two moneyers are assigned to both Wareham and Shaftesbury and one 'in the other boroughs': the *Quadripartitus* text gives one moneyer to Dorchester. Warne attributed a coin of the moneyer Torhtelm to Dorchester (1872, 315), but Symonds was of the opinion that no coins of that mint were known (1907, 162). Brooke, however, had attributed five moneyers to Dorchester (1950, 59), but these have now been assigned to Canterbury (Dolley 1964, 31; Blunt 1974, 74).

Blunt's survey of Aethelstan's coinage records that coins of the Wareham mint (mint signature WERHA, PERHA[M]) are of the greatest rarity, but the two moneyers of the Grateley decrees have been identified as Aelfred and Wulfsige (Blunt 1974, 73). The two moneyers assigned to Shaftesbury (SCEFTES, SCEFT) are Aethelwine and Aethelwold (ibid., 70). Although coins of Aethelstan can no longer be attributed to Dorchester, Bridport now emerges as a borough with one moneyer during the reign of Aethelstan. Symonds had questioned Maitland's identification (1897, 503) of Bridian in the Burghal Hidage (911–919) as Little Bredy, since Bridport was a more likely candidate and the existence of a mint there in the reign of Aethelred II was demonstrated by the assigning to Bridport of coins of Aethelred and Cnut, previously assigned to Bridgnorth (Symonds 1922, 38–9). Dolley has since identified Wihtulf as the Bridport moneyer active in the reign of Aethelstan, whose coins have the mint-signature BRIDIAN (Dolley 1964, 31).

No Dorset mints are known for King Edmund (939–46), Eadred (946–55), nor is a Dorset mint-signature found among the coinage of Eadwig (955–59). Coins were struck at Shaftesbury during the reign of Eadgar (959–75), both of the 'Reform' type of c. 973 and of one earlier type (moneyers Byrhtwold and Leofstan). Coins were struck at Wareham after 973 by the moneyer Byrhtric, but since this mint was active in Aethelstan's reign it might have struck in the interval (Dolley and Metcalf 1961, 144–5). Within seven or eight years of the 'Reform' coinage coins from Bridport are known, and it is likely that this mint was striking earlier (ibid., 146). Dorchester has been added to the list by c. 979–85, the period of Aethelred II's 'First Hand' type, but it is likely that it had a mint in operation at an earlier period. Dolley and Metcalf have shown that the geographical distribution of the mints gives a clear picture of the royal monetary policy and claim that a network of mints was a well-conceived plan so that men should be no more than 15 miles from a mint (Dolley and Metcalf 1961, 148–9).

Surviving coins from the reign of Aethelred II (978–1016) are numerous and the list of moneyers long. Shaftesbury (SCEFTE, SEFTSBRI and many variants) has Aegelric, Aelfwine, Aethelgar, Aethelmaer, Aethelric, Aethelwig, Aethestan, Byrhtwold, Goda, Lufa, Saewine and Wulfric. Wareham (WER, WERHAM and variants) has Aelfgar, Aelfsige, Byrhsige, Byrhtric, Oda, and Wulfric. Dorchester (DORES or DOR) has Aelfred and Wulfnoth, while Bridport has Eadnoth, Godric and Wine. All four mints remained in operation during the reign of Cnut and it is interesting to note the same moneyer names, suggesting that the same moneyers remained in work. Dolley has removed to Derby the moneyers Osbern and Osgar, previously entered under Dorchester (1955, 155), but has suggested that since the Dorchester moneyer Swet(a), unrecorded except at Dorchester, appears on two coins with the mint-signature EANBYRI, a new, probably emergency, mint for the reign of Cnut, not very far from Dorchester remains to be identified (ibid., 156). Hill has suggested that this mint perhaps has the same relationship to Dorchester as South Cadbury had to Ilchester, or Cissbury to Chichester (1978, 223).

Two other mints, perhaps emergency mints also, Brygin and Niwan operated during the reign of Aethelred II. The moneyer Aethestan appears on coins from both mints, which are die-linked. Since a reverse die of Æthestan's has been found with the same obverse with the mint-signature CAFT, an unusual abbreviation of Shaftesbury, the mints are probably not far from Shaftesbury (Lyon 1970, 202)*

It is recognised that moneyers may sometimes have operated at more than one mint and Stewart has shown that the evidence for this happening in the West Country is impressive (Stewart 1978, 102). However, for the Dorset mints the only ones which might have had such connections are Dorchester and Wareham, which had the moneyer Blacaman; Dorchester and *Eanbyri* which had Swet(a) in the reign of Cnut; and Dorchester and Bridport which had Hwateman in the reigns of Harthacnut and Edward the Confessor.

In the Domesday Book, two moneyers are recorded for Dorchester in 1066: one for Bridport, two for Wareham, and three for Shaftesbury—all paying one mark of silver and 20s. *quando moneta vertebatur* (Darby and Finn 1967, 118–21). Surviving coins show that Blacaman, Godwine and Hwateman struck at Dorchester during the reign of Edward the Confessor. Hwateman is recorded for Bridport. For Wareham, Biorn and Sideman occur as moneyers. At Shaftesbury, Ælfwerd, Godric, Wydecoc and Wulfric are recorded.

The known history of the four Dorset mints throws light on the history of those towns in which they operated, although the limited evidence for the three emergency mints needs further investigation. If the number of moneyers working is any guide, Shaftesbury emerges as the most important mint throughout the period, followed by Wareham. Dorchester appears to have increased in importance, while Bridport's role seems to have been less significant. The surprise must be that Sherborne appears never to have had a mint. Whether this impression of ranking is reinforced by more detailed discussion of mint output remains to be established. Certainly, it is premature to consider the economic role of the mint centres within their regions until the basic data is available. Similarly, the potential of the study of moneyers' personal names is yet to be undertaken, but the importance of such an exercise is ably demonstrated by the study of moneyers' names for the reign of Edgar (von Feilitzen and Blunt 1971).

*I owe this reference to Mr. Lean.

TABLE VII

Activity of Dorset Mints by Reign

			Aethelstan	Edmund	Eadred	Eadwig	Edgar	Edward the Martyr	Aethelred II	Cnut	Harold I	Harthacnut	Edward the Confessor	Harold II
G	TRE	Shaftesbury	X				X	X	X	X	X	X	X	X
G	TRE	Wareham	X				X		X	X	X	X	X	X
G	TRE	Dorchester	X?						X	X	X	X	X	?
	TRE	Bridport	X						X	X		X	X	X
		Eanbyri								X				
		Brygin							X					
		Niwan							X					

Key: X—coins recorded of mint for reign
G—mint mentioned in Grateley decrees
TRE—mint referred to in Domesday Book

Conclusion

The synthesis attempted in this essay, undertaken at a time when the study and investigation of Anglo-Saxon towns is still in its early stages, may be considered premature. But at this stage the identification of the problems may be more useful than their solution. Inevitably, since this essay has relied heavily on a topographical approach and a presentation of the available documentation, there has not been scope to consider the social, economic and political aspects of the settlements. The brief references to these aspects, which are of course essential to the understanding of urban centres, have been amplified, however, by the results which the essentially topographical approach has produced. We may be no nearer to suggesting when certain places should be called towns, or to understanding why some sites were chosen in preference to others for the construction of burhs. But the most conspicuous fact is that every settlement considered has its own marked individuality.

It is only for Dorchester that a suggestion of continuity of occupation from the Roman period can be made, and this tenuous continuity is in contrast to the more substantial body of evidence for British ecclesiastical settlements at Sherborne, Shaftesbury, Wareham, and possibly also Christchurch. The settlements within their estates, perhaps earlier than the 7th-century evidence available, are potentially of great importance in understanding the later urban centres into which they each developed. Furthermore, the connection between the royal estate of the West Saxon kings and the earlier British estates is still largely unexplored.

The significant presence of the Church at Sherborne, Shaftesbury, Wareham, Christchurch, Wimborne, and to a lesser degree at Lyme and Beaminster, undoubtedly acted as a focus for settlement and so provided a basis for expansion into major centres. Significantly, too, at Dorchester and Gillingham, the development of the settlements are linked directly with royal interest. For all these settlements the evidence suggests that a significant population was already in existence by the early 9th century. Of great interest is the complementary nature of Sherborne and Dorchester, both with evidence for associated field systems which may be of middle Saxon date.

In the 9th century the construction of the burhs must be seen as part only of the process of urban development. Apart from Bridport, where the burh seems to have been placed on a completely unoccupied site, the other burhs were sited over or near existing settlements with defensive properties much in mind: Christchurch, like Bridport, between two rivers; Shaftesbury on a promontory next to the existing settlement; and Wareham placed strategically between two rivers and defended on three sides.

Dorchester appears to have had its walled area made into a burh in the 10th century. It also, with Shaftesbury, Wareham, and Bridport, perhaps had a mint, surely a good indication of importance as a centre. The emergency mints of *Eanbyri,* near Dorchester, and *Brygin* and *Niwan,* near Shaftesbury, were no doubt in well-defended places. Their identification is vital to the understanding of the burhs during the reigns of Aethelred II and Cnut.

Significantly, the burhs and mints of Dorchester, Bridport, Wareham, and Shaftesbury are entered together as 'boroughs' on the first folio of the Domesday Book. Wimborne and Christchurch, with no mints, are recorded as having burgesses, but are not listed as 'boroughs'. With the Domesday Book and all the information it provides, another stage in the investigation of towns is reached. However, by the time the Domesday details were collected it seems clear that all 10 settlements studied in this essay, despite the slightly later references to Sherborne and Shaftesbury being villages, and despite the selection of Dorchester, Bridport, Wareham, and Shaftesbury as 'boroughs', were significantly important centres. If not all of them were then fully urban places, they were soon so to become.

ACKNOWLEDGEMENTS

This essay owes its origin to a seminar on the Anglo-Saxon settlement of Dorset held in Dorchester in May 1976. Now, as then, I owe much to C. E. Bean, Esq., F.S.A., who was aware of the problems long before I was aware that there was a question to attempt to answer. To him particularly I owe much, but especially for many hours discussing Sherborne. I have benefited greatly from the advice and encouragement of J. H. P. Gibb, Esq., F.S.A., and owe to him my involvement with Dorset. For thought-provoking discussions and for information generously given I must thank C. J. S. Green, Esq., on Dorchester; P. Woodward, Esq., on Wimborne; K. Jarvis, Esq., on Christchurch; Katherine Barker on Sherborne; and P. R. White on his excavations at Sherborne Castle. Special gratitude is owed to Bill Lean, who most generously amended the draft text on moneyers and mints; to Julian Munby, who read the text and offered many useful suggestions; to the long-suffering staff of the Dorset County Record Offices, Miss Margaret Holmes, Miss J. Hofmann, and Mrs. P. Smith; and to John Hopkins, librarian of the Society of Antiquaries of London. The editor's patience has been unbounded and to him I am most grateful.

Fig. 83 has been re-drawn from Mrs. C. Wells's original and is published by permission of the Dorset Archaeological Committee.

BIBLIOGRAPHY

ABBREVIATIONS

A.S.C.	*Anglo-Saxon Chronicle, E.H.D.,* 135–235.
Asser	*Asser's Life of King Alfred,* Stevenson, W. H. (ed.), Oxford 1959.
B.L.	British Library.
B.C.S.	Birch, W. d. G., *Cartularium Saxonicum: a collection of Charters relating to Anglo-Saxon History,* 3 vols., London, 1885–93. Index, 1899.
D.C.R.O.	Dorset County Record Office.
Dugdale i	Dugdale, W., *Monasticon Anglicanum,* Caley J., Ellis, H., Bandinel, B. (ed.), 1817.
vi	ditto, 1830.
E.H.D.	Whitelock, D. (ed.), *English Historical Documents c. 500–1042,* London, 1955.
Gesta Pont.	Willelmi Malmesbiriensis, *De gestis Pontificum Anglorum,* Hamilton, N.E.S.A., (ed.), Rolls Series 52, 1870.
Itinerary	*Leland's Itinerary in England and Wales,* Smith, L. T. (ed), 5 vols., reprint Centaur press 1964.
K	Kemble, J. M. (ed.), *Codex Diplomaticus Aevi Saxonici,* 6 vols., 1839–48.
P.D.N.H.A.S.	*Proceedings of the Dorset Natural History and Archaeological Society.*
R.C.H.M.	Royal Commission on Historical Monuments (England).
S.D.N.Q.	*Somerset and Dorset Notes and Queries.*
V.C.H.	*Victoria County History.*

Bailey, J. (1976), 'Excavations in the Glebe, Bridport', *P.D.N.H.A.S.* 97, 63.
Baring Gould, S. and Fisher, J. (1913), *The Lives of the British Saints,* iv.
Barker, K. (1977), 'The Origins of Sherborne: a preliminary note', *P.D.N.H.A.S.* 99, 127–8.
Barker, K. (1980), 'The early Christian topography of Sherborne', *Antiquity* 54, 229-31.

Bartelot, R. G. (1915), *The History of Fordington*, Dorchester.

Bateson, M. (1899), 'Origins and early history of double monasteries', *Transactions of the Royal Historical Society* n.s. 13, 137–98.

Bean, C. E. (1951), in Farrar, R. A. H., 'Archaeological fieldwork in Dorset in 1951', *P.D.N.H.A.S.* 73, 85–115.

Bean, C. E. (1955), in Farrar, R. A. H., 'Archaeological fieldwork in Dorset in 1955', *P.D.N.H.A.S.* 77, 123–54.

Biddle, M. (1974), 'The development of the Anglo-Saxon town', *Topografia urbana e vita cittadina sull'alto medioevo in occidente*, (Settimane di studio del Centro italiano di studi sull'alto medioevo, 21), Spoleto, 203–312.

Biddle, M. (1976), 'Towns', in Wilson, D. M. (ed.), *The Archaeology of Anglo-Saxon England*, London, 99–150.

Biddle, M. (ed.) (1976), *Winchester in the Early Middle Ages*. (Winchester Studies 1.)

Biddle, M. and Hill, D. H. (1971), 'Late Saxon planned towns', *Antiquaries Journal* 51, 70-85.

Bloch, M. (1962), *Les Caractères Originaux de l'Histoire Rurale Française*, Oslo 1931 edn., Paris.

Blunt, C. E. (1974), 'The coinage of Athelstan, 924–939, a survey', *British Numismatic Journal* 42, 35–158.

Bowen, E. G. (1954), *The Settlements of the Celtic Saints in Wales*, Cardiff.

Brooke, G. C. (1950), *English Coins*, 3rd edn.

Brooks, N. P. (1971), 'The development of military obligations in eighth- and ninth-century England', in Clemoes, P. and Hughes, K. (eds.) 1971, 69-84.

Brooks, N. P. (1979), 'England in the ninth century: the crucible of defeat', *Transactions of the Royal Historical Society*, 5th ser. 29, 1–20.

Campbell, J. (1979), 'The church in Anglo-Saxon towns', in Baker, D. (ed.), *The Church in Town and Countryside*, (Studies in Church History, 16), Oxford, 119-35.

Carpenter, R. H. (1876–77), 'On the Benedictine abbey of St Mary, Sherborne, with notes on the Restoration of its Church', *Transactions of the Institute of British Architects*, London, 137–51.

Clemoes, P. and Hughes, K. (eds.) (1971), *England before the Conquest. Studies in primary sources presented to Dorothy Whitelock*, Cambridge.

Cramp, R. J. (1976), 'Monastic sites', in Wilson, D. M. (ed.), *The Archaeology of Anglo-Saxon England*, 201–252.

Darby, H. C. and Finn, R. W. (eds.) (1967), *The Domesday Geography of South-West England*, Cambridge.

Dolley, R. H. M. (1954), 'A note on the mint at Wareham under Cnut', *P.D.N.H.A.S.* 76, 56–7.

Dolley, R. H. M. (1955), 'An important unpublished coin of the Dorchester mint', *P.D.N.H.A.S.* 77, 155-6.

Dolley, R. H. M. (1955-7), 'An alleged *Agnus Dei* penny of the Wareham mint', *British Numismatic Journal* 28, 412–4.

Dolley, R. H. M. (1956), 'The Shaftesbury hoard of pence of Æthelred II', *Numismatic Journal* 6th ser. 16, 267-80.

Dolley, R. H. M. (1964), 'A probable fourth Kentish mint of Æthelstan', *British Numismatic Journal* 33, 30–33.

Dolley, R. H. M. and Metcalf, D. M. (1961), 'The reform of the English coinage under Eadgar', in Dolley, R. H. M. (ed.), *Anglo-Saxon Coins*.

Douglas, D. C. and Greenaway, G. W. (eds.) (1953), *English Historical Documents 1042-1189*, Oxford.

Drew, C. D. (1952), 'The Forests of Blackmoor and Gillingham', in Roscoe, E. H. (ed.), *The Marn'll Book—Some particular history, some general topography, a number of photographs, and some maps, of the Blackmore Vale*, Gillingham.

Ennen, E. (1979), *The Medieval Town*, Europe in the Middle Ages Selected Studies No. 15, Translation of *Die europäische Stadt des Mittelalters*, Göttingen, 1972.

Farrar, R. A. H. (1952), 'Archaeological fieldwork in Dorset in 1952', *P.D.N.H.A.S.* 74, 85–110.

Farrar, R. A. H. (1962), 'Some Roman *tessarae* under the nave of Wimborne Minster', *P.D.N.H.A.S.* 84, 106–9.

Finberg, H. P. R. (1964), *Lucerna: Studies of some problems in the Early History of England*, London.

Fowler, J. (1951), *Medieval Sherborne*, Dorchester.

Fox, H. S. A. (1970), 'The boundary of Uplyme', *Transactions of the Devonshire Association* 102, 35–47.

Gallyon, M. (1980), *The Early Church in Wessex and Mercia*.

Gem, R. D. H. (1975), 'Documentary evidence of the early history of the buildings of Sherborne Cathedral: 705 to 1122', *Archaeological Journal* 132, 105–110.

Gem, R. D. H. (1976), 'The Early Church in the Diocese of Sherborne', (lecture given at Dorchester, 1 May 1976).

Gibb, J. H. P. (1975), 'The Anglo-Saxon Cathedral of Sherborne', *Archaeological Journal* 132, 71–105.

Godfrey, J. (1976), 'The place of the double monastery in the Anglo-Saxon minster system', in Bonner, G. (ed.), *Famulus Christi. Essays in Commemoration of the Thirteenth Centenary of the Birth of the Venerable Bede*, London, 344–9.

Green, C. J. S. (1977), 'Poundbury. A Summary of Excavations at Poundbury, Dorchester, Dorset, carried out between 1966 and 1976', typescript, Dorchester.

Green, C. J. S. (1979), 'Poundbury. A Summary of Recent Excavations at Poundbury, Dorchester', typescript, Dorchester.

Greenaway, G. (1980), 'Saint Boniface as a man of letters', in Reuter, T. (ed.), *The Greatest Englishman: Essays on St Boniface and the Church at Crediton*, 33–46.

Grierson, P. (1958), *Fitzwilliam Museum, Cambridge*, pt. 1, Sylloge of Coins of the British Isles.

Grundy, G. B. (1930), 'The Saxon charters of Somerset', *Proceedings of the Somerset Archaeological and Natural History Society*, 76, Appendix, pt. iii, 97-128.

Grundy, G. B. (1933), 'Dorset charters', *P.D.N.H.A.S.* 55, 239-68.

Grundy, G. B. (1934), 'Dorset charters', *P.D.N.H.A.S.* 56, 110-30.

Grundy, G. B. (1938), 'Saxon charters of Dorset', *P.D.N.H.A.S.* 60, 75-89.

Grundy, G. B. (1939), 'The ancient highways of Somerset', *Archaeological Journal* 96, 226-97.

Gunstone, A. J. H. (1977), *Ancient British, Anglo-Saxon and Norman Coins in West Country Museums*, Sylloge of Coins of the British Isles, 24.

Haase, C. (1965), *Die Entstehung der westfälischen Städte*, Münster.

Haddan, A. W. and Stubbs, W. (1871), *Councils and Ecclesiastical Documents*, iii, Oxford.

Hardy, T. (1929), *The Life and Death of the Mayor of Casterbridge. A Story of a man of character*, London.

Harmer, F. E. (1952), *Anglo-Saxon Writs*, Manchester.

Harrison, B. P. and Williams, D. F. (1979), 'Sherborne old castle, Dorset: medieval pottery fabrics', *P.D.N.H.A.S.* 101, 91–102.

Harvey, P. (1965), 'An Elizabethan map of manors in north Dorset', *British Museum Quarterly* 29, Nos. 3–4, 82–4.

Hart, C. (1965), 'Some Dorset Charter Boundaries', *P.D.N.H.A.S.* 86, 158–63.

Hase, P. H. (1975), 'The development of the parish in Hampshire, particularly in the eleventh and twelfth centuries', Ph.D. Thesis, University of Cambridge.

Herbert, J. A. (1920), 'Introduction', *The Sherborne Missal*, Roxburghe Club, Oxford.

Hill, D. H. (1969), 'The Burghal Hidage: the establishment of a text', *Medieval Archaeology* 13, 84-92.

Hill, D. H. (1978), 'Trends in the development of towns during the reign of Ethelred II', in Hill, D. H. (ed.), *Ethelred the Unready*, B.A.R. 59, 213-25.

Hinton, D. A. (1974), *A Catalogue of the Anglo-Saxon Ornamental Metalwork 700–1100 in the Department of Antiquities, Ashmolean Museum*, Oxford.

Hinton, D. A. (1975), 'Late Anglo-Saxon metal-work: an assessment', *Anglo-Saxon England* 4, 171–80.

Hinton, D. A. (1977), *Alfred's Kingdom. Wessex and the South 800-1550*, London.

Hinton, D. A. and Hodges, R. (1977), 'Excavations in Wareham, 1974-5', *P.D.N.H.A.S.* 99, 42-83.

Hubert, J. (1959), 'Evolution de la topographie et de l'aspect des villes de Gaule du 5e au 10e siècles', in *La Citta nell'alto medioevo*, Settimane di studio del Centro italiano di studi sull'alto medioevo 6, Spoleto, 529-58.

Hutchins, J. (1861-70), *The History and Antiquities of the County of Dorset*, 3rd edn., Shipp, W. and Hodson, J. W. (eds.) i (1861), ii (1863), iii (1868), iv (1870).

Jarvis, K. (1980), 'An Anglo-Saxon cemetery at Bargates, Christchurch, Dorset', in Rahtz, P., Dickinson, T. and Watts, L. (ed.), *Anglo-Saxon Cemeteries 1979, The Fourth Anglo-Saxon Symposium at Oxford*, B.A.R., 82, 307-9.

Jarvis, K. (1983), 'A review of the Anglo-Saxon *Burh* and Medieval Town of Christchurch', in Jarvis, K. (ed.), *Excavations in Christchurch 1969-1980*, Dorset Natural History and Archaeological Society, Monograph Series 5, Dorchester, 7-21.

Jesson, M. (1971), 'Saxon *Sceattas* of Southampton', unpublished B.A. dissertation, University of Southampton.

John, E. (1964), *Land Tenure in Early England*, Leicester.

John, E. (1970), 'The social and political problems of the early English church', in Thirsk, J. (ed.), *Historical Review* 18, supplement, 39-63.

Keen, L. (1975), ' "*Illa Mercimonia que dicitur Hamwih*": A study in early medieval urban development', *Archaeologia Atlantica* 1, 2, 165-90.

Keen, L. (1976), 'Dorset archaeology in 1976', *P.D.N.H.A.S.* 98, 54-62.

Keen, L. (1977), 'Late Saxon pottery from St Peter's church, Shaftesbury', *P.D.N.H.A.S.* 99, 129-31.

Keen, L. (1979), 'Dorset archaeology in 1979', *P.D.N.H.A.S.* 101, 133-43.

Lapridge, M. and Herren, M. (1979), *Aldhelm. The Prose Works*.

Leech, R. H. (1977), 'Romano-British rural settlement in south Somerset and north Devon', unpublished Ph.D. Thesis, University of Bristol.

Lennard, R. (1959), *Rural England 1086-1135, A Study of Social and Agrarian Conditions*, Oxford.

Lean, W. (forthcoming), *The Anglo-Saxon and Norman Mints of Dorset*, B.A.R.

Lyon, S. (1970), 'Historical problems of Anglo-Saxon coinage—(4) The Viking Age', *British Numismatic Journal* 39, 193-204.

Maitland, F. W. (1897), *Domesday Book and Beyond* (reprinted 1960).

Mayo, C. H. (1908), *The Municipal Records of the Borough of Dorchester, Dorset*, Exeter.

Mills, A. D. (1977), *The Place-names of Dorset*, part 1, (English Place-Name Society 52).

Mills, A. D. (1980), *The Place-names of Dorset*, part 2, (English Place-Name Society 53).

Nelson, J. (1979), 'Charles the Bald and the church in town and countryside', in Baker, D. (ed.), *The Church in Town and Countryside*, Studies in Church History 16, 103-18.

Nevill, E. R. (1911-12), 'Tenants of Sherborne, 1377', *S.D.N.Q.* 12, 341-6.

Nevill, E. R. (1913-14), 'Tenants of Sherborne, 1377', *S.D.N.Q.* 13, 171-6.

Niermeyer, J. F. (1976), *Mediae Latinitatis Lexicon Minus*, Leiden.

O'Donovan, M. A. (1972), 'Studies in the history of the diocese of Sherborne', unpublished Ph.D. thesis, University of Cambridge.

Padel, O. J. (1976-77), 'Cornish names of parish churches', *Cornish Studies* 4-5, 15-27.

Parker, J. H. and J. (1859), *Some Account of Domestic Architecture in England, from Richard II to Henry VIII*, 3, part ii.

Penn, K. J. (1980), *Historic Towns in Dorset*, Dorset Natural History and Archaeological Society, Monograph Series 1, Dorchester.

Petrie, H. (1848), *Monumenta historica britannica*, i.

Radford, C. A. R. (1970), 'The later pre-Conquest boroughs and their defences', *Medieval Archaeology* 14, 83-103.

Radford, C. A. R. (1978), 'The pre-Conquest boroughs of England, ninth to eleventh centuries', *Proceedings of the British Academy* 64, 131-53.

Reynolds, S. (1977), *An Introduction to the History of English Medieval Towns*, Oxford.

Rigold, S. E. and Metcalf, D. M. (1977), 'A check-list of English finds of *sceattas*', *British Numismatic Journal* 47, 31-52.

Robertson, A. J. (1959), *Anglo-Saxon Charters*, 2nd edn., Cambridge.

Rollason, D. W. (1978), 'List of saints' resting-places in Anglo-Saxon England', *Anglo-Saxon England* 7, 61-93.

Royal Commission on Historical Monuments (1952), *An Inventory of the Historical Monuments in Dorset*, i *West Dorset*; (1970), ii *South-east Dorset*; (1972), iv *North Dorset*; (1975), v *East Dorset*.

Royal Commission on Historical Monuments (1959), 'Wareham west walls', *Medieval Archaeology* 3, 120-38.

Rumble, A. R. (1977), 'Saxon Southampton', *Medieval Archaeology* 21, 186-88.

Short, E. B. (1976), 'The bounds of Bridport', *P.D.N.H.A.S.* 97, 62–3.

Smith, C. T. (1978), *An Historical Geography of Western Europe before 1800.*

Stenton, D. M. (ed.) (1970), *Essays preparatory to Anglo-Saxon England*, Oxford.

Stewart, I. (1978), 'The Sussex mints and their moneyers', in Brandon, P. (ed.), *The South Saxons*, 89–137.

Symonds, H. (1907), 'Coins struck in Dorset during the Saxon, Norman and Stuart periods', *P.D.N.H.A.S.* 28, 159–67.

Symonds, H. (1922), *Numismatic Chronicle*, 5th ser. ii, 144–5.

Tait, J. (1936), *The Medieval English Borough.*

Talbot, C. H. (1954), *The Anglo-Saxon Missionaries in Germany.*

Taylor, C. (1970), *Dorset*, (The Making of the English Landscape).

Taylor, H. M. and J. (1965), *Anglo-Saxon Architecture.*

Thomas, C. (1967), *Christian Antiquities of Camborne*, St Austell.

Thomas, C. (1981), *Christianity in Roman Britain to A.D. 500*, London.

Tysacke, S. and Huddy, J. (1980), *Christopher Saxton and Tudor map-making*, British Library Series, No. 2.

von Feilitzen, O. and Blunt, C. (1971), 'Personal names on the coinage of Edgar', in Clemoes, P. and Hughes, K. 1971, 183-214.

Wainwright, G. F. (1979), *Mount Pleasant, Dorset: Excavations 1970–71*, Society of Antiquaries Research Report 37.

Warne, C. (1871), *Ancient Dorset, The Celtic, Roman, Saxon, and Danish antiquities of the County, including the early coinage*, Bournemouth.

Watkin, Æ. (1956), *The Great Chartulary of Glastonbury*, iii, Somerset Record Society 64.

Wells, C. R. (1981), 'The Archaeological Implications of the Dorchester By-Pass', Dorset Archaeological Committee, typescript.

Wheeler, R. E. M. (1943), *Maiden Castle, Dorset*, Society of Antiquaries Research Report 12.

Chapter Eight

THE TOWNS OF DEVON

By Jeremy Haslam

Introduction

THERE ARE FOUR PLACES IN DEVON which are generally accepted as being towns in the pre-Conquest period, namely Exeter, Barnstaple, Lydford, and Totnes. Exeter, considered elsewhere in this book, was by far the largest urban place in the south-west peninsula by the time of Domesday Book, and is not discussed further in this chapter. The other three are described in Domesday Book as *burgi* having burgesses, were witan centres in *c.* 1018 (Tait 1936, 42), and were mints in the 10th century. Only Lydford is mentioned in the Burghal Hidage of *c.* 919 (Hill 1969).[1]

It is probable, however, that these places, which owe their origin to specific historical causes in the late 9th or early 10th centuries, were by the time of the Norman Conquest not the only urban places in the county, despite the silence of Domesday Book. It is still often taken for granted that, since references in Domesday Book are in their own way a useful and fortunately early general survey of existing boroughs, they represent a complete list of towns existing in *c.* 1086. For Devon, the Domesday references to boroughs have always been regarded as being exclusive (e.g., Finberg 1947, 129; Hoskins 1954, 104–5), and the assumption that there were only five urban places (including Okehampton) in the county at that time has never been questioned. Yet Darby has pointed out, with regard to towns in general, that the information in Domesday 'is as unsystematic as it is incomplete' (1977, 289). There are therefore good reasons for enquiring whether there is any independent evidence which can be used to indicate the presence of other early urban centres, without being too concerned as to whether they are or are not described as such in Domesday Book.

With these reservations in mind, it will be argued in detail below that Plympton and Kingsbridge, and possibly also Kingsteignton, were (with Barnstaple and Totnes) new burhs of Edward the Elder, set up in all probability as both fortresses and urban places in the first decade of the 10th century. Plympton, as well as Okehampton, have hitherto been considered as being entirely new urban creations around a Norman castle (Hoskins 1954, 447; Beresford 1967, 425–6), and Kingsbridge has not even been considered to have existed before the early 13th century (Beresford 1967, 422). The general view of the creation of a new town on a new site, espoused, for instance, by Professors Beresford, Hoskins and Finberg, presupposes the assumption that there was no earlier settlement in the same locality or on the same site, with any urban characteristics. It is engendered by a reliance on the further premise that the granting of a market or borough charter marks, or is the prelude to, the beginnings of a place as an urban community. In some cases this may be so, but this view by its nature

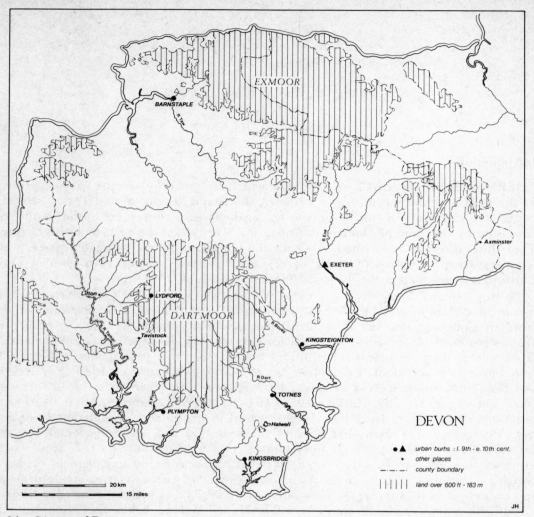

84. County of Devon

excludes the possibility of a more gradual development of proto-urban or urban characteristics in certain places, which may be suggested by other evidence (topographical, geographical, or historical), or by the application of models attempting to describe and explain general historical developments.[2]

A further case besides Plympton, Kingsbridge and Kingsteignton where these arguments have been applied is Tavistock. The town there is suggested to have developed around a monastery founded probably in the 970s. Finberg's discussion of its origin and growth (1947, 131) assumes both that the town was founded at one point in time by the monastery, and that this is a post-Conquest phenomenon, probably connected with the grant of a market in *c.* 1105 (*ibid.,* Finberg 1950–51, 204). He thus gives no consideration to the possibility that it could in fact be pre-Conquest. The 'rural economy' of the abbot's demesne is thus contrasted sharply with the specifically urban economy of the town from the 12th century onwards. This assumption—or series of assumptions—should in the writer's view be examined very critically.[3]

There are other places which, as royal centres from an early date, as heads of hundreds and with minster churches, might well have shown proto-urban characteristics in the same way and for the same reasons as have been discussed in more detail in the chapters in this volume covering Wiltshire and Berkshire. The study of these places in Devon has hardly begun, but amongst them might be included Axminster, Plympton, Tavistock, Kingsteignton, and Lifton. Plympton and Kingsteignton are discussed in more detail below. Axminster is particularly interesting as it was sited very near the junctions of three Roman roads, one of which bridges a river near the town. It was the centre of a hundred which was ancient royal demesne, and was also the site of a minster church and a princely burial place in 757 (Whitelock 1979, 176). It seems likely, therefore, that its borough charter of *c.* 1209 (Finberg 1950–51, 205) marks the culmination rather than the beginning of a long process of proto-urban and urban development which must have begun well before the Norman Conquest. Tavistock could also be put forward as an example of these developments. It was the head place of its hundred, very probably being the site of an early minster church (Radford 1975, 7) and *villa regalis,* and was the centre of routeways (Finberg 1947, 130). It is thus likely to have developed proto-urban if not truly urban characteristics at an early date, its charter of 1105 merely reflecting a status acquired as a result of a long process of urban growth, which was probably not so much initiated but rather actively encouraged by the abbey from the later 10th century onwards. There is clearly a considerable need for a more detailed examination than has been attempted here both of the possibility of early proto-urban development at other similar sites, and of their relationship to Roman and later pre-Saxon developments.

Barnstaple

The town of Barnstaple cannot be considered without studying its topographical and historical relationship to Pilton (Fig. 85). This has been discussed in detail by H. and T. Miles (1975), though there are some aspects of the topography of the areas which require further analysis. Miles and Miles argue (*ibid.*) against the identification of the Burghal Hidage fortress of *Pilletune* with a fortress either at the present Pilton itself or at the nearby hill-fort of Burridge (or Roborough) camp, and see the fortified site of Barnstaple as the original Alfredian fortress. Arguments against this, and in support of the more traditional view of the secondary origin of Barnstaple (Tait 1936, 18, n. 7) are, however, set out below.

These arguments are certainly not contradicted by the relationship between the parishes of Barnstaple and Pilton. The former is very much the smaller of the two, and appears to have been divided off from a larger unit comprising both parishes. This would support Miles's view (1975, 269–70) that Pilton was originally the

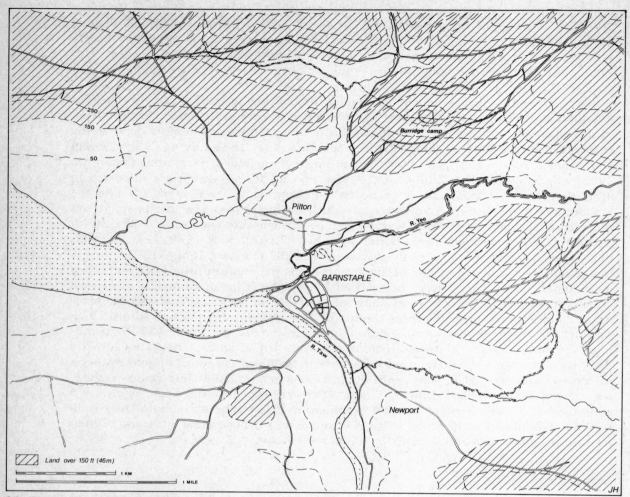

85. Barnstaple and Pilton parishes

primary (village) settlement, with Barnstaple being added to it (at whatever date) as a new settlement.

That the latter was a new urban foundation is shown both by its siting and by the details of its topography, as well as by its name.[4] Its site has clearly been chosen with a view to its defensive potential, its accessibility to both land and water transport and, not least, its position as probably the lowest possible crossing-point on the Taw estuary. Its defences utilise a low spur of dry land (roughly defined by the 25ft. [7.6m.] contour) which is surrounded on two sides by the tidal Rivers Yeo and Taw. The valley of the sharply meandering River Yeo would in the Saxon and medieval periods have been a wide tidal marsh (Miles and Miles 1975, 276).

The position of the defences is clearly shown in the surviving pattern of street and property boundary lines (Fig. 86). The core of the town is surrounded by two concentric streets, Boutport Street and Green Lane, both of which enclose the church and the main street of the town. The name Boutport derives from *Butan-port,* 'outside the town' (P-N.D. 1969, 26): on the supposition that Green Lane marks the line of an original intra-mural or wall street, the defences are likely to have occupied the strip between this lane on the inside and a nearly continuous line running in between and parallel to both streets, and formed by the rear boundaries of properties fronting on to Boutport Street. The core formed by these boundaries is consistently between 30m. and 35m. in width, and allows for defences consisting of a bank with probably multiple exterior ditches. The line of the defences runs between, and probably includes, both ends of the main street, where there were probably gates. It is uncertain whether the defences continued south-westwards along the bank of the River Yeo beyond the northern gate, though this is not improbable. It is unlikely that there would have been defences on the south-western side of the town, its location on the bank of the Taw estuary rather suggesting that it was a trading shore where boats could be either beached or moored. Subsequent alterations and additions to this area, in particular the building of the Norman castle on the western end of the town, and more recently the construction of the railway as well as the road (North Parade) along it, have altered its original topography beyond recognition. It is, however, reasonable to suggest that the defences of the town were laid out so as to include the maximum length of this shore line which was kept free for commercial use.[5]

There are various reasons for suggesting that there was also a gate in the centre of the defences. The excavation by the writer of an area on the eastern side of Joy Street in 1973 located part of the surface of this street,[6] which consisted of small stones and gravel, smoothed on their upper surfaces, laid on to the natural subsoil. The edge of the street was defined by the frontages of the earliest structures on the site. If, as seems likely, this was the laid surface of the original street, it must have formed part of the primary lay-out of the town. This being so, its position both midway between the two gates at the ends of the High Street and opposite the access point of the straight road approaching the town from the east, would suggest the existence here of an original gateway.

It has also been suggested as a result of recent excavations (Miles 1977, 9)[7] that Paiges Lane is only a more recent addition of the 15th century, a conclusion which could by inference be extended to Tuly Street to its west. The same excavations have shown the presence of properties laid out in the pre-Conquest period, defined by boundary ditches at right-angles to Holland Street. This suggests an early origin for the street itself, which is therefore a probable element in the earliest lay-out of the town. The original lay-out of the Saxon burh thus seems likely to have consisted of a single main spinal street with various streets or lanes at right-angles to it,[8] the most important being Joy Street and Holland Street. All of these streets would have been connected at their extremities by an intra-mural or wall street. The main properties must have been those fronting on to the High Street, with probably smaller ones laid out to front on to the subsidiary side streets. The excavations at Joy Street showed that what must have been the original property boundaries remained unchanged until recent times. The regular boundaries of properties fronting on to the High Street,

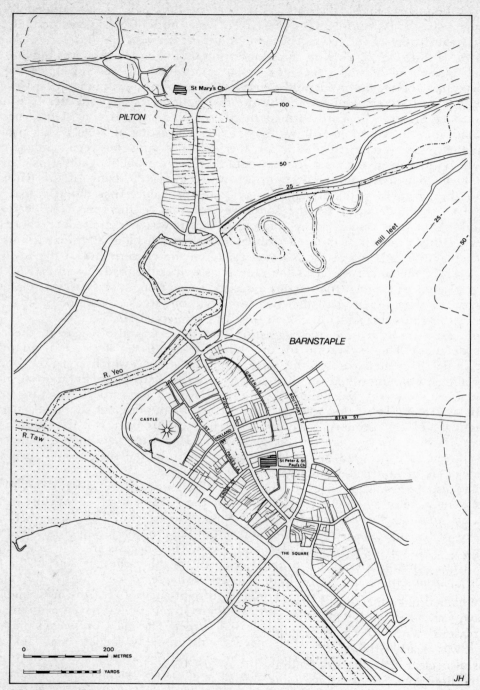

86. Barnstaple

which can still be recognised along most of its length, must also, therefore, reflect the original lay-out. This plan is identical in its essentials to those of Totnes and probably Plympton and Kingsbridge (discussed below), as well as to other burhs in southern England suggested (below) as being of early 10th-century date.

There is some evidence to suggest that the church of St Mary Magdalen, founded in all likelihood as the church of the burh in the early 10th century, is not now in its original position. Shortly after the Norman Conquest the existing minster church was 'refounded' as a priory of the monastery of St Martin of Paris (Radford 1975, 8). At this time the priory was described as being 'outside' the castle, being moved to its present site at a later date (*ibid.*, n. 30), presumably at some stage in the growth of the castle. Archaeological evidence of this seems to be provided by the excavation in 1973 by T. Miles of a cemetery sealed underneath the bank of the castle bailey (*see* Fig. 95). It seems likely that this was part of the cemetery of the original pre-Conquest minster church, and that the church itself lay to the south-west of this (nearer the motte of the Norman castle) under what is now the Castle Green, occupying an area distinct from the commercial area fronting the High Street.

The immediately extra-mural parts of the town are also of some importance in a discussion of its origin and early development. If it is considered that a bridge was built at the same time as the burh, its position outside the defended *enceinte* might at first sight appear anomalous. It is placed, however, at the point on the river which combines both proximity to the town and the shortest distance to the higher ground on the south side of the river (see Fig. 85), a position which also, perhaps most importantly, leaves free on its downstream side the whole length of trading shore within the town. The presence of a chapel dedicated to St Thomas à Becket on its northern end suggests that the bridge is at least as early as the later 12th century,[9] and there is no reason why its origin should not in fact be contemporary with the burh itself, to function with the defended burh as a defence of the river against inland penetration by Viking ships, and to provide access from the south and south-west to the new trading centre on the north bank.

There are several other topographical features whose origin can possibly be placed within the early years of the town's development. To the north of the town, the north gate is joined by a long causeway associated with a bridge over the tidal River Yeo leading to the higher ground around the village of Pilton to the north. Miles and Miles (1975, 268) see this causeway as being only a secondary element in the Barnstaple–Pilton geographical relationship, and suggest an origin in the medieval period.[10] However, as Fig. 85 shows, all the routeways to Barnstaple from the north-west, north and north-east converge at Pilton (whose earlier existence has already been postulated above) before leading to Barnstaple along this causeway and bridge. Since it seems somewhat unlikely that the early trading centre at Barnstaple would have remained unconnected to these routeways, this causeway is, like the bridge over the Taw, very likely to be as early as the burh itself, and constructed for precisely the same reasons. Without it there would have been little point in having the north gate where it was clearly situated.[11]

It is also clear that the intra-mural area of the town has been bypassed at some time by Boutport Street which joins the southern end of this causeway over the Yeo to the northern end of the Taw bridge. It is, furthermore, connected with an open area outside (east of) the east gate and immediately north of the Taw bridge, which must at an early stage have been a large market area. This is also approached from the south-east by what must have been an important routeway.[12] The lack of any concrete evidence makes it difficult to determine the date of development of this complex of features. However, the pattern of property boundaries to the east of Boutport Street already discussed suggest that these, with Boutport Street itself, were fixed while the early line of the defences was still visible. The relationship of this street to the Taw and Yeo crossings, which it is suggested were built with the burh, and the early, possibly pre-Conquest, origin of its name (P-N.D. 1969, 26) all suggest at least the possibility that both Boutport Street and the extra-mural market area were both of pre-Conquest origin, developing in response to the early success of Barnstaple as a town and port. The postulation of the pre-Conquest origin of this market area seems to be strengthened furthermore by the reference in the Domesday account to nine 'burgesses outside the borough'. As in the case of extra-mural burgesses at various other towns recorded in Domesday Book, these may merely have been working on the borough lands (Stephenson 1930, 179–80; 1933, 78–81; Tait 1936, 68–77, 83–4), but in view of the topographical evidence already discussed, as well as of the importance of Barnstaple as a coastal port, it seems more probable that they were rather the inhabitants of the area around the extra-mural market area. It is furthermore possible to see parallels to Boutport Street in the *twicene* or lanes at Winchester running around the outside of the defences, for which a pre-Conquest origin seems very likely (Biddle [ed.] 1976, 274, 303). These lanes were separated by a rectangular distance of about 45m. from the front of the wall (*ibid.*, 274), a figure remarkably similar to the equivalent space at Barnstaple.[13] As at Winchester, this space at Barnstaple could have been royal land in the same sense as the defences and streets of the town (*ibid.*, 275).

The existence of the extra-mural market area provides a parallel to one outside the west gate at Totnes (discussed below), as well as providing yet one more example of a general phenomenon shown by the larger burhs in Midland England (Haslam 1980; Haslam forthcoming). Its presence, however, does raise questions about the developing role of the burh in the royal control of trading activities during the 10th century. On a purely physical level its growth can be seen either as an organic and uncontrolled development in response to the unsuitablility of the narrow streets of the burh as market areas for rural produce such as livestock;[14] or else conceivably as an original element in the lay-out of the burh itself, provided as a space (still presumably under royal control) in which these very needs could be met,[15] thus leaving the defended area free for controlled settlement, for craft and industrial activities, and as a defended river port.

Lydford

The choice of the site of the fortress was clearly governed by the defensive potential of the marked interfluvial spur of land, which is defined on all sides except the north-west by precipitous gorges (Fig. 88). Its early topography has been considerably clarified by a series of excavations by P. Addyman,[16] from which it appears that the defences of the fortress followed the edge of the spur on all sides, except where they completed the enclosure over the crest of the promontory to the north-west. The original internal lay-out of what is inferred as being a new urban foundation of King Alfred (see below) took the form of side streets or paths and burgage plots laid out at right-angles to the single spinal street. As Biddle has pointed out (1976b, 131) the surviving pathways behind (south-west of) the cross-promontory rampart to the north-west are probably the remnants of an original intra-mural or wall street, though there is no evidence for its continuation around the inside of the rest of the defences. His further suggestion that an original back street, similar to those at Winchester, can be recognised to the north of the main street is less convincing.

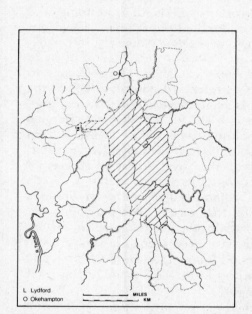

87. Lydford parish and adjacent parishes   88. Lydford

It is clear that this street, whose alignment is in any case governed by the position of the Norman castle, carries on out of the burh to the north through the corner of the defences, which cannot have been an original gateway. Its course thus suggests a comparatively recent origin.

The plan of Lydford is similar to those other places defined by Biddle (1976b, 126) as promontory burhs, in particular Shaftesbury and Malmesbury.[17] In many respects, however, the structure of the defences at Lydford offers a close parallel to those of Cricklade (Wilts.), described elsewhere in this volume. In particular the multiple ditch system at Cricklade is reflected in the arrangement of the two (?) external ditches outside the north-east defences of Lydford (Biddle 1976b, 129 and n. 243) (though precise details of this are unfortunately not available) which must have occupied the space, about 50m. in width, between the gateway and the V-shaped division of the main street outside the defences. Similarly, stone walls were added to the front of the earth banks of both burhs, probably in the late 10th or early 11th centuries, replacing presumed earlier timber revetments. As with the more certain case of Cricklade, it is also possible that this wall has been deliberately slighted, possibly in the early 11th century by Cnut.[18]

The size of Lydford, together with the archaeological evidence for an early and regular lay-out of property boundaries and streets, all suggest that it was set up as a fortress which was probably from the beginning intended to be an urban place. It is not, however, sited on any pre-existing routeways, nor could it have had a very productive hinterland. One function it may well have had, which will be discussed further below, would have been as a market centre for tin from Dartmoor, and as a place set up by royal initiative to control both its production, refining and distribution. This would provide a context for the undoubted importance of Lydford as a Stannary town from the later 12th century onwards (Finberg 1949, 157; Saunders 1980, 127–133).

The origins of the burh at Lydford has posed some problems. The reference to *Hlidan* in the Burghal Hidage is generally thought to refer to Lydford, although the late date of any name-form resembling the modern name (*Lydanford* or *Hlidaforda*, 979–1016: P-N.D. 191) has suggested to Hill (1969, 90 n. 17) that the Burghal Hidage entry refers to a fortress near the neighbouring royal vill of Lifton. Lifton itself lay on a Roman road, and was the head of its hundred. It included the enormous parish of Lydford which covers most if not all of the royal forest of Dartmoor (Fig. 87). It was the site of a witan in 931, and its church is very probably of Saxon origin. It seems clear, therefore, that it was the administrative centre of the area in the time of Alfred and the site presumably of a *villa regalis*. The possibility has furthermore been suggested that a nearby small earthwork to the east of Lifton, between the Rivers Lyd/Lew and Thrushnell, could have been a small fortress created or re-used as a burh by Alfred, comparable in type and function to those at Pilton and Halwell. It has also been suggested that the regularities in the lay-out of Lifton itself are the result of rectilinear planning as an urban place.[19]

There are, however, difficulties with both of the last two suggestions. In the first place, although the fortress to the east of Lifton commands good views in almost every direction, as well as being placed near the end of a ridgeway road approaching from the east (now the modern A 30), it is only a few metres across and would seem far too small to act as a centrally-placed gathering point for the *fyrd* for the whole of central Devon. There is anyway some doubt in the writer's mind that the surviving remains represent an embanked fortress—as was clearly the case with the fortress at Halwell. Secondly, the suggestion that the plan of Lifton reflects a lay-out associated with an episode of urban planning does not fit the evidence on the ground: although the church is built on the end of a narrow spur, the main part of the present village is situated in a shallow valley overlooked, especially on the north, by steep slopes. It is therefore quite unsuitable as the site of any fortress, let alone a relatively large fortified town.

It must be concluded, therefore, that for lack of any evidence of suitable fortifications at Lifton (whether urban or non-urban) which could be attributed to the time of Alfred, that Lydford itself is the Alfredian burh. This conclusion would be quite in accordance, firstly with the not infrequent siting of an Alfredian fortress near to but not at the estate centre or *villa regalis*,[20] and, secondly, with the topography and siting of Lydford itself, in both aspects of which it bears a remarkable resemblance to the urban fortresses at Malmesbury and at Shaftesbury.

Totnes

The origins and early development of Totnes are clearly shown both in its siting and in the details of its topography, as well as in its name.[21] The early defended nucleus of the town is sited, as its name implies, on a low promontory of land on the west side of the tidal River Dart, which forms an ideally defensible site (Fig. 90). Its peculiar importance to the Saxon town builder, however, lies in the physical association of this spur with a smaller more precipitous promontory on the opposite side of the river, jutting out into the flat valley to the edge of the river. The existence of this pair of promontories on either side of the river was clearly the primary reason for the choice of the site on the western bank as a defended settlement. This choice was not, however, governed solely by the convenience of the crossing-place. The precipitous nature of the eastern promontory (not adequately shown by the contour lines in Fig. 90) suggests that this crossing can only have been effected by a bridge, which must have been a permanent structure substantial enough both to withstand a strong tidal flow and to reach the lowest edge of the rocky eastern spur. The general configuration of the site thus suggests that the burh and the bridge, connected by a single spinal street, formed a single unit from their inception. The significance of this conclusion lies in the important role which such burh-bridge units played in blocking access to major rivers to Viking ships in the wars of Edward the Elder in the early 10th century in both the Midlands and in southern England, a consideration which in itself provides strong evidence for the date of the foundation of the town in the first decade of the 10th century, argued below.

Nor is this the only consideration. There is a possibility, suggested by the utilisation of double burhs associated with a bridge in Edward the Elder's Midland campaigns, that the eastern promontory was itself developed in this way, possibly being fortified by a bank and ditch across the neck of the spur. This could of course only be confirmed by archaeological means. A further indication of this could, however, be provided by the development of this area (Bridgetown Pomeroy) as an urban place in its own right in the 13th century (Finberg 1950-51, 205), which could reflect an earlier status as an urban foundation in the early 10th century, as a twin to the larger urban burh on the western bank.

There is every reason to believe that the present topography of the town reflects its original lay-out. Since the bridge must have been part of this lay-out, the single street running up the centre of the promontory was clearly the spine around which the other elements of the burh were built. The course of the defences can be inferred from the present topography (see Fig. 90), and must have formed an irregular oval enclosure divided internally by spaces occupied by the church and burgage plots, the

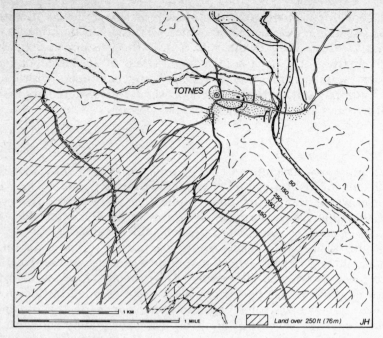

89. Totnes parish
90. Totnes and Bridgetown Pomeroy

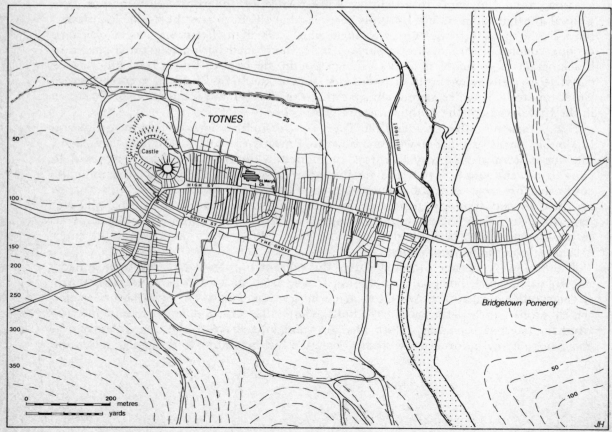

latter presumably with houses fronting on to the street, their gardens backing on to the rear of the bank. It seems possible that the present lane running parallel to the north of the High Street is all that remains of an original intra-mural or wall street, its existence elsewhere as an element in the burh's lay-out being inferred. The presence of a ditch or ditches may be indicated by the anomalous pattern of property boundaries on the eastern and south-eastern sides of the burh, which form a distinct strip some 20–25m. in width from the probable front of the bank. The topography of the western end of the burh has clearly been modified by the insertion of the early Norman castle. The south-eastern part of the outer ditch of the motte has made a considerable encroachment upon the western end of the High Street, possibly necessitating a wholesale re-alignment of its western end, and has also apparently modified the positions both of the road leading from the High Street to the north gate, as well of the north gate itself—if, as seems probable, they formed part of the original pre-Conquest lay-out. It is likely, however, that the west gate, immediately south of the castle, is in its original position. It is the meeting point of several presumably early routeways from the west and south-west, which as the contours show approach the town over the narrow neck of land joining the promontory to the higher ground to the south. There are, furthermore, indications of a former open area on the ridge where these roads meet, which could be interpreted as an early, possibly even pre-Conquest, extra-mural market area similar to that postulated for Barnstaple (above).

By analogy with Barnstaple, it may even be doubted whether the present church is in the same position as it was before the Conquest. A similar process of re-foundation of an earlier burh minster as a cell of a Continental monastery (in this case SS. Sergius and Bacchus at Angers) (Radford 1975, 8), and the similar construction of a Norman castle within the burh, might suggest that the old minster was moved at this time from the castle site to its new position near the east gate. A site for the original church at the highest point of the burh, occupying an area which would not have been a hindrance to the fullest use of the valuable area fronting on to the High Street nearest the river, would also seem more appropriate to the intentions of the burh's founder.

From its position, it can be inferred that the burh was intended to function as an inland port from its inception. The west bank of the river forms a relatively flat area for the beaching or wharfage of boats, although the details of the original topography of this area must have been largely obscured by later developments. It is possible, however, that the western branch of the river, followed by the parish boundary, was its original channel, and that the eastern, wider, branch is a canalisation effected at the time of the building of the burh to provide a quiet harbour in the former. It is also likely that streams flowing from the north-west and west were canalised at this time to power a town mill.[22]

The regularity of the property boundaries along the present Fore Street, between the river and the eastern gate of the burh, suggest that there have been episodes of regular planning, though at what period is not clear. However, this extra-mural area is one which would be expected to have been developed at an early date, a process which could well have begun relatively soon after the burh was built. Some indication of this may be provided by the record in Domesday Book of the presence of 15 'burgenses extra burgum terram laborentes' (Darby 1977, 364). Whether these were agricultural labourers or not, it seems at least a possibility that they would have formed part of the population either of the Fore Street area, or of the extra-mural market area outside the west gate.

Discussion

The question of the origin of Barnstaple, Lydford and Totnes, all of them demonstably new urban foundations in the later Saxon period, has given rise to a certain amount of discussion. One particularly important aspect of the main historical source for their origin, the Burghal Hidage document, lies not only in the fact that Barnstaple is mentioned in some versions as being in some way connected with a fortress at Pilton (*Pilletune*) (and is the only place to be so associated in the document), but also in the fact that a fortress at Halwell (*Halganwille*) is mentioned, while Totnes itself is not. It has commonly been assumed (e.g., Reichel 1906, 397; Tait 1936, 18, n. 7) that the fortified towns of Barnstaple and Totnes have replaced at some later date the temporary fortresses at Pilton and Halwell, because they were more favourably situated for land and sea trade. It is clear, however, that the Burghal Hidage references cannot by themselves provide a clear solution to the problem of when, or indeed whether, this process took place.

There have been two lines of argument, producing divergent results, which have been put forward to explain the origin of these places. The first is that of Dr. David Hill, who has argued that the creation of new urban places at Barnstaple and Totnes to replace fortresses set up by King Alfred must be attributed to King Athelstan. The establishment of these places is seen as part of a policy of the foundation of fortified market towns in southern England, a policy also reflected in his well-known law directing that mints should be systematically established in boroughs (Hill 1974, 217–21).[23] It has been suggested that the same factors operated widely throughout southern England, embracing, for instance, both Guildford (as successor to Eashing), and Southampton (as successor to *Clausentum*) (Biddle and Hill 1971, 84; Hill 1978, 187), as well as Barnstaple and Totnes.

The second alternative explanation is that of Henrietta and Trevor Miles, who have suggested, in relation to Barnstaple alone, that the present town is the original Alfredian burh, acting both as the original defensive centre for its region and as a protected urban place (Miles and Miles 1975, 267–70).

There are in the writer's view serious and ultimately insurmountable difficulties in both these hypotheses, and it is proposed here to put forward an alternative suggestion which overcomes many of these problems. This hypothesis both provides a scheme for the development of urban places in the whole of southern England, and elucidates the relationships between other pairs of fortresses and towns in this area. An extended treatment of all the relevant evidence must be reserved for another occasion; since, however, both Barnstaple and Totnes (and, as will be suggested below, Plympton and Kingsbridge) are in many ways type sites for this wider development, the main elements in this hypothesis at least must be discussed here.

It is suggested that shortly after his accession to the throne in 899, Edward the Elder created a series of fortresses or burhs, many connected with bridges, at strategic positions around the coastline of southern England and the Thames valley, which was designed as a systematic attempt to block access to all the major rivers and estuaries by the Viking fleet. It is suggested further that these were not merely fortresses but also fortified towns, and were, in fact, new urban foundations which replaced a more skeletal system set up by Alfred, which consisted in the main of non-urban fortresses. There are various reasons for suggesting that the construction of this series of fortifications was begun in c. 904, and that it was essentially completed by the beginning of Edward's extended campaign against the Danes in the Midlands from 911.

Apart from topographical and other evidence from the places themselves, there are four general historical considerations which can be called in support of this hypothesis:

(1) It is well known, because minutely documented in the *Anglo-Saxon Chronicle*, that probably the most important element in Edward's military strategy during his highly successful Midlands campaign was the building of a succession of burhs, which functioned as instruments both of offence and defence. An analysis of their situation suggests that in most cases these places comprised either a single burh associated with a bridge across a river, or else the secondary element of a pair of burhs defending both sides of an already existing bridge. It has already been pointed out that this burh-bridge unit was the essential means whereby movement up (or down) a river was to be denied to the mobile Viking warships (Hassall and Hill 1969, 191–4; Biddle 1976b, 136; Haslam 1983; Haslam forthcoming). It is furthermore quite clear that these tactics were employed from the beginning of Edward's Midlands campaign with the full knowledge both of their effectiveness and practicability; there are therefore good grounds for suggesting that the efficacy of this strategy had already been tested before 911 in a functioning system. The obvious context for this is in the 'blank' years of 899–911 in southern England.

(2) It seems unlikely that Edward would have conducted his Midland campaign without ensuring that his southern flank—the whole of the south of England and the Thames valley—was protected.

(3) The accounts in the *Anglo-Saxon Chronicle* of the abortive Viking raids of 914 into the Bristol Channel not only suggests that the whole of the south coast was by this time adequately protected; it also explicitly states that the southern side of the Severn estuary (though not South Wales) was similarly protected, by inference with fortresses preventing passage up all the major rivers. The failure of the raid is in itself testimony to the effectiveness of the defensive system in at least the south-western part of England.

(4) Edward's law codes themselves indicate that trading transactions should be limited to market towns (*ports*) and should have official witness there.[24] This implies that such towns were widely distributed over southern England.

It should already be apparent that the situation and topography of the burhs at both Barnstaple and Totnes suggest that their primary military function was to block their respective estuaries to river-borne attack and subsequent inland penetration—considerations which would in the light of the arguments given above suggest that they were creations of Edward the Elder. With these considerations in mind, the two alternative explanations put forward for the origin of these places—as urban creations of King Alfred, or of King Athelstan—must be examined carefully.

There are two main arguments to set against an identification of Barnstaple with the initial Alfredian fort:

(1) It is clear, as Miles and Miles have pointed out, that one MS. of the Burghal Hidage document (the Nowell version: Hill 1969, 85–6) mentions Pilton alone, whereas the rest (Hill's group B) include Barnstaple. That Barnstaple is a somewhat later addition inserted to explain Pilton (see Note 1) suggests that it is the latter which must be regarded as the primary fortress.

(2) Miles and Miles argue that since Barnstaple is the most suitable defensive site to control the Taw estuary, it must have been that initially chosen by Alfred. This of course assumes various premises: that the siting of Alfred's fortifications does, in fact, show an appreciation of the strategy of blocking estuaries by means of urban burhs and bridges, and that his choice of fortifiable sites was governed by considerations as much of their accessibility to traffic as of their defensive potential. The purpose of the present discussion is, however, to suggest that the strategies of Alfred and Edward were different both in scale and in kind, and were carried out by the construction of quite dissimilar fortresses and fortress systems.

From a detailed analysis of the topography and siting of all the late Saxon fortresses and burhs[25] it is clear that the key points in Alfred's defensive system were places with strong natural defensive potential whose refortification required a minimum of work.[26] These included various topographical types such as former Roman towns, with defences standing at least in part; strong hill-spur sites (e.g., Shaftesbury, Malmesbury, Lewes, and Lydford); already fortified hill-forts (e.g., Halwell, Chisbury, Old Sarum);[27] or islands (e.g., Athelney, Sashes). The large-scale fortress-towns on flatter sites (Wallingford, Wareham, and Cricklade) which may be considered to be of Alfredian origin, merely emphasise the contrast with the largely non-urban fortresses. Few of these fortresses near coasts were specifically sited to block estuaries, their function being rather to act as regional defence centres. An Alfredian fortress at the hill-fort near Pilton (Burridge or Roborough camp) fits into this wider pattern very neatly.

On the other hand, those burhs for which an Edwardian origin is suggested[28] were placed at points clearly chosen to block or control estuarine or river navigation, while at the same time being accessible both to inland and water-borne traffic. They are, compared say to Cricklade and the other Alfredian urban fortresses, generally conceived on a more modest scale, and usually occupy slightly elevated but accessible spur sites. They are, wherever the situation permits, always associated with bridges over the major rivers. Their topography suggests that they were always urban in character (i.e., they show regularly laid out patterns of streets, defences, burgage plots, and often church and market areas), and were the foci of routeways. They show, furthermore, a common characteristic in having been laid out along the length of a single axial street, with a few side streets of lesser importance, which usually followed the length of the spur on which they were built.[29]

An examination of the relevant evidence relating to all the examples of this type of burh cannot be given here, but it is clear that both Barnstaple and Totnes (as well as Plympton and Kingsbridge, discussed below) fit into this topographical type, which contrasts in many fundamental ways with the characteristics shown by known Alfredian forts and towns.[30] It is also clear that in a number of cases some of the Alfredian fortresses were replaced by new urban places, it is suggested here of

Edwardian origin, on more accessible (but still defensible) sites. Apart from the suggested move from Pilton to Barnstaple, the clearer examples of these include:

Halwel	Totnes and Kingsbridge
Langport (hilltop)	Langport (valley)
Bredy	Bridport
Clausentum	Southampton
Burpham	Arundel
Eashing	Guildford
Sashes	Cookham
Chisbury	Bedwyn/Marlborough
Old Sarum	Wilton

Some of these observations have been used in the alternative view of D. Hill, who has suggested that the origin of Barnstaple and Totnes must be sought in a programme of urban foundation by King Athelstan. The evidence for this assertion has at the time of writing not yet appeared in print, though it is stated as an established fact in four places (Addyman and Hill 1969, 89–90; Biddle and Hill 1971, 84; Hill 1978a, 187; Hill 1978b, 219). Hill's basic arguments, as set out in his unpublished Ph.D. thesis (1974, 217-21), are as follows:

(1) The laws of Athelstan associate together for the first time those functional aspects of the Anglo-Saxon town of defence, minting place, and market. All burhs were to have at least one mint.

(2) Since the small forts of the Burghal Hidage (such as Burpham, Eashing, Sashes, Chisbury, Halwell, and Pilton) were presumed to be in use in *c.* 919 (the presumed latest date of the document), and are not found as mints, or otherwise recorded as burhs, later than this, it is inferred that they were replaced in Athelstan's reign by a series of towns on new sites 'which were compact and mercantile in character'.

(3) The similarity of the topography of Totnes and Guildford, neither places mentioned in the Burghal Hidage, yet both replacing small fortresses (Halwell and Eashing respectively) and both minting places by Edgar's reign, is argued as suggesting a similar date of foundation in the reign of Athelstan.

(4) William of Malmesbury's account of the expulsion of the West Britons from Exeter by Athelstan records that he 'fortified it with towers and surrounded it with a wall of squared stone' (Whitelock 1979, 307–8), thus implying a process of urban creation.

There are several lines of reasoning which may be put forward against these arguments:

(1) The inference that the reform of the coinage and the limitation of mints to burhs which is shown in Athelstan's laws necessitates the concurrent reform of urban institutions, cannot be sustained. These facts merely demonstrate that such burhs were in existence at that time, not that they were necessarily created by Athelstan for this purpose. Indeed, it could be rather more plausibly argued that a wide distribution of small towns must have been a feature of the landscape for some time for it to have been thought necessary to create a network of minting places. Although a mint could not have existed without a burh, there is nothing to demonstrate that a burh must, before the reign of Athelstan, always have had a mint. In other words, the presence of a mint may demonstrate that a place had urban functions, but its absence

cannot demonstrate that a place was not urban, particularly in view of the minute sample of those coins actually produced in the earlier 10th century which the known coin finds must represent.

None of the evidence of the laws would therefore conflict with the assertion that in Athelstan's reign mints were merely added to a system of urban burhs already in existence. That this is so seems to be implied by a law of Edward the Elder limiting trading to market towns already quoted—a regulation which was merely repeated by Athelstan (Whitelock 1979, 419, n. 5).

(2) The general argument that the Burghal Hidage document is a complete list of burhs in existence at one time (if only it were possible to establish the 'original' text, or to fix its production in time) is one which has been advanced by Hill himself (1969, 88–92). Yet there are a number of counter-arguments suggesting that it is not complete (implied by the construction of burhs built at Plympton and Kingsbridge, discussed below), and that its various surviving versions merely encapsulate stages in a rapidly-changing system of fortress and town formation. It is, therefore, not legitimate to argue that the fortress burhs (Burpham, Eashing, etc.) were not abandoned before c. 919, the latest probable date of latest version of the document, and were, therefore, not replaced until Athelstan's reign. Nor, by the same token, can it be concluded that the exclusion of a place from the so-called 'list' means that it was not in existence by c. 919. Indeed, no certain conclusion can be drawn from the document concerning the date either of the construction, use, or abandonment of any of the burhs listed, except insofar as it supplies a *terminus ante quem* for only those mentioned in it. Indeed, the writer would venture to suggest that the existence of the Burghal Hidage document (while having many obvious benefits) has up till now been the greatest single obstacle in establishing a complete list of burhs in use in southern England in the late 9th to early 10th centuries. In short, the exclusion from the list of the two similar topographical types of Totnes and Guildford (not to mention Plympton and Kingsbridge) is not a demonstration that their foundation must be put no earlier than the reign of Athelstan.

(3) The episode of urban foundation at Exeter by Athelstan is in reality only an inference from the fact that he restored the walls. His expulsion of the British from Exeter must, however, be seen in the context of the similar treatment given, firstly, by Edward the Elder to the British at Chester in c. 924 (for which there is positive evidence of an earlier episode of foundation or restoration in 904); secondly, by Athelstan himself to the Danes at York in 927; and, thirdly, to the British again by Athelstan at Hereford (Whitelock 1979, 307), which was already reckoned as a burh from 912 (Lobel 1969, 2). In the case of neither Chester, York nor Hereford can it be inferred that these incidents were followed by episodes of urban foundation.

There is, in conclusion, no positive evidence that Alfred was responsible for the creation of new urban burhs either sited in positions similar to that at Barnstaple, or laid out in a similar way, nor is there any evidence that Athelstan was responsible for the creation of any of the new urban places so far mentioned. The ascription of this series of new urban burhs to the early years of the reign of Edward the Elder is, however, quite in accordance with all the positive evidence so far considered, and is supported by the general historical considerations already outlined. The wider topographical evidence of burhs outside Devon must though await a more extended discussion.

*   *   *   *   *

It remains to consider three further places which were also probably early urban centres: Plympton, Kingsbridge, and Kingsteignton. A combination of historical, geographical and topographical evidence suggests the hypothesis that Plympton and Kingsbridge, and possibly also Kingsteignton, were the sites of new burhs of Edward the Elder, founded as defended urban places for precisely the same reason as have already been adduced for the creation of Barnstaple and Totnes: namely to prevent penetration by Viking ships up major estuaries. The suggestions outlined below can only be substantiated (or refuted) by detailed fieldwork and archaeological excavation. However, the topographical and historical evidence alone amounts in the writer's view to an experimental verification of the general hypothesis put forward above.[31]

Plympton

The earliest documentary reference to Plympton comes from a charter of Edward the Elder, dated between 899 and 910, in which the king granted to Bishop Asser 23 hides in Somerset in exchange for the minster at *Plymentune* (Finberg 1953, 9, No. 17; Sawyer 1968, No. 380). It has already been suggested by Susan Pearce (1978, 118) that this transaction was one of several organised to 'secure and defend strategically important stretches of coastal areas'. The probable role of Barnstaple and Totnes as well as of other towns in southern England in this scheme indicates at least the possibility that this transaction was the preliminary to the building of a burh at Plympton.[32] As will be shown, the hypothesis of the creation of a burh here does indeed make intelligible many aspects of its topography and earlier history, and also provides the context within which many of Plympton's later developments can only be fully understood.

The grant of Plympton minster demonstrates the earlier importance of the site. At Domesday (and presumably considerably earlier) it was the head place of its hundred, the whole of which was the *parochia* of the minster (Reichel 1928, 246). Reichel has, in fact, suggested (*ibid.*, 281) that the estate or hundred was given by King Alfred to Asser. It was then, by the end of the 9th century, a place of central importance on the Tamar-Plym estuary.[33] It is reasonable to infer therefore that the minster must have been associated with a settlement of some importance, and possibly also originally with a royal residence.

The geographical location of this settlement is equally remarkable. Its site must be presumed to have been centred on the church of St Mary.[34] It thus lay on the edge of a low spur of land at a point in the Tory estuary which certainly in the medieval period was approximately the highest point to which tides came (Worth 1887, 372), and which was the lowest convenient crossing point of the whole estuary (Fig. 91). It lay, furthermore, at the end of a ridgeway running from the east, and was the focus of routeways from all directions except the west. Since the lowest crossing point of the River Plym (at Plym Bridge)—like that at Plympton on the 25ft. contour—is in a steeply sloping valley (Fig. 91), the site of the early settlement at Plympton is thus uniquely placed at what is in many ways an ideal geographical situation,

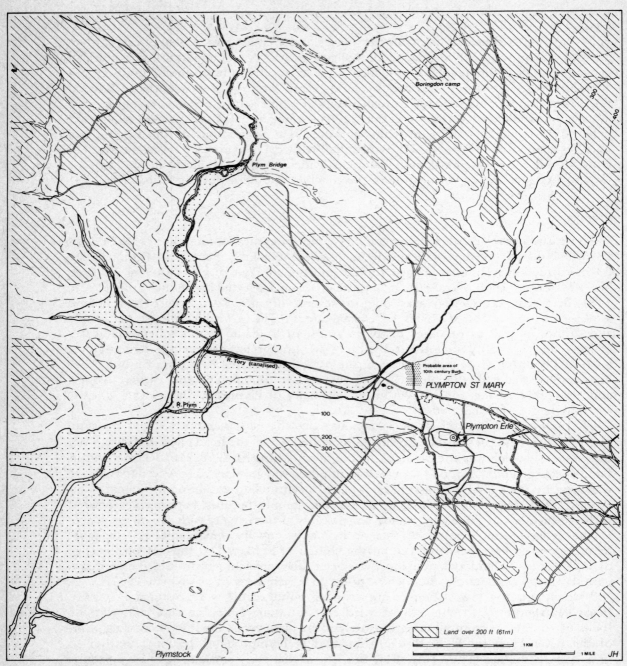

Land over 200 ft (61m)

1 KM

1 MILE

JH

91. Plympton parish (part of)

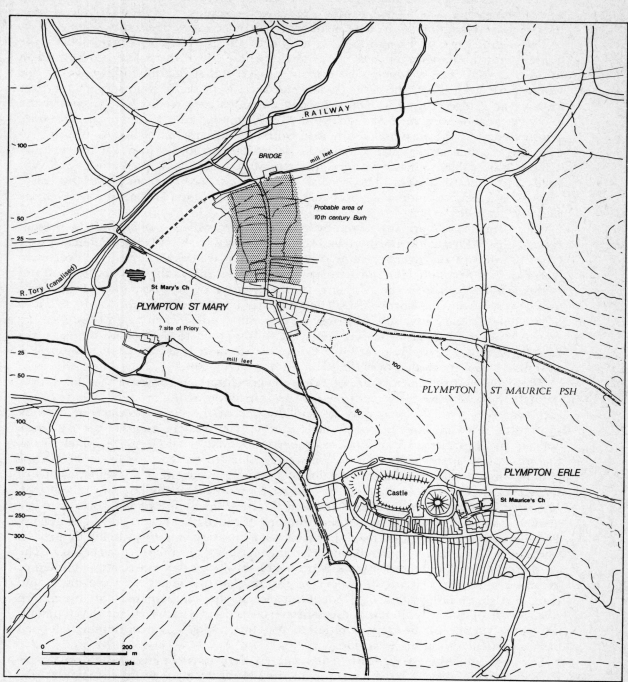

92. Plympton and Plympton Erle

occupying a low-lying but dry site which was accessible to both land and water transport. These factors mark it out as being of potential importance as a trading site in the earlier Saxon—and possibly pre-Saxon—periods,[35] as they provide at least part of the explanation for its demonstrable importance in later periods.

The significance of Plympton by the end of the 9th century provides both the context and the underlying cause of its choice as the site of the postulated Edwardian burh in *c.* 904. The topographical evidence suggests that the most likely site of this would have been along the road leading northwards from the ridgeway to the river crossing at Bridge (Fig. 92). The suggested defended area would have occupied the end of a pronounced spur of land, with steeply sloping sides to the north and more gentle slopes to the west and south, and would have consisted of houses fronting on to a single spinal street—plan characteristics similar to those shown, for instance, by Totnes, Barnstable, and Kingsbridge. Its suggested area would, furthermore, be very similar to that of Totnes. The central street would have continued to the north through a gateway leading to probably a combined bridge and causeway over the river and its valley.

These conclusions are supported by a number of significant aspects of the present topography.[36] Firstly, the northern end of the suggested burh is placed at the narrowest crossing point of the river for some way upstream as well as all the way downstream (see Fig. 91). Secondly, the northern end of the bridge marks the termination point of routes leading both from the north and (in the evidence of field boundaries following a hollow-way) from the north-west. (The latter has been diverted southwards to a new bridge near St Mary's church, probably in the 18th century when a new turnpike road system was constructed—Beresford 1967, 425). This road to the north-west leads to a crossing over the River Plym (at Plym Bridge) which there is every reason to suppose is of similar antiquity to that over the River Tory at Plympton.

The likelihood of the existence of a defended enclosure, as shown in Figs. 92 and 95, is furthermore substantially confirmed by an inspection of the ground, in spite of the fact that the original topography around the site of the burh has been masked by substantial later infilling of the former estuary. The western edge of the enclosure appears to be preserved in a modern property boundary wall (Fig. 92), which lies at the crest of an appreciable slope to the west. Inside (to the east of) this wall is a low mound which could well be the remains of the defensive bank. The northern slope of the enclosure is particularly steep, its lower edge marked by the line of the mill leet. The road running down this slope through the (presumed) site of the north gate is a marked hollow-way which recalls that running through the north gate at Wareham. The defensive bank could have been at any position on this slope, though its steepness would have rendered any elaborate system of ditches unnecessary. The southern line of the defensive bank is probably shown by the appreciable build-up of ground against the rear of the properties fronting on to Ridgeway to the south, and there are slight indications of a possible bank on the southern part of the eastern side. Much of this circuit must already have been destroyed by recent development, but there would still be opportunities to test this hypothesis in a number of open places, particularly on the west side.

The suggested site of the early 10th-century burh thus commanded all routeways from the north and south, which met along its central street, in addition to controlling traffic along the whole of the estuary of the Plym by a bridge over its lowest and most convenient crossing point. These considerations, however, do not by themselves demonstrate that this fortified centre was also an urban place, though it is suggested by the topographical and other parallels with Barnstaple and Totnes, by its potential as a trading site shown by its prime geographical location, and by its relatively large size. That it was so is, however, strengthened by two further observations. Firstly, a priory of Austin canons was founded by Bishop Warelwast at Plympton in 1121 in succession to the early minster. That such priories were founded often (though not exclusively) to serve urban communities (Dickinson 1950) goes some way towards strengthening the case for the existence of an urban community at Plympton in the early 12th century, with the inference that this community was the direct successor to one brought into being by the establishment of the burh in the early 10th century— the silence of Domesday Book notwithstanding. Secondly, the creation of the castle at Plympton Erle as the seat of the earls of Devon in 1107 must have reflected both the importance of the site and its central place in a network of communications.[37]

Kingsbridge

That the settlement at Kingsbridge originated in the Saxon period has never been seriously considered. Its development as an urban place is thought to be no earlier than the early 13th century (c. 1219), when it received its market charter and is described as a borough (Finberg 1950–51, 205; Beresford 1967, 422).[38] It is perhaps, therefore, not surprising that the possibility of its origin as a planned urban burh of the 10th century has not so far been examined.

Kingsbridge is first mentioned in a charter of 962, in which it is given as the start and finish of a perambulation of the bounds of an area of land to its north (Rose-Troup 1929). Its name-form (*to cinges bricge,* P-N.D., 305) demonstrates not only the existence of a bridge there, but also, perhaps more significantly, its royal associations. This may of course mean no more than that it was on a royal estate; however, the awkward site of the bridge in relation to the physical topography of the estuary head (described below), the fact that the estuary can have been no barrier to long-distance land traffic, and the fact that it would anyway have been crossed more conveniently just 300m. to 400m. to the north, all suggest that the bridge was built by one of the earlier 10th-century kings for more than mere geographical convenience. Given the arguments already set out in this chapter for the implementation by Edward the Elder of a systematic programme of construction of burhs associated with bridges, it must be asked whether the bridge at Kingsbridge was associated with a contemporary burh, the burh and bridge together forming a defensive unit of the kind argued for Barnstaple, Totnes and Plympton.

A detailed examination of both the site and the built topography of Kingsbridge (Fig. 94), as well as its relationship with surrounding parishes (Fig. 93), provides in the writer's view an unequivocal demonstration that this was indeed the case (although this hypothesis has yet to be tested archaeologically). The place is situated at the head of a large estuary, the bridge (underlying the present Mill Street) established at a point which is somewhat below the reach of normal tides (Davies 1913, 146-7). The later focus of the town (as shown on the O.S. map of 1886—see Fig. 94) appears

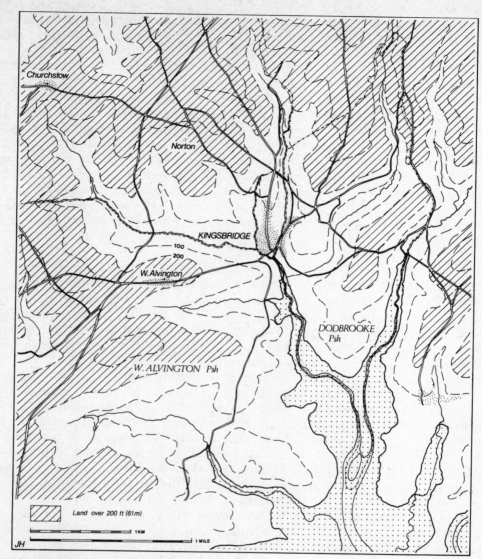

93. Kingsbridge and surrounding parishes

to have been in the valley immediately east of the bridge. The western part of the
town, however, is built along a single street which runs the length of the crest of a
pronounced—and, indeed, dramatically sited—spur of land, defined on its western
and eastern sides by streams and on its southern side by the estuary itself. The
considerable defensive potential of this spur in its relationship to the estuary, taken
with the evidence already argued above for the existence of a defensive policy based
on the construction of burhs on elevated by accessible sites at estuary heads, at once

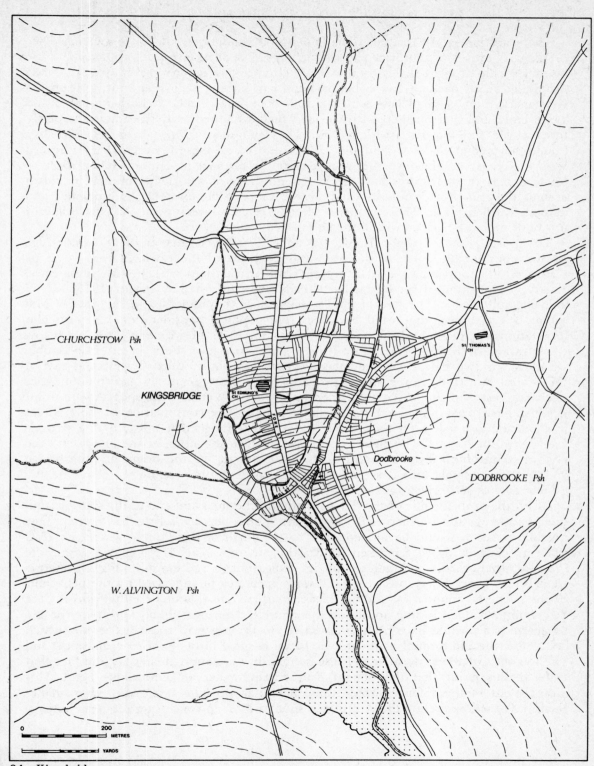

94. Kingsbridge

mark out this site as a possible burh of similar lay-out to those at Totnes and Barnstaple.

There are indeed clear indications in its built topography of the former existence of such a burh. The southern end of the spur is divided into long properties whose boundaries lie at right-angles to the single street along its crest (Fore Street). These properties reach back to two common boundary lines at their rear ends, that on the west marked by a small lane which is joined to Fore Street at both its north and south ends, and that on the east by a line which is marked partly by a lane and partly by a single line on its southern end. The lay-out of the main street, property boundaries and back lanes, and the relationship of all these features to the physical topography, is so similar to the arrangement for instance at Totnes, that it must be inferred that these features have preserved the lines of a former bank and ditch(es) around the end of the spur. Its total pattern suggests the existence of a planned and defended urban place. The arguments already given above suggest that the origin of this burh should be placed within the period 904 to 911.

The postulation of the existence of an early 10th-century burh at Kingsbridge throws considerable light on the rest of the lay-out of the town, as well as on its historical and topographical relationships with surrounding settlements and parishes. Firstly, the position of the bridge has already been suggested by Davies (1913, 146–7) as being reflected in the line of (and possibly surviving underneath) the present Mill Street, a conclusion supported by other topographical considerations, in particular its relationship to the burh immediately to its north. The bridge was sited just below the position of highest tidal flow (*ibid.*), and must have been in effect a double structure, its two halves spanning the two tidal stream mouths to west and east of the central spur (their lower courses probably marked by the present parish boundaries —see Fig. 94), and supported at the centre on the very end of the spur. At this point it must have been joined on its northern side by the continuation of Fore Street just outside a gateway on the defences. Such an arrangement must, to the writer's knowledge, be unique. The clear association between the siting of the bridge and the lay-out of the burh is furthermore a strong argument for the origin of both bridge and burh as a single unit designed to implement a military strategy—to defend the estuary against seaborne attack.

Given the probable line of the defences around the sides and end of the spur of land, their course on the northern side across the spur is perhaps a little less certain. One possible position would be immediately to the north of the church, where the 75ft. (22.8m.) contour shows a marked constriction, thereby placing the church within the burh—a situation not contradicted by its dedication to St Edmund, king and martyr (d. 870). A more likely position, however, appears to be indicated by the behaviour of the property boundaries, and the existence of two small lanes on either side of Fore Street immediately to the south of the church. The most likely position for the defensive bank would have been immediately to the north of the western lane (which could thus be interpreted as a survivor of an original intra-mural or wall street) and to the south of the eastern lane. These conclusions are strengthened by the fact that it is at this point that the line of Fore Street makes an appreciable bend. This arrangement of the defences would thus enclose an irregular oval area, rather smaller than at Totnes, encircling the end of the spur of land and enclosing about 26 burgage plots. The exact courses of the defences shown on Fig. 95, while open to modification by further work, are based on both observations made on the ground and deductions made from the large-scale first edition O.S. map. It is probable that the steepness of the slopes, particularly on the eastern side of the spur, would have made any elaborate system of ditches outside the bank unnecessary except on the northern side.

The exclusion in this arrangment of the church from the defended area does, in fact, fit in with what can be deduced about the wider relationships of the town. The parish of Kingsbridge (Fig. 93) is remarkably small, and includes merely the length of the spur, with its boundaries between the parishes of Dodbrooke on the east and Churchstow on the west following the course of the streams on either side. It is clear, however, from later medieval practices that the mother-church of Kingsbridge was always regarded as being Churchstow (Davies 1913, 147), and the town a part of the manor of Norton (*ibid.*, 143) (see Fig. 93). Although King Edward was, as both Barnstaple and Totnes show, quite capable of modifying local parochial arrangements by the building of burh churches, the example of Plympton, where the burh inhabitants used a pre-existing minster church outside the burh, suggests that at Kingsbridge, too, the burh church with associated burial rights would have continued to be that at Churchstow. These relationships furthermore demonstrate that the town was a new settlement, artificially fitted into already existing parochial and tenurial arrangements, thus strengthening the arguments already made for its origin as an early planted town.[39]

These observations suggest therefore that the church of St Edmund is an addition to the townscape after the first decade of the 10th century. A possible context for its foundation is the acquisition of the surrounding royal estate (which, of course, included Kingsbridge up to the boundary with Dodbrooke parish) by Buckfast abbey in the 960s or 970s.[40] It is not unreasonable to suppose that the acquisition of the burh by the abbey encouraged further urban development (as has been suggested above for Tavistock), which must have been concentrated along the extra-mural part of Fore Street to the north of the defences, with the consequent acquisition by the community as a whole of its own chapel.

The peculiar relationship of Kingsbridge to Dodbrooke to its east is also revealing. The latter was granted a market charter in 1257 (Finberg 1950–51, 206). It probably, therefore, represents, in an economic sense, an extension around the eastern end of the bridge of the earlier pre-Conquest urban centre at Kingsbridge in the 13th century, although in a tenurial sense it constitutes a new urban foundation in a different parish. It must, therefore, have replaced an earlier village, the parish centre, around the present church of St Thomas on the hill to the north-east. There is every reason to suppose that this village was in existence (as was W. Alvington) rather earlier than the date of the foundation of the burh at Kingsbridge, and that it probably therefore supplied at least some of the latter's inhabitants.

Kingsteignton

There is a further possibility that Kingsteignton was the site of another burh of the early 10th century. Its site, adjacent to a bridge crossing a wide estuary at its lowest convenient crossing-place, at a point just below the highest point of tidal flow, as well as its position midway between the two burhs of Totnes and Exeter, all provide strong reasons for suspecting the presence here of a further element in the system of burhs and bridges set up by Edward the Elder discussed above. It is described in Domesday Book as *Taignbrige,* and was the head place of a hundred which was ancient demesne of the king (Reichel 1897, 225). The *Anglo-Saxon Chronicle* also records its destruction by the Danes in 1001. It has furthermore been suggested by Rose-Troup (1929, 260) that its church, and, therefore, presumably an associated settlement, was in existence by 909. As at Plympton, it seems possible, therefore, that it was even before this the minster church of the whole of the hundred.

It is clear that the *-brige* element in its name at the time of Domesday indicates the presence of a bridge across the estuary in 1086. The archaeological evidence, while from a chronological point of view rather unspecific, certainly shows that it has had a long and eventful history (Taylor 1821). It has, however, been argued (Davidson 1884) that the existence of the name-form *Teigntone* in 1083–4 shows that the bridge was not then in existence, being constructed in 1085. This argument is, however, quite unconvincing.[41]

It would, therefore, be quite in accord with the historical and geographical evidence to postulate the existence at Kingsteignton of an early-10th-century burh associated with a bridge. The topographical evidence of the place itself is somewhat equivocal, but its position on the crest of a spur of land which must in the 10th century have been readily defensible does seem to strengthen this hypothesis. The church lies at the southern end of this spur, with the early *villa regalis* and associated settlement situated probably nearby to its north. Any further discussion must, however, await a closer examination of the evidence than is possible here.[42]

What is possible, however, is that Kingsteignton is likely to have been an early proto-urban settlement, associated with royal administrative functions, of a similar character to those proposed by the writer in Wiltshire (see Chapter IV). It is also not improbable that it could have acted as an early coastal trading centre, performing the same role as is suggested above for Plympton.

Conclusions

It has been the intention in this chapter to propose hypotheses or historical models to describe the long (and to us near-invisible) process of urban development in Devon up to the end of the 11th century. It is suggested that the development of towns in the Saxon period has been influenced by two general processes. The first of these is the gradual development before the 9th century of proto-urban settlements growing up around royal centres as a result of their administrative, ceremonial, economic, and redistributive functions, of very much the same character as been argued in more detail in this volume for both Berkshire and Wiltshire (Chapters III and IV). Instances of this development have been suggested at Tavistock, Plympton, Lifton, Kingsteignton, and Axminster. It has not, however, been possible either to examine this process systematically for the whole of the county, or to relate these developments to the wider pattern of royal estates, or even of Roman (or earlier) settlement or administrative foci. There is clearly a considerable scope for a more detailed consideration of all these aspects. Nor should the effects of pre-9th-century coastal and inland trade be minimised in this development. It is surely no accident that two of the places so far mentioned—Plympton and Kingsteignton, which were heads of hundreds, the sites of early minster churches and *villae regales*—were situated at the heads of large estuaries at ideal meeting places of water and land traffic.

It is furthermore possible that a factor in the location and growth of some of these places, as of the towns from the later 9th century onwards, was their function as trading ports, distribution points and administrative and industrial centres for a Dartmoor tin industry. The evidence for tin mining in Devon before the 12th century has been reviewed by Hatcher (1973, 14–18) who has suggested that in the period from the 3rd to the 13th centuries the mines of the south-west peninsula were virtually the sole source of supply of tin for the civilised world. They must have produced tin throughout this period, though not necessarily continuously in any one place, with Devon, at least in the early medieval period, producing more than Cornwall (*ibid.*, 153). The pre-Saxon open trading site of Bantham on the south coast has already been suggested as a possible port from which tin was exported (Fox 1955, 64), and the close proximity of Plympton to sources of tin on Dartmoor raises the possibility of its role at an early date as an industrial and administrative centre for the industry.[43] At the present time, however, the lack of relevant evidence does not enable these functions to be any more than speculative.

A similar function can also be postulated for Lydford, although again there is little direct evidence which can be called in its support. Its role as a fortress and an urban place, by no means the smallest of those built or utilised by King Alfred, must have been sustained by some economic activity. It clearly remained important enough to merit refortification with a stone wall, probably by Ethelred soon after A.D. 1000. Its situation at a high altitude in a poor agricultural district, yet near (if not actually on) Dartmoor, raises the possibility that it functioned both as an administrative centre from which royal control of the tin industry was to be exercised, as well as an industrial and market centre for the industry's products—functions which were all certainly well developed there when detailed documentation becomes available in the 12th century.

The second observable factor in the general urban development was, it is suggested, the implementation of policies of King Alfred and his son, Edward the Elder, which, although they differed in both scale and conception, were designed to secure the defence of southern England against the Vikings by the building of burhs. In the former case this seems to have been carried out in Devon by the refortification and construction respectively of two non-urban hill-top fortresses—Pilton and Halwell—near to but not on the coast, with probably new urban foundations at Lydford and Exeter. This arrangement was augmented, it is suggested, by the construction by Edward the Elder, between *c.* 904 and 910, of a system of small burhs (Barnstaple, Totnes, Plympton, Kingsbridge, and possibly Kingsteignton) associated with bridges at the heads of estuaries, as part of a policy for the systematic defence of the whole of southern England against Viking seaborne attack and inland penetration via the larger estuaries and rivers. They can best be understood as forming a unified system which, with the exception of Exeter, essentially replaced the old Alfredian arrangement. Thus in Devon Pilton was replaced by Barnstaple, and Halwell by both Totnes and Kingsbridge.

The lay-out and siting of these new places, as well as their geographical, ecclesiastical and tenurial relationships to wider landscape and settlement patterns, suggest that

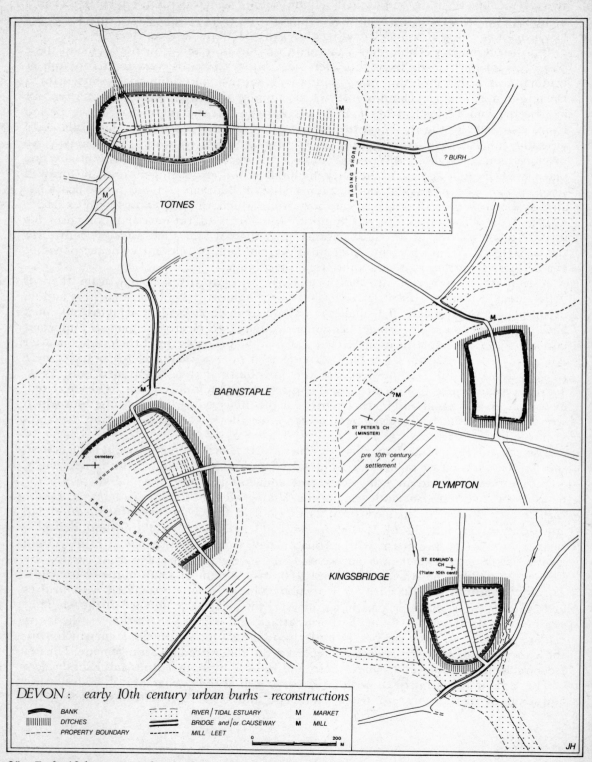

95. **Early 10th-century urban burhs—reconstructed topography**

these were all new urban foundations, set up by royal initiative as commercially viable communities in order both to secure the physical upkeep of defences and bridge and to ensure their effectiveness as garrisoned fortresses. They must be seen as the prototypes of the usually larger burhs set up by Edward in the Midlands after 911, for which the same functions can be postulated. Some of these (such as Barnstaple and Totnes) were clearly more successful as towns than others, their differences in scale (shown in Fig. 95) possibly reflecting the original aspirations of their builders.

It is clear, however, that all these places were planned on the same pattern, with a single street forming the axis of an elongated sub-rectangular or oval defended enclosure, with properties set out at right-angles to this street and (in the case of Barnstaple and Totnes) with space reserved for a presumably newly-created burh church. In all cases, the axial street was clearly laid out along the crest of a convenient spur of land, the position of other features determined by, rather than imposed upon, the immediate physical topography of the chosen site. It is doubtful if these places could have (as must have, for instance, Cricklade, Wallingford and Wareham) provided room for the protection of a large rural population. There can furthermore have been no space in these places, except insofar as it was provided in the wide main street, for large markets for livestock or other rural produce—a factor which, as has been suggested for both Totnes and Barnstaple, may well have led to the growth of extra-mural market areas.

As small and relatively early urban foundations, therefore, these places provided the framework around which later Saxon and medieval urban developments were to evolve. Given the contention of Professor Sawyer that England was as wealthy in the 11th century as it was in the 14th (Sawyer 1965), it need come as no surprise to realise that by the beginning of the 11th century there were in all probability at least twice as many urban places in Devon as have previously been thought.

POSTSCRIPT

Some of the arguments concerning the date and context of the Burghal Hidage document on pages 262–67 have been overtaken by the recent article by R. H. C. Davis ('Alfred and Guthrum's frontier', *English Historical Review* xcvii [1982], 803–810), which suggests that this document refers to a situation existing in the later 9th century (just before 866)—a conclusion which strengthens many of the arguments given here. If most of the burhs listed in the Burghal Hidage are of Alfredian origin at the latest (though there are problems posed by the inclusion of Wilton and Portchester amongst others), this provides both the context and the reason for the development of a new and arguably superior system of burhs by Edward the Elder in the years 899–911. It clearly explains why many of the burhs in this new system are not mentioned in the document (e.g., Barnstaple, Totnes, Kingsbridge and Plympton), which up till now would have perhaps been the major argument against the acceptance of a date for this new system of the first decade of the 10th century.

ACKNOWLEDGEMENT

I am grateful to Susan Pearce and Dr Nicholas Brooks for reading through and commenting on an earlier draft of the text.

NOTES

1. The 'B' version of the Burghal Hidage, which is a late form of the document, explains Pilton by adding 'that is Barnstaple'. Later versions of the 'B' version corrupt this to 'with Barnstaple'. I am grateful to Dr. Nicholas Brooks for these observations.

2. A similar argument has been set out with regard to Cornish towns by M. Witherick (1967, 52–4).

3. A case can, in the writer's opinion, be made for suggesting that the eastern part of the town represents a planned urban lay-out by the new abbey in the later 10th century. It is hoped that this thesis will be developed at a later date.

4. The earliest name form is *Beardastapol*, Bearda's staple or market (P-N.D., 25).

5. This is characteristic, for instance, of several other burhs of Edward the Elder in the Midlands and eastern England, such as at Bedford and Cambridge (Haslam 1983; Haslam forthcoming), and one which is suggested as having been built on the northern bank of the river at Thetford, none of which was apparently defended along the side facing the river. An excavation by K. Markuson on the line of the defences to the north of Joy Street in 1979, published after the above account was written (Markuson 1980), has provided evidence which would support the suggestion that the burh may originally have had a triple ditch system outside a wall located immediately outside (east of) Green Lane, which would then have acted as an intra-mural or wall street (*ibid.*, 78–9). This would parallel the triple ditch systems outside the banks at both Lydford and Cricklade.

6. The completed report of the excavation was handed by the writer to the Barnstaple Excavation Committee in July 1977.

7. I am grateful to Susan Pearce for providing me with this reference. The results of these excavations are otherwise unavailable.

8. The present streets south of the 19th-century market, and south of the church (Paternoster Street), are probably later additions to the original street pattern.

9. As suggested by the inclusion of a chapel of St Thomas on the new stone bridge at London, started in 1176 (Brooke and Keir 1975, 110).

10. The view originally stated by T. M. Hall (1867–8, 94) was that Pilton and Barnstaple were until the 15th century separated by an 'almost impassable marsh' crossed only at low water by a 'dangerous ford'.

11. The bridge over the Yeo and road to the west over very low ground must be post-medieval creations.

12. Along it developed the quite sizeable medieval suburb of Newport, immediately to the south of the early parish boundary (Fig. 85).

13. Boutport Street is consistently about 48m. to 50m. outside Green Lane; allowing for a thickness of the bank of about 5m., the space between the front of the bank and Boutport Street would have been 43m. to 45m. in width.

14. Further examples of this process are discussed by Keene (1976, 73–5).

15. Some support for this interpretation could be cited in the inclusion of the western suburb of Winchester, much of it in royal ownership, within the urban area probably by the first half of the 10th century (Biddle [ed.] 1976, 265).

16. Brief details of these have been published in *Medieval Archaeology* 8 (1964, 232); 9(1965 , 170–1); and 10 (1966, 168–9). Further details are included in Saunders (1980, 149–53).

17. It is argued below, however, that a number of these promontory burhs, such as Wilton, Bridport, Langport and Twyneham (Christchurch) are probably foundations of Edward the Elder, and are not strictly comparable.

18. This suggestion, at the moment a hypothesis, also fits the known archaeological evidence from excavations on the defences at Cricklade (Wilts.), Christchurch (Hants.), South Cadbury (Somerset), and Wareham (Dorset), and will be discussed by the writer at a later date.

19. I am indebted to Susan Pearce for much of the information in this paragraph. The suggestion of a fortress to the east of Lifton derives from an observation by Bob Silvester.

20. Such as Old Sarum, near Wilton, Chisbury, near Bedwyn, Malmesbury, near Brockenborough (Wilts.), and Langport, near Somerton (Som.), discussed in the appropriate chapters in this volume.

21. *Totanaes*, c. 979—'Totta's naess', referring to the promontory of land on which the town stands (P-N.D., 334).

22. The writer has suggested similar episodes of canalisation to facilitate both river-borne trade and the construction of a mill for an Edwardian burh at Cambridge (Haslam, forthcoming). The provision of a mill for the town would have been a similar process as that described for Tavistock in the 12th century (Finberg 1947, 136).

23. II Athelstan 14, issued at Grately, 926–30 (Whitelock 1979, 418).

24. I Edward I: 'And my will is that every man shall have a warrantor [to his transactions] and that no-one shall buy [and sell] except in a market town; but he shall have the witness of the port reeve or other men of credit, who can be trusted.

'And if anyone buys outside a market town, he shall forfeit the sum due for insubordination to the king . . .' (Attenborough 1922, 115).

25. This cannot be set out in detail here, but will be exhaustively treated elsewhere.

26. These have been examined by Biddle (1876b, 126–7), though this analysis does not take account of the differences suggested here between Alfredian and Edwardian burhs, or of the military strategies which these differing topographical types imply.

27. It is suggested in Chapter IV that Malmesbury was an earlier hill-fort with probably strong surviving defences. The re-use of Old Sarum is also discussed further in this chapter.

28. As will be argued below, the Burghal Hidage does not give a complete list of these places. A fuller description and discussion of these burhs must await another occasion.

29. Christchurch (Twyneham), Hants., has the strongest claim of all the burhs of this type to be considered an Alfredian foundation, but there are in the writer's view several independent arguments which suggest that its foundation belongs to the period of burh formation suggested for the early years of Edward the Elder's reign.

30. There is, of course, an element of circularity in these arguments; the postulation of the distinction between Alfredian and Edwardian burhs cannot by itself demonstrate the origin of any particular instance. But it does elucidate many of the historical and topographical peculiarities of these places (e.g., Old Sarum and Wilton, discussed in Chapter IV), and it is also supported by the occurrence of similar types in the known Edwardian burhs in the Midlands.

31. The preceding sections relating to the origins of Barnstaple and Totnes were written before the detailed evidence from Plympton, Kingsbridge, and Kingsteignton was examined.

32. Earlier writers (e.g., Birch *Cart. Sax.* No. 610; Worth 1887, 364; Reichel 1928, 245) have suggested that this transaction can be dated to 904. This is significantly the same year as a similar transaction involving the acquisition by King Edward of the estate centred on the future burh of Portchester (Finberg 1964, 36, n. 39; Sawyer 1968, n. 372).

33. Thus obviating the necessity to employ tortuous arguments (Worth 1887, 368–9) to explain the fact that it is not situated on the modern River Plym. The river name is anyway regarded as a back-formation from the name Plympton (P-N.D., 252).

34. The Domesday church is that of St Peter, which was presumably the dedication of the original minster church. After the replacement of this by a priory of Austin canons in 1121 (see below) a new church was built and dedicated to St Mary in 1311 (Worth 1887, 372). The precise relationships of the sites of these three establishments are not entirely clear, but must have been close.

35. A similar function has already been suggested for the 'Dark Age' trading site at Bantham, 10 miles (16km.) to the south-east (Fox 1955), which is in a similar topographical situation to Plympton.

36. Figures are based on the 1:2500 O.S. map of 1866 (1st edn.), as well as on the results of fieldwork.

37. Beresford states (1967, 425) that in 1194 the fifth earl 'made a borough here and gave the town a market and fair'. This episode can be dated so closely only on the questionable assumption that it happened at the same time as the granting of the charter in 1194 (Finberg 1950–51, 205). The laying-out of the town is likely to be earlier, though probably no earlier than 1170, the date of martyrdon of Thomas à Becket, the original patron saint of the church (Beresford, *op. cit.*).

38. Beresford, in fact, explicitly states that there was no settlement there until c. 1219, though, as argued below, is undoubtedly correct in suggesting an earlier origin for Dodbrooke, immediately to its east. Finberg, however, had already stated in 1952 that the town of Kingsbridge had been created by the abbot of Buckfast in the 13th century, at the same time as the creation of the church of Churchstow to its west (Finberg 1969, 27). These assertions are unsupported by any concrete evidence and are at variance in every respect from the course of settlement development proposed here.

39. That such arrangements were already in force in the early 10th century is suggested by the fact that the church at W. Alvington was already in existence by *c.* 909 (Reichel 1913, 170), and therefore presumably the settlement as well.

40. Frances Rose-Troup (1929, 257) has suggested that the area of the Hiwisce, whose bounds in the charter of 962 include Kingsbridge, was made over to Buckfast abbey (? in 962) by the king as an endowment. The question is further discussed by Finberg (1969, 26-7), who, however, asserts that Buckfast abbey was founded in 1018.

41. It is based on the manifestly dubious premise that the absence of a reference to a phenomenon in documents demonstrates the absence of that phenomenon.

42. It is possible that these topographical indications of the former existence of a burh have failed to survive through its partial desertion in favour of the 'Nova Villa' of *c.* 1200 at Newton Abbot (Beresford 1967, 423), on the opposite side of the estuary. The parallel with Plympton, where the suggested 10th-century burh at Plympton St Mary was all but deserted for Plympton Erle in the later 12th century, is particularly relevant. A lane leading to the church from the north is named Berry Lane, which could preserve the memory of the existence of either the 10th-century burh or the smaller burh around the king's residence and (presumably) the church.

43. A similar association in the early 9th century of a large-scale industry (iron smelting) with an early *villa regalis* has been argued in the case of Ramsbury, Wilts. (Haslam 1980).

BIBLIOGRAPHY

ABBREVIATIONS

P.D.A.S.   *Proceedings of the Devonshire Archaeological Society.*
P-N. D.   *The Place-Names of Devon,* ed. J. E. B. Gover, A. Mawer and F. H. Stenton (English Place-Name Society 8, 1931-2).
T.D.A.   *Transactions of the Devonshire Association.*

Addyman, P. and Hill, D. (1969), 'Saxon Southampton: a review of the evidence', pt. 2, *Proceedings of the Hampshire Field Club* 26, 61-96.

Attenborough, F. L. (ed.) (1922), *The Laws of the earliest English kings.*

Beresford, M. W. (1967), *New Towns of the Middle Ages.*

Biddle, M. (ed.) (1976a), *Winchester in the Early Middle Ages,* (Winchester Studies, 1).

Biddle, M. (1976b), 'Towns', in Wilson, D. M. (ed.), *The Archaeology of Anglo-Saxon England,* 99-150.

Biddle, M. and Hill, D. H. (1971), 'Late Saxon planned towns', *Antiquaries Journal* 51, 70-85.

Brooks, C. N. L. and Keir, G. (1975), *London 800-1216: the Shaping of a City.*

Darby, H. C. (1977), *Domesday England.*

Davidson, J. B. (1884), 'Remarks on old Teign Bridge', *T.D.A.* 16, 444-52.

Davies, W. (1913), 'Buckfast abbey and its relation to Kingsbridge', *T.D.A.* 45, 143-51.

Dickinson, J. C. (1950), *The origins of the Austin Canons and their introduction into England.*

Finberg, H. P. R. (1947), 'The borough of Tavistock: its origin and early history', *T.D.A.* 79, 129-53.

Finberg, H. P. R. (1950-51), 'The boroughs of Devon', *Devon and Cornwall Notes and Queries* 24, 203-9.

Finberg, H. P. R. (1953), *The early charters of Devon and Cornwall,* Leicester Univ. Dept. of English Local History, occasional paper No. 2.

Finberg, H. P. R. (1964), *The Early Charters of Wessex.*

Finberg, H. P. R. (1969), 'Two Acts of State', in *West Country Historical Studies,* 11-28.

Fox, A. (1955), 'Some evidence for a Dark Age trading site at Bantham, S. Devon', *Antiquaries Journal* 35, 55-67.

Hall, T. M. (1867-8), 'Notes on the priory of St Mary at Pilton', *T.D.A.* 2, 93-7.

Haslam, J. (1980), 'A middle Saxon iron smelting site at Ramsbury, Wiltshire', *Medieval Archaeology* 24, 1-68.

Haslam, J. (1983), 'The origins and topography of Bedford', *Bedford Arch. Journal.*

Haslam, J. (forthcoming), 'The origins and topography of Cambridge', *Proc. Cambs. Antiq. Soc.*

Hassall, J. and Hill, D. (1969), 'Pont de l'Arche: Frankish influence on the West Saxon burh?',

Archaeological Journal 127, 188–95.

Hatcher, J. (1973), *English tin production and trade before 1550.*

Hill, D. H. (1969), 'The Burghal Hidage: the establishment of a text', *Medieval Archaeology* 13, 84-92.

Hill, D. H. (1974), 'The Anglo-Saxon town', unpublished Ph.D. Thesis, University of Southampton.

Hill, D. H. (1978a), 'The origins of the Saxon towns', in Brandon, P. (ed.), *The South Saxons*, 174-89.

Hill, D. H. (1978b), 'Trends in the development of towns during the reign of Ethelred II', in Hill, D. (ed.), *Ethelred the Unready* (B.A.R., 59).

Hoskins, W. G. (1954), *Devon.*

Keene, D. J. (1976), 'Suburban growth', in Barley, M. W. (ed.), *The Plans and Topography of medieval towns in England and Wales*, C.B.A. Research Report No. 14.

Lobel, M. D. (1969), 'Hereford', in Lobel, M. D. (ed.), *Historic Towns Atlas*, i.

Loyn, H. R. (1971), 'Towns in late Anglo-Saxon England: the evidence and some possible lines of enquiry', in Clemoes, P. and Hughes, K. (eds.), *England before the Conquest*, 115-128.

Markuson, K. W. (1980), 'Excavations on the Green Lane access site, Barnstaple, 1979', *P.D.A.S.* 38, 67-90.

Miles, T. (1977), 'Excavations at Paiges Lane/Holland Street, Barnstaple—interim note', Devon Committee for Rescue Archaeology, *Annual Report*, 8-9.

Miles, H. and Miles, T. (1975), 'Pilton, N. Devon: excavation within a medieval village', *P.D.A.S.* 33, 267-95.

Pearce, S. M. (1978), *The kingdom of Dumnonia.*

Radford, C. A. R. (1975), 'The pre-Conquest church and the old minsters in Devon', *The Devon Historian* 11 (1975), 2-11.

Reichel, O. J. (1897), 'The hundred of Teignbridge', *T.D.A.* 29, 225-74.

Reichel, O. J. (1906), 'The Domesday Survey', in *V.C.H. (Devonshire)* 1.

Reichel, O. J. (1913), 'The hundred of Stanborough and Dippeforde in the time of Testa de Nevil 1243', *T.D.A.* 45, 169-97.

Reichel, O. J. (1928), 'The hundred of Plympton in early times', *T.D.A.* (extra volume), 245-303.

Rose-Troup, F. (1929), 'The new Edgar charter and the South Hams', *T.D.A.* 61, 249-80.

Saunders, A. D. (1980), 'Lydford Castle, Devon', *Medieval Archaeology* 24, 123-86.

Sawyer, P. H. (1965), 'The wealth of England in the 11th century', *Trans. Royal Historical Soc.*, 5th ser. 15, 145-64.

Sawyer, P. H. (1968), *Anglo-Saxon Charters.*

Stephenson, C. (1930), 'The Anglo-Saxon borough', *English Historical Review* 45, 177-207.

Stephenson, C. (1933), *Borough and town.*

Tait, J. (1936), *The Medieval English Borough*, Manchester.

Taylor, P. T. (1821), 'An account of some discoveries made in taking down the old bridge over the river Teign . . .', *Archaeologia* 19, 308-13.

Whitelock, D. (ed.) (1979), *English Historical Documents* I (2nd ed.)

Witherick, M. E. (1967), 'The medieval boroughs of Cornwall—an alternative view of their origins', *Southampton Research Series in Geography* No. 4 (University of Southampton), 41-60.

Worth, R. N. (1887), 'Beginnings of Plympton history', *T.D.A.* 19, 363-76.

Chapter Nine

SAXON LONDON

By Tony Dyson and John Schofield

BETWEEN 457, WHEN LONDON served as a refuge for the fleeing British (Whitelock 1961, 10) and 604, when the Kentish King Ethelberht founded St Paul's cathedral, there is no historical evidence for the city of London, and even these two notices were compiled at much later dates. Material evidence of any kind is lacking for occupation beyond the mid-5th century, or before the late 6th and early 7th centuries, and no structures earlier than the 8th century have been found.[1] On the other hand there is little to suggest any deliberate destruction, least of all by fire, which might account for this vacuum. The consequent impossibility of drawing any firm conclusions about the condition of London during the period of Anglo-Saxon invasion and settlement is further underlined by uncertainty as to the character of the late Roman city itself. It is now apparent that by as early as the end of the 2nd century well-established domestic or industrial occupation was abandoned—with existing buildings dismantled in some cases—and the sites covered by a layer of 'dark earth' up to a metre thick, on which there is no evidence of any subsequent habitation before the 9th or 10th centuries (Dyson and Schofield 1981, 41–3, 48) (Plate 11). This widely attested process, together with a general diminution in the quantity of locally-produced pottery, might well suggest that the settlement was in decline, were it not for the evidence of reconstruction elsewhere in the city, notably at the waterfront. Down-stream of the bridge, for example, elaborate timber quays were installed, while a bath-house and other stone buildings were in occupation from the 3rd to 4th, or 5th, centuries (Hobley and Schofield 1977, 34–7, 54–6); upstream, where evidence of further timber quays is beginning to appear, public buildings were demolished, perhaps to make way for prestigious new development of Severan date (Merrifield 1980, 201–4).

It is not easy to reconcile these costly and confident innovations, and several other indications of a high standard of living, with the evident widespread abandonment of the type of settlement on which a truly urban economy depended, and there is little to show that the new quays, once built, were extensively used.[2] The problem is accentuated in the later 4th century with the construction of the riverside wall and the addition of bastions to the existing land wall (Hill, Millett and Blagg 1980, 67–9), for it is far from clear what sort or scale of settlement they were intended to protect. By this date the surface planking of one of the quays was no longer intact (Tatton-Brown 1974, 127–8), while another had silted up by the 5th century (Hobley and Schofield 1977, 35); and in any case the river wall, built across the head of the quays, must have severely restricted any continuing activity upon them. These considerations need not rule out the possibility of a still significant urban population, but they might well suggest that the city's economic basis had greatly contracted. If so, the defences might be seen as the assertion of an official or formal status, but they certainly had one practical benefit which might throw light on the reason for their construction: London, according to the *Anglo-Saxon Chronicle,* was still in British control by 457 and provided a refuge for forces in flight from the invaders. In these circumstances the same geographical advantage which had once favoured the city as a great *emporium* would now emphasise its strategic potential.

Topography, though properly stressed in the context of the origins of Roman London, has received only incidental consideration in the case of late and post-Roman settlement. Nevertheless, there are indications that its importance was fully understood at the time. The Thames valley offered an obvious line of approach to invaders, and it is perhaps no coincidence that the Roman bastions of London seem to have been confined to the eastern sector of the city wall (Merrifield 1965, 68–72; 1969, 126–7; Maloney 1980, 58–9), facing the North Sea. The discovery at Shadwell of a military site of the late 3rd century, apparently a signal station, raises the possibility of a whole series of such installations extending to the mouth of the Thames (Johnson 1975, 278–80), while the late 4th- and early 5th-century settlement at Mucking (Essex), apparently manned by German mercenaries, was carefully sited

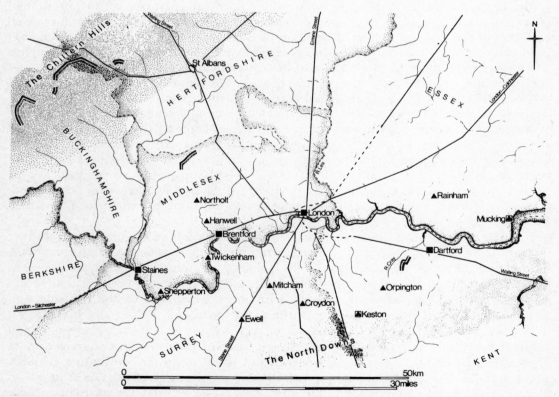

96. The city of London and its region in the immediately post-Roman period. Sites of early Saxon burials or cremations (triangles) or structures (squares) in the area are shown, together with earthworks and pre-L.C.C. county boundaries

on a bend commanding the estuary (Jones 1968, 222–8) (see Fig. 96). Both these provisions seem to underline the importance of securing control of the estuary and valley at large as much as the protection of London itself. No doubt either purpose was interdependent: enhancing the accessibility of the river valley were the major land routes which converged on London from east to west, and from north-east and north-west (Fig. 96), at the lowest point at which the river could be bridged. This accessibility gave London a tactical advantage, demonstrated by the British in 457, as well as a strategic significance of which the advancing Saxons were unlikely to have been long unaware. Whoever held London also controlled established communications along the Thames valley and the readiest access to much of south-eastern Britain.

Whether or not the late 4th-century defences can be wholly explained in these terms, it is unlikely that in any unsettled period of movement and migration these routes did not continue in constant use both inside and outside the walls of London. It is certainly the case that the modern main roads entering the city do so at exactly the same point as their Roman predecessors, and a modern excavation across Aldersgate Street revealed that its post-Roman usage was probably never significantly interrupted (Haslam 1973, 79). Aldersgate, moreover, was of late Roman date and its street of comparatively minor and local character; a proportionately greater degree of continual use might be expected in the cases of the major roads which also maintained their original courses. In the immediate vicinity of the walls these roads would tend to be fixed by the positions of the gates, but it is notable that for distances of several miles further afield, where no such constraints existed, they appear to have held their courses substantially intact: the only significant exception being a stretch of the Colchester road between one and four miles distant from Aldgate (Merrifield 1969, 41–56) (see Fig. 96). At the same time, the possibility that the city was bypassed to any significant extent in the post-Roman period is reduced by the fact that an existing road which linked the Silchester and Colchester routes with Ermine and Watling Streets is notably less well preserved by the lines of modern streets. That continuity of route denotes continuity of use is further suggested by a comparison with conditions in the Southwark area on the south bank of the Thames. Here, outside the main area of settlement, the lines of the Roman approach roads have either been entirely lost or exhibit an appreciably smaller degree of adherence in their modern counterparts (Sheldon 1978, Figs. 1, 5–10). On this analogy, the approach roads to Southwark would seem to have undergone less continuous use as lines of long-distance communication, a role which in any case would have largely depended upon the survival of the bridge, about which there is, to say the least, little certainty.

Roads which survived intact as far as the gates of London were liable to have been employed within the walls also. In this case, however, that use is apparent in a relative disregard for their original courses. It is true that the general articulation of the Roman street plan is insufficiently understood, but where established, as at Newgate Street, Cheapside and part of Cannon Street, it recognisably conformed with the present pattern (Fig. 97): the survival of the gates would have ensured that. It is also true that the plan of walled London was not rectangular and could never have presented a regular symmetry in which the gates were directly interlinked. Nevertheless, the sinuous sweeps of the modern roads between Newgate on one hand,

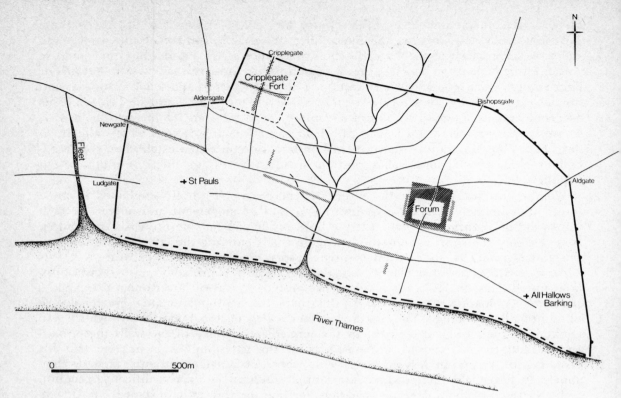

97. Plan of the city to show the relation between medieval and modern main routes and the Roman
street plan (as known), walls and gates

and Bishopsgate and Aldgate on the other reveal a conspicuously non-Roman lack of
linearity, which is most likely to have arisen over a period of constant use in which
corners could be cut and local obstacles avoided in the interests of establishing the
shortest routes through the city. It certainly implies that there was minimal occupation
in the areas immediately adjacent to these streets.

An instructive parallel is available from Winchester which, before its formal
re-settlement in the late 9th century, had survived as a royal and episcopal centre in
which there was little characteristically urban occupation. It stood, nevertheless, on
an important route represented by the High Street which ran directly between two
opposed gates, and the constant use of that route by through traffic was revealed
by its gradual encroachment of the former Roman properties which adjoined it
(Biddle 1976b, 107-9). At London an interesting exception to the degradation of the
Roman street plan is presented by the site of the Cripplegate fort where until recently
the lines of the internal streets were remarkably closely preserved by Wood and Silver
Streets, and, to a lesser extent, by Addle Street (Grimes 1968, 29, 32-7). The fort,
however, lay well away from the major routes and, though the dates of the removal

of its southern and eastern walls is unknown, its compact enclosure may have recommended itself for some purpose which involved a greater degree of control than is apparent elsewhere in the city (see below).

Unlike the major routes, the present minor streets of London would appear to be of considerably later origin and seem to mark a definite replacement of the Roman pattern. In the admittedly small number of sites from which evidence is available it seems possible that earlier streets survived to the 9th century in some cases, but had elsewhere long since been covered by thick deposits of dark earth (see below). In either case there is a consistent absence of any previous post-Roman activity alongside them: while it remains possible that in the later 5th and 6th centuries the intra-mural area of London served as a temporary refuge for those passing through it, the evidence for this or for any other more permanent form of occupation is still to be found.[3] It is nevertheless notable that most cases of probable structural survival are recorded near the waterfront. *Hwaetmundestan* (Fig. 101), mentioned in the late 9th century as an ancient stone building serving as a courtyard, seems to have lain immediately north of Queenhithe, on the site of the Roman bath-house at Huggin Hill (Dyson 1978, 209-10). The O.E. element *stan* often denotes former Roman buildings (Smith 1956, 143-4), and such names presumably arose in a period when stone buildings were exceptional. Another case, *Wifladestan,* recorded in the 12th century, was located near the waterfront on the boundary of the parishes of All Hallows, Barking, and St Dunstan in the East (Hodgett 1971, No. 199). Close by were late Roman stone buildings which survived into the 5th century, including Billingsgate bath-house, where sub-Roman pottery and an early Saxon brooch have been recovered (Merrifield 1976, 55; Hobley and Schofield 1977, 56). A Roman wall at the foot of Lambeth Hill survived long enough both to receive a dump of late Saxon or early medieval pottery, and to determine the line of a parish boundary (Merrifield 1965, 221).

Cases of this kind certainly do not prove continuity of occupation, but their incidence is consistent with the general locations of early stratified finds. The only such finds of early Saxon date were recovered from a dump layer which preceded the collapse of the Roman riverside wall at Blackfriars (Rhodes 1980, 97-8); of later date, at least 10 stratified sherds of middle Saxon Ipswich ware have been recovered at Peninsular House (see below), and other cases are recorded at New Fresh Wharf and Baynards Castle. Outside the walls a comparable riverside location was shared by similar finds at Arundel House (Haslam 1975, 221) and the Savoy (Wheeler 1935, 139-41), both south of the Strand, and at Whitehall (Green 1963, 1,004-7), and Battersea (Webster and Cherry 1978, 148).[4] A relative proximity to the Thames is also a characteristic of many of the early and mid-Saxon settlements recorded further afield in the London area (Fig. 96). The earliest Saxon occupation of all is represented by a group of late 4th- to early 5th-century date in the Croydon area, of which the most important is Mitcham. Settlements of similar date, where the presence of mercenaries was also indicated, were sited at Ham, on the Surrey shore of the Thames, and at Mucking on the Essex bank. Occupation of the early to middle Saxon periods is recorded at Ham and Blackheath (Surrey) (Hurst 1976, 61) and at Northolt (Hurst 1961, 211-99; 1962-3, 309), Hanwell (Wheeler 1935, 136-9), Staines (Crouch 1976, 82-134), and Shepperton (Middlesex) (Canham 1979, 109, 115). Though the date and precise nature of settlement at these sites is not always clear, it is notable that with the exception of the Croydon area, most are located on the river, and all within five miles (8km.) of it. A similar predilection might be expected within the microcosm of the city itself, and is certainly not contradicted by the available evidence, slight though it is.

Allegedly found in London, though without specific location, are two biconical rouletted pots, tentatively attributed to French and German provenances of the late 6th to early 7th centuries (Evison 1979, Figs. 14f and 15h). Both in respect of date and place, these attributions are of interest in the context of Bede's statement that in 604 Ethelberht of Kent founded the church of St Paul's at London, the metropolis of the province of the East Saxons (Colgrave and Mynors 1969, 142-3). Bede makes it clear that Augustine's mission depended upon recognition by the English kings in the main centres of their kingdoms. For his own part, Ethelberht seems to have exercised a general dominion over the kingdoms of southern England for some two decades (Stenton 1971, 60), and though his nephew was nominally king of Essex his own intervention at London suggests that he was the effective ruler. Thus it is possible that his support for the London mission was motivated by the desire to consolidate his own authority, while the choice of London as the site of a bishopric —or even, as late as 601, of an archbishopric (Colgrave and Mynors 1969, 104-5)— implies a renewed appreciation of London's geographical and political potential.[5] Moreover, the people of Kent were closely connected by language, culture and institutions with their Christian Frankish and Merovingian neighbours across the Channel, and Ethelberht's own marriage to a Frankish princess was clearly of crucial importance at the outset of Augustine's mission. The use of money values in his own laws, themselves based on Merovingian models, implies the introduction of money in Kent, and Frankish coins were circulating in southern England from the second half of the 6th century (Sutherland 1948, 23-30). Some forty Merovingian coins of early 7th-century date were found as far north as Sutton Hoo (Dolley 1976, 35), where fragments of Ipswich ware are also recorded (Hurst 1976, 301). The existence of the harbour at Ipswich by this date (West 1973, 8), stimulated by such cross-Channel trade,[6] would favour the probability that the superior site of London was also involved. Certainly by the mid 7th-century Merovingian *solidi* and *tremisses* were being copied in England, some of them bearing the name *Londuniu* (Dolley 1976, 351-2). The presence of the biconical pots of Continental origin mentioned above seems consistent with the re-establishment of London as a port at the turn of the 6th and 7th centuries, a process in which Ethelberht's founding of St Paul's might be seen as symbolising his roles as overking, patron of the Christian mission, and trading partner of his Frankish relatives.

Bede's remark that St Paul's cathedral was intended to serve the 'province' of the East Saxons, of which London was the chief town (*metropolis*), calls into question the political context of Ethelberht's intervention and of the city's apparent re-emergence as an urban centre. Though London lies just beyond the south-western extremity of Essex proper, and was not ideally placed to serve as its chief town, it was more centrally placed in the medieval diocese of London which was composed of Essex, Middlesex, and part of Hertfordshire. Since early dioceses, whose boundaries appear to have been formally defined by the time of Theobald (668-90), were frequently coterminous with existing English kingdoms, it looks as if Essex had already absorbed Middlesex by the beginning of the 7th century (Brooke and Keir 1975, 16–17, 198). The original extent of Middlesex presents an interesting problem: its name does not appear before the beginning of the 8th century, and no kings are recorded, so that the Middle Saxons, though evidently a separate people or group of peoples, appear never to have had any coherent political identity. On the other hand, Middlesex had a definite geographical identity, possibly extending south of the Thames. In c. 690 the laws of Ine of Wessex referred to the bishop of London as 'his' bishop (Whitelock 1979, 339), a description which presumably derived from the ancient West Saxon pre-eminence in Surrey. Moreover, the eastern and western boundaries of both Middlesex and Surrey face each other across the Thames (Fig. 96), while the name Surrey—'southern district' (Gover 1934, xiv-v)—implies a status subsidiary to a more distinctive territory north of the Thames. In the Domesday Survey a conspicuous number of Surrey landowners held property in London (Stenton 1970, 33), an uncommon arrangement in the late 11th century and suggestive of arrangements pre-dating the creation of Surrey as a separate shire. In the mid-12th century, moreover, the citizens of London claimed hunting rights over an area extending between the Chilterns, the south and west borders of Surrey, and the River Cray (ibid., 24–5). Stenton pointed out that these rights were unlikely to have arisen in any political circumstances known from the 7th century, while the existence of an early entity which included both sides of the Thames in the vicinity of London would help to explain Eorcenwold's foundation of monasteries at both Barking (Essex) and Chertsey (Surrey) in the 660s and 670s (Dyson 1980, 89). Both houses claimed to have been endowed by the Mercian King Wulfhere, who had the bishopric of London at his disposal in 670 (Colgrave and Mynors 1969, 234–5), and was temporarily in control of Surrey by 672–4; both men may have been acting within some residual political framework—or vacuum.

It may thus be that the historical Middlesex represents only a remnant of a larger area, which was encroached upon by the 7th century by Essex, Wessex, and, perhaps, Kent, but which originally extended as far north as the Chilterns and as far south as the North Downs (cf. Brooke and Keir 1975, 18, 197–9). Except to the east this area forms a well-defined geographical entity which coincides in part with a system of dykes to the north-west and south of the Chilterns, and also just beyond the River Cray in Kent (Wheeler 1935, 59–74).[7] It is possible, though unprovable, that such a coherent region, dominated by London, invited settlement by an early Saxon people distinct from the East and West Saxons outside it—perhaps contributing to that distinctiveness —just as it may also have determined the pattern of Roman local administration.[8]

The activities of Wulfhere and Eorcenwold c. 670, alluded to above, roughly coincide with the earliest certain knowledge of two important themes in the development of Saxon London: its role as a port, and its political status as part of Mercia which persisted until at least the late 9th century. The first mention of London as a port occurs in a charter of 672–4 by which the sub-king of Surrey, on the authority of his Mercian overlord, confirmed the endowments of Chertsey abbey. These included 10 hides 'near the port of London, where ships tie up' (Birch 1885, No. 34; Dyson 1980, 83–95), and the charter thus corroborates the implication of Bede's reference to the sale of slaves to a Frisian merchant in 679 (Colgrave and Mynors 1969, 404–5). It also lends further significance to the statement in the laws of the Kentish kings Hlothere[9] and Eadric (? *c.* 685) that a hall (*selde*) existed in London where Kentish merchants could obtain warranty for their purchases, and that a royal reeve was in attendance (Thorpe 1840, 14–15). Thus Bede's further statement that the London of his day was a mart of many nations who came to it by land and sea (Colgrave and Mynors 1969, 142–3) was equally applicable some 60 years earlier. Moreover, Chertsey's property near London, like parallel grants made to Eorcenwold's other foundation at Barking, itself seems to reflect the contemporary importance and prosperity of London, which was doubtless also an important factor in the location of the two houses. The presence of a royal reeve, an official active at Lincoln as early as *c.* 630 (Colgrave and Mynors 1969, 192–3), indicates that the Kentish kings were alive to the need for regulating, and taxing, the trade of the port. Furthermore, the casual way in which the Chertsey charter alludes to the port suggests that it was no new thing and was already well established by the 670s. Thus the likelihood is increased that the port had originated by the turn of the 6th and 7th centuries, probably under Ethelbert: the provisions of the Kentish laws of the 680s would themselves bear out that early connection.

By the 670s Kent was no longer the only, or the most important, external influence in London. The Mercians, who always had an obvious geographical advantage, appear to have gained effective control of the city by 670, when they were able to dispose of its bishopric. That authority was temporarily extended to Surrey by 672–4, and to Essex by 685; by the early 8th century Aethelbald of Mercia confirmed to the bishop of London land at Twickenham originally granted by East Saxon kings, and subsequently confirmed by his own Mercian predecessors (Birch 1885, No. 111). These developments roughly coincide with the emergence of a silver *sceatta* coinage based, like the earlier *thrymsas* and *tremisses* which it replaced, on Continental antecedents. The earliest types, from *c.* 680–725, predominate in East Kent and the Thames estuary and some are inscribed with the name of London (Rigold 1961, 6–53): it has recently been suggested that a distinctly Mercian coinage, issued and circulated under royal control, commenced as early as *c.* 715–20 at two mints, one conjecturally in south Mercia, and the other in London (Metcalf 1977, 102). Other local types have been found at *Hamwih* and, presumably originating from Ipswich, in East Anglia (*ibid.,* 102). Both these settlements, flourishing in the second half of the 7th century, have produced evidence of trading links with the Rhineland and bear a physical similarity to the undefended trading centres at Dorestad and Quentovic. Little archaeological evidence of this trade has yet been found at London, but Bede's reference to the presence of a Frisian merchant in 679 would confirm a presumption that London was included in this extensive trading area. In this respect it is significant, too, that London appears in the Kentish laws of the 680s as *Lundenwic,* and this compares with Ipswich, *Hamwih, Eoforwic,* Quentovic and Dorestad (*Wijk bij Duurstede*) (Biddle 1976b, 115). An indirect indication of growing prosperity in late 7th or early 8th-century London is provided by part of the fabric of the church of All Hallows, Barking. Bombing in the last war revealed an archway 2.4m. high and 1.4m. wide, set in a wall 3m. long. Its head was formed of large tiles sloping slightly outwards (Plate 2), an arrangement closely paralleled at Brixworth, erected *c.* 670 (Cherry 1976, 166, 175).

Some further indication of the scale, and also of the organisation, of seaborne trade in London is supplied by three charters of Aethelbald which date from the period of

Bede's famous reference to the *emporium*. In 733 Mildred, abbess of Thanet, received toll belonging *iure publico* to Aethelbald and his predecessors in the port (Sawyer 1968, No. 86), and the following year the bishop of Rochester was granted the toll which previous kings had taken *iure regis* from a shop *in portu Lundonie* (*ibid.*, No. 88); while in *c.* 743 the bishop and church of Worcester were similarly endowed with toll on two ships 'in Lundentunes hythe' (*ibid.*, No. 98). The exaction of toll by Aethelbald and his predecessors implies the presence of royal officials comparable in function with the Kentish reeve of the 680s, while the Worcester charter refers specifically to tax-collectors. Until at least two centuries after the Norman Conquest the mooring of ships, the levying of tolls, and the subsequent sale of goods, were privileges kept under strict royal surveillance (Dyson 1981, 37–38). London at large was described as a royal town (*loco praeclaro oppidoque regali Lundaniae vicu*) in 811 (Sawyer 1968, No. 168), and a grant of 889 refers to the commercial shore (*ripa emtoralis*) as if it was a limited and well-defined section of the waterfront, and carefully distinguishes between royal profits and those of the recipient (see below). Another grant of the same period pointedly restricts the mooring privileges to the river frontages of two properties near Queenhithe, while a charter of Ethelred II to Chertsey, dated 1006–10, concedes the right of mooring, trading, and, for one year only, toll (Kemble 1845, No. 718).

It is probable that similar conditions applied in the 7th and early 8th centuries, but for the location of the 'port' or 'hithe' of this early period there is little certain evidence. There is, as will be seen, documentary evidence for the existence of havens at Queenhithe by the late 9th century, at Billingsgate by *c.* 1000, and at Dowgate by 1066. Though excavation south of Thames Street has produced no clear indication of activity on the New Fresh Wharf/Billingsgate waterfront earlier than the late 9th century, recent investigations at Peninsular House on the opposite side of the street have revealed a distinctive re-development of apparently middle Saxon date (Figs. 98 and 99). Below the earliest levels of the present Botolph Lane and within the apparently contemporary brick-earth floor surfaces of buildings to the west of the lane were sherds of Ipswich ware. No external walls were recorded, but variations in individual floor sequences and a fairly regular interval of *c.* 4m. between the hearths excavated suggest a strip development comprising several separate building plots (Dyson and Schofield 1981, 53–55). The site presents the only indication so far of urban occupation of mid-Saxon date in London, and the absence of any trace of a Roman Street below the lane or the buildings raises the possibility that this development marks a re-planning of pre-Alfredian date, perhaps comparable with that at Tamworth and Hereford (Biddle 1976b, 120–22), and at Bedford (Haslam, forthcoming). Its proximity to the waterfront is of particular interest, since the Billingsgate area, like the other two Saxon centres of riverside activity at Queenhithe and Dowgate, maintained a marked pre-eminence as landing places throughout the medieval period. That the Billingsgate and Dowgate areas in particular were of early date is further suggested by the sitings of local churches. Of 17 waterfront parishes only in four cases were their churches positioned south of Thames Street: St Magnus and St Botolph between the bridge and Billingsgate, and All Hallows the Great and the Less, near Dowgate. In these instances there was presumably a more marked concentration of early activity on the waterfront than was the case elsewhere along the Thames.

None of this establishes that the Mercian port was based in these particular areas, but, not least in view of the evidence from Peninsular House, they remain the likeliest locations.

For the remainder of the 8th century, after the reign of Aethelbald, and for much of the early 9th century, documentary sources maintain a silence virtually as profound as that of the 5th and 6th centuries, so that there is little with which to substantiate the description of London in 811 as a 'famous place' (Sawyer 1968, 168). In view of Offa's concern with coinage and trade, and of his relations with the Continent—notably with Charlemagne—it might be presumed that London was of at least comparable importance to his economy as it had been to Aethelbald's. Direct Mercian access to other major ports was limited. The *sceattas* of East Anglia and Ipswich are of a local, rather than recognisably Mercian type, and it is significant that few Mercian coins have been found at the even more distant site of *Hamwih* (Metcalf 1977, 102). Apart from Chester, which was less than ideally placed for the purposes of Continental trade and was in any case apparently waste until the end of the 9th century, only London was directly accessible as an outlet: for much of the period Mercia had little, if any, control over the Kentish coast. The attempt by Offa's successor, Cenwulf (798–821), to have the seat of the southern English archdiocese moved from Canterbury to London (Stenton 1971, 226) confirms the importance of the city to Mercia. In this connection also Matthew Paris's reference, apparently derived from a late 11th-century source, to Offa's palace seems far from improbable (Riley 1867, 55), and the stated location of the palace next to the church of St Alban Wood Street, which allegedly served as its chapel, is consistent with the date of the excavated church fabric (Grimes 1968, 206–7), and, as will be seen, with other circumstantial evidence for the existence of a palace in the area of the former Cripplegate fort.

What size of population, or what extent of settlement within the walls, was required to sustain London as a 'famous place' or an international emporium is far from clear. In the north-western area of the city, at least, excavation has produced minimal evidence of occupation before the 9th century, and it is unlikely that further east conditions varied significantly. As late as the 14th century much of the area between

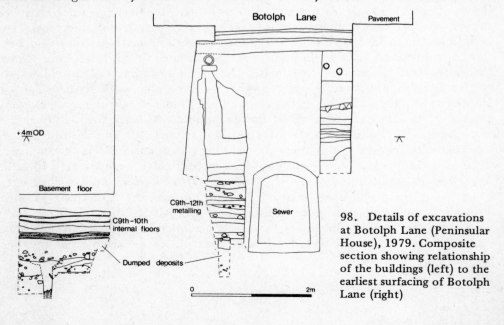

98. Details of excavations at Botolph Lane (Peninsular House), 1979. Composite section showing relationship of the buildings (left) to the earliest surfacing of Botolph Lane (right)

Coleman and Old Broad Streets was known as the *Mora* and was subject to flooding from the Walbrook and its tributaries (Dyson 1977, 15). Still further east, the district between Bishopsgate and Aldgate was sufficiently vacant at the beginning of the 12th century to accommodate Queen Matilda's foundation of Holy Trinity, Aldgate. Moreover, the quantity of imported pottery, almost exclusively Ipswich ware, remains negligible by comparison with the quantities found at *Hamwih* and Ipswich itself. There is, in fact, no evidence of any substantial local pottery manufacture before the mid-9th century, and even of residual pottery in Saxon contexts, the relative quantities of recovered Saxon and Roman material is of the order of one to six.[10]

The Mercian decline which followed the death of Offa in 796 was epitomised by the West Saxon victory at *Ellandun* in 825. In 829 Egbert struck coins in London bearing the inscription *Lundonia Civit*, presumably to assert his authority over the city, but within a year Mercia appears to have recovered, and there are indeed indications that the traditional rivalry between the two kingdoms was abated. Helmstan was consecrated bishop of Winchester at London in 839, while Berkshire, restored to Wessex by negotiation in *c.* 850, continued to be governed by a Mercian ealdorman.

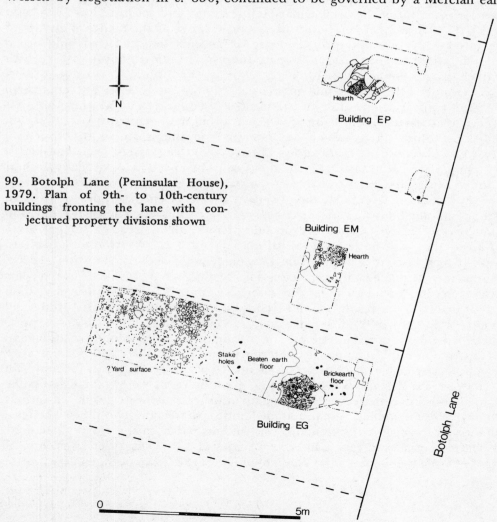

99. Botolph Lane (Peninsular House), 1979. Plan of 9th- to 10th-century buildings fronting the lane with conjectured property divisions shown

It has been suggested that a coin bearing the heads of kings Beorhtwulf of Mercia, and Aethelwulf of Wessex was struck ·to mark this compact (Stenton 1971, 244-5). No doubt Danish activity was a significant factor in this: London itself was first attacked in 842 and again, with greater severity, in 851. By the 860s at the latest a formal alliance was contracted between Mercia and Wessex in which the latter was clearly the dominant partner. Both the strength of this alliance and the essentially Mercian character of London were acknowledged by Alfred's concession of the custody of the city to the Mercian ealdorman Ethelred, later his son-in-law, when it was recaptured from the Danes in 886 (Whitelock 1961, 52).

The insistence of the English sources which record the events of 886 on the need for the 'restoration' and 'strengthening' of London seems deliberately to imply its destruction during the previous 15 years of Danish occupation (Campbell 1962, 46; Stevenson 1904, 69). Yet the Danes, once in possession, had as great an interest as anyone in maintaining its defences and amenities, and the evidence of Viking York demonstrates their familiarity with urban life. In this connection the survival of the Norse term *husting,* denoting in *c.* 990 (i.e., before the period of Danish occupation under Cnut) an institution by which matters of weight and measure were regulated (Stenton 1970, 30 and n. 1), and later the principal court of the medieval city, is of particular interest. It provides early evidence of the link between trade and urban administration, while the name itself strongly suggests a Viking innovation for which the most likely date is the period 871-886.

There is certainly little doubt that in the years immediately after 886 commerce was an urgent consideration, and the importance of Queenhithe at this time has recently been re-assessed in the light of two purported land grants to Alfred (Dyson 1978, 200-215). Both texts, which are late in date and irregular in form, have frequently been dismissed as fabrications, though they have rarely been considered together at any length and, until recently, no attempt had been made to relate both of them to the existing topography. The earlier of the two grants, dated 889, conferred on Waerferth, bishop of Worcester, the use of an enclosure (*curtem*), described as an ancient stone building known as *Hwaetmundes stan,* for a market. There is a stipulation that it any of the bishop's men trade outside in the public street or trading shore (*ripa emtoralis*) they will be liable to royal dues as much as they would be liable to the bishop's if they bought or sold within the courtyard. No specific location is given, but measurements in perches are provided. The text (Birch 1887, No. 561) appears in an early Worcester cartulary compiled at the beginning of the 11th century, soon after and probably as a result of the reorganisation of the diocesan estates by Archbishop Oswald (961-992). The later grant, dated variously 898 or 899, purports to have been issued as a consequence of a discussion of the restoration of London and conferred on Archbishop Plegmund of Canterbury and Bishop Waerferth of Worcester two adjacent plots of land at *Aethereds hid,* identified with Queenhithe in the mid-12th century (Hodgett 1971, No. 977). In addition, mooring rights were granted across the width of their respective properties; this time no measurements were given, but various lanes (*semita*) were mentioned which bounded and separated the two plots. The text, so unorthodox as to suggest an internal memorandum rather than a forgery, let alone a formal charter, survives in four Canterbury copies of 12th-century or later date, of which three observe a common form dated 899 (Birch 1887, No. 578), while a fourth, dated 898, stands apart (*ibid.*, No. 577). While it is impossible to authenticate either, a detailed comparison strongly suggests that the 898 text originated no later than 924, and thus considerably increases the probability of a genuine basis. The two grants of 889 and 898/9, each deriving from entirely separate sources, can, therefore, be shown to date respectively within a century and 40 years of the events they record.

The involvement of both Plegmund and Waerferth, both better known in connection with Alfred's propagandist activities, indicates that there was nothing random about these grants, the later of which was issued in the context of the restoration of London, and that they were directly concerned with the promotion of river-borne trade. Of particular interest is the role of Bishop Waerferth both in the fortification of his own town of Worcester and with the establishment there of a market on terms which closely resemble the arrangements at London, which are evident in a charter which presents the only documentary evidence for the interdependent military and economic role of the late 9th-century burhs (Birch 1887, No. 579). At Worcester, moreover, Waerferth was collaborating with the Mercian ealdorman Ethelred, the son-in-law to whom Alfred entrusted London, who attended the restoration council of 898/9 and whose name, perhaps not altogether by accident, was then shared by Queenhithe. Finally, the *a priori* likelihood that the bishop of Worcester's plots of 889 and 898/9 were identical is borne out by the measurements provided in the earlier documents; from these the proportions of the plot can be shown to correspond most closely with the medieval 'insula' immediately north of Queenhithe. On that basis, the western, Canterbury, plot of the later grant should be identified with the 'insula' between Fish Street Hill and Bread Street Hill (Fig. 103), which lies in the parishes of St Michael Queenhithe and St Mary Somerset. This seems to be confirmed by the fact that in the early 13th century Canterbury cathedral held rents from a series of riverside tenements immediately west of Queenhithe, while property in St Michael's parish owed socage to the bishop of Worcester (Hassall 1949, No. 231). Of comparable importance to the demonstration that London, and, in particular, its waterfront, was directly involved in Alfred's general programme of urban restoration, this identification invites the conclusion that the several north–south lanes of 898/9 had come into existence since 889. This inference may have a significant bearing, as will be seen, on comparable developments elsewhere in London.

Though the relevant area of modern Queenhithe does not survive archaeologically intact, excavations and observations at New Fresh Wharf, just downstream of London Bridge, in 1974–9 have indicated substantial modifications to the waterfront in the late 9th or early 10th centuries. Here the Roman timber quay, partially dismantled, formed the back of a bank of timber-laced rubble which extended 13m. into the river from the line of the Roman riverside wall, observed below the southern edge of Thames Street (Fig. 100; Plate 3). At one point the bank was covered by birch logs dated by C14 to 760 ± 100, and these in turn supported layers of planks, some of them from a clinker-built boat, to form a surface or 'hard' which extended eastwards for some 19m. towards Billingsgate. Mainly to the west of the bank, though partly overlapping and apparently contemporary with it, a large number of vertical oak posts, arranged in 14 rows from north to south and in nine from east to west, formed a grid of stakes which may have extended farther out into the river beyond the southern limit of excavation. The stakes, which were chamfered and bore pointed tops, were

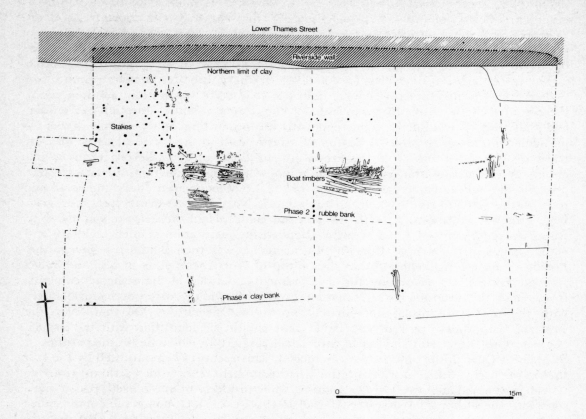

100. New Fresh Wharf, 1974–8: south of the Roman riverside wall, the two main phases of activity in the Saxon period: Phase 2 (stakes and rubble bank incorporating boat timbers), and Phase 4 (clay bank), with deposition of river silts between (Phases 1 and 3). Phase 2 is provisionally 9th- or 10th-century in date; Phase 4 is 10th-century

comparatively short to the north, but towards the river projected up to 2.5m. from the contemporary shore. They were dated by C14 to 870 ± 60 and though only one was suitable for dendrochronological analysis it was seen to be *c.* 65 years older than samples from a succeeding embankment (see below), dated absolutely to felling dates in the second half of the 10th century, and to the early years of the 11th century and by C14 to 940 ± 80. Thus a date in the late 9th to mid-10th century seems to be indicated for the stakes and for the bank contemporary with them. In some respects the stakes are analogous with similar installations at Hedeby, for which both defensive and anti-erosive purposes of comparable date have been suggested.

One of the most interesting aspects of the New Fresh Wharf excavations was that the 19m.-long embankment was evidently only the extremity of an amenity which continued beyond the eastern limit of investigation. It now seems possible that it extended 40m. further east, as its late 10th-century successor certainly did, to a point within 30m. of the site of medieval Billingsgate, first recorded in *c.* 1000 (Robertson 1925, 71 ff). Though in need of confirmation, this may mean that Billingsgate itself originated at the turn of the 9th and 10th centuries. While no definite archaeological evidence of pre-late 9th-century activity has been found south of Thames Street, the Peninsular House site to the north would suggest that the general area was well developed by then. The proximity of the western edge of the embankment and of the stakes to London Bridge is also suggestive: both bridge[11] and Billingsgate are first mentioned in the same context of Ethelred II's trading regulations, and it is unlikely that the relationship was entirely fortuitous.[12] There is some indication that both Alfred and Edward the Elder (899–924) were concerned with the need to control important river crossings by establishing double defences on either bank, an arrangement which implies—and in the case of Nottingham specifically involved—linking by bridges (Biddle 1976b, 135–6). Under Edward in particular these 'works' were constructed at several places in the east Midlands, occasionally (as at Hertford and Buckingham) where there had previously been no occupation on either side, but more often (as at Nottingham) where a settlement already existed on one side. Since the name Southwark first occurs in the Burghal Hidage, essentially a list of recently fortified West Saxon strongpoints (Hill 1969, 84–92), it is at least tempting to attribute the construction of London Bridge to the period of Alfredian or Edwardian restoration (Dyson 1980, 90–93). It is, at any rate, far from clear what useful purpose would be served by fortifications on the Surrey shore if they were not to secure a southern bridgehead, and there is certainly no evidence of any earlier post-Roman settlement on the site (Sheldon 1978, 48). The failure of a charter of 672–4 to provide any place-name in connection with land on the south bank of the Thames near London which could hardly be situated elsewhere than at Southwark is highly suggestive, while the text, understandably at pains to indicate some sort of location by the use of elementary landmarks, mentions nothing as definitive or distinctive as a bridge (Dyson 1980, 90–91).

There is thus reason to suppose that, as might be expected, London was directly involved in the dual economic and defensive reformation characteristic of other urban centres in the period of Alfred and Edward the Elder. Such a context may also be of relevance to a consistent pattern of development beginning at this period and involving the laying-out of new streets and adjacent buildings, evidence for which is beginning to emerge from a series of recent excavations in the western half of the the intra-mural city (Fig. 103). As yet it is too early to draw any firm conclusions: the dating relies upon pottery evidence which requires further analysis. At present, however, dates in the 9th or 10th centuries seem to be indicated at most of these sites. It has already been noted that charter evidence for activity at late 9th-century Queenhithe involved the appearance in 898/9 of numerous lanes which do not appear to have existed in 889, and the subsequent occupation of properties at Peninsular House, provisionally dated to the 10th century, was matched by contemporaneous variations in the composition of the street surfaces of the adjacent

Botolph Lane. While the lower, possibly mid-Saxon, levels incorporated a high proportion of ragstone and *tegulae* fragments, the upper levels revealed a preponderence of large,
water-worn flint cobbles. The use of cobbles suggests the exhaustion of locally available
material, and is paralleled in the new street grid at Winchester attributed to the
Alfredian refounding (Biddle 1976a, 450); accumulations of silt representing mud
or rubbish deposited upon the early metallings at Botolph Lane were conspicuously
absent from the later levels, perhaps indicating a higher and more consistent standard
of maintenance.

Further away from the waterfront, excavations at Milk Street produced evidence of
a sunken structure on the eastern side of the site, represented by a pit, *c.* 4.5m. north
to south by 3m. east to west, which was cut *c.* 0.5m. deep into the existing stratigraphy
to reach a stable, late 2nd-century surface (Fig. 101). The eastern side of this building

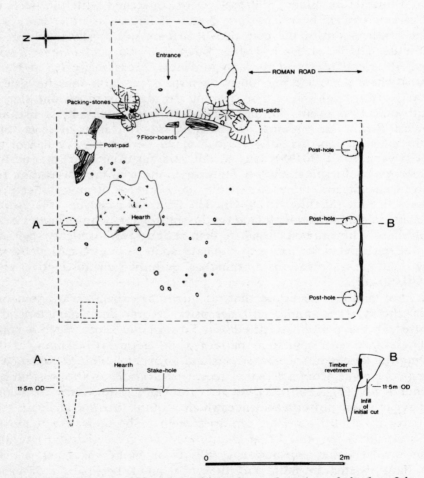

101. Milk Street, 1977: composition plan and section of the late 9th-
century sunken featured building

coincided with the inner edge of the ditch on the western side of a Roman street, from which an entrance into the pit was represented by a sloping hollow and a step. On present evidence, this structure is of probable late 9th-century to early 10th-century date. The position of the building suggests that the Roman street was still in some kind of use, even if only locally, but that usage was finally terminated by the replacement of the building by another of similar type which occupied the centre of the street. On the western side of the site, against the present Milk Street, the dark earth covering the 2nd-century stratigraphy was overlain by traces of cellarless buildings of the 10th and 11th centuries (Plate 1 [C]), dated by pottery which indicates a change from shelly wares to the hand-made, sand-tempered products which predominated in the 11th century. Their alignments, so far as they can be deduced from the patterns of successive pits, would suggest that they were served by Milk Street, and although the property divisions could not be traced across the full width of the site, these arrangements strongly suggest that in the 10th century a Roman street to the east had been replaced by the present Milk Street to the west. In the 13th century, tenements fronting on to Milk Street extended back to the boundary between the parishes of St Mary Magdalene and St Lawrence Jewry; this boundary, common with that between Cheap and Cripplegate wards, coincides with the line of the Roman street which in the late Saxon period appears to have provided an enduring topographical determinant.

A similar case seems to be indicated by current investigations at Ironmonger Lane where an east-west Roman street, c. 80m. north of Cheapside, was apparently encroached in the 9th century by a building[13] whose successor apparently fronted west, presumably on Lawrence Lane, rather than (at this period) east on Ironmonger Lane itself. Yet another case at Well Court, on the east side of Bow Lane, provides a clearer impression of the process by which a Roman street came to be superceded by a new thoroughfare, while also indicating the need for caution in the matter of dating. Here the Roman street was located c. 4m. to the east of the present Bow Lane, and on a markedly different orientation. The street and the area to the west of it were covered by a layer of dark earth 0.6m. deep so that, unlike the Roman streets at Milk Street and Ironmonger Lane, this had gone out of use and was apparently forgotten at a much earlier period. Above the dark earth were two phases of ground level buildings, both aligned upon the present Bow Lane, and both dated to the 9th century. The earlier was represented by two parallel lines of stake holes, slightly bowed in plan, which coincided with the edge of road gravelling c. 1.6m. to the east of the present lane frontage; whereas the second phase of the building extended further west to the modern lane itself. The lane was not dated, but the fact that the two distinct phases of 9th-century date exhibited a notable difference in frontage admits the possibility that the first phase is of pre-Alfredian date, while the lane itself may indeed be of pre-9th-century date.

*   *   *   *   *

Thoroughfares such as Milk Street and Botolph, Lawrence and Bow Lanes typify the majority of the minor streets of London, and offer a contrast with the main streets which lead between the gates and which appear to be modifications of essentially Roman predecessors (Fig. 97). In the recent excavations at least, these minor streets were seen to be of non-Roman origin, while there was ample evidence for the neglect or abandonment of their Roman equivalents by the 10th century. Moreover, the modern Bow and Botolph Lanes were seen to have preserved their original frontages virtually intact to the present day, and the minor streets in general are characterised by a more consistent linearity, particularly where orientated north to south (Fig. 102). In many cases, though not in all, their alignments continue more or less exactly across the prevailing east to west orientation of the main streets. This pattern would seem to suggest some definite policy, or policies, of overall planning at specific periods, rather than casual evolution. A decade ago it was suggested, on the basis of comparable developments at Winchester and elsewhere, that it arose from an Alfredian urban restoration (Biddle and Hill 1971, 83); the excavations and other work at London lend support to that suggestion, although more definitive dating evidence is required.

*   *   *   *   *

The single most important archaeological discovery of late Saxon date is the second of the two embankments at New Fresh Wharf (Fig. 100). The stakes and bank of its probable late 9th- or early 10th-century predecessor were consolidated by two layers of clay dumped around a core of logs (Plate 3) which was laid upon the brushwood matting of the existing bank. These dumps extended south from the surviving fabric of the Roman river wall, below the southern edge of the present Thames Street, for a distance of some 20m. Further dumps of clay, stone and timber raised the bank by some 2m., and in form as well as date closely resembled the Anglo-Scandinavian embankment along the River Foss at York, which prevented flooding and possibly served for unloading boats (Richardson 1959, 59–66). The London bank extended across the width of at least five properties, distinguishable both by the posts and planks of fences aligned north to south, and by slight differences in individual construction. Dendrochronological analysis of samples of timber from the boundary fences indicates felling dates of 964 ± 9, 976 ± 9 and $1,000 \pm 9$, compared with 940 ± 80 as a radio carbon date. This would imply the existence of separate, private wharves by the early 11th century, and it is notable that one of the property divisions was seen to coincide with the line of a medieval alleyway for which there is documentary evidence by the mid-12th century (Dyson and Schofield 1981, 61). Whatever the case with its predecessor, this embankment appears to have extended to within 30m. of the site of medieval Billingsgate, first recorded in c. 1000, and closely compares in construction with an embankment and revetment found 400m. upstream at Dowgate in 1959–60, in front of which large quantities of Pingsdorf ware were found scattered over the foreshore.[14]

By the mid-12th century, and probably by 1066, Dowgate had come to be associated both with the German merchants who in c. 1000 already shared the same privileges as the English, and with the French merchants from Normandy, Flanders, Ponthieu and the Île de France who also feature in Ethelred's ordinance (Robertson 1925, 71 ff) in connection with tolls levied at Billingsgate. Apart from this document, in which the scale of charges varied in accordance with the size of vessel, nothing is known of the handling and distribution of this trade, or, indeed, of the Viking element of the early 11th century attested by the five churches dedicated to St Olaf, and perhaps earlier by St Bride (Brooke and Keir 1975, 138–42). Nevertheless, even this much far exceeds the evidence available from any other English town (Stenton 1970, 42), and London's contribution of an eighth of the tribute levied from the country at large in 1018 gives some impression of the relative volume and importance of its trade, as does the fact that 24 per cent. of surviving coins of the period 959 to 1066 were minted at London, more than twice as many as recorded from York, and more than three times as many as from Winchester (Petersson 1969, 140–1). It seems likely that, at least in the late 9th century, seaborne trade was conducted on the shore (*ripa emtoralis*) at Queenhithe, and a similar practice may be indicated at a later date by the Dowgate and Billingsgate embankments.

The role of Thames Street at this period is uncertain; by the early 14th century it ran along the whole length of the intra-mural waterfront, connecting individual wharves with each other as well as with the hinterland of the city. At the western

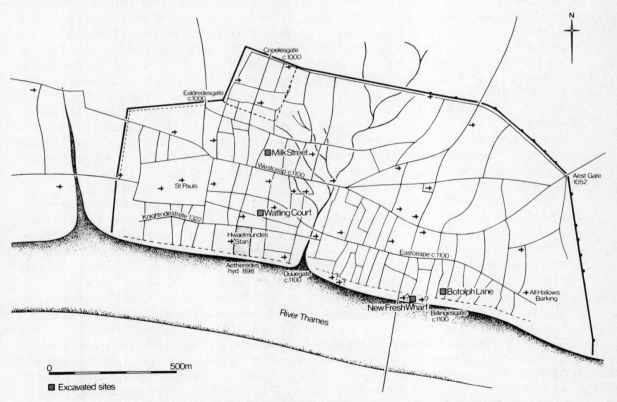

102. Later Saxon London, with the medieval street plan superimposed, and including churches of probable pre-Conquest origin, relevant excavations and other features mentioned in the text

extremity of the city, however, it has been shown to be no earlier than the 12th to 13th centuries (Hill, Millett and Blagg 1980, 16–17), while at the eastern end it may well not have existed until the late 13th century (Dyson 1975, 110). There is certainly no mention of such a thoroughfare in the Queenhithe charters of 889 and 898/9, where the properties granted were separated from the river only by the 'city wall'. On the other hand, both documents refer to a street at the northern end of the properties, apparently corresponding with Knightrider Street, from which the later of the two texts specifies three roads leading to the river. Until the mid-19th century Knightrider Street, together with Old Fish Street and Trinity and Cloak Lanes, existed as a continuous thoroughfare which led along the crest of the hillside behind the river and c. 150m. to the north of it, across the western half of the city (Figs. 102, 103). On the eastern side its equivalent was represented by Cannon Street, Eastcheap and Tower Street; Cannon Street roughly coincides with the line of a major Roman street, and the antiquity of Tower Street (the original access to the Tower of London) seems to be suggested by the position of the 7th- or 8th-century church of All Hallows on its north side. Eastcheap, so named in distinction from Westcheap (Cheapside), is recorded in c. 1100 (Ekwall 1954, 185) and was evidently one of the two major markets of London; it is interesting that it lies parallel with the waterfront between the bridge and Billingsgate further south. Botolph Lane, one of the streets linking Eastcheap with this sector of the waterfront, has recently been shown to be of possibly mid-Saxon date (see above), while the streets leading uphill from Queenhithe were in existence by the end of the 9th century. It thus seems at least possible that the more northerly street alignment served as an early arterial route in place of Thames Street. If so, the fact that Bread Street Hill and Garlick Hill extend across the line of Knightrider Street as far as Cheapside (Fig. 103), and Botolph Lane and St Mary Hill continue across Eastcheap as far as Fenchurch Street may provide a clue to the basis of the street grid pattern as a response to London's river-borne trade.

Cheapside, essentially a continuation of the Roman road which entered the city at Newgate, and the western equivalent of Eastcheap, appears to have developed as a collection of food markets commemorated from the 12th century in the names of several of the streets which lead into it: Honey Lane, Bread, Milk, and Friday (fish) Streets, and by Poultry, its eastern extension. With the exception of fish, these commodities would seem to have been less dependent upon the river and overseas trade, and the suggestion has been made that Cheapside may have originated with the sale of surplus food rents rendered to the chapter of St Paul's, at the western end of the street, by its estates in the London area (Brook and Keir 1975, 171–7, 286). Most of the recent excavations in the general area of Cheapside suggest that it was reoccupied by the late 9th to late 10th centuries.

Structurally the buildings in question fall into three main types: cellarless ground-level buildings dating between the late 9th century and the 11th century, and no doubt under-represented at London as a consequence of ubiquitous Victorian cellars; sunken floored buildings (up to c. 0.5m. below the contemporary ground level), which appear to predominate in the late 9th and early 10th centuries, but may also persist as an archaic type at later dates; and large-cellared buildings (floors up to c. 2m. below ground surface), some of which are distinguished by double linings of horizontal planks, affixed to either side of the vertical posts, and joisted floors, and which

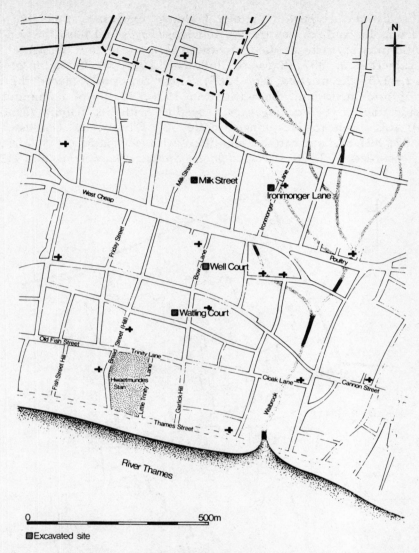

103. Detail of western half of later Saxon London, with the medieval
street plan and relevant excavation sites superimposed

consistently date from the (? late) 10th and 11th centuries. So far, no direct relation
has been determined between different types where they appeared on a single site, so
that questions of contemporaneous use or of whether or not such cases represent
different parts of a single property have yet to be settled. What has emerged from the
present sample, however, is that sites immediately adjoining street frontages (as at Bow
Lane, Botolph Lane and Milk Street) favoured ground-level buildings, and that the
deep cellared type, perhaps designed for ancillary storage, have invariably been found
well away from these frontages (Dyson and Schofield 1981, 58–59).

No doubt distinct from the humbler buildings excavated, there are occasional references from the mid-9th century to individual *hagas* and burhs in London, some given specific names such as *Ceolmundingachaga*, near the 'Westgate', given to Worcester cathedral in 857 (Sawyer 1968, No. 208), or the 'burh of St Paul's' mentioned *c.* 975 (Birch 1893, No. 1288). These apparently record the residences or estates of prominent individuals (Stenton 1970, 35) or of communities, some based outside the city. *Staeningahaga*, together with its parent manor Staines (Middlesex), was given to Westminster abbey by Edward the Confessor (Harmer 1952, No. 97; 327–8), and can be identified with the parish of St Mary Staining (Fig. 104), recorded in 1190 as *ecclesiam de Stanningehaga* (Hassall 1949, No. 6).

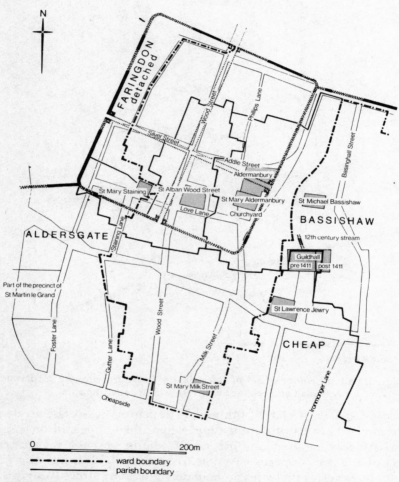

104. Map to show the relationship of the tenement of Aldermanbury to its parish, to the ward of Cripplegate (broken line), to the eastern gatehouse of the Cripplegate Fort and to the medieval Guildhall

Staeningahaga, a district large enough to accommodate 40 burgesses in 1086, would seem to represent a case, very common by the time of the Domesday Survey, of a rural estate holding property in the local urban centre. So also might *Basingahaga,* first mentioned in the period 1160 to 1180 (H.M.C. 9 1883, 206) and now represented by the uniquely coterminous ward and parish of Bassishaw (Fig. 104), except that the name apparently derives from Basing in Hampshire (Ekwall 1954, 12–3, 94), two counties distant from London: it may, therefore, be of earlier than 10th-century date. *Staeningahaga* and *Basingahaga* are moreover the only two names of this type recorded in London, and they are linked by two curious coincidences. Both Basing and Staines lay on, or close to, the course of the Roman road which led from Newgate, close to the *hagas,* to Silchester, and the *hagas* themselves lay just outside the lines of the east and south walls respectively of the Roman Cripplegate fort. The Silchester road was evidently an important line of early communications, and the position of the *hagas* emphasises the general interest of the fort site. Its enclosure (assuming that the internal walls survived) has often been suggested as a likely location for the Saxon royal palace which, according to two very late but independent medieval traditions, lay in the Aldermanbury area, close to the east wall of the fort (Riley 1867, 55; H.M.C. 9 1883, 44a; Biddle, Hudson and Heighway 1974, 19–20).

The potential interest of the fort site in the post-Roman period, and the subject of burhs and *hagas* generally, is currently being re-assessed in the course of documentary work on the medieval tenement of Aldermanbury, 'the fortified manor of the alderman' (Ekwall 1954, 13, 195), which gave its name to the present street, and to the parish at whose centre it stood, immediately to the north of the church of St Mary, Aldermanbury (Fig. 104). It is clear that the church originally belonged to the tenement, and as late as the 14th century the two were directly connected by a postern. In *c.* 1127 Aldermanbury was described as a soke, or private jurisdiction,[15] in a context which shows that it ranked in size or importance with the city wards (Davis 1925, 56–7), while in the mid–13th century the local ward, later to be known as Cripplegate, was referred to as *Aldermanesgarde* (Rigg 1902, 46). The extensive privileges attached to the tenement at this period (Davies 1957, No. 339), exceptional for any secular property, can only be compared with a handful of franchises granted to such specially favoured religious institutions as St Paul's cathedral and the priory of Holy Trinity, Aldgate: they would appear to be equivalent to those of the wards themselves.

This unusual prominence may perhaps be related to two further circumstances, themselves probably connected. The frontage of the tenement, which still projects conspicuously into the street of Aldermanbury, corresponds precisely with that of the assumed east gatehouse of the Roman fort (Grimes 1968, Fig. 4). Moreover, whereas elsewhere modern streets within the former enclosure closely followed the lines of the Roman streets, Addle Street had by the late medieval period been re-directed by some 30m. from the gatehouse site to run along the north side of the tenement. This would suggest that at some date after the demolition of the wall the gatehouse still survived to serve some purpose which justified the diversion of the street. No date can be put to this development, but Roman gatehouses are known to have survived the Dark Ages as residences for local dignitaries—for a bishop at Trier and, it would seem, for kings and earls at York (Hall 1978, 13).

A possible link between the fort area and a London palace is strengthened by the fact that in the years during and after the completion of Edward the Confessor's new palace at Westminster, a considerable amount of land in the Cripplegate area was awarded to various beneficiaries including Westminster abbey (which received *Staeningahaga* and Staines) and the royal college of St Martin le Grand. A late 11th-century source quoted by Matthew Paris notes that the liberties of the former palace site adjacent to St Alban Wood Street were preserved by a 'small house' (Riley 1967, 55), an interesting statement in view of the exceptional early medieval soke of Aldermanbury, its name and its proximity to the Guildhall, 90m. to the south-east, where the medieval aldermen convened at the court of Husting. A comparison with Winchester, where the *gihalda* of 1148, supervised by a royal official, was also established on the boundary of a recently-abandoned royal palace (Biddle 1976a, 336), perhaps at one of its gates, provides an analogy for the close institutional—and topographical—connection between royal and civic government in the late 11th and early 12th centuries. While decisive evidence is lacking, it could be suggested on circumstantial grounds that when a new palace was built at Westminster much of the old site was disposed of, but that part of the area, with its eastern gatehouse and the palace liberties, was reserved for a royal official, the alderman, needed to supervise the king's interest in London. This might be considered as an intermediate stage before the establishment of the Guildhall on its present site, probably in the 1120s when the citizens also won the right of electing a sheriff, as a centre of medieval government for the leaders of the wards, themselves now called aldermen.

POSTSCRIPT

The archaeological data in this chapter was based on a provisional pottery dating scheme using as its earliest fixed point the collection of pottery associated with the first Saxon structure at New Fresh Wharf, which was assumed to be of Alfredian date on the basis of a radio-carbon date (Rhodes 1980, 139). A very recent re-examination of the pottery from the site, and an analysis of all other Saxon assemblages from the city has shown that this chronology may be too long (Vince and Hurman, forthcoming). The first structure at New Fresh Wharf is now thought to be of mid-10th-century date, whilst pottery at first thought to be associated with its construction or earlier is now seen to belong to the succeeding phase, now dated to the early years of the 11th century.

Apart from a single archaeomagnetic date from a bread oven from Well Court, provisionally given as 10th century (A. Clark, A.M. Lab., *pers. comm.*), there is now no external dating from the late Saxon sequence in London. Applying this revised scheme to the Botolph Lane (Peninsular House) sequence, and allowing *c.* 25 years for each rebuilding phase, one arrives at a late-9th or early-10th-century date for the construction of the lane and the first buildings along it (Hurman and Vince 1983). Taking the combined evidence from Botolph Lane and New Fresh Wharf the following conclusions can be made: (1) There are only a handful of pot sherds from the city which definitely pre-date the 10th century. These are chaff-tempered sherds, which have yet to be found in a pre-late Saxon context. Some doubt has been cast on the identification of the Ipswich Ware sherds mentioned in the text. (2) The earliest pottery used in the post-Alfredian town was all made in Oxfordshire. No regional or Continental imports are known. (3) Hand-made squat cooking pots, probably of more local manufacture first appear at the end of the 10th century, but still without imported types. It is to this period that the second and third phases of the Milk Street sunken-featured building belongs. (4) A much wider variety of pottery types, including regional and Continental imports, appears c. A.D. 1000. (5) The famous Dowgate foreshore assemblage, with its high quantity of red-painted ware, blue-grey ware, and Andenne ware imports is probably post-Conquest (Dunning 1959).

A re-examination of non-ceramic finds from the city would probably show a similar pattern. Indeed, most of the late-Saxon finds are probably of 11th-century date. It follows that an 'Alfredian' date cannot be sustained on this evidence for the latest phase of the Milk Street hut, for which a late 10th-century date is indicated, and is less certain at Well Court where a 10th-century date should be preferred. The earliest embankment at New Fresh Wharf would now appear to point to a mid 10th-century date, although it is notable that at Botolph Lane, close to the New Fresh Wharf area, a late 9th- or early 10th-century date is indicated. Since it is hardly conceivable that occupation of this intensity at this location was not accompanied by activity on the adjacent waterfront, some explanation other than the simple absence of earlier activity on the riverside would seem to be required. A similar conclusion is suggested by the recovery along the waterfront outside and to the west of the city of a far fuller range of pottery, especially from the mid-Saxon period for which definite evidence is so far almost entirely lacking from within the city.

The effect of these modifications is to attribute the earliest evidence of the redevelopment of streets and adjoining buildings, and of New Fresh Wharf, more generally within the 10th century, while confirming a more specifically late 9th- to early 10th-century date, consistent with the documentary evidence from Queenhithe, for the early phases of Milk Street and Botolph Lane. Despite the evidence of New Fresh Wharf (partly redressed by that of Botolph Lane) it remains most likely at present that Alfred and/or Edward were responsible for these innovations, which were to be continued and extended by their successors.

NOTES

1. No attempt has been made in this chapter to give an even treatment of all aspects of London at this period: for more general conspectuses see Biddle, Hudson and Heighway (1974), Brooke and Keir (1975), and Clark (1980). Schofield and Dyson (1980) includes an account of Saxon London which contains supplementary information. The present purpose is to give particular consideration, within a chronological framework, to aspects on which significant light has been thrown in recent years. Thanks are due to Richard Lea for the illustrations.

2. A recent report by Ralph Merrifield on the Roman coins from the New Fresh Wharf site points to a virtual absence of issues of the late 3rd and 4th centuries. Communicated by Michael Rhodes, Archaeological Finds Officer, Museum of London.

3. It might be noted that Wheeler, who convincingly argued the continued use of the main roads within London (1935, 80–82), insisted that this was symptomatic of a 'sub-Roman' population (or 'slum') which persisted in the city throughout the 5th and 6th centuries, cultivating 'a continuing, if unexalted, civic consciousness'. There is little to bear out this contention, apparently based partly on Dark Age finds (to a catalogue of which his essay was an extended introduction), which have subsequently been re-dated, and partly on the absence of early Saxon sites in the immediate vicinity of London. There is some force to this latter observation, though hardly sufficient

to warrant the hypothesis of a 'sub-Roman triangle', obligingly avoided by the English. For the evidence of dykes in the Chiltern area and by the River Cray adduced as further support for this theory, see below, p. 291 and Note 7.

4. Communicated by Michael Rhodes, Museum of London.

5. In view of the considerable correspondence between Augustine and Gregory from 597, the Pope's conclusion, as late as 601, that London was a suitable site for an archbishopric is at least as likely to have been based on the missionaries' direct knowledge as on surviving guide books, the memory of Roman traditions, or of the 4th-century bishops of London (*cf.* Brook and Keir 1975, 16).

6. We are grateful to Keith Wade of the Suffolk Archaeological Unit for the information that a pre-'Ipswich ware' phase, characterised by considerable Merovingian imported pottery of the early 7th century, has recently been identified at Ipswich.

7. More recently the finding of Iron-Age pottery in the context of the Harrow earthwork has thrown some doubts on the dating of Grim's Dyke (Celoria and Macdonald 1969, 75–6), but its relevance to the question of early geo-political boundaries remains. We do not accept Wheeler's contention, based partly on these earthworks, that a sub-Roman population centred on London persisted after the mid-5th century.

8. It is notable, for example, that of the major Roman urban centres closest to London, Colchester is 50 (80km.), Rochester 27 (43km.), Silchester 45 (72km.), and St Albans 20 (32km.), miles distant. With the exception of the last, which barely intrudes within it, all lie beyond the limits of this area.

9. It is possible that the street name Lothbury, 'the manor of Lotha's people or descendants' and probably of Old English formation, commemorates the personal name Hlothere (Ekwall 1954, 197). The only recorded instance of this name is Hlothere of Kent (see pp 291–2), a contemporary of Eorcenwold the founder of Barking abbey which held the advowson of St Margaret Lothbury in the medieval period. Did Hlothere share the role of patron of Eorcenwold's foundations, played by Wulfhere, king of Mercia, a little earlier? The conjectural nature of this association will be obvious, but it is interesting that in the late 13th century the present Broad Street ward was known as Lothbury ward (Ekwall 1954, 196). A direct parallel is provided by the cases of Aldermanbury (see below, pp. 307-8) and Bassishaw (*Basingahaga*) (p. 307); both were evidently properties of considerable importance and, especially in the latter case, antiquity.

10. Communicated by Michael Rhodes, Museum of London.

11. An earlier reference to London Bridge in 963–75 has been convincingly re-attributed by Dr. David Hill (1976, 303–4) to a bridge on the road to London, near Ailsworth (Northants) with which the charter in question is immediately concerned.

12. In 1052 Godwine's navy anchored below London Bridge until a high tide enabled them to pass through it (Whitelock 1961, 123). Access interrupted by ebb tides may well have encouraged the establishment of a haven for large ships just downstream of the bridge.

13. This building overlay the two interconnecting oval sunken structures cut into the Roman road. In the western structure, two successive occupational phases were provisionally dated to the 9th century.

14. Communicated by Peter Marsden, Archaeological Field Officer, Museum of London.

15. Of the two early 12th-century surveys of Winchester, the first, of *c.* 1110, mentions three churches in private ownership (Biddle 1976a, 340; 34 [No. 10]; 37 [No. 23]; 45 [No. 71]). The second, of 1148, mentions two groups of properties with churches whose advowsons were later recorded as belonging to the owners of the rents (*ibid.*, 341; 106 [No. 510]). In the cases of Godbegot and Chapman's Hall, the landlords also exercised a private jurisdiction over their tenants, and sake and soke is mentioned in connection with another house in Southgate Street (*ibid.*). The surveys seem to preserve the outline of an earlier arrangement in which the 'urban manor' with the territorial lordship and private church of its rural counterpart, may have been a common and conspicuous feature of the refounded city of the late 9th century (*ibid.*, 451). Godbegot, with the church of St Peter, covered an area of 19,668 square feet; Aldermanbury, with the church and churchyard, covered some 20,000 square feet (0.18h.).

BIBLIOGRAPHY

ABBREVIATIONS

L.M.A.S.: London and Middlesex Archaeological Society.
H.M.C. 9: Historical Manuscripts Commission. Ninth report, i, London, 1883.

Biddle, M. (ed.) (1976a), *Winchester in the Early Middle Ages* (Winchester Studies 1), Oxford.

Biddle, M. (1976b), 'Towns', in Wilson, D. M. (ed.), *The Archaeology of Anglo-Saxon England*, London, 99–150.

Biddle, M. and Hill, D. (1971), 'Late Saxon planned towns', *Antiquaries Journal* 51, 70–85.

Biddle, M., Hudson, D. and Heighway, C. (1973), *The Future of London's Past* (Rescue Publication No. 4), Worcester.

Birch, W. (ed.) (1885–93), *Cartularium Saxonicum*, 3 vols., London.

Brooke, C. N. L. and Keir, G. (1975), *London 800–1216: The Shaping of a City*, London.

Campbell, A. (ed.) (1962), *The Chronicle of Aethelweard*, Edinburgh.

Canham, R. (1979), 'Excavations at Shepperton Green, 1967 and 1973', *Trans. L.M.A.S.* 30, 97–124.

Celoria, F. and Macdonald, J. (1969), 'Archaeology: the pagan Saxon period', *Victoria County History (Middlesex)*, i, 74-9.

Cherry, B. (1976), 'Ecclesiastical architecture', in Wilson, D. M. (ed.), *The Archaeology of Anglo-Saxon England*, London, 151–200.

Clark, A., Hurman, B. and Vince, A. (1983), 'Saxon London: the evidence of the artefacts', *Popular Archaeology*.

Clark, J. (1980), *Saxon and Norman London* (Museum of London).

Colgrave, B. W. and Mynors, R. (eds.) (1969), *Bede's Ecclesiastical History of the English People*, Oxford.

Crouch, K. (1976), 'The archaeology of Staines and the excavation at Elmsleigh House', *Trans. L.M.A.S.* 27, 71–134.

Davies, J. C. (ed.) (1957), *Cartae Antiquae Rolls 11–20*, Pipe Roll Soc. 33.

Davis, H. W. C. (1925), 'London lands and liberties of St Paul's, 1066–1135', in Little, A. G. and Powicke, F. M. (eds.), *Essays in Medieval History presented to T. F. Tout*, Manchester, 45–59.

Dolley, R. H. M. (1976), 'Coins', in Wilson, D. M. (ed.), *The Archaeology of Anglo-Saxon England*, London, 349-372.

Dunning, G. C. (1959), 'Anglo-Saxon pottery: a symposium', Dunning, G. C., Hurst, J. G., Myres, J. N. L., and Tischler, F. (eds.), *Medieval Archaeology* 3, 1-79.

Dyson, T. (1975), 'The topographical development of the Custom House area, in Tatton-Brown, T. (ed.), 'Excavations at the Custom House site, . . . Part 2', *Trans. L.M.A.S.* 26, 110-113.

Dyson, T. (1977), 'Historical survey', in Blurton, T., 'Excavations at Angel Court, Walbrook, 1974', *Trans. L.M.A.S.* 28, 15-16.

Dyson, T. (1978), 'Two Saxon land grants for Queenhithe', in Bird, J., Chapman, H. and Clark, J. (eds.), *Collectanea Londiniensia: Studies . . . presented to R. Merrifield*, L.M.A.S., Special Paper 2, 200–215.

Dyson, T. (1980), 'London and Southwark in the seventh century and later: a neglected reference', *Trans. L.M.A.S.* 31, 83–95.

Dyson, T. (1981), 'The terms "quay" and "wharf" and the early medieval London waterfront', in Milne, G. and Hobley, B. (eds.), *Waterfront Archaeology in Britain and Northern Europe*, C.B.A. Research Report 41, 37-38.

Dyson, T. and Schofield, J. (1981), 'Excavations in the City of London: Second Interim Report, 1974-1978', *Trans. L.M.A.S.* 32, 24-81.

Ekwall, E. (1954), *The Street-names of the City of London*, Oxford.

Evison, V. I. (1979), *A Corpus of Wheel-thrown Pottery in Anglo-Saxon Graves*, Royal Archaeological Institute, London.

Gover, J. E. B. (ed.) (1934), *The Place-Names of Surrey*, (English Place-Name Society 11), Cambridge.

Green, H. (1963), 'Evidence of Roman, Saxon and medieval Westminster', *Illustrated London News* 242, 1,004.

Grimes, W. (1968), *The Archaeology of Roman and Medieval London*, London.

Hall, R. (1978), *Two Thousand Years of York: The Archaeological Story*, York Archaeological Trust.

Harmer, F. (1952), *Anglo-Saxon Writs*, Manchester.

Haslam, J. (1973), 'The excavations of a section across Aldersgate Street, City of London, 1972', *Trans L.M.A.S.* 24, 74–84.

Haslam, J. (1975), 'The Saxon Pottery', in Hammerson, M. J., 'Excavations on the site of Arundel House . . . W.C.2 in 1972', *Trans. L.A.M.S.* 26, 209-51.

Haslam, J. (forthcoming), 'The origins and topography of Bedford', *Beds. Archaeological Journal.*

Hassall, W. O. (ed.) (1949), *The Cartulary of St Mary Clerkenwell*, Camden Society, 3rd ser., 71, London.

Hill, D. H. (1969), 'The Burghal Hidage: the establishment of a text', *Medieval Archaeology* 13, 84–92.

Hill, D. (1976), 'London Bridge: a reasonable doubt?' *Trans. L.M.A.S.* 27, 303–4.

Hill, C., Millett, M. and Blagg, T. (eds.) (1980), *The Roman Riverside Wall and Monumental Arch in London*, L.M.A.S. Special Paper 3.

Hobley, B. and Schofield, J. (1977), 'Excavations in the City of London, 1974–5: First interim Report', *Antiquaries Journal* 57, 31–66.

Hodgett, G. A. J. (ed.) (1971), *The Cartulary of Holy Trinity, Aldgate*, London Record Society 7, London.

Hurman, B. and Vince, A. (1983), 'Peninsular House Saxon pottery' (unpublished Level III report in Museum of London archive).

Hurst, J. (1961), 'The Kitchen area of Northolt Manor, Middlesex', *Medieval Archaeology* 5, 211–99.

Hurst, J. (1962-3), in 'Medieval Britain in 1961', *Medieval Archaeology* 6-7, 309.

Hurst, J. (1976), 'Anglo-Saxon and medieval', in *The Archaeology of the London Area: Current Knowledge and Problems*, L.M.A.S. Special Paper 1, 60–67.

Johnson, T. (1975), 'A Roman signal tower at Shadwell, E.1—an interim note', *Trans. L.M.A.S.* 26, 278–280.

Jones, M. (1968) 'Crop-mark sites at Mucking, Essex', *Antiquaries Journal* 48, 222–28.

Kemble, J. M. (1945), *Codex Diplomaticus Aevi Saxonici*, Vol. 7 (London).

Maloney, J. (1980), 'The defences of Roman London', *Current Archaeology* 7, 55–60.

Merrifield, R. (1965), *The Roman City of London*, London.

Merrifield, R. (1969), *Roman London*, London.

Merrifield, R. (1976), 'Romans', in *The Archaeology of the London Area: Current Knowledge and Problems*, L.M.A.S. Special Paper 1, 80–89.

Merrifield, R. (1980), 'The contribution to our knowledge of Roman London', in Hill, C., Millett, M. and Blagg, T., *The Roman Riverside Wall and Monumental Arch in London*, L.M.A.S. Special Paper 3, 200–205.

Metcalf, D. M. (1977), 'Monetary affairs in Mercia in the time of Æthelbald', in Dornier, A. (ed.), *Mercian Studies*, Leicester, 87-106.

Petersson, H. B. A. (1969), *Anglo-Saxon Currency: King Edgar's Reform to the Norman Conquest*, Lund.

Rhodes, M. (1980), 'The Saxon pottery', in *The Roman Riverside Wall and Monumental Arch in London*, L.M.A.S. Special Paper 3, 97-8.

Rhodes, M. (1980), 'Saxon Pottery', in Jones, D. M., *Excavations at Billingsgate Buildings 'Triangle', Lower Thames Street, 1974*, L.M.A.S. Special Paper 4, 139-41.

Richardson, K. M. (1959), 'Excavations in Hungate, York', *Archaeological Journal* 116, 51–114.

Rigg, J. (ed.) (1902), *Select Pleas, Starrs, and other Records from the Rolls of the Exchequer of the Jews, 1220-84* (Selden Society), London.

Rigold, S. E. (1961), 'The two primary series of *sceattas*', *British Numismatic Journal* 30, 6-53.

Riley, H. (ed.) (1867), *Gesta Abbatum Monasterii Sancti Albani*, Rolls Series i, London.

Robertson, A. (1925), *The Laws of the Kings of England from Edmund to Henry I*, Cambridge.

Sawyer, P. (1968), *Anglo-Saxon Charters: an Annotated List and Bibliography*, London.

Schofield, J. and Dyson, T. (1980), *Archaeology of the City of London*, Museum of London.

Sheldon, H. (1978), *Southwark Excavations 1972-74*, eds. Bird, J., Graham, A. H., Sheldon, H., and Townend, P., L.M.A.S. and Surrey Archaeological Society Joint Publication 1, 2 vols., London.

Smith, A. H. (1956), *English Place-Name Elements*, English Place-Name Society 25 and 26.

Stenton, F. M. (1970), 'Norman London', in Stenton, D. M. (ed.), *Essays Preparatory to Anglo-Saxon England*, Oxford, 23-47.

Stenton, F. M. (1971), *Anglo-Saxon England* (3rd edn.), Oxford.

Stevenson, W. H. (ed.) (1959), *Asser's Life of King Alfred*, Oxford.

Sutherland, C. (1948), *Anglo-Saxon Gold Coinage in the light of the Crondall Hoard*, Oxford.

Tatton-Brown, T. W. T. (1974), 'Excavations at the Custom House site, City of London', *Trans. L.M.A.S.* 25, 117-219.

Thorpe, B. (ed.) (1840), *Ancient Laws and Institutes of England*, Record Commission 66, London.

Vince, A. and Hurman, B. (forthcoming), 'Saxon pottery from London: a type series'.

Webster, L. and Cherry, J. (1978), 'Medieval Britain in 1977', *Medieval Archaeology* 22, 142-88.

West, S. (1973), *Ipswich: the Archaeological Implications of Development*, Ipswich.

Wheeler, R. E. M. (1935), *London and the Saxons*, London Museum.

Whitelock, D. (1961), (ed., with Douglas, D. C. and Tucker, S. I.), *The Anglo-Saxon Chronicle*, London.

Whitelock, D. (ed.) (1979), *English Historical Documents I* (2nd edn.), London.

Chapter Ten

SAXON CHICHESTER AND ITS PREDECESSORS

By Julian Munby

THE COLLECTED STUDIES in *The South Saxons* (ed. Brandon 1978) provide a new and authoritative background to the early history of Sussex towns, and there is no need to repeat what is discussed there. Writing on 'The origins of the Saxon towns', David Hill has placed the growth of urban centres into the context of the West Saxon response to Viking attacks in the 9th century, and sees Chichester as being 'organised for defence, for trade and for refuge, by 894', which is the date of the first mention of it in the *Anglo-Saxon Chronicle* (Hill 1978, 182). Precursors of late Saxon town development have to be sought in the evidence for sub-Roman survival and amongst the sites which may be considered 'central places' in earlier Saxon times.

The purpose of this paper is to consider evidence which comes mostly from a much later period, to see what light can be thrown on the early form of Chichester, and to examine the suggestion that Selsey, the site of the pre-Conquest cathedral, may have been a 'central place' at a time when Chichester was a place of little significance. As the available historical evidence is slight, and the amount of archaeological evidence small (though growing), attention is here directed to the landscape as a source for the study of town origins. The landscape setting of towns is an aspect conspicuous by its absence from urban history ever since Maitland's pioneering work on Cambridge and its fields (Maitland 1898). Indeed, the world 'field' is rarely found in the indices of books on urban history, and the boundaries of parishes, boroughs and their adjacent rural communities are more often than not omitted from published plans. And yet the potential for reading back from the late medieval landscape (as apparent in maps and written records) into early medieval times is a dimension that is ignored at peril. To be sure, there are dangers in anachronistic interpretation, but it is perhaps better to risk these rather than leave a large body of evidence completely out of consideration.

The Region of Chichester (Fig. 105)

The administrative geography recorded for the first time in Domesday Book shows Sussex organised round the six rapes into which it was divided. Unlike the others, which were held individually, the western pair of rapes, Chichester and Arundel, were held together by Earl Roger. The boundary between them is not respected by the distribution of places with appurtenant holdings in Chichester, shown in Fig. 105 B (Ballard 1904; Darby and Campbell 1962, 464); but the greater concentration lies within the rape of Chichester. The origins of these links between town and country are disputable, but it seems fair to see the overall pattern as reflecting at one level the sphere of influence of Chichester as a market centre (Biddle 1976, 382).

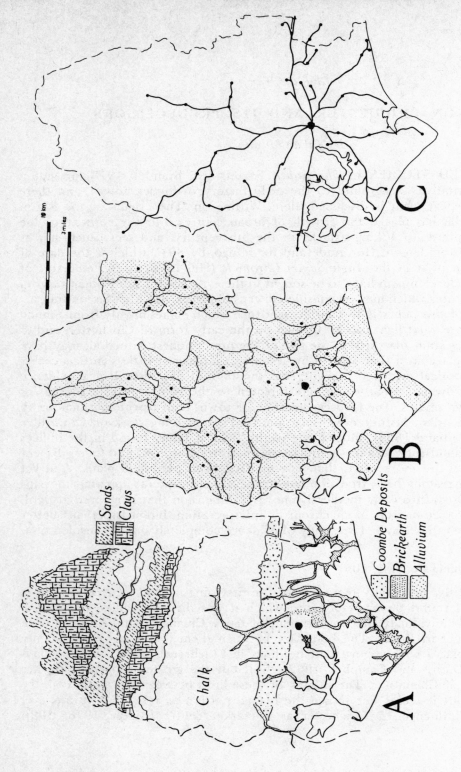

105. The Rape of Chichester: A. Principal geological divisions, B. Domesday Book manors with property in Chichester, 1086, C. Carriers plying to and from Chichester (from Kelly's 1910 Sussex Directory)

Comparing 1086 with 1910, and mapping the places sending carriers to Chichester market at the later date (Fig. 105 C), it is possible to see the fundamental continuity of the centre in its region.

The physical characteristics of the region can be briefly described. Lying between Surrey and the sea, its geology is made up of a series of contrasting east-west zones: a wide coastal plain of alluvium, brick-earths and Coombe Deposits, the chalk downland, and beyond the scarp of the Downs the Upper Greensand, clays and sands of the western end of the Weald (Fig. 105 A). North of the Downs landscapes have been investigated at Harting (Yates 1972), and around Elsted (Bell and Tatton-Brown 1975); on the broad dip-slope of the Downs the area surrounding Chilgrove Roman villas has been studied by Tittensor and Aldsworth (Down 1979, 1–30), the coastal plain in the Iron Age and Roman period is the subject of work by Cunliffe and Bradley (Cunliffe 1971), and Pitts has mapped the Roman finds (Pitts 1979). These localised studies can now be seen in a general framework, in *Archaeology in Sussex to A.D. 1500* (ed., Drewett 1978), but there remains a need to consider areas larger than the local study and yet smaller than the whole county. It is not intended to do this here beyond what appears in Fig. 105, but it is an approach that would seem to be appropriate for studying towns and their hinterlands.

The Environs of Pagham Harbour (Fig. 106)

The lack of any positive evidence for the continuity of town life in Chichester after the Roman period suggests that the establishment of the late Saxon town there may simply have been the choice of a suitable defensive site which had been abandoned. For the earlier Saxon period, Hill has discussed the possibility of there having been centres of population and trade in the South Saxon kingdom, which were 'central places' if not recognisable towns. He points to the part played by Selsey in the story of St Wilfrid and the Conversion, and to the distribution of coin find-spots that may indicate 'a central-place for some sort of trade at Selsey' (Hill 1978, 178–9). This suggestion will now be examined and developed, looking not only at Selsey, but also at Sidlesham and Pagham, two adjacent parishes also bordering on Pagham Harbour; it is this harbour (also known as Wythering) as much as any one place on it that can perhaps be seen as a feature of central importance in the early Saxon landscape.

Selsey

The persistent myth that the old cathedral at Selsey lies under the sea is probably no older than Camden, who refers only to 'some obscure remains of that ancient little city, in which those Bishops resided, covered at high water, but plainly visible at low water' (Camden 1695, 169). In reality, there is no reason to seek any further than the site of the old parish church at Church Norton and its associated earthwork (Aldsworth 1979). For quite apart from the probability that the church remained on the same spot (and that at some distance from the present village of Selsey), there is the explicit statement in the will of Bishop William Reed (dated 1382) that he wished to be buried before the high altar of the church at Selsey 'once the Cathedral Church of my Diocese' (Powicke 1931, 87). It may also be noted that the one

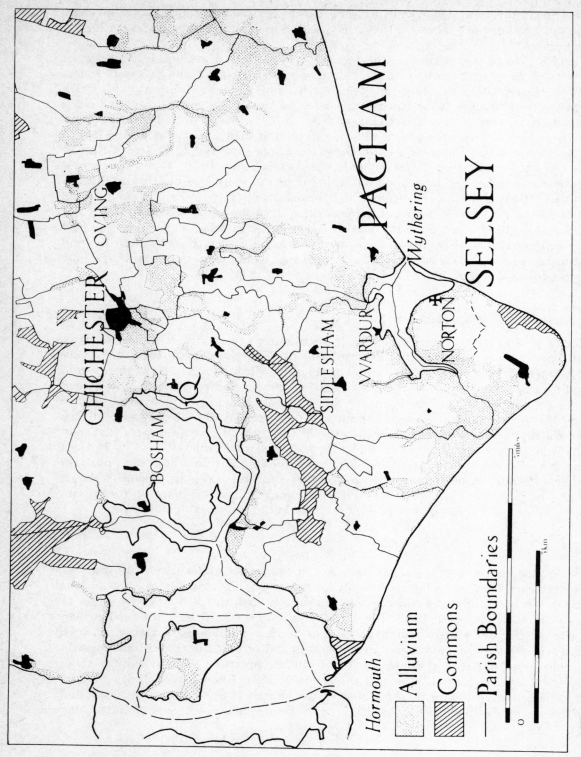

106.   The environs of Pagham Harbour, and Chichester: The ancient parishes, and aspects of land-use in 1778 (from Yeakell and Gardner's map)

late Saxon object found in the 1911 excavations of the 'mound' was a bronze tag of a type frequently found in ecclesiastical contexts (Heron-Allen 1911, 196, Pl. xxxvi; Peers and Radford 1943, 55–8; Waterman 1959, 76–7). The question can only be settled by excavation, but at present it seems more reasonable to assume that the cathedral precinct is mostly or partly on dry land rather than being at some distance out from the shore. This assumption is strengthened by a consideration of the topographical evidence discussed below.

The foundation history of Selsey is not without difficulties since the two accounts of its origin, in Bede's *History*, and Eddius's *Life of Wilfrid*, show conflicting details (Welch 1978, 29–32; Kirby 1978, 166–71). Further confusion is supplied by supposed land grants from King Caedwalla of Wessex (Sawyer 1968, Nos. 230 and 232) for Selsey and Pagham. What cannot be doubted is that the exiled Bishop Wilfrid founded a monastic house at Selsey in *c.* 680 with the support of King Aethelwalh of the South Saxons, amongst whom Wilfrid was evangelising. Eddius states that the king gave Wilfrid his own vill for the episcopal seat, later adding a territory of 87 hides in Selsey: *villam suam propriam, in qua manebat, ad episcopalem sedem cum territoribus postea additus lxxxvij mansionum in Seolesiae* (Colgrave 1927, 82–3). This is somewhat ambiguous, implying either that Selsey was a royal vill (and the grant being in two stages) or that the vill and the land in Selsey were in different places; the former is perhaps the more likely. A further question to be considered is the extent to which Selsey was a community 'in retreat from the world' (Eddius) apart from the sense in which it would have been so to the cosmopolitan and exiled Wilfrid.

Bede accurately described the situation of Selsey 'surrounded on all sides by the sea except on the west where it is approached by a piece of land about a sling's throw in width' (Colgrave and Mynors 1969, 375). Although erosion has nearly removed the western approach, and modern reclamation has masked the estuarine marshes that almost cut off the peninsula from the mainland, the original topography can easily be appreciated on the soil map (Hodgson 1967) or from the areas of pasture indicated by Yeakell and Gardner's survey of 1778 (see Fig. 106). It is apparent from historical records that the parish contained two divisions, Norton and Sutton, and although the distinction between them is not clear (Heron-Allen 1911, 12) the former is known to refer to the area near the church, and the latter part must refer to the main body of the village in the southern part of the peninsula. Fortunately, a map of Selsey in 1672 enables the topography to be better understood (Heron-Allen 1911, at end); it amplifies the information given on Yeakell and Gardner's map of 1778. Round much of the peninsula was a fringe of waste or common, the main common being on the east coast. The common arable fields (which were not enclosed until the 19th century) surrounded 'Sutton' except on the north-east, where the demesne of the bishop's manor lay. Beyond the demesne, and north of the common, the outline of the Bishop's Park can be traced against the coast (it gave its name to the offshore anchorage here). All this was in the southern end of the peninsula; the 'Norton' end shows a completely distinct pattern of small fields, perhaps representing late medieval enclosure of a separate field system. In the north-east corner near to the church lay the rectory with its glebe lands; other prebendal lands lay nearby. The division between these two field systems is marked on Fig. 106, but whether they exactly represent the tenurial division between Norton and Sutton cannot be determined, though the topographical difference is clear enough. It will not be stretching the evidence too far to propose that there may have been a shift in the focus of settlement away from an initial concentration on Pagham Harbour, with the church and northern group of fields, towards the southern part of the peninsula with its own fields. The belated removal of the parish church in 1866 to the centre of the village from Church Norton represents the last stage of a change that must have taken place many centuries before.

Coastal erosion round Selsey is an aspect of its topography that must be considered here, as it has played a large part in previous accounts, and it must be seen whether it affects the scheme that has been outlined. There is no doubt that erosion has been severe, particularly along the south-western coastline where the observable change since 1672 is greatest (Heron-Allen 1911, 291–9 and maps). But if the erosion is related to the medieval settlement pattern, it can be seen to have had only a marginal effect. Apart from the loss of much of Medmeney Farm on the south-west, and most of the South Field that lay below the village, nearly all the erosion on the east coast was of the Common and the Bishop's Park. The 'built-up' area of the village was not affected, and if there had been some feature out at Selsey Bill, it is notable that no medieval road led directly to it. Inside Pagham Harbour there has been a limited amount of erosion immediately east of the church, but for the most part the north and west sides of the peninsula have hardly been diminished. It can therefore be argued that whatever the prehistoric landscape may have been, and whatever may have been lost from Selsey Bill, the medieval landscape as perceived in the map of 1672 was only marginally altered by coastal erosion, leaving the two centres and their field systems largely intact.

Sidlesham

This large parish lies north and west of Pagham Harbour, and contained important estates of the bishop and cathedral. Divided by tidal streams penetrating far inland, the parish had centres at Sidlesham and Ham (Salzman 1953, 212), and by the 18th century a number of scattered farms and hamlets. The common was at the north end of the parish. The church and village are set back from the harbour, but near the road from Chichester to Selsey. This road divides south of the village, part continuing to the ferry over to Selsey and part skirting a creek down to the sea where there was a mill (in modern times a large tide-mill). It was here that Bishop Stephen Bersted (1262–87) founded the new town of Wardur (Peckham 1946, No. 971) on the north shore of Pagham Harbour. Although it has been supposed that there was no evidence for the place after its foundation (Beresford 1967, 497) there are, in fact, several references to it at later periods. It had a court of its own, and appears as 'Newhaven' in episcopal rentals of the late 14th century.[1] The significance of the new town is that, together with another foundation in Pagham, the use of the harbour in later medieval times can be used to throw light on what may have been the early medieval importance of the harbour.

Pagham

This large parish lies on the east side of the harbour. It was a manor of the arch-bishops of Canterbury, having been transferred to them from Selsey at an unknown date, perhaps in the 10th or 11th centuries (Brooks, 1968, 24, 249; Du Boulay 1966, 25). The supposed charter of King Caedwalla to Wilfrid (Sawyer 1968, No. 230) records pre-Conquest bounds that are apparently the same as the parish bounds shown on Fig.106; in 1334 these include the tithings of South Mundham, Pagham, Charlton, Shripney, North and South Bersted, Bognor, Aldwick, and Crimsham (Glasscock 1975, 307). The parish of Bersted was separated from Pagham in the 15th century, and Bognor only in the 19th century (Salzman 1953, 225–6). Until these sub-divisions were made Pagham remained as an estate fossilised in its early form, escaping the usual changes that might have taken place had it not been under distant ecclesiastical lordship. Together with other estates in the Chichester area (Slindon, Tangmere, Lavant, and land in Chichester), Pagham was a western outlier in the distribution of Canterbury lands, which was naturally concentrated in Kent (Du Boulay 1966, 196). This small group of estates could in some respects be seen as a parallel to the 'multiple estate' of Malling in the vicinity of Lewes to which attention has recently been drawn (Jones 1976, 26–35). It is of interest to note that the Canterbury manor of Tarring (near Worthing) is almost equidistant from Pagham and Malling—a day's ride from each.

Turning from the external relationships between the Canterbury manors in Sussex to the internal organisation of Pagham, it is possible to make out some similarities between it and the other manors round the harbour. In the first place, although it was a large parish with several tithings, each of which appears to have had its own field system and a fairly central settlement, Pagham itself and the parish church were located at the western extremity, at the head of a small inlet on the edge of the harbour (Fig. 106; Fleming 1949, map of 1786).[2] In addition to this there seems, as at Sidlesham, to have been an attempt to develop a borough, appropriately named Wythering after the harbour. References to it occur between the mid-13th and the late 15th centuries, and it was perhaps in association with the town that a market and fair were granted to Pagham.[3]

Pagham Harbour, the 'Port of Wythering'

Having considered the three parishes adjoining the harbour, the harbour itself must now be dicussed, as its use in the later medieval period may throw light on its potential in earlier times. It was a member of the port of Chichester, which was the name given to the accounting unit for the collection of customs from a number of landing places in the vicinity of the city. As to Chichester itself, in the words of an inquisition of 1339 'there is no landing place for ships; there are no men of that city who have ships, barges or boats, and no mariners dwell there' (Pelham 1937a, 202). The principal landing places were at Dell Quay, to the south-west of the city ('Q' on Fig. 106) on Chichester Harbour (known as Hormouth), and in Pagham Harbour (known as Wythering). A charter of Henry II confirmed to the citizens of Chichester the customs and liberties they had held in the time of Henry I in the ports of Wythering and Hormouth (Steer 1956, 6; *Cal. Pat. R.* 1374–7, 289). In 1212 the city, complaining that the archbishop of Canterbury had appropriated Wythering, claimed that it had belonged to the city since the Conquest (Salzman 1935, 101; *Book of Fees* ii, 73). Wythering had its own bailiffs, to whom writs were addressed in the 13th century (Fleming 1949, 46–8). Evidence for the activity of the port is to be found in the earliest accounts relating to the port of Chichester (1287–90), when the shipmasters, Andrew and Ciprian 'de la Wardur de Sidlesham' were operating for Chichester wool merchants (Pelham 1935, 102). In 1319 the archbishop made a 'loan' of wheat to Edward II at Newcastle, which having been milled at Chichester was conveyed to Sidlesham and shipped to Shoreham (Pelham 1931, 169). There are several cases of smuggling from the harbour, and one occasion in 1344 when a ship having been arrested in Sidlesham and broken out to Normandy returned to Pagham where it was apparently able to avoid the authorities as it was in the archbishop's liberty (Fleming 1949, 54). The proximity of Canterbury and Chichester lands on either side of the harbour provided many occasions for disputes, especially over the taking of porpoises and wrecks (Peckham 1946, No. 897). There seems to have been a decline in trade passing through the harbour in the 15th century (Fleming 1949, 190), though the 1587 'Armada Survey' mentions Sidlesham mill 'unto which a Barcke of 40 tonne may flete' (Salzman 1953, 210). Finally in 1680 the sole wharf of the port of Chichester seems to have been limited to Dell Quay (Salzman 1935, 100).

Conclusion

What should be apparent from the foregoing description of the parishes round the harbour is that here are three large ecclesiastical estates of which two had their churches, and, arguably, their primary settlement on the harbour, and that the harbour was the scene of sufficient commercial activity in the 13th century for it to be thought worthwhile founding boroughs in two of the manors. Without forcing the retrospective argument, it would seem fair to propose that if the harbour was well used in the post-Conquest period, its suitability is likely to have been realised long before then, and that the harbour may well have influenced the location of Selsey/Norton and Pagham.

From this modest suggestion it would, of course, be possible to speculate that Pagham Harbour was the focus of a developing commercial centre, possibly centred at Selsey, and that this was the reason for the location of Bishop Wilfrid's church, and for the gift to him of land there. The importance of Selsey has also been suggested from the evidence of coin distribution, if the small concentration of *sceatta* findspots near Selsey can be taken as an indicator of trade (Hill 1978, Fig. 12, 179). But whilst it would probably be going too far to suggest that Selsey was to the South Saxon Kingdom what Saxon Southampton was to Wessex (Biddle 1973, 246–7; Keen 1975, 182–7), it will not be unreasonable to think of Wilfrid establishing his church on an active port rather than a place 'in retreat from the world'. The harbour itself, surrounded by large estates on one of which was a royal vill, can surely be seen as a 'central place', at a time when there is simply no evidence for any activity in Chichester itself.

Chichester (Figs. 107 and 108)

Apart from an extraordinary single find, a gold *solidus* of Valentinian III (A.D.425–55) (Down 1974, 33), there is no hard evidence of sub-Roman activity in Chichester. The earliest post-Roman material from excavations is a small amount of 'mid-Saxon' hand-made pottery, which is difficult to date, but could possibly be 8th or 9th century (Down 1978, 341). At the least then, it could be said there is virtually no evidence for continued occupation between the Roman *civitas* and the late Saxon burh. What information therefore can the topography of the medieval borough provide about the early state of this burh?

A first approach may be through an examination of the parochial divisions of the area surrounding the city, which as so often have preserved down to modern times an

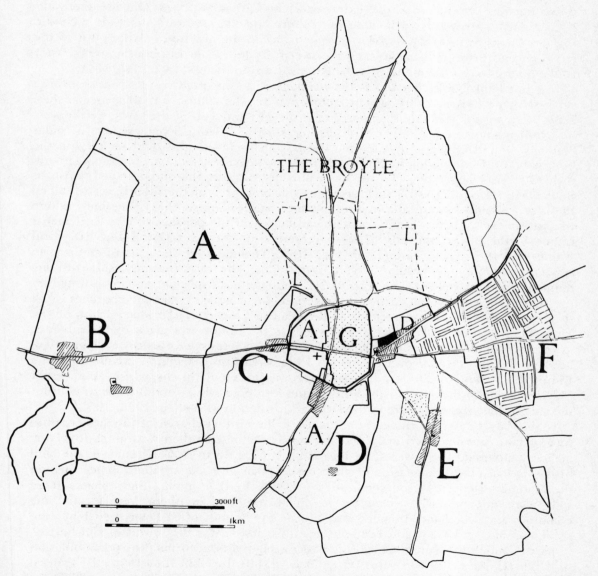

107.   Chichester and its extra-mural parishes: A. St Peter the Great; B. New Fishbourne; C. St Bartholomew (Holy Sepulchre); D. St Pancras; E. Rumboldswyke; F. Portfield and Guildenfield, in Oving (showing arable strips before enclosure); L bounds of City Liberty

indication of the primary arrangements. The parish of St Peter the Great is apparently the survivor of the pre-Conquest mother-church of Chichester, remaining as a parochial altar in the nave of the cathedral (and later in the north transept) after the cathedral had moved from Selsey to Chichester in 1075 (Salzman 1935, 105, 164–5; Peckham 1933, 69–72). The parish boundary is particularly instructive, including a large area both inside and outside the walls. It comprised the whole of the less densely occupied north-west corner of the city and a small area inside the southgate, leaving out the eastern part of the intra-mural area where the small urban parishes developed, and the south-west corner with the extra-parochial Cathedral Close. Outside the walls it continued southwards to include the suburb and the meadows alongside the main road as far as Stockbridge (which gave its name to the hundred on the south of the city), and northwards to include a wide sweep of land, from Fishbourne on the west to the bounds of Westhampnett on the River Lavant to the east (A on Fig. 107).

It is not improbable that this is the remnant of a large pre-Conquest parish, whose original shape it is not difficult to reconstruct by the addition of adjacent parishes. First there are the two suburban parishes at the east and west of the town. To the west lies St Bartholomew (C in Fig 104), earlier known as Holy Sepulchre.[4] Its irregular common boundary with St Peter the Great, and its meeting at right-angles with the boundary of Donnington to the south make it a likely candidate for a parish sub-divided from a larger one. To the east, outside the gate, the oddly-shaped parish of St Pancras (D on Fig. 107) includes only the built area of the suburb, a strip along the city wall and Lavant, and in addition the road leading south to Kingsham, where the parish encircles the farm. To these can be added the parishes of two settlements rather further from the city: New Fishbourne to the west (B on Fig. 107) and Rumboldswyke to the east (E on Fig. 107). Together, all these parishes form an almost complete and regular circuit surrounding the city (leaving aside for one moment the east fields (F on Fig. 107). Topographical speculation is confirmed by the scant records of ecclesiastical jurisdiction, for it appears that the churches of all these parishes were in the peculiar of the dean of Chichester (Peckham 1933, 65–7). Thus the collection of Peter's pence payable to the bishop was made by the sub-dean in the intra-mural parishes and the extra-mural ones mentioned above (Peckham 1946, 336), whilst in a dispute over Bosham in 1324 when Bishop Langton excommunicated Bishop Stapledon of Exeter, the sentence was read out 'in the parish churches of Chichester and in the churches of Fishbourne, Rumboldswhyke and St Pancras without the gate of the city, which are in the Dean's Jurisdiction' (Peckham 1946, 305).

If this large area was the early *parochia* of the mother-church of Chichester, what sort of land was included in it? To the south of the city there was much low-lying meadow alongside the Lavant (see Fig. 106). On the north of Chichester, as the land begins to rise, the brick-earths of the coastal plain give way to the stonier soils on the Coombe Deposits (Hodgson 1967, 11, 96). In their more flinty phases these soils were not primarily attractive to arable use, and on them were located the commons and woodland. Immediately outside the bounds of St Peter the Great were the commons of Lavant and Fishbourne, whilst inside was the 'forest of Chichester', in part of which the men of Chichester had grazing rights, according to a perambulation of 1225 (Holmes 1968, 70; *Rot. Litt. Claus.* ii, 80). In 1229 King Henry III granted the 'broyles of Chichester' to his chancellor, Bishop Ralph Neville, after which the area was disafforested and became the bishop's home farm (Peckham 1946, 31; 1925, 128; Pelham 1937b, 210). Other land nearby passed to the dean and chapter, and eventually ecclesiastical lordship was established over the whole area of St Peter the Great outside the city liberty (L–L on Fig. 107).

Inside the liberty boundary were pastures, several of which belonged to the city, and a certain amount of arable. The great arable fields lay to the east of the city, Portfield and Guildenfield, shown on Fig. 107 as they were in 1848, divided into strips. As indicated by their names, and the few surviving deeds of land transfers (Peckham 1950), these were the town fields of Chichester. However, for much of the medieval period these fields were outside the liberty of the city in the parish of Oving, and were only re-united with the city in the late 19th century (Salzman 1935, 71). This is puzzling, but may be explained by the report of the citizens of Chichester in 1212 that they had lost certain lands in the reign of Henry I, including Shopwyke and *terras cultas extra Cicestriam* which had been granted away by the king (*Book of Fees* ii, 72–3). Shopwyke lies immediately east of the Chichester fields; the other places that were lost, Martinsgrove, Drayton, *Orrea Regis* (Kingsham), and Egley, were all in Oving (except Kingsham). It is open to speculation how far east the parish of St Peter the Great may have extended, but it does at least seem likely that it once included the borough fields.

The land included in this reconstructed *parochia* of Chichester, which would have been the primary land unit of the Saxon borough, included a variety of meadow, arable, pasture and woodland, much as would be found surrounding an ordinary village. It also included two discrete communities, at Fishbourne and Rumboldswyke, within its bounds. Consideration must now be given to how this area of land related to the surrounding settlements. First it should be noted that the borough, presumably itself extra-hundredal, lay between the Domesday hundreds of Box (east), Singleton (north), and Stockbridge (south) (Morris 1976). In 1086 Fishbourne and Rumboldswyke lay in Stockbridge hundred, with the borough indenting its northern boundary; but if at an earlier date they, too, had been extra-hundredal, and the boundary of *parochia* and hundred had marched together, then Chichester could be seen as a discrete unit which was respected by the initial lay-out of the hundreds. As far as parish bounds are concerned (Fig. 106), the Chichester *parochia* in no way impinges on any of the surrounding parishes, nor does it have the appearance (as with some new boroughs) of having been cut out of any other parish. It looks much like any of the other large parishes of the coastal plain—Westbourne, Bosham or Aldingbourne. It can, therefore, be argued that its origin is possibly contemporary with the creation of the parochial system of the coastal plain. The date at which this process took place cannot be firmly established, but the relationships described above suggest two alternative modes of origin. The church of St Peter could on the one hand be seen as a central minster church serving at an early date a scattered group of settlements round the ruins of a Roman town: Fishbourne, Rumboldswyke and the suggestively named Kingsham. On the other hand, St Peter's could have been the church of a nascent urban community within the walls, established by King Alfred as founder of the borough (see Hill 1978, 180–1). A decision between the two is a matter which could perhaps be resolved by a comparison with the ecclesiastical topography of other former Roman towns and boroughs, but must take into account the (as yet) limited evidence for middle Saxon occupation within the walls, and the possibly overriding importance of the area round Pagham Harbour in the 7th to 8th centuries. The further possibility, that there might be some element of survival of the Roman *territorium* of Chichester, should perhaps be mentioned, though the area under consideration here is smaller than that apparently preserved round Silchester, or the area of the Chilcomb estate round Winchester which is another possible candidate (Biddle 1976, 255–8).

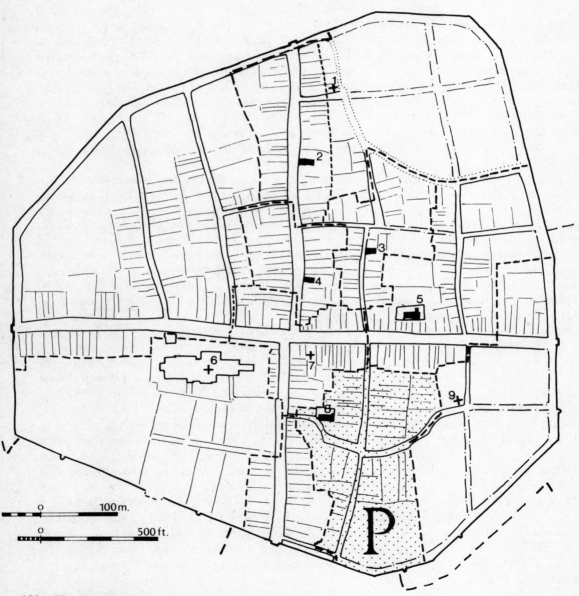

108. The intra-mural parishes of Chichester, with selected tenement boundaries: (1) St Peter sub castro; (2) St Peter the Less; (3) St Martin; (4) St Olave; (5) St Andrew in the Ox-Market; (6) St Peter the Great (situated in the extra-parochial Cathedral Close); (7) St Mary (or St Peter) in the Market; (8) All Saints in the Pallant; (9) St Andrew in the Pallant. P = the Liberty of the Archbishops of Canterbury.

Chichester Inside the Walls (Fig. 108)

The intra-mural topography of Chichester is the final aspect to be considered. Here there is little documentary evidence from the medieval period to go on, though the later material is now being collected (Down 1974, 7–15; Down 1978, 22–40). Hence it is necessary to work back from relict features that have survived long enough to appear on maps, adding to them features that can be reasonably supposed to have been present.

The street lay-out has now been shown to bear little relationship to that of the Roman town (Hill 1978, 181). Apart from the principal cross of the main streets, the predominant pattern is of north-south streets, with less regular east-west routes, and an intra-mural road that is even today well preserved on the north and west. The original lay-out has been obliterated in two places, by the Norman castle in the north-east corner, and by the Blackfriars' precinct in the south-east. Quite enough remains, however, to relate the plan of Chichester to other similar planned towns of the late Saxon period (Biddle and Hill 1971). One point that does emerge from this comparison is that it was quite normal to have a central 'Carfax' at the road junction, and the local myth that there was once an open market-place here should be discounted. Encroachments referred to in documents are likely to have been minor ones.

Tenement boundaries given on Fig.108 are selected from those on the early editions of the Ordnance Survey 1:2,500 plan, and though subjective this should not be wildly misleading, granted that work elsewhere has shown such boundaries to be fairly conservative features. They certainly fit in well with what is known of the parish boundaries.

Owing to the work of the late W. D. Peckham it is possible to map the boundaries of the late medieval parishes with a fair degree of accuracy (Peckham 1933). They are typical of small urban parishes, containing blocks of properties on opposite sides of the street and with the boundaries running along the backs of the tenements. Their distribution probably reflects the concentration of population and commerce in the city, with its emphasis on the north-east quadrant. It is impossible to say how many of the churches were in existence before the Conquest, though some of them certainly were. One interesting feature which must have arisen from their secondary status in relation to the mother-church is that the churches either have no burial grounds or very small ones (indeed, several of the churches were built on narrow tenement plots at right angles to the street). Burials seem to have taken place either in the cathedral cemetery or in The Litten, the graveyard with its chapel of St Michael in the east suburb, next to the site of the Roman cemetery (Down 1971, 55).

Two areas in the city are distinct from the general pattern described above: the Close and the Pallants. The Close was obviously laid out after the removal of the cathedral from Selsey to Chichester, the south-western corner being reserved for the Bishop's Palace, and the remainder, to the south of the cathedral cloister, divided into large plots for houses of the principal officers of the cathedral. This may represent considerable replanning of this quarter of the town, or it may, like the north-west quadrant, have been only thinly occupied. The Pallants, or rather the parish of All Saints (P on Fig.108), is a different matter. Here was a discrete liberty in the middle of the city, which belonged to the archbishops of Canterbury. It appears in Domesday Book as a 'Church in Chichester' in the entry for Pagham (Morris 1976, 2,5), and is a rare instance of the survival of a compact urban soke throughout the medieval period. The area of the parish can be seen to include the curious irregularity in the street lay-out where East and West Pallant bend to the south. It has been suggested that this is a re-alignment of an earlier street that ran directly east-west (Hill 1978, 181, Fig. 14), but it should be observed that there is a remarkable rectilinear arrangement of tenement boundaries here, almost as if there had been a large square enclosure east of the church. If this were so, then the road might have turned to avoid it. Whatever the explanation, it is notable that the shape of tenements is different within the archbishop's soke.

Beyond this consideration of the topography of pre-Conquest Chichester there is little than can be said about life in the town. The evidence of land resources may point to agrarian interests of the early inhabitants, though the arrangement of tenements and the development of parish churches would be indicative of a thriving urban community with a wider range of economic activities. No doubt the borough soon became established as the regional market centre as demonstrated above, and from the reign of Aethelstan it was one of the Sussex mints, though it never seems to have been as active as the mint at Lewes (Brandon 1978, 89-137; Drewett 1978, 70-77). Archaeological material from within the walls has been found in increasing quantities, especially in the series of excavations conducted in the north-west quadrant. Evidence for structures is slight, but the rubbish pits associated with domestic occupation have provided much pottery (Down 1978, 45, 83-6, 158, 341-53). The ceramic sequence from the 9th and 10th centuries is well established, and there are also small quantities of hand-made pottery, possibly dating from the 8th century (though usually in residual contexts). Further excavations hold the greatest potential for adding to the early history of medieval Chichester. But meanwhile, despite the limited amount of archaeological and historical evidence, the attempt has to be made to derive as much as possible from all sources, particularly the topography of the town and its environs. Above all, as Maitland wisely remarked, 'I have been endeavouring to suggest to you that those who would study the early history of our towns . . . have fields and pastures on their hands' (Maitland 1898, 9).

ADDENDUM

The following have appeared since this paper was written: F. G. Aldsworth *et al.* Excavations on 'The Mound' at Church Norton, Selsey, in 1911 and 1065, *S.A.C.* 119, 1981, 217-21; H. Mayr-Harting, St Wilfrid in Sussex, in M. J. Kitch (ed.), *Studies in Sussex Church History*, 1981, 1-17; and M. G. Welch, *Early Anglo-Saxon Sussex*, Brit. Archaeol. Reports 112, 1983.

ACKNOWLEDGEMENT

I am grateful to the staff of the West Sussex Record Office for their patient assistance, and to Michael Coker for aiding field work in the environs of Chichester. Dan Chadwick pointed out the connection between St Wilfrid and St Andrew, and Jeremy Haslam the reference to Holy Sepulchre (in addition to helping re-work an earlier draft of this paper). The original research for this study was mostly done in association with work for the History Department of Bishop Otter College, Chichester.

NOTES

1. Evidence for the location of Wardur, unknown to Beresford, is to be found on the plan of Sidlesham manor in 1755 (W.S.R.O. Add. MS. 1990), where 'Wardur Green' is marked by Rookery Farm (GR SZ 861977) and 'New Haven' is written along the coast to the east of the mill. The main source for medieval references is the cartularies of Bishop William Reed (1369–85), now in W.S.R.O. Liber P contains the foundation charter (f. 167v–8), and an undated rental of Sidlesham (? c. 1350) which lists 23 holdings of the 'free tenants at Newhaven'. A later rental of 1379 gives 40 holdings (Liber C, f. 110–11). In Liber A f. 5 is an undated list of courts which includes the 'free court of Newhaven' belonging to the manor of Sidlesham which also had its separate hall-moot (see S.N.Q.2 [1928–9], 82–3). Evidence for the 15th-century is lacking, but there are references to 'franchise land' in Newhaven in a manorial survey of 1552 (W.S.R.O. Ep. VI/2/1, f. 10–11) and in later courts (W.S.R.O. Add. MS. 752).

2. In addition to the parish church, dedicated to St Thomas, there was a chapel of St Andrew to the west of the church on the edge of Pagham Rife (GR SZ 878976; indicated by Fleming on map of 1786). This, if genuine, must be the one mentioned in Caedwalla's charter, the 'church of St Andrew on the eastern shore of the harbour' of Wythering (Salzman 1953, 227, 233). It is notable that St Andrew was held in special veneration by Wilfrid (Levison 1946, 262). There is also a church of St Andrew in Chichester (on the north side of East Street).

3. The township is first mentioned in the Assize Roll of 1248 as 'Wyteringe', and it occurs in the Canterbury Custumal of 1279x88, where some 35 messuages are listed in the 'port of Wytheryng'. It had a court of its own, at least from 1382 to the 1450s, and there are several references to burgage tenements from the early 15th century (Fleming 1949, 184–9). The market and fair were granted in 1204 and again in 1314 to the archbishop, though there is little further evidence for them (Salzman 1953, 229). The one burgage tenement that can be traced down to the estate maps was by the road junction to the east of the church, by present Church Farm (GR SZ 886975), No. 461 on the map of 1786 (Fleming 1949, 189; map at end).

4. The church was until the 17th century a round church (Salzman 1935, 165; Bodleian Gough Maps 31, f. lv). Its dedication suggests that it is unlikely to have been founded before the early 12th century (see the discussion of London's extra-mural Holy Sepulchre in Brooke and Keir 1975, 144). More could be said of the dedications of Chichester churches. That of St 'Andrew's has been mentioned above (n. 2); several were dedicated to St Peter (Peckham 1933 passim), whilst St Olave is another instance where a fairly close terminus post quem can be proposed for its foundation (Brooke and Keir 1975, 141, suggest after the death of Cnut in 1035). St Pancras was near the Roman cemetery, but too much need not be made of that.

BIBLIOGRAPHY

ABBREVIATIONS

S.A.C.	Sussex Archaeological Collections.
S.N.Q.	Sussex Notes and Queries.
W.S.R.O.	West Sussex Record Office (Chichester).

Aldsworth, F. G. (1979), ' "The Mound" at Church Norton, Selsey, and the site of St Wilfred's Church', S.A.C. 117, 103-7.

Ballard, A. (1904), The Domesday Boroughs.

Bell, M. and Tatton-Brown, T. W. T. (1975), 'A field survey of the parish of Elsted and adjacent areas, West Sussex', Bulletin of the Institute of Archaeology 12, 58–64.

Beresford, M. W. (1976), New Towns of the Middle Ages.

Biddle, M. (1973), 'Winchester, the development of an early capital', in Jankuhn, H., Schlesinger, W., and Steuer, H. (eds.), Vor- und Frü-formen der Europäischen Stadt im Mittelalter, Göttingen, Vol. I, 229-61.

Biddle, M. (ed.) (1976), Winchester in the Early Middle Ages (Winchester Studies 1).

Biddle, M. and Hill, D. H. (1971), 'Late Saxon planned towns', Antiquaries Journal 51, 70-85.

The Book of Fees (H.M.S.O.), 1921-31.

Brandon, P. (ed.) (1978), The South Saxons.

Brooke, C. N. L. and Keir, G. (1975), *London 800-1216: the Shaping of a City.*

Brooks, N. P. (1968), 'The Pre-Conquest charters of Christ Church Canterbury', unpublished Oxford D. Phil. Thesis.

Calendar of Patent Rolls, (H.M.S.O.) 1891 onwards.

Camden, W. (1695), *Britannia* (ed. Gibson, E.).

Colgrave, B. (ed.) (1927), *The Life of Bishop Wilfrid by Eddius Stephanus.*

Colgrave, B. and Mynors, R. A. B. (eds.) (1969), *Bede's Ecclesiastical History of the British People.*

Cunliffe, B. W. (1971), *Excavations at Fishbourne.*

Darby, H. C. and Campbell, E. M. J. (eds.) (1962), *The Domesday Geography of South-East England.*

Down, A. (1971), *Chichester Excavations 1.*

Down, A. (1974), *Chichester Excavations 2.*

Down, A. (1978), *Chichester Excavations 3.*

Down, A. (1979), *Chichester Excavations 4.*

Drewett, P. L. (ed.) (1978), *Archaeology in Sussex to A.D. 1500,* C.B.A. Research Report 29.

Du Boulay, F. R. H. (1966), *The Lordship of Canterbury.*

Fleming, L. (1949), *History of Pagham in Sussex.*

Glasscock, R. E. (1975), *The Lay Subsidy of 1334.*

Heron-Allen, E. (1911), *Selsey Bill: Historic and Prehistoric.*

Heron-Allen, E. (1934), 'The 1672 map of Selsey Bill', *S.A.C.* 75, 200–5.

Hill, D. H. (1978), 'The origins of the Saxon towns', in Brandon, P. (ed.), 174-89.

Hodgson, J. M. (1967), *Soils of the West Sussex Coastal Plain,* Soil Survey of Great Britain Bulletin No. 3.

Holmes, J. (1968), 'The Chichester dykes', *S.A.C.* 106, 63–72.

Jones, G. R. J. (1976), 'Multiple estates and early settlement', in Sawyer, P. H. (ed.), 15-40.

Keen, L. (1975), ' "*Illa Mercimonia que dicitur Hamwih*" a study in early medieval urban development', *Archaeologia Atlantica* 1, 2, 165-90.

Kirby, D. P. (1978), 'The church in Saxon Sussex', in Brandon, P. (ed.), 160-73.

Levison, W. (1946), *England and the Continent in the Eighth Century.*

Maitland, F. W. (1898), *Township and Borough.*

Morris, J. (ed.) (1976), *Domesday Book: Sussex.*

Peckham, W. D. (1925), *Thirteen Custumals of the Sussex Manors of the Bishops of Chichester,* Sussex Record Society 31.

Peckham, W. D. (1933), 'The parishes of the city of Chichester', *S.A.C.* 74, 65–97.

Peckham, W. D. (1946), *The Chartulary of the High Church of Chichester,* Sussex Record Society 46.

Peckham, W. D. (1950), 'Chichester city deeds', *S.A.C.* 89, 117–62.

Peers, C. and Radford, C. A. R. (1943), 'The Saxon monastery of Whitby', *Archaeologia* 89, 27–88.

Pelham, R. A. (1931), 'Studies in the historical geography of medieval Sussex', *S.A.C.* 72, 157–84.

Pelham, R. A. (1935), 'Sussex wool ports in the thirteenth century: Chichester', *S.N.Q.* 5, 101–3.

Pelham, R. A. (1937a), 'The wool trade of Chichester, 1377–80', *S.N.Q.* 6, 201–4.

Pelham, R. A. (1937b), 'The Agricultural Geography of the Chichester Estates in 1388', *S.A.C.* 78, 195–210.

Pitts, M. W. (1979), 'A gazetteer of Roman sites and finds on the West Sussex Coastal plain', *S.A.C.* 117, 63–83.

Powicke, F. M. (1931), *The Medieval Books of Merton College.*

Rotuli Litterarum Clausarum, ed. Hardy, T. D., Record Commission, 1833-4.

Salzman, L. F. (ed.) (1935), *Victoria County History (Sussex),* 3.

Salzman, L. F. (ed.) (1953), *Victoria County History (Sussex),* 4.

Sawyer, P. H. (1968), *Anglo-Saxon Charters: An Annotated List and Bibliography.*

Sawyer, P. H. (ed.) (1976), *Medieval Settlement.*

Steer, F. W. (ed.) (1956), *Chichester City Charters,* Chichester Papers No. 3.

Waterman, D. M. (1959), 'Late Saxon, Viking and early medieval finds from York', *Archaeologia* 97, 59–105.

Welch, M. (1978), 'Early Anglo-Saxon Sussex: From *civitas* to shire', in Brandon, P. (ed.), 13-35.

Yates, E. M. (1972), *A history of the landscapes of the parishes of South Harting and Rogate.*

Chapter Eleven

SAXON SOUTHAMPTON

By Philip Holdsworth

The Geographical and Topographical Background (Figs. 109 and 110)

SOUTHAMPTON STANDS ON A PENINSULA at the head of the Solent estuary and at the confluence of the Rivers Itchen and Test. It is surrounded by an agriculturally rich hinterland, which can be divided into several distinct areas on the basis of the varied surface geology (Finn 1962, 287–360).

In the south of the county lies the Hampshire Basin, composed of Tertiary clays and sands, and mainly under 200ft. O.D. A narrow belt of heavier London clay extends around the northern edge of the basin. The most common soils in the southern areas are sand and gravel based, and, consequently, are very light and occasionally infertile. North of the Hampshire Basin lies the chalk downland, rising in the north and east to 800ft. O.D., into which are incised the valleys of the Test, Itchen and Meon with their rich alluvial soils, suitable as both arable and meadow land.

The area is also rich in natural resources. Salt-pans existed all along the Hampshire coast and were particularly numerous around Portsmouth and Southampton; ironstone occurs as nodules and blocks in the Tertiary formations; charcoal was burnt in the New Forest; chalk was used as fertiliser and burnt for lime; and the Downlands have been noted since the Saxon period for the production of honey.

Southampton has always possessed good communications by both land and water. The valleys of the Test, Itchen, Avon, and Meon rivers provide relatively easy routes to the Thames valley and beyond into Midland England. Southampton Water allows easy access to the English Channel and the Continent beyond; it also has strikingly good features as a harbour. The Solent provides sheltered waters for ships driven up Channel by the predominating south-westerly winds. The Isle of Wight protects Southampton Water from rough weather and plays an important part in the creation of Southampton's unique tidal regime. As a result of the variations in hydraulic gradient between the two entrances to Southampton Water at Spithead and The Needles, quarter-diurnal tides are experienced with a very long period of rising or standing water. This, combined with a halt on the flood tide and the naturally small tidal range of about five metres, provides very favourable conditions for shipping in the harbour area of Southampton Water (MacMillan 1964, 51–65). It is possible that the large amount of anchorage and wharfage space available played some part in the town's unusual history, for the Roman, middle Saxon and late Saxon settlements were each at a different geographical location.

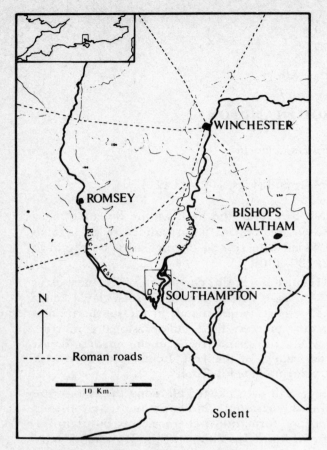

109. Southampton in its regional setting

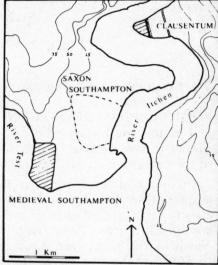

110. Southampton: the three sites

Roman Period (Fig. 111)

The Roman predecessor of Southampton, *Clausentum*, was situated on a neck of land formed by a bend in the River Itchen. It was built on flat land below the 25ft. (7.6m.) contour and on well-drained river gravel. *Clausentum* possessed great potential, both as a harbour and as a defensive position. Surrounded on three sides by water and defined on the eastern landward side by two lines of banks and ditches, the area enclosed was 27½ acres (11 hectares). The fort was linked by road to Chichester to the east and to Silchester, Mildenhall and Old Sarum, via Winchester, to the north. *Clausentum* functioned as a small fort from the Flavian period until the first quarter of the 5th century (Cotton and Gathercole 1958, 12-24). The discovery there in 1918 of two lead pigs stamped with the Emperor Vespasian's name, shows that the products of the Mendip mines were shipped to the Continent from here (*ibid.,* 14, n. 4), while slabs of marble imported from Tuscany are evidence for some trade in the opposite direction.

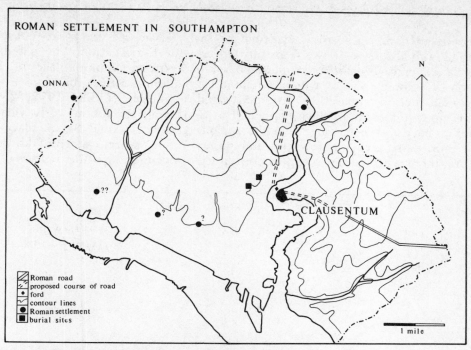

111. Southampton: known and suspected Roman sites

The cemetery to *Clausentum* was probably located at Portswood Hill on the other side of the River Itchen where three stone sarcophagi were found in 1852 (Crawford 1942, 37). Other Roman settlements nearby are known at Nursling and South Stoneham, while at Eastleigh there was a villa. In addition there are suspected farm sites at Four Post Hill, Freemantle, and Millbrook; together these form a distinctive settlement pattern, all three being located at the foot of stream valleys flowing from the plateau gravel and overlooking the Test estuary.

The end of *Clausentum* must, on coin evidence, have occurred sometime after A.D. 390 when building works can be shown to have been started but never completed. Nothing certain is known of the fort after the Roman withdrawal until the 11th century, when the manor house of the bishop of Winchester was built there. No pagan Saxon levels were found at *Clausentum* during excavation, and not one sherd of Saxon pottery has been found on, or near, the site. Nevertheless, there is evidence of some post-Roman activity in this area. A *sceatta* of B.M.C. type 7 was discovered in 1908 when new roads were being laid (Cotton and Gathercole 1958, 29), and a 5th- or 6th-century disc-brooch, decorated with ring and dot motif, occurred as an unstratified find in 1951 (*ibid.,* 45 and Fig. 12). In 1805 no fewer than 50 skeletons were discovered buried in wooden coffins held together with nails and recorded as possibly post-Roman (Englefield 1805). In 1939 burials accompanied by iron knives with short blades and tangs were found in graves cut through the via Principalis (Cotton and Gathercole 1958, 30), and, in 1951 and 1953, single burials were discovered which had been cut into the latest levels of Roman occupation (*ibid.*, 142).

There is then no substantial evidence of early Saxon settlement at *Clausentum*. The coins and the brooch were unstratified and the burials cannot be dated. Such a dearth of early Anglo-Saxon material is, however, a commonplace of British archaeology. Some places which retained an administrative function into the post-Roman period apparently attracted satellite villages (Biddle 1972, 239–41), but this does not seem to have happened at Southampton, for no early villages or cemeteries have yet been found in the region. The early Anglo-Saxon place-names of the immediate area are few and ambiguous. In the current state of knowledge, therefore, there is no reason to expect continuity of occupation at *Clausentum*.

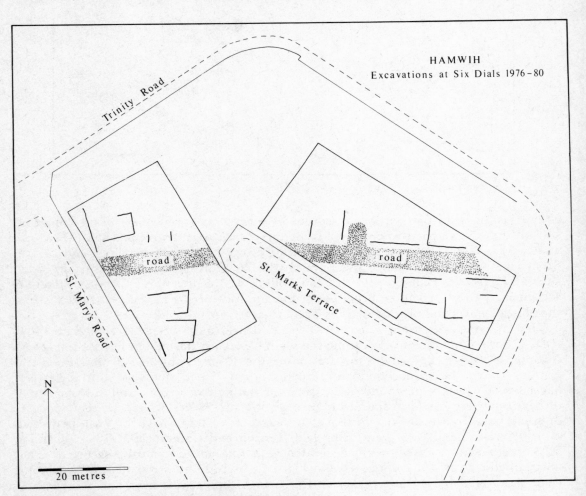

112. **Southampton: phase two building plans at Six Dials**

The Middle-Saxon Period (Fig. 112)

Saxon Southampton, or *Hamwih* as it has become incorrectly known in modern literature,[1] was founded on a new site on flat, low-lying brick-earth half a kilometre south-west of the Roman fort. It functioned as an international port-of-trade and was of fundamental importance to the developing foreign and economic policies of the Wessex and Mercian kings during the 8th and 9th centuries. The archaeological evidence from *Hamwih* demonstrates that commercial life was in full swing by the early 8th century. It is by now generally accepted that *Hamwih* was founded in a period of increasing political stability and prosperity in Wessex during the reign of King Ine (688–726) (Loyn 1972, 138). The presence of only a very few sherds of grass-tempered ware recovered during excavation, support the date of *c.* 700 by analogy with Portchester, where vessels of this type seem to have ceased being manufactured by the early 8th century (Cunliffe 1976, 191).

At its apogee the town covered an area of some 37 hectares, the occupation deposits being co-extensive with the brick-earth soils. The settlement never extended on to the gravels which enclosed it to the north and east, whilst to the south was marshland.

The earliest documentary reference to Saxon Southampton occurs in the life of the 8th-century monk St Willibald, who is said to have set sail for the Continent from Hamblemouth, a place 'juxta illud mercimonium quod dicitur Hamwih' (Golder-Egger 1887, 91). The regional importance of the town is underlined by the county name as given in the *Anglo-Saxon Chronicle* for 757—*Hamtunscire* (Garmonsway 1953). Shires generally took their names from the pre-eminent town within their area, and the fact that it was Saxon Southampton and not Winchester which lent its name to the county also provides some indication of the relative importance of these two places in the 8th century.

The results of excavations at *Hamwih* from 1946 to 1976 have been summarised elsewhere (Addyman and Hill 1968, 1969; Holdsworth 1976, 1980) and will not be repeated here. However, before considering the preliminary results from excavations currently taking place it will be useful to briefly outline the major characteristics of the town. *Hamwih* was possibly the largest and most densely populated town in 8th-century England. There the products and produce of the English kingdoms were exchanged for goods from the Continent, specifically the Carolingian empire. The resident population of the town, which was never defended or enclosed, were engaged mainly in service industries such as metal-working, bone-working, weaving, and other artisan activities. The people were supplied with their foodstuffs from the rural hinterland of the town and presumably at no great distance, as the archaeological evidence reveals the animals were brought in on hoof to slaughter. *Hamwih* can probably be regarded as a boom town, born as a response to an expanding economy and to changing market forces. Despite the constraints imposed upon the wider interpretation of the results from individual excavations by the limited sizes and wide spacing of past sites, all the available evidence suggests that *Hamwih* was laid out to a regular plan. Martin Biddle pointed out the importance of the Southampton evidence when he wrote: 'should the reality of a planned lay-out of the seventh century be established at Hamwih, there would be no need to look much farther for the source from which the regularly planned street lay-outs of eighth- and ninth-century Mercia or Alfredian Wessex were derived' (Biddle 1975, 22). By far the most convincing evidence for an orderly internal arrangement of the town has come from excavations at a three-acre site, known as Six Dials, on the north-west edge of the settlement. Work began here in 1977 and is continuing on neighbouring sites. The dominant archaeological feature on the site is an east-west road to either side of which are aligned buildings and groups of pits, which can be broken down into three phases of occupation. The alignments established by the earliest features are faithfully adhered to by the latest.

In the first phase the road was unmetalled and only one insubstantial building and an oven enclosed by a lean-to structure stood on the site. During the second phase activity became much more intense (see Fig. 112). The road was metalled with flints and pebbles and at least 14 buildings erected, although not all of these stood at the same time. A variety of structural techniques were employed: some houses had their side walls set in continuous or intermittent bedding trenches; others used large individual post-holes or double post-holes. A few of the buildings showed the use of more than one of these techniques in their construction.

The road was re-metalled on two occasions, and it was noticeable that although the quality of the individual surfaces varied, each was consistent along its entire length. This strongly suggests the firm administration of a civic works programme by a central authority, for if the repair of the road had been left to individuals, each house owner for example having responsibility for that outside his property, the quality would have been variable.

Where property boundaries have been found, abrupt changes in the nature of industrial activity from one plot of land to the next have been observed. It is becoming increasingly clear that in order to appreciate the orderly nature of land apportionment it is the plots which must be mapped and measured, for the buildings which lay within them can vary in attitude to, and distance from, the road.

In the third phase the area underwent a considerable change. The road continued in existence, but only as a narrow path, and the metalling was allowed to deteriorate without further repair. The most striking feature of this phase was the large number of pits which were dug—more than 200—although they did preserve the alignments recognisable in the first and second phases.

The evidence recovered from this site gives a strong impression of it having been part of a planned and centrally maintained town. The undisturbed continuity of the road and its wholesale re-metalling point to this conclusion as clearly as does the alignment of the features. The intense activity of the second phase activity reflects the need for more land as economic and social pressures increased with the growing success of the town as a port of trade. The change of land use in the third phase would be consistent with the withering away of the northern part of the town prior to the abandonment of its commercial hub. In all, the area presents a picture of growth and decline which probably mirrors the history of the entire town.

*   *   *   *   *

The events which led to the decline of trade at *Hamwih* and the date at which the consequent transfer of settlement took place have been subjects of much debate. Crawford postulated a salt-water lagoon which he believed to have formed *Hamwih's* harbour, and thought that it was the silting of this lagoon which brought about the demise of the town (Crawford 1949, 45-6). Addyman and Hill suggested a deepening of the draught of trading vessels in the 10th century made the lagoon unusable, and that the settlement shift occurred *c.* 940 (Addyman and Hill 1968, 77). A recent analysis of river sediments, however, has shown that a lagoon was not a topographical feature of the Itchen shore in the Saxon period (Shackley 1980, 3-7).

Cherry and Hodges have suggested a date in the second half of the 9th century for the abandonment of *Hamwih,* as a result of computer analyses concerned with the seriation of a sample of 20 pits, on the basis of the variable quantities of local pottery they contained (Cherry and Hodges 1979, 299-307). Although their findings agree with this author's proposal made some years earlier that occupation of *Hamwih* ended *c.* 870 (Holdsworth 1976, 60), there are a number of objections which can be raised to assumptions implicit in the study undertaken by Cherry and Hodges. Firstly, one of the features described as a pit was in reality a well. The pottery from this well was considered as a single assemblage despite the fact that it came from three separate contexts in the structure: the construction pit to the well; the primary sediments at the bottom of the shaft; and the infill of the shaft. Secondly, four pits at site XIV contained abnormally high quantities of sawn bone fragments and pieces of glass (Holdsworth 1976, 45), and three pits at site XI contained large amounts of animal dung (Buckland, Holdsworth and Monk 1976, 61-9). These two groups of features obviously reflect rather specialised and totally unrelated activities which renders any direct comparison of their contents invalid. By failing to take into account the sum total of archaeological evidence from the 20 features used in the analysis, and by ignoring the effects on the data of social and functional variations, Cherry and Hodges violated a fundamental principle of seriation; that only like and like should be compared.

The reasons for the abandonment of *Hamwih* are most certainly related to the collapse of the economic system which had flourished throughout Europe during the 8th and the first half of the 9th centuries. This collapse was hastened by the increasing amount of Viking activity which disrupted the established trading networks along the North Sea littoral. From the 850s onwards the ports which had been newly established in the post-Roman period were one by one abandoned. When the trade at *Hamwih* ceased, probably by the last quarter of the 9th century the *raison d'être* for the settlement ceased. *Hamwih* had been a place where wealth was created; profits were not re-invested in the town, as was the case in the later medieval period. There was no reason for the settlement to continue either in the same form or at the same location. The resident population moved away, some perhaps to Winchester, which began to emerge as a true urban centre at about that time, others perhaps returning to rural activities. But one group remained and it was they who laid the foundations to the late Saxon town.

The Late Saxon Period (Fig. 113)

The number of hides belonging to Southampton in the Burghal Hidage is 150 which gives a length of 206 yards (188m.) for the defences of the fort. This measurement corresponds very closely to the length of the inner fosse at *Clausentum* and not at all to the settlement on the bank of the River Test that became the

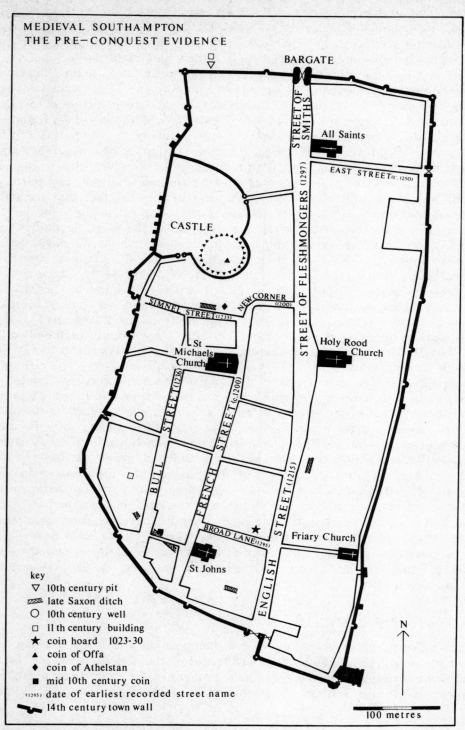

MEDIEVAL SOUTHAMPTON
THE PRE-CONQUEST EVIDENCE

BARGATE

STREET OF SMITHS

All Saints

EAST STREET (c.1250)

STREET OF FLESHMONGERS (1297)

CASTLE

NEW CORNER (1200)

SIMNEL STREET (1235)

St Michaels Church

Holy Rood Church

BULL STREET (1226)

FRENCH STREET (c.1200)

ENGLISH STREET (1215)

BROAD LANE (1295)

Friary Church

St Johns

key
▽ 10th century pit
▨ late Saxon ditch
○ 10th century well
□ 11th century building
★ coin hoard 1023-30
▲ coin of Offa
◆ coin of Athelstan
■ mid 10th century coin
(1295) date of earliest recorded street name
▬ 14th century town wall

N

100 metres

113. Southampton: evidence for the late Saxon burh

medieval port. But no evidence of late Saxon activity within the walls of the Roman fort has been found. Perhaps the best explanation of this anomaly, if one discounts the possibility of scribal error in the recording of the hides for Southampton as most scholars do (Hill 1967, 59–61), is that the Saxons utilised the site and surviving defences of Roman *Clausentum* during the troubles of the 870s. There may even have been a tradition of the use of *Clausentum* as a place of refuge stemming from the middle Saxon period; indeed, it would have been odd if the inhabitants of *Hamwih* had not made use of the fort, which survived reasonably intact until the 16th century, particularly at the times of the Viking raids in 840 and 842. The Burghal Hidage could, therefore, have been referring to the traditional place of refuge.

Whatever the correct explanation may be, the town which was recorded in the Domesday Book was built on a gravel ridge about half a mile (1km.) south-west of *Hamwih.* This site was some 30 feet (9m.) higher than the low-lying area to the east and north-east, and 20 feet to 40 feet (6–12m.) above mean sea level. It was bounded to the west by the River Test and to the south by Southampton Water.

It has been argued (Platt and Coleman-Smith 1975, 18) that the medieval town expanded southwards from an area of primary settlement located outside the later town walls. In recent years, however, a growing body of archaeological evidence has suggested that a late Saxon settlement was founded on the south-western tip of the Southampton peninsula and that it was this which was the origin of the medieval town.

Lengths of a ditch have been excavated to the north of Simnel Street, east of High Street, north of Porters Lane and west of Bugle Street. At each of these locations the absence of silts in the bottom of the ditch suggests that it could not have stood open for any appreciable length of time. The lower fillings were generally loams and clays, frequently interspersed with charcoal lenses—the hearths of squatter occupation. The upper fillings comprised mainly gravels and contained few finds. This sequence probably reflects a fairly long period during which the defences were neglected, followed by a deliberate infilling of the remainder of the ditch. The filling may well have been derived from an internal bank; indeed a platform for such a bank was recorded during excavations at Simnel Street.

The pottery recovered from these excavations is, with one exception, all locally produced and could belong to any part of the late Saxon period. At the Simnel Street site, however, fragments of Beauvais red-painted ware were found in association with a contemporary forgery of a penny of King Athelstan (924–39). These finds were located in the upper fillings of the ditch. The coin, which is retrograde, reads 'EDELSTAN EX' with a two-line reverse 'EMD INNV' which is probably meaningless (*pers. comm.* Michael Metcalf). Excavations immediately east of Bugle Street, by R. G. Thomson, produced a lead forgery of a mid 10th-century halfpenny; this was also found in the upper filling.

When the positions at which the ditch has been located are plotted on to a map of Southampton as it existed in the 15th century, it can be seen that they outline the only regularly laid-out street pattern within the circuit of the town walls. Inside this area apparently enclosed by the ditch further evidence of pre-Conquest occupation has been found. A wicker-lined well in an excavation north of Westgate Street by R. G. Thomson yielded a carbon-14 determination of A.D. 930 ($1020^{\pm}$ 80 bp, HAR-568). Excavations south of Westgate Street (Blackburn and Holdsworth, forthcoming) revealed one of the earliest features on the site to have been a gravel road aligned north-south and on the western edge of the gravel ridge. It may have been an intra-mural road, for it ran just inside the projected line of the ditch which was not found here because of terracing of the ridge which took place in the 13th and 14th centuries. Belonging to the same period as the road, and lying inside the defences, was the partially preserved ground-plan of a pre-Conquest timber building. Amongst the unstratified finds from this site was an ansate (or caterpillar) brooch. Such brooches are relatively common on the Continent, but are infrequently found in this country, and are rarely dated to later than the 9th century (Evison 1966).

*   *   *   *   *

There is then a substantial amount of archaeological evidence to suggest that by the late 9th century or early 10th century a Saxon settlement, enclosed by a bank and ditch, existed on the west side of the Southampton peninsula. The ditch would appear to have been backfilled no later than the middle of the 10th century on the dating provided by the coins found in its upper fillings. This event must have occurred as the town expanded northwards, a conclusion supported by the discovery of a 10th-century pit and an 11th-century building immediately north of the line of the later town wall (Platt and Coleman-Smith 1975, 18). The infilling of the ditch reflects the growing success of the town, for the rights conferred upon it by the king were only applicable within the defences. As it prospered, new defences enclosing a larger area would have been necessary. No such earthworks have been found, but the reason for this could be that the Norman and later defences followed the same line. The street pattern within the area defined by the ditch assumes a different emphasis from that of the medieval period, with French Street (as it was to become known in the 13th century) being the main thoroughfare of this early nucleus.

Alongside this excavated evidence for a later Saxon town must be placed certain topographical details of the developed medieval town which can be interpreted as corroborative data. Holy Rood church, the foundation date of which is unknown, did not always stand on its present site, but was once in the middle of English Street (modern High Street); the first reference to it having been moved occurs in 1230 (Platt 1973, 88). At that point the street takes up a different alignment on its course to the Bargate and changed in name from English Street to Street of the Fleshmongers. This point of coincidence in what must have been the north-east corner of the Saxon town suggests that the northern part of the street was a later extension to a road which originally terminated at that point. Also of interest is that the earliest documented street named is that of New Corner in 1200.[2] That it is New Corner, and not, for example, New Lane, suggests the alteration of a previously existing alignment—one perhaps brought about by the construction of the defences to the Norman castle.

Until very recently knowledge of the early history of the castle site has been slight; it is first referred to in 1153 as a *munitio* (Stone 1934, 243), and a coin of King Offa was reportedly discovered in 1818 during levelling of the castle mound (Shore 1911, 130). However, excavations initiated by the author in 1980 within the castle bailey have revealed a late Saxon hall at least 24m. long and 12m. wide (*pers. comm.* Steve Rollo-Smith). The building appears to be surrounded by a ditch, or possibly a double ditch, and as such may well be an early motte-and-bailey fortification comparable with Sulgrave (Davison 1968, 305–7). Such an interpretation would explain the otherwise peculiar siting of the Norman castle in relation to its town defences. Normally, as at Winchester, Chichester, Wareham, and Wallingford, for example, those Wessex burhs which received a castle after the Conquest had it positioned in a corner angle of the town defences. Such a location allowed for control of the settlement whilst at the same time providing direct access to the countryside beyond. At Southampton the castle is well inside the town. If, however, as now seems likely, a motte-and-bailey already existed at the Conquest, the siting of the Norman castle at the established political and administrative centre of the town would make great sense, being a visual takeover of the seat of power.

Almost nothing is known of the economy of the late Saxon town, although at an agrarian level the small sample of animal bones so far recovered clearly shows some setback. The mean heights of the main domestic species drop when compared with the earlier *Hamwih* stock. This tendency towards smaller animals may be a reflection of greater land pressures or a lessening concern for successful production; alternatively it could be that the conspicuous success in animal husbandry at *Hamwih* is a yardstick by which no late Saxon settlement could fairly be measured (Bourdillon 1980, 186). However, a further explanation of the diminution of animal sizes is that the middle and late Saxon settlements exploited different populations as the shift in settlement site led to a change of immediate hinterland from the Itchen to the Test valley. Larger samples of animal bone from the late Saxon town and from contemporary settlements in the river valleys will be necessary to check this hypothesis.

* * * * *

The proposed sequence of events, therefore, omitting for the moment just when in the late Saxon period they may have happened, is that a town was established by the River Test and surrounded by a bank and ditch. It had a regular internal arrangement of streets of which the main thoroughfare was French Street. A motte-and-bailey earthwork was erected outside the northern arm of the defences. As the town prospered it needed to grow in size; after a period of neglect the ditch was backfilled and the defences moved farther out. French Street was lengthened, as was English Street, although the latter extended on a slightly different alignment. At the Conquest the Norman castle was built on the earlier earthwork, truncating French Street and causing the construction of New Corner.

The question of when the late Saxon town was established remains open to question, although, as argued above, a date close to 900 would seem to be suggested by the archaeological evidence so far recovered. However, such an early date would be in contradiction to Hill's proposal (Hill 1974) that *Clausentum* was not abandoned by the Saxons for the new site until the reign of Athelstan, at which time the town was granted a mint. Yet, as has been noted above, excavations at the Roman fort have failed to produce conclusive evidence of late Saxon occupation.

The new town with its defences and regular street pattern could be attributed to the period of consolidation in Wessex under Edward the Elder. Indeed, Edward was in Southampton in 903 to attend a meeting of the witanagemot. The plan of the town is more consistent with the lay-outs of the late 9th century and the first quarter of the 10th century than it is with any that came later (*cf.* Biddle and Hill 1971, 70–85). The main argument against such an interpretation is provided by the Burghal Hidage which alone has been taken to demonstrate a post-919 date for the town; yet for the archaeological evidence to be accommodated by this view it would have to be telescoped into an unacceptably short period.

ACKNOWLEDGEMENTS

I would like to record my indebtedness to the many colleagues and friends with whom I worked during the time I was Director of Excavations in Southampton. I am grateful to David Devereux for the information on Fig. 111, and to Alan Morton on whose field drawings Fig. 112 is based. All line drawings were prepared by Margaret Holland. My thoughts on the development of the late Saxon town have benefited from the helpful advice and criticism of a number of individuals, but particularly Sheila Thompson, Bob Thomson, and John Walker. Finally, I would like to thank my secretary, Jasmin Vaccari, for transliterating the handwritten drafts into the final text.

NOTES

1. Despite Alexander Rumble's demonstration (1980, 7–20) that the settlement was known to contemporaries as *Hamwic* or *Hamtun,* the term *Hamwih* has been retained because it can be regarded as having established itself as a satisfactory modern name tradition among archaeologists. Furthermore, to change the name now with an increasing amount of evidence for Saxon occupation on the Test side of the Southampton peninsula, and with the possibility of Saxon utilisation of the Roman fort, would cause great confusion.

2. The dates of the street names as shown on Fig. 113 and quoted in the text were provided by Miss Sheila Thompson, City Archivist, Southampton.

BIBLIOGRAPHY

Addyman, P. V. and Hill, D. H. (1968, 1969), 'Saxon Southampton: a review of the evidence', *Proc. Hampshire Field Club and Archaeological Society,* 25, 61–93; 26, 61–96.

Biddle, M. and Hill, D. H. (1971), 'Late Saxon planned towns', *Antiquaries Journal* 51, 70–85.

Biddle, M. (1975), 'The evolution of towns: planned towns before 1066', in Barley, M. W. (ed.), *Plans and Topography of Medieval Towns in England and Wales,* C.B.A. Research Report 14, 19–31.

Biddle, M. (1972), 'Winchester: the development of an early capital', in Jankuhn, H., Schlesinger, W. and Steuer, H. (eds.), *Vor-und Früh-formen der europäischen Stadt in Mittelalter,* 218-28.

Blackburn, P. and Holdsworth, P. (forthcoming), 'Excavations at Westgate Green, Southampton', *Southampton Archaeological Research Committee Reports.*

Bourdillon, J. (1980), 'Town life and animal husbandry in the Southampton area, as suggested by the excavated bones', *Proc. Hampshire Field Club and Archaeological Society* 26, 181–91.

Buckland, P. C., Holdsworth, P. and Monk, M. (1976), 'The interpretation of a group of Saxon pits in Southampton', *Journal of Archaeological Science* 3, 61–9.

Cherry, J. F. and Hodges, R. (1979), 'The dating of Hamwih: Saxon Southampton reconsidered', *Antiquaries Journal* 58.

Cotton, M. A. and Gathercole, P. W. (1958), *Excavations at Clausentum, Southampton 1951-54,* London.

Crawford, O. G. S. (1942), 'Southampton', *Antiquity* 16, 36–50.

Crawford, O. G. S. (1949), 'Trinity chapel and fair', *Proc. Hampshire Field Club and Archaeological Society* 27, 45–55.

Davison, B. K. (1968), 'Excavations at Sulgrave, Northamptonshire, 1968', *Archaeological Journal* 125, 305-7.

Englefield, H. C. (1805), *A walk through Southampton* (2nd edn.), 119–20.

Evison, V. I. (1966), 'A caterpillar brooch from Old Erringham Farm, Shoreham-by-Sea, Sussex', *Medieval Archaeology* 10, 149–51.

Finn, R. W. (1962), 'Hampshire' in Darby, H. C. and Campbell, E. M. J. (eds.), *The Domesday Geography of South-East England*, Cambridge.

Garmonsway, G. N. (ed.) (1953), *The Anglo-Saxon Chronicle*, London.

Golder-Egger, O. (ed.) (1887), *Vita Willibaldi Episcopi Eichstentetensis*, in Mon. Germ. Hist. Scriptorum XI, pt. i, Hanover.

Hill, D. H. (1967), 'The Burghal Hidage—Southampton', *Proc. Hampshire Field Club and Archaeological Society* 24, 59–61.

Hill, D. H. (1974), 'The Anglo-Saxon Town', unpublished Ph.D. Thesis, University of Southampton.

Holdsworth, P. (1976), 'Saxon Southampton: a new review', *Medieval Archaeology* 20, 26-61.

Holdsworth, P. (ed.) (1980), *Excavations at Melbourne Street, Southampton, 1971-76*, C.B.A. Research Report 33.

Loyn, H. R. (1962), *Anglo-Saxon England and the Norman Conquest.*

MacMillan, D. H. (1964), in Monkhouse, F. J. (ed.), *A Survey of Southampton and its Region*, Southampton.

Platt, C. (1973), *Medieval Southampton*, London.

Platt, C. and Coleman-Smith, R. (1975), *Excavations in Medieval Southampton 1953–1969*, Vol. 1, Leicester.

Rumble, A. R. (1980), 'Hamtun alias Hamwic (Saxon Southampton): the place-name traditions and their significance', in Holdsworth, P. (ed.).

Shackley, M. (1980), 'The Hamwih brickearths', in Holdsworth, P. (ed.), 1980.

Stone, P. G. (1934), 'A vanished castle', *Proc. Hampshire Field Club and Archaeological Society* 12, pt. 3, 241–70.

Chapter Twelve

SAXON BATH

By Barry Cunliffe

IN 577, SO THE *Anglo-Saxon Chronicle* tell us, the Saxon war-leaders, Cuthwine and Ceawlin, killed three British kings at a place called Dyrham, and captured three cities, Gloucester, Cirencester, and Bath. More than 500 years later, in 1088, the same chronicle records the ravaging of the city of Bath by partisans led by Robert de Mowbray in rebellion against the king, William Rufus. The first date (or one thereabouts) marks the passing of the old sub-Roman city of *Aquae Sulis* into Saxon hands; the second is a convenient point to symbolise the end of the Saxon city, for a few months after the rebellion, John of Tours, chaplain and physician to the king, was consecrated bishop of Bath and was granted the abbey of St Peter at Bath, with all its possessions in which to set up his chair. Soon afterwards John acquired the rest of the city by grant from the king—a transfer which was later confirmed by Henry I in 1101 in return for 500 pounds of silver—and proceeded to transform it totally.

The development of the city throughout the half millennium is obscure in the extreme, but isolated documentary references, chance finds, and a growing body of archaeological evidence, held together by controlled hypotheses, allow certain generalisations to be made which future work will enable us to test, and eventually to modify and expand. The present essay is an attempt to summarise what is known and to point the way to future possibilities.

The Sub-Roman City: the Fifth to Seventh Centuries A.D.

By the beginning of the 5th century A.D. the Roman town of *Aquae Sulis* had become divided into two parts. Around the main religious sites and the springs an enclosing wall had been erected, dividing a core area of some 10 hectares from an unenclosed settlement area which spread north and north-east along the valley side, flanking the Fosse Way, and spilling over to the low-lying land to the east of the River Avon.[1] The existence of the wall, later to become the basis for the late Saxon and medieval defences, is well known, but its precise date of construction is still uncertain though a late Roman date seems reasonably established (Cunliffe 1969, 165–73; O'Leary 1981). In all probability it was erected in response to the same stimuli which saw other small settlements in the area such as Gatcombe and Mildenhall (*Cunetio*) protecting themselves with new stone-built defences. An alternative possibility, that the wall was a temenos boundary for the religious buildings should not, however, be totally rejected.

The walled area was dominated by three massive public buildings—a huge vaulted chamber enclosing the central sacred spring, the temple of Sulis Minerva to the west of

345

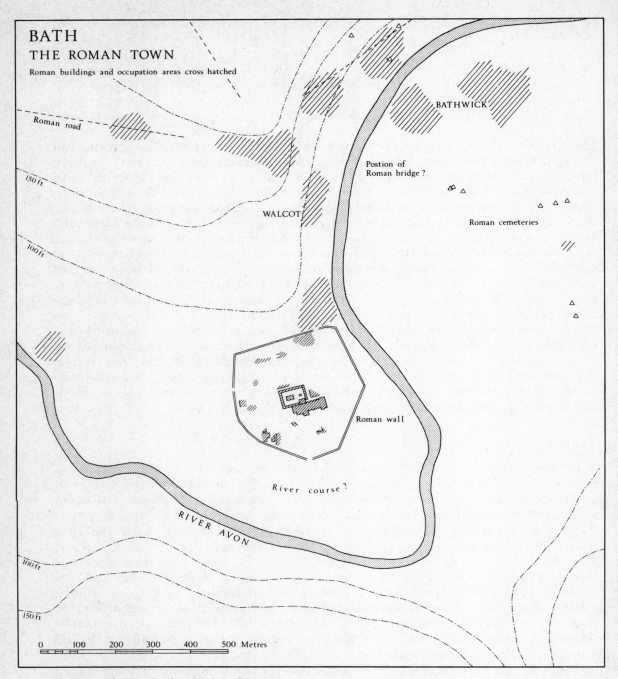

114. Roman settlement in the vicinity of Bath

it, and the main bathing establishment to the south (Cunliffe 1969, *passim*.; 1981). By the end of the Roman period there is evidence to suggest that part of the original temple precinct had been pulled down and that occupation of a more secular nature was impinging upon the once sacred area. This may have been the occasion when the temple building was enclosed by a new and far more restricted perimeter wall.

At some stage, presumably in the 5th century, but undated, the Roman drainage system, which allowed the quarter of a million gallons of spring water daily to drain away, started to break down with the result that the low-lying central area began to flood. Trial excavations immediately to the north of the spring have shown that the resulting marsh deposits, augmented by tumbled Roman masonry, accumulated to a depth of more than two metres during the Saxon period. How extensive was the flooding and how impenetrable the marsh are matters about to be considered in a new campaign of excavation; but one trial trench (dug in 1978 beneath the Pump Room) showed that after 30–40cm of black organic silt had accumulated over the temple precinct floor an attempt had been made to consolidate the ground with a layer of rough stone paving. The position of the paving in the stratified sequence would suggest a date some time in the 5th or 6th centuries. Significantly, the latest object found in the sacred spring nearby was a fine enamelled penannular brooch for which a 5th-century date would seem appropriate (Cunliffe 1981).[2] Continued, if sporadic, use of the sacred spring is therefore likely.

Elsewhere in the town evidence of sub-Róman occupation is sparse, but at a site in Abbey Gate Street a lengthy sequence of Roman occupation was seen (Cunliffe 1969, 159) ending with the construction of a substantial building in which, still later, a crude oven was inserted. After it was abandoned a human skull was thrown into the flue. Once more dating evidence is unavailable, but the last events of the sequence quite possibly took place in the 5th century. Thereafter a thick layer of sterile black organic soil developed.

Within the western part of the walled area another sequence of deposits was examined under modern conditions (Greene 1979). After the collapse of the masonry building which occupied the site, alignments of stone blocks, stone-packed post-holes, and a clay floor or yard attest continued occupation (periods 9 and 10), extending into the sub-Roman period, but without any distinctive material culture associated with them other than residual Roman artifacts.

The impression given by these three sites is of continued human activity on a rapidly diminishing scale. The springs would have continued to flow, and no doubt people would have been attracted to them and to the protection of the walls, but of organised urban life there is no trace.

The Saxon Masonry: Seventh to Ninth Centuries

In a 12th-century copy of the foundation charter dated 6 November 675, Osric, king of the Hwicce, a sub-kingdom of Mercia, granted estates outside Bath to the Abbess Berta for the establishment of a convent of Holy Virgins (Sawyer 1968, No. 51). The establishment may well have been a double monastery served by monks and nuns, and it has recently been suggested that the founding nuns probably arrived from a group of Frankish monasteries in the Paris region (Sims-Williams 1974). A few years later, in 681, a further grant of land, close to the River Cherwell, was made by Aethelmod, with the consent of King Aethelred, to the Abbess Bernguida and to Folcburg, who probably performed a function equivalent to that of a later prioress. By this date, as her name would imply, the abbess was English, but her deputy was evidently a foreigner.[3]

The location of the 7th-century monastery is a matter of debate. Most recent writers have assumed that it lay within the walled area on or close to the site of the later Saxon church of St Peter. There is, however, no positive proof that this was so, and Hamilton (1978, 22–4) has gone so far as to suggest that Osric's nunnery lay outside the walls in the vicinity of St Werburgh's chapel (now at the bottom of Landsdown Road). This would place it well within the outer, unenclosed, Roman settlement—the area significantly called Walcot.[4] Such a siting, though by no means impossible, is less likely than a location within the walls. The use of old, and largely

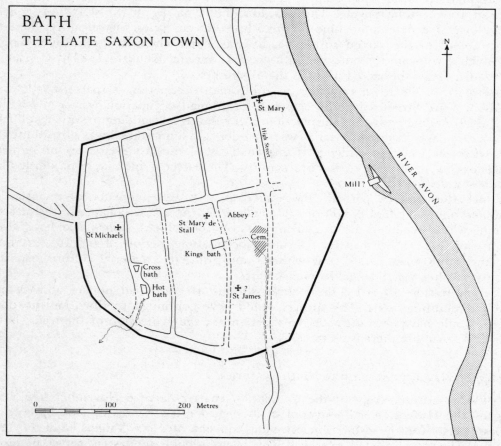

115. Saxon Bath—a tentative reconstruction

derelict, Roman walled enclosures for early religious establishments is a widely recognised phenomenon (Rigold 1977), the walls bestowing prestige and protection on the community. The issue, however, must remain unresolved, but it may be worth noting that both Leland and Camden, relying no doubt on local tradition, imply that the nunnery and St Peter's were adjacent or successive on the same site.[5]

The next charter, belonging to the years 757–8, records a grant of land in North Stoke (just north-west of Bath) to the brothers in the monastic church of St Peter. The grant was made by the West Saxon King Cynewulf and was confirmed by Offa (Sawyer 1968, No. 265). Either the charter marks an endowment to a newly-established community of monks occupying a site in the centre of the walled area, or it represents continued support for the community founded by Osric which by this time had become an all-male establishment. In any event the monastery of St Peter now became the dominant religious establishment in Bath. At the Synod of Brentford, held in 781, the monastery, described as 'most famous', was transferred to Offa having for some while been dependent upon the bishops of Worcester (Sawyer 1968, No. 1,257). It is worth noting that at the same time Offa was compensated by the church of Worcester with 30 hides of land on the south side of the Avon, acquired by purchase from the West Saxon King Cynewulf. The incident is a reminder that Bath was now seen as a frontier post of some significance on the boundary between Mercia and Wessex: its control by the Mercian royal house, together with a bridgehead of land on the Wessex side of the river, was something for which Offa evidently considered it worth bargaining. Henceforth the royal interest in the military potential of the walled enclosure and its river crossing becomes a recurring theme.[6]

The growing importance of Bath is reflected in two subsequent documents. In 796 King Ecgfrith of Mercia issued a charter from 'that celebrated town which is called in Saxon tongue *æt Baðun'*, and in the next century, in 864, the last Mercian king, Burhred held a gemot at Bath attended both by Queen Ethelswith and his nobles and bishops at which another charter was prepared. The royal presence on these two occasions, and no doubt on many others unrecorded, is an indication of the changing status of the town.

The archaeological record of Bath has, as yet, little to contribute to our understanding of the town in the 7th and 9th centuries, but, fortunately, there survives a fragment of a poem called *The Ruin* which describes, in contemplative mood, the towering remnants of shattered Roman buildings in an ancient city. The poem was written in the early 8th century, and it has been convincingly argued that the ruins described were those of the Roman bathing establishment and temple complex which were still standing in the centre of the Saxon town. 'Wondrous is this masonry shattered by the Fates . . . The buildings raised by giants are crumbling . . . the roofs have collapsed . . . the towers are in ruins . . . And so these courts lie desolate and the structure of the dome with its red arches sheds its tiles . . .' These extracts give something of the quality of the vividly emotive language, but it is the details which have convinced modern writers that the poet was expressing his feelings having visited Bath and seen its monuments for himself. The arguments are extensive and have been set out fully elsewhere (Leslie 1961, 22–8). One point, however, deserves particular emphasis for the significance thrown upon it by the most recent excavation of the Roman spring and reservoir in 1979. The poem ends with these words, 'There stood courts of stone and a stream gushed forth in rippling floods of hot water. The wall enfolded within its bright bosom the whole place which contained the hot flood of the baths'. Excavations have now shown conclusively that the massive late Roman wall built to enclose the reservoir was still standing well above ground level in the medieval period and was indeed utilised by the medieval builders (Cunliffe 1981). Thus, however much of the rest of the Roman structure had fallen or was buried beneath the marsh, a visitor to the site in the 8th century would have been confronted by a rectangular enclosure some 15m. by 24m., standing many metres in height and possibly even retaining some part of its vaulted roof built of tiles and concrete. It was within this enclosure that the gushing hot mineral water broke through to the surface. Such a remarkable phenomenon is likely to have claimed attention. Together the poem and the excavation throw an interesting light on the appearance of the town in the 8th century.

The Re-birth of the Town in the Tenth and Eleventh Centuries

Following Alfred's successes against the Danes in 878 the kingdom of the Hwicce, and with it Bath, came under the overlordship of the kings of Wessex. It was probably at about this time that the old Roman defences were improved and a militia assigned to their defence, for Bath is listed in the Burghal Hidage, prepared in the reign of Alfred's successor, Edward the Elder. By strict arithmetic, Bath, assessed at 1,000 hides, was allowed a garrison sufficient to man a defensive circuit of 1,375 yards: the actual circumference of the old Roman defences was a very close approximation at 1,250 yards (Hill 1969). Whether or not the wall itself was repaired at this time is uncertain, but recent excavations along the line of the northern defences have shown that the fronting ditch underwent clearing and modification at some post-Roman date possibly to be equated with the Alfredian period.[7]

The reign of Alfred and his immediate successors was a period of urban and monastic revival in the country as a whole, and it is evident that Bath shared in these developments. In 901 the witan met in the town, presided over by Edward the Elder, who was also responsible for establishing Bath's first mint,[8] while a few years later, in 906, the death at Bath of the king's reeve, Alfred, was thought worthy of recording in the *Anglo-Saxon Chronicle*. These isolated events, of little significance by themselves, taken together are an indication of the town's growing administrative importance.

It is worth considering what, if any, topographical changes were brought about at this time. Increased military and administrative functions are likely to have encouraged a growth in the resident urban population, while the presence of the abbey, the mint and no doubt a growing number of manufacturing and trading activities must have increased the services which the 'urban' community could now offer to its hinterland. Growing socio-economic complexity and rising populations are factors likely to require territorial reorganisation. It is tempting to suppose that Bath, along with other Wessex towns, was replanned at about this time with a framework of streets dividing up parcels of newly-measured burgage plots (Biddle and Hill 1971, 82–5). It should be stressed that at Bath there is no positive archaeological or documentary evidence that this was so. However, the street plan, stripped of its 18th-century improvements, offers scope for speculation.

Town Plan (Figs. 115 and 116)

The town was divided by an east–west street, now called Westgate Street, into two unequal parts, of which the northern part was sub-divided into five areas by streets at right-angles to the east-west axis. One of these, the High Street, led to the North Gate. The others opened on to the intra-mural road, now Upper Borough Walls. The southern part of the town plan is more confusing, but here, too, the germs of a regular pattern can be traced, with the present Hot Bath Street and the much-truncated Bilberry Lane serving to divide the south-western quadrant into areas of roughly equal size. The pattern in the south-eastern section is obscure in the extreme, but if it is accepted that the creation of the Norman monastic precinct in and after 1090 has largely obliterated the late Saxon plan, then it is possible to offer some attempt at reconstructing the pre-Norman topography. The simplest explanation would be to suppose an initial regularity with a southwards continuation of the High Street, passing beneath the present abbey to the vicinity of Ham Gate on the south wall, and a

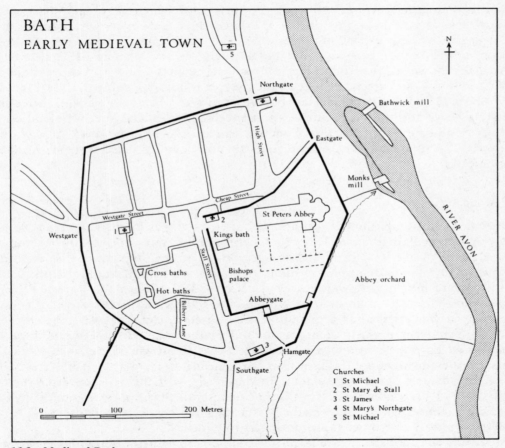

116. Medieval Bath

southern continuation of what is now Union Passage passing along the east side of the King's Bath to the site of South Gate. The hypothetical plan is illustrated in Fig. 115 and comparison with Fig. 116 shows how the Norman precinct may have distorted the supposed Saxon arrangement. It suggests that the desire to include the King's Bath spring within the precinct caused the line of one north–south street to be thrust westwards to become the medieval Stall Street, while the need for space for the enlarged establishment led to the abandonment of all but the southern extremity of the easternmost street. The suggestion is, of course, purely hypothetical, but two small observations may be called to its support. First, the supposed line of the missing eastern street was the line which we can be reasonably certain was in part followed by the drain taking the overflow from the King's Bath spring. Such a long-established topographical feature may well have dictated the position of a street in the late Saxon lay-out. Second, the original church of St James lay within the Norman precinct and was only later re-sited outside (p. 354), a fact which suggests that it belonged to an earlier town lay-out subsumed within the Norman precinct. One further observation may tentatively be offered: if the supposed eastern street existed as a southerly continuation of the surviving High Street it may have exited through the city wall at the site of the later Ham Gate where excavations have shown a gap to have existed through which the open drainage ditch flowed. It was blocked in the early medieval period and partially opened again in 1279, after which it became known as the Ham Gate. Several early maps show a winding trackway making its way south from the gate to the river. It is not impossible that the precursor to the Ham Gate was the original late Saxon south gate which was blocked and re-sited in its medieval position when the Norman precinct and Stall Street were laid out. If so then Southgate Street, leading from the gate to the bridge, would be a Norman creation. The argument is plausible, but tenuous, and, at the moment, incapable of proof.[9]

The Monastery

The monastic establishment, presumably sited in the vicinity of the later Norman abbey, continued to flourish. Numerous benefactions were received throughout the 10th century,[10] and William of Malmesbury described the building of 957 as 'known to be a wondrous workmanship'—a statement which must surely imply that the church at least was of masonry. It was here on 11 May 973 that Edgar was crowned king of England by Dunstan, archbishop of Canterbury, and Oswald, archbishop of York, in a ceremony which served as a prototpye for subsequent coronations. The choice of Bath for this event must to some extent reflect the grandeur of the buildings, but it must also have been influenced by the fact that the town still retained something of its frontier quality—politically a town with strong Mercian as well as Wessex links was a wise choice for the ceremony, taking place as it did so soon after the two kingdoms had been united. It is a distinct possibility that the royal interest in Bath may reflect the intention of the late Saxon kings to create a second capital in the western extremity of Wessex as a counterpart to Winchester.

No doubt the monastery would have benefited from these prestigious events, and from the religious revival of the times. Under the influence of Dunstan the community began to follow the rule of St Benedict and in *c.* 975 Dunstan appointed the renowned Aelphege as abbot. But even so the monastic establishment was not large: something of its size and influence in the local community can be gleaned from the Domesday Survey. At this time the church of St Peter held a manor within the city listed as 24 burgesses, a mill and 12 acres of meadow. Compared to the king's dependents, 64 burgesses of the king and 90 burgesses 'of other men' (presumably the king's barons), the church-owned land was comparatively meagre—roughly equivalent to about 13 per cent. of the total.[11]

Little is known of the physical form or exact location of the monastic buildings, but the presumption must be that they occupied a site coincident with or close to the Norman abbey. The only direct archaeological evidence for the Saxon establishment is its cemetery, first recorded in 1755 during the removal of the Abbey House which occupied the site of the medieval western claustral range. At that time a number of burials were seen cut down into the ruins of the Roman east baths. Beneath the head of one of them a hoard of coins dating to the mid-10th century was found. Further excavation in 1968 brought to light a charcoal-lined grave of late Saxon type. In the same general area late 19th-century excavations produced part of a 10th- or 11th-century stone cross-head and an inscribed leaden disc or coffin plate, recording the interment of 'Eadgyvu . . . a sister of the community'. Remembering the problem of the location of Osric's nunnery the plate is of some potential interest, but since the script is much later than the 7th- or 8th-century date one would expect for such a burial it may reflect the translation of a body from an earlier grave to the monastic cemetery. The period of the move remains uncertain because the lettering cannot be closely dated.[12]

Taken together, the finds enable the late Saxon cemetery to be located with some precision and they show that much of the Roman bathing establishment had by now disappeared from sight, but the cemetery gives no direct clue to the siting of the monastic church. Major Davis claimed to have found the remains of the building when he cleared the Roman baths in the 1880s, but sadly his records were pitifully inadequate. The fragments of wall that were recorded by his clerk-of-works, Richard Mann, give little scope for speculation (Cunliffe 1979, Fig. 36). It is, however, possible that the current excavation beneath the Pump Room may throw some further light on the problem.

Two hints of the style of the building survive. The first is provided by the small two-light window preserved as an isolated find in the *lapidarium* in the present abbey. It is superficially of late Saxon style and may well have come from Davis's excavation, but nothing is recorded of its archaeological context. This single dubious fragment is a poor reflection of the building of 'wondrous workmanship'. The other indication is on one of the early seals of the abbey which depicts the triple apses of the abbey church (Pl. 7), each apparently decorated with fluting and pilasters. If the 10th-century date conventionally ascribed to the seal matrix is correct then the seal may provide a stylised impression of the late Saxon building.[13]

Parish Churches

Of the rest of the late Saxon town little is yet known. It is, however, likely that the four early medieval churches were pre-Conquest foundations. St Mary intra muros

lay just inside the North Gate commanding the entrance to the city in a position
favoured by late Saxon churches elsewhere, for example, those on the north gates
at Wareham and Oxford. St Michael and St Mary de Stall are more or less where
parish churches serving the urban community might have been expected to have been
built following the laying-out of the new street grid, but this implies nothing of their
foundation date. St James's is of some interest. The original church probably lay to
the west of the present Abbey Green. In a charter of 1279 Bishop Robert granted the
prior and convent of Bath land close to the South Gate for them to 'construct a
parish church of St James in lieu of the Church of St James adjoining the Bishop's
chamber the chancel of which the Bishop has thought fit to remove reserving to
himself and his successors the nave or body of the church as a site for a chapel'.[14]
Since Leland makes clear that the bishop's palace lay within the close, to the
south-west of the abbey, the original parish church of St James must have stood
somewhere in the south-west corner of the Norman precinct. It is tempting to
speculate that some of the property boundaries in this region, which are set askew
to the modern frontages, may possibly reflect pre-Norman boundaries associated
with the early parish church: they would be more or less at right-angles to the
proposed dismantled late Saxon street—the precursor to the re-aligned Stall Street.

Baths

The three springs would have continued to have formed major topographical
features. The Cross Bath spring and Hot Bath spring no doubt influenced the
siting of the westernmost north–south street which ran past them and followed the
line of their drainage ditch as far as the city wall through which the drain passed.
Nothing is known of their superstructure in this period. Nor is there any evidence
of the form of the King's Bath, although the Roman enclosure wall was still substantially intact and must have contained the spring. The exact line of the drain which
carried away the constant flow of hot water is unknown, but it must have run
southwards, across what is now Abbey Green, to the city wall in the region of Ham
Gate where the wide open ditch was discovered. As has been argued above the ditch
may well have been followed by one of the streets.

The Archaeology of the Late Saxon City

Apart from the archaeological evidence discussed in the paragraphs above finds of
late Saxon date have been few. Among the small collection of chance finds recorded,
fragments of late Saxon crosses are comparatively numerous. In addition to those
from the monastic cemetery, one fragment was found in the vicinity of the Cross
Bath, one came from the *Pump Room* Hotel, one was found built into the Norman
precinct wall in Abbey Gate Street, and one was found in Chalcombe Lane to the
north of the city. It may possibly be relevant that, but for the last, all were found
close to parish churches—St Michael, St Mary de Stall, and the original St James
respectively.[15]

A gold ring of 10th- or 11th-century date was found beneath the new guildhall in
1893 where graves were also recorded. The records are poor, but since the area was

the monks' cemetery in the early Norman period the possibility remains that the ring may have been a post-Conquest deposit (Hinton 1979).

On a more secular level a clear indication of the increasing economic standards of the community is given by a comparatively large collection of late Saxon pottery from the town. The commonest types were the well-made cooking pots and pitchers decorated with a variety of geometric stamped designs. Contemporary with them were finer, harder-fired pitchers covered in pale green or orange glaze. Both classes can be shown to be of late-10th- or 11th-century date and are essentially a local manifestation of the greatly improved pottery techniques being developed at this time in southern Britain.[16]

Much of the pottery came from rubbish pits found on the Citizen House site in 1970. The same late Saxon layers produced a few bone objects, including a single-sided composite bone comb and bone thread pickers, providing a reminder of the importance of wool to the economy of the city.

The Norman Transition

The rapidly-changing political situation in the 11th century began to have its effect on the fortunes of the city. The summer campaign of the Danish King Swein in 1013 ended at Bath where the king formally received the submission of the western thegns. The *Anglo-Saxon Chronicle,* which records this event, gives no indication of violence and it is probable therefore that the city accepted the king without resistance.

A more serious event was the revolt, in 1088, of the Norman bishops, led by Odo, in support of the king's brother, Robert of Normandy. The rebels using Bristol as a base 'ravaged Bath and all the surrounding area'. Bath was singled out for attack partly because of its strategic position and partly because the king held substantial estates in the city. The extent of the damage is unrecorded, but its severity is hinted at by the apparent willingness with which the king was prepared to part with his Bath estates in 1091. The deal was the culmination of a series of acts which began with the appointment of John de Villula, one-time chaplain and physician to the king, as bishop of Wells in July 1088. Soon afterwards the king granted John 'the Abbey of St Peter with all the possessions belonging thereto' and sanctioned him to transfer the bishopric from Wells to Bath. Three years later in 1091 the bishop obtained the rights of all the king's holdings in the city, a grant he was careful to confirm with William's successor in 1101 at the price of 500 pounds of silver.[17]

John was now in full possession of the Saxon city and promptly set about its total transformation.

The Future

The skeleton of Saxon Bath, both historical and topographical, is tolerably intact, but is desperately in need of flesh. That flesh can be provided only by archaeological research. Fortunately (or, unfortunately, depending on one's viewpoint), Bath is a city of outstanding architectural significance and as such is not likely to be extensively re-developed: opportunity for large-scale rescue excavation is therefore slight. But as small sites become available they are avidly examined under the auspices of the

Bath Archaeological Trust. Our early results have already been published in full up to 1977 (Cunliffe 1969; Cunliffe [ed.] 1979). Since then an opportunity has been taken to carry out work in the Orange Grove (1979), the King's Bath spring (1979), and Upper Borough Walls (1980). Each evacuation has added significantly to our understanding of the archaeology of the city. The Trust has now embarked upon an ambitious programme of work in the city centre beneath and adjacent to the Pump Room. Much that is new will be revealed, and although the post-Roman levels are likely to be sadly truncated by cellar digging one suspects that at least some of the questions raised in this paper about the Saxon city will begin to see the glimmerings of answers.

POSTSCRIPT

The above paper was written and submitted to the Editor in November 1980, in anticipation of speedy publication. The pace of archaeological work in Bath and the very considerable delays which this volume has suffered means that much of what is said has now been superseded.

NOTES

1. It may be significant that the northern settlement area became known as Walcot while that on the east of the river was called Bathwick. Both names may be of early Saxon origin referring to existing communities on the outskirts of the walled area. For discussion of Walcot place-names see Cameron 1980. He does not list the Bath Walcot as a name referring to communities of Welshmen, in sub-Roman settlements, but this is probably because no early spellings are known. Bathwick appears as *Wiche* in Domesday. A Roman connection, while possible, cannot be substantiated. I am grateful to Margaret Gelling for advice on these matters.

2. Information from David Brown.

3. A full discussion of these two charters together with a consideration of their authenticity is given by Sims-Williams (1974). It is he who corrects the spelling of the name of the first abbess to *Berta* from the usually quoted *Bertana* (*ibid.*, 2). Transcripts of the original texts are conveniently provided in Hunt 1893. There has been much subsequent derivative discussion, some of it inaccurate. The principal references are given in Sims-Williams's paper.

4. See Note 1.

5. A further point which may be worth noting is that it was probably the same Osric who founded St Peter's abbey in Gloucester in *c*. 679. If so it is possible that his dedication in Bath was to the same saint. It is tolerably certain that the monastic church of St Peter existed in Bath, beneath or close to its Norman successor, from the mid-8th century.

6. The relationship of Bath to the kingdoms of Wessex and Mercia is given extensive consideration in Taylor (1900).

7. The excavation was carried out on a site in Upper Borough Walls in 1980. Work was directed by Tim O'Leary on behalf of the Bath Archaeological Trust.

8. A full description of the Bath mint is given by Grinsell (1973). At least five moneyers are known to have worked in Bath during the reign of Edgar (959–75). Under Aethelred II and Cnut three moneyers were working from 979 to 991, five from 991 to 1023, and seven from 1023 to 1029. For the rest of the Saxon period no more than three are recorded.

9. The archaeology of this area was briefly examined and published by Wedlake (1966). The open drainage ditch was clearly seen and was said to contain early medieval pottery. When the gap was blocked the overflow was canalised in a culvert. Insufficient of the city wall was examined to give much idea of the form of the late Saxon/early medieval opening, and whether or not a gatehouse existed, but it remains a possibility that the opening was originally Roman. The crucial area is now largely preserved beneath the floors of the Woolworths and Marks and Spencers structure.

10. The Wessex kings were significant benefactors of St Peter's monastery. One land grant is recorded by Athelstan (931); four by Eadwig (956, 957, 961 [? for 956] and 955 x 957); three by

Edgar (961, 970 and 972); and one by Æthelred (984). In addition the abbey benefited from bequests in the wills of Ælfgifu and Ælfheah. Details are summarised in Sawyer 1968, Nos. 414, 610, 643, 661, 664, 694, 777, 785, 854, 1,484 and 1,485.

11. The figure of 13 per cent. supposes that the burgesses of the church are not included in the 90 'of other men' who also paid tribute to the king. The total of 178 burgesses at the time of Domesday is interesting to compare with the poll tax figures of Richard II listing 197 households within the city and 129 in the north and south suburbs. The 12 acres of meadow lay outside the city wall between the south-east sector of the wall and the River Avon. The position of the 'monks mill' is recorded on later city maps. See Fig. 116.

12. The archaeological data is scattered and often ill-recorded. For a general summary with references to earlier accounts see Cunliffe 1979, 88–93. The lead disc has been discussed by Okasha (1971), and more recently by Hinton (1979). The late Saxon coins were considered by Metcalf (1958). Grinsell (1974) draws attention to an inscription on a memorial stone at Növelsjö in Smaland, Sweden, which records in Runic 'Gunnkel set this stone in memory of Gunnar, his father, Rode's son. Helge laid him, his brother, in a stone coffin, in England, in Bath' (Jansson 1962, 52–3).

13. The seal is No. 1,437 in the *Catalogue of Seals in the MS. Department of the British Museum*, where it is surely incorrectly described as 'an edifice of three towers without windows'. The actual seal was used on a manuscript of 1159–75 (Harl. ch. 75A.30) and could, if the early date proposed for the matrix is rejected, be a representation of John de Villula's church.

14. *Calendar of Charter Rolls* 2, 219.

15. For a listing of the cross fragments with references see Cunliffe 1979, 140. Not all survive and the early records are confusing.

16. A reasonable body of late Saxon pottery has now been published from Bath. The largest stratified collection came from the excavation of Citizen House in 1970 (Greene 1979, Figs. 15–19, with a discussion of the fabric types by Alan Vince, pp. 27–31). Finds from elsewhere in Bath are summarised by Cunliffe (1979, 140–49).

17. The events are discussed with full references in *V.C.H. Somerset* II (1911), 70–1.

BIBLIOGRAPHY

Biddle, M. and Hill, D. H. (1971), 'Late Saxon planned towns', *Antiquaries Journal* 51, 70-85.

Cameron, K. J. (1980), 'The meaning and significance of O.E. *walh* in English place-names', *Journal of the English Place-Name Society* 12, 1-53.

Cunliffe, B. W. (1969), *Roman Bath*, Society of Antiquaries Research Report 24, London.

Cunliffe, B. W. (ed.) (1979), *Excavations in Bath 1950-1975*, C.R.A.A.G.S. excavation report 1, Bristol.

Cunliffe, B. W. (1980), 'The excavation of the Roman Spring at Bath, 1979', *Antiquaries Journal* 60 187-206.

Greene, J. P. (1979), 'Citizen House (Westgate Buildings), 1970', in Cunliffe, B. W. (ed.) 1979, 4-70.

Grinsell, L. V. (1973), *The Bath Mint*, London.

Grinsell, L. V. (1974), 'A Viking burial in a stone coffin in Bath', *Somerset and Dorset Notes and Queries* 30, 67.

Hill, D. H. (1969), 'The Burghal Hidage: the establishment of a text', *Medieval Archaeology* 13, 84-92.

Hinton, D. (1979), 'Saxon Finds', in Cunliffe, B. W. (ed.) 1979, 138-40.

Hunt, W. (1893), 'Two Chartularies of the priory of St Peter at Bath', *Somerset Record Society* 1.7, 6-7.

Jansson, S. B. F. (1962), *The Runes of Sweden*.

Leslie, R. F. (1961), *Three Old English Elegies,* Manchester.

Metcalf, D. M. (1958), 'Eighteenth-century finds of medieval coins from the records of the Society of Antiquaries', *Numismatic Chronicle* 18, 73-96.

Okasha, E. (1971), *Hand List of Anglo-Saxon Non Runic Inscriptions*, Cambridge.

O'Leary, T. (1981), 'Excavations at Upper Borough Wall, Bath, 1980', *Medieval Archaeology* 25, 1-30.

Rigold, S. E. (1977), 'Litus Romanum—the Saxon forts as mission stations', in Johnston, D. E. (ed.), *The Saxon Shore*, 70-76.

Sawyer, P. H. (1968), *Anglo-Saxon Charters: an Annotated List and Bibliography*.

Sims-Williams, P. (1974), 'Continental influence at Bath monastery in the seventh century', *Anglo-Saxon England* 4, 1–10.

Taylor, C. S. (1900), 'Bath, Mercian and West Saxon', *Transactions of the Bristol and Gloucestershire Archaeological Society* 23, 129–161.

Wedlake, W. J. (1966), 'The city walls of Bath, the church of St James, South Gate, and the area to the east of the church of St James', *Proceedings of the Somerset Archaeological and Natural History Society* 110, 85-107.

Chapter Thirteen

SAXON GLOUCESTER

By Carolyn Heighway

THE HISTORY OF Anglo-Saxon Gloucester must begin with an account of the Roman colony of *Glevum,* even though it failed to survive as a town beyond the Romano-British period. There are, it is true, slight hints of administrative continuity, but the main influence of the Roman town was physical. The stone-built defences and public buildings were enduring even as ruins, and were bound to effect the Saxon administrative centre which grew up in the shelter of the Roman walls.

Gloucester is sited in the border country between England and Wales, at a controlling point of the fiercely tidal River Severn. Until modern times the town was the lowest bridging place. The river has been vital to Gloucester's history, and some changes in its course need to be understood.

In Fig. 117, only the eastern two of three arms of the river are shown. It is possible that in Roman times all three streams met above the sites of the bridges.[1] The most important channel was the easternmost one, which once provided a considerable river frontage in the west suburb of Gloucester (Hurst 1974, 46-7). The silting of this eastern channel caused the quays to shift south, so that they are today a less central part of the townscape.

The first settlement at Gloucester was built at Kingsholm in the A.D. 60s: a fortress or fort set beside the old eastern channel, a little to the north of the present site of Gloucester (Green 1942, 40-1; Richmond 1962; Webster 1970, 186; Hurst 1975, 267-9). The position of this fort, on lower ground than the present town, may have been related to a pre-existing ford.

The later fortress was founded on higher ground further south in the A.D. 70s. This was in turn converted into a Roman colony, perhaps in the period A.D. 96 to 98 (Hurst 1976, 66-9). The colony used the fortress defences, but it also had extensive suburbs (*ibid.,* 73-4), both to the north, and in the waterfront area, where there were large stone-built houses with mosaics (Bryant 1980; Knowles 1938, 167). A most important discovery has been of a massive wall about 1.4m. wide along the river frontage, with a masonry platform to the west of it (Hurst 1974, 46-7). It now seems likely that the platform was part of the Roman quay, and that the wall was a revetment or flood wall along the waterfront. The wall may also have been defensive, and it could, as I suggest, have extended east to join the city wall, thus enclosing the west riverside suburb just as the lower colonia was enclosed at Lincoln. The original west wall may have remained; it is only known that it was demolished at some time between the 4th and 10th centuries. What is more certain is that the riverside wall was a feature of Anglo-Saxon Gloucester, for it was not demolished until the early 12th century.[2]

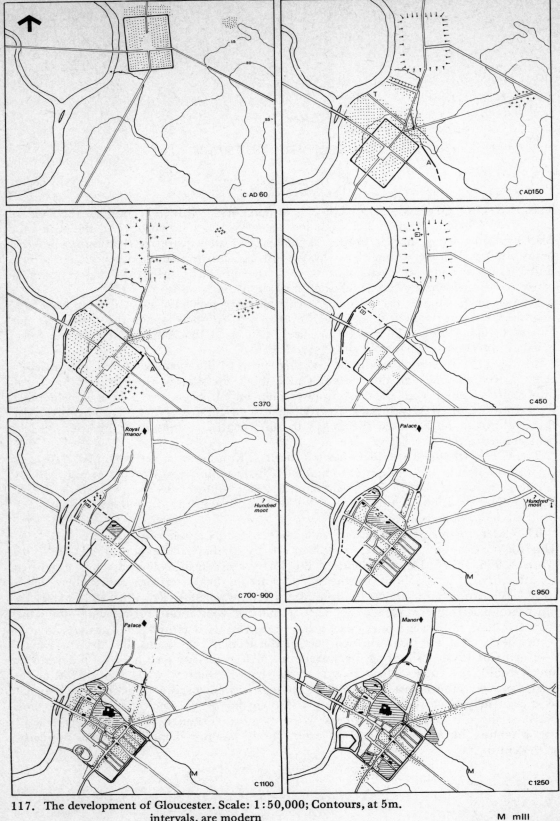

117. The development of Gloucester. Scale: 1:50,000; Contours, at 5m. intervals, are modern

Map labels by panel:

C AD 60

C AD 150 — T, A

C 370 — A

C 450

C 700-900 — Royal manor, ? Hundred moot

C 950 — Palace, Hundred moot, M

C 1100 — Palace, M

C 1250 — Manor, M

Legend:

∴ burials

▦ known occupied areas

⊡ burial chapel or mausoleum

▨ religious precinct

▬ church or chapel

ı 9th and 10th century stone crosses

M mill

A aqueduct

T tilery

The Roman colony was rebuilt in the early 2nd century, with large stone public buildings including the central *forum*. The new town retained much of the fortress street grid (Hurst 1976). Four cemeteries existed outside the town. Two were on municipal sites originally in use for other purposes: the Kingsholm fort became a cemetery, and so did the municipal tilery, which was no longer in industrial use after the 3rd century (Heighway 1980b).

The high building density of the initial colony was short-lived. Later, from the mid-2nd century onwards, there was a tendency towards construction of fewer and larger buildings, suggesting that wealth was concentrated in fewer hands (Hurst 1976, 78). The town was sufficiently well organised for its inhabitants to be able to refurbish the defences in the early to mid-4th century (Heighway *et al.* forthcoming). A 40m. stretch of wall on each side of the gates was rebuilt, and external bastions were added (Hurst 1972). Not much other 4th-century rebuilding seems to have taken place, and by the latter part of the century, if not before, the town's civic organisation was showing signs of strain. Public buildings were in industrial use and one, possibly the baths, was demolished (Heighway and Garrod 1980).

In the early 5th century the town centre at Gloucester underwent considerable change. The area north of the *forum* was re-metalled and extended across the *via principalis* (Heighway and Garrod 1980). It is not clear why this was done. Perhaps more space was needed for massing of troops or penning of cattle during a period of crisis. The elimination of the main east-west street shows that this routeway was already shifting northwards. The new street, Westgate Street, which presumably dates from this period, passed through two ruined public buildings, following the line of their colonnades. With the Roman street so altered, the Roman west gate must have been blocked, and a new opening made further north in the western wall. On the other hand, if there was a defended western suburb, a considerable section of the west wall may already have been obsolete.

Late Roman Gloucester may have been defended by local levies, wearing the dolphin belt-buckles of which two have been found in and near Gloucester.[3] Possibly a warrior aristocracy was already emerging. At Kingsholm, in the early 5th century, a warrior of high rank was buried in his own mausoleum (Hurst 1975). Other sub-Roman burial areas are known. At St Mary's church, in the western suburb, a large courtyard house was demolished and its site used for a 5th- to 8th-century mausoleum or chapel which was set out on the Roman alignment. The same alignment was later used for the Saxon church. Other cemeteries, which ostensibly belong to the 'late Roman' period, are so identified by the presence of inhumation graves, often with hobnailed footwear, but they also contain simple inhumations without any grave-goods at all, which could belong to the 5th century or later (Rahtz 1977, 55).

The only ceramic evidence of this period is the presence of occasional sherds of 'grass-tempered' pottery, whose date range extends from the 5th to the 8th centuries (Fowler 1970). Its find spots in Gloucester enable a few areas of occupation to be tentatively indicated (Fig. 117), but there are surprisingly few sherds, especially when compared with the dozens which derive from the villa site of Frocester (Gracie and Price 1979). Are we to believe that Frocester was more important, perhaps a rural market centre? Certainly the evidence of much activity in Gloucester is far from convincing. Presumably there was some occupation around the metalled extension of the *forum* already mentioned. On the New Market Hall site it was shown that some Roman buildings remained occupied into the 5th century; a group of pottery, the latest Roman ware found at Gloucester, may indicate still later activity—'. . . The impression gained . . . is of pots deliberately preserved and perhaps salvaged long after their date of manufacture . . .'. Bronze working is also suggested by the presence of metal objects and scrap metal of 5th- or even 6th-century date (Hassall and Rhodes 1974, 30, 36–91).

The history of 4th- and 5th-century Gloucester has probably been unduly distorted by the fact that the dating evidence ceases abruptly *c.* 400. In fact, there may not be a great deal of difference in the appearance of the town between the 4th and 5th centuries. The plans of both (Fig. 117) show a decrease in settlement, but it is difficult to say whether this is because 4th- and 5th-century levels have been destroyed by later activity, or whether it is the true expression of urban decline. The evidence seems contradictory. On the one hand 4th-century public buildings were used for domestic and industrial purposes, and timber buildings were constructed in the town centre; on the other hand the defences were repaired, and stone houses and services were maintained up to the end of the 4th century.[4] Presumably the decline was a long process, during which stone buildings were being gradually replaced by buildings wholly of timber (which would not have looked too different from their predecessors, many of which had timber superstructures). The presence of well maintained stone or stone-founded buildings does not in itself necessarily imply a flourishing urban context, and it may be that we must go some way towards Reece's view (1980) that the cities of Britain were already failing in the 3rd century.

By the time Saxon political conquest occurred, as a result of the battle of Dyrham in 577, Gloucester may only have had a relatively small population. However, it seems to have been, with Bath and Cirencester, the head place of a district, for 'kings' of each of the three places were killed at the battle (A.S.C. s.a. 577). The three districts may be identical with administrative arrangements in the 10th century, when Bristol (previously Bath) and Cirencester both controlled seven hundreds (Slater 1976, 82–3). The area controlled by Gloucester may have been smaller (see below).

By the mid-7th century, Gloucester lay within the territory of the Hwicce, a sub-kingdom of Mercia (Wilson 1969). Finberg (1972, 167–80) suggested that the area first came under the control of Mercia at the time of the battle of Cirencester in 628, perhaps as the result of an alliance between Mercia and Northumbrian war lords, who were established as the ruling family of the Hwicce.

It is probably safe to say that in the 7th century Gloucester was not a town. Its end is symbolised by the fact that the Roman street grid vanished completely, except where the principal Roman streets passed through the north and east gates. There is, however, some indication that the minor streets, no longer thoroughfares, had acquired another purpose: that of defining the limits of estate plots. The most important of these was the enclosure of the minster of St Peter, founded 679 x 81 (Finberg 1972, 153ff.). The south corner of this enclosure coincides with the crossing of two minor Roman streets (see Fig. 118). The north–south Roman street on the east side of the precinct survived into the post-Roman period after adjacent stone buildings had collapsed on to it, for rubble lying in the street was worn by the passage of traffic. Thus the street was probably still visible in the late 7th century.

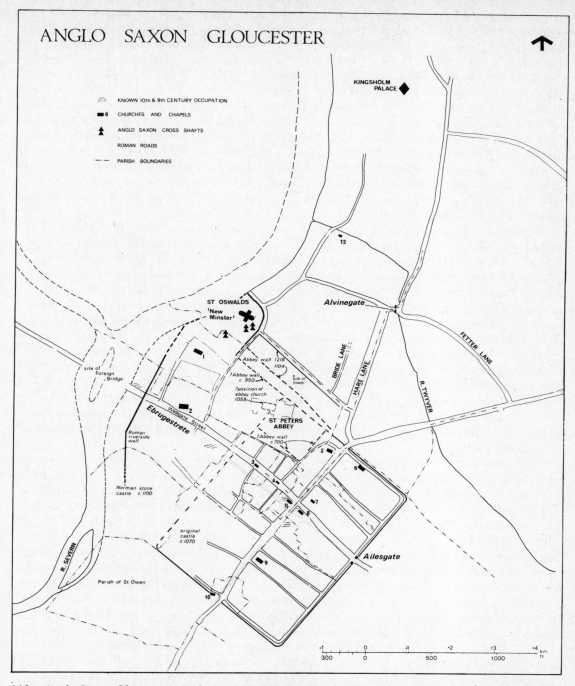

118. Anglo-Saxon Gloucester. Scale 1:5,000. Old English names in bold italic type; modern names in bold Roman type. Churches and chapels: (1) St Mary de Lode; (2) St Nicholas; (3) Holy Trinity; (4) St Mary de Grace; (5) St John; (6) St Aldate; (7) St Martin's chapel; (8) St Michael; (9) St Mary de Crypt; (10) St Kyneburgh's chapel; (11) All Saints'; (12) Chapel of St Thomas the Apostle at Kingsholm. Parish boundaries as in 1852. Drawn by L. Marley and C. Heighway.

After Roman buildings in the area were demolished, a 'desire path' was created, running obliquely on a slightly more easterly line towards the north gate (Heighway *et al.* forthcoming). It appears that the precinct, originally laid out on Roman streets, encroached across these when the movement of pathways gave an opportunity.

A further example is the 10th-century parish of St Aldgate, which formed a compact block of land, less than two acres in extent, in the north-east corner of the city. Its south boundary followed for much of its course the line of a minor Roman street (Fig. 118). It is possible that the parish unit represents an early urban estate or *hagae* originally laid out on a Roman street. By the time this block of land became a parish in the 10th or 11th centuries, the south boundary had moved away from the Roman street in places, and followed instead the backs of tenements. It need not be surprising that the 8th-century boundary had shifted, at a time when there must have been plots of unclaimed land. The process recalls a 20th-century phenomenon: the uneven colonisation by some householders of derelict railway land at the bottom of their gardens.

Whatever the validity of the preceding two examples, it is likely that many of the *hagae* of Gloucester originally followed obvious Roman features, particularly the streets and walls; it is also likely that the first *hagae* were several acres in extent (Tait 1936, 7). One is even led to ask whether there is a difference of quality rather of kind between the well spaced, large Roman houses that characterised much of late Roman Gloucester, and the *hagae* of the 8th century and later.

Other more certain deductions can be made about the 7th and 8th centuries. One is that large Roman ruins were still a feature of the landscape. The Roman walls, the north and east Roman gates, and the riverside wall, still stood and could have been in use. The Roman columns marking Westgate Street had once been 30 feet high and probably still stood to a considerable height. Nennius, writing early in the 9th century, described Gloucester as a great city ('magnem urbem' [*sic.*]; Morris 1980, 33, 74). Even though this remark was made in the context of a legendary foundation story, it implies that Gloucester still presented an impressive appearance in Nennius's own day.

At most sites where excavations have taken place, the period between Roman and the 10th century is represented archaeologically by a layer of dark loam which so far has defied analysis. The most likely explanation is that this was the result of cultivation (Hurst 1974, 23; Hassall and Rhodes 1974, 30). If this is so, then considerable areas of the Roman town were put to arable use. But in some areas there is evidence of different activity, for the 'dark loam' is not ubiquitous. It is replaced at the town centre by a sticky plastic layer of organic material, containing little pottery, but much bone and many wooden artefacts, and preserving fences and buildings made of wattle. At 1 Westgate Street, these organic levels were dated to the 9th century (Heighway, Garrod and Vince 1979). At 11–17 Southgate Street they contained 10th-century pottery (Hurst 1972, 61), but the earliest levels produced a consistent range of radio-carbon dates of the 8th century.[5] Similar levels at St Michael's church were two metres thick; their importance was not recognised at the time and no dating was available (Cra'ster 1961). A section excavated under the Shire Hall (Abbott 1967) uncovered 'silt and peat' and preserved wood at about 12m. A.O.D., above Roman strata.

It is clear that the preservation of these organic levels was not due to waterlogging (they are all, excepting the Shire Hall deposits, above the water table), but rather to anoxic conditions caused by the rapid accumulation of organic matter (Biek 1979). Their preservation was a direct result of intense human and animal activity. The evidence at 1 Westgate Street shows that in the 9th century animals were stabled at the town centre, and craft manufacture, including leather working, was carried out. Very little pottery was used. Domestic objects were all of wood, and pegged rather than nailed. The remains are few because of the limited size of the excavation, but it is obvious that the manufacture of wooden items, often highly complex, was a common industry. In contrast to 8th-century mercantile centres such as *Hamwih*, Gloucester seems to have received very few imports from far afield, although one of the few pottery vessels found came from the Oxford area. The economy was clearly strongly agricultural and intensely provincial (Heighway, Garrod and Vince 1979).

These dense organic levels have so far only been found at the town centre (except for the Shire Hall deposit, just outside the west gate of the Roman fort). The range of dating evidence from the organic material, spanning the late 7th to the 10th centuries, may suggest that not all these areas were in use simultaneously; possibly different parts of the town were occupied at different times, although the emphasis would always have been on the principal street frontages.

It is therefore clear that 9th-century Gloucester was occupied, though probably not densely. In 877, the remnants of the Danish army found room to camp in the town (A.S.C., 48, fn. 13). Present information suggests that the topography of the town in the 6th to 9th centuries was an echo of the Roman lay-out, but with a reduced population occupying a series of small estates rather than the unified town which had been the Roman ideal. It is interesting that, of four Roman cemeteries, three were to be significant sites in the Anglo-Saxon town. At Kingsholm the Roman cemetery area became, as in some Frankish towns (Böhner 1977), the focus for an extra-mural royal manor with its own hundred of Barton Regis. It is possible that there was a hundred-moot north-east of the town on or near the site of another Roman cemetery. The area now known as Wotton Pitch was called 'Dudstone' in the Middle Ages (Stevenson 1890, 90, 98), the name of the local hundred. The name means 'Dudda's stone'—'from the O.E. personal name . . . the stone doubtless marked the site of the hundred meeting-place' (Smith 1964, 137). By odd coincidence, a carved late Saxon stone has been found nearby.[6] Both the stone and the hundredal name may be 11th century, but the possibility must remain that the hundred is considerably older.[7] A third Roman cemetery was to become the site of the late Saxon minster of St Oswald (Heighway 1980a). Presumably the cemeteries remained as entities in the administrative records inherited from the Roman period; there is no reason why loss of urban status should imply the breaking of all links with the past. Finberg claimed that in 679 the old Roman land tax may still have been in operation, and that this became the basis of the hundredal system (Finberg 1957, 14–16).

The most significant event in these centuries was probably the foundation of the minster at Gloucester in *c.* 679. It seems to have begun as a double minster, that is, a mixed house of nuns and clerics, headed by ladies probably of the royal house of the Hwicce. The first abbess, Kyneburgh, was either the sister of the minster's founder, Osric, or she may conceivably have been the Kyneburgh who was wife of St Oswald of Northumbria (Finberg 1972, 165). The double monastery ceased to exist after the death in about 757 of Abbess Eafe. It has been held that it then lay derelict, although Finberg argues convincingly that the minster continued in being, as a college of secular priests (*ibid.*, 161).

The appearance and even the position of this early church are unknown. The only hint is in a document recorded by Dugdale, but now lost, called the 'Memoriale' (Dugdale, i, 563). It is obviously a post-medieval compilation, and includes many legendary elements no longer regarded seriously, but it provides the information that in 1058 Aldred rebuilt the church 'a little nearer the side of the city'.[8] This kind of information usually derives from a genuine tradition. Unfortunately, we do not know where 'the side of the city' was in the 11th century, nor even whether the minster started life inside the city limits (although this seems likely). However, since the expansion of the abbey precinct in the 12th and 13th centuries took place in a north-westerly direction, as described below, the original precinct was evidently a smaller area in the south-east of the present precinct. Indeed, the original enclosure may have been confined within the original Roman west wall (as shown in Fig. 117).

The beginning of the 10th century seems to mark a watershed in the fortunes of Gloucester. Evidence suddenly becomes much more abundant. For one thing, a local pottery industry appears, with kilns established in the town centre, which puts archaeological evidence on a firm footing for the first time in five centuries (Vince 1979, 175). For another, dramatic physical changes occurred which have been attributed to the influence of Aethelflaed, daughter of King Alfred, and her husband, Aethelred of Mercia. Although never specifically listed as a Mercian burh, Gloucester was clearly organised for defence, since the men of the city took part in a campaign which beat off a Danish attack in 914 (A.S.C.). Most remarkably, as Hurst pointed out, its street plan bears a very close resemblance to that of Alfred's Wessex burhs (Hurst 1972, 66–8), and it seems likely, in view of Aethelflaed's connections with Gloucester, that she would have laid it out as a burh in the pattern of her father's works elsewhere (Biddle and Hill 1971). At the same time she established the new minster of St Oswald, founded before 909 close to the old minster of St Peter. The town by now had a mint and a royal palace, and it almost certainly had a market (Heighway 1978, 121).

Only a little conversion would have been needed to create in the town a street pattern of the 'Alfredian' design. The axial streets already existed, and all that was required would have been the addition of the side streets in the eastern area of the town, where the Roman wall already provided a defence. No archaeological evidence relating to these streets has been obtained which could confirm this hypothesis, but on the other hand there has been no evidence to contradict it.

The development of the western part of the town is more difficult to understand. As in the sub-Roman period, the position of the western defence is uncertain. It would be logical if the Saxon burh had used all the walls of the fortress (Lobel 1969; Hurst 1972, 36–7; Hurst 1974, 13). Yet evidence is accumulating to suggest that this was not so. The burh obviously used the east, south, and part of the north walls of the Roman fortress, but it is not clear that it used the western wall. For one thing, if the western wall survived as late as the 10th and 11th centuries, it seems inconceivable that some part of it should not have been incorporated into tenement boundaries or other topographical features. The parish boundaries which ignore the western wall completely, could be 12th century (Fig. 119), but tenement boundaries usually remained unchanged from the earliest foundation of the burh (Biddle and Hill 1971, 82). The frontage at least of Westgate Street must have been occupied before the 10th century, yet the wall line, which is known from excavations in Berkeley Street (Hurst 1972, 35) has not influenced the lay-out of a single tenement (Fig. 119).

There is also the matter of the intra-mural street. The principal Wessex burhs had intra-mural streets which were an essential part of their function as military strongpoints (Biddle and Hill 1971; Biddle 1975b, 103). At Gloucester this street is still clear on the east side, the east part of the north side, and can be traced on the south, though colonised in the later Middle Ages (Hurst 1972, 67). Yet on the west side, no such street survives. Instead there is Berkeley Street, which crosses over the line of both wall and ditch and clearly came into existence when all elements of the western defences had gone.

For the investigation of city streets, which cannot generally be dug up by archaeologists, the watching of service trenches is invaluable. A trench in Berkeley Street (see Fig. 119), across the line of the wall, located the robbing trench of the wall (Garrod forthcoming, site 19/79, trench II). Above it were 14 metalled surfaces of the street. Under the third surface from the bottom was a late Saxon decorated scramasax sheath, which cannot be

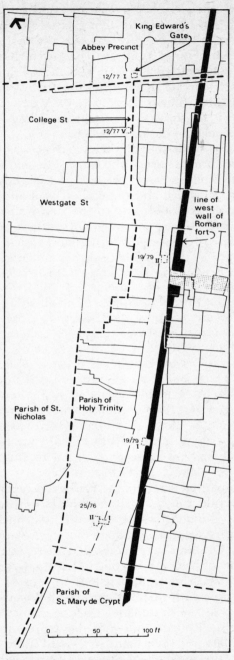

119. Gloucester: the west wall of the Roman fortress and town in relation to the tenement boundaries of 1852. Heavy broken line denotes 1852 parish boundaries. Scale: about 1:2,000

later than the 11th century, and pottery of the late 10th to early 11th centuries. It is hard to believe that Saxon streets were resurfaced particularly frequently, and an early 10th-century date for the first street is very possible.[9] Further south, another trench (Fig. 119, 25/76 II) showed that the street had 15 surviving metalled surfaces. An adjacent trench sectioned the possible west defensive ditch which had 11th-century pottery in its upper fills; the first streets could, however, have been laid before the last ditch fillings accumulated. A trench at the north end of Berkeley Street (Fig. 119, 19/79 II) showed 10 street metallings over the Roman ditch, but the earliest streets produced no dating evidence.

It is clear that Berkeley Street was in existence by the 11th century, and it may have formed part of the early 10th-century burh lay-out.

In College Street the site of King Edward's Gate, an entrance to the abbey precinct, was excavated and the earliest wall and gate located (Garrod forthcoming, site 12/77). The gate should date to the first walling of the abbey in 1104–13.[10] It was preceded by five streets, of which the earliest contained 10th-century pottery. (These streets apparently belonged to the land which surrounded the precinct wall, for rubbish pits of the 11th to 12th centuries underlay the first metalled surface of College Street, which may not have come into existence until later [Fig. 119, 12/77 V]). The site of King Edward's Gate is west of the line of the Roman west wall, so the indications are that the abbey precinct had already crossed the wall by the 10th century.

Recent work by A. P. Garrod in the area west of the cathedral cloisters uncovered the Norman west cloister range. Underneath this were human burials, aligned east–west, and many disturbed bones, showing that the burial ground was in use for several generations before the west range was built (site 11/80). This must be a late Saxon cemetery, but it is well outside the Roman west wall.

All the evidence available so far tends to suggest that the 10th-century city had crossed its Roman boundary to the west and extended down to the river. It is inherently likely that there was at least a Saxon suburb in this area, which was close to the quay frontage and to the churches of St Mary de Lode and St Oswald. Indeed, historians have already pointed to this area as a significant part of the Saxon burh (Lobel 1969, 3; Fullbrook-Leggatt 1952, 4). There was certainly 10th-century occupation here, for A. P. Garrod recorded a timber house 15m. west of the Roman quayside wall, associated with 10th-century pottery.[11]

It is inconceivable that this riverside area should have had no defence in the 10th century, especially when the town had the 'Wessex burh' type pattern in its eastern half. It seems very likely that there was, as suggested above, a western Roman circuit some of which was still in use, as were the rest of the Roman defences, in the 10th century. This wall, if it existed, should have left some mark on property boundaries. On the south side of the town all the evidence for such a wall was in the Norman castle area, so the boundaries became distorted in the 12th century. On the north, the line of this Roman wall may be represented by part of the parish boundary between St Mary de Lode and St Oswald's. By the 10th century, however, it is possible that that the precinct of St Oswald was enclosed and defended, so as to form part of the defensive circuit, as it did in the later Middle Ages. There are also property boundaries in the Cathedral Close which could represent the line of this Roman wall, which may have formed the limit of the abbey precinct in the mid 10th century (Figs. 117 and 118).

There is no need to postulate deliberate planning for the western part of the town, which is evidently less regular than the eastern area. Berkeley Street, as has been shown, is only possibly part of the early 10th-century plan. Most of the other streets in the western suburb appear to be essential routes which probably developed naturally and could have had very early origins; for instance, the road leading to St Oswald's church and Kingsholm, both of which sites have pre-10th-century origins, could have been in use a century before the burh was refounded by Aethelflaed. It is possible that the road leading direct to St Mary de Lode church was an intra-mural street built in the early 10th century to facilitate access to the riverside wall, but it is 20m. inside the wall, considerably further from it than the other intra-mural streets. In view of the early origins of St Mary's, it is likely that a track led to the church from Westgate Street well before the 10th century. Indeed, nothing whatsoever is known of the Roman streets in this area, and they may yet turn out to have been more influential on the topography than elsewhere in the town.

To the north of the Saxon town lay the royal palace at Kingsholm, and the suburb on this side of the town should have been important. No extensive archaeological excavation has been carried out in this area, which is unfortunate, since the street pattern is very curious. Hare Lane is the common Old English 'here straet' or 'military road' (Smith 1964, 129), and it is often assumed to occupy the line of the Roman road to the north, although this is by no means certain. Hare Lane is a double street which in the later medieval period acquired houses down its centre, dividing it into two streets, so that it resembled a colonised market. At the head of this 'market' was Alvin Gate, another Old English name—'Aelwine's gate' (Smith 1964, 126). Wide market streets outside town gates are known elsewhere: for instance, St Giles, Oxford (Keene 1976, 71-3). But there is no documentary reference to a market in Hare Lane, and in the 13th century it was the Tanners' Street.[12] By 1455 the lane and the strip down the centre were occupied by well over 41 properties, of mixed character, of which some were tenements and some were 'tofts, crofts and curtileges' (Stevenson 1890, 78-87). By the 18th century there was little here but gardens (Hall and Pinnell 1780). Parallel to Hare Lane was Bride Lane, first mentioned between 1195 and 1205 (Smith 1964, 127), already disused in 1597-8,[13] and leased out as a garden in 1743 (Woodman 1966, No. 2,043A). These streets have a very regular appearance and it is possible that they represent what remains of a planned, late Saxon suburb and extra-mural market which had declined long before the 12th century, when records in Gloucester begin.

Other streets which have Old English names may claim to derive from the late Saxon period. The most important of these are marked on Fig. 118 (medieval versions of such names in italic type). Fetter Lane, from the O.E. female name 'Feta' (Smith 1964, 128-9) formed a convenient 'bypass' from one approach to the city to the other. Several other streets which have Old English names, whose exact position is not certain (Powke Lane, Meinde Lane) were in the western suburb,[14] and there were doubtless Saxon streets under the original castle and perhaps the later castle as well (Hurst 1974, 12, and forthcoming).

The full extent of occupation in the late Saxon town is not known. The distribution of late Saxon pottery indicates that occupation was along the principal street frontages (Vince 1979, 175); it is likely that it took some time for the frontages of the subsidiary streets to become built up. Another indication of population distribution in the original burh should be given by a plot of those tenements which paid land-gavel (Langton 1977, 267–8; Tait 1936, 89). A convenient index of the land-gavel is that of the Rental of 1455, where about the same number of tenements rendered this tax as in 1100 (Stevenson 1890, x). The incidence of this tax is plotted in map form by Langton (*ibid.*). Most of the payments derived from properties along the frontages of the main streets, outside the north gate, and along Westgate Street to beyond the site of Foreign Bridge. In spite of the name 'Foreign' which implies this once marked the borough limit (Smith 1964, 133), the land-gavel payments suggest the Saxon burh extended as far west as did the later medieval town. Presumably there was, even in the 10th century, a suburb beyond the eastern arm of the river. There was certainly a suburb along Northgate Street. Hare Lane, according to the 1455 Rental, paid no land-gavel, except at its southernmost end, but there are indications that the payments had lapsed.[15]

The abbey of St Peter underwent a Benedictine reform in about 1022,[16] and in 1058 the abbey church was rebuilt by Aldred (A.S.C.). This church was rebuilt again by the Norman abbot Serlo, who began a new church 'from the foundations' in 1089; it was dedicated in 1100 (Florence of Worcester, ii, 44). Serlo also considerably restored the fortunes of the abbey.

The lay-out of the precinct before Serlo's time has to be deduced from the slight documentary evidence. When Serlo's church of *c.* 1100 was finished, the abbey built a wall on land which belonged to St Oswald's priory. The position of this wall is made clear in documents of 1218, when still more land was ceded by St Oswald's to St Peter's. This last area was used 'for enclosing with a wall, extending the court towards the north next to the Priory of St Oswald's'.[17] The abbey records carefully describe the land so acquired, which lay 'below the wall of the abbey [presumably the earlier wall of *c.* 1100] from the garden in a straight line descending by the refectory, larder and bakery as far as the new wall [i.e., that of 1218] next to St Oswald's' (Hart, i, 25). This describes a tract of land north-west of the then abbey complex, as the references to the abbey refectory and to St Oswald's make clear (Fig. 118). Since the wall of 1100 was built on land of St Oswald's (Hart, i, 82) there was obviously an even earlier wall further south. The fact that there is a pre-Norman burial ground (mentioned above) under the west range of the Norman cloister suggests that this area was already part of the abbey precinct in the 10th century. A wall has, therefore, been drawn in Fig. 118 which coincides with the hypothetical western Roman circuit.

The stream which flows through the abbey precinct was an artificial diversion which also served to water the town ditches. Mr. Fullbrook-Leggatt (1964, 80) thought this was done by the Norman monks to provide a water supply. It seems to coincide roughly with the line of the wall of 1104.

The discovery of the Saxon cemetery suggests that the church of 1058 was not too far away. The Norman abbey begun by Serlo in 1089 was more than 20 years in the building, and worship must have continued in the old church for some years.[18] If Aldred's church were on the same or a similar site as the Norman church, it would have to be under or partly under the nave for it to be usable whilst building on the Norman crypt and choir could begin. The 7th-century church could then have been south of the present cathedral, inside the original Roman circuit. However, it is equally possible either that the 7th-century church was under the Norman east end and crossing, and Aldred's church beneath the present cloisters, or that both churches were outside the original Roman west wall, which may have been taken down even before the 7th century.

Finally, it should be mentioned that one or two accounts state with apparent confidence that the ancient abbey was near the 13th-century infirmary, and was marked until the 16th century by a tower in the Monks Orchard.[19] These statements seem to derive from the 'Memoriale', which describes a tower near the infirmary, which, 'together with the monastery in the time of the nuns', was depicted in a window in the cloister. The tower is thus ancient only by implication. An 8th- or even 10th-century church in this position is very difficult to accommodate with the known abbey extensions of 1104 and 1218. It seems more plausible that this was a detached bell-tower of 12th- or 13th-century date.

Another late Saxon building of great importance was the palace at Kingsholm. It is reasonably well documented in the 11th century (Hurst 1975, 284) and from the 13th century onwards there are frequent references to the 'Aula Regis' in the Kingsholm area.[20] Kingsholm was a royal manor, the centre of a wealthy estate, which governed its own hundred (Barton Regis). It is likely to have been the place where Aethelflaed and Aethlred stayed, whether or not it was already dignified with the title of 'palace', and it is likely, too, as Hurst pointed out (1975, 284) that the assembly of the Mercian council in 896 (Finberg 1972, 50, No. 85) was held at Kingsholm (the abbey, the only other likely venue, probably not being sufficiently large or flourishing to support a gathering of several hundred people). Presumably the many royal councils that Edward the Confessor held at Gloucester (Oleson 1955, 159–60) were also held in the royal hall there. Excavations at Kingsholm have uncovered the traces of timber structures in the form of flat-bottomed trenches for timber sill beams, as well as large post-holes. These are likely to be part of the manor/palace complex (Hurst 1975). There is every chance that more extensive excavation could locate the superimposed buildings covering many centuries of occupation, and even establish a physical link between buildings relating to the late Roman cemetery and those of the early manor. However, much of the immediate area of the palace is in private ownership as back gardens; the available open space is quite small, little more than 300 square metres. It is now a scheduled ancient monument.

Closely related to the palace or manor at Kingsholm was the minster of St Oswald, founded in c. 900 by Queen Aethelflaed and Earl Aethelred of Mercia.[21] It is the most significant memorial of the queen's favour to Gloucester. In 909 the bones of Aethelflaed's saintly ancestor, Oswald of Northumbria, were moved to the new church at Gloucester, which became a famous place of devotion and pilgrimage.[22] It was described as the 'new minster' not much more than a century after its foundation, and it may be compared with the new minster of Winchester, founded at about the same date and possibly for the same purpose, to provide for the anticipated increased population in a newly-restored town.[23]

The new church was sited on land which probably then belonged to the royal palace; it was certainly in a spot where there were already a number of carved stone crosses. One of these was found in the 19th century, and has been cited as an example of 9th-century work (Cramp 1977, Fig. 62, i). Another is of two parts which were found in 1957 and 1966, and is also of the 9th century (Cramp 1975, 191). A third was found in 1977 built into the fabric of Aethelflaed's church, and so must have been on or near the site when building began (Heighway 1980a, p. 212 and Plate XXIII). A group of stone cross-shafts of such fine workmanship indicates a cemetery, and if the royal connections of St Oswald's are recalled, it is possible to suggest that it was a cemetery intended for members of the royal house of the Hwicce. If this were so, there is also likely to have been a mausoleum or chapel nearby. The chantry chapel of St Thomas, which was later in the care of the canons of St Oswald, could have originated in the 9th century. Alternatively, there is a building to the east of the church of St Oswald (described below) which could have been an early chapel.

The new church was built, at least in part, of re-used Roman stone, which suggests that sufficient Roman ruins were visible in the early 10th century to prompt extensive quarrying. A startling innovation was the western apse, on shallow foundations, and therefore possibly of timber, but nevertheless a reminder that the rulers of Mercia were not too provincial to be uninfluenced by Carolingian examples. The church was probably richly decorated. Only a few architectural fragments survive, but this is not surprising in view of the amount of stone which was taken from the site in post-medieval times. The decorated pieces include a door-head decorated with twisted cable and pellet ornament (illustrated in Heighway 1980a, Plate XXIa), an altar front of similar design, part of a fluted capital, and a magnificent grave-slab with foliate ornament. This last piece is worthy of the remains of St Oswald himself, although it dates to about 930 and therefore could not have covered the saint's remains until two decades after his translation. It is interesting that some of the parallels for this stone can be found in the designs of the Cuthbert embroideries, which may have been commissioned by Aethelflaed's sister-in-law, Edward's wife, Aelflaed (West 1980).

The east end of Aethelflaed's church remains unexcavated, but work so far has shown that east of the chancel was a separate square or rectangular building. This is of the same date as, or earlier, than, the first church. It could have been an earlier chapel or mausoleum which was later incorporated into Aethelflaed's building (Heighway 1980a).

The church of St Oswald was later reckoned to be a royal free chapel, and perhaps it had this status from its foundation. It housed secular canons, and seems to have been unreformed until converted into a college of Augustinian canons in the 12th century. Its floruit spanned the 10th century, the time when barely anything is known of its rival, St Peter's abbey, and it does seem that for a short while the new minster usurped the fame and wealth that by right of antiquity belonged to St Peter's. No doubt the bones of St Oswald contributed to this. The ancient abbey could boast no relics having anything like as much prestige, for Oswald had been both a ruling monarch and one of the great founding saints of Anglo-Saxon Christianity.

An intriguing problem is the origin of the parish of St Oswald. Like all royal free chapels, it had its own parish in the 13th century, which it presumably controlled from its inception. The parish included the area of the royal parish and was extremely large. It was also very oddly shaped, making a kind of jigsaw puzzle with the equally ancient parish of St Mary de Lode (Fig. 120). St Mary's parish was almost certainly

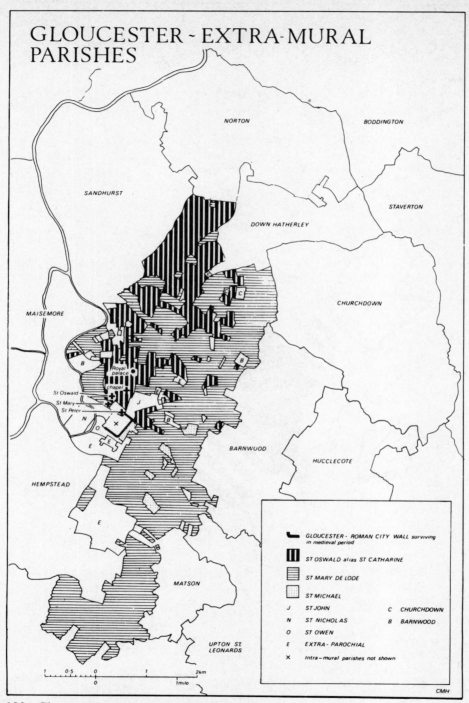

120. Gloucester: extra-mural parishes

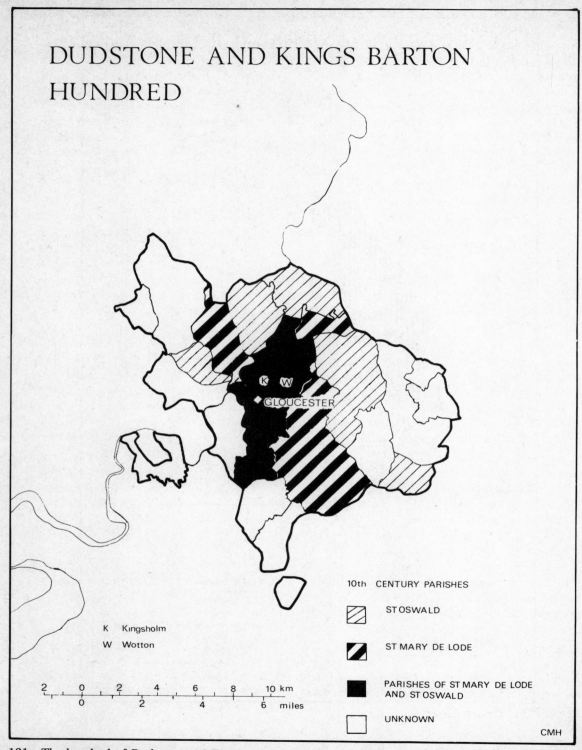

DUDSTONE AND KINGS BARTON HUNDRED

K Kingsholm
W Wotton

10th CENTURY PARISHES

ST OSWALD

ST MARY DE LODE

PARISHES OF ST MARY DE LODE AND ST OSWALD

UNKNOWN

CMH

121. The hundred of Dudstone and King's Barton, showing the hundredal boundary in 1824, parish boundaries at about the same period, and possible spiritual jurisdictions of the 10th century. Scale: 1:20,000

originally part of the parish of St Peter's abbey. I have suggested elsewhere (Heighway 1980a) that this pattern was of 8th- or 9th-century origin and represented the competition for tithes from the old minster (St Peter's) and the royal chapel (wherever this was). If the two parishes (St Oswald's and St Mary's) are put together, and those parishes are included which were anciently part of one or the other (Fig. 121) the resulting territory approximates to the hundred (once two hundreds) of Dudstone and Kings Barton. Possibly all this territory was once under the spiritual jurisdiction of St Peter's abbey, and it may even have been identical with those 'three hundreds' given to Osric in 679 to found his minster. The three hundreds could have been Dudstone, Kings Barton, and Gloucester itself.[24] This is an area of about 69 square miles—incidentally not much more than the area (47 square miles plus an unknown area of pasture and woodland) which has been calculated as being the size of the Roman *territorium* (Hurst 1976, 76).

The primacy of St Peter's abbey soon reasserted itself. Aldred of Worcester, on becoming archbishop of York, appropriated several of St Oswald's manors. York later acquired other St Oswald's manors also, and in 1093-4, William Rufus gave the church of St Oswald itself to Archbishop Thomas, with the result that St Oswald's remained a peculiar, under the jurisdiction of York, until the Dissolution (Thompson 1921). The loss of its estates, as well as its neglect by the Norman kings, accelerated its decay, and when Serlo rebuilt and revivified St Peter's abbey, St Oswald's sank into relative obscurity.

St Mary de Lode church is the most interesting of Gloucester's parish churches. First, it had a very large parish which, as Fosbrooke long ago remarked (1819, 172) testifies to its antiquity. Since it is closely connected with St Peter's abbey, which has no surviving parish of its own, it is likely that St Mary de Lode was the parish church of the old minster (Heighway 1980a) and that it had, as a result of this function, acquired the abbey parish. It was certainly the church of the abbey demesne, the Abbot's Barton (Taylor 1889, 175).

Excavations in 1978 and 1979 uncovered part of the Roman private house already known to have existed here. When this house was demolished, in or after the 4th century, its rubble was levelled over and a timber building on rough sleeper walls was erected on the Roman alignment. Inside this building were two burial pits and one decapitated burial, sealed by the floor of the building. The floor sealed late Roman pottery. The burials, though east-west, were not necessarily Christian, but the presence on the same site of the later Saxon church does suggest the possibility that the church developed directly from an early Christian burial place. If the church had been a place of Christian worship, however humble, since sub-Roman times, it would not be surprising if it had been appropriated by the abbey as a parish church (Bryant 1980a and b).

Other churches in Gloucester have not yet been thoroughly studied. Although Domesday Book mentioned only one priest in Gloucester, it is clearly an incomplete record, for by the time of the survey of 1096-1101 there were 'ten churches in the King's soke' (Stevenson 1890, xiv). Later medieval Gloucester boasted 10 churches and three chapels (excluding the various religions houses and castle chapels, so it is apparent that most of these 13 were in existence by the late 11th century.

Many of the parish churches were probably then not very old. The oldest are likely to have been those with the largest parishes and with 'town land' (Rogers 1972, 50), that is, St Mary de Lode, St Mary de Crypt, St John, and St Michael.

The parish of St Aldate, although it may as a unit have been an early urban estate (see above), has a south boundary which follows the backs of tenements fronting on one of the side streets, showing that the tenements were already in existence when the parish boundary was drawn (Rogers 1972, 61)—presumably well after the foundation of the burh, and perhaps in the late 10th century. The parish seems to have housed the 30 burgesses who pertained to the church of St Denys. Deerhurst, which later appears as owning St Aldate's church, was a cell of St Denys (Taylor 1898, 129).

Other similar parish boundaries are probably rather later than this: St Mary de Grace and Holy Trinity, and perhaps also All Saints, are typical examples of the formation of proprietory market churches, perhaps in the late 11th century. All Saints church may have been a little earlier and have been the original market church. Of course, any of the churches may be older than their parishes, and have begun their life as private chapels.

The parish of St Owen was extra-mural, but included a tiny area inside the south gate. By the 14th century the parish was built up.[25] The church of St Owen was founded by the first constable of the castle (Dugdale vi, 127) who endowed it with both the parish and the chapel of St Kyneburgh. St Kyneburgh's chapel must, therefore, be of Saxon date, notwithstanding the legendary flavour of its dedication (Hart, i, lxv–lxix), and its Saxon parish was presumably the small area inside the wall, and possibly included the whole area later claimed by St Owen. It is very likely that there was a Saxon suburb outside the south gate. St Kyneburgh's, together with the church of St Owen, was later given to the canons of Llanthony, who built a new chapel dedicated in 1147. The chapel was on the line of the city wall and ditch[26] and was not demolished until 1825 (Langston 1957). The exact position of the chapel can be reconstructed from various documentary references (*ibid.*). It seems to have stood on the Roman wall, approximately on the site of the Roman gate. Its alignment, however, as it appeared in 1780, was definitely not Roman.

Numerous examples could be cited of gate-churches in Saxon burhs. There was one over the East Gate at Winchester (Biddle 1976, 330), over many of the Roman gates at Canterbury (Tatton-Brown 1980, 93), and by the north gate to the Alfredian burh at Wareham.

The parish of St Nicholas appears to have been taken out of that of St Mary de Lode, again at a time when tenements were fairly densely built up. In 1203 St Nicholas's revenues were used for building a new Westgate Bridge (Furney), and some of its fabric belongs to the first half of the 12th century. If the dedication is to be trusted, the church was not founded before the mid–11th century, when the cult of St Nicholas was introduced to western Europe (Brooke and Kier 1975, 138).

There is no doubt that excavation could provide much more information about Gloucester's churches. The excavation of St Mary de Lode has already been described; St Oswald's also has proved well worth the expense of investigation. St Michael's has been excavated and produced tantalising remains of what may have been the Saxon church (Cra'ster 1961). Medland (1895) excavated All Saints in 1893, extracting the plan of a tiny church, possibly late Saxon, and producing a stone bear's head which is late Saxon in date. The chapel of St Thomas belonged to St Oswald's priory, and as described above, may have had a pre-10th-century origin as a royal burial chapel or chapel for the royal palace. Its site is now occupied by private gardens. Many other churches (St Kyneburgh, St Aldate, Holy Trinity, St Mary de Grace) are covered by city streets, whilst still others (St Mary de Crypt, St John) are in use and one, St Nicholas, is vested in the Redundant Churches Fund. Not many of the parish churches are therefore available for any archaeological investigation. However, still more important initially is the work that needs to be done on the documentary evidence. Both St Mary de Crypt and St Kyneburgh, for instance, were possessions of Llanthony priory, whose records are still being studied.

The physical appearance of Gloucester in the 10th and 11th centuries will also become clearer with future archaeological excavation. Domestic buildings were of timber: at 11–17 Southgate Street, and in 9th-century levels at 1 Westgate Street, the buildings were of posts hammered into the ground with interwoven wattle (Hurst 1972, 58–61). A 10th-century building at 1 Westgate Street incorporated an undercroft constructed of a series of upright posts linked by sill-beams (Heighway, Garrod and Vince 1979). The timber undercrofts are more familiar in the 11th century (Hurst 1972, 44); there may have been many of 10th-century date. The houses above these cellars were undoubtedly timber-framed and, like buildings of similar type in other urban centres, could have had more than one storey (Addyman 1979, 70; Rahtz 1976, 85).

There were abundant crafts and trades in 10th- and 11th-century Gloucester. There were certainly shoemakers and repairers, and there is evidence of silver and glass working, cloth weaving (probably on the horizontal treadle loom), and extensive smithing using iron from the Forest of Dean, giving rise to the render of iron nails enumerated in Domesday Book (Taylor 1899, 126). Wood-turning and working must have been a common craft, since most everyday objects were of wood. Working of bone and horn would have been another common trade. There were also pottery workshops in the town centre, producing a ware which was traded to Worcester and Hereford. As in the earlier periods, however, there is little sign of overseas trade and from the mercantile point of view, 10th-century Gloucester still had the character of a local market (Heighway, Garrod and Vince 1979).

That it was, however, more than this is suggested by historical and numismatic evidence. One obvious point of importance was Gloucester's status as the shire town: a status which it may have gained very soon after it was revived by Aethelflaed and Aethelred, when the shire was created by Edward the Elder (Stenton 1971, 337). The choice of Gloucester rather than Cirencester might have been due to the fact that the latter was less flourishing commercially (Slater 1976, 86–7); in addition Gloucester seems to have been favoured by Aethelflaed, and it was certainly a strategic as well as a ready-fortified centre.

There are coins from the Gloucester mint from the reign of Alfred onwards (Dolley and Blunt 1961) showing that the town was one of the privileged burghal centres licensed to mint coins (Stenton 1971, 536–7). Gloucester must also have had commercial importance as a market for the rural manors, many of which, by Domesday and probably long before, had estates in the town (Stenton 1971, 531).

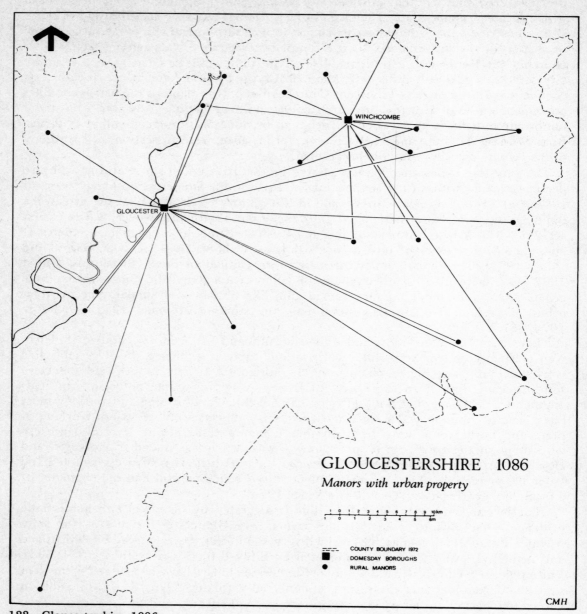

GLOUCESTERSHIRE 1086

Manors with urban property

COUNTY BOUNDARY 1972
DOMESDAY BOROUGHS
RURAL MANORS

CMH

122. Gloucestershire, 1086

The extent of Gloucester's influence in this respect is shown in Fig. 122. There may
have been a borough court as early as the 10th century (*ibid.*, 532–3). Gloucester was
also one of the principal towns in which royal councils were held. Although the
evidence for these in the 10th century is very thin (Stenton 1971, 352), Æthelstan

died at Gloucester (A.S.C., D), and there must have been other less inauspicious visits. Evidence is more copious in the 11th century: Oleson has shown (1955, 71, 159–60) that for Edward the Confessor, Gloucester was a favoured place, since his councils were held there nine times between 1043 and 1062. These gatherings, some of considerable size, must have been held in the hall at Kingsholm.

The Norman Conquest imposed new lords, the Norman tenants-in-chief, and a new royal authority, represented by the superimposition on the town of a motte-and-bailey castle. The castle destroyed 16 houses (Taylor 1889, 127) which suggests that by the Conquest, the city was occupied up to the circuit of the walls. By that time the population of the city may have been between 2,000 and 3,000 (*ibid.*, 129).

One of the changes brought about by the Conquest was the concentration of royal attention on the castle, to the detriment of the old Kingsholm palace, which became simply a royal manor. It was now to the castle that the kings came, though they do not seem to have worn the crown at Gloucester every Christmas, as the chronicles stated (Biddle 1975a). The town continued to flourish, particularly aided by its waterborne trade and the Severn fisheries; its contribution in the reign of Henry II places is amongst the 10 wealthiest towns in the kingdom (Lobel 1969, 4). The final significant additions to the topography of Gloucester were the 13th century religious houses, which took up much remaining space in the walled circuit.

*　*　*　.　*　*

It will be evident, from the foregoing account, that archaeological research has only just begun to elucidate the economy and topography of Anglo-Saxon Gloucester. Yet other lines of research are equally important. The documentary evidence for Gloucester's history is abundant. Though most of it is 13th century and later, it can still be used to illuminate the history of the early town. Quite apart from the published deeds and other records of the City Corporation and of St Peter's abbey (Stevenson 1893; Hart), there are three unpublished registers of St Peter's abbey (Kirby 1967, 1–2) dating from 1510–38, and an astonishing 13 books—eight cartularies and five registers—from the priory of Llanthony, which owned a considerable amount of property in the city (Jack 1972). These have not been studied in detail since Archdeacon Furney used them in the early 18th century to make notes for his history of Gloucester. Archdeacon Furney's manuscript is still a mine of information, from which stems every important city history produced since his time. In addition to all this there are large numbers of deeds and other documents which have been only incompletely transcribed by Stevenson (1893), and which would repay further study.

Until some attempt has been made to utilise all the topographical material that is available, any history of Anglo-Saxon Gloucester can only be a hesitant beginning.

ACKNOWLEDGEMENTS

I am grateful to Mr. J. F. Rhodes for allowing me to make use of unpublished material in the museum's archive.

I have benefited greatly by discussion with many people, especially Richard Bryant, Patrick Garrod, Michael Hare, John Rhodes, and Margaret Richards. I wish to thank all these people for their help, whilst acknowledging that any deficiences in the above account are all my own.

Gloucester, October 1980

NOTES

1. Rowbotham 1978. Mr. Rowbotham considers that the Roman river crossing was not by a bridge but by a ferry, which utilised the cross-tides in the channels. The western channel today joins the other channels much further down river, perhaps as a result of 16th-century canalisation (*ibid.*, 9).

2. Recent information is from A. P. Garrod's excavation (Garrod forthcoming, site 28/79). If Mr. Rowbotham is correct that the Roman minimum water level was at about 3m. A.O.D. (Rowbotham 1978, 7) then the 'quay wall' must have been on dry land except in exceptional floods. In the 11th century there was certainly dry land west of this wall at 7.6m. A.O.D., even though the water level generally had risen (Garrod, *op. cit.*).

3. Hawkes and Dunning 1961, Type IIA. The significance of these belt-buckles has been questioned: for a useful summary of the arguments see Hills 1978. Type IIA probably still signifies a military presence. The Gloucester finds are from New Market Hall (Hassall and Rhodes 1974, 67, No. 35) and Saintbridge (Garrod forthcoming, site 98/75).

4. Hassall and Rhodes 1974, 32; unpublished section at 33 Southgate Street (site 18/66).

5. Cited in Heighway 1978, f.n. 58.

6. Gloucester Museum A 2654. The museum catalogue gives its date as late 10th century; D. P. Dobson (1933, 266) suggests 9th or 10th century, and wrongly states that it comes from Wotton-under-Edge.

7. Finberg 1957, 14–16. The old name of Dudstone Hundred ought to have been the Hundred of Abbots Barton, for it must have consisted of the hundred (or 120) hides given to the abbey for the Abbots Barton in 777–90 (Finberg 1972, No. 45, 41). An eminent Dudda, a founder of Tewkesbury abbey, had a brother, Almaric, who was buried at Deerhurst (Dugdale, ii, 59). This may be the same Dudda or Dodda who witnessed charters in the mid–11th century (Robertson 1956, 201, 448). The latter two references were kindly provided by Dr. Richard Gem.

8. The 'Memoriale' gives the wrong date, 7 Edward Confessor: the correct date of 1058 is provided by the *Anglo-Saxon Chronicle.*

9. The pottery is type fabric 41A; see Vince 1979. Saxon streets at Winchester showed eight re-surfacings between *c.* 900 and 1067; once every 20 years, which would date Berkeley Street to about 1000 at the latest (Biddle 1970, 285–7).

10. Hart, i, 13. The pottery evidence confirmed this: the first wall cut levels with late-11th-century pottery.

11. Hurst 1974, 48: pottery re-assessed by Alan Vince. It includes 10th-century 'Chester ware'.

12. Ross 1964, 391; the Tanners Guildhall was also here: G.R.O./D 105; D.C./H, 149.

13. Gloucester Borough Records, 1406/1521, 17.

14. Fullbrook-Leggatt 1952, 2. Mr. Fullbrook-Legatt misplaced Powke Lane: see Stevenson 1890, 50b, where the lane is clearly further east than postulated by Fullbrook-Leggatt. I am grateful to A. P. Garrod for pointing this out.

15. Stevenson 1890, 2. The rents and land-gavel are omitted by Stevenson and at least one of the Hare Lane deeds summarised in his *Calendar* includes a render for land-gavel (Stevenson 1893, No. 368), although the property did not render the tax in 1455.

16. Hart, i, 8. The date of 1022 is problematic. The foundation is ascribed to Wulfstan, bishop of Worcester, with the consent of Cnut. Wulfstan was jointly archbishop of York and bishop of Worcester from 1002 to 1017, but after 1017 was archbishop of York only. Whatever the truth of this issue, there can be little doubt that a Benedictine reform took place between 1015 and 1025. I am grateful to Michael Hare for providing me with these notes from his forthcoming publication on 'The church in Anglo-Saxon Gloucester'.

17. *Register of Archbishop Gray*, Surtees Soc., 56 (1870), 276–7.

18. The 15th-century Abbey *Historia* (Hart, i, 80) says that the old church was burnt down in 1089. The statement is probably based on a lost chronicle, whose reliability is uncertain; *see* C. N. L. Brooke, 'St Peter and St Cadoc' in *Celt and Saxon* (Cambridge 1964), 263–4. Florence of Worcester, a near neighbour and contemporary, does not mention the destruction of Gloucester (Freeman 1883–4, 103).

19. Dugdale, i, 531; Fosbrooke 1819, 80. Leland (*Antiquarii Collectanea* iii, 159) said the 'ancient buildings' were standing in his time, but he was surely referring to the Norman abbey.

20. Kirby 1967, I/18, III/16, V/21, VI/8; translated in G.R.O. D 1609. In view of the Deerhurst Odda's chapel inscription where 'aula regis' referes to the chapel, some of the references may be to the royal chapel and not to the hall.

21. William of Malmesbury *Gesta Pontificum Anglorum*, Rolls Series, ed. N. E. S. A. Hamilton, London 1870, 293.

22. A.S.C., *sub anno* 909; *Reginald of Durham* Rolls Series 75, 369–70. *Aelfric's Lives of the Saints*, ed. Rev. Walter W. Skeat, London 1890, 143.

23. Biddle 1976, 314. I suggested originally (Heighway 1978, 119, f. n. 46) that it was the church of St Mary de Lode which was built at Gloucester for this increased population; but St Mary's is probably of earlier origin (Bryant 1980). It may have been appropriated to the abbey at this time.

24. Finberg, on the other hand (1957, 55) thought that Gloucester's 'three hundreds' might be Berkeley, Whitstone and Kings Barton. But he omitted Dudstone, which is Gloucester's 'out-hundred'. The town itself was certainly a separate hundred in 1086 (Taylor 1889) if not before. The original limits of the hundred of Kings Barton do not seem to be discoverable. Smith (1964, 114) seems to have reversed the position of Kings Barton and Dudstone. In 1316 the hundred of Kings Barton contained one vill, Barton Regis (Feudal Aids, ii, 264, 74) which, judging by the vills mentioned for Dudstone, was that of Kingsholm, which one would expect to be the centre of the hundred and royal estate. The post-medieval common fields in Kings Barton manor were concentrated in the Kingsholm area (G.R.O. 936 M.11) but certainly by post-medieval times the *jurisdiction* of Kings Barton hundred extended much further than this (Furney, 154). Doubtless this was a result of the two hundreds being for so long considered as one.

25. *Nonarum Inquisitiones* Record Commission 1807.

26. *Cal. Inqu. Misc.* i, 1219–1307, 115; *Cal. Pat. Rolls* 1485–94, 46–7, The sources say it was the castle ditch that was being dug, but they must be mistaken as the then castle was much further west. The city ditch was enlarged by the king's orders in the same year: *Cal. Close Rolls* 1264–8, 414. I am grateful to Mr. J. F. Rhodes for providing these references.

BIBLIOGRAPHY

ABBREVIATIONS

A.S.C.   *Anglo Saxon Chronicle*, ed. Dorothy Whitelock (London 1961).
T.B.G.A.S.   *Transactions of the Bristol and Gloucestershire Archaeological Society.*

Abbot, R. (1967), 'Excavations at the Shire Hall site Gloucester 1965', *T.B.G.A.S.* 86, 95-101.

Addyman, P. V. (1979), 'Vernacular buildings below the ground', *Archaeological Journal* 136, 69-75.

Biddle, M. (1970), 'Excavations at Winchester 1969: Eighth Interim Report', *Antiquaries Journal* 50, 277-326.

Biddle, M. (1975a), 'Seasonal festivals and residence: Winchester, Westminster and Gloucester in the tenth to twelfth centuries' (text of a paper presented to the Council for British Archaeology Conference on the Archaeology and History of the European Town, Oxford 1975).

Biddle, M. (1975b), 'Excavations at Winchester 1971: Tenth and Final Interim Report', *Antiquaries Journal* 55, 96-126; 295-337.

Biddle, M. (ed.) (1976), *Winchester in the Early Middle Ages* (Winchester Studies 1), Oxford.

Biddle, M. and Hill, D. H. (1971), 'Late Saxon planned towns', *Antiquaries Journal* 51, 70-85.

Biek, L. (1979), 'A note on preservation', in Heighway, C. M., Garrod, A. P. and Vince, A. G. (eds.) 1979, 205-10.

Böhner, K. 'Urban and rural settlement in the Frankish kingdom', in Barley, M. W. (ed.), *European Towns: their archaeology and early history*, 185-201.

Brooke, C. N. L. and Keir, G. (1975), *London 800-1216: the Shaping of a City*, London.

Bryant, R. M. (1980a), 'Excavations at St Mary de Lode Church, Gloucester, 1978-9', *Glevensis* (The Gloucester and District Archaeological Research Group Review) 14, 4-12.

Bryant, R. M. (1980b), 'St Mary de Lode Church, Gloucester', *Council for British Archaeology Churches Bulletin*, 13, 15-18.

Cramp, R. (1975), 'Anglo-Saxon sculpture of the reform period', in Parsons, D. (ed.), *Tenth Century Studies*, Chichester.

Cramp, R. (1977), 'Schools of Mercian Sculpture', in Dornier, A. (ed.), *Mercian Studies*, Leicester.

Cra'ster, M. D. (1961), 'St Michael's church, Gloucester 1956', *T.B.G.A.S.* 81, 59–74.

Dobson, D. P. (1933), 'Anglo-Saxon buildings and sculpture in Gloucestershire', *T.B.G.A.S.* 55, 271–76.

Dolley, R. H. M. and Blunt, C. E. (1961), 'The Coinage of Alfred the Great', in Dolley, R. H. M. (ed.), *Anglo-Saxon Coins* (London), 77–94.

Dugdale, Sir W. (1846), *Monasticon Anglicanum*, eds. Caley, J., Ellis, H. and Bandinel, B., London.

Finberg, H. P. R. (1957), *Gloucestershire Studies*, Leicester.

Finberg, H. P. R. (1972), *The Early Charters of the West Midlands*, Leicester.

Florence of Worcester, *Chronicon ex Chronicis*, ed. Thorpe, B., London, 1848.

Fosbrooke, Rev. D. (1819), *An Original History of the City of Gloucester*, London.

Fowler, P. (1970), 'Grass-tempered pottery', in Gracie, H. S. (ed.), 'Frocester Court Roman Villa, Gloucestershire', *T.B.G.A.S.* 90, 50-52.

Freeman, E. A. (1883-4), 'Gloucester and its Abbey', *Records of Gloucester Cathedral* 2, 18-37.

Fullbrook-Leggatt, L. E. W. O. (1952), *Anglo-Saxon and medieval Gloucester*, Gloucester.

Fullbrook-Leggatt, L. E. W. O. (1964), 'The River Twyver and the Fullbrook', *T.B.G.A.S.* 83, 78-84.

Furney, Archdeacon R., *History of Gloucester*, c. 1740. MS. Gloucester Records Office D 327.

Garrod, A. P. (forthcoming), *Excavations in Gloucester 1974–9: The Evidence of the Watching Briefs*.

Gracie, H. S. and Price, E. G. (1979), 'Frocester Court Roman Villa: second report', *T.B.G.A.S.* 97, 9-64.

Green, C. (1942), 'Glevum and the Second Legion', *Journal of Roman Studies* 32, 39–52.

Hall, R. and Pinnell, T. (1780), *A Plan of the City of Gloucester*.

Hart, W. H., *Historia et Cartularium Monasterii Sancti Petri Gloucestriae*, Rolls Series, Vol. I 1863; II 1865; III 1867.

Hassal, M. and Rhodes, J. (1974), 'Excavations at the New Market Hall, Gloucester 1966-7', *T.B.G.A.S.* 93, 15-100.

Hawkes, S. C. and Dunning, D. C. (1961), 'Soldiers and settlers in Britain: 4th to 5th century', *Medieval Archaeology* 5, 1–70.

Heighway, C. M. (1978), 'Excavations at Gloucester: fourth interim report: St Oswald's Priory 1975-6', *Antiquaries Journal* 58, 103-32.

Heighway, C. M. (1980a), 'Excavations at Gloucester: fifth interim report: St Oswald's Priory 1977-8', *Antiquaries Journal* 60, 207-26.

Heighway, C. M. (1980b), 'The cemeteries of Roman Gloucester', *T.B.G.A.S.* 98, 57–72.

Heighway, C. M. (1983), 'The Roman municipal tilery at Gloucester', *Britannia* 13, 25-77.

Heighway, C. M., Garrod, A. P. and Vince, A. G. (1979), 'Excavations at 1 Westgate Street, Gloucester', *Medieval Archaeology* 23, 159-213.

Heighway, C. M. and Garrod, A. P. (1980), 'Excavations at Nos. 1 and 30 Westgate Street, Gloucester', *Britannia* 11, 73-114.

Heighway, C. M., *et al* (1983), *The North and East Gates of Gloucester*, Bristol.

Hills, C. (1978), 'The archaeology of Anglo-Saxon England in the pagan period: a review', *Anglo-Saxon England* 8, 297-330.

Hurst, H. (1972), 'Excavations at Gloucester 1968–71: first interim report', *Antiquaries Journal* 52, 24–69.

Hurst, H. (1974), 'Excavations at Gloucester 1971-3: second interim report', *Antiquaries Journal* 54, 8-52.

Hurst, H. (1976), 'Gloucester (Glevum): a colonia in the West Country', in Branigan, K. and Fowler, P. (eds.), *The Roman West Country*, Newton Abbot.

Hurst, H. (forthcoming), 'Gloucester Castle'.

Hurst, H., *et al.* (1975), 'Excavations at Gloucester: third interim report: Kingsholm 1966-75', *Antiquaries Journal* 55, 264–94.

Jack, R. I. (1972), 'An archival case history: the cartularies and registers of Llanthony priory in Gloucester', *Journal of the Society of Archivists* 4.5, 270–83.

Keene, D. J. (1976), 'Suburban growth', in Barley, M. W. (ed.), *The Plans and Topography of Medieval Towns in England and Wales*, C.B.A. Research Report, 14.

Kirby, I. M. (ed.) (1961), *A catalogue of the Records of the Dean and Chapter including the former St Peter's abbey*, Gloucester.

Knowles, W. H. (1938), 'Gloucester Roman Research Committee Report 1938-9', *T.B.G.A.S.* 60, 165-8.

Langston, J. N. (1957), 'Old Gloucester Churches': bound typescript in Gloucester Library. Unpaginated. 2 vols.

Langton, J. (1977), 'Late medieval Gloucester: some data from a rental of 1455', *Transactions of the Institute of British Geographers* n.s. ii, 3, 259-277.

Lobel, M. D. (1969), 'Gloucester', in Lobel, M. D. (ed.), *Historic Towns Atlas* 1.

Medland, H. (1895), 'An account of Roman and medieval remains found on the site of the Tolsey at Gloucester in 1893-4', *T.B.G.A.S.* 19, 142-58.

Morris, J. (ed.) (1980), *Nennius: British History and the Welsh Annals*, Arthurian Period Sources, 8, Chichester.

Oleson, T. J. (1955), *The Witenagemot in the Reign of Edward the Confessor*, Oxford.

Rahtz, P. (1976), 'Buildings and rural settlement', in Wilson, D. M. (ed.), *The Archaeology of Anglo-Saxon England*, London.

Rahtz, P. (1977), 'Late Roman cemeteries and beyond', in Reece, R. (ed.), *Burial in the Roman World*, C.B.A. Research Report, 22.

Reece, R. (1980), 'Town and country: the end of Roman Britain', *World Archaeology* 12.1, 77-92.

Richmond, Sir I. (1962), 'The earliest Roman occupation of Gloucester', *T.B.G.A.S.* 81, 14-16.

Robertson, A. J. (1956), *Anglo-Saxon Charters*, Cambridge.

Rogers, A. (1972), 'Parish boundaries and urban history: two case studies', *Journal of the British Archaeological Association*, 3rd series, 34, 46-64.

Ross, C. D. (ed.) (1964), *The Cartulary of Cirencester Abbey*, London and Oxford.

Rowbotham, F. W. (1978), 'The River Severn at Gloucester with particular reference to its Roman and medieval channels', *Glevensis* 12, 4-9.

Slater, T. (1976), 'The town and its regions in the Anglo-Saxon and medieval periods', in Macwhirr, A. (ed.), *Studies in the Archaeology and History of Cirencester*, B.A.R. 30, 81-108.

Smith, A. H. (ed.) (1964), *The Place-Names of Gloucestershire*, English Place-Name Society, 39, Cambridge.

Stenton, F. M. (1971), *Anglo-Saxon England* (3rd edn.), Oxford.

Stevenson, W. H. (ed.) (1890), *Rental of all the Houses in Gloucester 1455, compiled by Robert Cole, Canon of Llanthony*, Gloucester.

Stevenson, W. H. (ed.) (1893), *Calendar of the Records of the Corporation of Gloucester*, Gloucester.

Tait, J. (1936), *The Medieval English Borough*, Manchester.

Tatton-Brown, T. W. T., 'Canterbury urban topography: some recent work', in Riden, P. (ed.), *The Medieval town in Britain*, Gregynog seminars in local history, Cardiff, I, 85-98.

Taylor, C. S. (1889), *Analysis of the Domesday Survey of Gloucestershire*, Bristol.

Thompson, A. H. (1921), 'The jurisdiction of the archbishops of York in Gloucestershire', *T.B.G.A.S.* 43, 85-180.

Vince, A. G. (1979), 'The pottery', in Heighway, C. M., Garrod, A. P. and Vince A. G. (eds.), 1979.

Webster, G. (1970), 'Military situations in Britain A.D. 43 and 71', *Britannia* 1, 179-97.

West, J. (1980), 'The sculpture', in Heighway, C. M. (ed.), 1980a, 220-23.

Wilson, M. (1969), 'The Hwicce', in Barker, P. (ed.), The origins of Worcester, *Transactions of the Worcester Archaeological Society*, 3rd series 2, 1-116.

Woodman, V. A. (1966), 'Supplement to Gloucester Corporation Records' (typescript in G.R.O.).

Chapter Fourteen

SAXON EXETER

By John Allan, Christopher Henderson and Robert Higham

ORDERIC VITALIS, in his account of the siege of 1068, described Exeter as a 'wealthy and ancient city (*urbs*), strongly fortified' (Chibnall 1969, II, 211 ff.).[1] In Hill's ranking of the Anglo-Saxon mints between 973 and 1066 Exeter is placed seventh, and at the beginning of the 11th century it ranked in fifth position (Hill 1974, 280–1).[2] The city's prominence in the 11th century is further attested by the proliferation of early churches (see below) and by the fact that in Domesday Book it paid geld only when London, York and Winchester did so. Domesday Book also records a total of 399 houses,[3] implying a population of perhaps 2,000 inhabitants in 1068. The Norman city was described by William of Malmesbury as 'magnificent and wealthy, abounding in every kind of merchandise' (Whitelock 1955, 277–83), and the author of the *Gesta Stephani* praised it as 'a large city (*civitas*) . . . the fourth place, they say, in England' (Potter 1976, 33).[4] In short, the Saxo-Norman city was almost certainly more prominent in national life than either its Roman predecessor or its late medieval successor.[5]

The Roman Background

The earliest Roman settlement at Exeter was a legionary fortress established in *c.* A.D. 55–60 on a virgin site of 15.4 hectares (38 acres) which occupied a broad, sloping, interfluvial spur overlooking the lowest early bridging point on the River Exe. The legion departed in *c.* 75 and a few years later the town *Isca Dumnoniorum* was founded within the defences of the dismantled fortress. The construction of public buildings, including the basilica and forum and the public baths, commenced in about A.D. 80. Towards the end of the 2nd century the earthen defensive bank which surrounded the early town was thrown down to be replaced by a stone wall enclosing the much larger area of 37 hectares (92.6 acres) (Bidwell 1980, *passim.*).

Although the central *insulae* in the late Roman town were evidently occupied by substantial stone buildings, extensive peripheral areas within the walls were apparently only sparsely built-up. Over 30 late Roman buildings are known from excavations or building site observations, but few of these are attested by more than odd fragments of stone wall foundations.

In the 4th century a courtyard house in Insula IV/V was flanked on two sides by probable stockyards (Bidwell 1980, 69–71). A town house such as this, within the protection of the walls might seem a likely candidate for survival into the 5th century; however a lack of closely datable finds allows the final phase of occupation to be assigned only to the last quarter of the 4th century or later.

Our knowledge of the end of the Roman town remains very poor. The latest Roman layers rarely survive undisturbed, especially in the central parts of the city where post-medieval cellars and modern re-development have destroyed most deposits. Where the relevant levels remain intact, however, the late Roman streets and buildings are invariably covered by a layer of dark gritty loam containing only residual Roman finds. Except in the forum area, no useful evidence has been found, either from demolition deposits or from the overlying dark soil, to indicate when the late Roman buildings were abandoned. The later 4th-century pottery from the town cannot be closely dated (Bidwell 1980, 86). Although North African amphorae and colour-coated pottery from south-western France (*céramique à l'éponge*) are relatively frequent finds in 4th-century contexts at Exeter, sub-Roman Mediterranean imported wares are absent. By the last decade of the 4th century fresh supplies of coinage had ceased to reach Exeter: the latest Roman coin is an issue of the house of Theodosius, dated 388–92. The 12 Byzantine coins which Shortt (1840, 79–109) recorded as Exeter finds cannot be regarded as securely provenanced (Bidwell 1980, 86–7). As with various other curiosities, such as an Egyptian *sistrum* of the 6th century B.C. and the Ptolemaic coins in his collection, it is likely that these were passed off as Exeter finds because Shortt was keen to buy local antiquities. No such finds are present among over 400 Roman coins recovered from recent excavations.

The Forum Area (Figs. 123 and 124)

There is as yet no evidence to suggest that the survival of any Roman buildings influenced the form of the medieval city. A probable thread of continuity between the Roman and later towns is, however, to be found in the area of the forum. The basilica was remodelled extensively in the mid-4th century and following this the floors were relaid on at least one occasion; the make-up of the latest surviving floor contained a well-circulated coin of Valens (364–78), suggesting that the building remained in use for some time. In the late 4th or early 5th centuries the basilica was taken down and the site systematically cleared of demolition rubble. Subsequently a number of features were dug into the latest Roman levels, including a quarry pit containing bronze-working debris in its fill (Fig. 124A) (Bidwell 1979, 108–10).

By the end of the 5th century a burial ground (Fig. 124, cemetery I) had been established on the forum site. Six sub-Roman graves were found in the excavations of 1971–6, two of which yielded radio-carbon dates of 420± 70 and 490 ± 80.[6] The burials were unaccompanied by grave-goods and orientated on the Roman alignment with their heads to the north-west. The arrangement of four of the graves close together in a neat row suggests that they belonged to an ordered cemetery. The other two graves, one of which was cut into the metalling of the street on the south-east side of the forum, were situated 24m. apart. These burials seem to be the remnants of an extensive cemetery, most of which must have been destroyed by later grave digging (*ibid.*, 111–13). The argument that this was a Christian burial ground has been presented in detail elsewhere by P. T. Bidwell (*ibid.*) who draws attention to the similarity of this cemetery to those associated with 5th-century Christian churches in the *fora* of certain towns in North Africa, as at Lepcis Magna and Sabratha. At Exeter, the orientation of the burials on the Roman line could have resulted from their

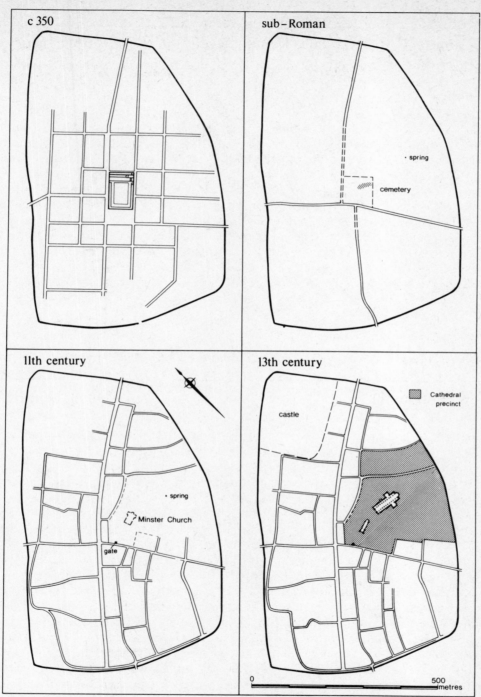

123. The development of the street plan and Cathedral Close at Exeter. The bounds of the 11th-century Close are uncertain, particularly on the north-east and south-east sides. The position of the 13th-century boundary is based (with amendments) on a sketch map of *c.* 1810 by R. Barnes, now in the Cathedral Library.

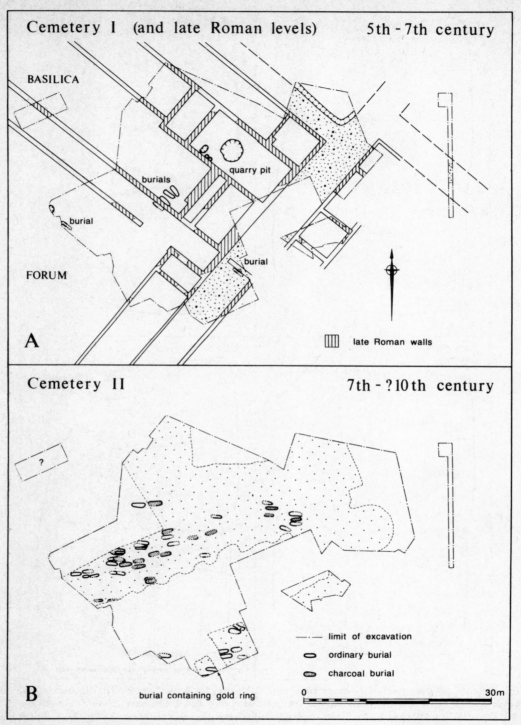

124. Plan of the sub-Roman and Middle Saxon burials excavated in the Cathedral Close at Exeter

alignment with an adjacent church,[7] or may simply reflect the survival of Roman walls or streets bounding the cemetery. A number of factors may have influenced the siting of the cemetery, which presumably served as the burial ground for the Christian inhabitants of Exeter and the surrounding area. The town may have had a bishop in the 4th century (*cf.* Thomas 1981, 193) and it is possible that a standing Roman church provided a focus for Christian burial in the following centuries. Exeter probably remained a seat of local administration even after the collapse of urban institutions (*cf.* Rodwell 1982, 49) and could perhaps have continued as an episcopal centre well into the sub-Roman period (but for a more cautious view see Frend 1982). Unfortunately we do not know when the cemetery was established, and this could have been as late as the 6th century.

The Minster (Figs. 123–125)

The area of the Roman forum which in the 5th century came to be occupied by cemetery I continued in use as a burial ground during Saxon and medieval times. The excavations in the Cathedral Close uncovered a total of 107 burials which can be assigned to the period after the use of cemetery I but before the construction of the Norman cathedral in the early 12th century. Many other pre-Norman burials must have been destroyed by medieval grave digging. The alignments of the graves ranged between 66deg. and 108deg. from true north, and it is possible to distinguish two successive groups of burials termed cemeteries II and III (Henderson and Bidwell 1982, 152–3). Cemetery II, which included a grave containing a middle Saxon gold finger-ring (Graham-Campbell 1982), is likely to represent the burial ground of the Saxon minster founded at Exeter in the 7th century (below). The mean alignment of this group of graves lies close to east–west, and this presumably approximates to the orientation of the middle Saxon minster church. No buildings of this period were found in the excavations, but it is possible that all trace of these had been obliterated by later activity on the site.

As well as 'ordinary' inhumations, which occur at all periods, cemeteries II and III contained interments of a type known as 'charcoal' burials, in which the bottom of the grave was covered with a layer of charcoal up to 0.1m. deep. This type of burial is also known from Saxon cemeteries at Winchester (Biddle 1964, 211; *idem* 1965, 257–8), Gloucester (Heighway 1980, 217) and elsewhere.[8] At Exeter, the charcoal burial rite appears to have been practised concurrently with ordinary inhumation from at least as early as the 9th century until the late 10th or 11th centuries. Twenty-three burials in the Saxon cemeteries contained iron nails and/or strappings indicating the presence of a wooden coffin. The incidence of such coffin 'fittings' appears to have been higher amongst the charcoal burials than the ordinary inhumations (Henderson and Bidwell 1982, 154–5; *cf.* Shoesmith 1980, 30–8).

The graves of cemetery III were aligned on a Saxo-Norman church whose fragmentary remains were preserved to the north and east of St Mary Major parish church, which stood 23m. to the west of the Norman cathedral and was demolished in 1970 (Fig. 125). The Saxo-Norman church was at least 34.2m. long with foundations belonging to three or more building periods (Henderson and Bidwell 1982, 159–62). Its apsidal east end lay 7m. to the east of the medieval chancel of St Mary

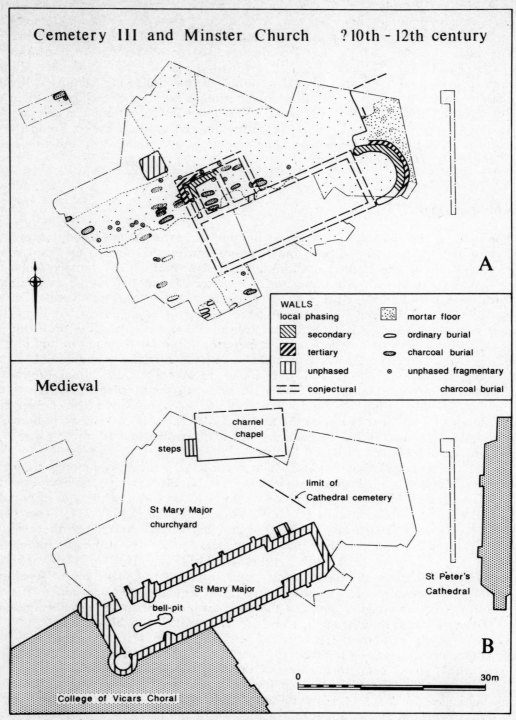

125. Plan of the late Saxon and medieval burials excavated in the Cathedral Close at Exeter

Major and shared the same axis as the later church. The apse was 7.8m. wide internally and had probably been built as an addition or modification to an earlier east end with shallower foundations. Around the head of the apse an extensive area measuring at least 18.5m. by 6.8m. had been terraced into the hill slope and furnished with a level mortar floor laid on a stone bedding 0.3m. in thickness. In the deepest part of the terrace, on the north side of the apse, the surface of the mortar floor was 0.45m. below the highest surviving Roman deposits. The exterior of the apse foundation was revetted with a narrow wall seated on the mortar floor of the terrace. It is not clear if the terrace formed an open courtyard or whether it was wholly or partially roofed.

No early floor levels survived inside St Mary Major, but a short length of foundation may represent the north wall of the Saxo-Norman nave. To the north of the medieval church were a deep-set rubble foundation 3.6m. square—perhaps the base of a tower— and two sets of poorly preserved wall footings representing *porticus* of two building periods. As these foundations had been dug through burials on the cemetery III alignment, none of them is likely to have formed part of the earliest fabric of the church.

The excavations did not produce any evidence to indicate when the Saxo-Norman church was constructed, but some datable finds were recovered from demolition deposits at its east end. Before the apse was taken down, the terrace to the east of it saw intensive use as a mason's working area, presumably during the construction of the Norman cathedral. The robbing trench for the apse cut through successive mortar mixing beds and layers of mason's debris. From its fill came finds including a 9th-century strap-end (Graham-Campbell 1983), a little-worn penny of William II (Shiel forthcoming) and local and imported pottery which must have been deposited before the late 12th century (Allan forthcoming).

St Mary Major church was pulled down in 1865 to be replaced by a massively founded Victorian structure. Only the chancel and the large Norman west tower of the medieval church were located in the excavations, but the full plan is known from a surveyor's drawing of 1850. This shows that the nave of St Mary Major corresponded in position with the western end of the nave of the Saxo-Norman church, implying that part of the latter was retained to form the nave of the medieval church (Henderson and Bidwell 1982, 164–6).

The size of the Saxo-Norman predecessor to St Mary Major, its association with an ancient cemetery, and its proximity to the Norman cathedral allow it to be identified with reasonable confidence as the minster church of St Peter to which Leofric, the first bishop of Exeter, transferred his episcopal seat from Crediton in 1050 (Barlow 1963, 212–15), and which served as the cathedral church of Devon and Cornwall until the consecration of the Norman cathedral in 1133 (Rose-Troup 1932, 3–4). The minster was probably the only church within the walls of the Saxon town to possess a cemetery, since the Chapter of the medieval cathedral claimed the sole right to bury the citizens of Exeter (*idem* 1923, 15), and their exclusive rights of sepulture are likely to have been inherited from their Saxon predecessors.

The documentary evidence relating to the minster has recently been discussed by Henderson and Bidwell (1982, 145–8). The history of the house is not well known, owing in part to the destruction by fire of its early charters. The 8th-century Life of St

Boniface provides evidence for the existence of a Saxon monastery at Exeter by about 680 (Levison 1905, 6). This is likely to have been a fairly recent foundation following the conquest of the region by the West Saxons. There are two questions which inevitably arise when the origins of the minster are considered. First, was there continuity of use between cemeteries I and II? There is a gap of about two centuries between the dated burials of cemetery I and the period around 680 when the Saxon minster is first attested. This gap may, however, be more apparent than real. The two radio-carbon-dated burials clearly represent only a very small sample of the graves in the sub-Roman cemetery, and it is quite possible that the cemetery continued in use for a considerable time. Equally, the use of cemetery II may have started a good deal earlier than c. 680 (Bidwell 1979, 113). In the absence of further radio-carbon dates, we cannot ignore the possibility that a recognisable Christian cemetery site, perhaps displaying grave markers, was re-adopted in the late 7th century after a period of abandonment. However, since the Christian church in Dumnonia apparently enjoyed an unbroken existence from at least the late 5th century, it seems reasonable to suppose that Christian burial grounds will have remained in continuous use once established. If this was the case at Exeter, then the change from cemetery I to cemetery II probably reflects merely the re-alignment of graves following the construction of a new church. Second, did the sub-Roman cemetery serve simply as the burial ground for the inhabitants of the surrounding area, or was there also on the site an early Christian monastery? This question cannot be answered at the moment, but we should certainly not rule out the possibility that the Saxon minster supplanted a British religious community.

*   *   *   *   *

Asser states in his *Life of King Alfred* that the king 'gave' him 'Exeter, with all the diocese (*parochia*) belonging to it, in Saxon territory and in Cornwall' (Stevenson 1959, 68; Whitelock 1955, 271). This passage was taken by Finberg (1964, 109) to imply that Asser was granted the income from the estates of the minster at Exeter while he served as a *chorepiscopus* or auxiliary to the bishop of Sherborne in Devon and Cornwall. Another possible interpretation of this statement is that the writer was made bishop of a short-lived diocese of western Wessex which was merged with Sherborne again when Asser was appointed to that see (Whitelock 1968, 14). The grant mentioned by Asser must have been made within a few years of 890 (*ibid.*, 5), and it is noteworthy that this is also probably the period when Exeter became a burh and when a mint was first established there. The diocese of Sherborne was divided permanently into three on the death of Asser in 909, and the minster at Crediton became the cathedral church of Devon and Cornwall. Why the see was not based on the urban minster at Exeter is not known.

There was a strong tradition current in the early 11th century that the minster at Exeter was founded by Athelstan. In the manuscript known as the Athelstan Donation it is stated that the king 'on one occasion came here to Exeter, so it was said of old in the sayings of the most righteous men' and 'commanded that . . . they should build a monastery to the honour of God and of . . . St Mary . . . and of St Peter' (trans. Swanton 1975, 15). The account goes on to say that Athelstan bestowed upon the monastery 26 estates and one-third of his collection of holy relics. This suggests that the minster may have been re-founded and newly endowed by King Athelstan (925–39). His reign must, therefore, be regarded as the most likely period for the replanning of the church reflected in the different alignments of the graves in cemeteries II and III. It should be emphasised, however, that at present there is no archaeological evidence to support an early 10th-century date for the construction of the Saxo-Norman church associated with cemetery III. The fragmentary remains of the church revealed in the excavations afford a glimpse of a large multi-cellular building which probably evolved over several generations by means of successive additions to the fabric of an original church of relatively simple plan (Henderson and Bidwell 1982, 162).

According to Florence of Worcester, King Edgar placed a colony of monks at Exeter in 968 (Thorpe 1848–9, I, 141). The monastery probably suffered in the Danish raid of 1003 (Whitelock 1955, 219), and this may be the occasion referred to in a charter granted to the house by Cnut in 1019 which states that the monastery's ancient royal charters had been burnt in an attack by heathens (Kemble 1839–48, No. 729).

In 1050, Bishop Leofric moved to Exeter and installed canons subject to the Rule of St Chrodegang. King Edward and Queen Edith attended the enthronement ceremony accompanied by an impressive assembly of earls and nobles (Chaplais 1966, 28–31; Barlow 1972, 6–9; Blake 1974, *passim*). William of Malmesbury believed that Leofric ejected nuns from the minster (Hamilton 1870, 201), but he was almost certainly mistaken (Barlow 1972, 9). It is unlikely that a truly monastic community still existed at Exeter by 1050, and the house may have become secularized following the setbacks suffered earlier in the century (Barlow 1963, 213). All Leofric found on his arrival was one set of mass vestments and five books (Chambers *et al.* 1933, 28), and there remained only one of the 26 estates given by Athelstan (Warren 1883, 2). But although the minster was undoubtedly impoverished and dilapidated when Leofric took it over, it was not derelict, since neither he nor his Norman successor undertook a complete rebuilding. No doubt for reasons of poverty, the Norman cathedral was not started until nearly 50 years after the Conquest. Nevertheless, the minster is likely to have undergone major alterations and additions in the years after 1050. The numbers of monks or clerks who had previously resided there are likely to have been much smaller than the establishment of canons and vicars introduced during Leofric's episcopate (Henderson and Bidwell 1982, 147, 163). Since the whole of Leofric's chapter was required to live in common, it will have been necessary for him to provide domestic accommodation on a considerable scale (*cf.* Hamilton 1870, 201; Radford 1973, 130). It is possible that the terraced area to the east of the apse formed part of domestic buildings erected by Leofric. At Wells, where Bishop Giso (1030–57) introduced the Rule of St Chrodegang, a possible cloister and domestic building of his period have been found in recent excavations at the east end of the minster church (Rodwell 1980, 9).

Leofric died in 1072 (Barlow 1972, 15–16) and was buried in the crypt of his cathedral (Warren 1883, 2). His successor, Osbern fitzOsbern (1072–1103), the first Norman bishop, was followed by William Warelwast (1107–37), who built the Norman cathedral. The work was started in 1112 or 1114 (Blake 1972, 32, n. 51) and the eastern arm of the church was probably completed in 1133 when the remains of Leofric and Osbern were transferred from the old to the new cathedral (Chambers *et al.* 1933, f. 56). Use of the Saxo-Norman minster as the cathedral church presumably ceased on 2 July 1133, the most likely date for the consecration of the Norman church (Rose-Troup 1932, 3–4).

The Early Topography of the Cathedral Close (Figs. 123, 127)

The recognition of the site of the Saxon minster church at the west end of the Close calls for a reconsideration of the early topography of the area. It had been suspected that the minster was in a quite different place, at the east end of the present cathedral, but this was not based on substantial evidence (Henderson and Bidwell 1982, 148). The idea did, however, appear to be supported when excavations by Sir Cyril Fox uncovered the site of an early spring beside the southern wall of the 13th-century cathedral quire (Fig. 123) (Fox 1956, 202–17). At least two phases of masonry surrounding the spring could be shown to precede early 13th-century work forming part of the adjacent Bishop's Palace. The second phase was attributable to the 12th century; Fox's suggestion that the earlier work represented a 7th-century adaptation of Roman masonry now seems distinctly optimistic: this masonry is on the same alignment as the Bishop's palace and therefore need be no earlier than the 11th or 12th century. The spring itself, perhaps one of several in the area, is likely to have been an early feature in the landscape.

There is sufficient evidence to allow at least a partial reconstruction of the bounds of the sub-Roman burial enclosure. The possibility that these approximated to the sides of the forum insula merits consideration, and on two sides—the north-east and north-west—there is, in fact, some reason to believe that this was the case. First, on the north-east side, the limit of the two Saxon cemeteries has been established by excavation, and was found to coincide roughly with the line of the external wall of the basilica (Bidwell 1979, 112).[9] As there was probably continuity of use between the sub-Roman and later cemeteries (above), the boundaries of the enclosure occupied by the successive cemeteries may have remained constant over a long period. Second, in the late medieval period the north-western edge of the Cathedral Close probably followed the present edge of the Close which runs along the border of the Cathedral Green (Lega-Weekes 1915, 187). Between South Street and Broadgate this runs at a distance of *c.* 20m. behind High Street. However it appears that the cemetery formerly extended nearer to High Street, since burials have been found below the tenements which lie between High Street and the Close. One of these was found on the site of the northern corner of the Roman basilica.[10] Clearly these tenements are in part at least encroachments upon the early cemetery. Since some of the bones came from a rubbish pit of the 12th century, the process of encroachment was evidently underway by that time. The recognition that the early cemetery formerly extended close to the High Street has important implications in considering the positions of Exeter's principal Saxon and medieval streets. A notable feature of the city's street plan is the pronounced north-eastward curve of High Street, which strays *c.* 80m. from the direct line from Eastgate to Westgate, and even runs as much as 12m. outside the edge of the Roman forum (Fig. 123). It seems probable that this curve resulted from the obstruction of the direct route between the city gates by the early cemetery. Two alternative explanations may be offered to account for the line taken by the High Street. In the first it is assumed that the sub-Roman cemetery was bounded by the Roman street leading from the east gate (Fig. 123), and that this street was shifted and partially re-aligned in the late 9th or early 10th century when Fore Street and the rest of the Saxon street system were laid out (below). This would have created space for burgage plots on the frontage next to the minster precinct. The second possible explanation is that the cemetery originally extended as far as High Street, which came to occupy its present course in the middle Saxon period or earlier. There is no firm evidence to support either hypothesis: in both cases encroachment on to the cemetery margin could have occurred at any time between the late 9th and the 12th century.

On the other two sides of the Close there is also a little evidence to suggest that the early cemetery occupied much of the forum plot. There seems little doubt that the cemetery once extended as far as South Street. The former extent of the cemetery is attested by the discovery of human burials or bones at various locations between South Street and the church of St Mary Major. Some were on the street frontage: Shortt (1841, 41) records that when the stretch of South Street outside the Vicars Choral was cleared in 1835, 'an immense number of human bones . . . amounting to many waggon loads' were removed from the site.[11] Pits full of human bones were found on the adjacent site of 11–12 South Street in 1946 (Fox 1952, 44) and charnel material has been noted periodically in neighbouring properties (Ashworth 1872, 26; Lega-Weekes 1915, 32; Shiel 1977, 256). The process of encroachment by housing in this area was remembered in a document of 1477 when the dean and chapter announced the annexation to the parish of St Mary Major of houses they had built on the frontage of South Street to the north of Kalendarhay, an area formerly within the enclosure of the graveyard (Lega-Weekes 1915, 188). Later, part of the cemetery behind these houses was enclosed as a garden and became built on only in the late 17th century (*ibid.*, 181). The apparent absence of buildings on at least part of the frontage in medieval times strongly suggests that this part of the Close boundary was established at an early date, probably before burgage plots were laid out in the late Saxon period. South Street was one of the main trading streets in Exeter and it is difficult to imagine the cemetery encroaching upon valuable house plots at the centre of the town once these had become established.

On the fourth side, to the south-east, the sub-Roman cemetery evidently spread beyond the edge of the forum, since one of the early graves was found to lie in the adjacent Roman street (above). Anglo-Saxon burials extended under some of the late medieval houses of the Vicars Choral in Kalendarhay (Fig. 125). However, since no human bones were found in the 1932 excavations in the Deanery garden (Montgomery-Neilson and Montague 1933–6, 72–8), at least part of the Deanery plot must have lain outside the sub-Roman and Saxon burial grounds. It is possible, therefore, that the north-western boundary of the Deanery follows a line close to the south-eastern limit of cemetery I and its successors.

One further feature of this part of the Close invites comment. In late medieval times the principal entrance to the Cathedral Close from the city was Broad Gate, next to the High Street. Its name (*porta lata*) had formerly applied to a different gate, that known until recently as Little Style, which stood next to South Street (Lega-Weekes 1915, 20). Before 1286, when Edward I granted licence for the construction of gates at each of the entrances into the Close, Little Style was apparently the only entrance to possess a gate.[12] This gate did not give direct access to the present cathedral; it did, however, stand directly in front of the west end of the Saxon minster church. It seems, therefore, that this was the principal early entrance to the minster precinct. Broad Gate probably became the main entrance into the Close when the Norman cathedral was built.

The Defences

The late Roman town was surrounded by a wall *c.* 3.2–3.4m. wide and perhaps 6m. high, backed by an earth bank *c.* 6m. in width (Bidwell 1980, 58–63). Excavations carried out since the 1930s have confirmed beyond reasonable doubt that the medieval city wall followed in all places the line of its Roman forerunner. Until recently it was generally assumed that a high proportion of the facework visible today was Roman (Burrow 1977, 32). However an excavation at Cricklepit Street in 1974 showed that a long stretch of wall, composed of neat volcanic ashlar which had previously been regarded as Roman work, was in fact of 15th- or 16th-century date (Griffiths 1974). Re-examination of the fabric elsewhere suggests that no facework is conclusively of Roman date, and there survive only two or three short stretches of possible Roman work. Most of the visible masonry is medieval or later, although the Roman core is probably preserved for the greater part of the circuit.[13]

When Exeter was occupied by a Danish army in 877 it was described in the *Anglo-Saxon Chronicle* as a *faesten*; it is first described as a burh in the entry under 893. The terminology of these references strongly suggests that Exeter was among the Wessex towns fortified by Alfred in the years between *c.* 880 and 892 (*cf.* Stenton 1971, 264–5; Biddle 1976, 273).[14] The Burghal Hidage entry for Exeter presents an unresolved problem: the 734 hides[15] assigned to the city provide for the defence of only about half the Roman circuit. Two explanations have been put forward to account for the discrepancy between the length of the Roman circuit (2,354 metres; 2,566 yards) and the Burghal Hidage figure of 1,009 yards. Hill (1974, 117) has tentatively suggested that the burh defences may have enclosed a corner of the Roman town which excluded the British population. The present writers prefer the alternative solution, proposed by Burrow (1977, 33), that provision was made for the maintenance only of those parts of the defences (the southern and eastern sides) which lacked steep natural slopes.

An indication of the strength of the late Saxon defences is to be found in accounts of the three attacks on the city in the 11th century. The Danish assault of 1001 was rebuffed, whilst that of 1003 was successful only because of the treachery of Exeter's French reeve (Thorpe 1848–9, I, 156; Whitelock 1955, 217). On the third occasion, in 1068, William besieged the city for 18 days before it fell, and then only after an attempt had been made to breach the wall with a mine (Hardy 1840, II, 421–2; Thorpe 1861, I, 340; Chibnall 1969, 2, 211 ff.).

Very little is known of the form of these defences. None of the surviving masonry can be securely ascribed to this period.[16] William of Malmesbury's record of the construction by Athelstan of a wall of squared stones (Hardy 1840, I, 214) has sometimes been dismissed (Radford 1970, 99), but on the false belief that the ashlar visible today is mostly Roman. There is indeed reason to believe that William of Malmesbury was well informed, as he was drawing on early, and probably near-contemporary, accounts (Whitelock 1955, 277–83). His mention of Athelstan fortifying the city with towers is perhaps a surprise, but Orderic Vitalis again mentions towers in the 1060s (Chibnall 1969, 210). It is not known whether the late Roman wall was provided with projecting towers.

An excavation in 1976 at Trinity Street, outside the city wall near the South Gate, located a substantial early medieval ditch c.10m. wide and 3m. deep at a distance of 33m. from the wall. This had been infilled in the early 13th century and presumably formed part of the defences in the 12th century and perhaps earlier.

It is now fairly certain that the four principal gates of the medieval city stood on or close to the sites of the Roman gates.[17] Of these, the South Gate retained until its demolition in 1819 a carriageway with a round head, but records of this are too poor to judge whether it was Roman or Romanesque (Fox 1968, 13).[18]

The Lesser Churches (Figs. 126 and 128)

Of the city's parish churches, the earliest attested, and arguably the most interesting, is St Sidwell's. 'Sydefulla virgo foras Exancaestre' is listed in an Old English record of the resting places of the saints (Liebermann 1889, 18).[19] The list is dated on the evidence of its earliest surviving manuscript to the first half of the 11th century; internal evidence indicates that the relevant section was compiled after 1013 (Rollason 1978, 61–8). Since only major cult centres are listed, St Sidwell's was evidently flourishing by that time, presumably with a church and a shrine. The minster is also known to have possessed relics of the saint by the early 11th century.[20] St Sidwell has been regarded as a local martyr who died in about 740 on the site of the church which bears her name (Kerslake 1873, 12). However her history is a matter of considerable obscurity, as no Life has survived, and even her very existence is not beyond doubt. It is not beyond the bounds of possibility that she was a martyr of the late Roman period. St Sidwell's church lies adjacent to one of the principal Roman roads into the city, some 280m. from the East Gate. This area was occupied by an early Roman cemetery (Fox 1952, 103) and is a likely site for a late Roman one. It is possible, therefore, that in St Sidwell's we have an example of a late Roman mausoleum developing into a shrine and eventually becoming a cult centre.[21] Nor is this the only extra-mural church which overlies a Roman cemetery. St David's stands on a hill some 450m. north-west of the city walls. There was an early Roman cemetery in its vicinity (Bidwell 1980, 44), but it is not known whether this was still in use in the 4th century. The church is first attested c. 1200 (Rose-Troup 1923, v).

The churches[22] within the walls have formed the subject of several antiquarian enquiries (e.g., Cresswell 1908; Rose-Troup 1923; Hoskins 1959). St Olave's in Fore Street is the best documented; it received grants of land from Countess Gytha between 1057 and 1065, and from King Edward in 1063 (Sawyer 1968, Nos. 1,037, 1,236).[23] The dedication of the church can hardly have taken place more than a generation earlier (cf. Brooke and Keir 1975, 141). It was granted to Battle Abbey shortly after the Conquest (Oliver 1840, 116) and was the only parish church mentioned by name in Domesday Book. The dedication of St Martin's in 1065 is recorded in a late 13th-century transcript of earlier material (Rose-Troup 1923, 9). Domesday Book records that the bishop of Exeter and Robert of Mortain held churches in the city; Reichel identified these as St Stephen's and St Lawrence's[24] respectively (Reichel 1898, 308; *idem* 1901, 630). However, the alternative suggestion of Hoskins (1959, 21) that the bishop's church was St Sidwell's seems more probable (Curtis 1932, 12–19; *cf.* Hamlin 1976, 93).

It is likely, however, that these scattered references identify only a minority of the city's late Saxon churches. St George's church in South Street incorporated masonry of Anglo-Saxon type, including long-and-short quoins, until its demolition after the last war (Fox 1952, 25–9), but received no early mention. The close proximity of churches to the four city gates is strongly reminiscent of Anglo-Saxon churches in similar positions elsewhere, as at Canterbury (Tatton-Brown, above), and probably Winchester (Biddle 1976, 333). None of these churches is demonstrably early, but St Mary Steps next to the West Gate retains a grand Norman font, and a very late source describes St Bartholomew's as 'built at the first erection of the eastgate' (Rose-Troup 1923, 25–6). A further probable late Saxon church, dedicated to Edward King and Martyr, was situated near St Mary Major in the Cathedral Close (*ibid.,* 34–7). This is likely to have been founded as a memorial chapel soon after the boy king's death in 978, and relics of St Edward may have been housed in it (Henderson and Bidwell 1982, 168). The chapel seems to have been demolished in the late 13th or early 14th centuries, and may have been replaced by the charnel chapel which stood in the cathedral cemetery a few metres to the north of St Mary Major (Fig. 125) (*ibid.,* 168–9).

It is probable that most of the city's churches were in existence by the time of William I: an entry in the part of the late 13th-century St John's Cartulary sometimes known as the St Martin's Missal records that there were in his reign 29 chapels in Exeter and its immediate vicinity (*ibid.,* 12). By the beginning of the 13th century only three new ones had been added to this total (*ibid.,* 11–14). One of these was probably St Edmund's, built *c.* 1200 as part of the fabric of Exe Bridge (Henderson 1981, 119), and another must have been St Mary Major, formerly the Saxon minster, which presumably assumed the status of a parish church upon the consecration of St Peter's cathedral in 1133 (Henderson and Bidwell 1982, 166).

Almost all the surviving churches within the walls appear to post-date the laying-out of the streets; they occupy plots on the frontages and in most cases the orientation of the church corresponds more closely to the line of the adjacent street or property boundaries than to an east-west alignment (Fig. 126). An exception is St Pancras', which lies in a back area to the north-west of High Street and is clearly earlier than Pancras Lane. Most of these churches are likely to have been founded in the 10th or 11th centuries as small proprietary chapels. Their distribution along the four main streets and within the northern part of the city corresponds with those areas which are believed to have been most intensively occupied in the 11th century (Fig. 128).

The parish boundaries await detailed study in the future. An early 14th-century document records the delimitation of the parishes by Bishop Simon of Apulia in 1222 (Rose-Troup 1923, 10–11). He probably rationalised the existing parishes, which may have been to some extent intermixed. Most of the boundaries ratified

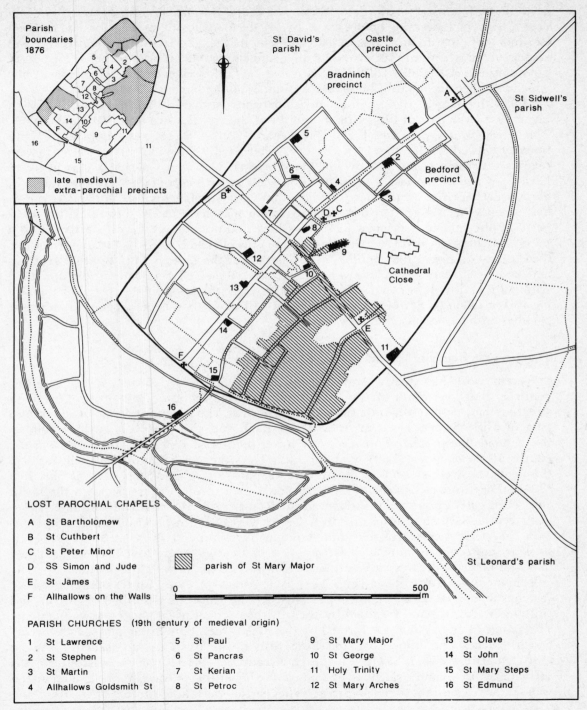

Parish
boundaries
1876

late medieval
extra-parochial precincts

St David's
parish

Castle
precinct

Bradninch
precinct

A

St Sidwell's
parish

Bedford
precinct

B

D C

Cathedral
Close

E

St Leonard's parish

LOST PAROCHIAL CHAPELS

A   St Bartholomew

B   St Cuthbert

C   St Peter Minor

D   SS Simon and Jude

E   St James

F   Allhallows on the Walls

parish of St Mary Major

0   500
                                      m

PARISH CHURCHES   (19th century of medieval origin)

1	St Lawrence	5	St Paul	9	St Mary Major	13	St Olave
2	St Stephen	6	St Pancras	10	St George	14	St John
3	St Martin	7	St Kerian	11	Holy Trinity	15	St Mary Steps
4	Allhallows Goldsmith St	8	St Petroc	12	St Mary Arches	16	St Edmund

126. The parishes and parish churches of medieval origin and the extra-parochial precincts of
Exeter in 1876, and the sites of 'lost' medieval parochial chapels.

by Bishop Simon must have been those of the chapelries carved out of the parochia of St Peter's minster in the late Saxon and early Norman period. Excavation of an area which includes the boundary between the parishes of St Pancras and St Paul showed that this division was already present in the 12th century when its line was respected by a row of Saxo-Norman pits, indicating that it was by then a property boundary at least (Collis 1972, 11). However at 197–8 High Street the tenement line which later became a parish boundary was underlain by large late Saxon pits.

Much the largest of the intra-mural parishes is that of St Mary Major, which occupies a large part of the southern quarter of the city (known as the 'West Quarter'). This area, which contains Rack Street and Preston Street, was apparently only sparsely settled before the 13th century, whereas the higher parts of the city were relatively densely populated by 1100 (see below). The West Quarter is thus likely to have been one of the last areas within the walls to be incorporated into the system of parochial chapelries which developed in the Saxo-Norman period. For this reason it has recently been suggested that St Mary Major may have received as its parish those parts of the minster's original parochia which had not already become attached to a parochial chapelry by 1133 (Henderson and Bidwell 1982, 166–8). In support of this idea it may be noted that until 1477, when part of the Close next to South Street was annexed to St Mary Major (above; Lega-Weekes 1915, 188), the church did not stand within its parish. It is conceivable that some other thinly-populated areas of the city may have fallen to St Mary Major parish in 1133 and then been assigned to adjacent parishes in the reorganisation of 1222.

The Street-system and Extent of Late Saxon Occupation (Figs. 127, 128)

Recent work has greatly amplified our knowledge of the Roman street plan; this confirms that very little of the Roman grid became incorporated into the medieval street-system, despite the retention of the gate sites. The exception is the north-eastern part of High Street, between St Martin's Lane and the East Gate, which follows the Roman line precisely; however the lower section of this street deviates from the course of the Roman street by about 14m. The other probable pre-burh elements in the medieval street system are North Street–South Street and Stepcote Hill–Smythen Street. The former is likely to have developed as a through route between the north and south gates upon the breakdown of the Roman grid. Stepcote Hill–Smythen Street is a steep lane which runs up the hill from the West Gate towards South Street as far as Milk Street. It seems probable that it originally continued as far as South Street; if so, it is interesting to note that the junction of the two would have been immediately opposite Little Style, the early entrance to the late Saxon minster precinct.

The medieval street plan (Fig. 127) is less regular than, for example, those of Winchester or Wareham, but displays most of the elements described by Biddle and Hill (1971, *passim*) and regarded by them as the product of late Saxon town planning. The spines of the system are formed by the High Street–Fore Street and North Street–South Street. The upper part of Fore Street was certainly in existence by the mid-11th-century when St Olave's church already occupied a plot on its frontage; it is sufficiently broad and straight to encourage the belief that it was laid out in a regulated way as an extension to High Street. The partial deviation of the latter from the

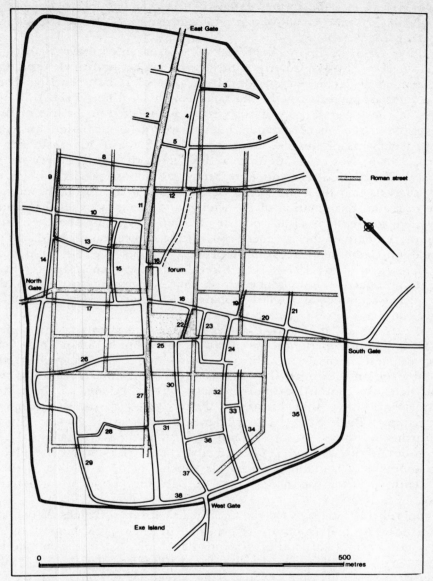

127. The Roman and medieval street plans of Exeter. The Roman street-
system is based on Bidwell 1980, Fig. 37, with some peripheral streets whose
positions have yet to be established by excavation omitted. Excavations in
1980–1 in Insulae I, II and XXX have necessitated a revision of the Roman
street-plan in these areas. It is not known whether any of the medieval streets
on the north-west side of the High Street originally extended as far as the city
walls. On the south-east side, there is documentary evidence to suggest that
Bampfylde Street, Chapel Street and St Martin's Lane all ran up to the
defences (Little and Easterling 1927, 32; Lega-Weekes 1915, 135–6)

(1) Castle Street; (2) Musgrave's Alley; (3) Bampfylde Street; (4) Bedford Street;
(5) Stephen's Street; (6) Chapel Street; (7) Catherine Street; (8) Gandy Street; (9) Upper
Paul Street; (10) Goldsmith Street; (11) High Street; (12) St Martin's Lane; (13) Pancras
Lane; (14) Paul Street; (15) Waterbeer Street; (16) Broadgate; (17) North Street;
(18) Little Style; (19) Bear Street; (20) South Street; (21) Palace Street; (22) George
Street; (23) Guinea Street; (24) Sun Street; (25) Milk Street; (26) Mary Arches Street;
(27) Fore Street; (28) Friernhay Street; (29) Bartholomew Street; (30) Smythen Street;
(31) John Street; (32) Preston Street; (33) Little Rack Street; (34) Rack Street;
(35) Coombe Street; (36) King Street; (37) Stepcote Hill; (38) West Street

Roman line may reflect the former extent of the cemetery or could have resulted from a re-alignment made to allow space for burgage plots on the frontage adjacent to the minster precinct (above).

Of the other elements in the system, back streets still survive to each side of High Street in the form of Waterbeer Street and Catherine Street; the latter until recently extended as far as Bampfylde Street. The plots between High Street and these back lanes are almost exactly the same length (c. 40m.; 131ft.). Moreover, a gentle curve in the lower section of High Street is reflected in the line of Waterbeer Street, suggesting that plots of a standard length were laid out beside the main street. In addition, tenements of this size are present along much of the north side of Fore Street (Nos. 182–5; Nos. 141–50 form a tidy block of slightly larger size), whilst those between Smythen Street and Fore Street are almost precisely of this length. This surely suggests that these properties were laid out in an organised way, probably on a single occasion. Examination of the widths of tenements or blocks of tenements has so far failed to yield any clear evidence of regular divisions. There are only a few indications of the date of the tenement blocks: the dedication of St Martin's church on one side of Catherine Street in the 1060s provides the earliest documentary evidence; an excavation at 197–8 High Street, lying between Waterbeer Street and High Street, produced a long sequence of Saxo-Norman occupation in the sixth phase of which was a coin of 1072–4 probably lost before c. 1084. Occupation here probably extends back into the 10th century.

Of the streets which lie at right-angles to the main streets, a few were clearly occupied from an early period. Concentrations of rubbish pits next to Goldsmith Street, for example, indicate that it was quite intensively occupied in the 11th century, and a site on the corner of Waterbeer Street and Pancras Lane also contained pits of this date. By contrast, extensive excavations in the area of Rack Street and Preston Street have shown that this part of the city was only sparsely occupied before the 13th century. Rack Street, a back lane to the rear of Preston Street, once extended further north-east towards South Street, but the section above Little Rack Street went out of use around 1300 or a little later. The earliest metalled surface overlaid a hollow way containing wheel-ruts which had been infilled in the mid- to late 13th century. There was no evidence to date the period of formation of the hollow way.

Biddle and Hill (1971, 82) used the Old English forms of names of two streets in Exeter, *Kalendarhaie* and *Irlesbyri,* as evidence of their pre-Conquest origin. This argument is not without difficulties. Kalendarhay took its name from the Kalendar brethren who moved to this area shortly after 1200 (Orme 1977, 153–6); the name must surely date from this time or later. Some street names containing the O.E. (ge) *haeg* element are later still: Friernhay, for example, must have been so called after the arrival of the Greyfriars in the 13th century. This street was earlier known as *Irlesbyri.* The name presumably referred primarily to a residence occupied or owned by a Saxon earl or *ealdorman* (P.N.D., 22); its application to the street may be secondary, and is therefore not conclusive evidence for the date of the street. In this instance, however, these is a suggestion from topographical evidence that the street may indeed be pre-Conquest. When the adjacent buildings of St Nicholas priory were laid out in the late 11th century, they were not orientated east–west, nor

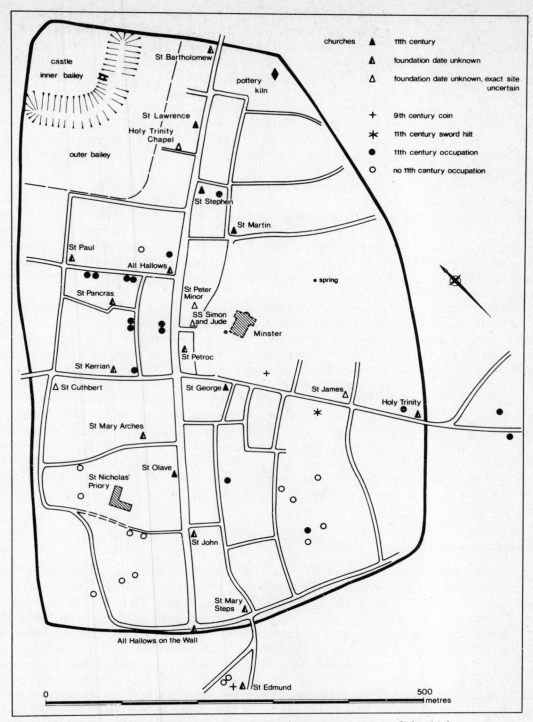

churches ▲ 11th century
▲ foundation date unknown
△ foundation date unknown, exact site uncertain

+ 9th century coin
✳ 11th century sword hilt
● 11th century occupation
○ no 11th century occupation

castle
inner bailey
St Bartholomew
pottery kiln
St Lawrence
Holy Trinity Chapel
outer bailey
St Stephen
St Martin
St Paul
All Hallows
St Pancras
St Peter Minor
SS Simon and Jude
Minster
● spring
St Petroc
St Kerrian
St Cuthbert
St George
St James
Holy Trinity
St Mary Arches
St Olave
St Nicholas' Priory
St John
St Mary Steps
All Hallows on the Wall
St Edmund

0   500
                     metres

128. 11th-century Exeter (with medieval churches). The provenance of the 11th-century sword-hilt described by V. Evison (1967, 171–2) is given by Shortt (1840, 143 and frontispiece). The 9th-century coin from the Deanery garden (Montgomerie-Neilson and Montague [1933-6, 56]) was destroyed during the last war

parallel with Fore Street, but on the alignment of Friernhay Street; they differ by about 26deg. from a true east–west orientation. This suggests that Friernhay/*Irlesbyri* is likely to be a pre-Conquest street. It is therefore interesting to note that a recent excavation along a sizeable stretch of its frontage produced little evidence of occupation before the late 13th century;[25] the laying out of the street must have preceded the occupation of most of the adjacent land by several centuries.

The street plan also exhibits elements of a possible circuit of intra-mural streets. West Street and part of Bartholomew Street skirt the wall overlooking the Exe; in addition, Hogenberg's map of 1587 depicts a lane, now lost, between properties in Paul Street and the wall to their rear. No further stretches of such a street have been located by excavation.

The identification of three classes of pottery which were in circulation in the late Saxon period and went out of use around 1100 has enabled some progress to be made in plotting the general distribution of settlement. The results are shown in Fig. 128. As already noted, there is a clear contrast between tenements in the High Street, which have produced evidence of a long sequence of occupation in the limited areas where excavation has been possible, and those in the lower parts of the city— such as Preston Street, Friernhay Street and Bartholomew Street—where early occupation was sparse.

Good evidence for 11th-century occupation has come from two sites in the suburb outside the South Gate, and a few sherds of Saxo-Norman pottery have been found in more outlying areas. The eastern suburb was much more extensive than the southern one, both from the end of the medieval period and, very probably, in Roman times; since this is likely also to have been the case in the Saxo-Norman period, it is most unfortunate that no excavation has taken place there.

Outside the West Gate lay the floodplain of the Exe. In later medieval times the area between the walls and the river, known as Exe Island, was crossed by a series of mill-leats. The earliest reference to one of these, the Higher Leat, occurs in the late 12th century.[26] There are indications that elsewhere in the lower Exe valley the reclamation of low-lying ground was already in hand by the mid-11th century (Alcock and Coombes 1977, 327), and it is probable that part at least of the Exe Island leat-system was a creation of the late Saxon period (*cf.* the leats at Winchester: Biddle 1976, 282–5).

Aspects of the Economy

In his brief description of Exeter in the 12th century William of Malmesbury drew a contrast between the wealth and magnificence of the city and the poverty of the local agricultural (Whitelock 1955, 277–83). He stated that there was in the city a great concourse of strangers who brought to it an abundance of every kind of merchandise. This was not a new phenomenon of the post-Conquest period. Orderic Vitalis recorded that in the siege of 1068 the foreign merchants were detained by the citizens to augment their fighting force; he also noted that Exeter lay beside the closest routes to Ireland and Brittany (Chibnall 1969, 211 ff.). Confirmation of the early trading interests of the port has come in recent years with the excavation of a sizeable series (nearly 200 vessels) of imported Saxo-Norman pottery. This collection has been the subject of recent analysis (Hodges and Mainmann forthcoming). The earliest finds are probably 10th century, but could be early 11th; there is a scatter of further imports attributable to the 11th century (about a dozen vessels) and larger numbers of these wares are present in the 12th-century deposits (over 50 vessels), although much of the collection is not closely datable. Since these wares are already present in the earliest levels excavated, it seems reasonable to suggest that the town's urban revival was closely related to the development of its foreign commerce. The collection offers some evidence regarding the directions of Exeter's early trade. The most common finds are Normandy gritty and glazed wares and *Hamwih* Class 11 cooking pots, together with red-painted pottery from both Normandy and the Beauvaisis. These suggest strong links with the coast of Normandy, and particularly with Rouen. There are in addition several examples of ceramics which are much more unusual in English contexts and seem to come from western or north-west France. One vessel is firmly attributable to a centre in Laval, another seems to come from the Loire valley, and the petrology of several strongly suggests a source in, or close to, Brittany. Since these areas were not major pottery-exporting centres like the Beauvaisis and Normandy, the Breton and western French wares probably reflect regular commercial contacts. Contrasting with the wealth of French wares, there is very little indeed from the major production centres of the Rhineland and the Low Countries, nor have the excavations yet produced any other evidence of north European contacts.

In addition, the ceramics give some indication of more local contacts. One class of coarse ware, for example, is heavily tempered with calcareous inclusions, the most accessible source for which is the south-east coast of Devon at Beer and Salcombe, about twenty kilometres away.

The emergence of Exeter as a central place serving much of Devon is more graphically illustrated by two pieces of documentary evidence. First, Domesday Book records some 114 houses in the city attached to rural manors. Only one of these is firmly located—that of Kenn, 6km. away. Others are listed under the entries for Tawstock (in north Devon), Bishopsteignton, and Ilsington (Darby and Welldon Finn 1967, 280–2). Second, a number of places had prayer gilds attached to the minster at Exeter. These provided for obits and masses for the dead, for which sizeable sums were paid to the minster. Gilds existed in Woodbury, Nutwell Colyton, Whitestone, Halsford, Exmouth, Clyst St George and Broadclyst (Thorpe 1865, 608–10; Barlow 1963, 196–8).[27] The most distant of these is 25km. from Exeter.

A variety of other evidence attests contacts with other parts of southern England. Two men with Exeter by-names were to be found among others from Devon at Winchester in the 1140s, and another Devonian was there in the reign of Edward (Biddle 1976, 194). At the time of the siege of Exeter in 1068, a Berkshire priest, Blaecman, may have been resident here.[28] Eleventh-century pennies recently found in the city were minted at Wilton and Wareham. The distribution of coins from the Exeter mint awaits full study, but finds from Somerset seem quite numerous. Moneyers working in the city also minted at Barnstaple, Ilchester, and the unlocated centre of *Gothaburgh* (Shiel 1980, 10). The dies used in the production of Alfredian coins at Exeter probably came from Winchester (Dolley and Blunt 1961, 87).

Evidence of a variety of trades has come from late Saxon deposits, supplementing the known activity of coinage. In Goldsmith Street and Waterbeer Street excavations produced concentrations of horn cores from sheep and goats; these must be the waste of local horners' workshops (Maltby 1979, 41-54). The small-scale working of metals on these sites and at 196 High Street is evidenced by small earthenware crucibles and waste slags. A rubbish pit in a neighbouring tenement on the High Street yielded a fragment of a delicate balance, perhaps used in commercial transactions. In the north-eastern corner of the city, a pottery kiln of elaborate construction produced high-quality wheel-thrown Saxo-Norman wares, a few of which are richly glazed.[29]

By contrast, structural evidence from the Saxon city has been disappointing. Only two or three fragments of the plans of timber buildings have been excavated. On two sites waterlogged structural timbers of oak gave dendrochronology dates in the early to mid-11th century; some of these appear to have come from a building of stave-type construction.[30] The two excavated stone churches attest a Saxon building industry whose only witness elsewhere in Devon is the crypt at Sidbury. The gatehouse of Exeter Castle also displays Anglo-Saxon architectural features, presumably reflecting the drafting of English masons. These may have been local men, but Orderic Vitalis mentioned that Englishmen were already to be found in the Norman army at the siege of 1068 (Chibnall 1969, 211 ff.), so masons could have been sent from Wessex to undertake the building.

The Composition of the Population

In an oft-quoted passage, William of Malmesbury described Athelstan 'compelling the British population of Exeter to leave the city, which they had until that time occupied with equal rights with the English' (Whitelock 1955, 281). This prompted several earlier researchers to attempt to identify a 'British quarter' in the town. It has been claimed (Hoskins 1960, 12–13) that the street known from the 13th century as *Bretayne,* now Bartholomew Street, marks the site of the 'British quarter', but the alternative explanation that this represents an area of later Breton settlement (*P.N.D.,* 21) is altogether more probable. William's remark has also been cited as evidence that the town's sub-Roman population was still to be found there in the 10th century (Frere 1974, 422), but clearly there must have been British inhabitants in the surrounding district who could have been drawn to the town following the re-establishment of urban life under Alfred. Similarly, the two churches with Celtic dedications have sometimes been regarded as evidence of pre-Saxon urban life, or even of a British quarter in the centre of the city (Kerslake 1873). However, as has recently been argued (Pearce 1978, 136), there are good reasons for placing the dedication of St Kerrian in the period between 1050 and the reign of Henry I, and that of St Petroc in the years shortly after 1050. In any case, both churches occupy plots on the street grid, and this very probably shows them to be of post-Alfredian origin. Suggestions that the nearby dedication to St Olave may reflect a Scandinavian settlement or patron are probably more firmly based (*cf.* Brooke and Keir 1975, 141).

The Environs of the City (Fig. 129)

Recent study of the bounds of Anglo-Saxon charters relating to lands near Exeter shows that the parish boundaries in these areas correspond closely with the boundaries of pre-Conquest estates (e.g., Alcock 1971; Alcock and Coombes 1977). The limits of the parishes for which charters do not survive are no doubt equally early, and this may well be true of the extra-mural parishes of the city. The bounds of Exeter were first accurately recorded in the Map Book of the lands of the City Chamber in the early 18th century.[31] The circuit there described enclosed the area which had received the status of a county two centuries earlier: it included the extra-mural parishes of St Sidwell's and St David's, but excluded the parish of St Leonard's to the south-west. The only aspect of the bounds of the County of the City which was post-medieval in date was the inclusion of Exe Island, recently gained from the Courtenays; the rest had belonged to the city in late medieval times. The line corresponds to the boundaries of the parish of Holy Trinity, whose church lies within the walls, and the extra-mural curacies of St David's and St Sidwell's. It is unlikely that these parish bounds have changed since the 12th century.

At the time of Domesday the burgesses had land for 12 plough-teams outside the city (*extra civitatem*), and the bishop of Exeter had 2½ acres of land which lay with the land of the burgesses (*jacent cum terra burgensium*). The extent and location of these lands were considered by Reichel (1902, 718–19); allowing 80 acres per plough-team, and interpreting the entry for the bishopric as meaning 2½ acres in each shoot, he believed the entry indicated a total of 960 acres cultivated by the city, of which 300 were held by the bishopric. More recent work suggests a figure of about a hundred acres per team (Darby 1977, 93–136), giving an arable area farmed by the burgesses of *c.* 1,200 acres, of which *c.* 360 acres belonged to the bishop. Since there is plenty of evidence for the rounding-off of ploughland totals in the south-west of England (*ibid.*), these figures will be very approximate.

Which were these lands? The obvious candidate for those of the bishop is St Sidwell's fee. This was an episcopal manor in the early 13th century, the earliest date at which this can be established.[32] Its bounds are first recorded in *c.* 1600;[33] the Tithe Apportionment of the 1840s records a total of 330 acres for the parish, of which all but a small block belonged in St Sidwell's fee in *c.* 1600. The correspondence between the size of the fee and that of the Domesday entry is sufficiently close to suggest that St Sidwell's was the land in question and that its bounds are probably of pre-Conquest date.

To the north of the city lies the ancient manor of Duryard. This was already the city's manor by 1186 x 1191 (Oliver 1840, 153), and it remained a city possession until its sale and subsequent division in 1703. Although no maps showing its boundaries have been found, the post-medieval extent of the manor can be established from an examination of surveys drawn up in 1688 and *c.* 1700.[34] It appears that the manor was then almost coterminous with St David's parish.[35] A scatter of 13th- and 14th-century references shows that some of the principal topographical features of Duryard belonged to the manor at that time (e.g., *H.M.C.* 71, 393). The likelihood that this manor is of pre-Conquest origin is strengthened by a comparison of its bounds with those of two Anglo-Saxon estates. First, the boundary along the Exe is also that of the Creedy Lands recorded in a document of the end of the 10th century (Finberg 1969, 45). The use of the River Exe as the shared boundary is, of course, unsurprising and need not imply contemporaneity. Of more interest is a spurious mid-11th-century charter[36] in which the bounds of *Hrocastoc*, now Stoke Canon, are

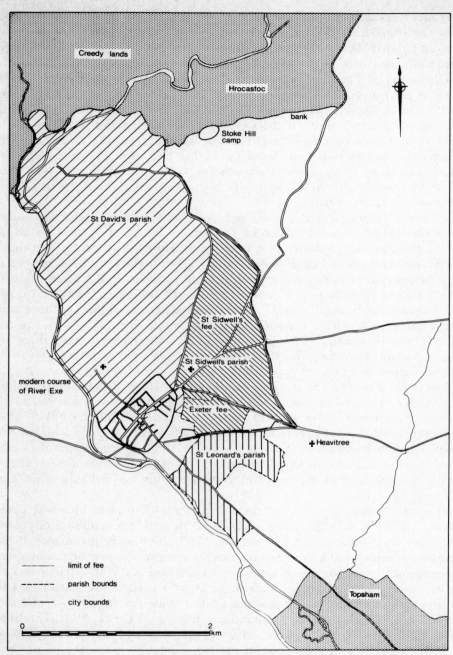

129. The environs of early medieval Exeter. The bounds of Topsham are those
recorded in the 11th-century charters and plotted by Alcock and Coombes (1977).
Those of the Creedy Lands follow Finberg (1969, 29–69). The bounds of
Hrocastoc follow *PND,* 447. Most of the roads shown are either of Roman origin
or form the boundaries of probable pre-Conquest estates

recorded; the land in question was claimed by St Peter's. The line of its boundary as it approaches Duryard is quite clear (*P.N.D.*, 447): it runs along a ridge to Stoke Hill camp, where it survives as a large hedge bank whose antiquity was emphasised by Hoskins (1960, 14), and then runs down to the Exe via a spring. The line between Stoke Hill camp and the Exe appears to follow the present city boundary. This boundary does not follow any obvious natural feature, and its probable correspondence with that of the city manor of Duryard, the parish boundary of St David's and the city bounds suggests that the city lands here occupy a land unit of a pre-Conquest date. Since the Exe will always have served as the west side of Duryard, and there is a little evidence to suggest that the shared boundary with St Sidwell's is pre-Conquest, it seems probable that Duryard's bounds are essentially pre-Conquest.

Most of the other land adjoining the city was attributed in Domesday Book to estates outside it, particularly the great royal estate of Wonford. There is, however, one probable exception. The parish of St Leonard's evidently belonged to the city in the mid-12th century (Reichel 1902, 718–19) although it was excluded from the later County of the City, and Reichel's suggestion that this was probably city land at Domesday is reasonable. The ploughlands held by the burgesses at Domesday amount to about 840 acres. The total arable acreage of St Leonard's and St David's would probably account for this figure. St Leonard's comprises some 174 acres, nearly all of which could be cultivated. This leaves say *c.* 680 acres for St David's. This parish has an area of *c.* 1,160 acres, though much of this must have been wooded, as it was in later medieval times. The figure of over 600 acres, in fact, seems quite a high arable total for this parish, but the surprisingly large extent of arable is a feature of the national totals recorded in Domesday Book (Darby 1977, 93–136).

In his popular history of the city W. G. Hoskins (1960, 14–15) suggested that these suburban parishes had formerly belonged to the great royal estate of Wonford. The attachment in the later medieval period of the chapels of St David and St Sidwell to Heavitree church, and the curious form of the small parish of St Leonard's, which may well have been a sub-division of a larger unit, perhaps led him to this conclusion. However, since the parochial chapelries were probably all city lands at Domesday, we suggest these may have been very ancient city possessions. In view of the evidence that other Saxon towns, such as Winchester (Biddle 1976, 255–8) and Gloucester (Heighway, in Chapter 13 above) possessed suburban estates comparable to Continental *territoria* of very early, and perhaps Roman, origin, these might even be pre-Saxon. However hardly anything is known of the Roman settlement of the environs of the city and nothing is known of their early post-Roman settlement, and so this possibility cannot yet be pursued.

Conclusion

Exeter lay far to the west of the early Anglo-Saxon settlements. There is nevertheless no clear sign of protracted sub-Roman urban occupation in the city. A small community, implicitly of Christian character, survived in or near the Roman town after the demise of urban institutions, and its life was perhaps continuous with that of the monastery known from the end of the 7th century. Both coin evidence and the references in the *Anglo-Saxon Chronicle* point clearly to the inclusion of Exeter among the burhs established by Alfred between *c.* 880 and 892. There is, however, hardly any archaeological evidence of urban life before the late 10th or early 11th centuries. This may in part reflect the destruction of the archaeological deposits along the city's principal streets, but the extent of 10th-century occupation appears to have been much more restricted than that of the next century. The *arx regia* from which Athelstan issued a charter in 928 (Sawyer 1968, No. 399) may still have been proto-urban rather than truly urban in character. The thriving city recorded in Domesday Book, with its large population and commercial life, its privileges and institutions, may well have been a product only of the preceding century.

ACKNOWLEDGEMENTS

We wish to thank Mrs. A. Erskine and Professor F. Barlow for reading and commenting on a draft of the text. Mrs. Erskine also provided us with help and advice regarding manuscripts in Exeter Cathedral Library. Miss B. Jupp drew the maps; Mrs. F. Silvester and Mrs. E. Holden typed the text.

ADDENDUM

Since the completion of this paper, doubt has been cast on the date of the supposed 10th-century source used by William of Malmesbury in his description of Exeter's defences. It now seems probable that the source is post-Conquest (Lapidge 1981).

NOTES

1. Although a 12th-century source, the account of Orderic Vitalis is a valuable one, since he appears to have used the lost ending of William of Poitier's *Gesta Guillelmi.*
2. Other methods of ranking the late Saxon mints may produce rather different results; Petersson (1969) offers no figures for Exeter. See also Metcalf (1978).
3. This is the figure adopted by Darby and Welldon Finn (1967, 281). The main entry in Domesday Book lists 285 houses; a further 114 are listed under the properties of tenants-in-chief. The latter may, however, have been included in the former entry. There were in addition 51 wasted houses; their devastation is often attributed to the construction of Exeter castle, but some houses, particularly in the suburbs, may equally have suffered during the siege of 1068 or the troubles of the following year.
4. Although the author was familiar with the West Country, this is probably an exaggeration. Exeter takes seventh place in the Borough Aids of Henry II (Biddle 1976, 501).
5. The city ranked twenty-seventh by wealth in the Lay Subsidy of 1334 (Glassock 1975).
6. H.A.R. 1614 and H.A.R. 1613 respectively (Bidwell 1979, 111). For the position of the graves, see Bidwell (1979, Fig. 32). These dates are uncalibrated.
7. Possibly a late Roman congregational church (Thomas 1981, 166–70), housed for example in the town house on the south-east side of the forum, or situated in the forum-courtyard (Bidwell 1980, 112).
8. In Devon, they have also been found beneath the bank of the Norman castle at Barnstaple.
9. It is possible that when the basilica and forum were demolished some of the outer walls were left standing to a reduced height to act as boundary walls.
10. In 1911 part of a skeleton was found during rebuilding (Lega-Weekes 1912, 485) and further human bones were recovered from an excavation in the vaults of the National Westminster Bank in 1977. Skeletons have also been found in the vicinity of St Petrock's church: 'The whole of the ground round this Church (now crowded with houses), appears to have been a cemetery; great

numbers of human bones having been discovered for the foundations of houses' (Jenkins 1806, 366).

11. Shortt believed that the human bones found in the 1830s may have been dumped there after the 'cleaning out of some ancient cemetery'; this possibility cannot be dismissed entirely.

12. D. and C. MS. 2118.

13. A survey of the wall fabric was undertaken by the Exeter Museums Archaeological Field Unit in 1978. The report on this work is unpublished, but copies are lodged in the Unit's archive and the West Country Studies Library, Exeter.

14. This section of the *Chronicle* appears to have been compiled during Alfred's reign, probably under the supervision of the king (Davis 1971). In an earlier part of the entry occurs the famous description of the division of Alfred's army.

15. All texts give this figure. It seems improbable that it is a textual error (Hill 1974, 114-6).

16. Burrow (1977, 20-2) thought that a stretch of wall next to 'Athelstan's Tower' was probably Anglo-Saxon. Re-examination of the sequence of masonry at this point suggests that a different interpretation is possible.

17. The Roman South Gate stood on the same site as the medieval gate (Fox 1968, 13). Recent excavations have demonstrated that Roman streets within the city led towards the medieval East and West Gates (Bidwell 1980, 68).

18. Exeter evidently had town gates by the year 1003. Florence of Worcester adds that Swein plundered the city and destroyed the wall from the East Gate to the West Gate (Thorpe 1848-9, I, 156). This account is almost certainly exaggerated.

19. We are grateful to Dr. Susan Pearce for drawing this source to our attention.

20. Swanton 1975, 19; St Sidwell is also included in the late 12th-century list D. and C. MS. 2861.

21. This possibility will be explored further by Dr. Pearce in a forthcoming paper.

22. The parish churches of Exeter were, strictly, parochial chapels, since they did not possess the right of sepulture (Rose-Troup 1923, 15).

23. The authenticity of the second document is not beyond doubt.

24. As he points out, however (*idem*, 1898, 276-8), mention of a church in Domesday Book is not conclusive evidence for the existence of a church building. His reason for identifying Robert of Mortain's church with St Lawrence's is not known (*cf.* Hoskins 1959).

25. Friernhay Street site, 1981.

26. D.R.O. ED/M/6. The surviving document is, in fact, of the early 13th century, but one of the witnesses died in 1194. Further mill leats close to the city are attested in the late 12th century (Jackson 1972, 58).

27. The last two places appear as *Cliftwike* and *Cliftune*. There was another gild at the unidentified *Lege*. The references are post-Conquest but reflect earlier conditions.

28. Freeman (1887, 34) makes this assertion on the basis of a statement in *Chronicon Monasterii de Abingdon* that Blaecman left England with Gytha, mother of Harold. The *Chronicle* does not, however, specifically state that Blaecman was in Exeter (Stevenson 1858, II, 283). According to Florence of Worcester, Gytha escaped from Exeter to Flanders when the city fell to William in 1068 (Thorpe 184, 8-9, II, 2).

29. For its location see Fig. 128. When the kiln was published it was believed to be of the 14th century, but it is now clear that it operated in the Saxo-Norman period (Allan, forthcoming).

30. This material came from Goldsmith Street, site 3 (1971) and Trichay Street (1972).

31. In the D.R.O.

32. D. and C. MS. 381.

33. In Hooker's view of St Sidwell's, in the D.R.O.

34. D.R.O. ECA S1/Box 1/Folders 3, 4; Book 185.

35. It did, however, contain a few areas of land north of the Exe.

36. D. and C. MS. 2517.

BIBLIOGRAPHY

ABBREVIATIONS

D. and C. MS.   Dean and Chapter manuscript, Exeter Cathedral Library.
D.R.O.   Devon Record Office.
H.M.C.   *Historical Manuscripts Commission Report on the Records of Exeter.* Prepared by J. H. Wylie (1916).
P-N.D.   The Place-Names of Devon, ed. J. E. B. Gover, A. Mawer, and F. M. Stenton (English Place-Name Society 8, 1931–2).
T.D.A.   *Transactions of the Devonshire Association.*

Alcock, N. W. (1971), 'The Clystwicon Charter', *T.D.A.* 103, 25–33.

Alcock, N. W. and Coombes, I. (1977), 'The Topsham Charter', *Devon and Cornwall Notes and Queries* 33, 324-7.

Allan, J. P. (1983), *Medieval and Post-Medieval Finds from Exeter, 1971-80.* Exeter Archaeological Reports 3.

Ashworth, E. (1872), 'Accounts of the church of St Mary Major, Exeter', *Trans. Exeter Diocesan Architectural Society,* 2nd ser. 2, 24–8.

Barlow, F. (1963), *The English Church 1000–1066: A Constitutional History.*

Barlow, F. (1972), 'Leofric and his times', in Barlow, F., *et al., Leofric of Exeter,* Exeter.

Biddle, M. (1964), 'Excavations at Winchester, 1962–3', *Antiquaries Journal* 44, 188–219.

Biddle, M. (1965), 'Excavations at Winchester, 1964', *Antiquaries Journal* 45, 230–64.

Biddle, M. (ed.) (1976), *Winchester in the Early Middle Ages (Winchester Studies I).*

Biddle, M. and Hill, D. H. (1971), 'Late Saxon planned towns', *Antiquaries Journal* 51, 70-85.

Bidwell, P. T. (1979), *The Legionary Bath-House and Basilica and Forum at Exeter.* Exeter Archaeological Reports 1.

Bidwell, P. T. (1980), *Roman Exeter: Fortress and Town,* Exeter Museums.

Blake, D. W. (1974), 'Bishop Leofric', *T.D.A.* 106, 47–57.

Brooke, C. N. L. and Keir, G. (1975), *London 800–1216: The Shaping of a City.*

Burrow, I. (1977), 'The town defences of Exeter', *T.D.A.* 109, 13–40.

Chambers, R. W., Förster, M. and Flower, R. (eds.) (1933), *The Exeter Book of Old English Poetry,* Exeter.

Chaplais, P. (1966), 'The authenticity of the royal Anglo-Saxon diplomas of Exeter', *Bulletin of the Institute of Historical Research* 99, 1-34.

Chibnall, M. (1969), *Historia Ecclesiastica* (Oxford Medieval Texts Series).

Collis, J. (1972), *Exeter Excavations: The Guildhall Site.*

Cresswell, B. F. (1908), *The Churches of Exeter.*

Curtis, M. E. (1932), *Some Disputes Between the City and the Cathedral Authorities of Exeter,* Manchester.

Darby, H. C. (1977), *Domesday England.*

Darby, H. C. and Finn, R. W. (eds.) (1967), *The Domesday Geography of South-West England.*

Davis, R. H. C. (1971), 'Alfred the Great: propaganda and truth', *History* 56, 169–82.

Dolley, R. H. M. and Blunt, C. E. (1961), 'The chronology of the coins of Alfred the Great, 871-99', in Dolley, R. H. M. (ed.), *Anglo-Saxon Coins.*

Evison, V. I. (1967), 'A sword from the Thames at Wallingford Bridge', *Archaeological Journal* 124, 160–89.

Finberg, H. P. R. (1964), *Lucerna.*

Finberg, H. P. R. (1969), *West Country Historical Studies.*

Fox, A. (1952), *Roman Exeter (Isca Dumnoniorum): Excavations in the War-Damaged Areas, 1945-7,* Manchester.

Fox, A. (1968), 'Excavations at the South Gate, Exeter', *Proceedings of the Devon Archaeological Society* 26, 1-20.

Fox, C. (1956), 'The siting of the Monastery of St Mary and St Peter in Exeter', in Harden, D. B. (ed.), *Dark Age Britain.*

Freeman, E. A. (1887), *Exeter* (Historic Towns Series).

Frend, W. H. C. (1982), 'Romano-British Christianity in the West: Comparison and Contrast', in Pearce, S. M. (ed.), 5-16.

Frere, S. S. (1974), *Britannia*.

Glasscock, R. E. (1975), 'The Lay Subsidy of 1334', *British Academy Records of Social and Economic History*, new ser. 11, 28-29.

Graham-Campbell, J. (1982), 'A Middle Saxon gold finger-ring from the Cathedral Close, Exeter', *Antiquaries Journal* 62, 366-7.

Graham-Campbell, J. (1983), 'A ninth-century Anglo-Saxon strap-end from the Cathedral Close, Exeter', *Proceedings of the Devon Archaeological Society* 41.

Griffiths, M. (1974), 'Recent work by the Exeter Archaeological Field Unit', *Proceedings of the Devon Archaeological Society* 32, 167-70.

Hamilton, N. E. S. A. (ed.) (1870), *William of Malmesbury: De Gestis Pontificum Anglorum*.

Hamlin, A. (1976), 'A painting of Norman work at St Stephen's church, Exeter', *Proceedings of the Devon Archaeological Society* 34, 92-4.

Heighway, C. M. (1980), 'Excavations at Gloucester, fifth interim report: St Oswald's priory 1977-8', *Antiquaries Journal* 60, 207–26.

Henderson, C. G. (1981), 'Exeter', in Milne, G. and Hobley, B. (eds.), *Waterfront Archaeology in Britain and Northern Europe*, C.B.A. Research Report 41, 119-122.

Henderson, C. G. and Bidwell, P. T. (1982), 'The Saxon minster at Exeter', in Pearce, S. M. (ed.), 145-75.

Hill, D. H. (1969), 'The Burghal Hidage: the establishment of a text', *Medieval Archaeology* 13, 84-92.

Hill, D. H. (1974), 'The Anglo-Saxon Town' unpublished Ph.D. Thesis, University of Southampton.

Hodges, R. and Mainmann, A. (1983), 'The Saxo-Norman imported pottery', in Allan, J. P. (ed.).

Hoskins, W. G. (1959), 'Early churches in Exeter', *Friends of Exeter Cathedral Annual Report* 29, 20–25.

Hoskins, W. G. (1960), *Two Thousand Years in Exeter*, Chichester.

Jackson, A. M. (1972), 'Medieval Exeter, the Exe and the earldom of Devon', *T.D.A.* 104, 57–80.

Jenkins, A. (1806), *The History and Description of the City of Exeter*.

Kemble, J. M. (ed.) (1839–49), *Codex Diplomaticus Aevi Saxonici*.

Kerslake, T. (1873), 'The Celt and the Teuton in Exeter', *Archaeological Journal* 30, 1–15.

Lapridge, M. (1981), 'Some Latin poems as evidence for the reign of Athelstan', *Anglo-Saxon England* 9, 61–98.

Lega-Weekes, E. (1912), 'An account of the Hospitium de le Egle, etc.', *T.D.A.* 44, 480–551.

Lega-Weekes, E. (1915), *Some Studies in the Topography of the Cathedral Close, Exeter*.

Leibermann, F. (1889), *Die Heiligen Englands*, Halle.

Levison, W. (ed.) (1905), *Vitae Sancti Bonifatii*, Hanover.

Little, A. G. and Easterling, R. C. (1927), *The Franciscans and Dominicans of Exeter*.

Maltby, M. (1979), *Faunal Studies on Urban Sites: The Animal Bones from Exeter, 1971–5*, Exeter Archaeological Reports 2.

Metcalf, D. M. (1978), 'The ranking of boroughs: numismatic evidence from the reign of Ethelred II', in Hill, D. H. (ed.), *Ethelred the Unready*, B.A.R. 59.

Montgomerie-Neilson, E. and Montague, L. A. D. (1933–6), 'Reports of the Exeter Excavation Committee', *Proceedings of the Devon Archaeological Exploration Society* 2, 224-37.

Oliver, G. (1840), *Ecclesiastical Antiquities in Devon*.

Orme, N. (1977), 'The Kalendar brethren of the city of Exeter', *T.D.A.* 109, 153–69.

Pearce, S. M. (1978), *The Kingdom of Dumnonia*.

Pearce, S. M. (ed.) (1982), *The Early Church in Western Britain and Ireland*, B.A.R. 102.

Petersson, H. B. A. (1969), *Anglo-Saxon Currency: King Edgar's Reform to the Norman Conquest*, Lund.

Potter, K. R. (1976), *Gesta Stephani: The Deeds of Stephen (1135-54)*.

Radford, C. A. R. (1970), 'The later pre-Conquest boroughs and their defences', *Medieval Archaeology* 14, 83–103.

Radford, C. A. R. (1973), 'Pre-Conquest minster churches', *Archaeological Journal* 130, 120–40.

Reichel, O. J. (1898), 'The "Domesday" Churches of Devon', *T.D.A.* 30, 258–315.

Reichel, O. J. (1901), 'The Devonshire Domesday: part 6: identifications', *T.D.A.* 33, 603–39.

Reichel, O. J. (1902), 'The Devonshire Domesday: part 6. Some notes on part 1 of Domesday identifications', *T.D.A.* 34, 715-32.

Rodwell, W. J. (1980), *Wells cathedral: Excavations and Discoveries*, Wells.

Rodwell, W. J. (1982), 'From mausoleum to minster: the early development of Wells Cathedral', in Pearce, S. M. (ed.), 49-59.

Rollason, D. W. (1978), 'Lists of saints' resting places in Anglo-Saxon England', *Anglo-Saxon England* 7, 61-93.

Rose-Troup, F. (1923), *Lost Chapels of Exeter*, Exeter.

Rose-Troup, F. (1932), *The Consecration of the Norman Minster at Exeter, 1133*.

Sawyer, P. H. (1968), *Anglo-Saxon Charters, an Annotated List and Bibliography*.

Shiel, N. (1977), 'Exeter hoards', *Numismatic Circular* 85, No. 6, 256.

Shiel, N. (1980), 'The Saxon and medieval Mint', in Andrews, J., Elston, W. and Shiel, N. (eds.), *Exeter Coinage*.

Shiel, N. (1983), 'The numismatic finds', in Allan, J. P. (ed.).

Shoesmith, R. (1980), *Hereford City Excavations, Vol. I: Excavations at Castle Green*, C.B.A. Research Report 36.

Shortt, W. T. P. (1840), *Sylva Antiqua Iscana*.

Shortt, W. T. P. (1841), *Collectanea Curiosa Antiqua Dumnonia*.

Stenton, F. M. (1971), *Anglo-Saxon England* (3rd edn.).

Stevenson, J. (ed.) (1858), *Chronicon Monasterii de Abingdon* (2 vols., Rolls Series).

Stevenson, W. H. (ed.) (1959), *Asser's Life of King Alfred*.

Swanton, M. (ed.) (1975), *Anglo-Saxon Prose*.

Thomas, C. (1981), *Christianity in Roman Britain to A.D. 500*.

Thorpe, B. (ed.) (1848–9), *Chronicon ex Chronicis* (2 vols., English Historical Society).

Thorpe, B. (ed.) (1861), *The Anglo-Saxon Chronicle* (2 vols., Rolls series).

Thorpe, B. (ed.) (1865), *Diplomatarium Anglicum Aevi Saxonici*.

Warren, F. E. (ed.) (1883), *The Leofric Missal*.

Whitelock, D. (ed.) (1955), *English Historical Documents* I (1st ed.).

Whitelock, D. (1968), *The Genuine Asser*, Reading.

LIST OF SUBSCRIBERS

Leslie Alcock
Arnold M. Allen, C.B.E., M.A.
John Allen
T. W. M. Anderson, M.C., T.D., B.A.
John E. Ayto
Keith Bailey
Harry M. Ball
James Barber
David Beard
A. F. Bennett
Alison M. Bennett
G. L. Bishop
W. J. Blair
P. W. Bollen
C. J. Bond
John Bosanko
Enid E. S. Bown
John Bradley
J. D. Brand
Dr. Rupert Bruce-Mitford, F.B.A.
W. T. F. Bult, A.R.I.C.S.
Paul Cannon
Alan Carter
Ian Caruana
Miss J. M. Charlton
Joan E. Collins
Stephen Cooper
Monica Cooper
E. A. Crossland, I.S.O.
Mrs. J. M. B. Counihan
T. H. S. Curry
K. Rutherford Davis
J. W. Day
Kenneth F. Dibben
C. H. Dalwood
Philip Dixon
Dorset County Library
Dorset Natural History and Archaeology Society
P. J. Drury, F.S.A.
Miss Janet P. Duke
Cyril Dyer
Dr. D. Eaves
Mrs. Jill Eddison
Ann Ellison
Kenneth Rainforth Emmett
Judie English
Mrs. Vivien Ettlinger
Irene A. M. Everett
Exeter City Museum
W. E. Fairhead
Anthony S. D. Farmer
Dr. G. S. Feggetter
Leola J. Fleming
Peter G. T. Fogg
John Mark Fothergill
H. S. A. Fox
Gillian Frost

R. A. E. Fursey
James B. Gale
Mr. and Mrs. J. B. Garrett
Dr. Richard Gem
J. H. P. Gibb, F.S.A.
Alasdair M. Glass
Janet Goldsbrough-Jones
John and Marian Gower
F. M. Griffith
E. N. Gummer
Haddon Library, Faculty of Archaeology and Anthropology
Mrs. Pamela Haines
Hikki Haines-Kälin
V. G. Hallett
Richard Halsey
Ralph B. Harrison
Cyril Hart
Ruth M. Haslam
Tom Hassall
Sonia Chadwick Hawkes
Dr. Martin Henig
Derrick Stuart Herbert
I. Hewitt
Michael B. Hill, A.L.A.
Brian Hobley, B.A., M.I.F.A. F.S.A., A.M.A., M.B.I.M.
Paul Trevor Hodge
N. A. Hooper, M.A.
Dr. N. P. Hudd, M.A., M.B., M.R.C.P.
Dr. T. P. Hudson
Miss E. P. Humphreys
John R. Hunt, B.A.
John G. Hurst
Christopher Roy Hussey
G. H. Huxley
Kenneth Huxley-Robinson
E. A. Huxter
Phyllis M. Jackson
Jude James, B.A.
Philip Jones
Laurence Keen
David H. Kennett
Kent Archaeological Rescue Unit
Alexander C. King
Dr. R. H. Leech
L. H. Le Mottee
Bruce Levitan
Lincoln Archaeological Trust
Graham C. Linington
David W. Lloyd
Julian E. Lloyd
Mr. and Mrs. D. G. Longden
Dr. Graham A. Loud
Lyme Regis Museum
Stewart Lyon
A. G. Mein

R. A. Merson
Denis E. Miles
Jeremy Milln
J. P. F. Mills
E. V. Mitchell
W. F. Moore
Mrs. Carole A. Morris
Rupert P. Morris, B.A.(Hons.)
H. H. Oak-Rhind
Oriel College, Oxford
A. E. B. and D. M. Owen
K. J. Penn
John C. Pentney, M.A.
Martin Petchey
D. C. Phipps
Keith Piercy
John S. Pile, B.A.
Poole Museums Service
Mrs. M. Priestly
Miss Clare Randall
Miss E. D. Roberts
Dr. David M. Robinson
Eve B. Robson
Dr. Warwick Rodwell
Roman Baths Museum
D. R. Rudling
J. G. T. Rutherford
Edward Sammes
Mrs. V. E. Satterthwaite
Jennifer M. S. Scherr
Stephen William Schlich
B. Selwyn
Shaftesbury Historical Society
Mrs. Muriel E. Shaw
R. Shoesmith
Dr. Neil Stacy
Michael A. Stokes, B.A.
Anthony Streeten
Philip Syret
F. H. C. Tatham
Janet Taylor
Mrs. B. M. Thirlaway
F. F. Thompson
W. W. J. Trollope
Frank Trelawny Underwood
Peter Vinter
Jane Wadham
M. C. Wadhams
Alan Ward
Oswald Barrett Ward
Weald and Downland Open Air Museum
Martin G. Welch
N. P. Wickenden
David Wilkins
Dr. Ann Williams
Edward S. Worrall
D. M. Wray